Residential Housing & Interiors

Clois E. Kicklighter, Ed.D

Dean Emeritus, School of Technology
Professor Emeritus of Construction Technology
Indiana State University
Terre Haute, Indiana

Joan C. Kicklighter, CFCS

Author of Instructional Materials in
Family and Consumer Sciences
Naples, Florida

Publisher
The Goodheart-Willcox Company, Inc.
Tinley Park, Illinois

Manufactured in the United States of America.

Library of Congress Catalog Card Number 2003060011

International Standard Book Number 1-59070-304-9

2 3 4 5 6 7 8 9 10 – 05 – 10 09 08 07 06 05

Library of Congress Cataloging-in-Publication Data

Kicklighter, Clois E.
Residential housing and interiors / Clois, E. Kicklighter, Joan C. Kicklighter.
p. cm.

Includes index.
ISBN 1-59070-304-9
1. House construction—Planning. 2. Dwellings—Materials. 3. Interior decoration. I. Kicklighter, Joan C. II. Title.
TH4808.K53 2005
690'.8--dc22 2003060011

Introduction

Homes are more than buildings; they are a reflection of the lives of the occupants. *Residential Housing & Interiors* provides practical information about planning, building, and decorating a home to enhance its use for living, working, relaxing, and entertaining. Principles of good design are applied to individual rooms, the structure as a whole, and the surrounding landscape.

The text explains how today's many housing options meet individual tastes and different family needs. With the help of charts, drawings, and illustrations, the specific housing topics addressed in the chapters can be applied to any housing environment.

Residential Housing & Interiors examines the basic building materials and structural components of housing to help you evaluate materials in terms of appropriateness, strength, versatility, maintenance requirements, and cost. Basic facts about electrical, plumbing, and climate control systems are covered with suggestions for conserving energy and water in the home. A chapter on computer applications discusses the many important ways that computers are involved in housing beyond their invaluable use as information-search tools. The text also explores home offices, ergonomic furniture design, and housing design adaptations for individuals with special needs.

The 2005 edition of *Residential Housing & Interiors* is a complete update of the earlier text, with new information on Twenty-First Century furniture design (Chapter 11), green building (Chapter 22), and career paths in the housing field (Chapter 29). Other chapter additions to the text include highlighted key terms, Internet resources, suggested activities, and summaries. This new text also includes three new chapters: "Communication, Security, and Home Automation" (Chapter 21), "Designing for Health and Safety" (Chapter 23), and "Keeping a Job and Advancing a Career" (Chapter 30). Over 250 new full-color photos are used throughout.

Finally, if the housing field interests you as a possible career path, the text discusses the wide range of jobs available and introduces the professional techniques you will use when presenting housing ideas.

Clois E. and Joan C. Kicklighter

About the Authors

Dr. Clois E. Kicklighter is Dean Emeritus of the School of Technology and Professor Emeritus of Construction Technology at Indiana State University. He is a nationally known educator and has held the highest leadership positions in the National Association of Industrial Technology including chair of the National Board of Accreditation, chair of the Executive Board, president, and regional director. Dr. Kicklighter was awarded the respected Charles Keith Medal for exceptional leadership in the technology profession.

Dr. Kicklighter authored or coauthored *Architecture: Residential Drafting and Design; Modern Masonry: Brick, Block, and Stone; Drafting for Industry; Upholstery Fundamentals;* and *Modern Woodworking.* His educational background includes a baccalaureate degree from the University of Florida, a master's degree from Indiana State University, and a doctorate from the University of Maryland. His 37 years of experience include industrial, teaching, and administrative positions.

Joan C. Kicklighter is the coauthor of *Architecture: Residential Drafting and Design, Upholstery Fundamentals,* and instructional materials in Family and Consumer Sciences. She taught classes in Business and in Family and Consumer Sciences at the high school and adult levels. Mrs. Kicklighter's educational background includes a baccalaureate degree from Indiana State University and graduate work at Eastern Michigan University.

Contents in Brief

Contents

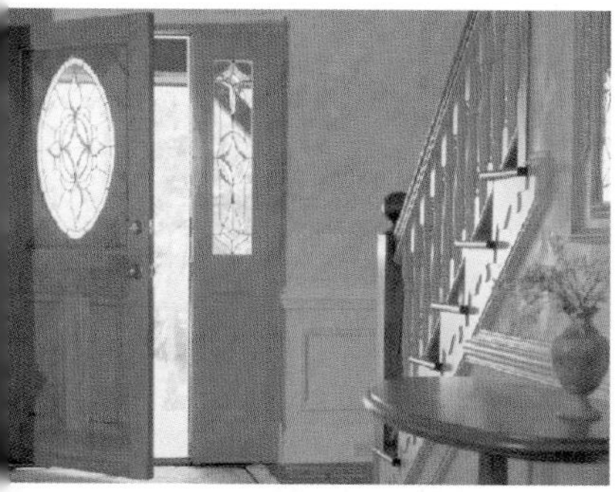

Part One Housing and Space Planning

Chapter 5
Planning Service and Work Areas 69

Part Two Design and Color

Chapter 6
Design 89

Chapter 7
Color 107

Part Three Materials Used in Housing and Interiors

Chapter 8
Wood, Masonry, and Concrete 126

Part Six House Systems

Part Seven Designing Exteriors and Remodeling

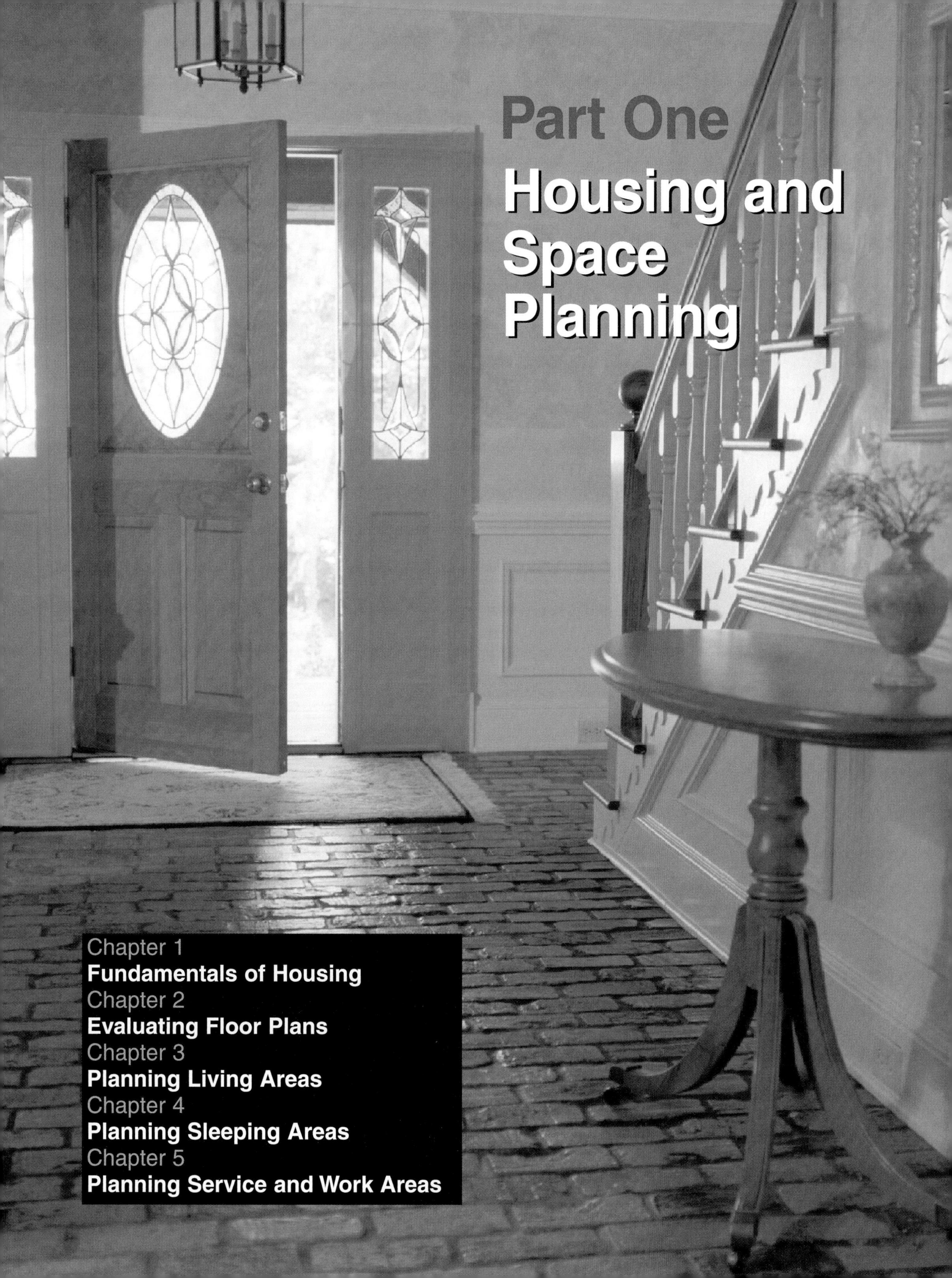

Part One

Housing and Space Planning

Chapter 1
Fundamentals of Housing

Objectives

After studying this chapter, you will be able to

- list physical factors outside the house that affect housing choices.
- explain the relationship between lifestyle and housing choices.
- describe the seven main types of housing.
- determine the strengths and weaknesses of the different types of housing.

Key Terms

housing
tract houses
custom houses
manufactured houses
prefab houses
kit houses
precuts
cooperative
condominium

The term **housing** refers to more than just a structural dwelling. It also includes all that is within the dwelling and all that surrounds it. Housing is the creation of a special environment in which people live and grow. Housing affects the way people feel and act, just as values and personality affect people's housing choices. People and housing are inseparable, and for that reason the term *lifespace* is sometimes used to describe housing. Lifespace, or housing, provides shelter, security, privacy, prestige, and a means of self-expression. Housing is an important part of people's lives.

Factors Affecting Housing Choices

Housing choices are affected by several factors such as location, climate, availability, cost, taste, and lifestyle. Each of these factors must be considered if a functional solution to the housing challenge is to be found. A brief examination of these factors will show the effect they exert on housing choices.

Location

Location refers to the specific placement of a home, 1-1. On a large scale, location choices range

Photo Courtesy of James Hardie® Siding Products

1-1 This attractive design is well suited to a hillside location.

from urban to suburban to rural. Location choices may also be categorized as seashore, mountain, desert, and so on. Homes in dissimilar locations often have distinctly different looks.

A home that takes advantage of its surroundings reflects the character of the area. For example, a home in Florida should differ in design and materials from a home in Minnesota, 1-2. A home located in the city should show an awareness of the characteristics resulting from its location. Since most city lots are small, most city homes are designed as compact, multilevel structures. A home designed for a mountain view should be oriented to take maximum advantage of its location.

Location, on a large scale, is thus an important consideration in the selection, design, or construction of a home. The materials used to build the structure as well as the furnishings used to decorate the interior can be affected by the location.

Location, on a smaller scale, also affects housing choices. A home is part of a neighborhood and should be viewed in the community setting. Each occupant has needs that must be met by the larger community. Facilities for education, transportation,

A WCI Communities, Inc.

B Photo Courtesy of James Hardie® Siding Products

1-2 Homes should fit their surroundings. The first home (A) has a light-colored exterior that is well suited to its Florida location. The second home (B) looks sturdy and warm enough for its Minnesota location.

worship, health care, shopping, and recreation are factors to consider when making housing choices.

Selecting the right neighborhood may be a bigger task than determining the basic requirements of the house or apartment. A tour of the area and visits with neighbors may reveal important characteristics about the community. While evaluating features that add to or detract from the quality of life in the area, the following questions should be considered:

- Has the community's growth followed a logical plan, or has its growth been uncontrolled?
- Is the desired home in the same price range as surrounding homes?
- Are the neighbors in a similar socioeconomic group as the prospective resident?
- Does the community have a high rate of turnover due to the resale of homes?
- Have property values increased as they have in similar neighborhoods elsewhere?
- Do the residents of the community take pride in the upkeep of their homes, or do the homes look rundown?
- Does the community have modern schools, several places of worship, quality shopping areas, and a variety of recreational facilities?
- Are there adequate services for health care, police and fire protection, utilities, and garbage collection?
- Is the home near the prospective resident's place of work? Is public transportation available?

These and other factors are important considerations in the selection of a neighborhood. When making housing choices, remember that a home cannot be separated from its location in a neighborhood.

Climate

Climate has always been a major consideration in housing choices. Climates vary from warm to cool and from dry to humid. Some areas receive more sunshine than others. Some climates are mild all year, while others have four distinct seasons.

The choice of a climate in which to live automatically affects the choice of housing design. A house built in northern Michigan should be designed for comfort during cold winters with lots of snow. It needs ample insulation and a tight shell to keep cold air out. The roof slope is important so snow will not accumulate to damage the structure. The amount of glass in a cold-climate home is also a concern since heat loss is greater through glass than through walls. The interior of such a structure should promote a feeling of warmth and friendliness to help its occupants endure the long winters.

Homes designed for desert climates should ideally have thick masonry walls. Such walls would shield the occupants from the high daytime temperatures and would release heat during the cool nights, 1-3. Homes in warm climates also should have wide overhanging roofs to shade the walls and light colors to reduce heat buildup, 1-4.

Climates that receive excessive amounts of rain, have high winds, or have an abundance of insects also affect the way a functional structure is designed. Adverse conditions must be considered when solving the housing problem.

Red Cedar Shingle and Handsplit Shake Bureau

1-3 Thick masonry walls and a wide overhanging roof make this home suitable for the hot, arid climate of the Southwest.

1-4 This south Florida home is particularly suited for a warm, moist climate.

Availability

Availability of desirable housing in a given area is often limited. Because of our growing, shifting population, housing is sometimes in short supply. Many apartments, 1-5, condominiums, and houses have been built in recent years to accommodate the rising demand for housing, but shifts in population do not always coincide with construction patterns. Therefore, availability is often the determining factor in acquiring housing.

Some people do not need to worry much about the availability of housing. They take their homes with them. Each year more people buy trailers, motor homes, mobile homes, and houseboats. These dwellings offer personalized comfort for their occupants while providing the ultimate in mobility.

Norandex/Reynolds Building Products

1-5 This modern apartment building is home to 36 families.

Cost

Cost is a crucial factor in housing choices for almost everyone. Cost becomes increasingly important as construction costs continue to rise. Not only is the initial cost of housing critical, but repairs, taxes, and insurance costs must also be considered. The total cost severely reduces the variety of choices open to the average person seeking housing.

Taste

Taste is the sense of what is fitting, harmonious, or beautiful. In other words, good taste is that which seems agreeable or pleasing. Taste reveals much about the personality of an individual. A person's taste is probably acquired through the sum of experiences and cultural influences.

Some people prefer to be surrounded with myriad colors or objects. Others choose just the opposite. Taste preferences vary not only from person to person, but also from time to time throughout a person's life. Taste changes as a person matures, meets new friends, and has new experiences. Group taste also affects individual taste. The "in" fashions and colors in clothing, home décor, and household furnishings set trends that influence individual taste preferences.

Another aspect of good taste in design is function. A reading area should be designed not just for beauty. In addition, it should have a comfortable chair and adequate light. A tasteful kitchen design, for example, is not only pleasant, but also efficient when frequently used dishes and appliances are within easy reach.

Personal taste must be considered when designing or purchasing a lifespace if that lifespace is to be functional, comfortable, and pleasing for its occupants. Like everyone, you have favorite objects, colors, and shapes that make you feel like being in familiar surroundings—in your own territory. In such a setting, you can relax and feel good. Thus, design that follows personal taste is likely to be pleasing, 1-6.

Lifestyle

A household's lifestyle is related to the values, social status, and activities of the household members. Their lifestyle influences their housing choices and dictates how their home is used. For some people, a home is merely a place to sleep and get ready for the next day. For others, it is a bustling center of activity. Some use their home as a peaceful retreat, while others use it mainly for social gatherings. However the home is used, it should be designed to complement the lifestyle of those who live in it.

A truly functional lifespace is a logical extension of a household's lifestyle. This is true of both the overall design of the structure and the use of the inside space. Space inside a home may be described as individual, group, and support space. All homes need all three types of space, but the amount needed of each type varies according to lifestyle.

- *Individual space* is needed for sleeping, dressing, studying, relaxing, and conducting business in privacy, 1-7. The amount needed varies depending on how many household members there are and how highly they value privacy.
- *Group space* is needed for family recreation, conversation, dining, and entertaining, 1-8. The amount needed varies with the household's lifestyle and social values.

Georgia Pacific Corporation

1-6 The pleasing design of this home reflects the personal taste of its occupants.

Manufactured Housing Institute

1-7 This individual space is for a young boy in the household.

Drexel Heritage Furnishings, Inc.

1-8 Group space is necessary for activities involving the interaction of two or more persons.

- The amount of *support space* needed in a home varies widely from household to household. Preparing food and doing laundry are two common support activities, 1-9. Many other types of work may also be done in the home, thus requiring more support space.

Space for individual, group, and support activities does not necessarily need to be divided into separate rooms. It is true that some activities are restricted to specific areas, but others can be performed in several locations throughout the home. In some cases, the spaces for different activities may

Wilsonart

1-9 The kitchen is a good example of support space in the home.

overlap. The main concern is to provide space for the activities of each member as well as those of the group. A home should be designed to achieve this goal.

Types of Housing Available

Several types of housing are available. These include: tract houses, custom houses, manufactured houses, mobile homes, and multifamily dwellings such as cooperatives, condominiums, and rental apartments.

Tract Houses

Tract houses are built by a developer who subdivides a large piece of land into lots. The developer then builds several houses using just a few basic plans. The number of different designs is limited to reduce the cost of each house and speed the work. The developer often provides financing or assistance in obtaining financing. An example of each house design is generally completed and displayed to entice prospective buyers.

Tract houses have several advantages. The buyer can see what he or she is buying, and a firm price can generally be negotiated even before construction begins. The fact that a subdivision has been planned as a whole may be another advantage—if it was planned well. A tract house usually costs less than a custom house, and it usually increases in value as the development grows. Therefore, those who buy early may realize a handsome profit on their investment.

Disadvantages are also associated with tract houses. They may be monotonous and have little individuality. They often look bare and unfinished for a few years until trees and shrubs grow. The lots are generally of minimum size so the developer can sell as many houses as possible. Also, a buyer takes the risk of not knowing how successful the development will eventually be.

The advantages and disadvantages of tract houses must be weighed on an individual basis. Some tract houses are well-designed and built with quality materials. Others are poorly designed and poorly constructed. The buyer must evaluate the variables to determine if a tract house is the answer to his or her housing needs.

Custom Houses

Custom houses are designed and built to meet the needs of a specific household. They may be designed by an architect, a home designer, or the prospective homeowner. A special designer or builder is not what makes a house a custom house. Rather, the fact that it is designed and built to meet the needs of a specific household distinguishes it as a custom house. It differs from all other houses, 1-10.

1-10 An architect designed this custom house. It is compatible with the site and climate conditions as well as the lifestyle of the occupants.

A custom house costs more per square foot than other types of housing, but it is the most functional housing for those for whom it is designed. Not only is the structure designed for specific individuals, but it is also tailored to a certain building site. This type of house is the dream of most people.

Those who want a custom house, but cannot afford to hire an architect, may purchase a stock plan from a magazine or other source and have it modified to fit their needs. This is usually done by the builder in consultation with the prospective homeowner. A house built from a stock plan will not be truly unique, but it should be functional if care is taken in choosing a good design. Thousands of available plans are well designed by professionals, and many include provisions for modification. An example is shown in 1-11.

Model: B90-2
From 912 sq. ft. to 1,062 sq. ft.

Sliding glass doors flood room with light and lead directly to outdoor living area. Compact L-shaped kitchen combines efficient work area with family dining room. Gracious living room has unbroken walls for easy furniture arrangement. Privacy of a quiet bedroom wing away from living-work area. Convenient closet and storage rooms for easy access.

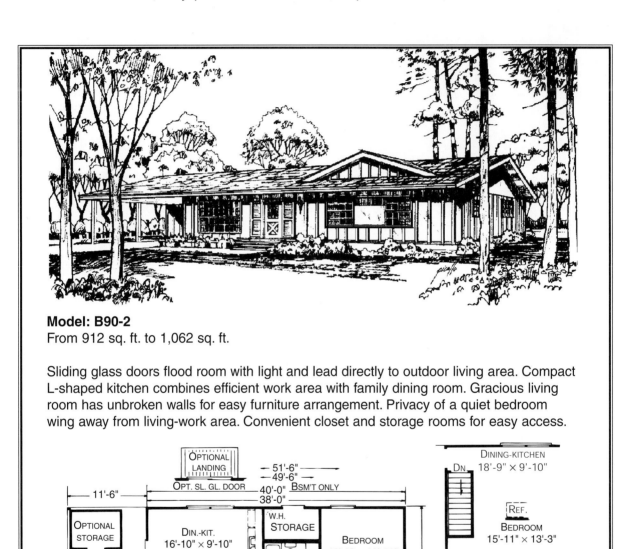

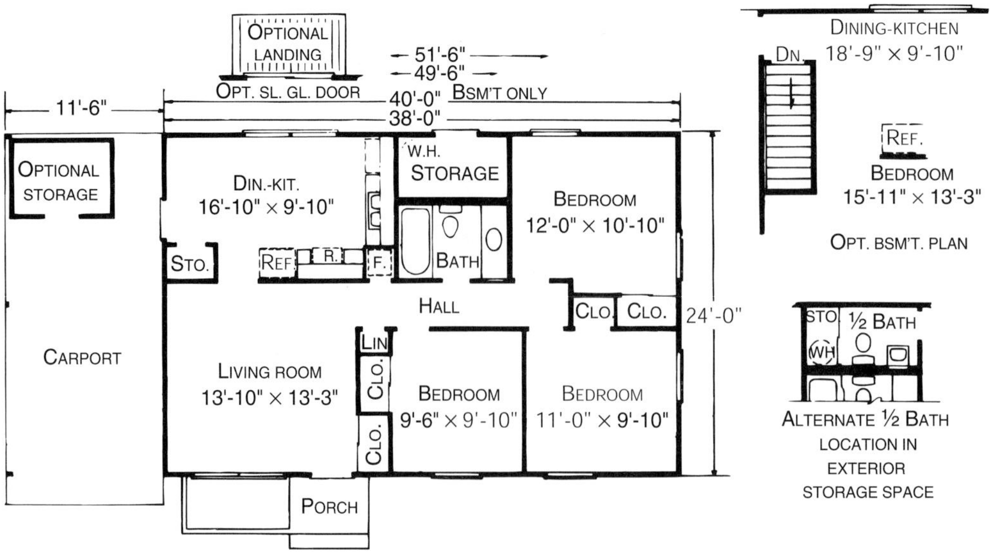

Kingsberry Homes

1-11 A stock plan can be modified to meet the needs of the prospective homeowner.

Many people desire the rewarding experience of designing and building their own homes. However, it may require skills they do not have. Design is probably the most important step in home building. Even good-quality construction, beautiful decoration, and creative use of materials will not be satisfactory if the basic design is poor. Those who are considering designing and building their own homes should look objectively at their skills. They should make honest decisions about what they can and cannot do, and get help if and when they need it.

A truly functional living space must complement the lifestyle of those who occupy it. A household should not have to alter its activities to fit the home. Rather, the home should be designed to accommodate the activities. A dwelling should also be designed to make the most of the site on which it is located, 1-12. The site is an integral part of the whole and will add to or detract from the appearance of the finished structure.

Advantages of designing and building one's own home include the great experience gained from such an endeavor, the savings in labor charges, and the satisfaction of having everything built to personal specifications. As with any other approach to acquiring housing, there are some disadvantages. Designing and building a home is complicated and requires a lot of patience and hard work. It is sometimes difficult to get a loan to cover the expenses of an owner-built house. Codes in some areas require a licensed contractor to perform certain tasks. This approach to housing will be ideal for some but not others.

Manufactured Houses

Manufactured houses are produced in a factory, shipped to the site, and put into place with a crane. They are available in several forms and degrees of completion. Modular components, prefabs, kit houses, and precuts are marketed by scores of companies throughout the country.

Most manufactured houses consist of modular components or building parts that are preassembled. Parts such as roof panels, floor panels, wall sections, kitchens, and baths are all produced as modules. A completed house may then be built from these modules, 1-13.

Some houses are virtually complete when they leave the plant as large, finished modules ranging in size from 12 by 20 ft. to 12 by 40 ft. and larger. See 1-14. Others are delivered as preassembled panels ready for erecting on the site. This option is generally referred to as **prefab housing**. Also available are **kit houses**, which are factory models of houses available in kits. Kit houses are similar to prefab houses, but many companies will make prefab houses of any design. **Precuts** are packaged materials already cut to size for a customer's plan, 1-15.

Manufactured housing has come a long way in recent years. In the past, manufactured houses were thought to be cheap, poorly constructed, and void of design. Today, this simply is not true. Many companies are producing houses that are well designed, well constructed, and beautiful. In most instances, it is impossible to recognize a factory-built structure once it is in place on the site, 1-16.

1-12 This custom house is well suited to its beach location.

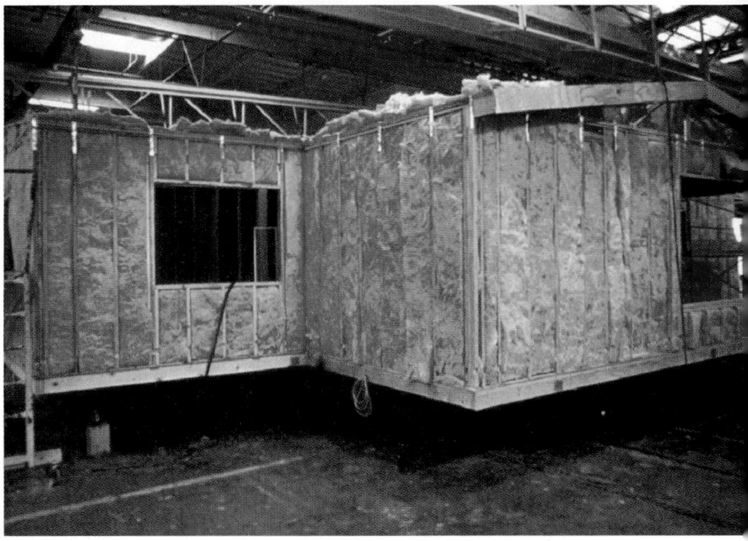

Manufactured Housing Institute

1-13 Standard modular components were used to assemble this manufactured house.

Manufactured Housing Institute

1-14 A factory-built module is placed on the foundation with a large crane.

Photo courtesy of Lindal Cedar Homes, Inc., Seattle, Washington

1-15 This striking chalet-style home was constructed using factory precut components.

Advantages of choosing manufactured houses include lower costs and reduced time in building. Quality is frequently better, and various components can be selected, as you would choose options for a new car. However, there are disadvantages. The selection is limited, and special equipment is necessary in some cases to install large modules. Shipping large modules can be expensive if the house is to be located far from the factory. The field of manufactured housing is continually growing and provides a viable solution to the housing needs of many people.

Manufactured Housing Institute

1-16 Who would ever guess this house is a manufactured house? It has the beautiful, detailed look of a custom house.

Manufactured Housing Institute

1-17 Mobile homes are generally more economical than other housing types and use space efficiently.

Mobile Homes

A mobile home is designed to be movable. It is constructed on a frame that has wheels attached for towing. One unit is sometimes joined to another to form a larger home. A mobile home can be placed on a temporary or permanent foundation. See 1-17.

Mobile homes are fully equipped with major appliances, furniture, carpeting, and even draperies included in the purchase price. Modern mobile homes are much larger, more convenient, and more adaptable than the "house trailer" of years ago.

Mobile homes should be moved by professionals who know the problems involved and have the necessary equipment, but moving is expensive. States have different laws relating to mobile homes, and it is important to know these laws before attempting a move.

The main advantage of a mobile home is economy. The purchase price is comparatively low, and very little upkeep is required. Monthly license fees are generally much lower than property taxes on a typical house. Another advantage is the exceptional recreational facilities and services offered at some mobile home parks. A mobile home has the additional advantage of being movable. A permanent site is not required.

There are some disadvantages, however, to mobile homes. They depreciate rapidly and may lose half their resale value in five years. Mobile homes are sometimes considered second-class housing. Many cities limit their location to a specific area. Furthermore, they are not really very mobile once they reach their final location. The cost of moving a mobile home, the need for professional movers, and highway restrictions all reduce their mobility.

The would-be purchaser should be aware of the moving, zoning, and taxing regulations as well as the facts about financing before choosing this type of housing.

Cooperatives

A **cooperative** is a dwelling that is managed and run as a corporation. The terms *cooperative* and *co-op* refer to the type of ownership, not the type of building. Cooperative ownership is available in many different types of housing, including single-family homes, mobile home parks, and multifamily dwellings. Cooperative ownership is most common in multifamily dwellings, and each family's living space is usually called an apartment. See 1-18.

Cooperative ownership combines the advantages of home ownership with the convenience of apartment living. The buyer purchases stock in the corporation that runs the building and, thereby, receives an apartment. The value of the apartment determines the amount of stock purchased. The buyer receives a lease granting exclusive right to possession of the apartment.

Since the buyer owns the apartment, he or she does not pay rent. The buyer does, however, pay a monthly fee that is used to pay the property taxes and maintenance costs of the building. The corporation takes care of maintenance and repairs with the money collected from the residing stockholders.

Photo Courtesy of James Hardie® Siding Products

1-18 Cooperatives are dwellings whose management is run as a corporation.

Owners have a voice in how the co-op is run, which is an advantage over a rental apartment. Owners can also express their opinions regarding who their future neighbors will be. Residents generally vote on which potential buyers should be allowed to purchase an apartment in the building.

The major disadvantage of a co-op is that each member must abide by the wishes of the total group. If the group makes a bad decision, then all suffer.

Condominiums

A **condominium** is a dwelling wherein the owner buys an apartment and a share of the common ground. The owner receives a deed to the apartment and pays taxes on it just as though it were a separate house. It is his or her apartment, 1-19. Owners of units in a condominium building have joint interest in all the shared property and facilities. These may include hallways, laundry areas, parking lots, sidewalks, lawns, tennis courts, and swimming pools. Common property is maintained with money collected from monthly assessments, as it is under cooperative ownership.

An owner of a condominium unit may sell the unit without consent or approval of other owners. In matters relating to common property, each owner has a vote in proportion to the original value of the unit he or she owns.

A condominium complex may consist of a single building or a group of buildings and surrounding property. It may even include a mixture of apartments, townhouses, and duplexes. The special feature of a condominium is that each unit is owned individually with a joint interest in the common property.

Rentals

Any type of dwelling can be rented, but apartments are by far the most common rentals, 1-20. Apartments are especially popular among people who prefer to be more mobile. Rental apartments usually require less initial expense and much less upkeep effort than other types of housing.

In many cases, several apartment buildings are planned and built at the same time in a group. This makes good use of the land and helps provide greater security.

Rental apartments have definite advantages for large segments of the population. They offer a variety of lifestyles and are readily available. In recent years, many new apartments have been built in attractive settings with conveniences to meet almost any need. Choices are unlimited in terms of style, size, price range, and facilities. Apartments are often conveniently located near public transportation, shopping centers, and recreation areas. Another advantage is they require little time or effort from the renter for upkeep and maintenance.

Disadvantages relate mostly to loss of control over the living space. Renters have little or no voice in how the apartment building is managed or maintained, although this has improved in recent years. Neighbors may move in and out so often that no true neighborhood spirit is developed. Also, money spent on rent is not applied toward ownership. After paying rent for years, renters have no property to show for their payments. In spite of the disadvantages, the rental apartment is the best answer to the housing needs of many people.

1-19 Condominiums look no different than cooperatives or rental apartments, but the owner may sell his or her unit without the consent of other owners.

1-20 Rental apartments are a viable choice for many Americans. They are available in many locations and in a wide range of prices.

Chapter Summary

Housing includes everything within a dwelling and surrounding it. Housing provides shelter, security, privacy, prestige, and a means of expression. It is where people live and grow, and it influences how they feel and act. Many factors affect housing choices.

There are several types of housing available such as tract houses, custom houses, manufactured houses, mobile homes, and multifamily dwellings. Multifamily dwellings include cooperatives, condominiums, and rental apartments.

The housing professional needs to understand how each of the factors presented in this chapter relates to matching a family to suitable housing.

Review Questions

1. What are the six main factors to consider when choosing a house?
2. What features in a community might keep individuals from buying homes they like?
3. How might a home in North Dakota differ from a home in Arizona?
4. What are the three types of space in a home and the common activities that take place in each?
5. How does a tract house differ from a custom house?
6. What factors need to be considered in designing a custom-built house?
7. What are some advantages and disadvantages of a manufactured house?
8. What problems may be involved in moving a mobile home?
9. How does a cooperative differ from a condominium?
10. What features might persuade a person to rent rather than buy a house?

Suggested Activities

1. Interview an architect, home designer, or building contractor in your area to determine what environmental factors most affect housing design in your region.
2. Using a city or county map, plot the location of your home to the closest location of each of the following: elementary school, high school, public transportation pick-up site, public library, public park, place of worship, health care facility, and shopping center.
3. Prepare a short essay on how the local climate affects residential dwelling construction in your community.
4. Prepare a list of the types of housing that are available in your neighborhood.
5. Make a list of the facilities that you would like to have in your personal lifespace.
6. Write an essay on the advantages and disadvantages associated with tract houses, custom houses, manufactured houses, and mobile homes.
7. Participate in a class discussion on the characteristics of cooperatives, condominiums, and rentals.

Internet Resources

American Institute of Architects
aia.org

Architectural Digest Magazine
archdigest.com

Architectural Ornament, Inc., a manufacturer of polyurethane architectural molding
architectural-ornamentation.com

Avis America, a manufacturer of modular homes
avisamerica.com

Better Homes and Gardens Magazine
bhg.com

Eric Crown Design Group, designers of the Palladian Design Collection
designgroupstudio.com

Insurance Information Institute
iii.org

Manufactured Housing Institute
manufacturedhousing.org

The Sater Design Collection, Inc.
saterdesign.com

U.S. Department of Veterans Affairs
va.gov

U.S. Environmental Protection Agency
epa.gov

Wausau Homes, a manufacturer of modular homes
wausauhomes.com

Note: Web addresses may have changed since publication. For some entries, reaching the correct Web site may require keying *www.* into the address.

Chapter 2
Evaluating Floor Plans

Objectives

After studying this chapter, you will be able to

- map a circulation pattern and evaluate its quality.
- identify the specific activities and areas involved in family, work, service, and guest circulation patterns.
- determine the utility of a floor plan in relationship to a family's needs.
- identify the seven types of drawings included in a set of house plans and explain their purposes.
- interpret the symbols on a plot plan, foundation/basement plan, floor plan, exterior elevation, electrical plan, and construction detail drawing.

Key Terms

circulation
circulation frequency
plot plan
foundation/basement plan
floor plan
exterior elevations
electrical plan
construction details
pictorial presentation
climate control plan
plumbing plan

The starting point for evaluating a floor plan is to make a list of your needs and wants related to housing. This list can help you decide which type of housing is most desirable for a specific situation. It can help you determine how much space is needed and how the space should be divided for the most effective use.

The first items on your list should meet absolute needs. These include bedrooms, baths, storage closets, and room for all necessary furniture and appliances. After listing all these needs, begin listing other features that are wanted in the home. Housing wants might include a fireplace, patio, or room for table tennis equipment. Try to be farsighted when making this list so changing needs can be met in the future.

Once you know what is needed and wanted in a home, begin examining floor plans. In each floor plan, identify the three main areas of the home. (Chapters 3, 4, and 5 provide in-depth analyses of these areas.) The three main areas are the living, sleeping, and service areas.

- The *living area* includes the living room, dining room, and family or recreation room. It also includes special rooms, such as a study, den, library, music room, or hobby room, as well as entryways, patios, and porches.
- The *sleeping area* includes the bedrooms, bathrooms, and dressing rooms.
- The *service area* includes other rooms, such as the kitchen, clothes-care center, utility room, basement, and garage.

As you study a floor plan, you may want to shade each of the three areas with a different colored pencil. This should help you visualize the location and contents of each area more easily. In most good plans, the rooms in each area are grouped to form a compact unit since they share similar functions. Compare the plans in 2-1 and 2-2 to see how the grouping of areas differs.

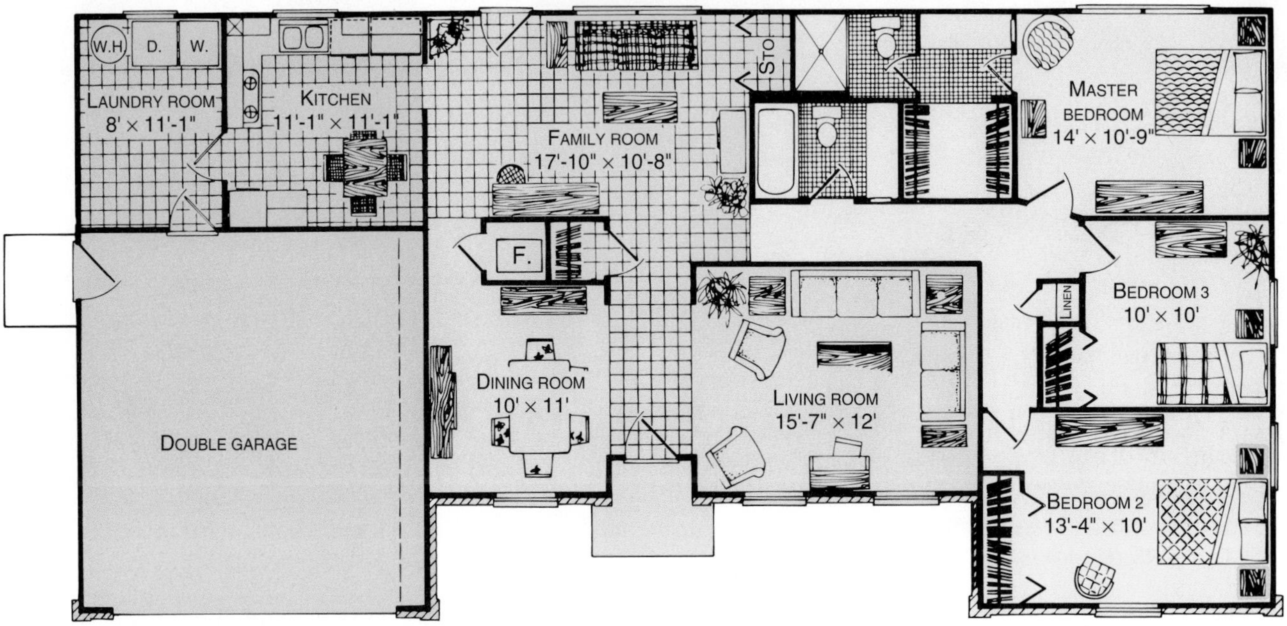

2-1 In this plan, the rooms in each area—service, living, and sleeping—are grouped together. This is usually a sign of a convenient, well designed floor plan.

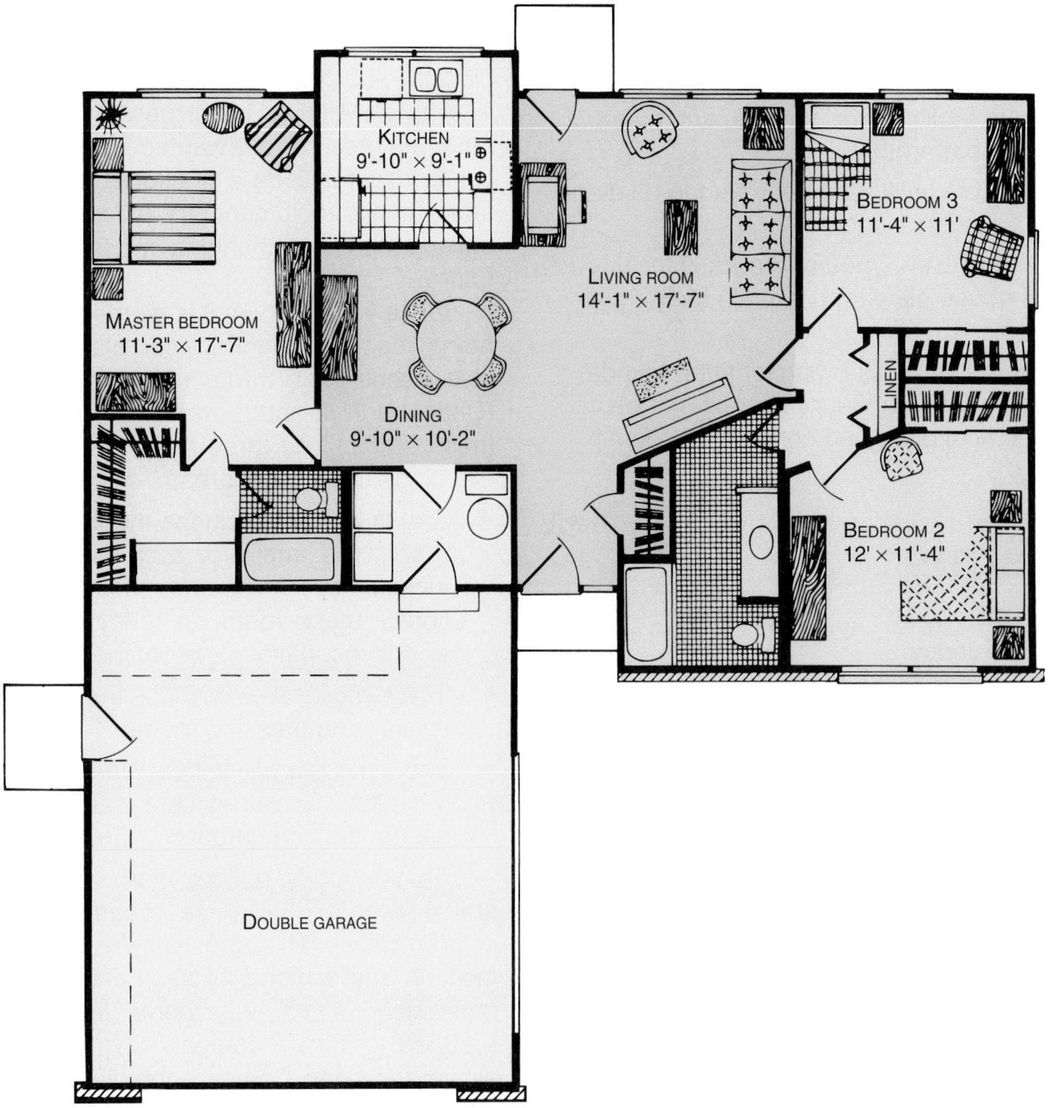

2-2 The sleeping and service areas are divided in this floor plan. Although some efficiency is lost as a result, many households would find the plan satisfactory.

Circulation

If you have identified the three areas of the home on a floor plan and you like how they are grouped, the next step is to map the circulation. **Circulation** is the route that people follow as they move from one place to another in the home. Circulation is not limited to hall space; it may pass through a room. Generally 3 to 4 ft. of space should be allowed for circulation paths.

When reviewing the circulation of a floor plan, it is important to check not only what routes are followed, but also how often they are followed. **Circulation frequency** refers to the number of times a route is repeated in any given period. Generally, routes with high circulation frequency are short and direct in a good floor plan. The habits, needs, and special considerations of a household also affect the quality of circulation. Therefore, a given plan may be good for one household but not another.

Types of Circulation

The four basic types of circulation patterns are family, work, service, and guest. Each type of circulation should be mapped and identified as you evaluate the floor plan. See 2-3. Use different colored pencils for the different patterns. This procedure should help you evaluate the efficiency of the floor plan.

Family Circulation

Family circulation is the most complex and difficult pattern to identify. Members of each household have different living habits that produce different circulation patterns. Try to map movements on a room-to-room

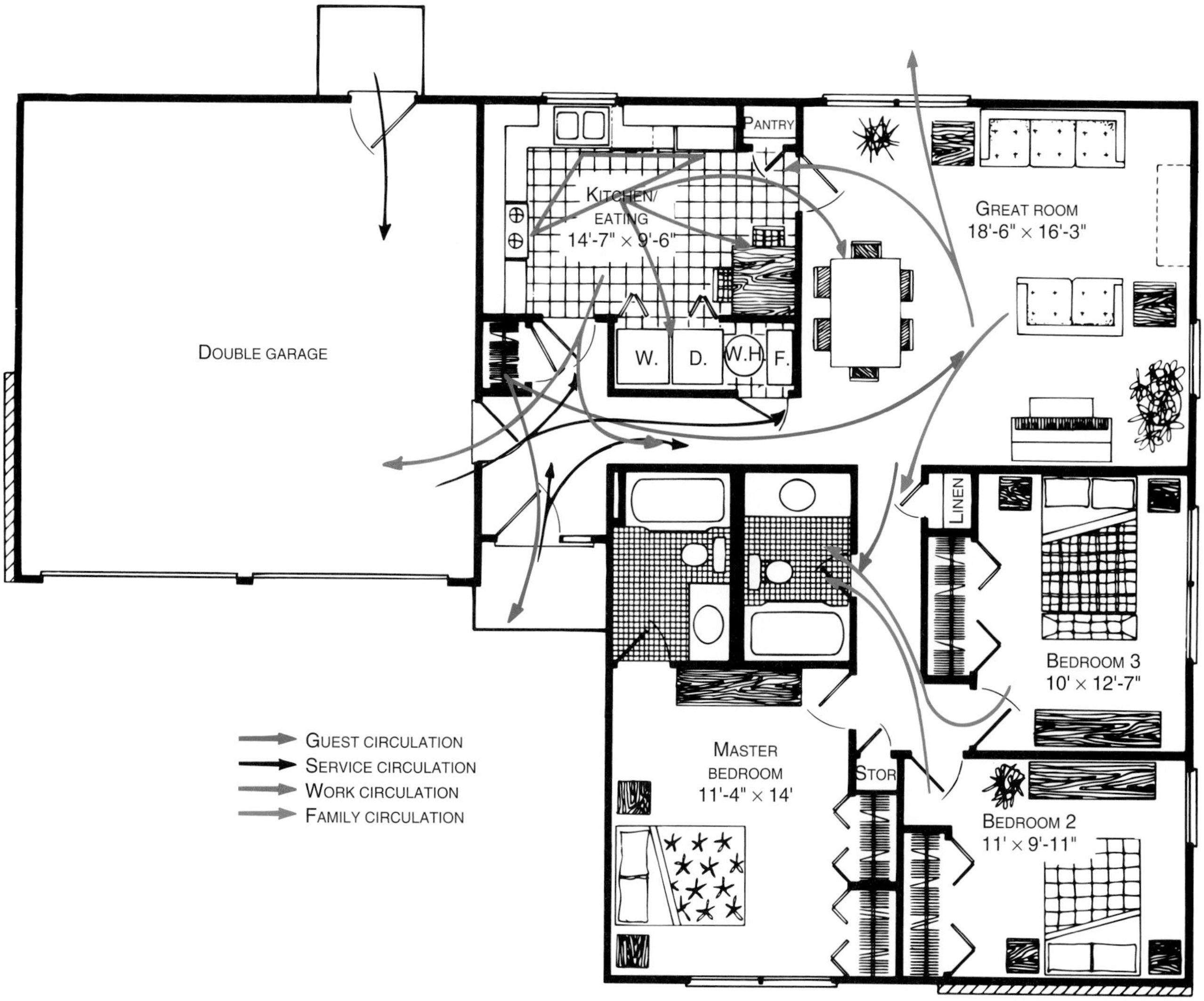

2-3 To evaluate the circulation efficiency of a floor plan, draw the family, work, service, and guest circulation patterns on the plan.

and activity-to-activity basis. A good family circulation pattern usually follows these principles:

- A bath is located close to the bedrooms.
- The indoor living area is readily accessible to an outdoor living area such as a patio or deck.
- Related rooms are close together.
- High-frequency circulation routes are short and simple.
- Excessive hall space is avoided.
- Rooms are not cut in half by circulation routes.

A floor plan that follows these principles is likely to be convenient for household members.

Work Circulation

The kitchen is generally the hub of the work circulation pattern. Circulation should move easily from the refrigerator to the sink to the cooking units and to the eating areas. Placing these areas relatively close together allows kitchen tasks to be done quickly and easily.

The kitchen should be located adjacent to the dining area. No cross traffic should be allowed to interfere with the circulation back and forth between the cooking and eating areas. This rule is intended to help prevent spills and broken dishes. The kitchen should also be located near the service entrance for convenience in many tasks. Good accessibility to other parts of the home such as bedrooms and baths is also desirable. Consider the number of trips that must be made from the kitchen to other rooms while cooking and cleaning.

Another aspect of a good work-circulation pattern is it provides easy access to the basement, garage, and storage areas throughout the home. The clothes care center also needs a convenient location since many trips are made to this work area. Any area of the home in which work is performed should be easily accessible to those who use it.

Service Circulation

Service circulation relates to the movement of people in and out of the home as they make service calls, deliver goods, read meters, take out garbage, and so on. It makes no difference whether household members do these tasks. The result is the same as it relates to the floor plan. In a good floor plan, no one should have to cross the kitchen to get to the basement or cross the dining room to carry groceries to the kitchen.

Locating a service entrance near the kitchen and basement enhances good service circulation. A good floor plan provides easy access to and from the kitchen, basement, garage, and other service areas.

Guest Circulation

This circulation pattern is the easiest to define. It simply involves movement from the entry to the coat closet and to the living room with access to powder room facilities. Guests should be able to move from the entry to the living area without passing through other rooms. A small house or apartment may not have a separate foyer or entrance area. In this case, guests may enter directly into the living room. They still should have access to a coat closet and powder room without having to pass through the main part of the living room.

Circulation Frequency

After the various circulation patterns are identified and analyzed, they should be evaluated in terms of circulation frequency. For example, how often does a family member walk from the recreation room to the kitchen compared to a guest walking into the living room? If dozens of family trips occur for each guest's visit, obviously the route from the recreation room to the kitchen should receive higher priority. It should be shorter and more direct than the guest's circulation route. This example shows that even though a floor plan may have a good circulation pattern, it may not meet the needs of household members because of their particular circulation-frequency patterns.

Realistically, all floor plans are compromises. One plan may have a perfect service circulation, while another has excellent family circulation. Still others may be average on all counts. The main goal is to judge how compatible the floor plan and circulation patterns are with the lifestyle of household members.

Room Relationships

The satisfaction household members receive from their living space is determined largely by the floor plan of their home. Other factors influencing satisfaction are the sizes and shapes of the rooms and the relationship of each room to the others.

The size of a room is not always an accurate indication of its usable space, 2-4. Poorly located doors, windows, and closets, or too many architectural features interrupting wall space can greatly reduce usable space. See 2-5. When evaluating floor plans, study the potential for furniture arrangement and circulation within each room.

The relationship of one room to another dictates how functional the space will be. For example, the dining area should be located adjacent to the living room for convenience in entertaining. The dining area should also be located next to the kitchen for ease in serving food. If the plan has more than one

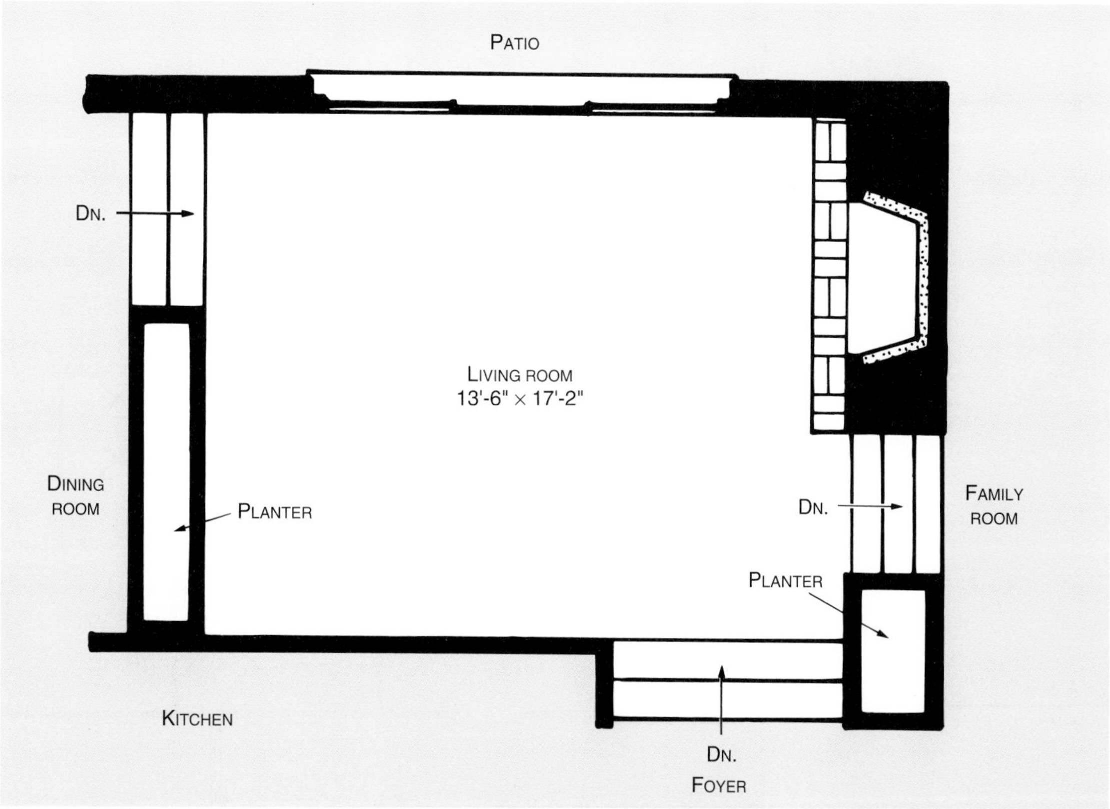

2-4 Although this living room is large, furniture placement is difficult because only one wall surface is free of architectural features. The design severely limits good space utilization.

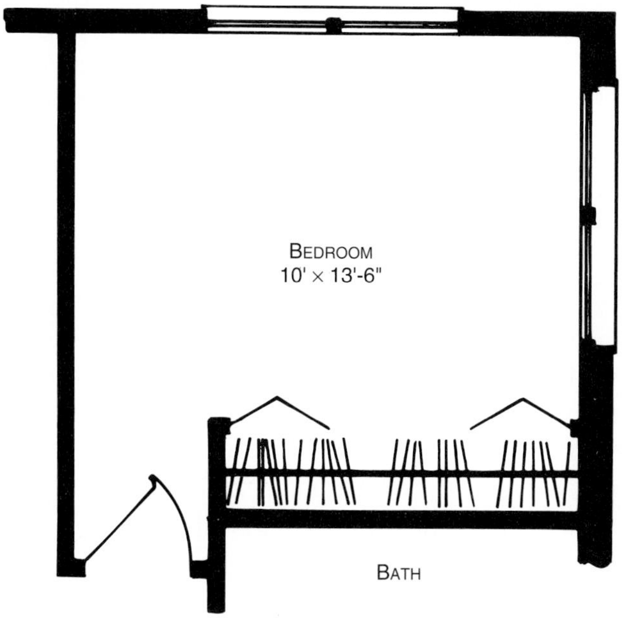

2-5 This bedroom has a desirable location, shape, and size, but it presents a problem for furniture placement. Large windows dominate the two exterior walls, while a closet is along the interior wall adjoining the bath. Only one wall, the one most visible from the doorway, is suitable for taller pieces of furniture.

dining area, the most frequently used area should receive priority. It should be closest to the kitchen. If food is often prepared or served on a patio or porch, that area should also be located near the kitchen.

The relationship between bedrooms and bathrooms deserves attention because convenience, accessibility, and privacy are important. These rooms should be close together for convenience. For good accessibility, at least one bathroom should be located where people can reach it without having to go through another room. Finally, privacy should be considered in terms of both sight and sound.

The floor plan in 2-6 shows logical and functional room relationships. The dining room is adjacent to both the living room and the kitchen. Another, smaller eating area is located in the kitchen itself. For added convenience, the kitchen has an access to the garage. The living room is large enough to accommodate several people. The walkway along one side promotes good circulation and adds space to the room. A coat closet and powder room are easily accessible to guests. All the bedrooms are near the bath and linen closet. The bath is centrally located, which is important since the plan includes only one bath. A second bath (for the master bedroom) could replace the current exterior storage.

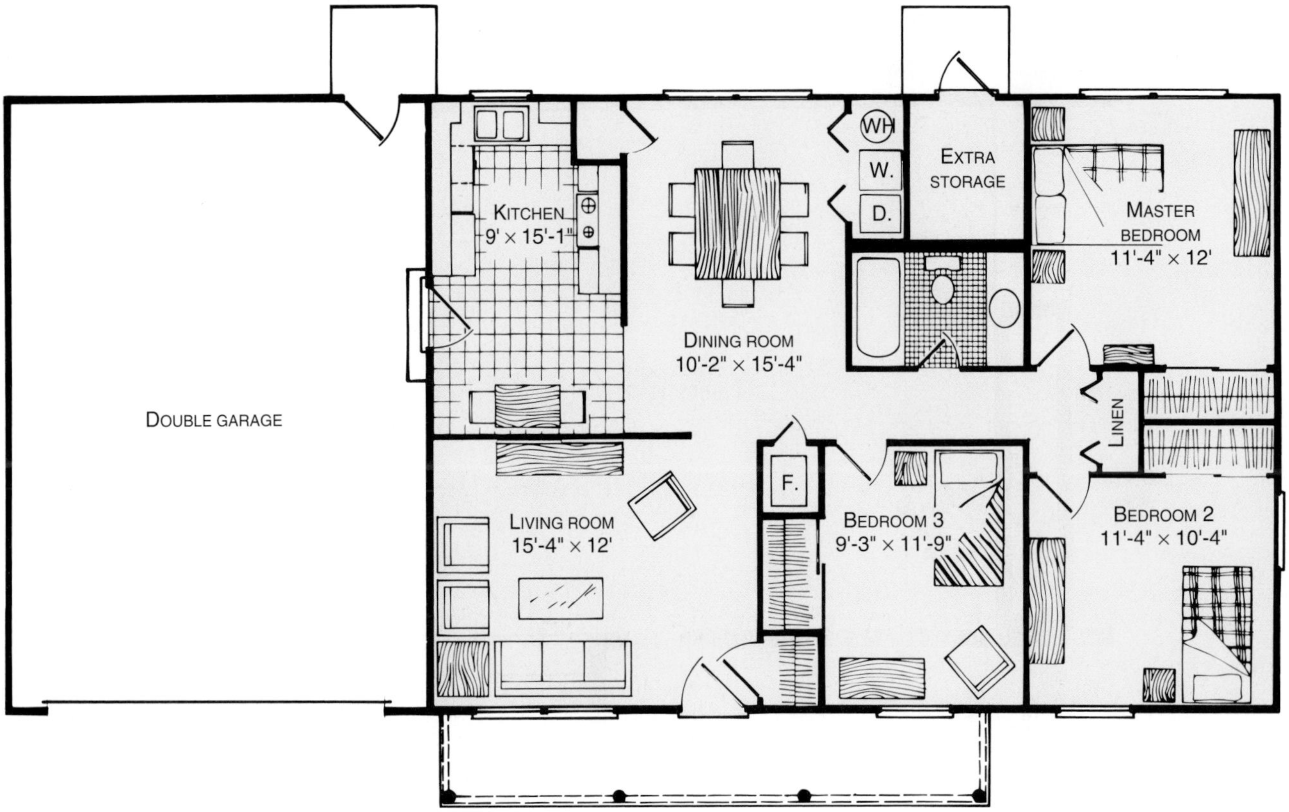

2-6 This 28 by 40 ft., three-bedroom home packs a lot of convenience into its 1,120 sq. ft. of living space.

Reading House Plans

A typical set of house plans, also called *construction drawings*, generally includes the following seven specific drawings:

- plot plan
- foundation/basement plan
- floor plan
- exterior elevations
- electrical plan
- construction details
- pictorial presentations

These drawings, together with a set of specifications, form the basis for a legal contract between the owner and builder. The specifications describe the quality of materials and construction techniques to be used. The specifications take precedence over the drawings in the event of a disagreement.

Description of Drawings

The following descriptions of the drawings generally found in a set of construction plans are intended to communicate the role that each drawing plays in the total plan.

The **plot plan** shows the location of the structure on the site. See 2-7. Its scale is generally *1 in. equals 20 or 30 ft.* A plot plan shows the following items:

- location, outline, and size of building(s) on the site
- streets, driveways, sidewalks, and patios
- location of utilities
- easements for utilities and drainage (if any)
- fences and retaining walls
- length and bearing of each property line
- contour of the land
- trees, shrubs, streams, and gardens
- elevation of property corners
- meridian arrow (north directional symbol)
- well and septic tank and field (if any)
- lot number or address of the site
- scale of the drawing

The plot plan is drawn using information provided by a surveyor and recorded on a site plan. The plot plan shows both the property and the proposed construction. Lending agencies, building inspectors, and excavators all need this drawing.

The **foundation/basement plan** shows the location and size of footings, piers, columns, foundation walls, and supporting beams of the structure. See 2-8.

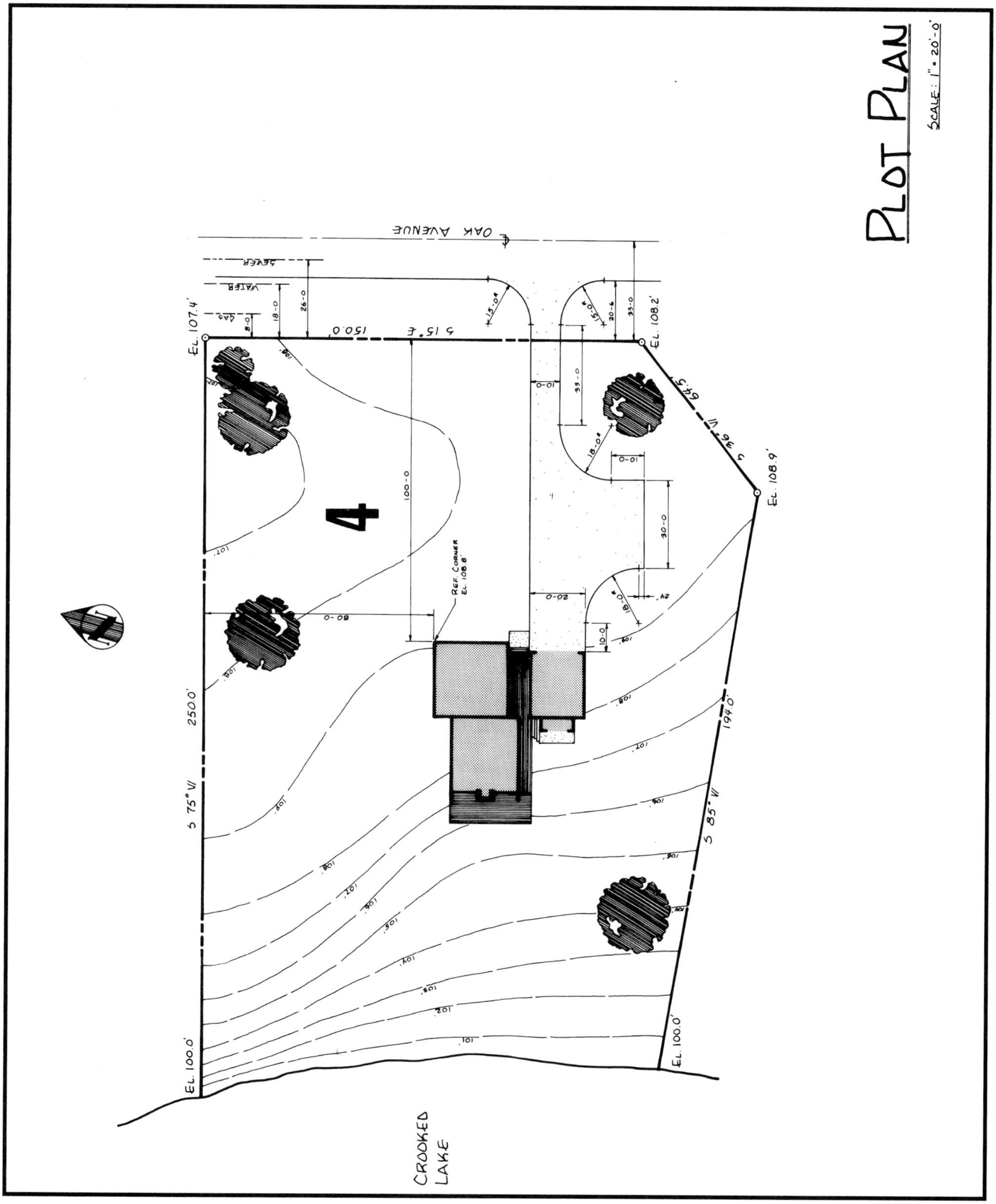

2-7 A typical plot plan shows the location of the structure on the site and other pertinent features.

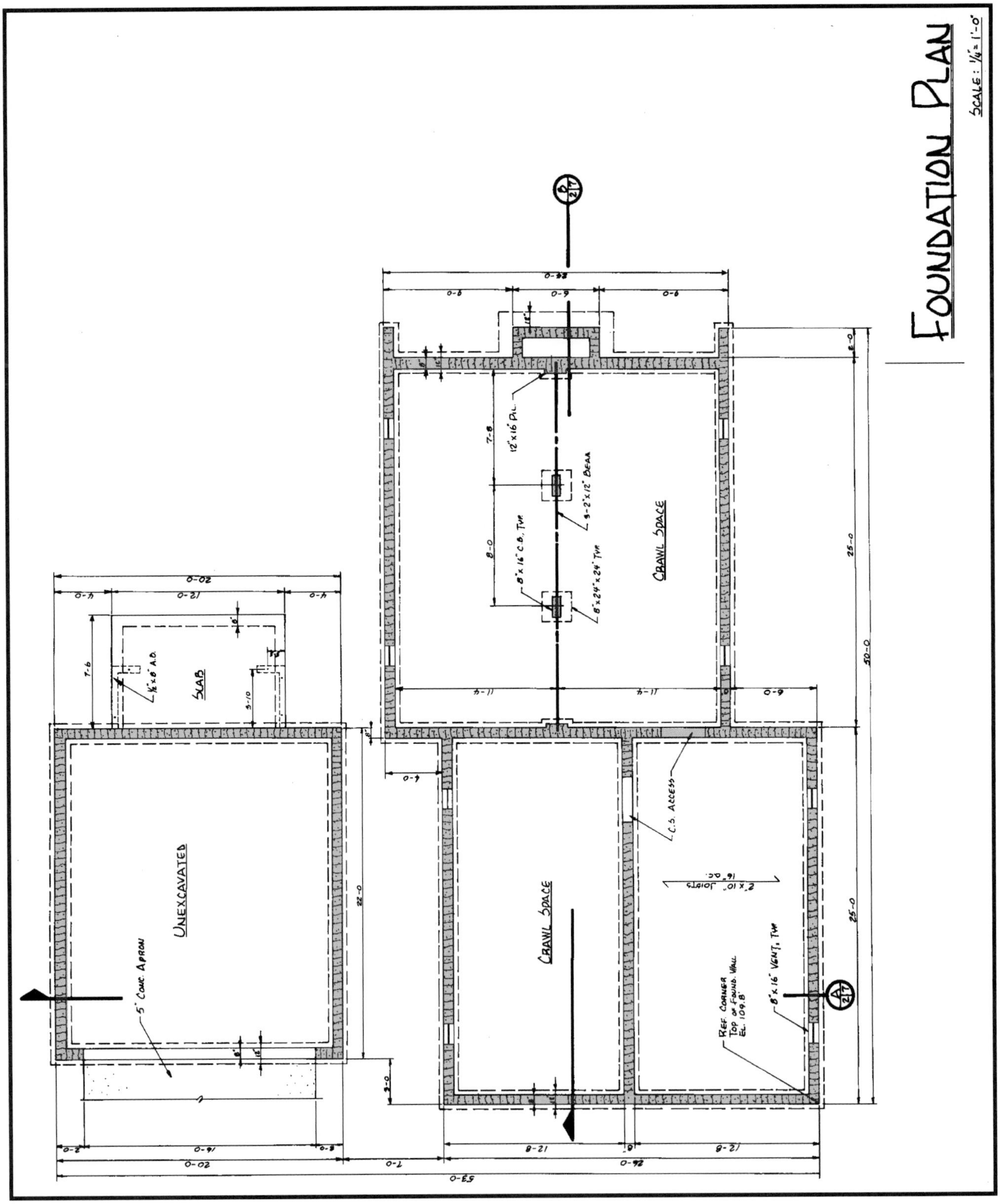

2-8 The foundation/basement plan is used for excavation and construction of the footings and foundation walls.

A foundation and/or basement plan ordinarily includes the following items:

- footings for foundation walls, piers, and columns
- foundation walls
- piers and columns
- dwarf walls (low walls)
- partition walls, doors, and bath fixtures
- furnace, water storage tank, water softener, hot water heater, and so forth
- openings in foundation walls such as windows, doors, and vents
- beams and pilasters
- direction, size, and spacing of floor joists
- drains and sump (in basement)
- details of foundation and footing construction
- grade elevation
- complete dimensions and notes
- scale of the drawing

The foundation plan is prepared mainly for the excavator, masons, and cement workers who build the foundation. Generally, a scale of *¼ in. equals 1 ft.* is used.

The floor plan is the heart of a set of construction drawings and is used by all tradespeople. See 2-9. The **floor plan** is actually a section drawing for each floor of the structure, taken about 4 ft. above the floor. A scale of *¼ in. equals 1 ft.* is used for the drawings. The floor plan generally includes the following items:

- exterior and interior walls
- size and location of windows and doors
- built-in cabinets and appliances
- permanent fixtures
- stairs and fireplaces
- porches, patios, and decks
- room names and approximate sizes
- material symbols
- location and size dimensions
- scale of the drawing

Exterior elevations are drawings that show the finished appearance and height dimensions of one side of a building. Each side of the building requires a separate elevation. See 2-10. The scale for these drawings is usually *¼ in. equals 1 ft.* Most exterior elevations include the following items:

- identification of the specific side of the building that it represents
- grade lines (level of the soil against the building)
- depth of foundation (in hidden lines)
- finished floor and ceiling levels
- location of exterior wall corners
- windows and doors
- roof features and materials
- roof pitch
- chimneys
- deck railings and outside steps
- patios, decks, and porches
- exterior materials
- vertical dimensions of features
- scale of the drawing

The electrical plan is similar to the floor plan in appearance. However, the purpose of the **electrical plan** is to show the locations and types of electrical equipment to be used in the structure. See 2-11. The plan is generally in a scale of *¼ in. equals 1 ft.* Most electrical plans include the following items:

- meter and distribution panel
- electrical outlets
- light fixtures
- switches
- telephone
- doorbell and chimes
- circuit data (optional)
- lighting fixture schedule (optional)
- appliances that use electricity
- home security system
- scale of drawing

Construction details are drawings that provide detailed information to fully describe the construction of special architectural features. See 2-12. Typical details include the following:

- foundation and footing details
- typical wall sections
- truss details
- fireplace and chimney details
- stair details
- kitchen and bathroom details
- window and door details
- flower planters
- decorative screens
- soffit details
- unique construction
- built-in cabinets, bookcases, and so forth

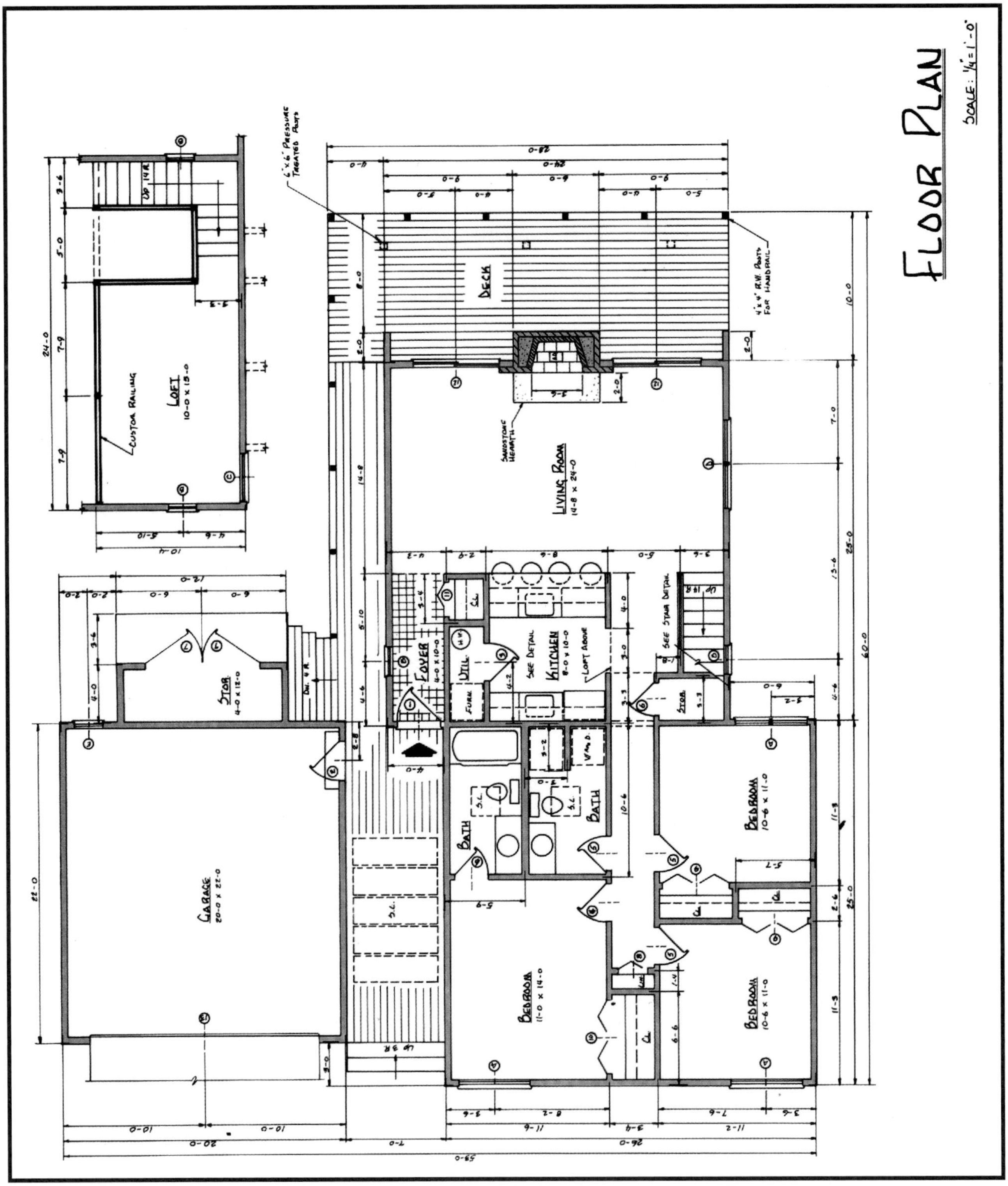

2-9 A floor plan is drawn for each above-grade level of the structure. The floor plan forms the heart of a set of construction drawings.

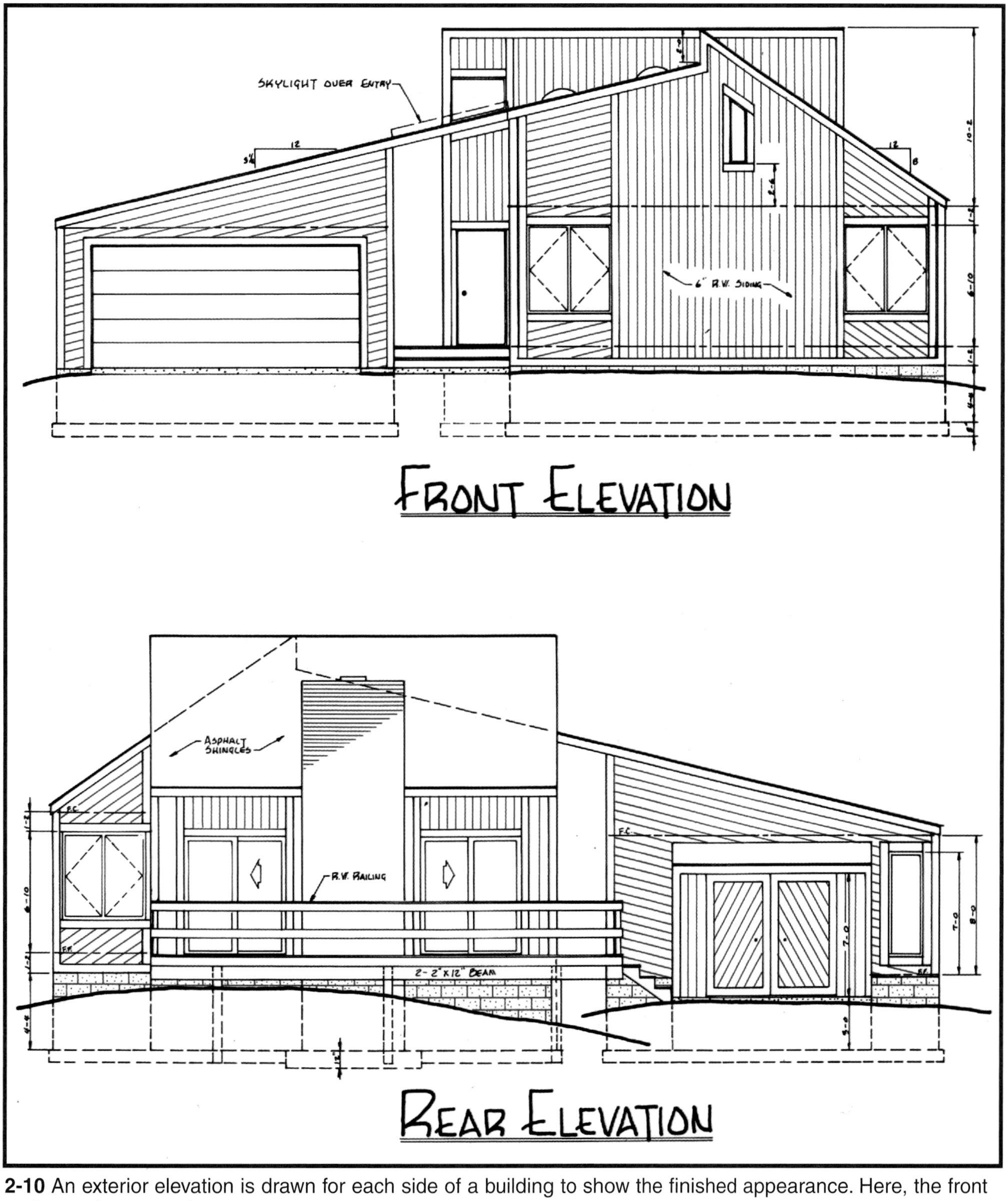

2-10 An exterior elevation is drawn for each side of a building to show the finished appearance. Here, the front and rear views are shown.

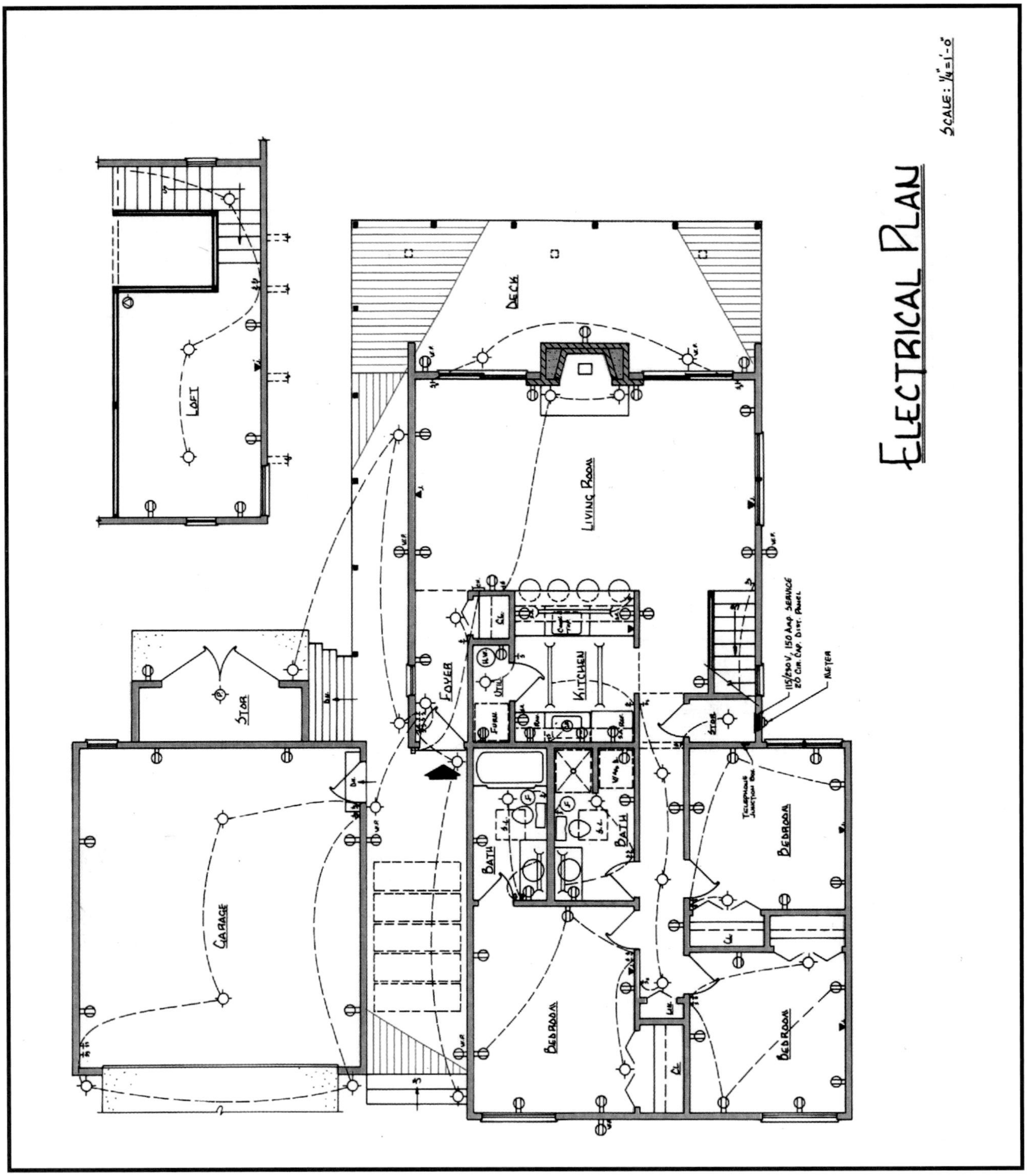

2-11 An electrical plan for each floor of the building is prepared to show the locations and types of electrical equipment to be used.

KITCHEN CABINET SCHEDULE

QUAN.	TYPE	HEIGHT - WIDTH	REMARKS
1	BASE	34½" - 24"	DRAWER BASE
1	BASE	34½" - 36"	
1	BASE	34½" - 36"	SINK BASE
1	BASE	34½" - 36"	SPECIAL FOR COOK TOP
1	WALL	12" - 24"	
1	WALL	12" - 36"	
1	WALL	24" - 24"	PENINSULA STYLE
1	WALL	24" - 36"	
2	WALL	24" - 36"	PENINSULA STYLE

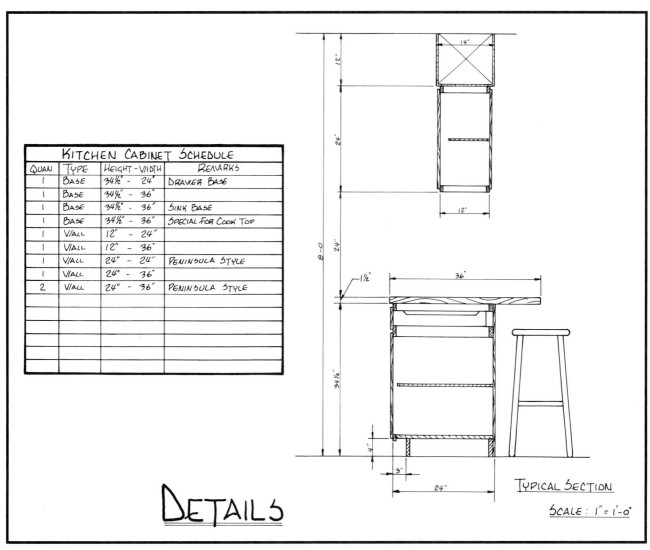

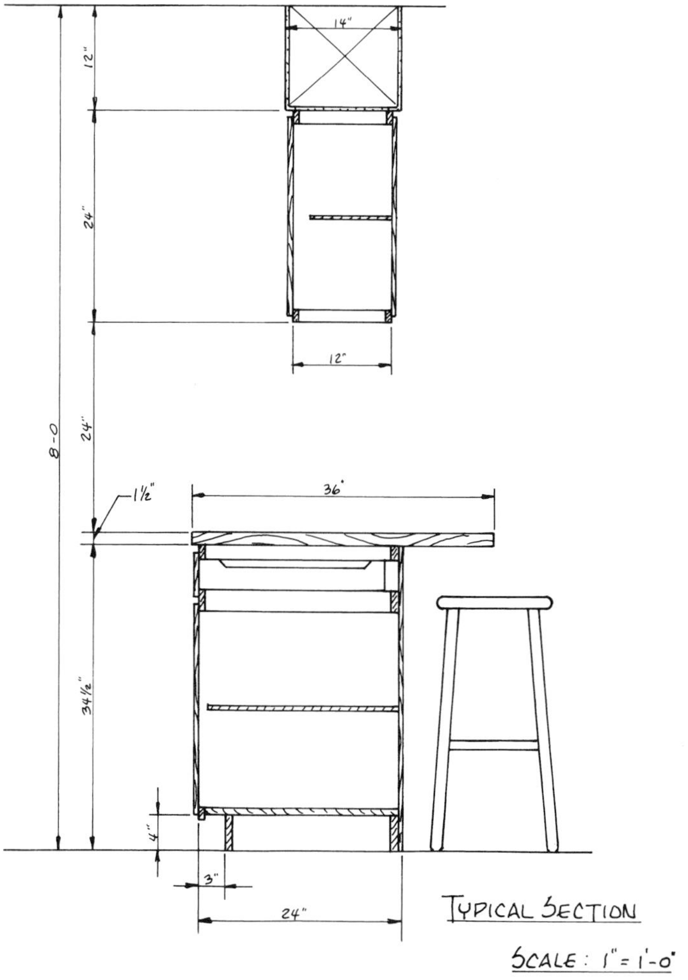

DETAILS

2-12 Several pages of construction details are often required for a typical structure. These details help to fully describe the intent of the designer.

The scale of these drawings is almost always larger than *¼ in. equals 1 ft.* Typically, *½ in., ¾ in., 1 in.,* or *3 in.* are used to represent *1 ft.*

Often included in the package of drawings are **pictorial presentations**. These are realistic renderings, often in color and proper perspective, used to better communicate the finished appearance of a structure. Presentation drawings rendered in color make the drawing more lifelike. These communication devices are intended primarily for those who cannot visualize the completed product from the construction drawings.

Other Drawings

In rare cases, a set of residential construction drawings may include a climate control plan and a plumbing plan. These, however, are more likely to be included in the construction drawings for a larger building such as an apartment or condominium complex.

A **climate control plan** shows the location of the heating, cooling, humidification, dehumidification, and air cleaning equipment. It also shows distribution routes and the means of transmitting the conditioned air to the various rooms.

A **plumbing plan** shows the freshwater supply lines to the water storage tank or house main as well as wastewater lines, water conditioning equipment, and plumbing fixtures. Such fixtures include sinks, water closets, showers, and tubs.

Construction drawings are very useful. Often, problems during the building process are avoided because they are solved on paper before the building begins. (For related information, see A-1 through A-6 of the Appendix.)

Chapter Summary

The area or space in a dwelling is represented by a floor plan. The way to begin evaluating the plan is to make a list of the needs and wants of those who will occupy the space. This is a very personal step that, if done well, will result in highly effective housing for the home's occupants.

A major consideration in evaluating the arrangement of space in a specific floor plan includes plotting the four basic types of circulation routes. Analyzing circulation frequency further defines the efficiency of the plan for a given household.

The size, shape, and relationship of one room to another largely determine the satisfaction that household members receive from their living space. Other factors include usable space, privacy, and accessibility.

A typical set of house plans generally includes at least seven basic types of drawings. Each contains specific information that is necessary to provide a complete picture of the new structure to everyone involved with it.

Review Questions

1. How does circulation frequency affect the type of path allowed for circulation?
2. What are the four basic types of circulation?
3. What principles should a good family circulation pattern follow?
4. Why is it important for work areas to be small and free of cross-traffic?
5. For the most efficient service-circulation pattern, where should a service entrance be located?
6. What parts of the house are involved in guest circulation?
7. What features may cause a large room to have a greatly reduced amount of usable space?
8. What rooms should be placed adjacent to the kitchen? far from the kitchen?
9. What specific drawings are included in a typical set of house plans?
10. If information in a house's floor plan conflicts with its specifications, which is considered correct?

Suggested Activities

1. Interview everyone in your household who is school age or older to record each member's needs and wants in terms of housing. Their needs might include items such as rooms, storage, furniture, and appliances. Their wants might include items such as a study, fireplace, patio, or room for table tennis. Prepare a chart that displays all the interview comments and identifies those points on which two or more members agree.
2. Sketch a floor plan of your residence and, using different colored pencils, shade the living, sleeping, and service areas. Study the efficiency of the plan and make recommendations for improving the arrangement.
3. Reuse the floor plan prepared for Item 2 or sketch a floor plan of your residence. Map the circulation routes using different colored pencils to distinguish the four types.
4. Find a floor plan in a newspaper or magazine and analyze the functionality of its room arrangement. List the strengths and weaknesses of the plan in terms of the principles covered in this chapter.
5. Secure a set of residential construction drawings or use a set provided by your instructor. Identify the features shown on the plot plan, foundation/basement plan, floor plan, exterior elevations, electrical plan, and construction details.
6. Collect several different types of housing presentation plans from the Internet, magazines, or other sources. Explain to the class the purpose of each.

Internet Resources

American Institute of Architects
aia.org

Architectural Digest Magazine
archdigest.com

Better Homes and Gardens Magazine
bhg.com

Design Basics, Inc., a home design service
designbasics.com

SoftPlan Systems, Inc. residential design program
softplan.com

Studer Residential Designs
studerdesigns.com

The McGraw-Hill Companies, Inc. construction products marketplace
sweets.com

The Sater Design Collection, Inc.
saterdesign.com

Note: Web addresses may have changed since publication. For some entries, reaching the correct Web site may require keying *www.* into the address.

Chapter 3
Planning Living Areas

Objectives

After studying this chapter, you will be able to

- list the rooms and activities involved in the living areas of a house.
- judge the appropriateness of a living room for a family according to its location, size, and arrangement.
- identify a dining room that meets the size and location needs of a specific family.
- determine the appropriateness of a family room's location, size, and arrangement for a family.
- recognize various types of entryways according to purpose and location.
- list possible uses and styles of patios, porches, and courts.
- identify living-area requirements for individuals with special needs.

Key Terms

living areas
closed plan
open plan
main entry
foyer
special-purpose entry
patio
grade level
porch
deck
court

The living areas of a home serve two groups of people: household members and guests. **Living areas** are places in the home for family members to relax, entertain guests, dine, and meet together. They are areas devoted to conversation, meals, company, recreation, and hobbies, such as the living room, dining room, family room. Several more "rooms" constitute the living areas of a home, including the entryway, foyer, patio, and porch, 3-1.

California Redwood Association

3-1 This private porch provides a pleasant area for relaxing and entertaining guests.

Rooms used for specialized activities are considered part of the living area. Such special rooms may include a study den, library, music room, and special hobby room. The number and types of rooms in living areas are determined by household size, lifestyle, and budget.

Living Rooms

The center of activity for many households is the living room. It may be used as a conversation area, TV room, or place to entertain guests, depending on the specific occasion. Reading, listening to music, playing indoor games, and pursuing hobbies are some of the other activities that may take place in the living room. The lifestyle of the household helps to determine the living room's location, size, arrangement, and functions.

Location

The living room in a newly built home is often located in the front or back of the home, depending on individual preference and the building site. If some parts of the building site are visually more pleasing than others, you may want to locate the living room so it overlooks the best view.

The location of the living room refers not only to the room's location on the building site, but also to its relation to the main entry and other rooms in the home. A living room should not serve as a main circulation route into and through the home. To avoid traffic directly into the living room, have the main entry open into a foyer or hallway, 3-2. A change in floor level can also help set the living room apart and eliminate heavy traffic through it.

Since entertaining and dining are two activities that often go together, the living room should be located near or adjacent to the dining room. A combined living room and dining room is sometimes planned to serve both entertaining and dining purposes. A screen, flower planter, dwarf wall, furniture arrangement, or fireplace can be used to separate the two areas. A change in floor levels can also set apart the two rooms.

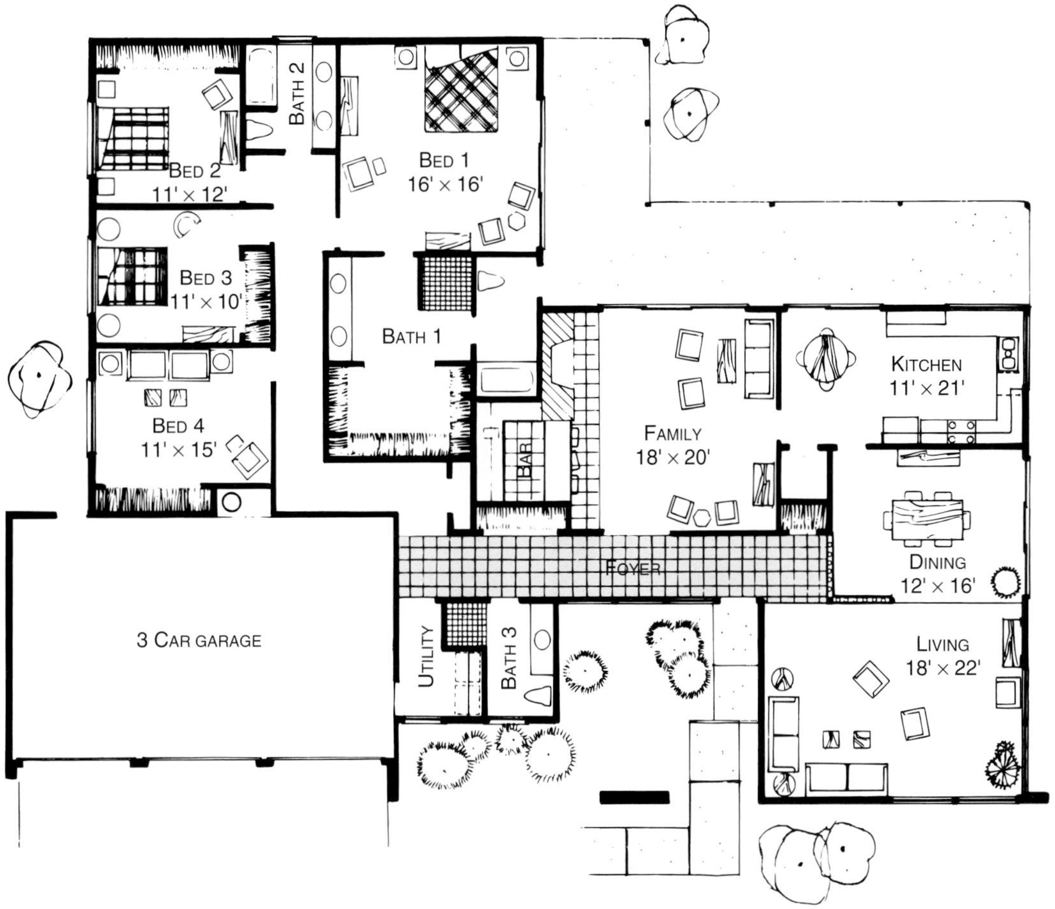

3-2 A foyer at the main entry prevents constant traffic through the living room.

Another factor to consider in the location of the living room is noise. The living room should be located so noise from the kitchen does not interfere with quiet activities in the living room. On the other hand, the living room should be located away from bedrooms so living room activities will not disturb family members using the sleeping area.

Size and Arrangement

Living rooms are designed in a variety of sizes and shapes. The ideal size of a living room is determined by the number of people who will use it, how and when it will be used, the furniture intended, and the size of the other rooms. Another factor that may influence the ideal size of a living room is the presence of an adjacent patio, porch, deck, or balcony. This added space can make a room appear more open and extend the use of the room.

Every living room requires an area for conversation. The dominant furniture grouping in the living room is called the *primary conversation area*, 3-3. This area occupies a circular shape, 8 to 10 ft. in diameter.

To accommodate an 8 to 10 ft. conversation circle, a living room needs to be 10 to 14 ft. wide. Living room widths greater than 14 ft. can be difficult to decorate. The solution is to use the extra space for circulation along one side of the room or for a secondary furniture grouping, 3-4. A *secondary furniture grouping* may consist of a small conversation area that seats two or three people. On the other hand, it may contain a piano, desk, or reading chair for one person, 3-5. (For common sizes of living room furniture, see A-7 of the Appendix.)

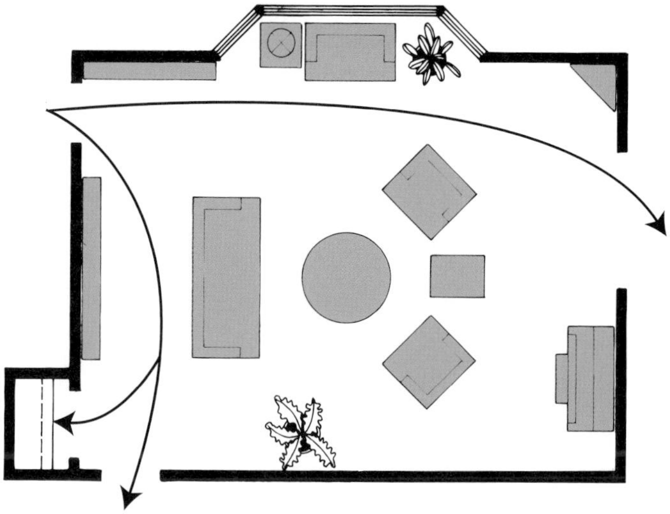

3-4 To accommodate circulation and a secondary furniture grouping, a living room width greater than 14 ft. is generally needed.

WCI Communities, Inc.

3-3 The seating in this living room defines the primary conversation area.

The ideal living room space allows enough area for the desired number of conversation circles and traffic. A length of 16 to 18 ft. is sufficient for a seated conversation area. A living room 18 to 22 ft. long can easily accommodate a primary conversation area and a secondary furniture grouping. Both examples allow enough space for people to move around easily.

A well-planned living room avoids circulation across conversation areas. Circulation problems can be avoided by strategically locating entrances. For example, in 3-6, two doorways are located at one end of the room, and the other doorway is located in the middle of the opposite wall. This causes circulation to pass across the living room, interfering with conversation and/or television viewing. In 3-7, the doorways are located at one end of the room so circulation passes along the unoccupied side.

If a living room has a fireplace, it should be located within view of the people seated in the conversation circle, 3-8. There should be no traffic between the fireplace and conversation circle.

Dining Rooms

Many homes built today provide at least two dining areas: an informal area in the kitchen and a more formal one in the dining room. Having a room set aside

3-5 This secondary furniture grouping allows an area for games away from the main conversation circle.

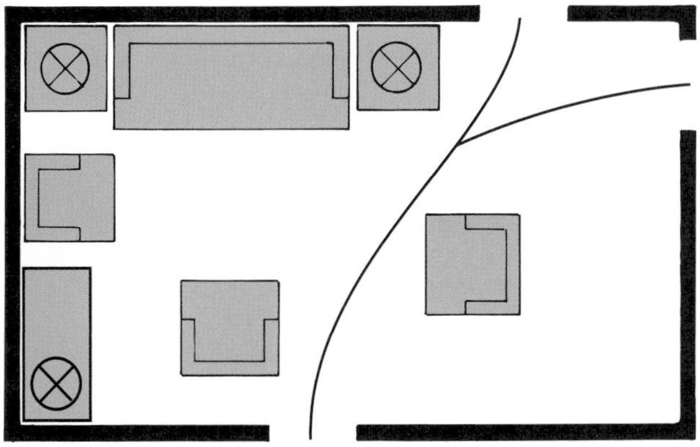

3-6 Poorly placed doors make it difficult to arrange a good conversation circle, one that is not interrupted by a circulation path.

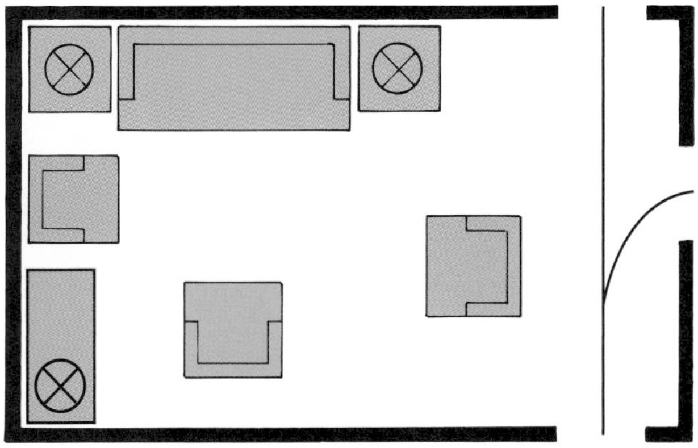

3-7 Well-placed living room entrances allow a direct circulation path that does not interfere with the conversation circle.

for dining is both functional and relaxing for many households. The decision to plan a separate dining room depends on the lifestyle of household members.

The primary purpose of a dining room is to set aside a place for eating, but it may serve other purposes. A dining room may be used to display a household member's special interest, such as a collection of unusual seashells or beautiful houseplants. Such displays make interesting topics for dinner conversation.

Manufactured Housing Institute

3-8 A fireplace can become the focal point of a conversation circle.

There are two basic types of space design plans that apply to dining rooms—closed and open. In a **closed plan**, rooms in the living area are basically cubicles that permit little sharing of activities between rooms. The dining room in a closed plan is set apart from the living room or kitchen.

In an **open plan**, rooms in the living area use minimal walls to encourage a sharing of activities across the space. The rooms are not closed off from each other. The dining area in an open plan is an extension of the living room or kitchen, 3-9. A home tends to appear more spacious with an open plan because there are fewer walls to divide the space.

Location

The dining room needs to be near the kitchen to permit the movement of food at serving time. It should also be near the living room so guests can move easily to the dining room. Therefore, an ideal location for the dining room is between the living room and kitchen. See 3-10.

Size and Arrangement

The ideal size for a dining room is determined by the number of people to be served at one time, the furniture intended, and the amount of space needed for circulation.

The minimum-size dining area for four people is 80 sq. ft. A dining room averaging 120 sq. ft. can comfortably seat four people and provide space for a buffet. A dining room measuring 180 sq. ft. seats four to eight people and has space for a hutch and a buffet, 3-11. A dining room over 200 sq. ft. is considered very large, with room for several pieces of furniture.

WCI Communities, Inc.

3-9 The open dining room plan gives a home a more spacious appearance.

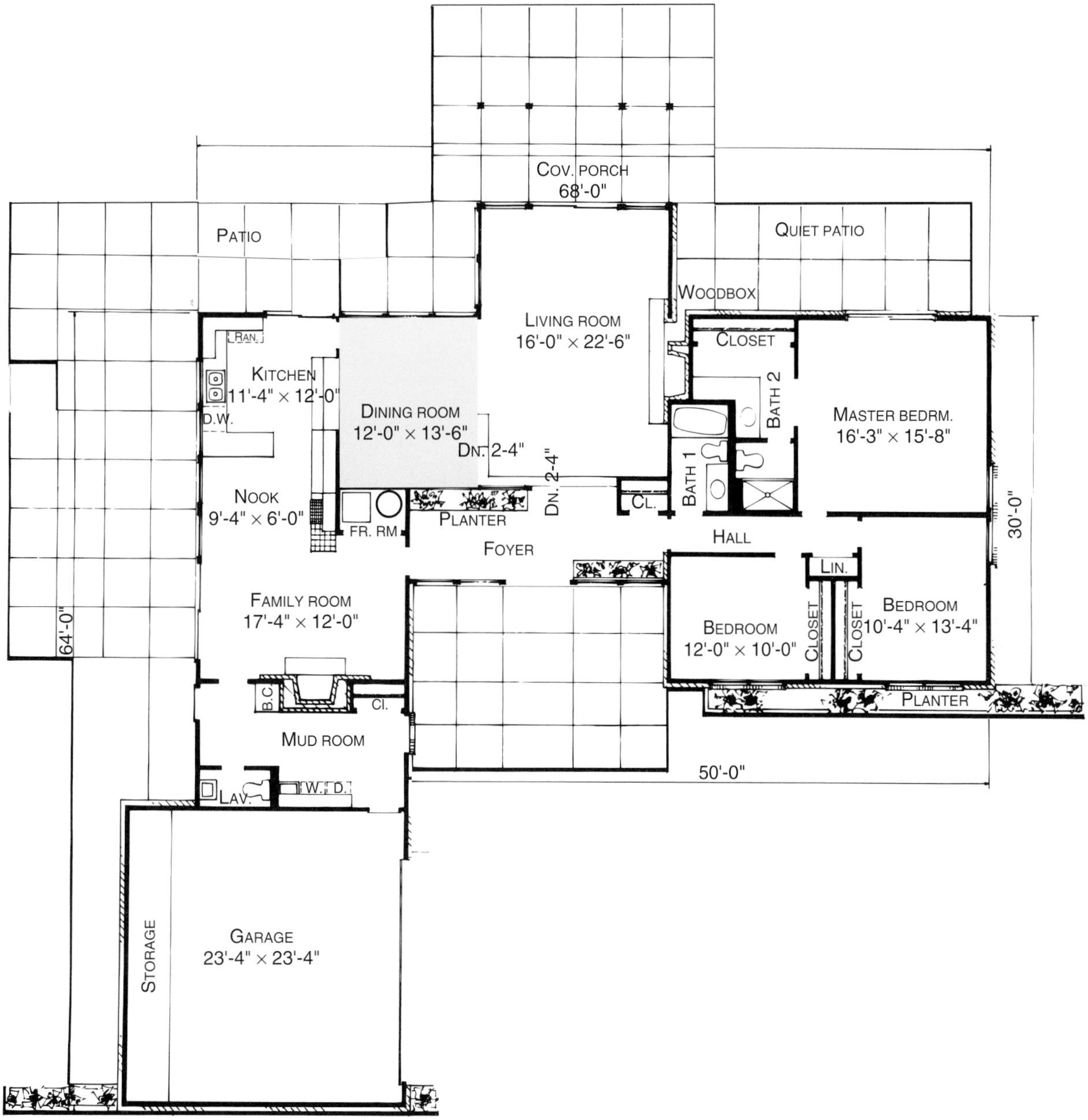

3-10 In this floor plan, the dining room is conveniently located between the living room and kitchen.

The basic pieces of dining room furniture are a table and chairs. The household size, number of guests, and size of the dining space are the factors that determine the size and shape of the table. Approximately 2 ft. of table length should be allowed for each seated person. A rectangular table measuring 3½ by 5½ ft. seats four to six people.

The required space for dining room chairs varies with chair sizes and styles. Large chairs and armchairs require more space. To easily move into and out of average-size chairs, there should be at least 32 in. of space between the table edge and the wall, buffet, or hutch behind. More space, about 36 to 44 in., allows enough space for walking around seated guests to serve food. See 3-12.

Other possible furniture pieces in the dining room are buffets, hutches, corner cabinets, and serving carts. They provide space for food and storage. Serving carts move wherever needed and take very little floor and wall space.

Family Rooms

Many households need space for action-oriented pursuits. Having a family room in addition to a living room makes possible the separation of

3-11 This medium-size dining room has ample space for a large dining room table, hutch, and buffet.

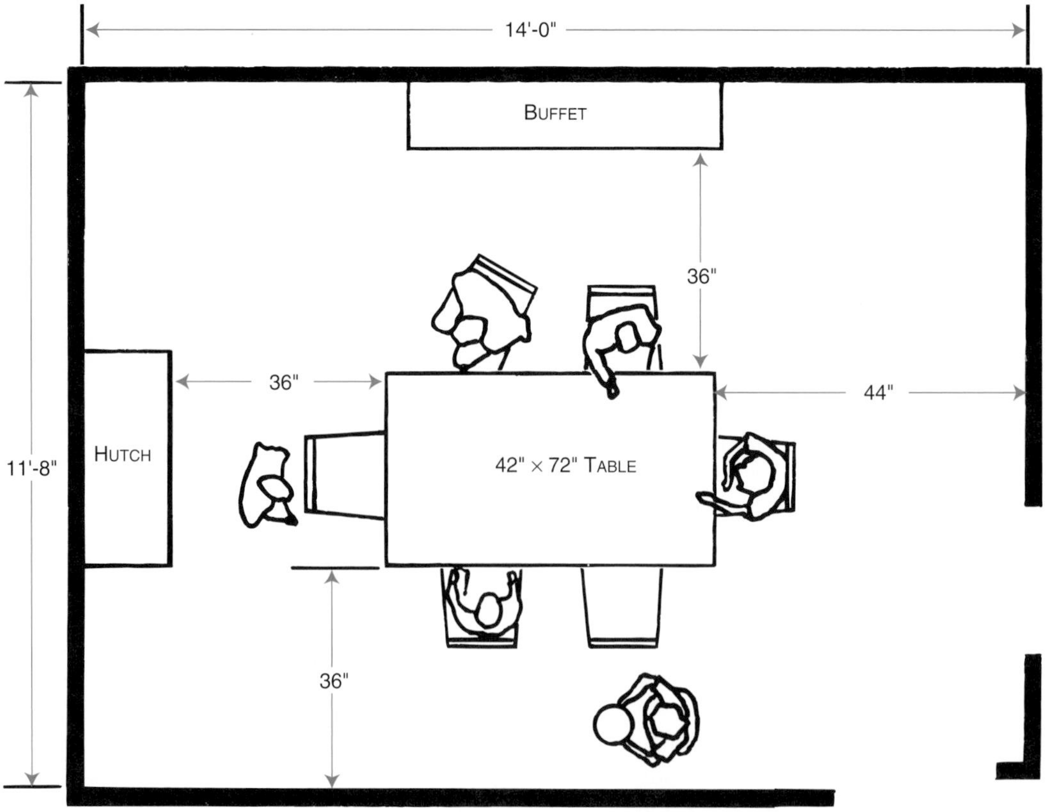

3-12 Ample clearance space for seating and service should be allowed around a dining room table.

active and passive activities. The living room can be used for conversation, reading, studying, listening, and TV viewing, while the family room can be the center for games, hobbies, dancing, exercising, and active play. Family rooms are distinguished from living rooms by informal decor and durable, easily maintained furniture.

Family rooms are also called great rooms, media rooms, playrooms, recreation rooms, and multipurpose rooms. See 3-13. With families increasingly interested in making their homes a refuge as well as a place for fun and entertainment, the size of family rooms is progressively increasing. In fact, family rooms are replacing living rooms altogether in some homes. In such cases, the family room is located centrally and often opens to the kitchen, allowing those working in the kitchen to communicate easily with the rest of the family. A centralized family room also facilitates the casual style of entertaining that is common today; it permits guests to socialize and participate in the food preparation together.

Location

No set rules exist for the location of family rooms. In some homes, the family room is separated from the rest of the home. For example, many basements and

Sauder Woodworking Co.

3-13 The family room may be used for special activities, such as hobbies or crafts. Family rooms generally have more casual furnishings than living rooms.

attics are converted into family rooms. Basements are often good locations for family rooms because they are usually large enough for a variety of activities. Basements also tend to contain noise well.

Family rooms can also be placed to provide an extension to living or service areas. For example, locating the family room near the living room provides overflow space. Locating the family room by the kitchen allows those preparing meals to share in family room activities. In some homes, the family room is combined with the kitchen and is called a *great room*. See 3-14. A family room may also be located near a pool or outdoor recreation area. This provides a convenient arrangement for entertaining outdoors while providing accommodations close to the outdoor activities for guests who prefer being indoors.

Size and Arrangement

The ideal size for a family room depends on the activities planned for it and the number of people who will use it. A minimum space of 12 by 16 ft. is recommended.

An important consideration for family rooms is storage, which is definitely needed for the many items that are used there. Storage units can be arranged to form a room divider that separates an activity area from the remainder of the room.

3-14 In homes with an open design plan, the family room is often an extension of the kitchen.

Furniture for family rooms should be comfortable as well as durable and serviceable. A sturdy table with comfortable chairs could serve as an area for game playing, dining, or a variety of hobbies.

Floors, too, need to be durable, easy to clean, and suitable for activities. If noise or warmth is a consideration, carpeting may be practical.

Entryways

Entryways control circulation to different parts of a home. From the entryway, people should be able to move to other parts of the home without interfering with activities in any area. Careful planning of entryways adds to the convenience and comfort that a family derives from the home. There are three basic types of entryways: main or guest entries, special-purpose entries, and service entries. (Service entries are discussed in Chapter 5, "Planning Service and Work Areas.")

The **main entry** opens to the living area of the house, often a foyer. It is the part of the home that most guests see first. An attractive main entry welcomes guests into a home and makes a good first impression.

To establish better circulation patterns inside a home, the main entry is usually located near the center of the dwelling. The floor plan in 3-15 shows how a well-located main entry provides access to various areas of a home.

A main entry that opens into a foyer is preferred over one that opens directly into a living room. A **foyer** is an entry hall that functions as a place to greet guests and, in colder climates, remove coats and boots, 3-16. The foyer lends privacy to the visitor and household.

The size of the dwelling and the number of people using the entry determine the space it needs. The minimum space required for one person to fully open a door is 3 by 5 ft., but 5 by 7 ft. is more convenient and comfortable. The minimum foyer size is 6 ft. square, not including closet space.

An entry closet is convenient for storing coats, hats, gloves, umbrellas, and other outdoor accessories. The minimum closet size is 2 by 3 ft., but a closet that is 2½ ft. deep and 4 ft. wide is more desirable. For convenience and easy access, the closet should be located 4 to 5 ft. from the doorknob side of the door, not directly behind the door.

The floor at the entry of the house should be durable, water- and soil-resistant, and easy to clean. Slate, ceramic tile, asphalt tile, and vinyl floor

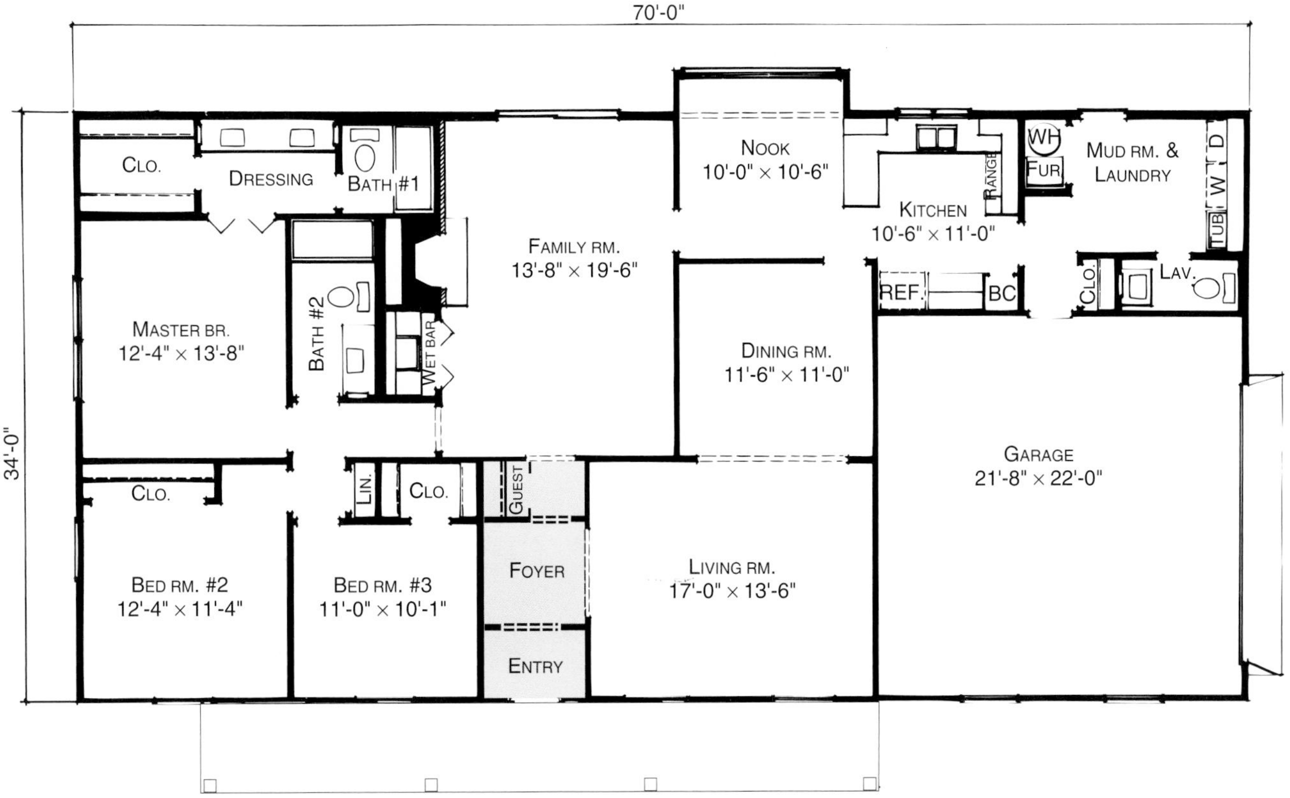

3-15 A centrally located main entry helps to establish good circulation patterns throughout a house.

Therma-Tru Corporation

3-16 The main entry opens into a foyer that provides ample space for greeting visitors.

coverings are popular and durable floor treatments. If carpeting is used, select a tight weave that is easy to vacuum. A doormat outside the door for cleaning shoes and boots reduces the amount of dirt carried indoors.

A **special-purpose entry** provides access to patios, decks, and courts. See 3-17. Sliding glass doors and French doors are often used for this type of entry. Special-purpose entries extend the use of the room to outdoor areas and make the room appear more spacious. Since these entries are infrequently used, usually by just one person at a time, less clearance space may be needed.

Patios, Porches, and Courts

Patios, porches, and courts extend the living areas of a home to the outdoors. They may be used for conversation, relaxing, playing, entertaining, dining, and cooking. The intended purpose of the space and the size of the home determine the design, size, and location of patios, porches, and courts.

States Industries Inc.

3-17 A special-purpose entry may provide access to a private garden or patio.

Patios

A **patio** is an outdoor extension of a home's living area usually built at grade level, but not structurally connected to the house. **Grade level** is the level of the land surrounding the building. Patio materials should be durable and maintenance free. Brick, concrete, stone, and redwood are among the materials often used, 3-18. Patios can be categorized by function as play, living, and quiet patios.

- *Play patios* are usually located adjacent to a family room or service area to provide an area for play activities.
- *Living patios* are located near the living areas of the home: the living room, dining room, and family room.
- *Quiet patios* are located on the quiet side of the dwelling, near the bedrooms. They are used for relaxing, reading, and even sleeping.

If the patio will be used for dining, access to the kitchen or dining room is necessary, 3-19. The living patio is usually the largest of the three types of patios and may be connected to, or serve as, a play patio as well.

Patios vary in size and shape. The size of the patio is determined by the activities planned for the area, the equipment and furnishings needed, and the size of the home. When an in-ground pool is designed for a home, it becomes an extension of the patio, 3-20.

Marvin Windows and Doors

3-18 This brick patio is very durable and maintenance free.

Brown Jordan Co.

3-19 A patio adjacent to the kitchen is convenient for outdoor dining.

3-20 A pool can be the center of activity for a patio.

3-22 A veranda is generally located one story above the ground.

The view as well as exposure to the sun should be considered in the design and planning of a patio. In cool climates, the sun is a desirable factor so the patio should be placed on the south side of the home. In warm climates, shade is preferred. Consequently, the patio should be placed on the north side of the dwelling.

Porches

Like patios, porches vary in shape, size, and purpose. A **porch** is an outdoor extension of a home's living area that is structurally connected to the house, built above grade level, and covered by a roof. See 3-21. An uncovered porch is called a **deck**. Porches built high off the ground are called *verandas* or balconies, 3-22. Screens, glass, or railings enclose some porches.

Porches are often located in front of the main entrance to provide shelter for guests and protection for the entry. A dining porch can be located off the kitchen or dining room.

The shape and size of a porch should fit the design of the dwelling. The lines and proportions of

3-21 The porch on this traditional home is a central design feature.

the porch should complement the lines of the house. A porch planned with the overall design of the house in mind appears as part of the house rather than a "tacked-on" addition.

Courts

Courts were an important part of early Spanish architecture and are still designed for homes today. A **court** is a patio-like structure that is partially or completely enclosed by walls. Courts are used for the same purposes as patios and porches: relaxing, entertaining, and dining. Courts are more prevalent in warm climates where heating is not a major consideration.

Adaptations for Special Needs

Attention to certain details can make the living area of the house accessible to everyone in the household, including small children, the elderly, and individuals with physical disabilities.

Living and Family Rooms

Placing the living areas at grade level enables people who use wheelchairs, crutches, walkers, or braces to easily move indoors, outdoors, and throughout the living space. Clearances at least 4 to 5 ft. wide should be allowed around furniture to permit turnaround space for a wheelchair, 3-23. Seats and cushions should be firm to provide the support needed by individuals in wheelchairs to transfer easily to a sofa or chair. Power-operated, elevating chairs are available to raise and tilt the seat forward, which helps people with weak leg muscles to a standing position.

Dining Rooms

Clearance for wheelchair armrests and sufficient leg space are the two primary conditions for making a dining room accessible to disabled family members and guests. Tables with widely spaced legs or pedestal supports provide the open legroom needed. A space at least 32 in. wide is necessary for guiding a wheelchair between furniture pieces or around furniture near walls.

In frequently used dining areas, flooring should be durable to withstand daily wear. Nonslip, hard-surface floors or low-pile carpeting are good choices for areas used by children, the elderly, or disabled individuals.

Entryways and Foyers

Entryways and foyers large enough to permit the door to open fully are needed to comfortably accommodate people with disabilities who use a wheelchair, crutches, or another aid. There should be 12 to 18 in. of space on the doorknob side of the entry and foyer to allow maneuvering room for the aids. Doors with lever handles instead of knobs are easier for everyone to open.

In wheelchair-accessible homes, the entry door should be at least 34 in. wide. This provides space for the wheelchair plus enough room for a person's arms to turn the wheels.

Patios, Porches, and Courts

Stairs present an insurmountable challenge to most physically disabled individuals. Consequently, elevated patios, porches, and courts are off-limits to them unless a gently sloping ramp provides access to the area. A ramp with a slope between 1:12 and 1:20 should be planned.

3-23 Allowing living and dining spaces to flow together in an open arrangement suits today's casual lifestyle and provides maneuvering space for a family member with a wheelchair or walker.

Chapter Summary

The living areas of a home serve two groups of people: household members and guests. The center of activity for many households is the living room, where family members enjoy TV, conversation, and entertaining guests. The location, size, and arrangement of the living room should accommodate the lifestyle of the household members. Dining areas can be formal or informal, and many homes have both. The size of the living and dining rooms should be large enough to comfortably seat everyone that uses them.

Family rooms allow action-oriented pursuits and can be used for dancing, hobbies, music, or games. A family room should be located away from the quiet area of the home. Size and arrangement should be considered for maximum usefulness.

Main entryways and foyers control circulation to other parts of the house. The design considerations for these areas include size, location, floor coverings, decor, and enough storage for coats and boots. Other types of entries provide access to patios, decks, terraces, or porches that extend the home's living space outdoors. Attention to certain details can make the entire living area accessible to all household members and guests.

Review Questions

1. What activities take place in the living areas of a home?
2. What rooms are included in a home's living areas?
3. How can circulation through a living room be minimized?
4. What items are usually placed in a secondary furniture grouping?
5. Why is it desirable to place the living room door(s) at one end of the room?
6. Should a closed or open plan be used for a dining room in a small home? Explain.
7. What is the ideal location for a dining room in a house?
8. What minimum size is recommended for a dining room for a family of three? of six?
9. What locations in a home are good for a family room?
10. What type of furniture is appropriate for a family room?
11. Where should the main entry of a house be located? Explain.
12. Which side of the house is the best location for a porch or patio in Texas? in Minnesota?
13. How much space is needed around furniture for wheelchairs to maneuver?
14. What types of flooring are recommended in dining rooms used by children or disabled or elderly members?

Suggested Activities

1. Using available sources, collect photos of rooms commonly associated with the living area of a residence. Be sure to identify the room or area that is represented in each photo.
2. Sketch an ideal living room for your family, and indicate how adjacent rooms connect to it. Explain the features, size, and arrangement of items you would plan for this room.
3. Create a floor plan for a dining room that will seat eight people and hold a china cabinet and buffet or hutch.
4. Plan a family or recreation room that allows family members to pursue their favorite individual and group hobbies. Identify the room's dimensions, furniture pieces, and other equipment.
5. List the considerations to make before designing a main entryway. Explain why each consideration is important.
6. Collect photos of patios, porches, and courts that you feel are attractive, functional, safe, and easy to maintain. Display them to the class.
7. Interview a person who has a physical disability to learn what types of housing features cause the greatest barriers to living independently in their homes.

Internet Resources

Architectural Digest Magazine
archdigest.com

Armstrong World Industries, Inc.
armstrong.com

HomeCrest Cabinetry
homecrestcab.com

James Hardie® Building Products, Inc.
jameshardie.com

Marvin Windows and Doors
marvin.com

National Gypsum Company
nationalgypsum.com

Owens Corning
owenscorning.com

Schulte Corporation, a manufacturer of storage solutions
schultestorage.com

Note: Web addresses may have changed since publication. For some entries, reaching the correct Web site may require keying *www.* into the address.

Chapter 4
Planning Sleeping Areas

Objectives

After studying this chapter, you will be able to

- describe the two main types of bedroom plans.
- recognize a well-designed bedroom.
- arrange bedroom furniture in a style that is attractive and functional.
- list the three main types of bathrooms and the fixtures they include.
- recognize the need for special features in the bathroom due to heat and moisture.
- identify sleeping-area requirements for individuals with special needs.

Key Terms

sleeping area
group plan
split-bedroom plan
ribbon windows
water closet
lavatory
half bath
three-quarters bath
full bath
ground fault circuit interrupter (GFCI)

All individuals, at times, require privacy. The purpose of the sleeping area of a home is to provide privacy for such activities as sleeping, bathing, and dressing. Bedrooms, bathrooms, dressing rooms, and nurseries constitute the **sleeping area**. For peace and quiet, these rooms need to be located away from circulation and noise.

Bedrooms

The number, sexes, and ages of family members determine the number and size of bedrooms needed. If possible, each individual should have his or her own bedroom or personal space within a bedroom. Each person requires sleeping space, storage space for clothes and personal items, and dressing space. Playing, studying, relaxing, and other activities may also need space. See 4-1.

Thomasville Furniture Industries, Inc.

4-1 This bedroom provides enough space for activities and storage in addition to sleep.

Location

Bedrooms may be located anywhere in the home as long as each bedroom has privacy of sight and sound. Bedrooms are usually grouped according to one of two plans. One plan, called the **group plan**, clusters all bedrooms in one area of the home, 4-2. The other plan, called the **split-bedroom plan**, separates the master bedroom from the remaining bedrooms to provide greater privacy, 4-3. A bedroom for overnight guests, live-in relatives, or employees may also be segregated from the remaining bedrooms.

A room that could be used as a bedroom should be considered for the first floor of a two-story home. Such a room would be convenient when caring for a sick or elderly person.

Another factor related to the location of bedrooms is accessibility. Ideally, each bedroom should open from a hallway instead of directly from another room. A person should not have to pass through one bedroom to reach another. Also, each bedroom should have its own bath or be located close to one.

Size and Arrangement

The size of a bedroom depends on the number of occupants, their ages, the intended functions of the room besides sleeping and dressing, and the necessary furniture. The more people sharing the room, the more activities will be performed in it. Likewise, the bigger the furniture, the larger the bedroom will need to be.

When arranging furniture in a bedroom, placing the bed is the first consideration since it usually is the largest and most-used piece. Allow 22 in. of space on three sides for room to make the bed from both sides. The exception is a twin bed, which can

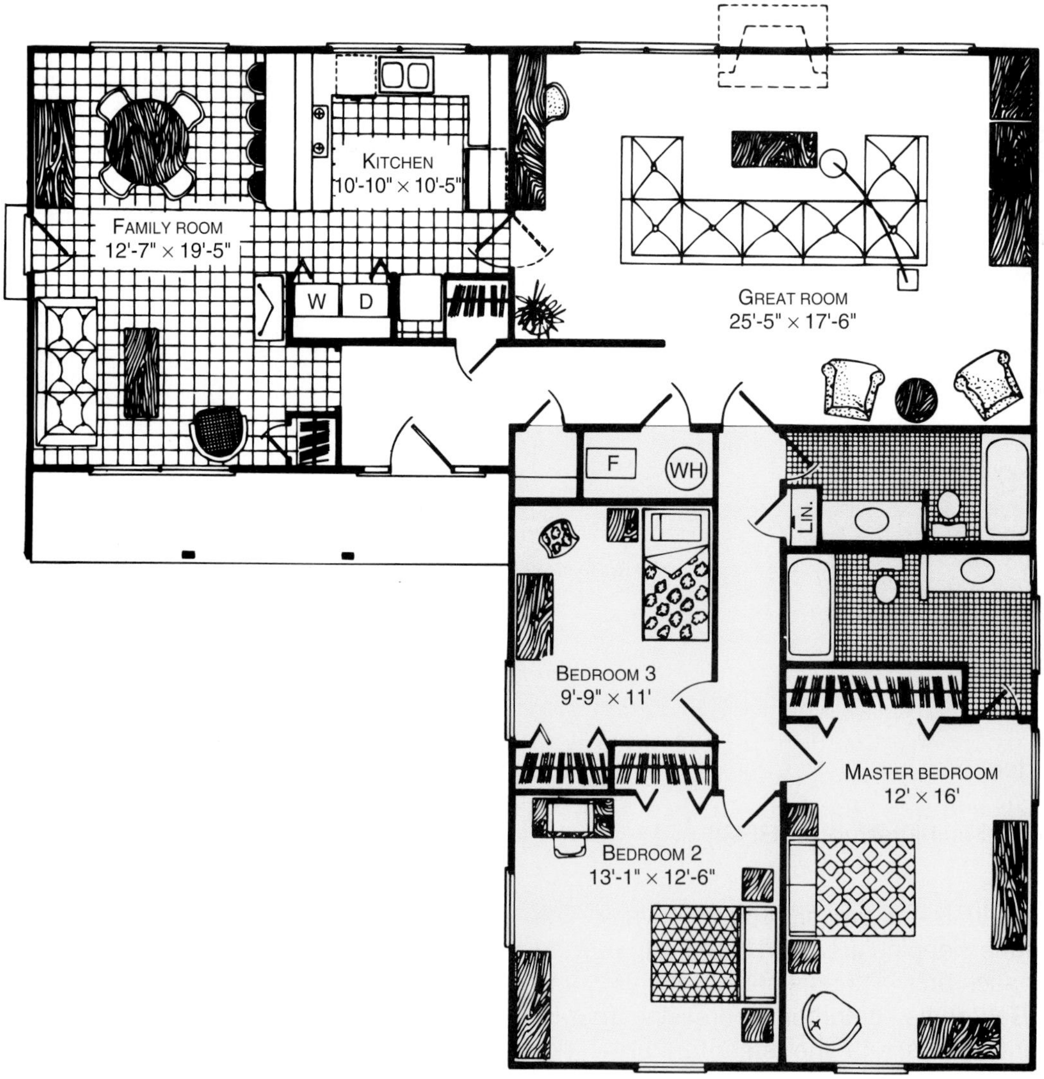

4-2 Bedrooms can be grouped together to form a compact sleeping area away from the noisier living and service areas.

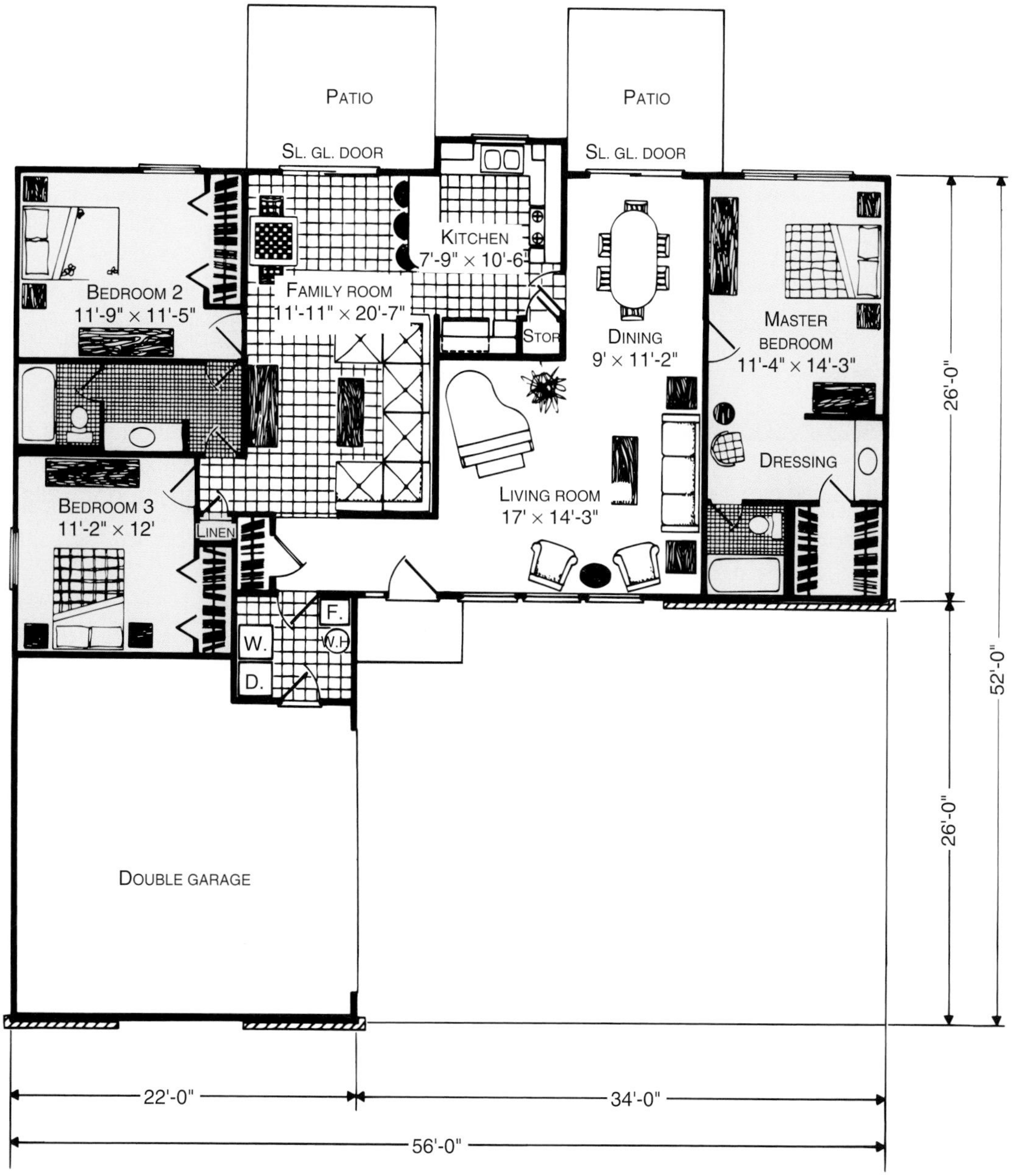

4-3 In the split-bedroom plan, the master bedroom is separated from the other bedrooms. This arrangement is desirable for many families.

be made from one side. Then, only a 6 in. clearance is needed next to the wall to allow the bedspread to drape over the side. The amount of space recommended between twin beds is 22 in.

Consider windows when positioning the bed. Early morning sun should not shine directly on the bed. Ventilation should be possible without causing a draft across the bed.

When arranging the bed and other furniture, consider circulation into the bedroom. Neither the bed nor the other pieces of furniture should interfere with circulation into the room and to the closet.

Guidelines for furniture arrangement and clearance space make bedrooms more convenient and functional. Bedside tables should be the same height as the bed's mattress. Lamps on the tables should be at an appropriate height for reading. Sufficient lighting should be available for using the dresser or makeup area.

In front of a dresser or chest of drawers, a space of 40 in. is recommended for pulling out the drawers. In front of a closet, the recommended clearance space is 33 in. For dressing, a 42 in. dressing circle is needed. See 4-4. These measurements are only

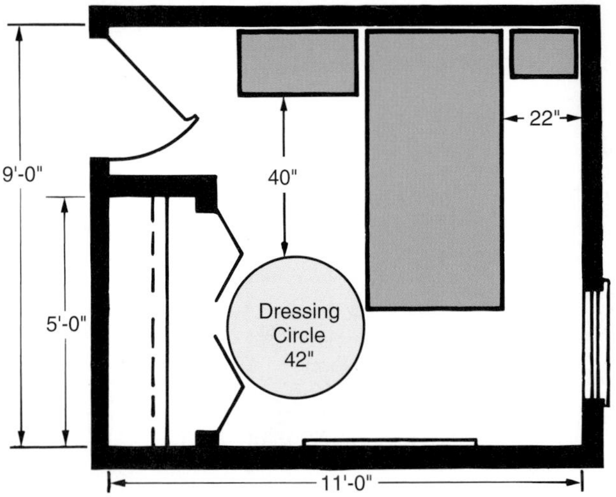

4-4 Space for a 42 in. dressing circle should be allowed in each bedroom.

guidelines. Some people prefer and can afford additional space and, thus, larger bedrooms.

The steps to follow when planning and arranging furniture in a bedroom are summarized in 4-5. The result of careful planning is shown in 4-6. (For more information on common sizes of bedroom furniture and minimum clearance requirements, see A-8 and A-9 of the Appendix.)

Closets, Doors, and Windows

Bedroom arrangement is affected by the location of closets, doors, and windows. The recommended location for a bedroom closet is adjacent to the room entrance. This location allows a person to reach the closet without walking around furniture. Closets can be placed along interior walls to provide insulation from noise between rooms and to allow

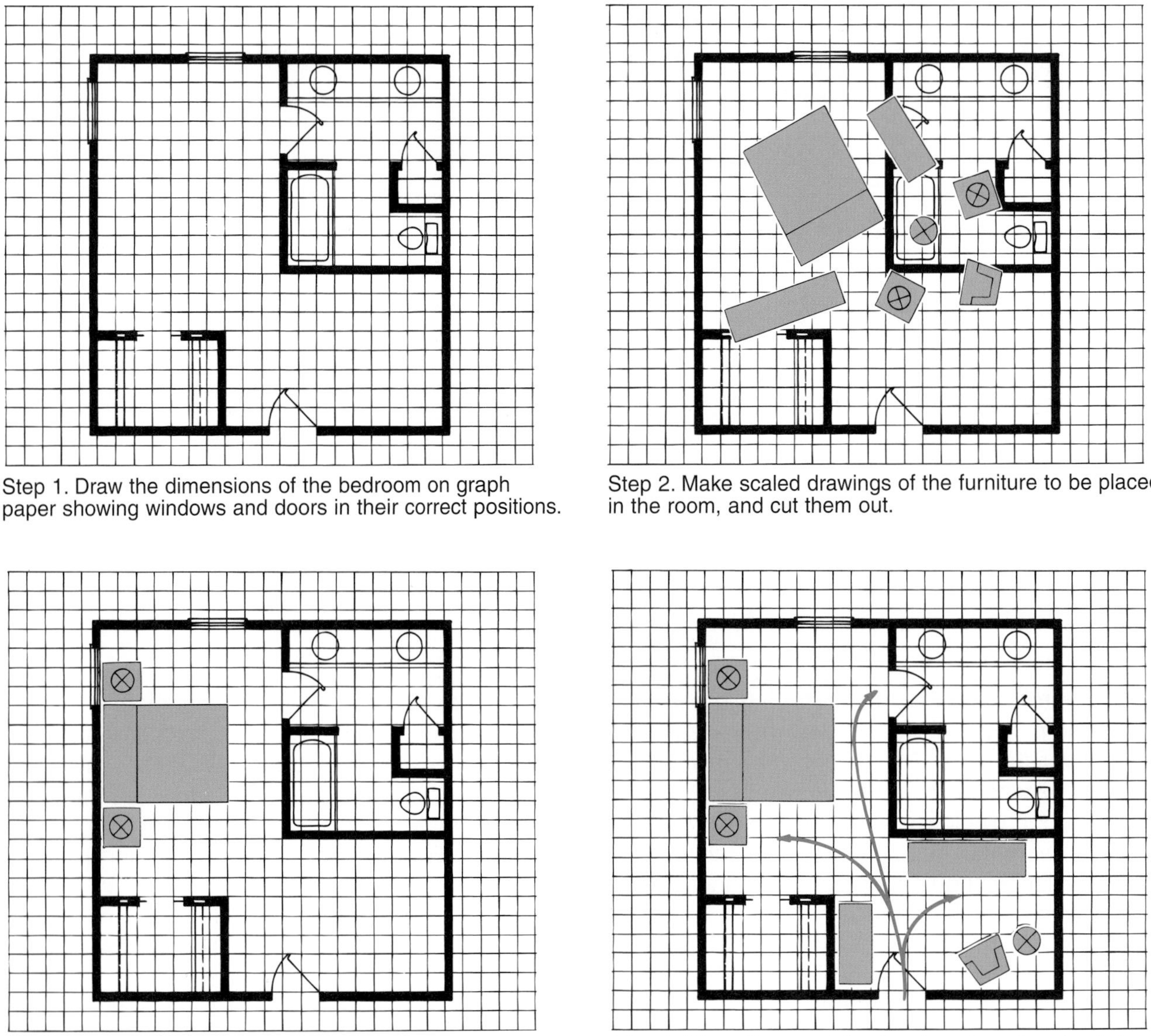

Step 1. Draw the dimensions of the bedroom on graph paper showing windows and doors in their correct positions.

Step 2. Make scaled drawings of the furniture to be placed in the room, and cut them out.

Step 3. Place the bed first.

Step 4. Place the remaining furniture, keeping circulation paths clear.

4-5 Follow these steps to plan the arrangement of bedroom furnishings.

Broyhill Furniture Industries, Inc.

4-6 Careful planning will produce a functional room layout like this.

more space on exterior walls for windows. When placed on exterior walls, closets provide insulation from outside temperatures.

The minimum closet space recommended per person is 4 to 6 ft. long and 24 to 30 in. deep. The two types of closets commonly found in homes are freestanding and built-in closets. Freestanding closets, also called wardrobes or armoires, are pieces of furniture, 4-7. They are not attached to or built into the walls. Built-in closets deeper than 4 ft. are usually considered *walk-in closets*. Some walk-in closets are large enough to accommodate a dressing area.

The recommended location for a bedroom door is in a corner of the room so it will not interrupt wall space. Each bedroom will have at least one entry door and possibly other doors leading to a bathroom, closet, or patio. The entry door should swing into the room, and space should be allowed for the door to fully open. To conserve space, a pocket door may be used for the entry; and sliding doors, for the closet or patio doors.

Windows placed on two exterior walls are ideal for cross ventilation. High **ribbon windows**, which are wide, short windows, are especially effective. While providing ventilation, high ribbon windows also provide privacy and unrestricted placement of furniture below. Ribbon windows also prevent drafts from blowing across the bed. Windows placed lower on the wall interfere with furniture arrangement. However, they allow a person lying in bed or sitting at a desk to see out, and they can be used as fire escapes.

Lexington Furniture Industries

4-7 This period armoire provides an ideal storage place for clothes. Storage space inside is adjustable to accommodate various requirements.

Master Bedrooms

The master bedroom may serve as a private retreat, 4-8. It may be personalized to accommodate activities other than sleeping. A conversation area, work area, or private garden may be part of the master bedroom. An adjoining master bath is convenient for private use. Sometimes the dressing

4-8 The master bedroom may provide space for reading, needlecrafts, or other quiet activities.

area is removed from the bedroom and placed between the bedroom and bathroom. Special equipment or space for hobbies may be a part of the master bedroom as well.

Children's Rooms

The bedroom needs of children change as they grow, so future needs should be considered when planning the room. A minimum-size bedroom should contain at least 100 sq. ft.—enough space to accommodate a single bed, chest or dresser, and bedside table or chair. This size is ideal for a nursery that can be converted to a child's bedroom in future years.

Young children need plenty of floor space for play. They also need child-high storage space for their toys and books. As children grow, their activities change. Older children may need higher shelves and more storage space as well as tables or desks for studying. They may have special needs if they have special hobbies.

Since children's bedrooms must accommodate change, flexibility and creativity are keys to planning. An L-shaped room or room dividers can provide privacy for each child when a room is shared. Twin beds offer flexibility in room arrangements, while captain's beds provide under-the-bed storage. Beds with bolsters can serve as couches for teenage children.

Bathrooms

The trend in homes today is to have bigger and more bathrooms. Besides being highly functional, today's bathrooms are also attractive and personalized, 4-9.

All include a **water closet**, or toilet, and a **lavatory**, or sink. Larger bathrooms may also include a shower and/or tub. More luxurious baths may have saunas or whirlpool baths added. The following are the three basic types of bathrooms and the fixtures in them:

- A **half bath** has only a water closet and lavatory.
- A **three-quarters bath** has a water closet, lavatory, and shower.
- A **full bath** includes a water closet, lavatory, and tub with or without a shower.

Location

Bathrooms need to be located near the living areas of the home as well as the sleeping areas. If a home has only one bathroom, it should be located in a place that is easily accessible to all areas of the home, 4-10.

Photo courtesy of Kohler Co.

4-9 This bathroom is designed to be attractive and functional. Bathrooms can be personalized regardless of size or budget.

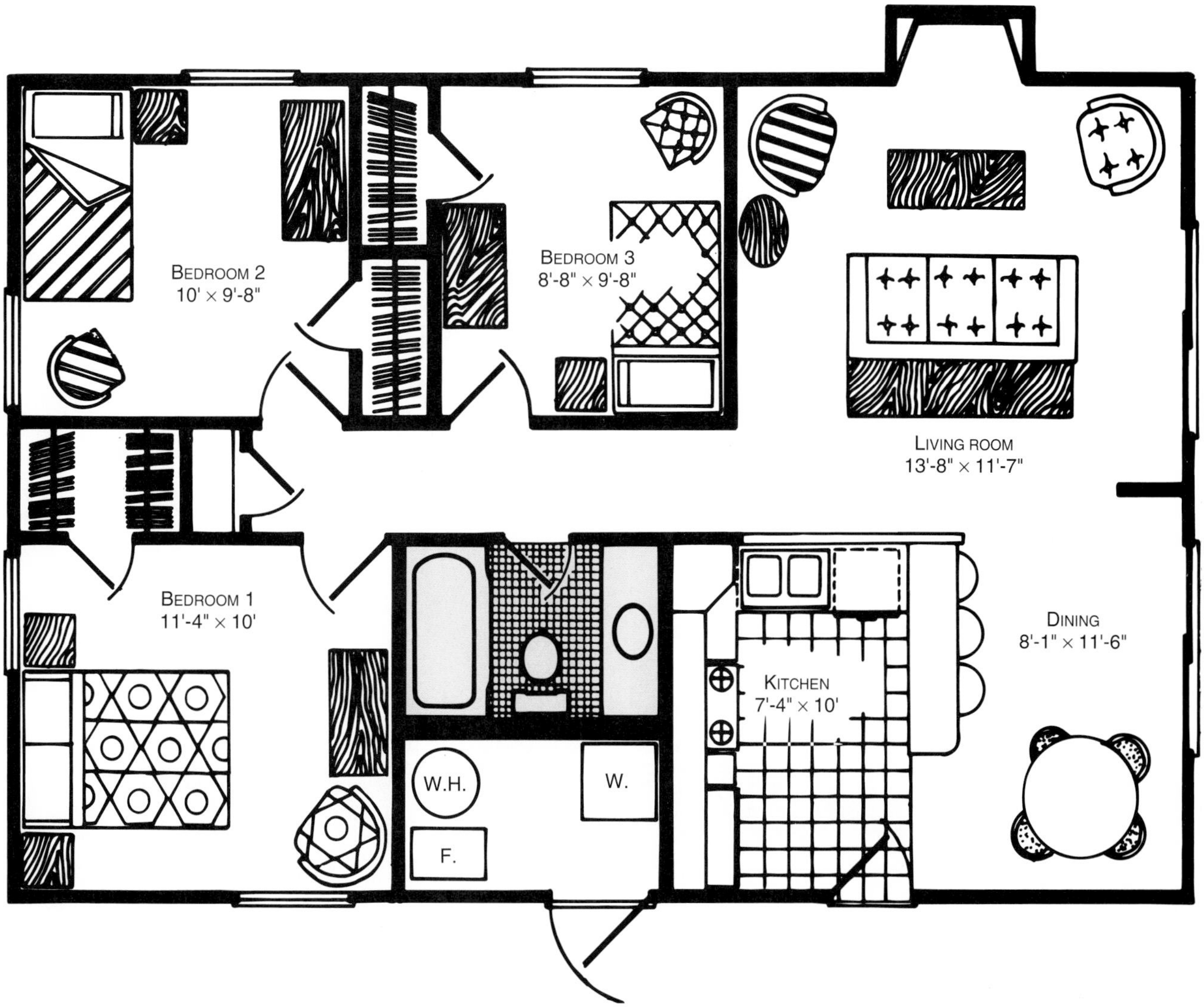

4-10 This three-bedroom cottage has just one bathroom, but its location is convenient to the living, sleeping, and service areas.

The architectural style sometimes dictates the number and location of bathrooms in a dwelling. Ideally, a two-story home needs at least one-and-a-half baths—a full bath upstairs in the sleeping area and a half bath downstairs near the living and service areas. A split-level home also needs one-and-a-half baths—a half bath on the lower level and a full bath on the upper level. A ranch home with bedrooms located away from the living and service areas also needs one-and-a-half baths. Houses with four or more bedrooms are more functional with two or more bathrooms.

Size and Arrangement

The minimum bathroom size depends on the number of people who will use it and the activities it will accommodate. Activities may include bathing, applying makeup, and dressing. More elaborate bathrooms may even provide space for exercising, sunbathing, or laundering.

The bathroom should be as comfortable and convenient as possible to meet the needs of those using it. For example, a bathroom that is shared by all family members should have ample storage and counter space for the grooming and hygiene supplies of each family member. A seldom-used guest bath would not require as much counter and storage space.

Water closets, like all bathroom fixtures, come in many sizes, shapes, and colors. They are available as floor-mounted or wall-mounted units. See 4-11. Clearance space around a water closet should be at least 16 in. from the center of the stool to the sidewall or another fixture, and 24 in. at the front of the stool.

A Eljer Industries

B Kohler Co.

4-11 Water closets are available as (A) wall-mounted or (B) floor-mounted units.

Lavatories are available in a vanity base or as a wall-hung unit. Twin lavatories are convenient when two or more people must share one bathroom. The common size for a bathroom lavatory is 18 in. A larger sink should be selected if it will be used for purposes beyond grooming, such as hand-washing clothes.

Bathroom tubs come in many sizes and shapes. They range in size from 54 to 72 in. long, and from 28 to over 48 in. wide. Common shapes are rectangular, square, and round. A clearance space of 30 to 42 in. is needed between the front of the tub and the opposite wall.

Tubs are available with different features. Most tubs have a showerhead installed above it. Some tubs have wide ledges that can be used as seats for leg or foot washing. For safety, some tubs have grab rails and nonskid bottoms.

Homes that have two bathrooms may have a tub/shower installed in one bathroom and just a shower stall in the other, 4-12. A shower stall requires less space than a tub and lowers the cost of building a home. Shower stall sizes range from 30 by 33 in. to 36 by 48 in.

Saunas and whirlpool baths may be placed in or near the bathroom, but should not interfere with general circulation in the bathroom. See 4-13. Saunas can be purchased as kits or custom installed. Some newer models are designed to accommodate one person and require no more space than a closet. Others contain a combination of a sauna, whirlpool, and steam bath. Whirlpool baths are available in ready-to-assemble wood kits or in precast units. Many are designed to double as a bathtub and a whirlpool. Skid-proof steps are generally placed outside the whirlpool bath for easy, safe access. At least 30 to 42 in. of clearance space should be allowed for entering and leaving a sauna or whirlpool bath.

4-12 This modern shower stall is enclosed with large panels of glass.

Photo courtesy of Kohler Co.

4-13 This whirlpool bath, though located in the bathroom, is placed outside the traffic pattern.

Storage space should be available in each bathroom. Storage may be needed for grooming supplies, medicines, grooming appliances, towels, and washcloths. A vanity and/or a bathroom closet can provide storage space. The proper arrangement of bathroom fixtures and adequate space clearances make a bathroom convenient to use. (For more information on minimum clearance requirements and common sizes of bathroom fixtures, see A-9 and A-10 of the Appendix.)

Heat and Moisture Considerations

An exhaust fan or a window can provide ventilation. Exhaust fans should be located near the water closet and tub. Electrical switches controlling fans and lights should be placed so they cannot be reached from the tub. To prevent electrical shock, all bathroom outlets should have a **ground fault circuit interrupter (GFCI)**. This is a safety device that continually monitors the amount of electricity flowing in the circuit and opens it if an imbalance occurs.

Heat, high humidity, and frequent cleaning are factors to consider when choosing materials to finish bathroom walls, floors, and ceilings, 4-14. Wall surfaces should be waterproof and easy to clean. If walls are finished with drywall or plaster, a type of paint that resists soil and water should be used on the surface.

Bathroom floors should not be slippery when wet. A bath mat or rug with nonskid backing can be used when exiting the tub or shower. Ceramic or vinyl tile floors are good for frequently used bathrooms. Nylon acrylic carpeting is popular in master bathrooms.

Adaptations for Special Needs

Attention to certain details can make the sleeping area of the house accessible to everyone in the household, including small children, the elderly, and individuals with physical disabilities.

Bedrooms

Adjustable shelves make ideal storage space because they can be placed at various heights from 18 to 45 in. above the floor. Shelving depth should not exceed 16 in. Clothing rods should be installed

Photo courtesy of Kohler Co.

4-14 The materials chosen for this bath are resistant to moisture and heat.

within reach, generally 40 to 48 in. high, and clothes hooks should be located no higher than 40 in.

To provide turnaround space for a wheelchair in front of a closet, a 5 by 5 ft. clearance is needed. Doorways should be at least 3 ft. wide.

Beds for wheelchair users should have firm mattresses to permit easy transfer between bed and chair. The bed's height can be identical to the seat of the chair, or it may be adjustable to allow different mattress positions. In both cases, a clearance of 10 to 13 in. underneath is necessary for the chair's footrests. A phone as well as controls for lights should be near the bed. For a person who is older or disabled, a bedroom is more convenient with its own bath.

Bathrooms

To make bathrooms accessible to wheelchair users, a 5 ft. sq. turnaround space is needed. Slightly tilting the mirror forward or mounting it lower allows children and seated adults full viewing. Installing a full-length mirror on a bathroom wall or door is another option. Medicine cabinets should be mounted so the top shelf is no higher than 50½ in. from the floor, but slightly lower if mounted over a counter or sink.

Wall-mounted and pedestal-type lavatories usually provide sufficient knee space for individuals in wheelchairs. Allow 26 to 30 in. of vertical clearance under the sink for the chair's armrests.

A 30 in. wide installation space is needed for most water closets, but a 36 in. space is recommended to comfortably accommodate wheelchair users. Generally, wall-mounted water closets are more accessible to these family members than are the floor-mounted types. The water-closet seat should be 20 in. high, which is about level with the seat of most wheelchairs.

Shower stalls with wall-mounted, foldaway seats are available for disabled individuals who can transfer from crutches or a wheelchair to the seat. Special-made shower stalls, however, can allow wheelchair users easy entry to the shower, 4-15. Placing a showerhead over the center of the shower instead of the drain provides better access.

Devices should be installed in tub and shower faucets to thermostatically control water temperature. They prevent the possibility of serious burns from scalding water.

Muscular Dystrophy Association

4-15 The entry to this shower is level with the bathroom floor to allow a wheelchair to enter easily.

Chapter Summary

The purpose of the sleeping area of a home is to provide privacy for such activities as sleeping, bathing, and dressing. These rooms need to be located away from circulation and noise. The number, sexes, and ages of family members determine the number and size of bedrooms needed. Each person needs sleeping space, storage for clothes and personal items, and dressing space.

Bedrooms can be located anywhere in the house so long as they have privacy of sight and sound, but each bedroom should be accessible from a hall. Guest bedrooms are frequently separated from other bedrooms. The size of a bedroom will depend on the number of people to use the room, the furniture to be included, and storage space provided. Location of doors and windows must be considered in a bedroom plan as well.

Bathrooms are larger and more numerous in new homes. The location, size, and arrangement of bathrooms should be planned using well-established principles. The basic bathroom fixtures include a water closet, lavatory, and tub/shower. Heat and moisture in the bathroom is a concern in bathroom design.

Bedrooms and baths should be accessible for those who will use these rooms. Considerations such as shelf height, turnaround space, door widths, mirror height, type of lavatories, and vanity height should become part of the planning process for bedrooms and baths.

Review Questions

1. What are the two main plans for bedroom arrangements and the advantages of each?
2. What are the steps to follow when planning a bedroom furniture arrangement?
3. How much space should be allowed for the following activities?
   A. making a large bed from one side
   B. making a twin bed from one side
   C. opening a dresser drawer
   D. opening a closet door
   E. dressing
4. If two bedrooms have the same dimensions, why might one have more usable space than the other?
5. What are the differences among freestanding, built-in, and walk-in closets?
6. What factors should be considered when planning a bedroom for two children?
7. What are the three main styles of bathrooms and the fixtures contained in each?
8. What is the ideal location for one bathroom in a small home? two bathrooms in a two-story home?
9. What is an advantage of a wall-mounted water closet?
10. What features might you add to a bathtub in the home of an elderly couple?
11. What items can be included in the bathroom to assure proper ventilation?
12. How much space is required to turn a wheelchair in front of a closet?
13. What type of device prevents scalding water from flowing from tub and shower faucets?

Suggested Activities

1. Search magazines and Internet sites for a good example of each of the two basic types of bedroom plans. Display them to the class.
2. Design a bedroom for yourself showing the room size, arrangement, type of furniture, storage, and other personal items you would select. Explain why the plan is a good one.
3. Prepare a list of clearance requirements needed for a highly functional bedroom arrangement. Consider circulation, safety requirements, code requirements, and comfort.
4. Secure product literature for bathroom equipment or check the product information provided on the Web sites of at least two manufacturers. Prepare a chart of standard sizes of lavatories, tubs, shower units, and water closets to serve as a guide for future design projects.
5. Write a short essay explaining the factors that should be considered when designing a functional bathroom for a residence.
6. Prepare a checklist of features to incorporate into a bathroom that will be accessible to small children and people with disabilities.

Internet Resources

A.O. Smith Water Products Company
hotwater.com

Jacuzzi, Inc.
jacuzzi.com

Kohler Company, a manufacturer of plumbing products
kohler.com

Masonite International Corporation, a door manufacturer
masonite.com

Owens Corning
owenscorning.com

Velux, supplier of roof windows and skylights
velux.com

Western Wood Products Association
wwpa.org

Note: Web addresses may have changed since publication. For some entries, reaching the correct Web site may require keying *www.* into the address.

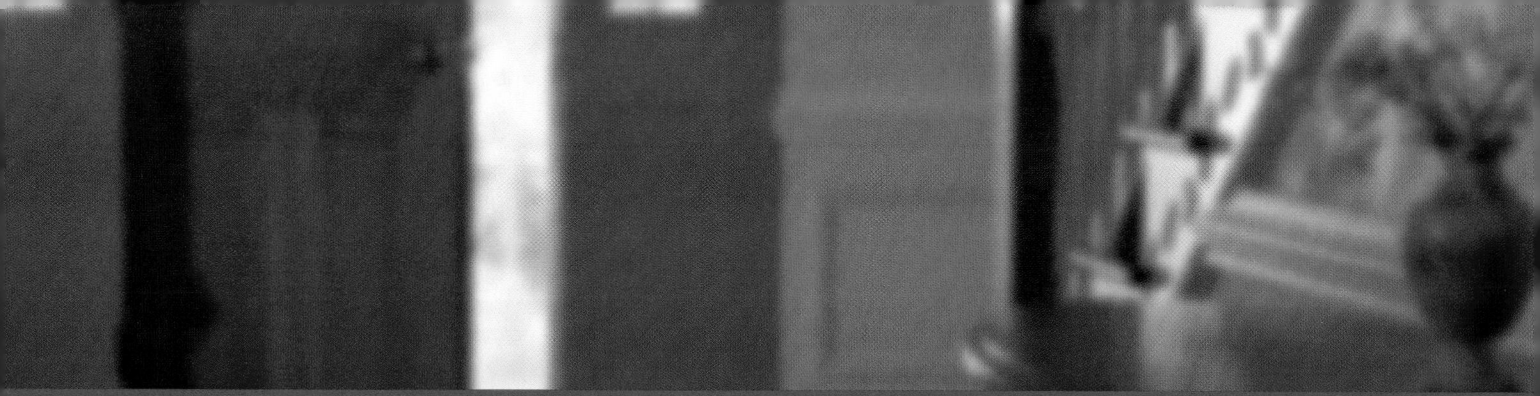

Chapter 5
Planning Service and Work Areas

Objectives

After studying this chapter, you will be able to

- describe the three centers of the work triangle and plan an efficiently arranged kitchen using any of the six common floor plans.
- evaluate the location, layout, and efficiency of laundry facilities in relationship to the lifestyle of various households.
- list possible uses and layouts of basements.
- determine the best location on a floor plan for the garage (or carport) and service entries.
- list the types and uses of special-purpose rooms, especially home offices, and storage units.
- identify requirements for service areas used by individuals with special needs.

Key Terms

service area
work center
work triangle
U-shaped kitchen
L-shaped kitchen
corridor kitchen
peninsula kitchen
one-wall kitchen
island kitchen
service entry
special-purpose room
ergonomics

The **service areas** are the parts of the home that sustain all other areas. The living and sleeping areas depend on the service areas for many activities. Consequently, much planning is necessary to make these areas as efficient as possible. Service areas include the kitchen, laundry facilities, basement, garage (or carport), service entries, special-purpose rooms, and storage.

Kitchens

The kitchen is the center for meal preparation and cleanup. Although many homes have the kitchen in a separate room, the kitchens in new homes usually extend into a family, living, or dining room, 5-1. Open kitchens are more convenient for supervising or joining nearby activities while working in the kitchen. The open design also helps small kitchens—like those in apartments or small homes—seem larger.

The kitchen itself may have facilities for dining, laundering, or doing office work in addition to preparing meals. A well-planned kitchen that meets the needs of household members should fit the lifestyle of the household. It should contain areas for each of the activities performed there, ample workspace, and adequate storage.

Location

Ideally, a kitchen should be located near the service entrance of a home as well as the dining area, 5-2. If the household often enjoys outdoor grilling, it is convenient to have the kitchen located near the patio

WCI Communities, Inc.

5-1 An open kitchen adjacent to the dining area uses the available space more efficiently.

or deck. If young children are in the home, it may be important to have the kitchen oversee the outdoor play area or the recreation or family room. The kitchen should also have access to the main entry and the living room, but be out of view from both. Circulation from the kitchen to other rooms, however, should not pass through the living room.

Size and Arrangement

The ideal size for a kitchen is determined by the type and size of meals to be prepared and the activities intended for the room. For example, the kitchen space needed by a couple that eats out frequently would never meet the needs of a family with teenagers who eat most meals at home. Smaller kitchens may vary in size from 60 to 130 sq. ft. Households that often prepare gourmet food may desire a more spacious and elaborately equipped kitchen, 5-3.

Extra space may be needed for eating areas, laundry facilities, or a home office. Kitchens that accommodate dining and nonfood activities may have as much as 300 sq. ft. of space. Households that rarely eat at home or never prepare meals from scratch may find a large, elaborate kitchen to be a waste of space.

Work Centers

A well-arranged kitchen is designed around work centers. A **work center** is an area for performing related tasks and storing the necessary

5-2 The dining area of a home should be adjacent to the meal preparation area.

5-3 This large kitchen contains all the necessary features for the serious gourmet—plenty of counter space, abundant cabinet storage, and a pleasant decor.

tools. Most kitchens have the following three basic work centers:

- The *food preparation and storage center* focuses on the refrigerator area.
- The *cooking and serving center* concentrates on the cooking surface.
- The *cleanup center* focuses on the sink area.

Larger kitchens may have additional centers such as a mixing, planning, snacking, dining, or laundry center. If more than one person in the home likes to cook, the kitchen may be equipped with an auxiliary food preparation area or a secondary cleanup center.

Food Preparation and Storage Center

The food preparation and storage center focuses on the refrigerator, usually a refrigerator-freezer. Cabinets and counter space beside the refrigerator are a part of this center. Wall and base cabinets are used for storing nonperishable foods, food containers, and serving dishes. A counter at least 18 in. wide is needed on the door-opening side of the refrigerator for setting out supplies and preparing food.

A small center for mixing is usually located beside the food storage area. Counter space at least 36 in. wide is needed for this activity. The area also stores mixing bowls, measuring tools, baking utensils, baking ingredients, and small appliances such as an electric mixer and food processor.

Cooking and Serving Center

The focal point of the cooking and serving center is the cooking surface, which can be part of a freestanding range or a separate appliance installed in a heat-resistant counter. The oven, too, can be part of a range or separately installed in a wall. Above or within the cooking surface, an exhaust system is needed to ventilate the air. A cooking surface should not be placed directly under a window since curtains are a fire hazard.

The cooking center requires at least 24 in. of heat-resistant counter space on each side of the range to hold ingredients and utensils needed for cooking, 5-4. The wall and base cabinets store the seasonings, cookware, cooking utensils, and potholders. Electrical outlets are needed for using countertop appliances such as a microwave oven, electric frypan, or toaster.

Cleanup Center

Activity in the cleanup center takes place around the sink. The cleanup center may also include a dishwasher

5-4 The cooking center in this home has plenty of cabinet space below the cooking surface because ovens are stacked to the right. Counter space is available on both sides of the cooktop.

and food waste disposer. In this center, foods such as fresh produce are cleaned, and dishes and utensils are washed. The sink should be placed no more than 3 in. from the front edge of the counter. To one side of the sink, 36 in. of counter space is needed for stacking dirty dishes. On the other side, at least 18 in. is needed for draining and stacking clean dishes. If the kitchen also has a secondary sink, it needs less counter space—at least 18 in. on one side and 3 in. on the other.

When a dishwasher is present, it is usually placed next to the sink to connect most directly to the water source. This placement also permits easy loading. See 5-5. The cabinet and drawer space in this center stores dishes, dishcloths, towels, and dishwashing detergent. Utensils for cleaning, cutting, and draining foods are usually stored nearby.

The Work Triangle

The focal points of the three work centers—the refrigerator, sink, and cooking surface—form a work triangle. Simply stated, the **work triangle** is the route that connects the refrigerator, sink, and range. The triangular route should total no more than 22 ft. when measuring from the midpoints of the three focal points. See 5-6. A larger triangle would require too much walking to perform a task.

The work triangle should follow the normal flow of food preparation. Food is taken from the refrigerator, cleaned at the sink, and taken to the range for cooking. Leftovers are returned to the refrigerator, thus completing the work triangle.

Appliances, Cabinets, and Counters

Kitchen appliances are available in a variety of types, sizes, shapes, and colors. When choosing appliances, the amount of usable space in the kitchen should be considered. Space should be allowed for clearance as well as for the appliance itself. In order to store and remove food from a refrigerator comfortably, 36 in. of clearance is needed.

For a conventional range, a clearance of 38 in. at the front of the range allows a person to use the oven in a standing position, while 38 in. at the front of an open oven door allows room for oven use when kneeling. To load and unload a dishwasher, allow 42 in. at the front of the dishwasher and 20 in. on either side. See 5-7.

Cabinets can be custom-made or manufactured. The standard size of base cabinets is 34½ in. high by 24 in. deep. Widths range in 3 in. increments from 9 to 48 in. Typical base cabinets include a drawer and two shelves.

5-5 This cleanup center has ample counter space by the sink for dirty and clean dishes. The dishwasher is placed beside the sink for ease in loading and unloading the dishwasher.

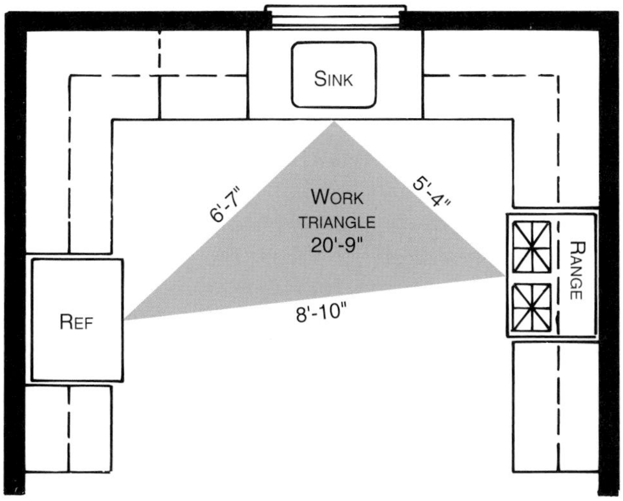

5-6 The sum of the three sides of the kitchen work triangle should not exceed 22 ft.

Wall cabinets generally range from 12 to 30 in. high and 12 or 13 in. deep. Those 12 to 18 in. high are useful over sinks, refrigerators, and ranges. Widths of wall cabinets generally range in 3 in. increments from 12 to 48 in.

A minimum run of 72 in. of cabinet space is recommended for ample kitchen storage. This does not include cabinet space under the sink since food products should not be stored there. Space under the sink could be used for storage of cleaning products and a container for waste. Using an L-shaped lazy Susan can maximize corner-cabinet space, 5-8. The shelves rotate outward for easy access to stored items. Many standard cabinets also have shelves that pull out, 5-9.

The space between countertops and the wall cabinets above is usually 15 to 18 in. This distance provides clearance for portable appliances such as toasters and mixers. Above a range, the minimum clearance is 30 in. to cabinets and 24 in. to a range hood. Cabinets over the sink should be placed above eye level. (For more information about common sizes of kitchen cabinets and appliances, see A-11 through A-13 of the Appendix.)

Countertops are prepared in made-to-order sections that generally measure 25 in. deep and 1½ in. thick. Countertops should be durable, easy to clean, and nonabsorbent. Suitable materials include ceramic, metal, wood, plastic, and stone. The cost of a countertop varies widely, depending on the type of materials used and installation charges. As a general rule, plastic laminate countertops are the most affordable. Ceramic, metal, wood, or solid surface countertops cost more. Finally, stone countertops are usually the most expensive. Decorative edges increase the cost and are priced per linear foot.

Kitchens should have sufficient outlets for electric appliances and lighting. General lighting should be provided in a central location as well as additional lighting above each work center.

Kitchen Designs

Work centers can be arranged into various kitchen designs that reflect six basic types: the U-shaped,

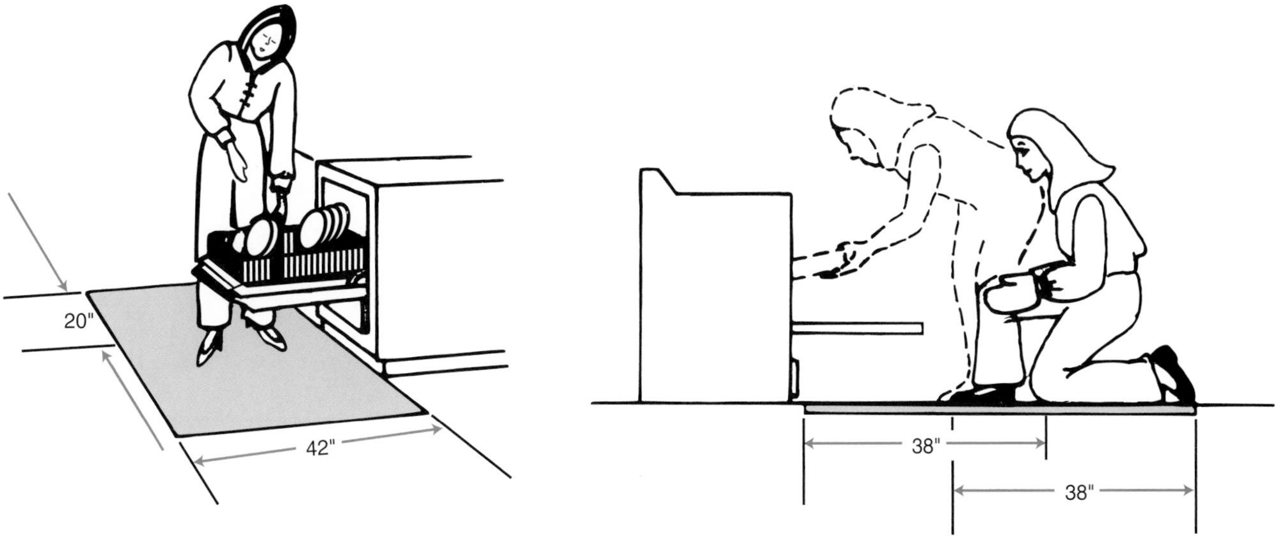

5-7 Space is needed for using a front-loading dishwasher and a conventional range.

Norcraft Companies Inc.

5-8 These lazy Susan shelves swing out for easy access to stored goods.

L-shaped, corridor, peninsula, one-wall, and island kitchen.

- The **U-shaped kitchen** has its work centers form a continuous line along three adjoining walls. See 5-10. The U-shaped kitchen is one of the most popular kitchen layouts and the most efficient. This design has two major advantages. It prevents circulation from passing through the work triangle and provides ample cabinet and counter space.
- The **L-shaped kitchen** has its work centers form a continuous line along two adjoining walls. See 5-11. The L-shaped kitchen is a popular layout because it adapts to a variety of room plans. In a large room, this design allows space for an eating area. Another advantage of this plan is it prevents circulation from interrupting the work triangle.
- A **corridor kitchen** has work centers placed along two walls that are divided by an aisle 4 to 5 ft. wide. See 5-12. A long, narrow room suits the layout of the corridor kitchen. A compact work triangle is its main advantage, but a very long room will create an extended work triangle that requires many steps. Another advantage of this kitchen design is it can be located between two eating areas, an informal dining area and a formal dining room. If the corridor is open at both ends, however, circulation through the corridor may interfere with the work triangle.

5-9 The heights of these sliding base shelves are perfect for storage of various dry goods. All items are within easy reach.

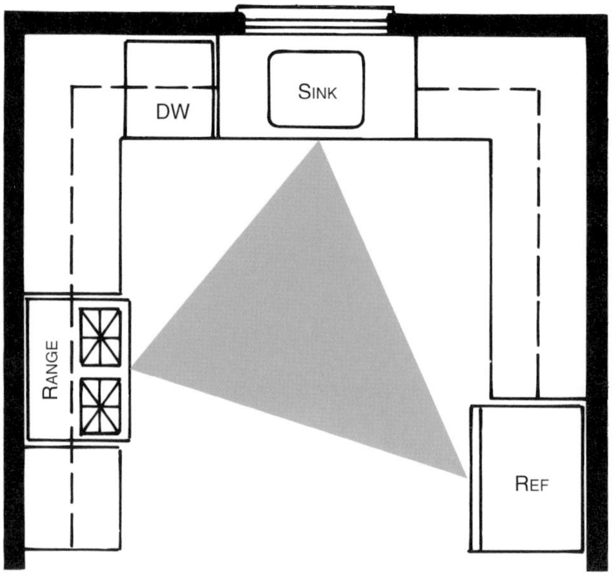

5-10 In the U-shaped kitchen the cleanup center is most functional at the base of the U, between the preparation/storage center on the right and the cooking center opposite.

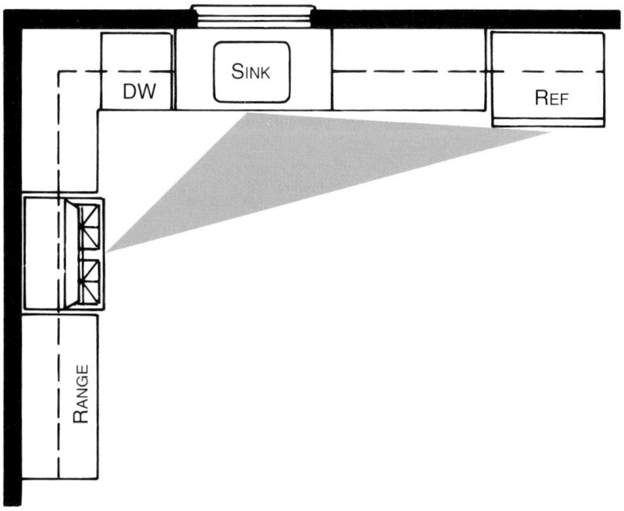

5-11 The L-shaped kitchen provides several alternatives for efficient layout.

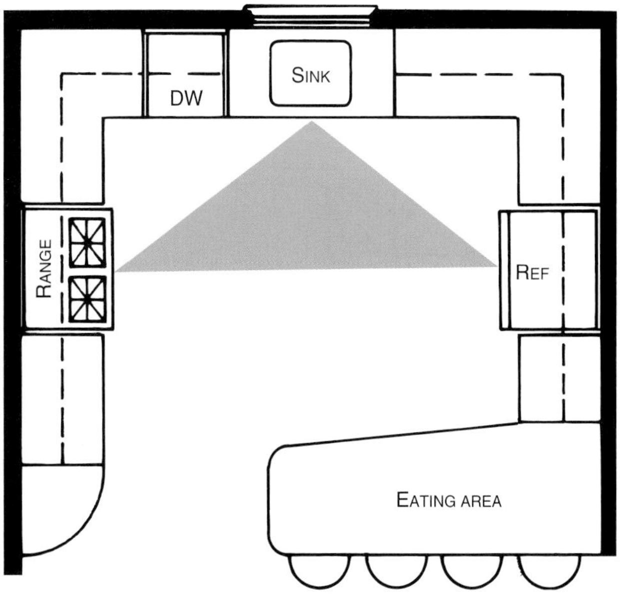

5-14 The peninsula kitchen adds extra counter and storage space in the peninsula, which is often used as an eating area. This plan prevents circulation through the kitchen to other areas of the home.

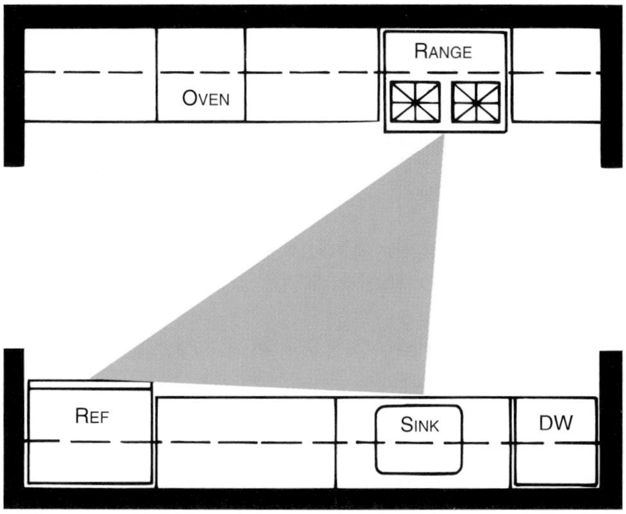

5-12 The corridor kitchen is most efficient when the preparation/storage and cleanup centers are on one wall with the cooking center opposite.

- A **one-wall kitchen** has all the appliances and cabinets located on one wall. See 5-13. This type of layout is often used where space is limited, such as in an apartment or summer cottage. When not in use, the one-wall kitchen is often closed off from other rooms by a folding door. This plan is generally the least desirable because it has a long, narrow work triangle with insufficient cabinet and counter space.
- A **peninsula kitchen** is a U-shaped kitchen with a counter extending from one end of the U. See 5-14. This type of layout is often used to separate the kitchen from an adjoining family room or a dining room. The peninsula can serve as a mixing center, a cooking and serving center, a cleanup center, a counter for informal eating, or just additional counter and storage space.
- The **island kitchen** has a separate counter unit that stands alone. See 5-15. This kitchen design may be a variation of the U-shaped, L-shaped, or one-wall kitchen. A clearance of 4 ft. should be allowed on all sides of the island. The island counter unit divides the food preparation area from the rest of the room and can serve all the same functions as the peninsula.

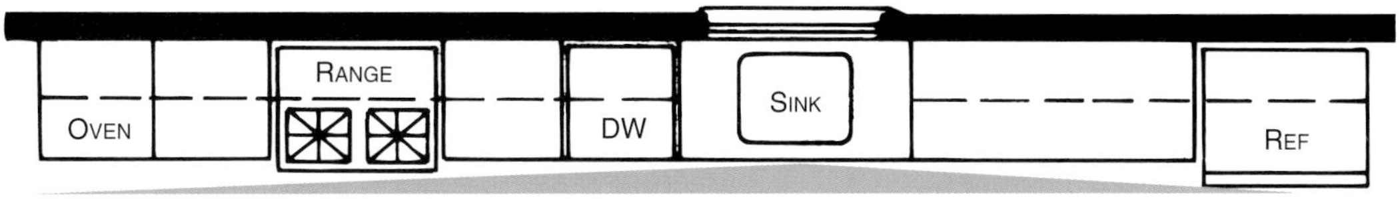

5-13 In this one-wall kitchen, work flows from right to left since the refrigerator is on the right. Notice that countertop space is provided in each of the work centers.

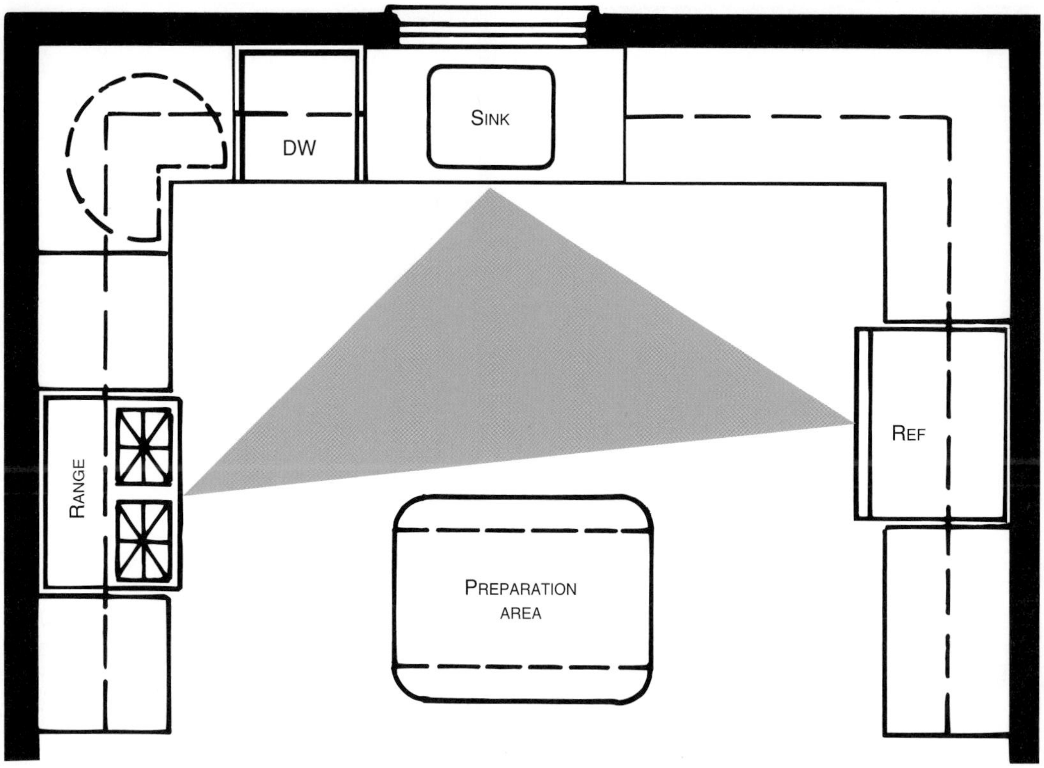

5-15 This island kitchen is a variation of the U-shaped layout. The island area can be used as a peninsula.

Laundry Facilities

Caring for clothes and linens is another important activity performed in the service area of a home. Laundry facilities may vary from a washer and dryer tucked in a closet to a separate laundry room with plenty of floor and counter space. See 5-16. The activities involved in laundering are: sorting and preparing clothes for washing, washing by hand or machine, drying (air drying or machine drying), folding, ironing, and possibly mending.

Location

No set rules exist for the location of laundry facilities in a home. However, the availability of hot and cold water lines, a 240-volt electrical outlet, possibly a gas line, and an outside wall for a dryer vent may limit the choice of locations. These features are expensive to install or move, so cost may outweigh other considerations.

Laundry facilities may be located in the kitchen, mudroom, utility room, sleeping area, basement, or a separate room. Each location has its advantages and disadvantages.

The advantage of locating the laundry facilities in or near the kitchen is the ability to supervise laundry duties and other tasks at the same time while saving steps. A disadvantage of a kitchen location may be the lack of adequate space for folding and ironing.

Locating laundry facilities in a mudroom or utility room near the service entrance is also convenient. This location allows soiled clothing to be removed immediately rather than walked through the house. See 5-17. If the household has a washer, but no dryer, close proximity of the washer to the service entrance is convenient for taking laundry outside to line dry.

The sleeping area is a practical location for laundry facilities since this is where soiled clothes are removed and clean clothes are stored. However, a washer and dryer can be noisy, making this location less desirable to some households.

Another location for laundry facilities is the basement. Although this location removes the noise from the other areas of the home, it can be inconvenient. Unless there is a laundry chute, extra time and energy is required to carry the laundry up and down stairs. In addition, doing laundry in the basement makes it difficult to combine that task with other household activities.

If space and expense are not limiting factors, a home could have a room just for caring for laundry. A good location for a laundry room is between the kitchen and bedroom area.

General Electric Company

5-16 A laundry facility should have counter space for sorting and folding clothes.

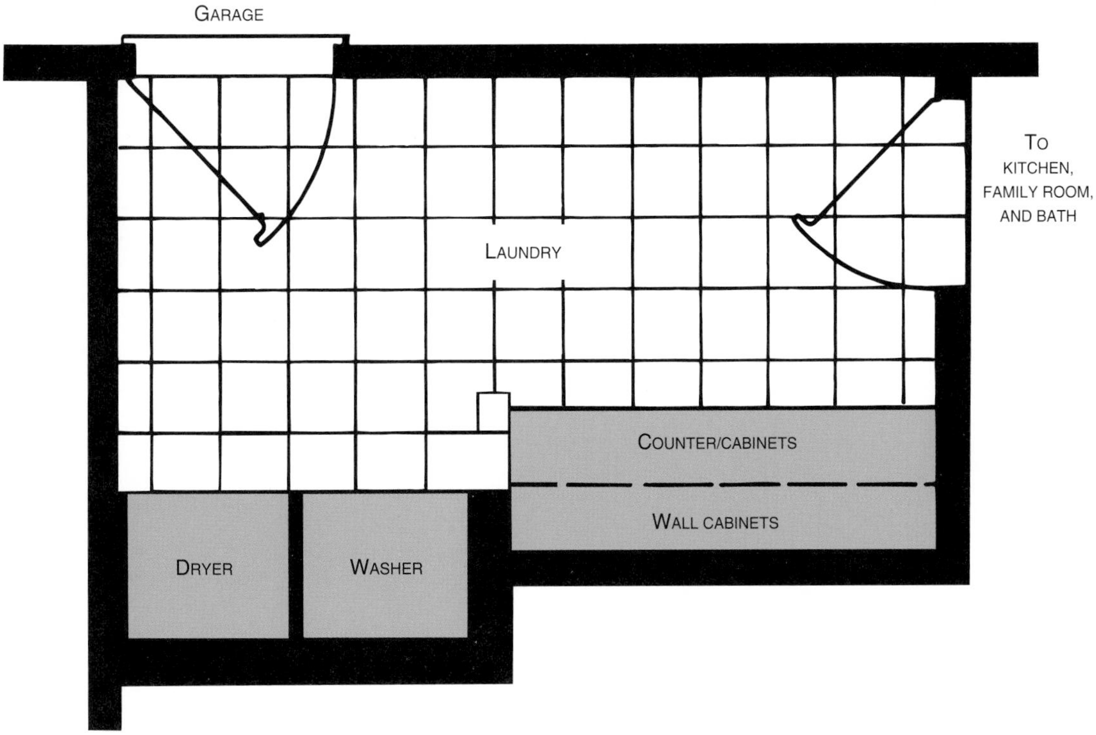

5-17 This laundry doubles as a mudroom. Located adjacent to the garage, it is also the service entrance.

Size and Arrangement

The ideal amount of space needed for laundry facilities depends on the number and ages of household members. The more family members there are, the more space is needed for sorting, folding, and hanging clothes.

The arrangement of laundry facilities should make the work flow in an orderly fashion, 5-18. Equipment required in the laundry area includes a sink or laundry tub, the washer, and in most parts of the country, a dryer. (Many residential areas do not permit clotheslines and line drying.) Counter space is needed in the sink area for pretreating stains and in the dryer area for folding clean clothes. Storage for laundry supplies is also necessary. Space should be allowed for ironing and hanging clean clothes.

Washers and dryers range from 24 to 34 in. wide. Top-loading washers require clearance above to open the door and to add and remove clothes. A washer and dryer can be placed side by side or at a right angle to each other. See 5-19. In the side-by-side arrangement, an area 3½ ft. deep and 5½ ft. long should be clear in front. In the right-angle arrangement, both appliances share a 3½ by 4 ft. clearance area.

The floor space required for ironing is an area about 5 ft. wide and 6 ft. long. On the working side of the board, a 30 in. space is required, and a 6 in. space is needed on the opposite side. At the point of the ironing board, an 18 in. clearance space is needed.

Basements

Although basements can be living or sleeping areas, they are more likely to be part of the service area. Laundry facilities, a furnace or utility room, a workshop, and storage are often located in a basement, 5-20.

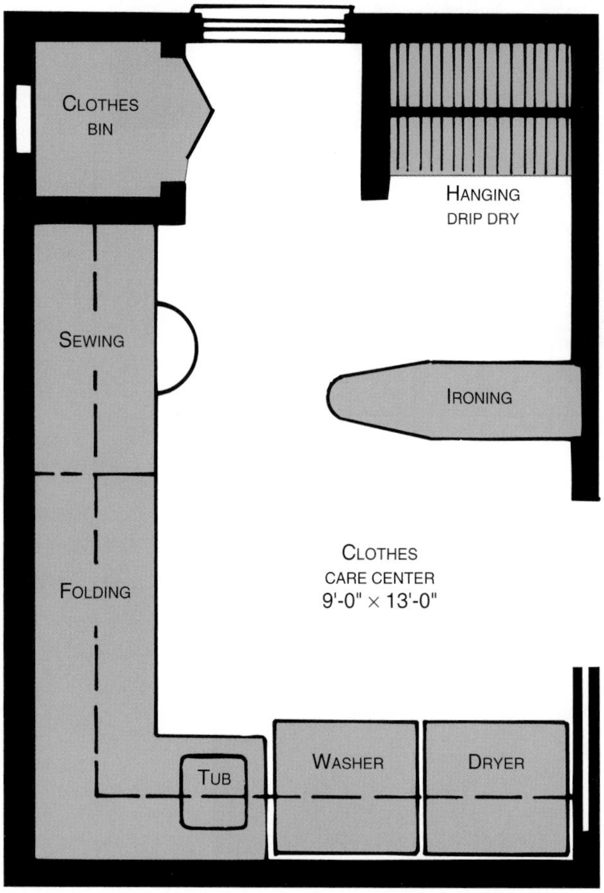

5-18 A well-designed clothes care center has facilities for collecting soiled clothes, sorting, pretreating, washing, drying, ironing, folding, mending, and storing. This center is 13 ft. long and 9 ft. wide.

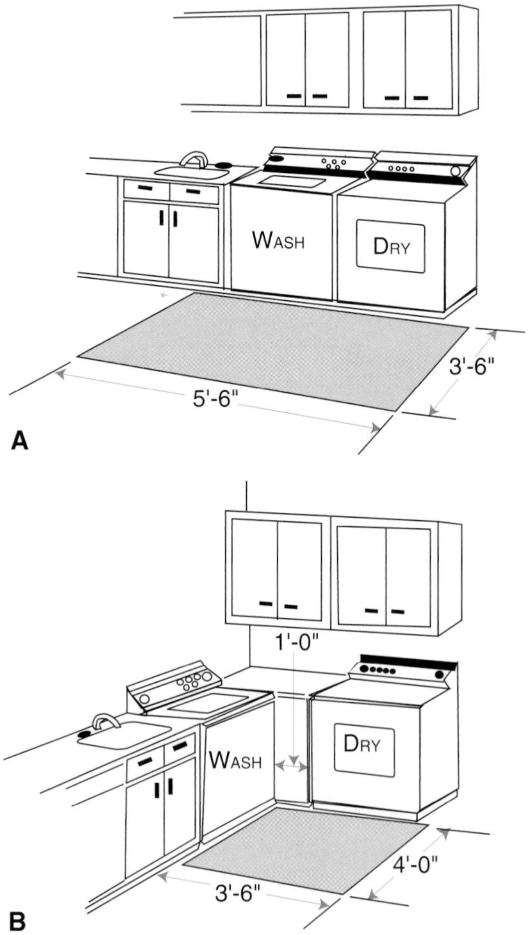

5-19 In the side-by-side placement of the washer and dryer (A), a 3½ by 5½ ft. clearance space is needed. In a right angle placement (B), both appliances share a 3½ by 4 ft. clearance area.

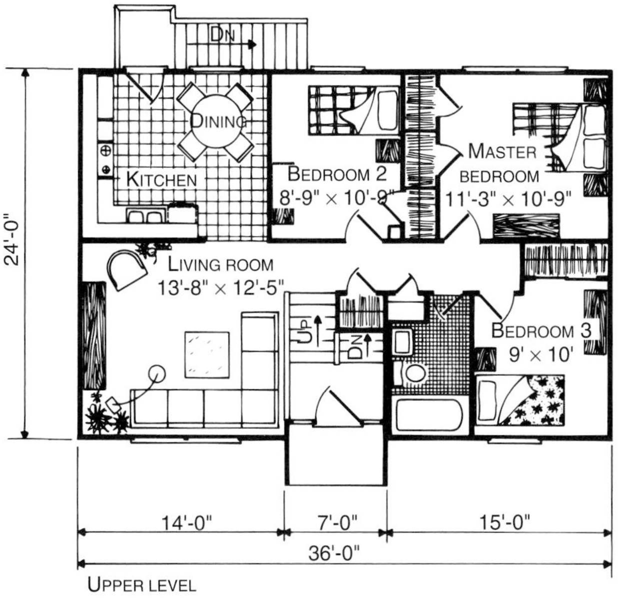

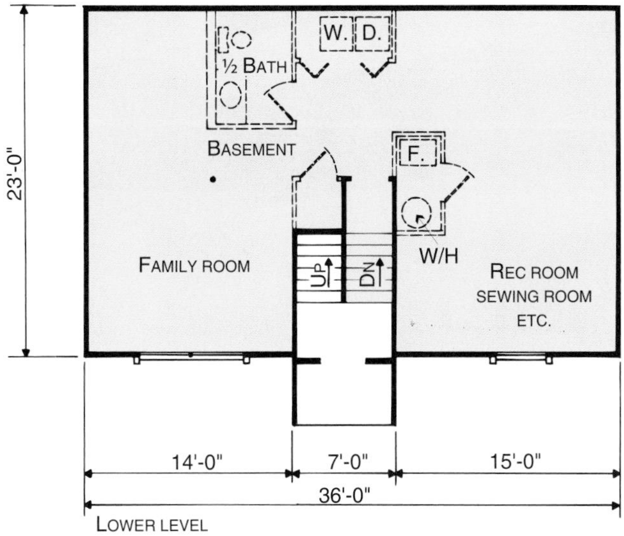

5-20 This small townhouse unit has a full basement with a family room, half bath, sewing or recreation room, utility area, and laundry area.

When part or all of a basement is used in a service capacity, an exterior entrance to the basement is helpful. An exterior entrance makes it easier to store outdoor tools and equipment, such as lawn mowers and garden tools. It also helps reduce traffic on the interior stairway.

The interior stairway to a basement should be located to accommodate the greatest amount of traffic that uses the basement. For instance, if the laundry facilities are the most-used area of the basement, the stairway should lead from the laundry area to the sleeping area. If the recreation room is the most-used room in the basement, the main floor's stairway entrance should be centrally located. The basement stairway should be 36 in. or more in width to accommodate large items such as water heaters, furniture, and equipment.

Because of its location and construction, moisture is a primary concern in the basement. Dampness and humidity can damage items stored in the basement and make the environment uncomfortable. This condition can be reduced by providing proper ventilation and using a dehumidifier. Insulating walls with moisture-resistant insulation also reduces the amount of dampness in a basement. In cool weather, heating can be used to dry the air and provide a more comfortable environment.

Garages and Carports

Shelter for an automobile is the fundamental purpose of a garage or carport. However, the structure may also provide space for storage, laundry equipment, or a workshop.

Location

The garage or carport should be located at the service entrance so packages and groceries can be carried directly from the car into the kitchen. If possible, orientation to the sun and wind should be considered in the location of a garage. In cold climates, a garage located on the north side of a home will help insulate the home against northerly winds. A garage facing the west or south would help shade a home from the sun.

Size and Design

How a garage or carport will be used determines the size needed. To store one car, a space measuring 11 by 20 ft. is needed. The storage space required for two cars is 21 by 21 ft. These dimensions include space for opening car doors and walking around each vehicle. Additional space is needed to store other large items such as campers, bicycles, motorcycles, or lawn mowers. Incorporating a workshop or laundry room requires additional space.

The design of the garage or carport should complement the design of the home. Garage designs that extend the lines of the eaves can make a house appear larger.

Garage doors should also complement the overall design of the home, 5-21. Various types of doors are available. Overhead doors either slide back into the garage or project out when opened.

5-21 These garage doors blend well with the design of the house.

For greater convenience and safety, automatic garage door openers can be used on almost any type of overhead door. Garage doors that swing outward, slide, or fold are also available.

A door for a one-car garage needs to be at least 8 ft. wide, but preferably 9 ft. For a two-car garage, a door 16 ft. wide is needed. If the approach to the garage is not straight, a door 18 ft. wide is needed. To increase the clearance between cars, two single doors can be used. A common height for a garage door is 7 ft., but a taller door may be necessary for recreational vehicles.

Service Entries

The **service entry** is a house entrance that usually leads to the work area, often the kitchen. Through this entry, groceries are brought in, and laundry may be carried in and out. Also, family members tend to use this entrance instead of the main entry, especially when their clothes are wet or dirty.

Preferably, the service entrance opens into a mudroom or utility room instead of directly into the kitchen. Such a room provides space for taking off and storing coats and other outdoor clothing. It also helps prevent the tracking of mud, snow, or dirt throughout the home.

Special-Purpose Rooms

After primary areas of the home are planned, consideration may be given to **special-purpose rooms**. These are separate rooms dedicated to a single purpose. Examples include a home office, exercise room, darkroom, library, sewing room, arts and crafts studio, hobby room, workshop, music room, greenhouse, and billiard room. See 5-22.

When planning a specialized area, the amount of space and privacy required should be considered. Some special-purpose areas may work well in the corner of another room. Adequate storage for the required materials must be provided.

Noise may be a consideration in determining a good location. A furniture restoration shop or music room may be more functional if located away from bedrooms. Rooms requiring great privacy, such as a darkroom, should be placed in a remote area to keep traffic away.

Suitable lighting is needed above all work areas. Ventilation is an important requirement in a workshop or craft area where harmful fumes may form.

Velux-America, Inc.

5-22 Special-purpose rooms can be designed to meet the needs and desires of any household. Solarium windows transformed this little-used area into a sunny, breakfast room.

Plumbing is a consideration in areas where water is needed, such as a darkroom or workshop. Electrical outlets should be available in all areas, and a 240-volt outlet should be placed in a workshop for using major equipment.

Home Offices

The workplace has changed significantly in recent years and so have worker values. Employees are much less willing to waste time with long commutes, endure highway and subway hassles, and sacrifice their personal lives for their jobs. Increasingly, people are searching for ways to make their homes a base for earning money, either part-time or full-time, while being closer to their families. For them, a home office is a must. Many others who work outside the home desire a home office just to keep family and household records organized.

The first consideration in planning a home office is determining the type of work you will do there. Do you need a full-time office where you can meet clients to discuss business? See 5-23. Will it be mainly used for record keeping and working alone? Will it be a space used for projects brought home from your regular place of business, or will this be your only office? Answering these questions will help you create a workspace better suited to the intended use.

Location is the next consideration in planning a home office. If it will be used daily for serious work, it should be isolated from common household distractions—possibly in the least-used part of the home or a separate structure. If you need to consult with clients, an outside entrance with direct access from the street may be necessary. A separate room (with a door) that can be furnished and equipped exclusively for work is best for these office needs. In fact, the U.S. Internal Revenue Service (IRS) requires this if you are self-employed and want to deduct the cost of a home office from your income taxes.

5-23 An entire room devoted to this home office with furniture made from cherry wood creates a luxurious workspace for professionals.

One solution for eliminating distractions is moving the home office outside the living space. The simple act of traveling even a short distance changes the perception of the site from "home" to "work." For instance, a guest cottage could be converted to a home office. Other structures such as garages or toolsheds can also become home offices, but they would require a much greater expense. Separate spaces within the home such as spare bedrooms, dens, and converted attics or basements probably offer better opportunities. Also, a screened-in porch could be made into a home office.

If the need for a home office is only occasional, look for rooms that can do double duty, such as a guest bedroom or family room. For example, a daytime workspace for an architectural design business could double as a family room in the evenings. Similar possibilities exist for the corner of a basement, bedroom, kitchen, dining room, or living room, 5-24. A workspace off the family room could be elevated a foot with a half wall added to separate the two areas. Other spaces that can be converted to offices include an alcove, dressing room, wide landing, foyer, coatroom, loft, walk-in closet, or space under a stairway.

Once the location for the office is decided, the next step is planning its interior. The type of work that will be done in the office will determine the furnishings, equipment, and type of storage needed, 5-25. If clients will be coming to the home office, comfortable seating for a consultation area is a must. Furniture such as a sofa, table, chairs, and lamps may be needed to make the home office comfortable both physically and emotionally.

Careful organization and planning is needed to turn a workspace into a convenient home office. All supplies and equipment must be within easy reach so the user can concentrate on his or her work. The ideal work surface may be a desk, table, counter space, or some combination. Be sure to plan sufficient surface space for spreading out, organizing, and collating items as well as keeping office equipment and references handy. Built-in storage such as bookshelves and portable storage such as filing cabinets may also be needed.

Seating in the form of adjustable, ergonomic office chairs is recommended, but side chairs may

A Broyhill Furniture Industries, Inc. **B** Broyhill Furniture Industries, Inc.

5-24 Incorporating an office into a living room (A) can be as simple as adding one piece of furniture to a little-used corner. (B) This self-contained office has room for a computer plus all its hardware, software, and additional reference materials.

5-25 Little space was needed for this well-planned office area, which includes ample storage and desk space plus comfortable seating for clients.

suffice. **Ergonomics** is the study of humans and their response to various working conditions and environments. An ergonomic chair is designed for human safety, comfort, and efficiency. It prevents the back pain and muscle fatigue associated with sitting in chairs unsuited for hours of deskwork.

The best way to begin equipping your office is to identify which items you will use most. Look for equipment that serves multiple purposes and items that save space. A computer can be used for business transactions as well as home safety and security when linked to a master computer network. In addition to a computer, a business may need a printer, telephone/answering machine, scanner, and copier as well as fax capabilities and Internet access. Specialized equipment or supplies may also be required for a particular business. Regardless of the type of office space planned, the equipment and supplies should meet the needs of the work that will be done there.

An energy audit from the utility company will tell you if you have enough electrical power to run the equipment planned for the home office. Requirements for power, electrical outlets, and for telephone jacks should be evaluated. A surge suppresser on every outlet that supplies power to office equipment should be considered. Electrical surges, spikes, sags, and line noise can create enormous problems with digital data. In addition, an uninterruptible power supply that provides about 25 minutes of emergency power to computers or other equipment may be needed. Home offices today generally require sophisticated telephone capability, and any new lines should be planned and installed before construction is completed. Local phone companies often provide new wiring with up to three separate lines (pairs) in one cable.

Sufficient lighting is an important factor in achieving maximum productivity. Specific tasks may require special lighting, and window coverings may be needed to prevent glare from natural light. Converted office spaces such as basements and attics may have unique lighting needs.

The furnishings and finishes of the workspace should reflect the style and professionalism of your business, yet be comfortable and inviting. If the home office is located in a space used for other purposes, the decorating style should be compatible with the style in the adjoining space. The type of flooring should be suitable for the type of business operated from the home office. For example, if carpeting will be used, then select a fiber that helps reduce static buildup around electronic equipment.

Security is important in a home office where costly equipment and important records are kept. An exterior door should have a keyed lock as well as a deadbolt, and interior doors should also have keyed locks. Adequate insurance coverage should be acquired to protect the equipment and furnishings.

The quality of air is a special consideration when planning a home office. High levels of airborne debris can hinder the performance and shorten the life of high-tech equipment. Such debris includes grease droplets in cooking fumes, smoke from cigarettes or fireplaces, and pet hair and dander stirred up by traffic or wind currents. Air with insufficient moisture can create static electricity that might cause a computer to lose data. High humidity can lead to condensation on computer chips and other electronic parts. For these reasons, adequate ventilation systems should be planned. Fresh-air exchangers can be used to provide ventilation to improve the air quality. Your goal in planning a home office is to work conveniently, comfortably, functionally, and safely.

Storage

Approximately 10 percent of the space in a house should be allocated for storage. Each family has different storage needs depending on family size and individual habits.

A good floor plan provides for sufficient and convenient storage throughout the home. Floor plans can be used to determine how much built-in storage is provided and how much space is available for additional storage. Storage space should be flexible so changes in space can be made as interests and family size change. See 5-26.

When planning storage for a specific activity, space should be allowed first for the larger pieces, then the smaller items. In a home office, for example, space for the desk and conference table should be planned first. The location of the file cabinets and shelving would be planned next.

The two basic types of storage in a home are: built-in and freestanding. Built-in storage units are attached permanently to the walls, ceilings, and floors, 5-27. They usually require less space than freestanding units and utilize space more efficiently. However, they limit furniture arrangement possibilities and cannot be moved as easily.

The main advantage of freestanding units is they can be moved easily. Freestanding units range in size from small, compartmental boxes to large wall units and are available in many styles and finishes. Some freestanding units used in the home might include cabinets, shelf units, wall units, wardrobe closets, trunks, and storage racks.

Adaptations for Special Needs

Attention to details can make the service areas of the house accessible to everyone in the household, including small children, the elderly, and individuals with physical disabilities.

5-26 This family room provides flexible storage for a variety of family activities.

Wilsonart

5-27 Built-in storage units can be tailored to hold many different items.

Kitchens

An accessible kitchen for physically disabled users may follow the same layout as any other plan with three important differences:

- Work areas should be lower.
- The height of sinks and cooking units need to be adjusted.
- Space must be provided for wheelchairs.

Nearly all kitchen designs can easily be adapted for a person who uses a wheelchair. Toe space that is 6 in. deep and 8 in. to 11 in. high is needed under cabinets for wheelchair footrests. The required knee space of 28 to 30 in. wide, 27 to 30 in. high, and 21 to 24 in. deep can be provided by an overhang or extended counter space.

An electric range or cooktop may provide more safety for some users because of the absence of the open flame in gas cooking. A wall oven installed at eye level is easier for people in wheelchairs to use, but depending on an individual's vision and range of motion, some other height may be more convenient, 5-28.

Adding compartmentalized drawers to base cabinets instead of shelves allows disabled users to access items stored in the back that would otherwise be unreachable. Also, rollout bins, racks, baskets, and shelf trays can be used to make base

Whirlpool Corporation

5-28 Installing a microwave oven waist high allows the user to see the food and remove it from the oven easily in spite of limited arm mobility.

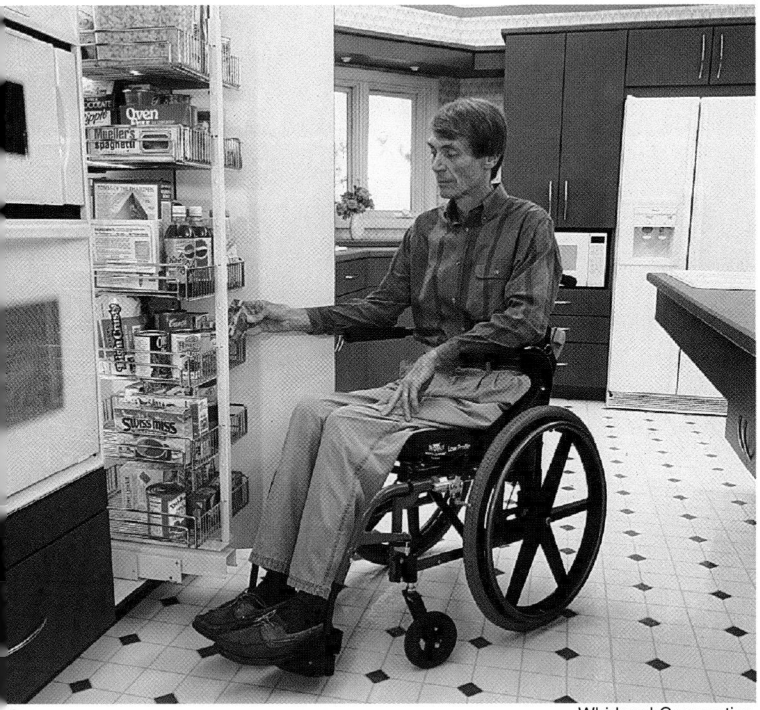

Whirlpool Corporation

5-29 Pull-out, open-bin storage systems are handy for everyone, but especially those with limited reach.

cabinets more usable. See 5-29. Lazy Susans are convenient for corner wall or base cabinets. It is difficult for people in wheelchairs to reach shelves higher than 48 in.

So they can be reached from a sitting position, the bottom shelf of a wall cabinet should be no higher than 17 in. above the counter. (Cabinets over stoves and refrigerators are the exceptions.) Shelves in wall cabinets should be adjustable.

Clothes Care Centers

For greater accessibility to individuals in wheelchairs, the washer and dryer openings should be slightly higher than the chair's armrests. Front-loading appliances can be placed on platforms to achieve the ideal height, 5-30. Individuals with canes, crutches, or walkers can comfortably use a stacked laundry appliance that has the dryer directly above the washer. All controls should be accessible.

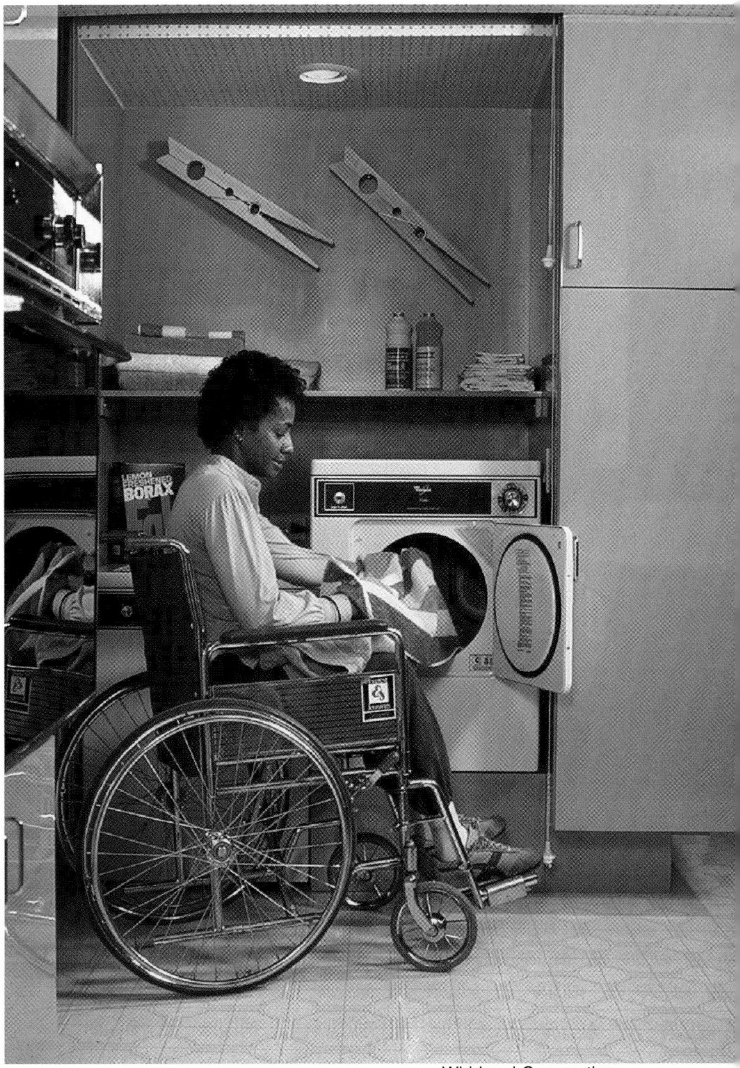

Whirlpool Corporation

5-30 This dryer is easily accessible for a person in a wheelchair.

Garages

To be accessible, a garage or carport should be at least 24 ft. long to provide space for walking around the front or back of the car. At least 5 ft. should be planned on the side of the car for a fully opened car door and adjacent wheelchair. A width of 12 to 14½ ft. is recommended for one car and a wheelchair.

Chapter Summary

The service and work areas of the home include kitchens, laundry facilities, basements, garages/carports, service entries, special-purpose rooms, and storage space. The kitchen is the center for meal preparation and cleanup, but may also serve dining, office, or laundering functions. Location of the kitchen should be near the service entrance, dining room, and living room. Its size, design, and furnishings should be suited to the many activities performed there. An efficient kitchen should have a relatively short work triangle connecting well-arranged work centers.

Laundry facilities may be as simple as a washer and dryer or as elaborate as a clothes care facility with space for sorting, cleaning, folding, ironing, and mending clothes. The location, size, and arrangement of a laundry facility will depend on a number of factors related to the lifestyle of the household and the basic house design.

Basements are generally considered part of the service area unless they are finished as living space. They often include space for the laundry, heating/cooling equipment, storage, and recreation. Special considerations such as high moisture levels and access must be addressed for basement locations.

Garages and carports provide storage for the vehicles and should be located near the service entrance of the house.

Special-purpose rooms address the special needs and interests of a household. The purpose each serves determines its size and location in the house as well as its furnishings and lighting. Home offices in particular are becoming an integral part of many new homes.

Attention to details can make the service areas of the house accessible even to family members and guests with physical disabilities.

Review Questions

1. What are the kitchen's three main work centers and their associated tasks and equipment?
2. What maximum length is recommend for the work triangle?
3. When would a 72 in. run of cabinet space *not* provide ample kitchen storage?
4. Why is a U-shaped kitchen preferred over a one-wall kitchen?
5. What tasks are performed in the laundry area?
6. What are some possible locations for laundry areas? What are the advantages and disadvantages of each?
7. For a basement, what types and locations of entrances are needed?
8. On what side of the house should a garage be located in warm climates? in cold climates?
9. How tall is the common garage door?
10. What is the best location for a service entrance?
11. What are eight possible types of special-purpose rooms that can be included in a home?
12. What are the advantages and disadvantages of the basic types of storage?
13. What factors should be considered if holding meetings with clients is one of the purposes of a new home office?
14. At what height should an oven be placed for a person using a wheelchair?
15. How much garage space should be provided beside a car to accommodate a wheelchair?

Suggested Activities

1. Obtain a floor plan and shade the areas that are considered part of the home's service area. Be sure that each is identified by name.
2. Sketch a U-shaped kitchen design of your own that meets the principles of good design and arrangement. Incorporate the three basic work centers and use standard-size cabinets and appliances. Show the work triangle's length.
3. Research the advantages, disadvantages, and costs of various types of countertop materials used in kitchens. Also find out what the installation cost is per square foot.
4. Interview the person(s) in your household responsible for handling the laundry to hear recommendations for improving the current laundry area. List their comments and draw sketches showing how their ideas could be incorporated.
5. Find a house plan in a magazine or newspaper real estate section that includes a garage. Compare the garage plan to the design suggestions presented in this chapter. Record the results of your comparison.
6. Sketch a plan for a special-purpose room that you or someone in your household strongly desires. Identify all furniture pieces and other equipment planned. Show dimensions using a scale of *¼ in. equals 1 ft.*
7. Summarize the design considerations presented in this chapter to make a kitchen accessible to individuals with disabilities. Add additional ideas you may have.

Internet Resources

Anchor Retaining Wall Systems
anchorwall.com

Hurd Windows and Patio Doors
hurd.com

Louisiana-Pacific Corporation, a manufacturer of building materials
lpcorp.com

Portland Cement Association
portcement.org

Raynor Garage Doors
raynor.com

Sterling Plumbing, a Kohler Company
sterlingplumbing.com

Whirlpool Corporation
whirlpool.com

Note: Web addresses may have changed since publication. For some entries, reaching the correct Web site may require keying *www.* into the address.

Chapter 6
Design
Chapter 7
Color

Part Two
Design and Color

Chapter 6
Design

Objectives

After studying this chapter, you will be able to

- describe the various uses and effects of space, line, shape, form, texture, and color.
- evaluate a room design according to its proportion, scale, balance, emphasis, and rhythm.
- use the elements and principles of design to create a room plan with appropriateness, harmony, variety, unity, and function.
- evaluate the selection and placement of functional and decorative accessories according to the elements, principles, and goals of design.

Key Terms

space
line
shape
form
texture
tactile
proportion
scale
balance
formal balance
informal balance
emphasis
rhythm
repetition
gradation
transition
radiation
harmony
unity
variety
function

A well-designed home provides a pleasant atmosphere for those who live there. It is both attractive and functional. The study of design may be divided into three main areas:

- elements of design
- principles of design
- goals of design

Elements of Design

The elements of design are space, line, shape, form, texture, and color. Each of these elements plays an important role in the overall success of a design, whether it is created for a home's exterior, a specific room, or a piece of furniture.

Space

Space is the area provided for a particular purpose. It may have two dimensions (length and width), such as a floor, or it may have three dimensions (length, width, and height), such as a room or dwelling. The elements of good design apply to both two- and three-dimensional space.

Walls, dividers, or other objects can define residential space. For example, in an open floor plan, the furniture and its placement define the interior space, 6-1.

Any space, no matter what size or shape, can be divided into distinct parts. For example, a room with two brightly colored rugs directs attention to the two separate areas rather than the total floor space of the room. Likewise, a walk from the entrance of a dwelling to the street divides the front lawn into two spaces.

Laura B. Trujillo, ASID, Illinois Chapter

6-1 Furnishings, not walls, define space in open plans. In this open kitchen, the wall cabinets and peninsula island define the storage and work areas, while the table and chairs define the eating area.

6-2 Soaring space creates a light, airy atmosphere in this living room.

Divisions of space can provide a sense of privacy and security. A fence or hedge outdoors is used to accomplish this purpose and screen out unwanted views and noises. Indoor objects such as furniture and partial walls accomplish the same goal.

Having too little space can create a feeling of being exposed. As building sites become smaller, homes are being built closer together. As a result, many people feel they are losing their privacy. Frequently, the solution is to plant shrubs or build privacy fences and use landscaping to create outdoor spaces. This extends the living area of the house beyond its walls while still maintaining privacy, and better utilizes the existing space.

Conversely, very large rooms or common areas designed for many people can produce a lonely feeling when a person is alone. Areas such as this can be made more intimate by providing dividers and clustering furniture and accessories into groups.

Space engulfs the area around objects, such as furniture. Too much furniture reduces the space in a room until it feels overcrowded. Space outside a building can also feel crowded, even if there is sufficient room for playing, cooking out, and handling services such as trash collection and deliveries. Try to sharpen your sense of space so you can use it to enhance a design, 6-2.

Space is affected by the number and size of objects in it. Many objects scattered throughout a room will most likely destroy the design effect because the space will have no apparent organization or unity. On the other hand, objects grouped into large units will create a more ordered space, 6-3.

When space changes gradually, it is more pleasing than when it changes abruptly. For example, plantings help soften the abrupt line where the house meets the grade level. When space changes suddenly, the eye shifts from one view to the other without making a smooth transition.

6-3 This large living room has furniture clustered to provide a quiet, conversation area near the window and group seating near the wall.

Line

Line is the visual direction of a design. It can be used to emphasize a pleasing element or disguise an undesirable one. Different types of lines have different effects on design.

Vertical lines lead the eye up, adding height, formality, and strength to a design. They can be seen in tall furniture; columns; pillars; striped wallpaper; and long, narrow draperies. Vertical lines can make rooms seem more spacious than they actually are and ceilings appear higher, 6-4. They can also make the exterior of a dwelling seem taller and narrower.

Horizontal lines lead the eye to the left or right, suggesting informality and restfulness. They are apparent in long, low roofs and furniture pieces, such as sofas and chests. Horizontal lines can make buildings, rooms, and furniture seem wider and shorter, 6-5.

Diagonal lines suggest action, movement, and excitement. Since diagonal lines can be overpowering and tiring, they should be used sparingly in design. Diagonal lines are evident in staircases, cathedral ceilings, and gable roofs, 6-6.

Curved lines add a softening, graceful effect to designs. See 6-7. However, too many curved lines create a busy look. Curved lines can be seen in

6-5 The horizontal lines on this residence makes the wall segments appear wider.

6-4 The strong vertical lines of this bed add visual height to the entire room.

Jayne Dranias, ASID, Illinois Chapter

6-6 The use of a dramatic ceiling treatment creates diagonal lines that add interest to the home's living area.

Lori Lennon, ASID, Illinois Chapter

6-7 The curved lines of the archways and wall niche soften the long linear path of the hallway.

doorway arches, ruffled curtains, curved furniture, and rounded accessories.

In design, one type of line should dominate. Others can be added for interest. For example, if horizontal lines dominate a room, accessories with diagonal or curved lines may be added.

Shape and Form

Shape and form are two elements of design that are sometimes used interchangeably. However, there is a distinct difference between the two terms, and they are used separately in this discussion.

Shape

Shape is a flat or silhouette image. It is an element of design with two dimensions: length and width. Shape is created by intersecting lines that form squares, rectangles, and triangles. Connecting one continuous line to make a circle also creates a shape. These are perfect geometric shapes, which are very pleasing to the eye.

Flat or silhouette images can also consist of imperfect geometric shapes, 6-8. Sometimes these images have no apparent geometric configurations and may even look random and irregular. Imperfect geometric shapes tend to create tension and attract greater interest. They should be used in small amounts so they do not detract from the total design.

Geometric shapes occur in nature in different degrees. For example, triangles appear in the petals of a flower, circles in the growth rings of a tree, and trapezoids on a turtle's shell. These shapes serve as a basis for emulation by designers and architects. Dwellings incorporate the shapes of squares and rectangles as well as triangles and circles, 6-9. Furniture, accessories, and other household items also incorporate geometric shapes.

The surface treatment of a shape can affect its overall appearance and its use in the design plan. Surfaces may be shiny and reflect images, such as mirrors, or transparent and create visual effects, such as window glass. They may also be brightly

6-8 Imperfect geometric shapes and diagonal lines are used in this stained glass window to create interest.

6-9 The arch shape of the roof tiles is repeated in the design of this Spanish dwelling.

Pittsburgh Corning

6-10 The carpeting on this attractive stairway has texture to absorb light and sound, while the texture of the window glass adds visual interest.

colored, smooth, and add interest, as in accessories. On the other hand, surfaces may be highly textured and absorb light and sound, such as window treatments, upholstery, and carpeting, 6-10. In addition, surfaces can be hard or soft, plain or patterned, and have color values ranging from light to dark. Application of these characteristics depends on the design function.

Form

Form is the outlined edges of a three-dimensional object. It has length, width, and depth (or height) as well as volume and mass. A square sheet of glass has shape, but when several pieces are joined together at right angles, a cube is created. Cubes, pyramids, cones, and spheres are some common geometric forms. Other examples of forms are found in furniture and architecture, 6-11.

Forms, such as furniture and accessories, should be chosen after considering how they will relate to the interior space and other forms within it. For example, placing a table in an empty room changes the space of the room. Adding a chair to the table not only changes the space, but affects the relationship of the table to the space as well.

The form of an object may convey a fragile or stable appearance, 6-12. Thin, delicate forms appear fragile, even when built of sturdy materials, while large, heavy forms provide stability to a design scheme.

Related forms tend to look better together than unrelated forms. A room is more pleasing if the form of the dominant piece is repeated in minor pieces and accessories within a room. The same is true for architectural features. See 6-13.

6-11 Columns are just one of the many types of forms used in architecture.

Texture

Texture is a surface's tactile quality. **Tactile** refers to the perception of touch. In design, texture involves how a surface feels to the touch as well as how it appears to feel. Thus, texture appeals to sight as well as touch. *Ribbed, crinkled, rough,* and *smooth* are some words used to describe various textures. Often patterns or colors are used to create the illusion of texture.

Texture can affect color by subduing or intensifying it. Smooth surfaces reflect more light than rough surfaces, making them look lighter and brighter. Rough surfaces absorb more light, making them look darker and less intense. Red carpet, for instance, looks darker and duller than red ceramic tile.

A balance of textures is needed in a well-designed room. A room with the same texture throughout is monotonous, but too many different textures can appear disjointed and distracting. Most well-designed rooms have a dominant texture with accents of contrasting textures, 6-14.

A Smithsonian Institution Photo No. 84-6235 B

6-12 Both chairs are made of sturdy, durable wood. However, the first chair (A), a Victorian style side chair by John Henry Belter, appears fragile because of its thin form. The second chair (B) appears sturdier because of its thick, stocky form.

6-13 Related forms are demonstrated through the use of similar roof pitches and window styles.

WCI Communities, Inc.

6-14 Several textures are combined in this living room, but they complement one another.

Color

Color is considered the most important element of design. For that reason, it is covered separately in Chapter 7.

Principles of Design

Principles of design are guidelines to follow when working with the elements of design. Together, they can be used to create an aesthetically pleasing design. Proportion, scale, balance, emphasis, and rhythm are the five main principles of design.

Proportion and Scale

Proportion and scale are two principles of design that are closely related, but different. Therefore, they are discussed separately.

Proportion

Proportion is the ratio of one part to another part or of one part to the whole. The most effective proportions have an uneven ratio of 2:3, 3:5, or 5:8. Even ratios of 1:1 or 1:2 are less pleasing to the eye. For example, a rectangle has more pleasing proportions than a square. A coffee table that is two-thirds the length of a couch is more pleasing than one that is the same length or half the length of the couch, 6-15.

A number of human designs as well as those found in nature seem to be based on mathematical ratios called the *golden section*, 6-16. These ratios, discovered by the ancient Greeks, are a series of numbers that progress by the sum of the two previous numbers: 2:3, 3:5, 5:8, 8:13, 13:21, and so forth. When a golden ratio is the underlying principle used to divide a shape or form into two parts, the smaller section has the same proportion to the larger section as the larger one has to the whole. Strictly speaking, the golden ratio is 0.618 to 1.0.

When selecting objects for the home, the designer pays careful attention to good proportion. For example, the parts of a chair—arms, legs, back, and seat—should be proportional to each other and to the chair as a whole. Each part should appear to belong to the whole.

When the proportions of an object are wrong, people often react negatively without really understanding why. For example, a low coffee table with large, massive legs does not look right because its parts do not have good proportions to each other or

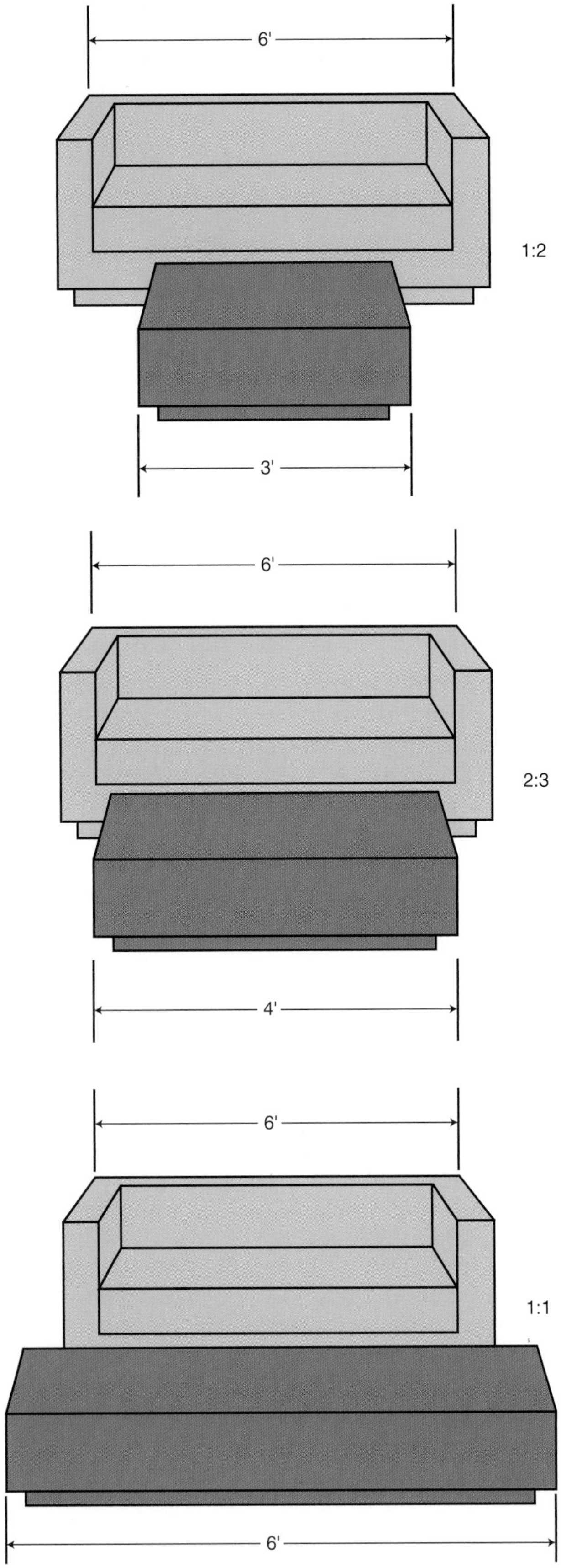

6-15 The pair of objects in the center, which have a 2:3 ratio, have the most pleasing proportion.

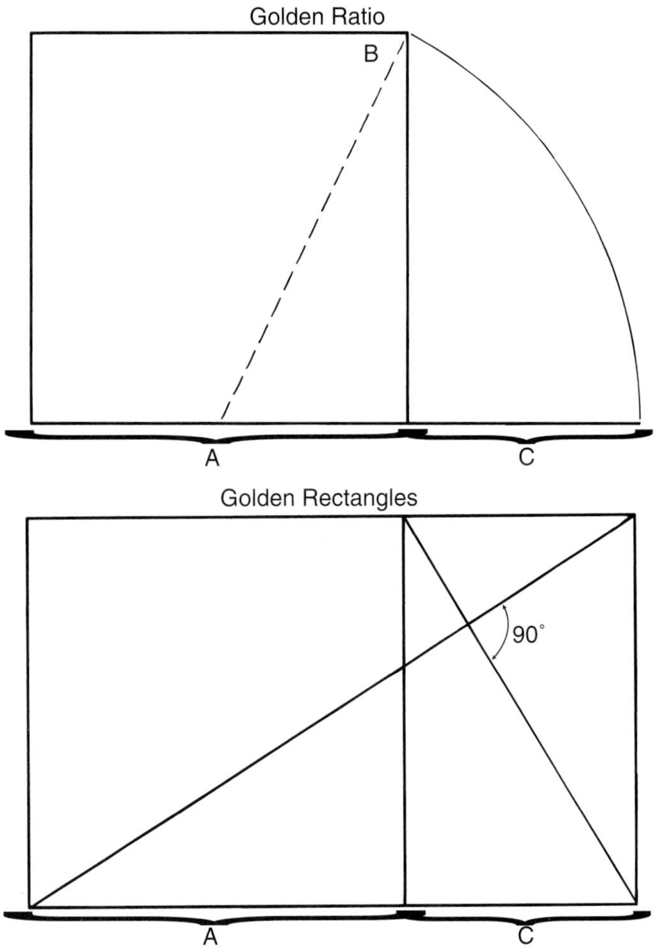

6-16 The golden ratio determines the most pleasing proportions for lines and forms. To find the golden ratio for Line A, draw a square with A as the base. Connect the midpoint of A to an upper corner of the square to form Line B. Sweep B down to A to form an extension, Line C. The relationship of A to A+C is the golden ratio of 0.618:1.0. Golden rectangles use the same pleasing proportions. When a square is removed from a golden rectangle, a smaller golden rectangle remains. Another mark of a golden rectangle is the creation of a right angle (90°) when the diagonals of the large and small rectangles intersect.

to the whole. The legs are too large for the remainder of the table. A tall, wide lampshade is too large for a lamp with a small base. Not only does it appear disproportionate, but its normal function will also be adversely affected.

One of the most important features of proportion in house design is the relationship between wall area and windows. To achieve good proportion, the openings should not equal the wall area. They should form a proportion of 1:3, 3:5, or 5:8, for example.

Scale

Scale refers to the size of an object in relation to a standard or familiar size, 6-17. When a design plan appears so right that scale does not come to mind, good scale has been achieved. To achieve good scale, choose objects that are appropriate for human dimensions and the proper size for the space they occupy. When choosing furniture, remember that large rooms require large-scale furnishings, 6-18. On the other hand, small rooms require small-scale pieces.

Dominant pieces of furniture should be in scale to the furnishings that complement them. For example, a large floor lamp would be out of scale placed next to a delicate loveseat, while a slender floor lamp would be the correct scale. Scale is also an important factor when designing dwellings. See 6-19. For instance, an attached, one-car garage is out of scale with a large, two-story home, but in scale with a small bungalow.

Furnishings should be in proper scale for people as well as the space they occupy. If a couch is intended for relaxation, it should be long enough for a person to lie comfortably. Kitchen counters should

Cultured Stone by Stucco Stone Products, Inc.

6-17 The large stones above the fireplace and the sculptured art piece are proper scale for the wide fireplace opening.

Roy Klipp, ASID, Illinois Chapter

6-18 A room with high ceilings needs properly scaled furnishings, such as this bedroom's tall bed and window treatment.

6-19 A chimney of lesser scale than this would appear lost on such a massive structure.

be the proper height for efficient work. Small, low chairs are a good scale for a young child's room.

The visual size of furniture and accessories is influenced by scale. For example, two objects may have the same dimensions, but one may appear larger than the other because of its design. A furniture piece of the same color with bold lines, coarse textures, and large patterns may appear larger than a piece with thin lines, smooth textures, and small patterns. Although the two pieces of furniture are the same size, the first piece will appear to use more space in a room. Keep this in mind as you choose furnishings.

The visual size of an object is also affected by its frame of reference. For instance, a sofa with a high back will seem too tall next to a low window, but perfect next to a high window. Curtains and upholstery with large patterns may look enormous in a small setting, but well sized in a large setting, 6-20.

F. Michael Kerley, ASID, Illinois Chapter

6-20 Bold patterns would overwhelm a small room, but look appropriate in this spacious, light interior.

Balance

In design, **balance** is a sense of equilibrium. Balance may be either formal or informal.

Formal balance is a visual equilibrium achieved through the placement of identical objects on both sides of a central point, 6-21. This type of balance is also known as symmetrical. Formal balance is used frequently in architectural designs and landscaping as well as in room designs, 6-22. Symmetrical balance gives a quiet, orderly feeling to a room.

Informal balance is a visual equilibrium achieved through the placement of different, but equivalent, objects on both sides of a central point. This type of balance is also known as asymmetrical. Various forms, textures, and colors can be used together to achieve informal balance. See 6-23. For instance, a large object can be balanced with a few smaller ones. Since asymmetrical balance involves the arrangement of varied objects, it usually requires more thought and creativity to achieve than formal balance.

Emphasis

In design, **emphasis** refers to the center of attention or interest. It is the feature that repeatedly draws attention. The center of interest in a room is usually a fireplace, window, work of art, or dominant piece of

Drexel Heritage Furnishings, Inc.

6-21 Here, formal balance is used to create a pleasing effect. The sectional sofa pieces, matching chairs, and glass-front cabinets on each side of the fireplace are identical.

6-22 Formal balance gives this house a stately appearance.

furniture. See 6-24. Emphasis is also an important design element for landscaping and exterior design.

To achieve effective emphasis, two guidelines are important. First, the point of emphasis should dominate, but not overpower the rest of the room or the design. Second, no other features should compete with the focal point.

Rhythm

Rhythm is a principle of design that leads the eye from one part of a design to another. Rhythm can be created through repetition, gradation, transition, and radiation.

Rhythm by **repetition** can be achieved by repeating color, line, form, or texture.

Gradation is rhythm created by making a gradual change in form or color value. One example is a sky painted in a child's room, with light blue at eye level and deep blue above. Another example of gradation is a change in form, such as large to small. See 6-25.

Curved lines that carry the eye over an architectural feature or rounded parts of furniture create rhythm through **transition**. See 6-26.

Drexel Heritage Furnishings, Inc.

6-23 The opposite sides of this room do not mirror each other, but they are balanced. The large flowered sofa is balanced by the two side chairs, a small table, and a lamp. Along the back wall, the tall plant on one side balances the chair on the other.

American Olean

6-24 The design and materials used in this large fireplace creates a point of interest in this very formal room.

6-25 Gradation is apparent in the two-bowl fountain. The eye is lead from the largest to the smallest bowl.

Radiation is rhythm created by lines flowing outward from a central point. It is found in the lines of a flower arrangement, a light fixture, or the leg supports of a table.

Goals of Design

The elements and principles of design can be used to meet the goals of design, which include the following:

- appropriateness
- harmony, variety, and unity
- function

Appropriateness

Good design should be appropriate for its intended function and for the lifestyle of the household. For example, the furniture and accessories in a living room should be conducive to relaxing, conversing, and entertaining. Comfortable chairs

Pozzi Wood Windows

6-26 The curves in this window unit provide rhythm through transition, leading the eye from one side of the room to the other.

and soft lighting would be appropriate for these functions, 6-27.

The appropriateness of the design for the lifestyle of a family should also be considered. Families with small children need durable, easy-care furniture and carpeting in their living rooms. A pottery display case in the living area is ideal for a household that collects or designs pottery as a hobby. Good design is appropriate when it addresses the personality, needs, and values of family members.

Harmony, Variety, and Unity

In design, **harmony** is an agreement among the parts. It results when unity and variety are combined. Harmony is achieved when the elements of design are used effectively according to the principles of design. A single design idea is executed, and similar shapes and forms are repeated, 6-28.

Unity in design is the appearance of all parts seeming to belong together, 6-29. It is achieved by repeating certain elements of design. A dominant type of line, shape, form, texture, or color should be apparent in designs that have unity. In a unified room design, the room is seen as a whole, not as a collection of unrelated furnishings, accessories, colors, and patterns.

In design, **variety** is the use of contrasting features to prevent monotony. Contrasting lines, forms, textures, and colors add variety to a unified design. However, the contrasts should not compete with the dominant elements of the design.

Variety and unity work well together when one or more design elements are held constant while the others change. Any element of design—space, line, shape, form, texture, or color—can remain unchanged to promote unity. For example, when light browns and beiges are used throughout a room for unity, splashes of blue will add variety. When curved patterns predominate in a room, rectangular patterns will provide the accent.

Function

The saying "form follows function" is a guideline for good design. In design, **function** refers to the intended use or purpose of a structure, room, or object. It should be the primary consideration in determining an item's form.

Designers should always consider how the object is expected to perform and what purpose it will serve. No matter how beautiful the form is or how perfect its balance, success will ultimately depend on whether the design enhances its function. For example, a chair should be attractive, but more importantly, its form should allow a person to sit comfortably.

Generally, a design that is commonly linked to a certain function should not be repeated in objects serving different functions, unless the resulting effect appeals to the individual. For example, a telephone and a radio are two very different and identifiable

WCI Communities, Inc.

6-27 The furniture and accessories in this room are appropriate for conversing and entertaining.

Pozzi Wood Windows

6-28 Curved and square forms are repeated in the windows, walls, and furnishings of this dining area.

Photo Courtesy of James Hardie® Siding Products

6-29 Unity is achieved through the combination of materials, color, and shape of this classic structure.

objects. Most people with a telephone at their bedside would want it to look like a telephone. Teens, on the other hand, may enjoy having a phone that looks like a radio or some other object. This is a matter of personal taste.

Accessories in Design

Accessories complete the total room design. Accessories should reflect the personalities of the household members and give individuality to a design, 6-30. Accessories can be functional, decorative, or both.

The elements, principles, and goals of design should be considered when choosing accessories. Items should repeat or accent the dominant line, shape, form, texture, and color in the room. Accessories should be in proper proportion to other items in the room. Accessories are used to achieve formal or informal balance. They may repeat patterns in other pieces for rhythm. Each accessory should be appropriate and contribute to the unity of the overall design.

Functional accessories include such items as lamps, mirrors, clocks, screens, and fireplace tools. These items should be chosen and placed for functional purposes first and decorative purposes second. See 6-31. For example, when selecting a lamp for reading, only those that provide enough light should be considered. Also, a lamp for reading should be placed near a chair or couch, not in a corner away from seating.

Decorative accessories include sculptures, figurines, pottery, crafts, plants, pictures, and other wall hangings. These items should express the personalities of household members and be pleasing in appearance.

Due to the decorative nature of these objects, they should be placed so they are enhanced by their surroundings and easily seen. Tabletops, shelves, display cases, and individual stands are often used for three-dimensional accessories.

Pictures and wall hangings should be carefully hung so they unify the room's design and their proportions seem pleasing. Unless a picture is large and dramatic enough to serve as a focal point, several pieces should be grouped with the furniture pieces in the room. Space between pictures and furniture should be small enough to make the

A Lynn Masters, ASID, and Diantha Harns, ASID, Illinois Chapter

B Anne Lise Lawson, ASID, Illinois Chapter

6-30 Accessories say a lot about the personality and lifestyle of a household. Bedrooms, for example, reflect the interests of adults (A) and children (B).

6-31 This decorative lamp chosen for this room provides ample light for reading. Its style and location blend well with the overall design of the room.

pictures and furniture look unified. The furniture then serves as an anchor for the pictures, 6-32. A picture without an anchor appears to float on a wall and never really blends into the overall design.

Picture groupings should be hung in a unified arrangement. The grouping should be based on one dominant horizontal line and/or vertical line. See 6-33. Hanging groupings in a stair-step fashion should be avoided; this arrangement carries the eye away from the grouping. One exception is on walls with a diagonal architectural feature, such as a stairway.

Spacing between pictures should be small enough to unify the grouping. Even spacing should be used between all the pictures in the grouping.

Groupings of pictures tend to be more interesting when an uneven number is used instead of an even number. Groupings also tend to be more pleasing if one picture dominates the grouping, such as a picture with bolder colors, larger size, unique shape, or a different theme. An example of a dominant picture is a formal portrait in a group of informal paintings.

A picture or grouping of pictures should be hung at eye level, with the center of the picture or grouping approximately 5 or 6 ft. from the floor. Pictures and groupings above furniture should be in scale to the furniture. Pictures mounted above chairs or sofas should be placed at least 6 to 8 in. above the furniture so the head of a seated person will not touch the frame.

WCI Communities, Inc.

6-32 The sofa serves as an anchor for the picture behind it. The picture is in good scale to the wall and sofa.

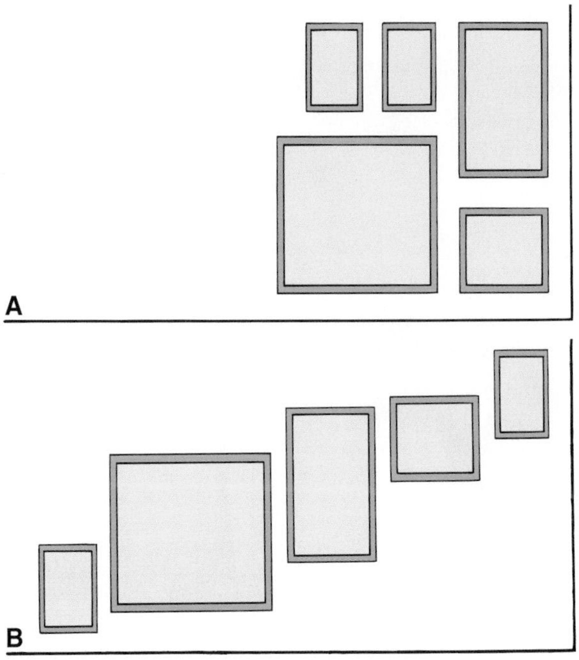

6-33 Picture groupings that are aligned on one or more sides (A) have a pleasing, unified appearance. Groupings that are not aligned (B) lead the eye away from the pictures.

Chapter Summary

The study of design focuses on three main areas: elements, principles, and goals. The elements of design are space, line, shape, form, texture, and color. Space is the area provided for a particular purpose. It can be two- or three-dimensional space. Lines give direction to a design and can emphasize or disguise a design element. Lines may be vertical, horizontal, diagonal, or curved. Shapes are flat, while forms contain volume and mass. Texture is how a surface feels to the touch or how the surface qualities look.

The principles of design—proportion, scale, balance, emphasis, and rhythm—are guidelines to follow when working with the elements of design. Proportion is the ratio of one part to another or of one part to the whole. The most effective proportions usually have an unequal ratio—2:3, 3:5, or 5:8. Scale refers to the relative size of an object when compared to other objects. Consider the human dimension when working with scale. Balance in a design projects a sense of equilibrium, whether formal or informal. Emphasis refers to the center of attention or interest in a design. Rhythm leads the eye from one part of the design to another.

Applying the elements and principles of design achieves the three goals of design. First, a good design serves its intended function. Secondly, the parts of the design agree but display variety. Finally, the intended use of the design determines a suitable form.

Accessories complete a room design, giving individuality and practicality to the space. Accessories can be decorative, functional, or both.

Review Questions

1. What guidelines should be followed when using the five elements of design?
2. How can internal space be utilized to provide privacy and protection?
3. In a small bedroom with a high ceiling, should the wallpaper have vertical, diagonal, or horizontal stripes? Why?
4. What effect do curved lines have on design?
5. What is the difference between shape and form?
6. How can texture affect color?
7. Which of the following room features reflect good proportion: an equal amount of wall and window area versus unequal amounts? Why?
8. Should a tall china closet or a low hutch be chosen for a dining room with a low ceiling?
9. How does formal balance differ from informal balance?
10. What are the two main guidelines for achieving emphasis in a room design?
11. What four methods can be used to create rhythm in design?
12. What are the three goals of design?
13. How can monotony be avoided in a design?
14. In design, what does *form follows function* mean?
15. How does the selection and placement of functional accessories differ from that of decorative accessories?
16. What are two guidelines to follow when hanging a picture above a sofa?

Suggested Activities

1. Select two elements of design—space, line, shape, form, texture, or color—and illustrate them with photographs or drawings of your choosing.
2. Describe the difference between shape and form and name examples of each.
3. Write an essay defining and identifying each of the principles of design.
4. Select two pictures: one with formal balance in design and one with informal balance. Identify the components within each picture that contribute to each room's type of design balance. In each case, describe what could be done to change the room to the opposite type of design balance.
5. Find an example that you believe shows the design goal of harmony with variety and unity.
6. Write a short essay describing what is meant by *form follows function*. Give examples.
7. Describe the purpose(s) of accessories in a design scheme selected by your teacher.

Internet Resources

American Institute of Architects
aia.org

American Society of Interior Designers
asid.org

American Society of Landscape Architects
asla.org

Architectural Digest Magazine
archdigest.com

Architectural Ornament, Inc., manufacturer of polyurethane architectural molding
architectural-ornament.com

Design-Build Institute of America
dbia.org

Modern Plastics
modplas.com

Reynolds Building Products
reynoldsbp.com

U.S. Department of Energy
energy.gov

Note: Web addresses may have changed since publication. For some entries, reaching the correct Web site may require keying *www.* into the address.

Chapter 7
Color

Objectives

After studying this chapter, you will be able to

- explain the perceptions linked to certain colors.
- describe the standard color wheel.
- evaluate a color according to hue, value, and intensity.
- use a color wheel to plan various color harmonies.
- describe three popular color systems.
- identify seven common color harmonies.
- explain the effect of light on color.

Key Terms

color spectrum
primary colors
secondary colors
intermediate colors
hue
value
intensity
tint
shade
complement
monochromatic color harmony
analogous color harmony
complementary color harmony
split-complementary color harmony
triadic color harmony
double-complementary color harmony
neutral color harmonies

Color is the most exciting tool of the designer. It offers unlimited opportunities for decorating. Color can help to create a mood within a room, 7-1. It can communicate excitement, romance, or solitude.

The Psychology of Color

How color influences human behavior is the subject of many research projects. The results show that certain perceptions are linked to certain colors.

Thomasville Furniture Industries, Inc.

7-1 The bright red sofa in this room, dominated by wood tones and neutrals, brings the room to life.

Many color perceptions affect the way people feel about a room, space, or object.

Red is associated with danger, power, love, passion, anger, fire, and strength. It is bold, exciting, and warm. See 7-2. Research has shown red to stimulate the nervous system and increase blood pressure, respiration rate, and heartbeat. It is conspicuous wherever it appears, and since it is so lively and stimulating, it should be used with care. A variety of popular colors may be derived from red when it is darkened, lightened, dulled, or brightened. For example, when red is lightened, it becomes pink. When it is darkened and muted, it becomes maroon.

Orange is cheerful, warm, and less aggressive than red. It expresses friendliness, courage, hospitality, energy, and hope. Orange has stimulating properties similar to red, but is not as intense. Orange mixes well with cool colors.

Yellow is cheerful, friendly, and warm. It is traditionally associated with happiness, sunlight, sympathy, prosperity, cowardice, and wisdom. Yellow rooms are light and airy. Pure yellows demand attention and should therefore be used with care. Gold provides a luxurious touch and is especially useful for accents or accessories. All yellows take on the tones of other colors and add flattering highlights.

Green is refreshing. The color of nature, it is cool, peaceful, and friendly, 7-3. Green is often associated with hope, envy, and good luck. Green mixes well with other colors and looks especially good with white. Dark green is a favorite color for floor covering.

Blue has the opposite effect of red. It is cool, calm, and reserved. Blue communicates serenity, tranquility, and formality, 7-4. However, too much blue in a room can be depressing. Blue, more than any other color, is affected by the different types of materials it colors. For example, lacquer, glass, and other shiny surfaces intensify blue.

Violet is the color of royalty, dignity, and mystery. It is dramatic and works well with other colors, especially pink and blue. Popular violet hues include plum, eggplant, and lilac. Violet is often used in small amounts as an accent.

Black is mysterious, severe, and dramatic, 7-5. It symbolizes wisdom, evil, and death. Small amounts

NMC/Focal Point

7-2 Red provides the excitement in this color harmony and presents a bold presence.

7-3 Lush greenery and deep green side chairs create a serene setting for this modern living room.

Manufactured Housing Institute

7-4 The blue in this room increases the formality of the setting.

Summitville Tile

7-5 Black provides drama in this hallway.

of black help other colors appear more vivid. Black and dark gray in accessories or furniture finishes make other colors crisp and clear. Large areas of black should be used extremely sparingly as it can be oppressive and claustrophobic.

White is the symbol of youth, freshness, innocence, purity, faith, and peace. Like black, white can make other colors appear cleaner and livelier. Creamy white creates a mellow background color and is effective in blending furniture of different woods and styles. It is used with traditional as well as modern styles.

When making color decisions for a home, the color preferences of all family members should be considered. The social area of a home should be decorated in colors that will make all members feel comfortable. Individual color preferences can be used in the sleeping areas and other personalized areas of the home.

The Color Spectrum

The **color spectrum** is the full range of all existing colors. It is composed of more than ten million identified colors. Each of these distinct colors is derived from a few basic colors, shown in 7-6. This array is found in the rainbow, which is one interpretation of nature's total color spectrum.

Even though the variations in colors are virtually limitless, they and their relationships to one another

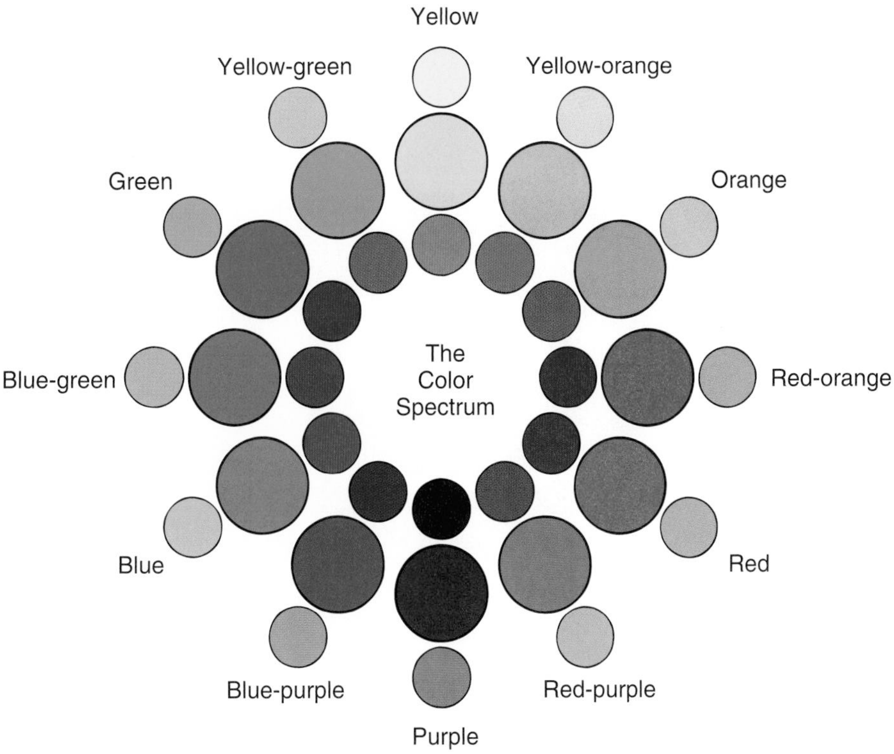

7-6 This is one visual representation of the color spectrum.

are easy to understand when they are reduced to a few basic principles. The standard color wheel best illustrates these principles.

The Color Wheel

The color wheel is the most commonly used tool for understanding color relationships in design, 7-7. The middle ring of the color wheel consists of three types of colors: primary colors, secondary colors, and intermediate colors.

Yellow, blue, and red are the **primary colors**, 7-8. Mixing, lightening, and darkening the primary colors can make all other colors.

The **secondary colors** are orange, green, and violet, 7-9. Mixing equal amounts of two of the primary colors makes these colors. Orange is made

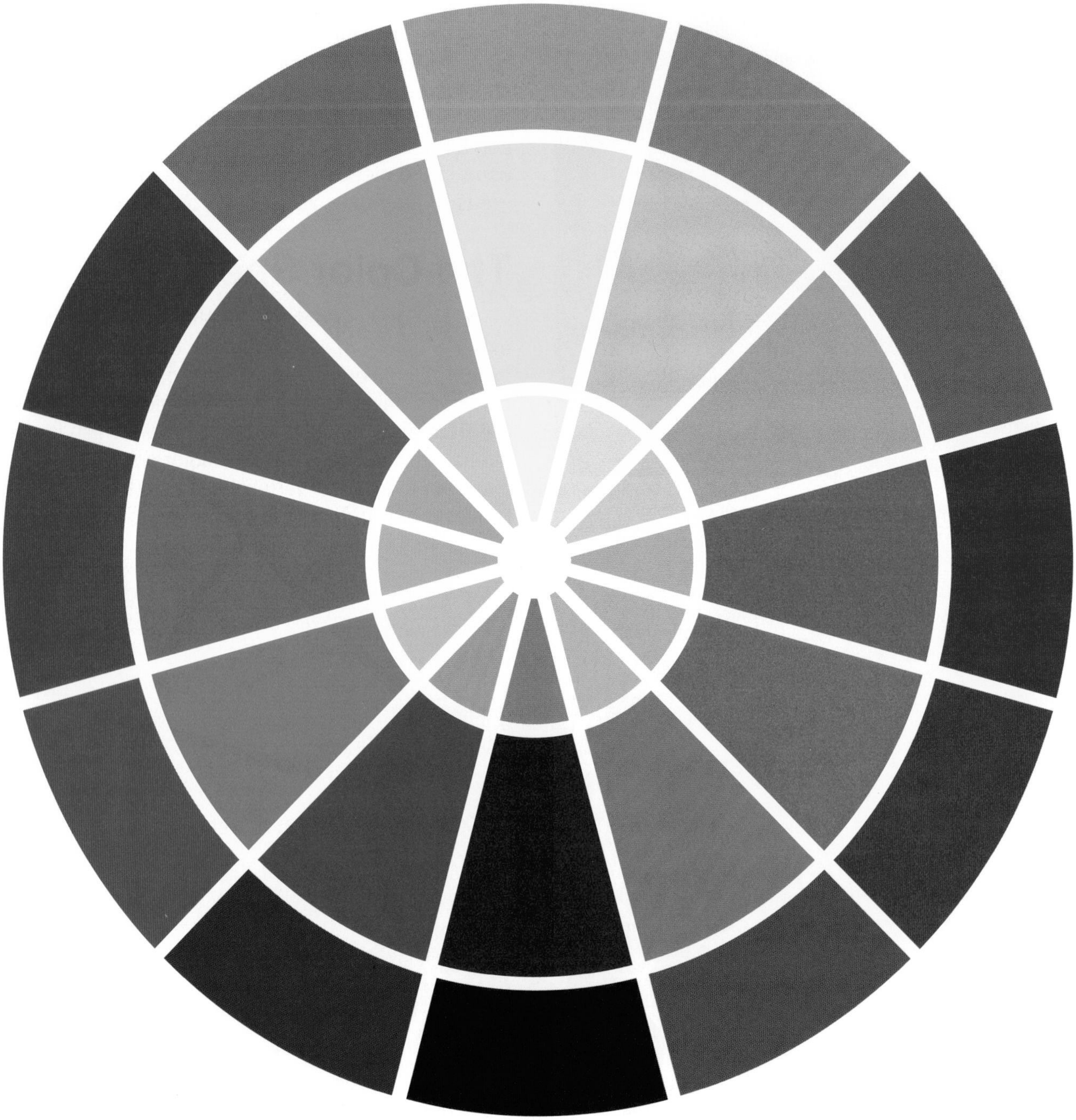

7-7 The color wheel shows the primary, secondary, and tertiary colors. The middle ring shows the normal values of these colors; the inner ring, tints; and the outer ring, shades.

by mixing yellow and red. Green results from mixing yellow and blue. Violet is made by mixing blue and red. On the color wheel, each secondary color is positioned between the two primary colors used to make it.

Colors made by mixing a primary color with a secondary color are the **intermediate colors**. These are the remaining colors on the color wheel—yellow-green, blue-green, blue-violet, red-violet, red-orange, and yellow-orange. See 7-10. These six colors are also called *tertiary colors*. Intermediate colors are named after the two colors used to make them. The primary color is always listed first.

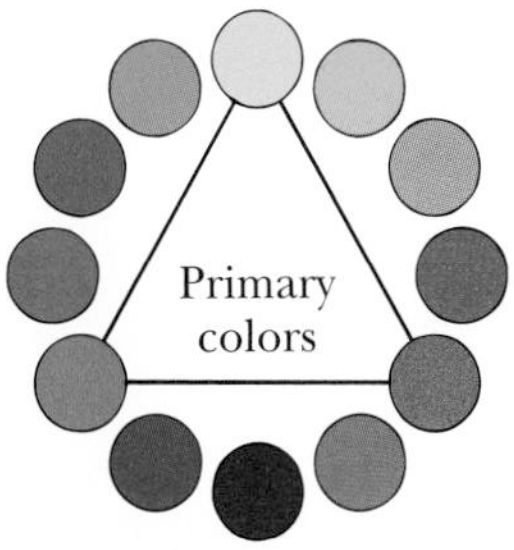

7-8 The primary colors are yellow, blue, and red.

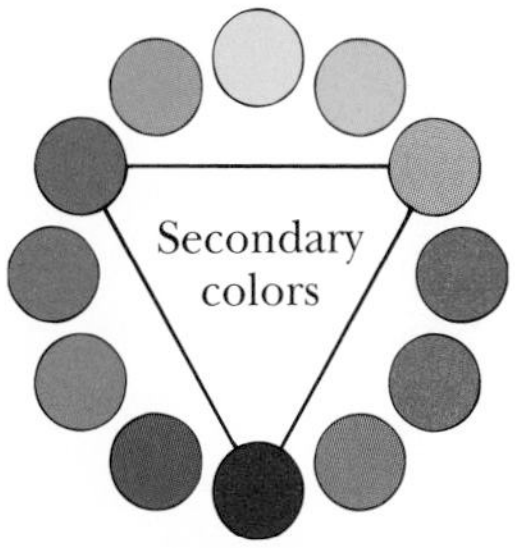

7-9 The secondary colors are orange, green, and violet.

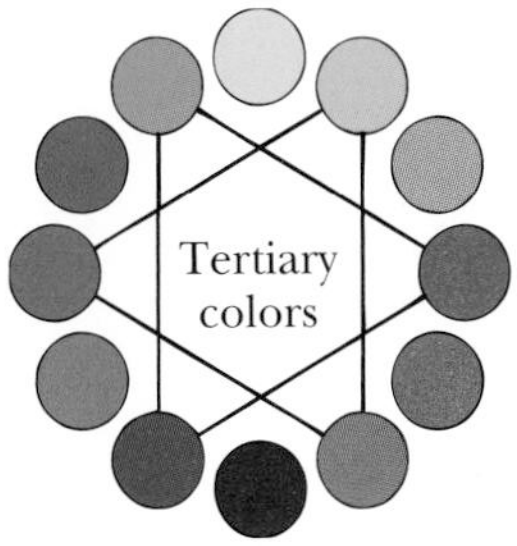

7-10 The tertiary colors are yellow-green, blue-green, blue-violet, red-violet, red-orange, and yellow-orange.

Color Characteristics

Each color has three characteristics: hue, value, and intensity.

- **Hue** is the name of a color.
- **Value** is the lightness or darkness of a hue.
- **Intensity** is the brightness or dullness of a hue.

Red, green, and blue-violet are examples of hues. The hue is the characteristic that makes red different from green. A color may be lightened or darkened, brightened or dulled, but the hue will remain the same.

The normal values of hues are shown in the middle ring of the color wheel. All colors do not have the same normal value; some are lighter or darker than others. For example, yellow has the lightest normal value of all the hues on the color wheel, while violet has the darkest value.

The value of a hue can be made lighter by adding white. This produces a **tint**. For example, pink is a tint of red, made by adding white to red. For lighter tints, more white is added. Tints are shown in the inner ring of the color wheel.

A hue can be made darker by adding black. This produces a **shade**. Maroon is a shade of red. Shades are shown in the outer ring of the color wheel.

A value scale is shown in 7-11. It shows the full range of values for a hue, from the lightest tint to the darkest shade.

The normal intensity of a hue is shown in the center ring of the color wheel. Adding some of its complement can lower the intensity of a hue. The

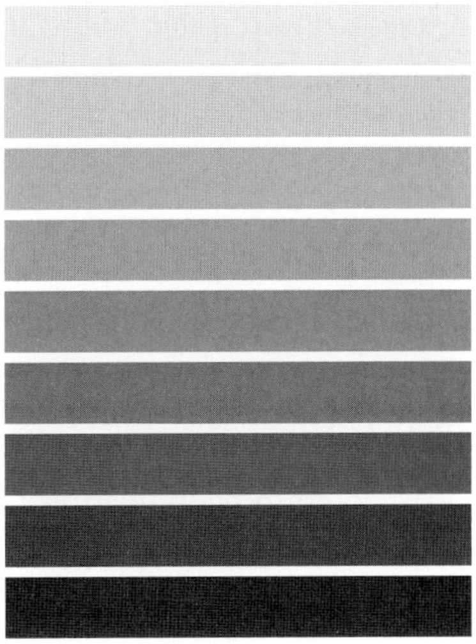

7-11 The value of a color can be changed by adding different amounts of black or white.

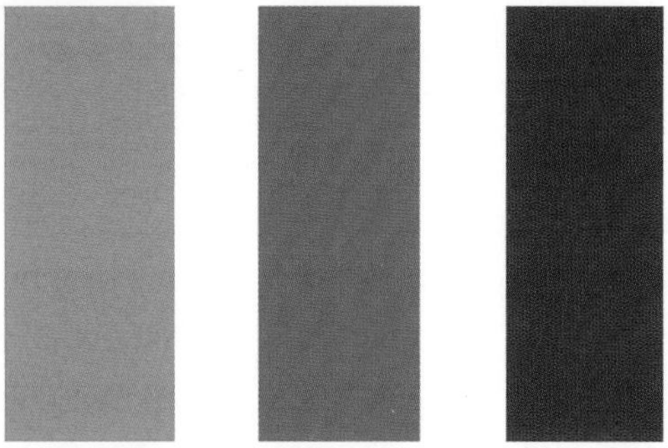

7-12 The intensity of a color is lowered by adding some of its complement.

complement of a hue is the color directly opposite it on the standard color wheel. For example, adding a small amount of its complement, green, can dull red. See 7-12. Examples of high intensity colors include hot pink and fire-engine red. Examples of low intensity colors include rust and smoky blue.

Warm and Cool Colors

Colors can be classified as warm or cool. Although the temperature throughout a home may be the same, some rooms may seem warmer or cooler because of the colors used in decorating. See 7-13.

Warm colors include orange, yellow, and red, which is the warmest. These are considered the warm colors because of their association with warm objects of the same color, such as the sun and fire.

Warm colors are also called *advancing colors* because they make objects appear larger or closer. They can make a room feel warm and cozy.

On the opposite side of the standard color wheel are the cool colors: green, blue, and violet. They are associated with water, grass, and trees.

Cool colors are called *receding colors* because they make objects seem smaller and farther away. A small room can appear larger if it is decorated in cool colors. Cool colors also make a room feel restful and peaceful.

Neutral Colors

The neutral colors are white, black, and gray. White is totally absent of color, black is a mixture of all colors, and gray is a combination of black and white. Neutral colors are often used as background colors in rooms because they blend well with other colors.

Brown, tan, and beige are considered near-neutral colors, 7-14. These also blend well with other colors. However, brown, tan, and beige colors are usually based on the red, orange, and yellow hues.

A Sauder Woodworking Company

B Shea Lubecke, ASID, Illinois Chapter

7-13 The apparent warmth of a room is affected by the colors decorating it. This family room seems cool because green dominates (A), while the living room seems much warmer because of the oranges and reds (B).

Color Systems

Several color systems or theories are recognized by students of color. Some incorporate both psychological and physical factors. The result has been a number of color wheels, each with a different group of basic colors. The three most common systems are the Brewster, Ostwald, and Munsell systems.

Thomasville Furniture Industries, Inc.

7-14 Near neutrals include brown, tan, and beige colors. They are often used in decorating because they blend well with each other and other colors. Touches of deep red serve as the accent color here.

The Brewster System

The Brewster system is the standard color wheel shown in 7-7. Developed by David Brewster, it is the best known and simplest of the color systems. It is also called the *Prang system*.

The Brewster system is based on three primary hues: red, yellow, and blue. These hues are called primary because they cannot be mixed from other pigments, nor can they be reduced into component colors.

When equal amounts of any two primary colors are mixed together, a secondary (binary) hue results. The Brewster system produces three secondary colors: green from yellow and blue, violet from blue and red, and orange from red and yellow. Each of the secondary colors can be mixed equally with a primary color to form a tertiary (intermediate) hue. The tertiary hues include: blue-green, red-orange, and red-violet. Together, these twelve hues make up the full Brewster color wheel.

The Ostwald System

Friedrich Wilhelm Ostwald developed the Ostwald system. His color wheel uses yellow, orange, red, purple, blue, turquoise, sea green, and leaf green hues plus white and black added to the hues. In theory, mixing these hues plus pure white and black can create 24 hues. In

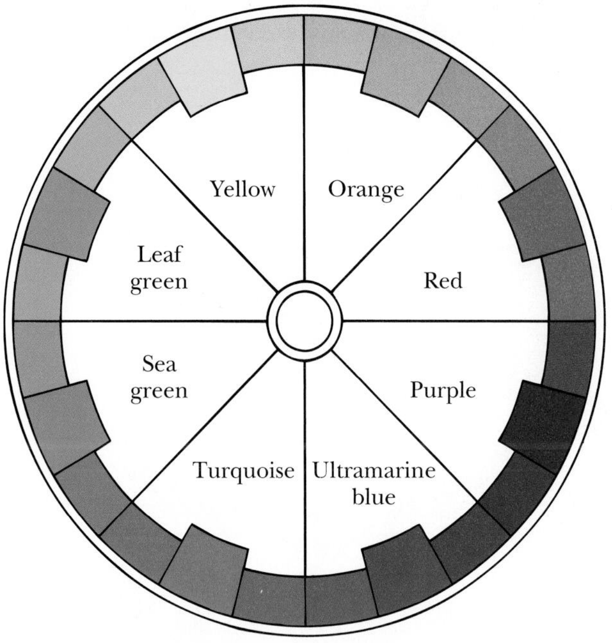

A

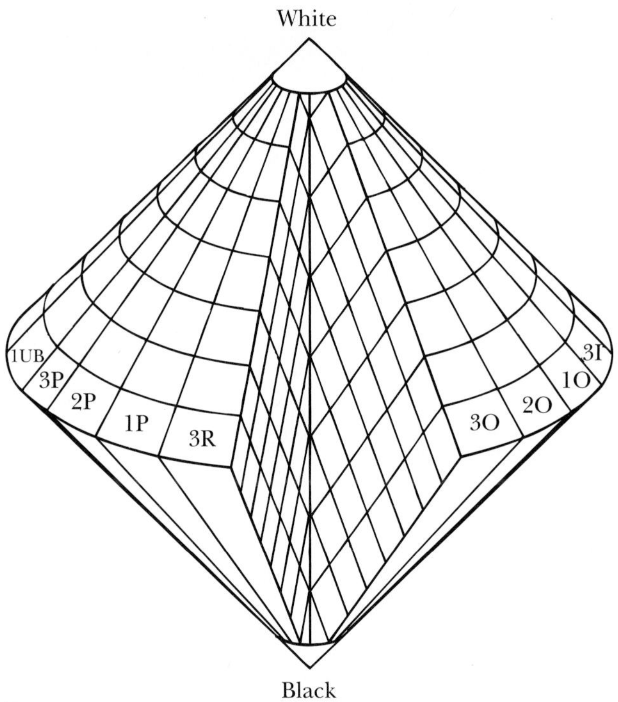

B

7-15 The Ostwald color system (A) is based on 24 hues that are either pure hues or black and white mixed with a pure hue. The hues used in this system are: yellow, orange, red, purple, ultramarine blue, turquoise, sea green, and leaf green. The other 16 hues are intermediate hues of these colors. The hues and their ranges of value and chroma are configured to form a three-dimensional double cone (B).

addition, there are 28 variations of these 24 hues that result in 672 hues and eight neutrals. On the Ostwald color wheel, cool hues are on half of the circle, while warm hues are on the other half. The overall configuration is a three-dimensional double cone, 7-15.

The color wheel is arranged with yellow, red, blue, and green spaced equidistant from one another. Between each pair of hues are five intermediate hues. The result is a circle of 24 hues plus six other hues that are required to complete the color range. In this system, no real distinction is made between value and intensity. The hues are lightened, darkened, or neutralized by adding varying amounts of white and black.

Colors are most saturated at the equator, where the two cones meet, and become increasingly neutralized toward the central axis of gray values. Pure white tops the central axis and black is at the bottom. Colors are lighter in the top cone and darker in the bottom cone.

The Munsell System

The Munsell system is a system of color notation that scientifically describes and analyzes color in terms of hue, value, and *chroma*, the Greek word for color. The chromatic colors are based on five principal hues: red, yellow, green, blue, and purple.

Hue is the color name and is indicated by the letter H, followed by a fraction. The fraction's top number, or numerator, represents the value, while the bottom number, or denominator, indicates the chroma.

Value, the lightness or darkness of a color, is shown on the central axis as nine visible steps. The darkest value is at the bottom and lightest value is at the top. The value of pure black is designated as 0/, and that of pure white as 10/. Middle gray is 5/.

The horizontal band extending outward from the value axis shows chroma. The chroma value shows the amount a given hue deviates from a neutral gray of the same value. The number of chroma steps varies because hues vary in their saturation strength. For example, red has the most steps while yellow has the fewest.

The Munsell color wheel has a total of 100 different colors. By using the correct letters and numbers, any one of the hues can be located on the color tree, 7-16. This method enables users to accurately communicate color information.

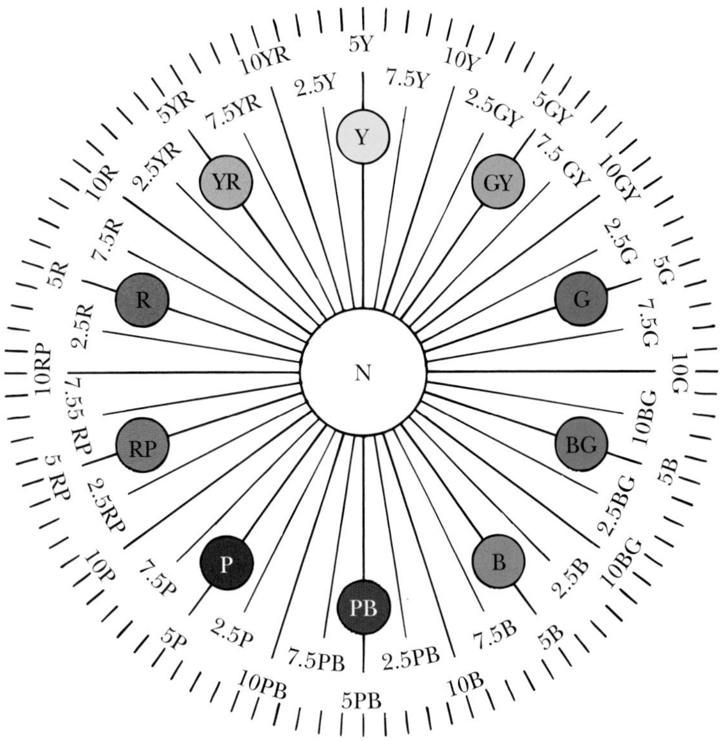

A

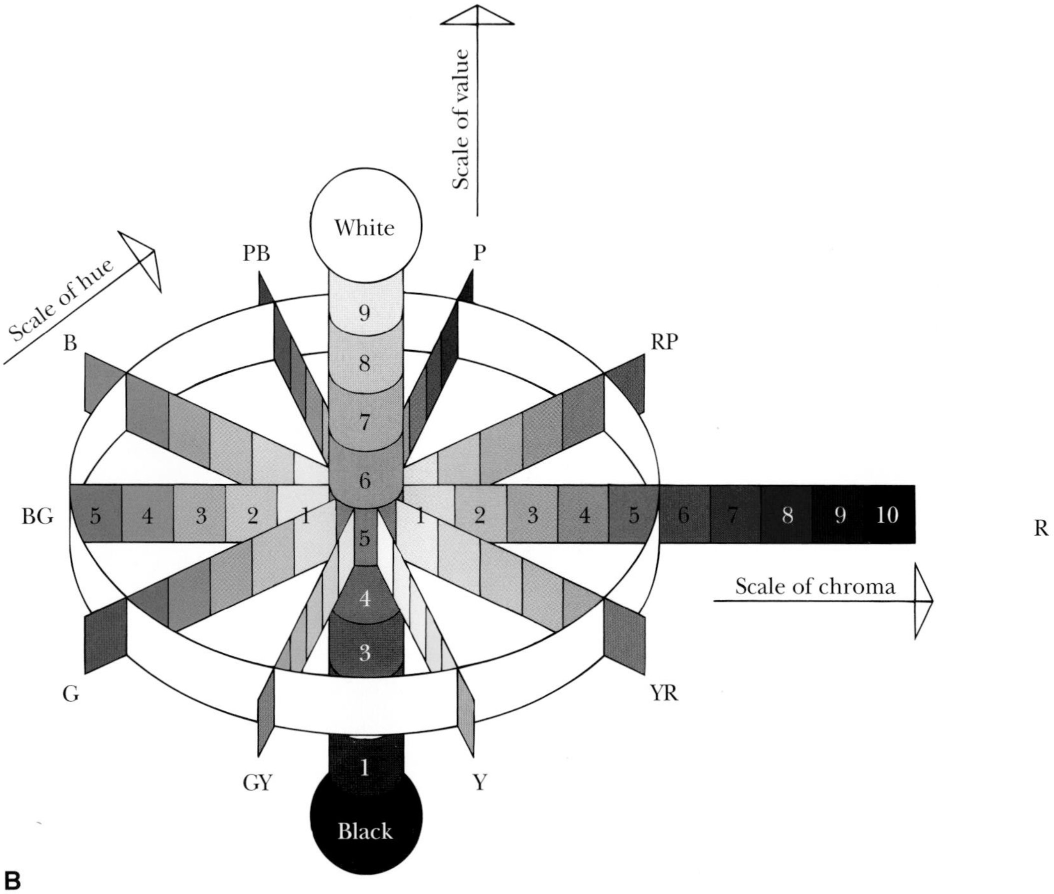

B

7-16 The Munsell color system (A) includes hue notations of the five principal and five intermediate hue families. Each hue family is broken down into four parts: 2.5, 5, 7.5, and 10. The outer circle markings represent the 100 hues included. The adjacent graphic (B) represents the relationship of hue, value, and chroma. The circular band represents the hues in their proper sequences. The upright center axis represents the scale of value. The ribbons pointing outward from the center show the steps of chroma, increasing in strength as indicated by the numerals.

Color Harmonies

When certain colors are used together in a pleasing manner, they create a color scheme or color harmony. Color harmonies provide guidelines for designing and decorating successfully with color. The seven basic color harmonies are: monochromatic, analogous, complementary, split-complementary, triadic, double-complementary, and neutral.

- A **monochromatic color harmony** is based on a single hue of the standard color wheel. It is the simplest color harmony, 7-17. Variation is achieved by changing the value and intensity of the hue and by adding accents of neutral colors. A monochromatic color harmony can make a room appear larger and unified.
- An **analogous color harmony** is based on combining three to five adjacent hues on the color wheel. It combines related hues such as yellow, yellow-orange, and orange, or green, blue-green, and blue. See 7-18. Analogous harmonies tend to look best when one color is dominant and smaller amounts of the related colors are used to add interest.
- A **complementary color harmony** is made by combining two hues that are directly opposite each other on the standard color wheel. Complementary colors make each other look brighter and more intense because they contrast, 7-19. When red is next to green, the green looks greener and the red looks redder. For less contrast, the values and intensities of the two colors can be varied. Generally, one color is allowed to dominate, and various values and intensities are used to lessen the contrast.
- A **split-complementary color harmony** is made by combining one hue and the two hues on both sides of its complement. See 7-20. For example, red-orange, green, and blue form a split-complementary color scheme. Red-orange would most likely be used as the dominant color, while green and blue would provide contrast.

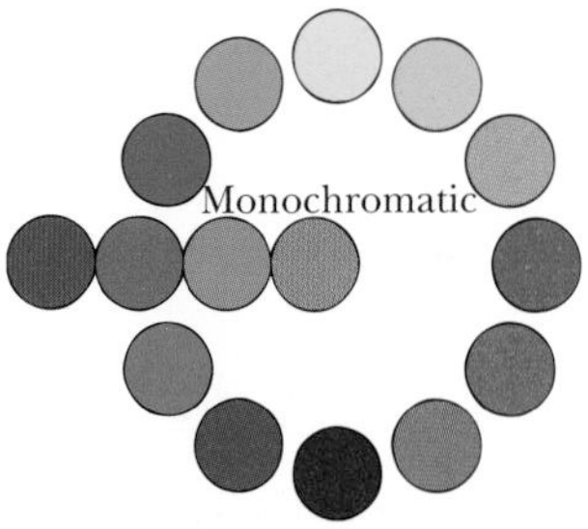

Lexington Furniture Industries

7-17 Monochromatic color harmonies combine various shades and tints of one color.

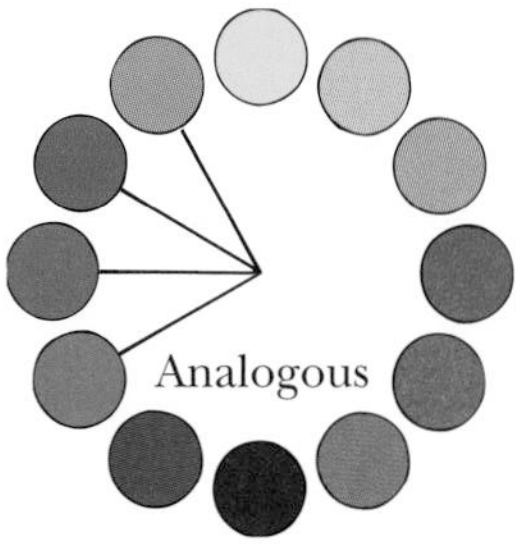

Lynn Aseltine-Kolbusz, ASID, Illinois Chapter

7-18 This analogous color scheme has yellow-green as the dominate color with green, blue-green, and blue as accent colors.

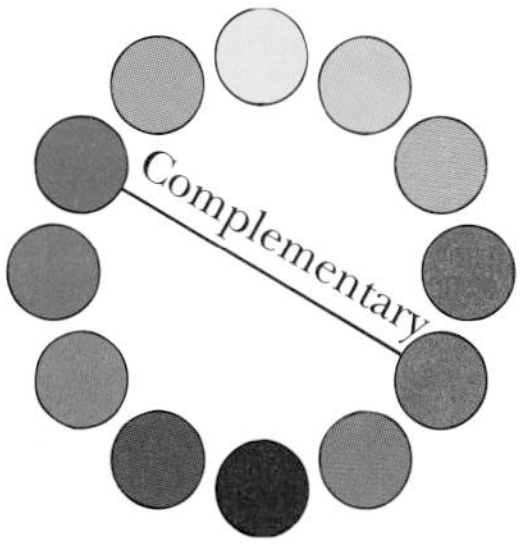

7-19 Complementary colors intensify each other. This pink and green color harmony enhances both colors.

- A **triadic color harmony** is the combination of any three colors that are of equal distance from each other on the standard color wheel. For example, yellow, blue, and red—the primary colors—form a triadic color scheme, 7-21. Any other three colors chosen the same way will also form the color harmony. Sharp contrasts result when intense values of the three colors are used, but changing values and intensities can lessen contrast. Skill is needed to achieve pleasing triadic harmonies.
- The **double-complementary color harmony** combines two sets of complementary colors together. An example is an interior that combines green and red with blue and orange. See 7-22. Any combination of pairs may be used as long as each pair is composed of complementary colors.
- **Neutral color harmonies** are made by using combinations of black, white, and gray. Shades of brown, tan, and beige may also be used, 7-23. Touches of accent colors are usually added for interest.

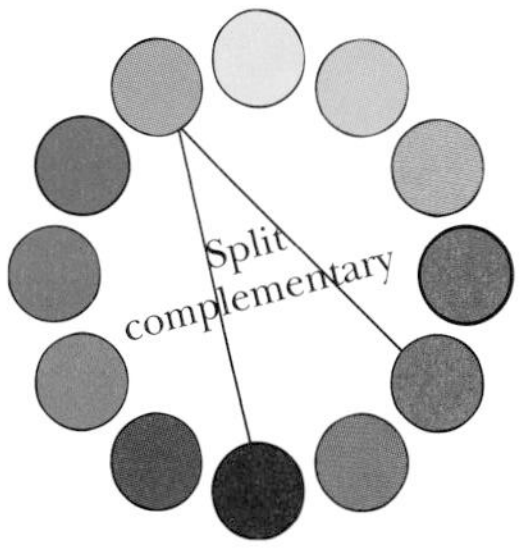

7-20 The split-complementary color harmony uses one hue and the two colors beside its complement.

Effect of Light on Color

Color as well as the other elements of design require light to make them visible. Light is important

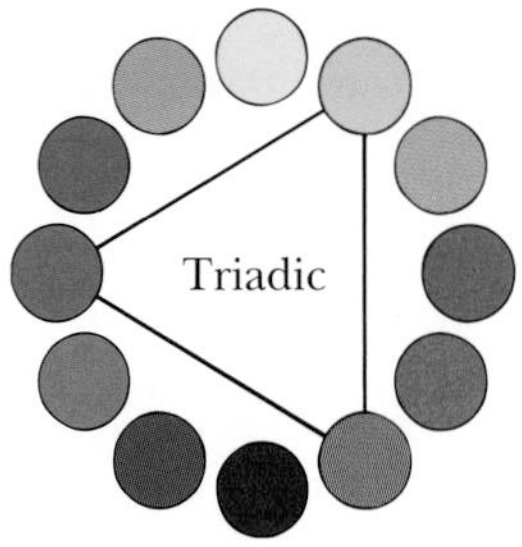

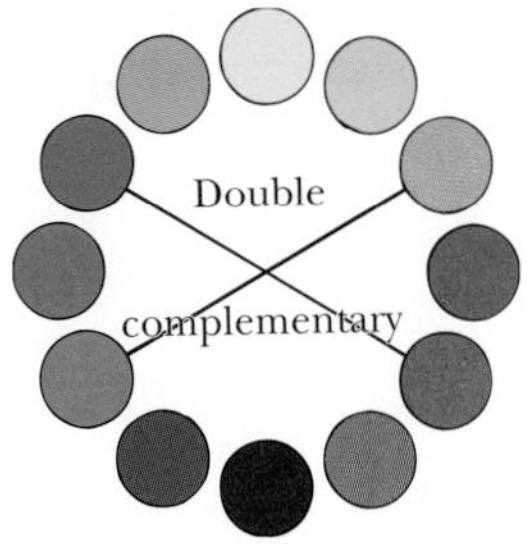

Suzanne Mauzey, ASID, Illinois Chapter

7-21 This triadic color harmony uses yellow-orange, red-purple, and blue-green with red accents. The color combination gives a lively appearance to this child's bedroom.

Paul Schlismann, ASID, Illinois Chapter

7-22 The complementary color pairs—red and green on the walls and furniture plus blue on the windows and pale orange on the floor—are used in this double-complementary color scheme.

because there is no sight without it. Light is available as natural and artificial light. Natural light is electromagnetic energy supplied mostly from the sun in wavelengths that range in size from very long (infrared) to very short (ultraviolet). Humans cannot see infrared or ultraviolet light. Between these two extremes, only a narrow visible band of light energy is visible. This visible light and its colors are seen by separating natural light into its light bands: red, orange, yellow, green, blue, and violet. White light, also called *colorless light*, is composed of equal amounts of these separate colors.

When light strikes an object, what we see depends primarily on the way the object reflects and absorbs light. For example, when light strikes an opaque object, some light rays are absorbed while others are reflected. The reflected rays give the object its color. A red object absorbs almost all colors of light except red. A blue object absorbs almost all the colors of light except blue. This is true of all colors. White objects reflect almost all the color in light, while black objects absorb most of it.

Natural light changes throughout the day. The midday sun is very nearly white or colorless, but early morning or late afternoon sun appears slightly colored, 7-24. Light from the moon is bluish, while light from a candle or typical incandescent lamp is yellowish. These effects can be modified using filters, reflectors, diffusers, translucent shades, tinted glass, or curtains. Cool light intensifies blue and violet and neutralizes red, yellow, and orange. Warm light does just the opposite. Knowing the effect of light on various colors enables designers to make maximum use of light and color in their designs. Working with light and color is an art as well as a science.

KraftMaid Cabinetry

7-23 This neutral color harmony uses shades of brown, tan, and beige to give this living room a crisp yet warm appearance.

7-24 The late afternoon sun adds a pink tint to the landscape.

The following are some commonsense rules regarding light that can help make color selection easier.

- Colors for large spaces, such as walls, floors, and draperies, should be chosen under the light source specified for the installation. Generally, warm sources of light should be used at low lighting levels; and cool sources, at high levels.
- Cool-color harmonies may need warm light sources when low lighting levels are used.
- Warm-color harmonies may appear too warm if lighted with a warm source at high levels. Use a cooler light source.
- Lighting that is shielded or in bracket lighting fixtures tend to cool a room. An added source of warm light, such as a table lamp, can counteract the effect.

Effect of Adjacent Colors

Colors appear to change when placed near other colors. For example, red appears to be red-violet when placed beside violet.

Some hues seem to produce unity or restfulness when placed next to each other. An example is blue next to blue-green or green. Using adjoining colors on the color wheel results in the analogous color harmony, which provides a blended, pleasing effect.

When that same blue is placed beside orange, however, a sense of contrast or excitement is created. Blue and orange, opposite colors on the color wheel, are sharply contrasting colors. Using these colors together emphasizes both and makes the hues appear to gain intensity, 7-25. This forceful use of color is an example of complementary color harmony. By mixing small areas of complementary colors, as in a tweed fabric, the original hues may appear to combine to form in-between colors.

Effect of Texture on Color

Textures affect the appearance of color. Flat, shiny surfaces reflect light and can enhance color brightness and intensity. Dull, soft, mottled, or heavily textured surfaces make a color seem less intense and darker, 7-26. These rough surfaces disburse the light and diffuse the color. Therefore, a bright red plush carpet is not as overpowering as a bright red shiny floor. Coarse or textured fabrics appear darker than smooth fabrics that are dyed with the same hue of equal intensity and chroma.

7-25 These complementary hues gain intensity when used in close proximity to each other.

If your decorating treatment calls for strong colors or a bold pattern, it is best to keep the textures subdued so they will accent the main theme without conflicting. A dull or matte surface absorbs color, so if using a dark color, much of the detail may not be visible.

Effect of Color on Space

Colors appear darker and brighter when closer than viewed at a greater distance. Therefore, bright or dark colors may be used in large rooms without appearing too demanding.

Colors seem to gain intensity when they cover large areas. For that reason, a color selected from a paint chip may appear too dark or intense when painted on a wall. Remember the area of the paint chip has been multiplied many times. Therefore, when using paint chips, it is wise to choose a color several tints lighter than the color desired for the room.

Another factor to consider when selecting the color for a given space is the natural tendency for some colors to appear either closer or farther away. Light or cool colors recede, while dark and warm colors advance. Therefore, a small room will appear larger if painted with light or cool colors. Conversely, a large room will appear smaller if dark or warm colors are used.

Color Decisions

Some of the best ideas for developing pleasing color harmonies may come from sources other than the standard color schemes. Make a practice of looking for and evaluating the color harmonies around you to develop a sense of the color harmony you prefer.

Myriad color harmonies appear in nature, created from natural elements. Consider the *earth colors*, which are obtained from pigments found in iron oxides and other minerals in rocks and soil 7-27. After washing and grinding the minerals, they are mixed with other substances to form paints or dyes. Typically, earth colors include ocher (yellow), sienna (reddish orange or reddish brown), red oxide (red), umber (brown), and terra verde (green). Earth colors have been used for centuries, primarily to protect against corrosion. They are nontoxic and very resistant to the forces of weather and erosion.

A beautiful painting or wall hanging can also be the inspiration for a harmonious blend of colors. Light or neutral colors can provide the background, stronger colors can be used in the room's furnishings, and bright or intense colors are perfect for accent pieces. Drapery and upholstery fabric, wallpaper, area rugs, carpeting, and art objects offer inspiration for creating color harmonies.

You can identify the color harmonies that are most pleasing to you by compiling a portfolio. Include photographs as well as pictures from magazines of color schemes that you like. Add samples of fabric and wallpaper, if possible. Periodically, weed out the items that no longer appeal to you, and in time, you will know which color harmonies most suit you.

When planning color harmonies, keep in mind the following guidelines:

- Color schemes look best when one color dominates.
- Your dominant color should cover about two-thirds of the room area. An equal split between areas of dominant and subordinate color is far less pleasing.

Lexington Furniture Industries

7-26 The rough textures in the carpeting and wicker seating make the colors appear darker than surfaces with smooth textures.

7-27 The colors in this natural sandstone contain minerals that provide some of the pigments used to make earth colors.

- Subordinate colors are not as lively as dominant colors and are generally used to blend large furniture pieces into the background.
- Accent colors add flair to the decor. Often bright focal points of color are drawn from the opposite side of the color wheel.
- Bold, warm, and dark colors appear to advance. Use them to lower high ceilings or create a feeling of closeness in a room, 7-28.
- Dark values and warm hues make rooms appear smaller.
- Cool, dull, and light colors recede. Use them to heighten low ceilings or widen a room.
- Light values and cool hues make rooms appear larger, 7-29.
- Neutrals enhance and strengthen the other colors around them.
- Large areas look best when covered with low-intensity colors. Large areas of space tend to enhance a color's intensity.
- Contrasting colors are emphasized when used together. For example, light colors appear lighter beside dark colors, and the reverse is true.
- Surfaces with rough textures make colors appear darker than surfaces with flat, smooth textures.

Armstrong World Industries, Inc.

7-28 The deep hue used on the walls of this home office creates a quiet, cozy atmosphere.

Southface Energy Institute, Atlanta, Georgia

7-29 Light colors used on the walls, ceiling, and chair coverings give this small dining room a spacious appearance.

- Exposure of a room affects color harmony choice. Rooms that face north or east and receive little sun can feel warmer with reds and oranges.
- Rooms that face south or west and receive sun will appear cooler with blues and greens.
- Colors appear different under different lighting conditions. Artificial light softens colors. Colors that appear attractive under artificial light may be too harsh in full daylight.
- Incandescent lighting normally adds a warm glow to colors. Fluorescent lighting changes the hue of colors in a variety of ways. For more details, see Chapter 18 on Lighting.

Chapter Summary

Color is the most exciting tool the designer has. Colors, or hues, influence human behavior and perception. Bold, exciting red is associated with danger, power, love, passion, anger, fire, and strength. Cheerful orange expresses friendliness, courage, hospitality, energy, and hope. Warm yellow is traditionally associated with happiness, sunlight, sympathy, prosperity, cowardice, and wisdom. Refreshing green is cool, peaceful, and friendly. It is often associated with hope, envy, and luck. Blue is cool, calm, and reserved, communicating serenity, tranquillity, and formality. Violet is the color of royalty, dignity, and mystery. Black, which symbolizes wisdom, evil, and death, can be mysterious, severe, and dramatic. White is the symbol of youth, freshness, innocence, purity, faith, and peace.

The color wheel is the most common tool for understanding color relationships in design. It shows primary, secondary, and intermediate colors in the middle ring; their tints in the inner ring, and their shades in the outer ring. Color intensity can vary from bright to dull. Colors are also classified as warm or cool.

The most common color theories are the Brewster, Ostwald, and Munsell systems. The standard color wheel reflects the Brewster system. The Ostwald system uses yellow, orange, red, purple, blue, turquoise, sea green, and leaf green hues plus white and black added to the hues. The Munsell system uses five principal hues: red, yellow, green, blue, and purple.

Color harmonies are formed when certain colors, based on their position in the color wheel, are used together. The seven basic color harmonies are: monochromatic, analogous, complementary, split-complementary, triadic, double-complementary, and neutral.

Knowing the effect of light on colors enables designers to make maximum use of color in their designs. Color is influenced by the amount and source of light, adjacent colors, surface textures, and its distance from the viewer. The principles and observations of nature should generally guide color decisions.

Review Questions

1. What three categories of colors are shown on the standard color wheel?
2. What are the three characteristics of color?
3. What is the difference between warm and cool colors? Name the three main examples of each?
4. List the three neutral colors and the three near-neutral colors.
5. Name the primary colors that serve as the basis for the Brewster color system.
6. What is the basic shape of the Ostwald color system?
7. How many different colors are included in the Munsell color wheel?
8. What is the simplest color harmony?
9. What color harmony is made by combining two colors that are directly opposite each other on the standard color wheel?
10. If an object absorbs most of the visible light rays that strike it, what is its color?
11. Give an example of two colors that, when paired, create a sense of contrast or excitement.
12. What type of hues make a room seem smaller?
13. What typical colors are considered earth colors?

Suggested Activities

1. Write an essay describing the common perceptions linked to the following colors: red, orange, yellow, green, blue, violet, black, and white.
2. Prepare the following three samples using pigments of a primary color, black, and white: the primary color, a tint of the color, and a shade of the color. Display your samples for the class to see.
3. Prepare two color pallets, one of warm colors and one of cool colors, for display. This comparison can be presented on a piece of illustration board.
4. Secure a picture of a room that clearly shows one of the major color harmonies. Identify it and the individual colors used.
5. Devise a demonstration that shows the effect of the following factors on the same color: light, adjacent colors, and surface texture.
6. Select two guidelines for planning color harmonies that are discussed in the chapter. Find photos or other materials to illustrate them.

Internet Resources

About, Inc.'s Color, Design, and Style Index
interiordec.about.com/cs/designcolorstyle

American Association of Textile Chemists and Colorists
aatcc.org

American Society of Interior Designers
asid.org

Interior Design Magazine
interiordesign.net

International Color Consortium
color.org

National Paint and Coatings Assn.
paint.org

Painting and Decorating Contractors of America
pdca.org

Professor J.L. Morton, Color Matters®—Design-Art
colormatters.com/colortheory.html

Society for Protective Coatings
sspc.org

Note: Web addresses may have changed since publication. For some entries, reaching the correct Web site may require keying *www.* into the address.

Part Three
Materials Used in Housing and Interiors

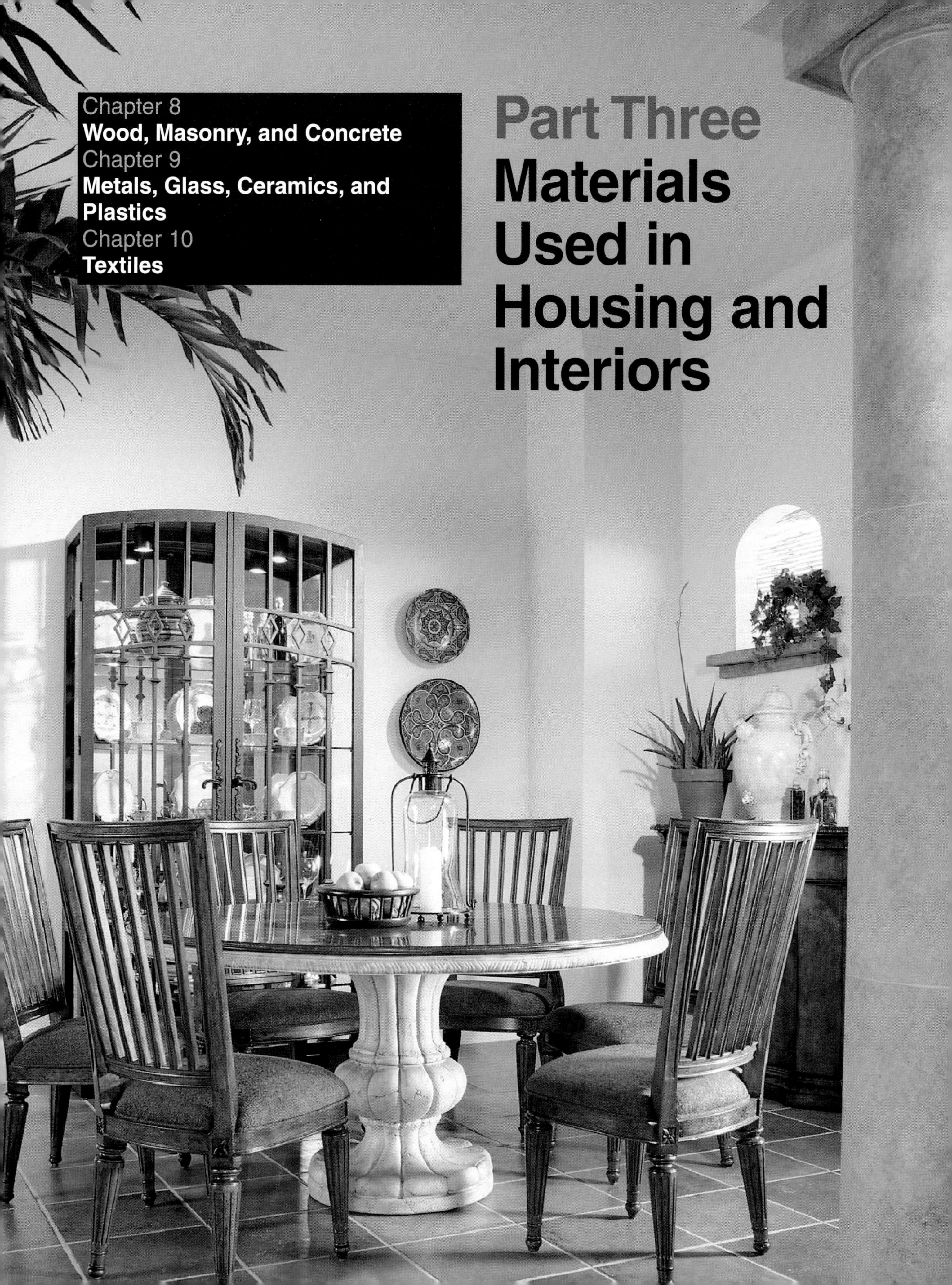

Chapter 8
Wood, Masonry, and Concrete

Objectives

After studying this chapter, you will be able to
- list the major characteristics and uses of hardwoods and softwoods.
- distinguish the various kinds of wood materials used in residential housing.
- list the main types of wood finishes and describe their characteristics and uses.
- list and describe the main types of masonry materials used in residential housing.
- describe the characteristics and uses of concrete and list types of decorative finishes that can be applied.

Key Terms

hardwoods
softwoods
grain
lumber
seasoned
timber
millwork
plywood
laminated timber
composite board
hardboard
particleboard
varnish
lacquer
polyurethane
building brick
facing brick
paving brick
firebrick
pattern bond
concrete building brick
slump brick
manufactured stone

Many different materials are used in a house. Some materials are part of the structure while others are used for furnishings and decoration. The eight families of materials most commonly found in modern dwellings are the following:
- wood
- masonry
- concrete
- metals
- glass
- ceramics
- plastics
- textiles

This chapter discusses the properties and residential applications of the first three families of materials. Chapter 9, "Metals, Glass, Ceramics, and Plastic," covers the next four materials, while Chapter 10 discusses textiles.

Wood

No other material is comparable to wood in its degree of workability, beauty, strength, durability, and versatility, 8-1. Wood has a higher strength-to-weight ratio than steel, concrete, or glass. Wood materials are easy to fabricate and repair. Wood is also one of the few housing materials that is replenishable.

Wood Classification

Woods are broadly classified as hardwoods and softwoods. **Hardwoods** are woods from deciduous or broad-leaved trees. These trees shed their leaves at the end of their growing season. **Softwoods** are woods from coniferous or cone-bearing trees. They typically keep their needle-shaped leaves all year long.

NMC/Focal Point

8-1 The dominant material used in this room is wood—in the furniture, paneling, and beams. Wood is a warm, durable, and interesting material with many applications.

Generally, hardwoods are harder than softwoods, but there are exceptions. For example, yellow pine and yew are classified as softwoods, but they are harder than many hardwoods. Basswood, balsa, and cottonwood trees are classified as hardwoods, but they have soft wood.

Several factors affect the appearance and use of various woods, such as color, strength, and grain. In wood, **grain** refers to the pattern of the fibers. The United States has almost 1,200 species of trees, but only 100 species have any real commercial value. See 8-2.

Of the commercially important species in the United States, about 40 are softwoods. Softwoods are strong and resilient, but they do not accept finishes as well as most hardwoods. Softwoods are generally used in construction. The remaining 60 species are hardwoods, and of these, oak is the most frequently used. Hardwoods tend to be more expensive than softwoods. However, they resist denting and scratching better than softwoods, and their surfaces yield smooth finishes with attractive grain patterns. Hardwoods are most often used to make flooring materials and furniture. The color and grain of several popular American woods are shown in 8-3.

Wood Materials

Wood is the hard, fibrous substance that forms the trunk, stems, and branches of trees. It can be processed to make lumber, plywood, or other wood products used in construction.

Lumber is wood sawed from logs into boards of various sizes. It is the product of the sawmill. The boards can be resawed or planed to standard

Physical Properties and Uses of Common Woods

Name	Wood Classification	Forest Region of Growth	Properties	Uses
Ash, White	Hardwood	Northern and Central U.S.	Hard, creamy white to light brown color; grain similar to oak; wears well; has medium tendency to warp	Furniture frames requiring bending, veneer, handles
Beech, American	Hardwood	Northern and Central U.S.	Hard and strong; white or slightly reddish color; good for natural finish; medium tendency to warp	Food containers, furniture, handles, veneer, curved parts, rocker runners, interior parts requiring strength
Birch, Red	Hardwood	Northern and Central U.S.	Hard, heavy, and strong; medium tendency to warp; dark reddish brown heartwood and white sapwood	Boxes, baskets, furniture, woodenware, flooring, veneer plywood

8-2 Most of the woods discussed in this chart are shown on the following pages.

Physical Properties and Uses of Common Woods

Name	Wood Classification	Forest Region of Growth	Properties	Uses
Cedar, Western Red	Softwood	Western U.S. and Alaska	Soft and weak; reddish brown to white color; close grained; lightweight and easily worked; low shrinkage and warping; resists decay	Shingles, siding, paneling, novelties, posts
Cherry, Black	Hardwood	Central U.S.	Strong, durable, and hard; light to dark reddish brown color; close grained; low tendency to warp	Furniture, carvings, woodenware, veneer
Cypress, Bald	Softwood	Southern U.S.	Strong; light yellowish brown color, but silver gray when exposed; weathers easily; resists decay; low warpage	Tanks, vats, gutters, siding, shingles, trims, posts
Elm, American	Hardwood	Northern, Central, and Southern U.S.	Hard and heavy; light grayish brown color tinged with red to dark brown; porous and open grained; high shrinkage and warpage	Baskets, boxes, crates, decorative veneers, curved parts of furniture
Fir, Douglas	Softwood	Western U.S.	Soft, strong, and heavy; yellow to reddish brown color; coarse grained	Plywood, framing, millwork, cabinets, low-cost furniture
Mahogany, Honduras	Hardwood	Central America	Medium hard and strong; almost white to light brown color; dense and hard to work; low shrinkage	Fine furniture, cabinets, veneer
Maple, Sugar and Hard	Hardwood	Central and Southern U.S.	Hard, heavy and strong; almost white to light brown color; dense and hard to work; low shrinkage	Furniture, flooring, handles, woodenware, veneer
Oak, Red and White	Hardwood	Northern, Central, and Southern U.S.	Hard and strong; pale gray to reddish color; open grained; workable and carves well	Furniture, flooring, millwork, handles, woodenware, veneer paneling.
Pine, Eastern White	Softwood	Northern and Central U.S.	Soft and relatively weak; white to cream color; close grained; uniform; easy to work; medium warping and shrinkage	Millwork, carvings, veneer, trim, cabinets
Pine, Sugar	Softwood	West Coast	Soft; white to cream color; close grained; uniform; easy to work; low warping and shrinkage	Cabinets, carvings, fancy woodwork, trim, doors, windows
Poplar, Yellow	Hardwood	Eastern U.S.	Moderately soft and weak; white to yellowish brown; uniform texture; easy to work	Siding, trim, inexpensive furniture, cabinets
Redwood	Softwood	West Coast (California)	Soft and moderately strong; reddish brown color, but weathers to a silver gray; splinters easily; resists rot and decay	Construction, millwork, vats, outdoor furniture
Walnut, Black	Hardwood	Central U.S.	Hard, heavy, and strong; light to dark chocolate brown color; low warpage; good finish	Fine furniture, veneers, cabinets, paneling

8-2 *Continued*

8-3 The native American woods on these four pages are used in housing construction and furniture making.

8-3 *Continued*

8-3 *Continued*

8-3 *Continued*

dimensions. Resawing and planing also help to give the wood a smooth, even surface. Lumber can be crosscut to various lengths.

After lumber is cut, it is **seasoned**. This term refers to a drying process that removes moisture from wood to help prevent shrinking, warping, splitting, and rotting in finished products. As moisture is removed, wood shrinks. To allow for shrinkage and machining, unseasoned wood, also called *green wood,* is cut into boards larger than the desired finished sizes. The size of seasoned, machined lumber, therefore, is smaller than the stated size. For example, a two-by-four is actually 1½ by 3½ in.

Processing lumber normally includes sawing, resawing, planing, crosscutting, and seasoning. Lumber can be used as is or processed further. **Timber**, or lumber that is at least 5 in. wide and thick, is used mainly as support posts or beams. Softwood lumber is frequently used for the construction of housing, especially for the structural framework. It can also be used to produce millwork. **Millwork** is processed lumber, such as doors, window frames, shutters, trim, panel work, and molding. Hardwood lumber is generally used to make furniture or produce millwork.

Plywood is a wood panel made from thin sheets of wood that are glued together with the grain of one layer at a right angle to the grain of the next. See 8-4. This adds strength to plywood and reduces warping, shrinking, and splitting. The thin sheets are called *veneers* or *plies*. The outer layers can be fine, attractive veneer or plain wood, depending on how the plywood is used. Plywood is used in construction, especially of floors and walls. It is also used to make furniture and paneling.

Laminated timber is constructed by combining layers of wood with the grain running in one direction. See 8-5. As a result, this type of timber can be produced in shapes and sizes that are difficult to achieve with solid timber. Arches and beams are custom fabricated by bonding wood layers together with glues stronger than the wood itself.

Composite board is a panel fabricated from wood particles. It can be covered with a thin veneer for some uses. The most common types of composite board are hardboard and particleboard. **Hardboard** is made from refined wood fibers that are pressed together. One or both sides can be smooth. **Particleboard** is made from wood flakes, chips, and shavings that are bonded together with resins or adhesives. Panels of particleboard can be produced thicker than hardboard panels. Also, particleboard is more readily covered with veneers and laminates than hardboard.

Composite board is less expensive than plywood, but it is strong enough to be used in many of the same ways. Left uncovered, composite board is suitable for floor underlayment and wall materials

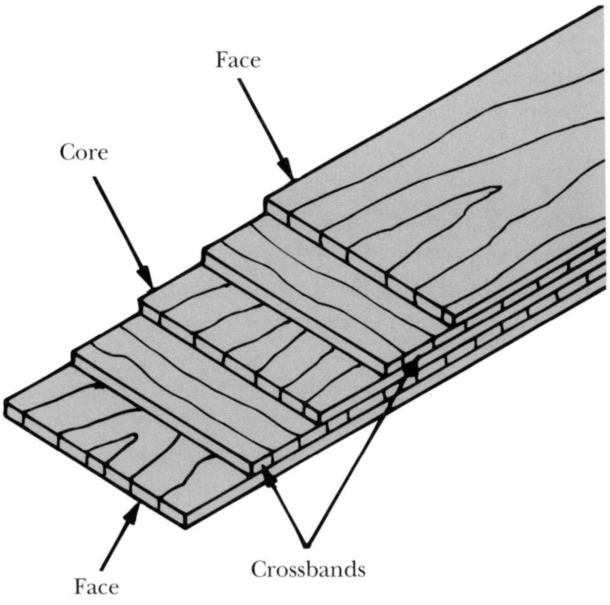

8-4 Plywood has an odd number of plies with the grain of each ply running at right angles to the next ply.

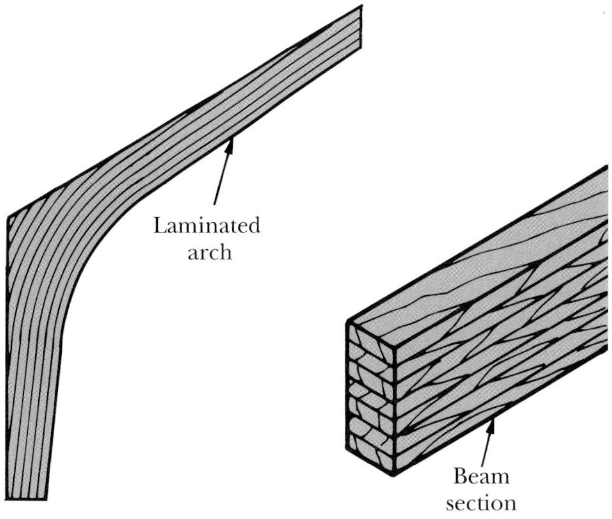

8-5 Laminated timbers can support wide spans because of their construction.

as well as for hidden parts of furniture. Laminated and veneered particleboard is popular for doors, counters, and exposed parts of furniture.

Wood Finishes

Most woods require a protective finish or treatment to retain their beauty and usability. Finishes and treatments keep wood surfaces clean. They reduce the hazards of rot, decay, weathering, and insect damage. They also help keep the moisture content of wood constant so the wood will not warp, crack, or shrink. Typical finishing materials include bleaches, fillers, stains, clear finishes, and paints. One of the following materials or a combination can be used to finish wood.

Bleaches

Bleaching removes the natural color of wood to give a pale or weathered appearance. It also evens the color of wood pieces having dark and light areas. Various acids or chlorine compounds are used to bleach wood. Bleaching must be done carefully, or the compounds may damage the wood. Instructions for using bleach should be followed carefully. Bleached wood can be treated with other finishes or left unfinished.

Fillers

Some types of wood, called *open-grain wood*, have large, open pores. These include such woods as walnut, oak, and mahogany. Filler is often applied to open-grain wood to fill the pores and even the surface. This prevents stains and other finishes from accumulating in the pores and leaves the finished surface with an even color and smooth texture. Paste filler is the most common type used, but liquid and latex fillers are also available.

Stains

Alcohol- and water-based stains and one type of oil-based stain add color to wood without masking grain patterns. Oil-based stains are classified as pigmented stains and penetrating stains.

Penetrating-oil stains, alcohol-based stains, and water-based stains contain soluble, organic dyes that penetrate the wood's surface. They have a clean, transparent appearance compared to pigmented stains, 8-6A. They produce brighter colors but fade more quickly than pigmented stains. Penetrating stains must be properly sealed, or color is likely to bleed into succeeding coats of varnish or lacquer. Penetrating stains are most commonly used on furniture and cabinets, but they can be used on any wood surface where a clear, bright color is desired.

A The Engineered Wood Association **B** The Engineered Wood Association

8-6 Penetrating oil stains (A) are less opaque than pigmented stains (B).

Pigmented-oil stains contain insoluble pigments that are permanent in color, like those in paint. They coat, but do not penetrate, the wood's surface. If applied too heavily, pigmented stain will obscure the wood grain. This product is especially useful in disguising the irregular grain pattern of softwoods and in covering trim to match stained siding. See 8-6B.

Clear Finishes

Clear finishes are used to protect wood, enhance the grain, and give a luster or gloss to the wood's surface. The finishes can be used on plain, stained, or bleached wood. One or a combination of clear finishes can be used. Varnish, shellac, lacquer, oil, wax, and other synthetic finishes are the most common clear finishes, 8-7.

Many kinds of varnishes are available for use as topcoats on wood surfaces. **Varnish** is a clear finish used to emphasize wood grain and deepen wood tones. See 8-8. Different types, ranging from a low luster to a high gloss, are available. Varnish is most often used on wood furniture and floors. Pieces with a good finish have several thin coats of varnish rather than one or two thick coats. The two main

A Carandon Doors and Windows, Inc.

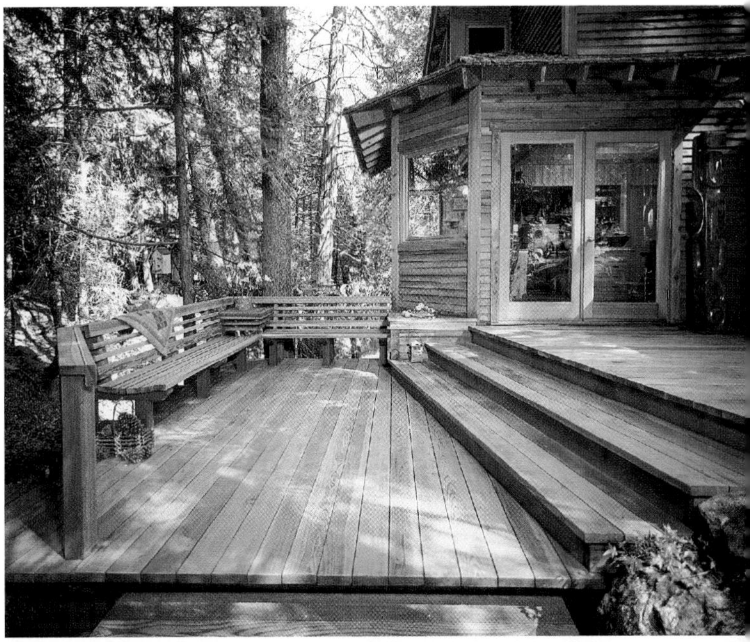

B California Redwood Association

8-7 Clear finishes enhance natural or stained wood surfaces (A). They are used on interior or exterior surfaces (B).

8-8 Varnish enhances wood-grain patterns and gives a luster to wood.

types of varnishes are oleoresinous varnishes and spirit varnishes.

- *Oleoresinous varnish* contains a gum or resin dissolved in a drying oil.
- *Spirit varnish* is made of a resin or gum dissolved in alcohol.

Shellac is technically a spirit varnish, but it is designed specifically for sealing wood. It changes the character of wood very little, but it prevents moisture from entering or leaving. Shellac is used on stained wood to prevent the stain from bleeding into the topcoat. It is used on plain wood to prevent topcoats from penetrating into wood. Shellac does not provide an acceptable topcoat, however, if used alone.

Lacquer is a wood finishing material that forms a tough, glossy finish. It is a complex finishing material containing nitrocellulose. Different formulas of lacquer are available to produce a finish ranging from low to high gloss. Lacquer-based sealers are also available; these should be used under lacquer finishes. Lacquer is used on furniture and other woodwork. See 8-9. It is especially popular as a finish for oriental style pieces because of its ability to produce a very high gloss. Lacquer is not intended for outdoor woodwork.

Everett Bramhati

8-9 Lacquer finishes are popular for most styles of furniture.

Oil finishes penetrate wood to highlight the grain, darken the color, and produce a soft luster. They are used mainly on fine wood furniture. The most commonly used oil finishes are boiled linseed oil and tuna oil thinned with turpentine. Between 5 and 30 coats are needed to produce a good finish. Oil must be reapplied periodically to renew the wood's surface.

Wax can be used over other finishes to produce a smooth luster or shine. It can also be used on plain wood to penetrate the surface, enrich the grain pattern, and darken the wood. Several kinds of wax are available from animal, vegetable, and mineral sources. Popular waxes include carnauba, beeswax, candelilla, Japan wax, and mineral waxes. Wax finishes are not very durable; they must be renewed frequently.

Many new finishes are made with synthetics for superior durability. Some are quickly replacing older finishes. **Polyurethane** is a clear finish that is especially popular as a floor finish. It dries more quickly than traditional varnish and resists wear and abrasions well. It also has high resistance to chemicals, alcohol, and grease.

Epoxy resin is another excellent floor finish because of its durability. It can also be used for furniture and exterior woodwork. Other synthetic coatings include polyester, polyamide, vinyl, acrylic, and silicone coatings. Most of these have excellent properties, but some are currently limited to few applications.

Paints

Paints are colored coatings that form opaque films. They contain pigment suspended in a liquid medium, called a vehicle. The pigment provides color and "hiding power." The vehicle provides the proper consistency for brushing, rolling, or spraying. A binder is also added to bond the pigment particles together to form a cohesive film during the drying process.

Paint is most commonly chosen to finish woods that do not have natural grain beauty, such as pine, gum, poplar, and fir. It is frequently used to cover exterior wood siding and trim. Some homes also have painted interior wood doors and molding, 8-10. Although paint is used on some styles of furniture, especially Early American and early Scandinavian, most modern furniture is stained, 8-11.

Paints are oil or water based, and designed for either interior or exterior use. When wood is covered

8-10 Paint is the primary surface covering in this room, which is being redecorated.

Lynn Keck Petty, ASID, Illinois Chapter

8-11 The unique, painted storage piece in this cozy sitting room captures the flavor of Early American furniture.

with paint, no other finishing material is needed. *Enamel* is a special kind of paint made by mixing pigments with varnishes or lacquers to produce a hard, smooth, long-lasting finish. Enamel is especially useful for surfaces that receive much wear.

Masonry

Through the years, the variety of masonry materials used in housing has greatly increased. Dozens of new shapes, textures, colors, and applications are now available. For example, brick alone is made in at least 10,000 different shape, color, and texture combinations. Masonry materials have grown in popularity because they are versatile, durable, and beautiful. Although masonry construction is often more expensive than wood construction, masonry products generally require less maintenance and last longer. The materials used in masonry construction include: structural clay products, concrete masonry units, glass block, and stone.

Structural Clay Products

Structural clay products, sometimes called burned clay products, are made from clay or shale. These materials are made naturally as rock weathers. Shale is very dense and harder to remove from the ground than clay. Shale products, therefore, are more costly. Structural clay products can be divided into three main groups: brick, tile, and architectural terra cotta.

Brick

Brick is fireproof, weather-resistant, and easy to maintain. It is popular for fireplaces, chimneys, walls, and floors. See 8-12. The four classes of brick most commonly used in residential housing are building brick, facing brick, paving brick, and firebrick.

- **Building brick**, also called common brick, is used mainly as a structural material where durability and strength are more important than appearance.
- **Facing brick** is used on exposed surfaces where appearance is more important.
- **Paving brick** is a harder brick that is highly resistant to abrasion and moisture absorption. It is used to pave walks and driveways, 8-13.
- **Firebrick** is used for places that become very hot. Examples are the inner linings of fireplaces, brick ovens, and outdoor barbecues.

Photo Courtesy of James Hardie® Siding Products

8-12 Brick is a popular building material because of its strength, ease of maintenance, and durability.

8-13 Paving brick is the ideal material for a long-lasting walk or driveway.

Bricks are available in a variety of sizes. The lengths of most new bricks are based on a module of 4 in., although some older styles of brick are not. Common nominal lengths are 8 or 12 in. A list of common brick sizes is provided in A-14 of the Appendix.

Like wood, bricks are smaller in actual size than in nominal size. The nominal size of a brick includes the brick's actual dimensions plus the thickness of mortar used in a wall built with that brick. Nominal dimensions make it easier to determine how many bricks are needed to build a wall of a certain size. For example, if a wall will be 9 ft. long and bricks with a nominal length of 12 in. are used, 9 bricks will be needed to form the length of the wall.

About all brick is produced in the color range of reds, buffs, and creams. Colors vary with the chemical makeup of the clay and the time and temperature used to fire the brick. Surface texture is created by the method used to cut and mold the brick. The two most common finishes are a smooth surface produced by water, called water-struck brick, and a sandpaper-like surface produced by sand, called sand-struck brick.

The appearance, durability, and strength of brick construction depend largely on the bond used. The term *bond* refers to three different types.

- The *structural bond* is the way bricks are interlocked to provide support and strength.
- The **pattern bond** is the pattern formed by the masonry units and mortar joints on the exposed parts of construction.
- The *mortar bond* is the adhesion of mortar to masonry.

A wide variety of designs result from using different structural, pattern, and mortar bonds.

Mortar is used between masonry units to bond units together and seal spaces between them, 8-14. It is also used to compensate for slight differences in the sizes of masonry units. Mortar joints provide different visual effects in a masonry wall, depending on the type of joint used. The seven main styles of mortar joints are shown in 8-15.

Hollow Masonry

Hollow masonry includes hollow brick and hollow clay tile. Hollow brick has the appearance of brick in a finished wall. Both have less cross-sectional area than solid bricks. Though the faces are solid, holes make up 25 to 40 percent of the unit's total volume. This makes hollow units lighter, easier to handle, and less expensive to transport than solid brick. Also, larger units can be used because of their relatively lighter weight.

Clay tile is available in structural and facing units and are used like brick. However, special construction may be necessary to make hollow clay tile construction as structurally sound as brick construction. Clay tile is produced in interesting shapes for use in decorative masonry screens.

Brick Institute of America

8-14 Uniform mortar joints are a mark of good workmanship.

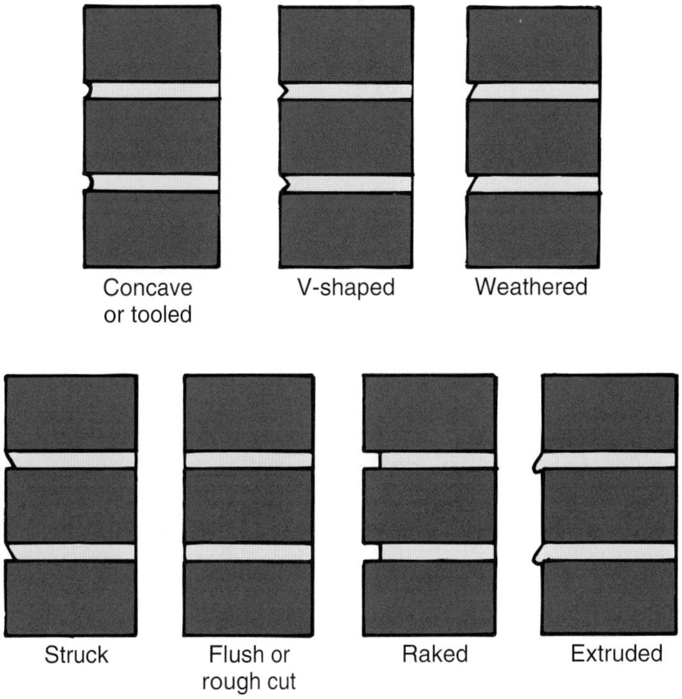

8-15 Several styles of mortar joints can be used in brick construction.

Architectural Terra Cotta

Architectural terra cotta is a custom-made product that can be produced in many shapes and colors. It is expensive and difficult to find, making it uncommon for modern homes. However, some older homes have masonry trim and chimneys of terra cotta. Terra cotta can be a desirable construction material for remodeling and restoring these homes.

Concrete Masonry Units

Concrete masonry units are a popular housing material for both aboveground and basement construction. Concrete masonry is less expensive than brick and fairly lightweight. It also is fire and weather resistant, and requires little maintenance. Over 700 different concrete units are made throughout the United States. There are three classifications of concrete masonry units: concrete brick, concrete block, and special units.

Concrete Brick

The two main types of concrete brick are building brick and slump brick. **Concrete building brick** is similar in size, function, and appearance to clay brick. See 8-16. **Slump brick** or block is a type of concrete brick with an irregular face that has the appearance of stone. See 8-17. Slump brick is produced from a wet mixture that causes the bricks to sag, or slump, when removed from the mold.

Concrete Block

Most of the concrete masonry units produced are concrete block. They are used mainly for foundations and basement walls. In some sections of the country, they are used for exterior walls as well. Concrete block are either solid or hollow. Most types are capable of supporting heavy loads, 8-18.

Portland Cement Assn.

8-17 Slump brick has the appearance of stone.

Portland Cement Assn.

8-16 Concrete building bricks have the appearance of clay brick, but they are lighter in weight and less expensive.

Concrete blocks are generally produced in larger sizes than concrete or clay bricks. The most common nominal size is 8 by 8 by 16 in. Half blocks and special application blocks are available for special uses.

Different pattern and mortar bonds can be used with concrete block to produce decorative effects. The most common patterns for concrete block are the running bond and stacked bond, 8-19. For decorative effects, some blocks can be projected from the surface. See 8-20.

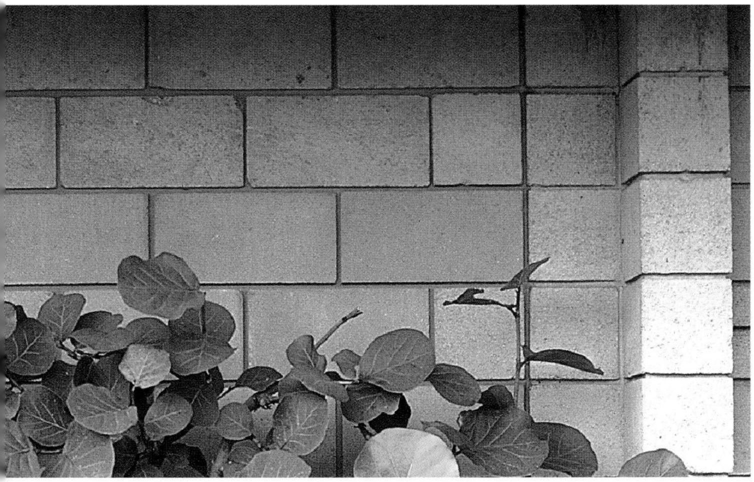

8-18 Concrete block has great support strength.

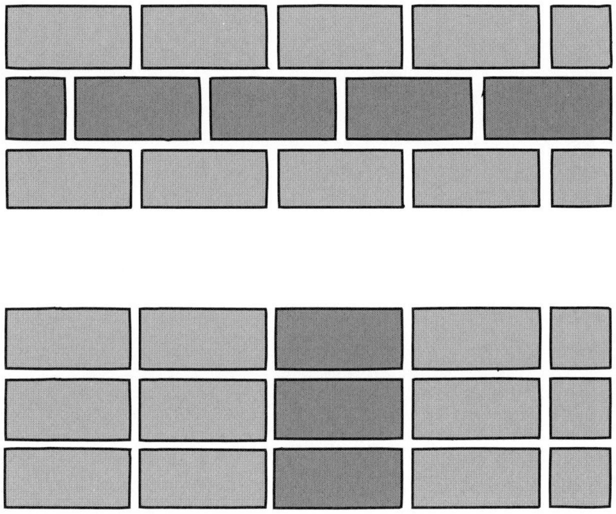

8-19 Concrete block is usually laid in a running bond (top) or stacked bond (bottom).

Portland Cement Assn.

8-20 Decorative effects can be produced by projecting concrete blocks in a pattern.

8-21 Split-faced concrete block has a rough, stonelike appearance.

Special Units

Many types of concrete block are designed for special purposes. Most have a more decorative finish than ordinary concrete block, but some have special, functional uses.

Decorative units include ribbed, fluted, and stri-faced units. These have parallel ridges or grooves that form patterns when used in a wall. Split-faced units are made by fracturing units to produce a rough, stonelike surface, 8-21. Other types of blocks have more complex designs in a variety of patterns and colors.

Faced blocks are both decorative and functional. They have a ceramic-type glaze finish on the surface. This surface is less porous than concrete, making faced block more stain resistant and easier to clean than standard concrete block. Faced block is used mainly in kitchens, schools, and hospitals.

Screen blocks are often used for outdoor fences and walls. They have an open design to provide privacy and ventilation, 8-22.

Sound blocks have special cavities designed to absorb sound. They are useful for interior walls of noisy areas.

Glass Block

Glass blocks are hollow units of clear, rippled, or frosted glass. They are *partially evacuated*, meaning

8-22 Screen blocks provide privacy but allow ventilation.

that some air has been removed to prevent condensation and improve insulation value. Standard glass blocks are produced in 6, 8, and 12 in. squares. Custom-made sizes are also available.

Glass blocks are often used in masonry walls where both privacy and natural light are desired. They are frequently used in place of basement, entryway, and bathroom windows, 8-23. Glass blocks are also useful as decorative screens.

Pittsburg Corning

8-23 Glass block allows light to enter adjacent rooms, creates sparkle, and provides the illusion of added space.

Stone

Stone is an ancient building material, once used as the main structural component of houses. Today it is almost always used in nonstructural applications such as facing, veneer, or pavement. See 8-24. The varied color and texture of stone provide visual interest. Stone is fireproof and resistant to decay, and it gives a feeling of permanence and stability.

Stone is, however, an expensive material. Also, it is more difficult to use in building, causing more expensive labor costs.

The types of natural stone most common in housing structures include: granite, sandstone, limestone, marble, and slate. Manufactured stone and terrazzo are two other stone materials that are used in residential housing.

Natural Stone

Granite is a hard, durable stone varying in color from almost white to black. It is also found in shades of pink, green, and yellow. Fine granite has a salt-and-pepper pattern. See 8-25. It can be polished smooth or left coarse. Granite is used for tabletops, windowsills, building stones, steps, paving, and wall veneers.

Sandstone is composed mainly of quartz grains cemented together with silica, lime, or iron oxide. Some sandstone is porous; it is prone to dampness and has poor insulation value. It may require a special treatment if it is used in cold regions. Colors

8-24 Stone construction adds variety and interest to a house.

8-25 This polished granite countertop has the customary salt and pepper pattern with some crystalline formation throughout the stone.

Heatilator, Inc.

8-26 Limestone has a fine grain, giving it a smooth appearance.

are in the brown, tan, rust, and gray ranges, and textures range from smooth to granular. Popular varieties include bluestone, brownstone, silica sandstone, and lime sandstone. Sandstone is used for fireplace hearths, decorative pieces, building stone, trim, and wall veneers.

Limestone consists mainly of calcite, a mineral, and compact shells or crystalline rocks. See 8-26. It varies widely in color from white to dark grays and tans. Probably the best-known type of limestone is

Bedford limestone from Bedford, Indiana. Limestone weathers more rapidly in humid climates than in dry climates. It is used for building stones, fireplaces, windowsills, trims, and ornamentation.

Marble is an expensive, luxurious looking stone formed from recrystallized limestone. It may be white, yellow, brown, green, black, pink, or a mixture of several colors. See 8-27. Marble is hard and durable, but not as durable as granite. Therefore, it is more frequently used for interior applications. Marble is generally polished for a smooth, shiny surface. It is used for wall veneers, floors, tabletops, bath fixtures, sculpture, and landscape chips.

Slate is a hard, somewhat brittle stone formed from compressed clay or shale. It is frequently blue-gray in color, but it may be green, red, brown, or black. Slate is split into sheets so the surface often has patterned grooving. Slate is used mainly for flooring stones and roofing shingles, 8-28.

Manufactured Stone

Manufactured stone is a veneer made from lightweight concrete to give the appearance of natural stone. See 8-29. Simulated stone is also produced from fiberglass. Manufactured stone is colorfast, weatherproof, and available in several colors and textures for interior and exterior use.

Manufactured stone is applied over stucco, concrete block, brick, cast concrete, or any other untreated masonry surface rough enough to provide a good mechanical bond. It can be applied over other wall surfaces, such as plaster or wood, but special preparation of the wall is needed. Manufactured stone can be cut to various shapes.

Terrazzo

Terrazzo is a very old material composed of marble chips bonded together with cement. It is expensive, but durable. It can be cast in place or precast into desired shapes. Terrazzo is primarily used as a floor finish. It is generally ground and polished to a smooth surface for interior floors, 8-30. Exterior patios and pathways are generally left rough, 8-31. Terrazzo with a rough surface is called *rustic terrazzo*. Terrazzo has become a popular material for precast shower receptors, windowsills, stair treads, and wall veneers.

Concrete

Almost every home has some concrete in its structure. Concrete is used for footings, foundations, exterior walls, floors, walks, and driveways, 8-32.

A Heatilator, Inc.

B Heatilator, Inc.

8-27 Marble is available in a variety of patterns and colors to match most any decor. These rooms were designed around warm (A) and cool (B) color palettes to coordinate with their marble fireplaces.

Lexington Furniture Industries

8-28 Slate floors have a sleek appearance and are easy to maintain.

Cultured Stone by Stucco Stone Products, Inc.

8-29 Manufactured stone looks like real stone, but it is lighter in weight and easier to use.

Before concrete hardens—when it is in *plastic* form—it can be formed into unlimited patterns and textures. Hardened concrete is economical, tough, weather resistant, and long lasting.

Concrete is made from a mixture of Portland cement, fine aggregate (sand), coarse aggregate (gravel or crushed stone), and water. Other materials can be added for special uses. The proportion of ingredients in a concrete mix determines its plastic and hardened qualities. Plastic concrete should be workable, consistent, and easy to finish. Hardened concrete should be strong, watertight, and wear resistant.

A wide variety of decorative finishes can be incorporated into concrete during construction. The basic types of decorative concrete include: colored concrete, exposed aggregate concrete, and concrete with textured finishes or geometric patterns.

Colored Concrete

Concrete can be colored by one of three methods. Color can be mixed into the dry batch before water is added to the concrete mix. Color can be added to a top coating of concrete placed on a regular concrete bed. As a third alternative, color can be added to a plastic concrete slab just before it is smoothed.

The National Terrazzo and Mosaic Association

8-30 Polished terrazzo has a smooth finish.

Exposed Aggregate Concrete

Exposed aggregate is one of the most popular decorative finishes for concrete. Aggregate, such as pebbles or stones, is available in an unlimited variety of colors and textures. Aggregate can be pressed into the surface of poured cement, or mixed into cement before pouring and then washed to expose the aggregate. Exposed aggregate surfaces provide slip resistance as well as an attractive, sturdy finish.

Textured Finishes

Textured finishes can be applied to concrete slabs used for walls or floors while they are still wet. Using a broom or putting rock salt on the surface to produce cavities can create texture. Applying a dash coat of mortar to the surface can also texture slabs, 8-33. Numerous other methods can be used to produce more varied textures.

Geometric Patterns

An endless variety of geometric patterns can be stamped, sawed, or scored into a concrete surface. Stone patterns are popular. Patterns of brick or tile can be applied with a stamping tool, 8-34. Wood or metal divider strips can also be used to form patterns, but the wood strips should be pressure treated lumber to resist decay.

8-31 Rustic terrazzo is used for exterior applications.

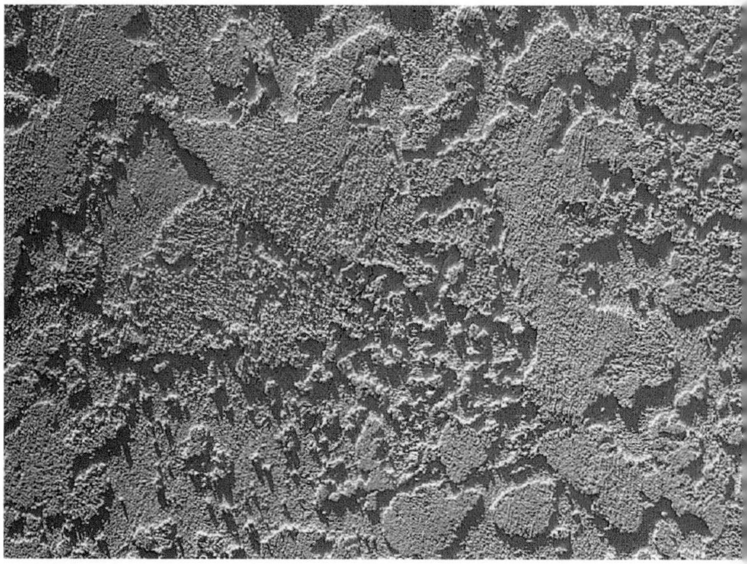

8-33 Mortar can be applied to concrete to produce a travertine finish.

8-32 This house is made almost entirely of concrete, which was used for the walls, floors, and roof tile.

8-34 Stamps can be used to give concrete the appearance of tile or brick.

Chapter Summary

Wood has no equal when its characteristics are considered together—workability, beauty, strength, durability, versatility, and replenishability. Wood, classified as hardwood or softwood, can be processed into the products used in construction. Most woods require a protective finish or treatment, which can include bleaches, fillers, stains, wax, clear finishes, and paints.

Masonry materials are available as structural clay products, concrete masonry units, glass block, and stone. Structural clay products are made from clay or shale. Brick, the most well-known structural clay product, is available in four common classes: building, facing, and paving brick; and firebrick. Brick units are made in modular and nonmodular sizes. Brick bond is important to the appearance, durability, and strength of brick construction.

Concrete masonry units are popular for above-ground and basement construction. Concrete brick is available as concrete building brick and slump brick. Concrete block represents the largest group of concrete masonry units. In addition, special units are designed for unique applications.

Concrete is used in most every type of dwelling. It is found in footings, foundations, exterior walls, floors, walks, and driveways. A wide assortment of decorative finishes can be applied to concrete.

Review Questions

1. How do hardwoods differ from softwoods?
2. What are the primary uses of hardwoods? of softwoods?
3. What steps are used to process wood into lumber?
4. How is lumber used?
5. How does seasoning affect wood?
6. Why are plywood and composite board becoming more common than solid wood?
7. Is pigmented or penetrating stain more commonly used on oak furniture? on yellow pine siding?
8. How does shellac differ from regular varnish? Which can be used alone on wood?
9. What qualities make masonry products popular building materials?
10. How does mortar function in masonry construction?
11. What options are available for producing a decorative wall from concrete masonry?
12. What types of stone are available for use in residential housing and how is each commonly used?
13. What kinds of decorative finishes are available for use on concrete?

Suggested Activities

1. Write an essay describing why wood is so popular as a material in housing.
2. Select a type of wood shown in Figure 8-3 in this chapter. Prepare a brief oral report including such things as its: name, wood classification, growth region, physical properties, commercial uses, and any other pertinent facts.
3. Collect one sample of as many different wood products as possible, such as lumber, millwork, timber, plywood, laminated timber, composite board, hardboard, and particleboard. Identify each and display them to the class.
4. Write a report describing one of the common wood finishes. Cover its strengths, weaknesses, resulting appearance, durability, and so forth.
5. Research the process of how clay bricks are made and present your findings to the class.
6. Prepare a list of the most common shapes and sizes of concrete block. Identify their use in construction.
7. Collect samples of common building stone and show them to your class. Identify each sample.
8. Research terrazzo as a construction material. Present a short history of its use and describe how the material is made.
9. Illustrate several typical decorative concrete surfaces, using photos, rubbings, sketches, magazine ads, or any other means.

Internet Resources

ASTM International, formerly the American Society for Testing Materials
astm.org

Eldorado Stone, a manufacturer of stone veneers
eldoradostone.com

National Hardwood Lumber Association
natlhardwood.org

Portland Cement Association
concretehomes.com and **portcement.org**

Southern Pine Council
southernpine.com

The Engineered Wood Association
apawood.org

U.S. Forest Products Laboratory
fpl.fs.fed.us

Western Wood Products Association
wwpa.org

Note: Web addresses may have changed since publication. For some entries, reaching the correct Web site may require keying *www.* into the address.

Chapter 9
Metals, Glass, Ceramics, and Plastics

Objectives

After studying this chapter, you will be able to
- list the main properties and housing applications of iron, steel, aluminum, copper, brass, bronze, and lead.
- describe the main properties of glass and list the different types of glass products that are used in housing.
- list the main properties and housing applications of ceramics.
- identify plastic products used in housing.

Key Terms

alloy
ductile
cast iron
wrought iron
malleable
weathering steel
stainless steel
gunmetal bronze
tensile strength
float glass
leaded glass
stained glass
glazed tile
ceramic mosaic tile
quarry tile
pavers
thermoplastic
thermosetting plastics

Metals, glass, ceramics, and plastics are used extensively in homes. They have unique characteristics that make possible a variety of applications. They are important materials although they are not used to the same extent in structures as wood, masonry, and concrete. Metals, glass, ceramics, and plastics may be used in construction, furniture, appliances, and accessories.

Metals

Over the years, the amount of metal used in residential structures has increased at a steady rate. Today's average "wood" home contains about 8,000 pounds of various metals. This seems impossible until all the metal products used in a residence are considered. Such a list includes the main supporting beam of a house, wood and masonry reinforcements, water pipes, heating ducts, electrical wiring, roofing materials, gutters, nails, plumbing hardware, appliances, window frames, and doors. Cooking utensils, furniture, tableware, and other accessories could also be included.

Metals are versatile housing materials because they can be shaped in so many ways. They can be cast into complex shapes, rolled into sheets, extruded into standard shapes, machined, welded, bent, sawed, drilled, hammered, and spun. Metals are available in a variety of natural colors. They can be coated with many materials for a wider variety of colors and for added protection. Metals are also strong, decorative, and good conductors of heat and electricity.

Although hundreds of different metals and **alloys**, or mixtures of metals, are produced today, not all of them are used in residential housing. The seven metals most commonly used in housing are iron, steel, aluminum, copper, brass, bronze, and lead.

Iron and Steel

Iron and the iron-containing alloy, *steel*, are frequently used in the housing industry. Pure metallic iron is soft, easily shaped, and **ductile**. This refers to the ability of a metal to be drawn into wire. Pure iron is too weak for most uses, however, so carbon is added to create an alloy with high strength, corrosion resistance, and wear resistance. Iron with carbon also has great resistance to warping and cracking at high temperatures.

Two types of iron are used in the housing industry: cast iron and wrought iron. **Cast iron**, made of iron and 2 to 3.75 percent carbon, is melted in a blast furnace and cast into different shapes. It is used for wood-burning stoves, bathtubs, sinks, skillets, sewer lines, waste disposal systems, and gas pipes. **Wrought iron** is nearly pure iron that is worked into various shapes. It is used in ornamental lawn furniture, lighting fixtures, fences, and railings, 9-1.

Steel contains elements other than iron to make it stronger, more ductile, less brittle, and more **malleable**. This refers to the ability of metal to be formed into sheets. One negative aspect of steel is that it corrodes. Copper, chromium, and other elements, however, may be mixed with steel to increase its corrosion resistance. Steel is used to make I-beams, appliances, cabinets, bathtubs, sinks, knife blades, and cooking utensils.

Copper-bearing steel is steel with copper added for improved corrosion resistance. It is used for sheet-metal products, such as siding, and roofing products, 9-2. Copper is also used for flashing, which is applied to roofs at joints to prevent leaking.

Weathering steel produces a protective oxide coating that resists rust and corrosion. The coating that forms is rusty brown in color. Weathering steel is generally used where accessibility is difficult, such as siding on multifamily structures. It is also used where the rust color is desired for architectural reasons, such as on a part of a roof to provide an accent.

Stainless steel is steel that contains chromium, which makes it hard and corrosion resistant over a wide temperature range. Stainless steel can be scoured repeatedly and still maintain a like-new appearance. Structurally, stainless steel is used for gutters, downspouts, architectural trim, windowsills, railings, tubings, and pipes. Interior items made of stainless steel include furniture, cooking and eating utensils, ranges and other appliances, countertops, and sinks, 9-3.

Stainless steel is more expensive than carbon steel. It is a better material for frequently used items,

WCI Communities, Inc.

9-1 Wrought iron is a popular material for outdoor furniture.

Photo Courtesy of James Hardie® Siding Products

9-2 Metal roofing is a popular roofing material because it resists corrosion.

Kohler, Co.

9-3 Stainless steel sinks are easy to maintain. They retain their original shine and do not show scratches over the years.

however, because it resists corrosion and tarnish, maintains a bright and shiny appearance, and holds a sharp edge longer than carbon steel.

Aluminum

Aluminum, produced since the 1800s, was accepted as a construction material only in the last 50 years. About 300 pounds of aluminum are used in a typical residence today. Aluminum's unique combination of properties makes it one of the most versatile metals used in housing. Aluminum is lightweight, highly resistant to corrosion, an excellent conductor of electricity, and a good reflector of heat and light. It is easily formed into many shapes and receptive to many finishes, which are added for decoration or extra corrosion resistance. Some alloys of aluminum are even stronger than structural steel.

The three main methods of processing aluminum are extruding, casting, and rolling. Extruded aluminum is heated to a plastic state and forced through a die opening to produce a desired shape. This process provides great flexibility of design shape and accurately sized, high-quality aluminum products. The most common use of extruded aluminum is the manufacturing of window and door frames, 9-4. Louvers, railings, grilles, solar collectors, and builder's hardware such as door and window hinges can also be made of extruded aluminum.

Cast aluminum products are made by pouring hot metal into molds. Cast aluminum is used for decorative panels, lamp bases, trivets, plant stands, electrical fittings, grilles, handles, and cookware.

Aluminum is rolled by running soft aluminum through steel rollers. Rolled aluminum products are generally not as straight or accurately sized as extruded aluminum products. Also, the surface finish of rolled aluminum is generally a poorer quality. Rolled aluminum may be used to make pipes, air ducts, appliance cabinets, range hoods, suspended ceiling supports, awnings, garage doors, and grilles, 9-5.

Copper

Copper is used in residential structures in sheet, roll, and wire forms. Its most important qualities are electrical conductivity, heat conductivity,

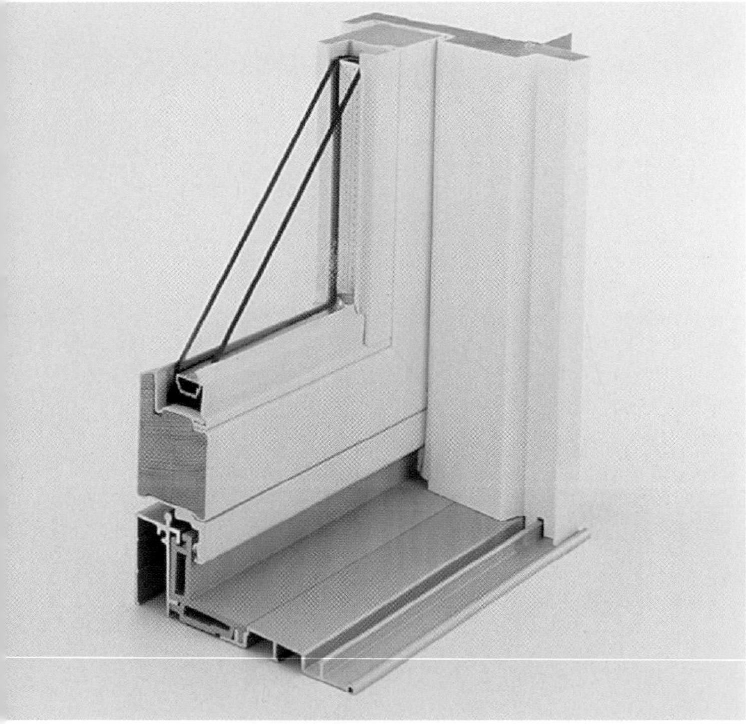

Andersen Corporation

9-4 Extruded aluminum is often used for window and door frames and threshold saddles.

9-5 This aluminum grille-type fence is attractive and resists corrosion well.

and resistance to corrosion. Its strength and ductility are affected by the mechanical and heat treatment that it receives. Copper heated and cooled slowly becomes brittle. Copper heated and cooled rapidly is malleable and ductile. When copper is exposed to moist air, it forms a thin coating of green carbonate. This coating protects copper against further corrosion.

Copper is used in housing construction primarily for wiring, tubing, pipes, roof flashing, and decorative nails and bolts. It is also an excellent, but expensive, roofing material, 9-6. Inside the house, copper may be used for cookware, range hoods, lamps, and decorative pieces. Since copper is a soft material, it lends itself to many finishes. It can be brushed, burnished, polished, sandblasted, or buffed.

9-6 The copper roofing over this bay window will last indefinitely. It forms an oxide coating that protects it from further corrosion.

Brass

Brass is an alloy of copper and zinc. Most brasses range in composition from 60 percent copper and 40 percent zinc to 90 percent copper and 10 percent zinc. Standard brass contains 67 percent copper and 33 percent zinc. Colors range from copper red to silvery white, depending on the copper content. Small amounts of tin can be added to help prevent corrosion or tarnishing. Brass can be coated with clear enamel or another coating to prevent corrosion.

Brass is formed by casting, hammering, stamping, rolling, or drawing. Brass is expensive, but its attractive color and strength make it a desirable housing material. It is used for weather stripping, screws, bolts, nails, and wire, 9-7. It is also popular for furniture and decorative pieces, 9-8.

Bronze

Bronze is an alloy of copper and tin. It usually contains 75 to 95 percent copper and five to 25 percent tin. Tin increases the hardness of copper. The strongest bronze, called **gunmetal bronze**, contains 90 percent copper and 10 percent tin. This composition was used to make cannons, resulting in the term *gunmetal*.

Bronze is a beautiful, stately material that weathers well. Although expensive, it is the highest quality material available for thresholds, glass sliding-door frames, windowsills, screens, screws, and bolts. High-quality plumbing valves and pipes are made of bronze, 9-9. Bronze is also used for interior decorative pieces, 9-10.

Baldwin Hardware Corp.

9-7 Brass hinges are attractive and less likely to creak with age than hinges made of other materials.

NMC/Focal Point

9-8 Brass is popular for decorative pieces such as this chandelier.

9-9 Cast-bronze plumbing hardware will last indefinitely because it almost completely resists corrosion.

9-10 Art objects made of bronze are attractive and can be used to enhance interior as well as exterior settings.

Lead

Lead is a heavy, yet workable, metal that is resistant to corrosion. Lead sheets are used extensively under showers, as liners for pools, and as flashing. It is sometimes used as a roofing material on curved or irregularly shaped surfaces. Lead is a very useful material for drainage pipes in earthquake-prone areas. Lead is also used to attach anchor bolts in concrete.

One disadvantage of lead is its high expansion and contraction rate in changing temperatures, which makes it difficult to fasten the metal into place. Other disadvantages are heavy weight and possible lead-poisoning problems, which limit the number of practical housing applications for lead.

Glass

Glassmaking has been an art for over 4,500 years. However, not until the early twentieth century could glass be produced in large, flat sheets. The availability of flat glass exerted a dramatic influence on modern lifestyles and architecture. While colonial homes had only a few small, divided windows, modern homes may have entire walls of glass. See 9-11.

Glass is the only housing construction material that allows the passage of light and permits a clear view. It does not conduct electricity, and it is almost completely corrosion resistant. Only a few chemical reactions can cause glass to break down.

Although strong, glass does break if enough force is applied to stretch or bend it past its breaking point. The **tensile strength** refers to the amount of force that glass can withstand before breaking. Tensile strength of glass can be increased by increasing its thickness or by applying certain production techniques to the glass. Scratches, imperfections, and improper production decrease tensile strength. Rapid temperature change also decreases the tensile strength of glass.

Flat Glass

Most of the glass used in housing structures is flat glass. It is used for window and door panes, tabletops, shelves, and mirrors, 9-12. About 95 percent of the flat glass in America is **float glass**. Floating molten glass over a bed of molten metal produces this glass. The process yields an even sheet of glass that is smooth and polished on both sides. Float glass is produced in several strengths and thicknesses to fit different needs. The glass is distortion free and available in sheets large enough to create a wall-sized window.

A Massachusetts Office of Travel and Tourism

B Janco Greenhouses

9-11 Older homes (A) had few windows with small panes of glass due to limited technology. Modern homes (B) can have entire walls of glass.

9-12 This Regency period mirror was a prized accessory in the early 1800s.

Sheet glass and plate glass are types of flat glass produced by other methods. Sheet glass is often rippled, causing distortion and poor quality. It may still be found in older houses. Plate glass is similar in quality to float glass, but it is much more expensive to produce. Float glass has almost completely replaced both types.

Decorative Glass

Types of decorative glass include patterned, etched, cut, and enameled glass. Patterned glass has a linear or geometric pattern embossed on one or both sides. This produces a translucent glass that allows privacy while admitting light. It is made in thicknesses of 1/8 and 7/32 in. and may be tempered to increase its strength. Patterned glass is used for partitions and bathroom windows, and in other areas where privacy is desired. Patterned safety glass is frequently used as a tub or shower enclosure.

Etched glass is treated with hydrofluoric acid to make it appear frosted. Various patterns can be used for a decorative effect, 9-13. Enameled glass has translucent or solid colors applied to its surface. Cut glass is produced by applying gem-cutting techniques, which break up light and make the cut edges sparkle.

Tinted Glass

Tinted glass is made by adding a coloring agent to a batch of molten glass. Bronze and gray are the most common colors, 9-14. The addition of a tint can reduce light transmission from 25 to 75 percent, depending on the color and thickness of the glass. This helps to reduce heat transmission and glare.

Tinted glass is used most frequently in warm, sunny climates to provide a more comfortable interior. In cool climates, tinted glass may be used for eastern or western windows to reduce glare. However, they are not recommended for southern windows in northern areas because they interfere

9-13 Frosted patterns can be etched on glass for a decorative effect.

9-14 Tinted glass is used for windows where hot sunlight and glare is a problem.

9-15 These large window panels are made from reflective glass to reduce interior heat gain in warm weather.

with the sun's ability to provide solar heat. Tinted glass can contribute to the architectural style of a house. It is also used for tabletops and shelves.

Reflective Glass

Reflective glass, also called environmental glass, is fairly new. It is even more effective than tinted glass in reducing heat gain, 9-15. The glass has a transparent metal or metal oxide coating bonded to one surface of the glass. Frequently, the reflective material is laminated between two thicknesses of glass to protect the coating from abrasion. The coatings used include cobalt oxide, chromium, copper, aluminum, nickel, and gold. Glass may be neutral, copper, bronze, blue, or golden in color. Reflective glass is used primarily in warm climates to reduce air conditioning costs.

Insulating Glass

Insulating glass is designed to reduce the transmission of heat. It consists of dehydrated air or a special dry gas sandwiched between two pieces of glass. Insulating glass units are produced with metal or welded-glass edges, 9-16. Metal-edge units are generally available in a wide range of sizes and glass thicknesses. Units with welded-glass edges are generally limited to smaller sizes. The typical air void in an insulated glass unit is ¼ to ½ in. wide. Insulated glass is widely used in housing structures and some appliances to reduce heat loss or heat gain.

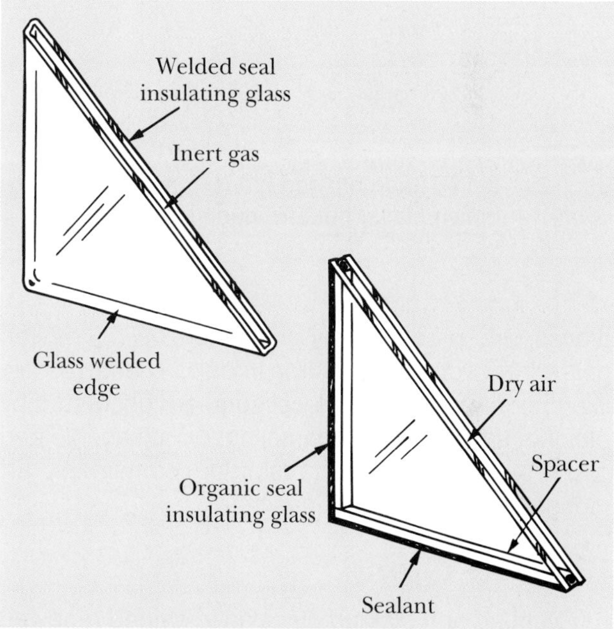

9-16 Both welded-edge and metal-edge insulating glass are more effective insulators than single-pane glass.

Handblown Glass

Handblown glass is expensive but desired for its beauty and individual character. It is produced by dipping a hollow metal rod into molten glass and blowing the glass into a bubble. The bubble is then formed into a shape by rolling, twisting, or shaping with tools while the glass is still hot and plastic. Handblown glass is used mostly for art pieces and vases, although it can also be used for fine drinking glasses.

Molded Glass

Molded glass products of excellent quality are available today, 9-17. They are less expensive and often more durable than handblown items. Molded

WCI Communities, Inc.

9-17 These molded glass candleholders are similar in quality and appearance to hand-blown glass, but are much less expensive.

pieces are produced by machine-blowing molten glass into wood or cast-iron molds. These pieces, like their handmade predecessors, are decorated by etching, sandblasting, enameling, or cutting. Molded glass is used for ornate storage containers, art pieces, and decorative dinnerware.

Leaded Glass

Leaded and stained glass have gained renewed popularity. They are made by setting small pieces of clear or colored glass into strips of lead or copper foil. **Leaded glass** usually refers to transparent or colorless glass. **Stained glass** refers to glass colored by pigments or metal oxides that are fused to the glass. Leaded and stained glass are used in doors, lampshades, and decorative windows, 9-18.

NMC/Focal Point

9-18 This beautiful stained glass window in the shower adds excitement and interest to the bathroom.

Ceramics

Ceramic products have been used from the beginning of civilization and remain popular today. Clay is hardened with heat to make a wide variety of ceramic products. These include wall, floor, roofing, and drain tiles; chimney flue liners; dishes; and sculptured objects.

Clay in its plastic form is easily shaped. When dried and fired, it is like porous stone. Firing clay in a kiln preserves its shape, color, and texture. Firing also makes clay resistant to heat, cold, moisture, acids, and salts. Clay can be glazed, colored, and textured for decoration. Glazing also increases clay's strength and seals its pores, making it waterproof.

Ceramic Tile

Ceramic tile is made from clay or shale that is fired at high temperatures. It is manufactured in modular unit sizes. All ceramic tile products possess good abrasion resistance and a high degree of resistance to moisture. These properties make ceramic tile a perfect choice for areas exposed to heavy foot traffic, water, or corrosive chemicals. Tiles are produced in a variety of dimensions, properties, and appearances, 9-19. The main types of ceramic tile produced are: glazed, ceramic mosaic, and quarry and paver tile.

Glazed tile is available for use on walls or floors. Tile designed for walls usually has one coat of glazing, while that for floors generally has two or three coats. Tiles designed for very heavy traffic areas should be finished with a special crystalline glaze. Glazing gives tile a smooth, glossy finish that resists stains. Many different colors and textures of glazes are used on tile, making tile a versatile decorating tool, 9-20.

Nominal sizes of standard 5/16 in. thick glazed tile include 4¼ by 4¼ in., 4¼ by 6 in., and 6 by 6 in. Some glazed wall tile is sufficiently abrasion resistant for use on floors in light traffic areas. All glazed floor tile can be used on walls, but floor tile is usually more expensive. Glazed tile is especially popular for bathrooms and kitchens, where high moisture resistance and ease of cleaning is especially important. However, new designs and colors have made glazed tile popular for other rooms, such as living rooms and bedrooms.

Ceramic mosaic tile is small, decorative tile made of porcelain or natural clay. It is smaller than standard glazed tile and generally available in vivid, solid colors. Areas covered with ceramic tile may display one color, a random combination of colors, or geometric or pictorial patterns.

Porcelain mosaic tiles are brighter, smoother, and more water repellent than clay tiles. The clay mosaic tiles are generally in muted, earthy colors. Mosaic tile is generally ¼ in. thick and is available in

Florida Tile

9-20 Plain ceramic tiles cover this kitchen countertop, while tiles of several colors and patterns are combined to create a one-of-a-kind wall.

9-19 Ceramic tile is available in a variety of styles to suit almost any purpose.

standard sizes of 1 by 1 in., 1 by 2 in., and 2 by 2 in. They are also made in hexagonal and round shapes. Mosaic tile is generally used on walls, floors, and countertops, 9-21.

The strongest of the ceramic tiles are quarry tile and pavers, which are made from natural clays and shales. Both are designed for heavy-traffic floors. **Quarry tiles** are large, squares of ceramic tile, while **pavers** are generally rectangular tiles. Although quarry tile can be glazed, these tiles generally derive their color from the type of clay used, 9-22. Glazing gives the tile great, long-lasting durability and prevents the surface color from wearing away. Quarry tiles may be ½ or ¾ in. thick and are available in 6, 9, and 12 in. squares. Pavers are ½ in. thick tiles that are available in rectangular sizes of 2 ¾ by 6 in. or 4 by 8 in.

9-21 The mosaic tile on this kitchen wall is both attractive and functional.

9-22 Quarry tiles are suitable for frequently used areas. Their colors are warm and earthy.

Roofing Tile

Clay tile roofs are characteristic of Spanish and Mediterranean architecture. See 9-23. Clay roofing tile is durable and attractive but very expensive. It is also more porous than other roofing materials.

Clay roofing tile is available in a flat or roll design. Flat tile is similar to shingles with interlocking edges. Roll-type tile forms a corrugated design. Clay tile is generally fastened to the roof with copper nails because copper resists corrosion and lasts as long as the tile. A waterproof membrane is required under clay tile to prevent leaking.

Pottery

Pottery refers to ceramic objects such as dinnerware, cookware, and vases. Pottery making is an old art, but most pottery pieces today are manufactured rather than handmade. There are three types of pottery: earthenware, stoneware, and porcelain.

9-23 Clay roofing tile is attractive and long lasting.

Earthenware is the most casual type of pottery. It is made of coarse-textured clay fired at a relatively low temperature (1800° to 2100°F). Earthenware products are porous, fragile, and opaque. Flowerpots, casual dinnerware, and folk pottery are examples of earthenware, 9-24. They are generally red or brown in color. If they are glazed, the glaze generally has a rougher texture than that on stoneware or porcelain.

Stoneware, which is usually gray or light brown in color, is made from finer clay than earthenware. The clay is fired at a medium temperature (2100° to 2300°F), causing the clay to lose its porosity. The heat also makes the clay *vitrify*, or fuse into a glassy substance. This clay is used primarily for high-quality, casual dinnerware, 9-25. Stoneware pieces are more durable and waterproof than earthenware pieces. Glazes on stoneware are generally in subtle colors with a matte finish.

Porcelain is fired at a high temperature (2250° to 2500°F) to a white, finely textured finish. The highest quality of pottery, porcelain is completely vitrified and very hard. A chipped area will not absorb moisture due to porcelain's nonporous nature. Porcelain items are often translucent, giving them a delicate appearance.

Expensive dinnerware and artwork are made of porcelain. Bathtubs, sinks, and other household fixtures may also be finished with porcelain, 9-26. Most porcelain is white, off-white, or pastel. Glazes on porcelain have a hard, glossy finish, and patterns are finely detailed, 9-27.

Plastics

Plastics are manufactured polymer materials. Plastic is a fairly new material; the first commercial plastic in the United States was developed around 100 years ago. Plastics are gaining use in housing due to their reasonable cost and wide range of properties. For

9-24 Earthenware has a rough, somewhat porous finish.

9-25 Stoneware is more durable than earthenware. It is popular for casual dinnerware.

9-26 Porcelain finishes are standard for bathroom fixtures. The finish is smooth, durable, and easy to maintain.

9-27 Decorative porcelain items like this vase often have finely detailed, painted designs.

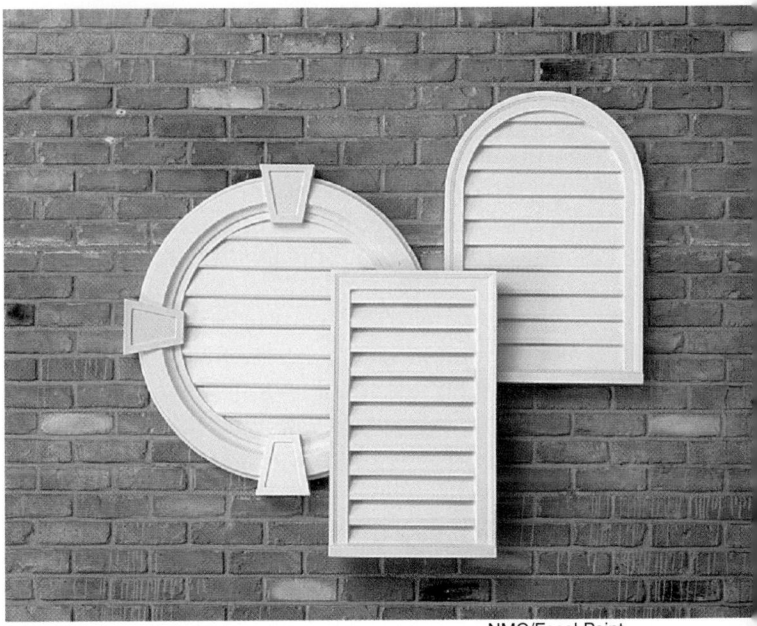

NMC/Focal Point

9-28 Plastics allow the inexpensive production of durable, lightweight construction details, such as these ventilation louvers.

example, plastics are generally moisture and corrosion resistant, lightweight, tough, and easily molded into complex shapes, 9-28. They possess characteristics found in other, more-expensive materials.

Plastics have a variety of uses in housing. They are replacing many natural building materials because of their low-maintenance requirements and durability. Plastics are used for floor coverings, window frame and door coatings, siding, countertop and tabletop laminates, safety windows, vapor barriers, insulation, furniture, and accessories.

Plastics are classified as thermoplastics and thermosetting plastics. **Thermoplastic** materials can be repeatedly softened with heat and hardened by cooling. Many thermoplastics are flammable. **Thermosetting plastics** are permanently shaped during the manufacturing process and cannot be softened again by reheating. They form a rigid, often brittle, mass that will not burn. Some characteristics and applications to housing of several commercial plastics are listed in A-16 and A-17 of the Appendix.

9-29 Solid-surface materials provide an excellent mar-resistant surface that is available in a variety of colors.

Plastic, solid-surface materials, such as Avonite, Corian, Fountainhead, Gibraltar, and Surell, are replacing high-pressure laminate materials for countertops. These materials are frequently made to look like natural stone, 9-29. They are also available in solid colors and flecked patterns. Countertops made with these ½ in. thick, solid-surface materials do not require a substrate as traditional plastic laminates do. These materials may also be cast into sinks or moldings at the factory.

Chapter Summary

Metal, glass, ceramics, and plastics have broad applications in the structure, furnishings, and decoration of a dwelling. These are important materials although they are not used to the same extent as wood, masonry, and concrete.

The use of metal in residential structures has increased steadily over the years. Some of the applications include: beams, reinforcement, pipes, ducts, wiring, roof coverings, flashing, gutters, nails, appliances, window and door frames, utensils, and furniture. The seven metals that are most commonly used in dwellings are iron (both cast and wrought iron), steel, aluminum, copper, brass, bronze, and lead.

Glass is the only housing material that allows the passage of light and permits a clear view. Glass is available in eight basic types: flat, decorative, tinted, reflective, insulating, handblown, molded, and leaded.

Ceramic tile is made from clay or shale fired at high temperatures. This family of products is hard and resistant to abrasion and moisture. Common tile forms include: glazed tile, mosaic tile, quarry tile, pavers, roofing tile, and pottery.

The use of plastics, which are manufactured polymer materials, is increasing daily in housing. Plastics are classified as thermoplastics and thermosetting plastics.

Review Questions

1. How does cast iron differ from wrought iron?
2. What are some uses of cast iron and wrought iron in housing?
3. What are the main properties of steel?
4. How are the properties of steel affected by the addition of copper? of chromium?
5. What are some uses of steel in housing?
6. What are the three main ways that aluminum is processed and examples of housing products that result from each?
7. How does copper differ from brass and bronze?
8. How are copper, brass, and bronze used in housing?
9. As a housing material, what qualities make glass desirable? undesirable?
10. If two windows made of the same type and thickness of glass were hit with the same amount of force, but only one broke, what might explain this?
11. What are the different types of glass used in housing and their main uses?
12. What types of ceramic products are used in housing?
13. What qualities make ceramic products popular?
14. What properties make plastics desirable housing materials?
15. What are some examples of plastics used in housing?

Suggested Activities

1. Write an essay describing the numerous ways that metal can be shaped into products, such as rolling and extruding. Identify housing products that lend themselves to each type of manufacture.
2. Identify where in a housing structure each of the seven most commonly used metals are generally found.
3. Prepare a list of the primary characteristics associated with the following metals—cast iron, wrought iron, weathering steel, stainless steel, and aluminum.
4. Explain how copper, brass, and bronze differ from one another in composition.
5. Describe the various types of glass used in housing, identifying their primary characteristics and applications.
6. Visit your local home center or floor covering store and ask for a sample of each basic category of ceramic tile. Display them in the classroom.
7. Research the many types of plastic building products produced and develop a list of product categories. Identify five local or regional businesses involved with producing or selling one or more of the products.
8. Collect as many samples of plastic building products as possible. Display them to the class.

Internet Resources

Aluminum Company of America (ALCOA) Building Products, Inc.
alcoahomes.com

American Iron and Steel Institute
steel.org

Ceramic Tile Institute of America
ctioa.org

House of Glass, worldwide glass trading site
glasschange.com

International Zinc Association
iza.com

Modern Plastics Magazine
modplas.com

Reemay, Inc., manufacturer of nonwoven, spunbonded products such as housewrap
reemay.com

The McGraw-Hill Companies, Inc. construction products marketplace
sweets.com

U.S. Department of Energy
energy.gov

Note: Web addresses may have changed since publication. For some entries, reaching the correct Web site may require keying *www.* into the address.

Chapter 10
Textiles

Objectives

After studying this chapter, you will be able to

- list the origins, qualities, and uses of natural and manufactured fibers.
- evaluate a yarn in terms of the method used to create it and its advantages, disadvantages, and uses.
- describe the various types of fabric construction in terms of their production, quality, and uses.
- evaluate the appropriateness of a fabric for a specific use within the home.

Key Terms

fiber
yarn
cellulosic fibers
protein fibers
microfiber
staple fibers
filaments
pilling
blend
combination
weft knitting
warp knitting
felt
nonwoven fabrics
films
foams
leather
stock dyeing
solution dyeing
roller printing
rotary screen printing
block printing

Textile products are used throughout the home to add color, texture, and comfort. Carpets, rugs, upholstery, and curtains are common textile products used in the home. Understanding the materials and methods involved in fabric construction will help you choose fabrics that are attractive, durable, and appropriate for use.

Fibers

The basic element of most textiles is called **fiber**, while fibers twisted together to form a continuous strand are called **yarn**. Yarns are woven, knitted, or fastened together to make fabric.

Fibers determine a fabric's strength, elasticity, texture, shrinkage, warmth, absorbency, and durability. They also determine a fabric's resistance to stains, fire, sunlight, mildew, and abrasion. The properties of a fiber depend on its source. Fibers originate from either natural or chemical sources. They are classified as natural fibers and manufactured fibers.

Natural Fibers

Natural fibers are derived from one of three naturally occurring substances: cellulose, protein, or mineral. See 10-1. **Cellulosic fibers** come from plants. Flax, the source of linen, and cotton are two common cellulosic fibers, but others include hemp, jute, and ramie. **Protein fibers** come from animals. Silk, wool, and hair fibers such as cashmere, camel hair, mohair, and angora are protein fibers.

The only natural mineral fiber is asbestos, found in rocks. This fiber was used for insulation and in products where a noncombustible material was

Natural Fibers	
Cellulosic	Cotton Flax Hemp Jute Ramie
Protein	Silk Wool Specialty hair fibers alpaca angora camel hair cashmere guanaco llama mohair vicuna
Mineral	Asbestos

10-1 Natural fibers are categorized as cellulosic (plant), protein (animal), or mineral.

required. Manufactured products, however, such as glass and novoloid have generally replaced asbestos because of health problems linked to its fibers.

Natural fibers are unique because they cannot be duplicated exactly by technology. Cotton, flax (linen), silk, and wool are the four common natural fibers. The common uses of these fibers in home furnishings, their characteristics, and the care methods recommended are described in 10-2.

Manufactured Fibers

Manufactured fibers are chemically modified materials derived from substances found in nature, such as wood pulp and petroleum. Unlike natural fibers, these substances are not fibrous in their natural form. They are transformed into fibers through chemical engineering. First, they are made into solutions. Then, fibers are extruded from the liquid and solidified.

Four Common Natural Fibers

Fiber	Uses	Characteristics	Care
Cotton	Sheets Towels Bedspreads Draperies Upholstery Rugs	Absorbent Easy to dye and print Does not generate static electricity Highly flammable unless treated with flame-retardant finish Wrinkles easily Shrinks in hot water unless treated Soils easily	Wash or dry-clean. Avoid damp storage to prevent mildew. Avoid prolonged exposure to sunlight.
Flax (Linen)	Draperies Upholstery Tablecloths Kitchen towels	Strongest of natural fibers Durable, withstands frequent laundering Ages well Lint free Wrinkles easily unless treated Flammable Expensive if good quality	Wash or dry-clean. Iron on wrong side to prevent creating a shine. Avoid damp storage to prevent mildew.
Silk	Draperies Upholstery Lampshades Wall hangings	Strong but lightweight Very absorbent Dyes well Smooth and lustrous Resists wrinkling Retains shape well Soil resistant Expensive Yellows with age Spotted by water unless specially treated	Dry-clean unless otherwise specified. Avoid prolonged exposure to sunlight. Avoid contact with silverfish, which attack the fiber.
Wool	Blankets Draperies Carpets Upholstery Rugs	Warmest of all fibers Very absorbent Wrinkle resistant Holds and retains shape well Creases well Expensive	Dry-clean unless otherwise specified. Press with low, moist heat. Avoid contact with moths and carpet beetles, which eat the fibers.

10-2 The four most common natural fibers are used in many household fabrics. Individual characteristics and care requirements help determine which uses are best for each fiber.

The two basic types of manufactured fibers are cellulosic and noncellulosic. See 10-3. Cellulosic fibers are derived from cellulose, the fibrous substance found in plants. Rayon, triacetate, and acetate are three cellulosic fibers.

Noncellulosic fibers are made from molecules containing various combinations of carbon, hydrogen, nitrogen, and oxygen. The molecules are linked into long chains called polymers, from which long strands of fibers are produced. Acrylic, nylon, and polyester are three common noncellulosic fibers.

Microfiber is the name given to ultrafine manufactured fibers. Such fibers are at least two times finer than a strand of silk, the thinnest natural fiber. The fiber's thinness creates a fabric with a more luxurious look and feel. Currently, four types are available: acrylic, nylon, polyester, and rayon microfibers.

The chart in 10-4 identifies the uses, characteristics, and proper care of common manufactured fibers used in home furnishings.

Yarns

The size and texture of a yarn depends on its fiber content, the tightness of the twist, and the number of *plies*, or strands, it has. Yarns are either made from short fibers called **staple fibers** or continuous strands of fibers called **filaments**. All natural fibers except silk are staple fibers. Silk and all manufactured fibers are filaments, but they can be cut into staple fibers.

Spun yarns are made from staple fibers. These yarns have a fuzzy appearance because tiny fiber ends protrude from these yarns. The tiny fiber ends of spun yarns may cause pilling. **Pilling** is the formation of tiny balls of fiber, called pills, that form on fabrics from abrasion.

Monofilament yarns are made from a single filament. Multifilament yarns are made from a group of filaments. Silk and most manufactured fibers are made into multifilament yarns.

Many textiles today are either blends or combinations of natural and manufactured fibers. Two or more different staple fibers spun together into a single yarn forms a **blend**. Two different single yarns twisted into one yarn forms a **combination**. Blends and combinations possess the best characteristics of the individual fibers they contain. For example, cotton/polyester is a blend commonly used for sheets. It combines the soft, absorbent properties of cotton with the wrinkle-resistant properties of polyester to produce comfortable, easy-care sheets.

Twist in yarns is necessary to hold fibers or filaments together. Twist can also increase yarn strength. As the degree of twist increases in a yarn, the yarn becomes firmer, more compact, and less lustrous. Average to high twist is used for most yarns made from staple fibers; a low twist is used for most yarns made from filaments.

Yarns are classified as single, ply, or cord. See 10-5. The twisting together of fibers or filaments forms a single yarn. Two or more single yarns twisted together form a ply yarn. Knitting yarn is an example of a ply yarn. Two or more ply yarns twisted together result in a cord yarn. Ropes are often made from cord yarns.

Manufactured Fibers	
Cellulosic	Acetate Rayon Triacetate*
Noncellulosic	Acrylic Anidex* Aramid Azlon * Glass Lastrile * Metallic Modacrylic Novoloid * Nylon Nytril * Olefin Polyester Rubber Saran Spandex Vinal * Vinyon
*Not currently produced in the United States.	

10-3 Manufactured fibers are broadly categorized as cellulosic and noncellulosic.

Fabric Construction

Fabrics can be made by various methods. Weaving, knitting, and tufting are the most common construction methods involving yarns. Other methods may be used to construct fabrics with or without yarns. Color and finishes may be added at several stages of fabric construction.

Weaving

Woven fabrics are made with two sets of yarns interlaced at right angles to each other. The two sets of yarns are called *warp yarns* and *filling yarns*, and

Common Manufactured Fibers

Fiber	Uses	Characteristics	Care
Acetate	Bedspreads Draperies Fiberfill Upholstery	Easy to dye Drapes well Soft and luxurious Inexpensive Resistant to pilling, moths, and mildew Nonabsorbent Melts under high heat	Dry-clean unless otherwise specified. Avoid contact with acetone and other organic solvents.
Acrylic	Awnings Blankets Carpeting Draperies Fiberfill Rugs Upholstery	Resembles wool Soft, warm, and lightweight Colorfast Retains shape well Nonabsorbent Generates static electricity Resistant to wrinkles, chemicals, moths, mildew, and sunlight Not resistant to abrasion, pilling, stretching, and soil Is available as a microfiber	Machine wash in warm water. Machine dry on low setting. Hand wash delicate items in warm water. Use moderately warm iron.
Glass	Curtains Draperies Insulation batting	Strong and relatively heavy Resistant to heat, flames, and most chemicals Nonabsorbent	
Metallic	Draperies Rugs Slipcovers Tablecloths Upholstery	Colorfast Very durable Resistant to moths, mildew, and shrinking	
Modacrylic	Awnings Blankets Carpeting Curtains Rugs Draperies	Warm, heavy, and bulky Retains shape well Flame resistant Resistant to chemicals, moths, mildew, and shrinking	For deep pile, dry-clean or use fur-cleaning process. For washable items, machine wash in warm water. Machine wash on low-heat setting. Use cool iron.
Nylon	Bedspreads Carpeting Curtains Draperies Outdoor furniture Mattress pads Rugs Slipcovers Tablecloths Upholstery	Very strong and durable Lustrous and lightweight Easy to dye Drapes well Retains shape well Resistant to moths, mildew, and oily stains Nonabsorbent Generates static electricity Not resistant to soil and pilling Is available as a microfiber	Machine wash in warm water. Machine dry on low setting. If ironing is necessary, use a warm setting.
Olefin	Awnings Carpeting Carpet backings Doormats Outdoor furniture Mattresses Slipcovers Upholstery	Very strong, yet lightweight Colorfast Very durable Quick drying Resistant to abrasion, chemicals, moths, mildew, oily stains, and shrinking Inexpensive	Machine wash in lukewarm water. Machine dry on low setting. Do not iron 100% olefin fibers.

10-4 Many manufactured fibers are used in the home. Each has unique characteristics and care requirements.

Common Manufactured Fibers

Fiber	Uses	Characteristics	Care
Polyester	Awnings Bedspreads Blankets Carpeting Curtains Draperies Fiberfill Mattresses Mattress pads Pillowcases Rugs Sheets Slipcovers Tablecloths Upholstery	Colorfast Very strong and durable Easy to dye Retains shape well Resistant to wrinkles, stretching, bleach, moths, and mildew Nonabsorbent Generates static electricity Not resistant to oily stains, soil, and pilling Is available as a microfiber	Machine wash in warm water. Machine dry on low setting. Use moderately warm iron. Most polyester items are also dry-cleanable.
Rayon	Bedspreads Curtains Draperies Sheets Slipcovers Tablecloths Upholstery	Resembles cotton Absorbent Easy to dye Colorfast Drapes well Resistant to moths and pilling Wrinkles easily unless treated with a special finish Shrinks in hot water unless treated Highly flammable unless treated Is available as a microfiber	Hand wash in mild, lukewarm sudsy water unless otherwise specified. Do not wring or twist. Air dry. Press on the wrong side while damp.
Saran	Awning Draperies Outdoor furniture	Colorfast Very durable Strong and heavy Flame resistant Resistant to chemicals, moths, mildew, oily stains, and sunlight Softens at low temperatures	Wash with soap and water.

10-4 *Continued*

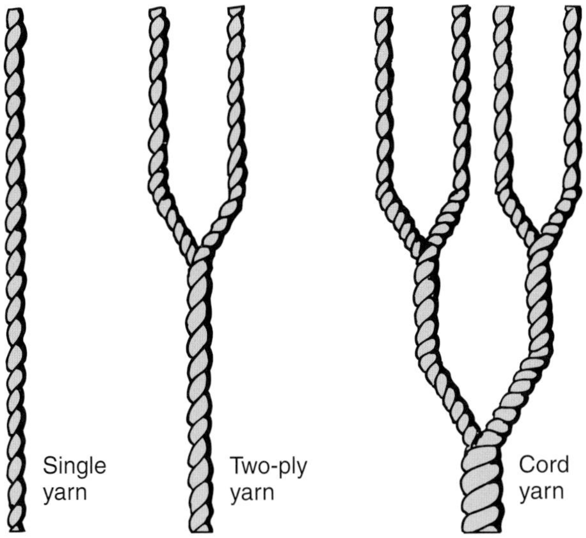

10-5 A single-ply yarn is formed by twisting together fibers or filaments. When two single-ply yarns are twisted together, a two-ply yarn is formed. Twisting together two or more ply yarns produces a cord yarn.

the direction they run is called the grain. Warp yarns run along the lengthwise grain; and filling yarns, the crosswise grain.

By passing the filling yarns over and under various numbers of warp yarns, different weaves are created. The five weaves often used to construct fabrics for the home are: plain, twill, satin, jacquard, and leno.

Plain Weave

The simplest form of weaving is the plain weave, formed by passing a filling yarn over and under one warp yarn. See 10-6. The plain weave produces strong, durable fabrics. Broadcloth, percale, gingham, and grosgrain are examples of plain weave fabrics.

A common variation of the plain weave is the basket weave. It is made by passing two or more filling yarns over and under the same number of warp yarns. Monk's cloth and hopsacking are woven in the basket weave.

American Textile Manufacturers Institute

10-6 A plain weave is formed by passing a filling yarn over and under one warp yarn. Combining thick warp yarns with thin filling yarns can make textured curtain fabric.

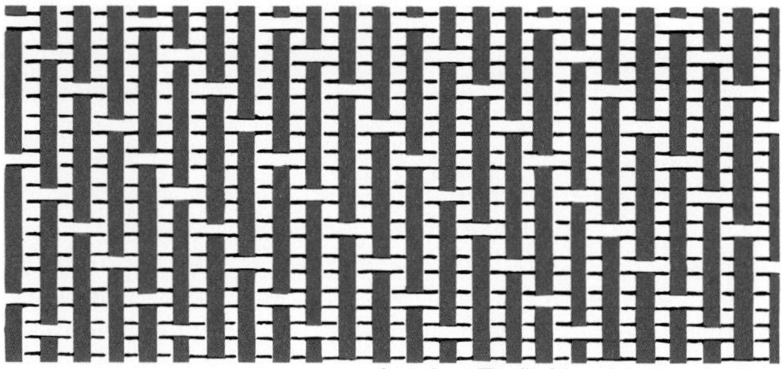

American Textile Manufacturers Institute

10-7 A twill weave has floats that form diagonal patterns. The weave resists wrinkles and hides soil.

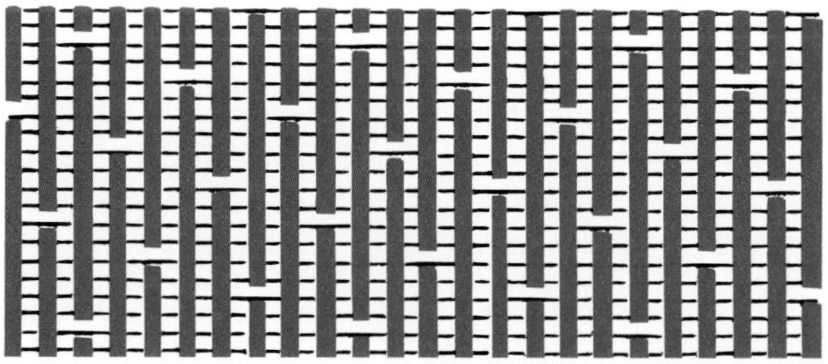

American Textile Manufacturers Institute

10-8 Satin weaves create long floats on a fabric's surface. The fabric is smooth and shiny, but not very durable.

Twill Weave

Fabrics woven in the twill weave display diagonal lines, or *wales*, 10-7. A wale is formed when a yarn in one direction passes over two or more yarns in the other direction. Each float begins at least one yarn over from the last one. Like plain weaves, twill weaves form strong, durable fabrics. They also resist wrinkles and hide soil. Denim and gabardine are two examples of twill weaves.

The herringbone twill is a common variation of the twill weave. In this design, the wale changes direction at regular intervals to produce a zigzag effect.

Satin weave

The satin weave produces smooth and lustrous fabrics. The smoothness and shine is the result of long floats on the surface of the fabric. A *float* is made by passing a yarn over four or more intersecting yarns, 10-8. Each float begins two yarns over from where the last float began.

The satin weave does not produce very durable fabrics because the floats tend to snag easily. However, durability can be increased if the yarns are woven closely together. The two fabrics woven in the satin weave are satin and sateen. In satin, the floats run in the warp direction. In sateen, the floats run in the filling direction.

Jacquard Weave

Jacquard fabrics are characterized by intricate patterns, 10-9. These patterns are made by different arrangements of the warp yarns, determined by cards attached to the Jacquard loom. The complex process required to manufacture Jacquard weaves makes Jacquard fabrics expensive to produce.

Fabrics made on a Jacquard loom are damask, brocade, and tapestry. These fabrics are used for upholstery, tablecloths, and wall hangings. Jacquard fabrics tend to be less durable if they have long floats or if fine yarns are used.

Leno Weave

The leno weave is characterized by paired warp yarns that are passed over and under the filling yarns in a figure-eight configuration. This type of weave produces a meshlike fabric. Fabrics made by the leno weave are used to manufacture curtains and some thermal blankets.

Knitting

Interlooping yarns create knitted fabrics. The two methods of knitting fabrics are weft, and warp knitting. In **weft knitting**, loops are formed by hand or machine as yarn is added in a crosswise direction. Weft knitting is also called filling knitting. In **warp knitting**, loops are formed vertically by machine, one row at a time.

A

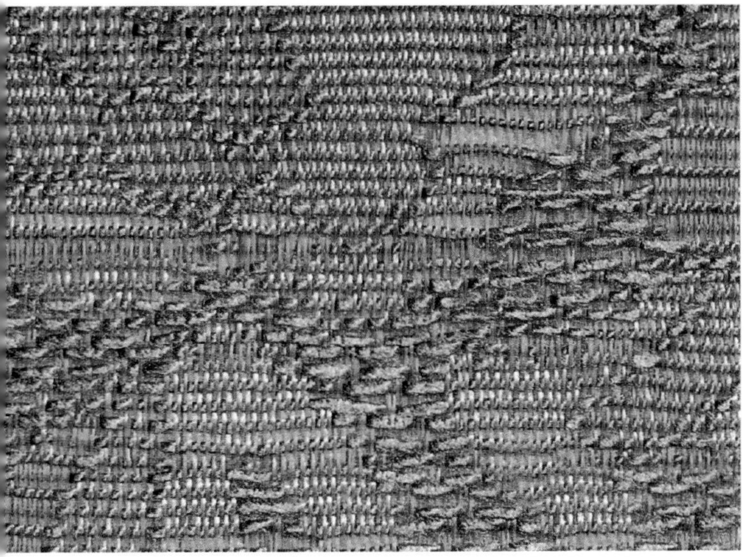

B

10-9 Jacquard tapestry (A) is a popular fabric for upholstery. Upholstery tapestry is durable if the warp and filling yarns are of similar quality. Jacquard brocade (B) has an embossed appearance that emphasizes the pattern.

The only knitted fabrics used to any great extent in home furnishings are the Raschel warp knits. Raschel knit fabrics are used in the making of curtains and draperies.

Tufting

Tufting is a construction method used to make carpeting. About 95 percent of all carpeting is tufted because tufting is an easier and less costly construction method than weaving.

Tufting machines produces tufted carpeting and fabrics. The machines have needles that loop yarns into a backing material. Since the needles go in and out of the backing in the same place, a latex coating is applied to the backing to hold the yarns in place. To give body, a second layer of backing is often added, 10-10.

Other Construction Methods

Some fabrics are made with methods other than weaving, knitting, and tufting. These include felt, nonwoven fabrics, films, foams, and leather.

Felt is a fabric made by applying heat, moisture, agitation, and pressure to wool fibers. Through a process called *felting*, the fibers shrink and interlock permanently. Industrially, felt is used for padding, insulation, soundproofing, filtering, and polishing materials. Felt is also used for wall hangings and other decorative items.

Saxony Carpet Co.

10-10 A strong second layer of backing is added to tufted carpets.

Nonwoven fabrics are made by bonding nonwool fibers, yarns, or filaments by mechanical or chemical means. Nonwovens are used to make many durable goods such as bedding, backing for quilts, dustcloths for box springs, carpet backing, and furniture upholstery. Nonwoven fabrics are also used for draperies and mattress pads.

Films are made from synthetic solutions that are formed into thin sheets. Most household textile films and film coatings come from vinyl or polyurethane solutions. Films may be used alone or as a coating applied to other fabrics. Products made from film and film-coated fabrics include shower curtains, draperies, upholstery, wall coverings, and tablecloths. See 10-11.

Foams are made from a rubber or polyurethane substance into which air is incorporated. Foams are useful for their bulk and sponginess. They are available in a wide range of weights, densities, and resiliencies. Foams are used as carpet backing, furniture padding, pillow and cushion forms, and foam laminates to fabric for household textiles.

Leather is a material made from the hides of animals for use as fabric. Cowhide and steer hide are the most common leathers. In higher-priced furniture, leather is often used as an upholstery fabric because of its beauty, durability, and moisture resistance, 10-12.

Dyeing Fabrics

Color is a major part of any textile product, and dyeing is one way to add it. Fibers, yarns, or fabrics may be dyed.

To dye fibers, different methods are used depending on whether the fiber is natural or manufactured. **Stock dyeing** involves adding dye to loose natural fibers. **Solution dyeing** involves adding dye to a solution for making manufactured fibers before extruding it into filaments.

In yarn dyeing, yarns are wound on spools and placed in a dye bath, 10-13. Plaid and striped fabrics are constructed from dyed yarns. Generally, yarn dyeing is less expensive than fiber dyeing, but more expensive than piece dyeing.

Piece dyeing is the most common method of dyeing. Dye is added after the fabric is constructed. Piece dyeing allows textile manufacturers to store undyed fabric and later dye it to order as fashion dictates, 10-14.

Printing Fabrics

Printing is another way to color fabrics. With printed fabric, one side appears much lighter than the other. This is different from dyed fabric, in which both sides are the same color. Three common methods for printing fabrics are: roller printing, rotary screen printing, and block printing.

Roller printing is a method of printing fabric in which color is transferred directly to a fabric as it passes between a series of rollers. Also called direct printing, roller printing accounts for the majority of fabrics printed. Roller printing is a simple process that produces large quantities of printed fabrics inexpensively. See 10-15.

10-11 Vinyl tablecloths can appear as attractive as fine linen, yet are sturdy enough to stay outdoors.

Herman Miller

10-12 Leather is a practical, yet attractive and comfortable, upholstery fabric.

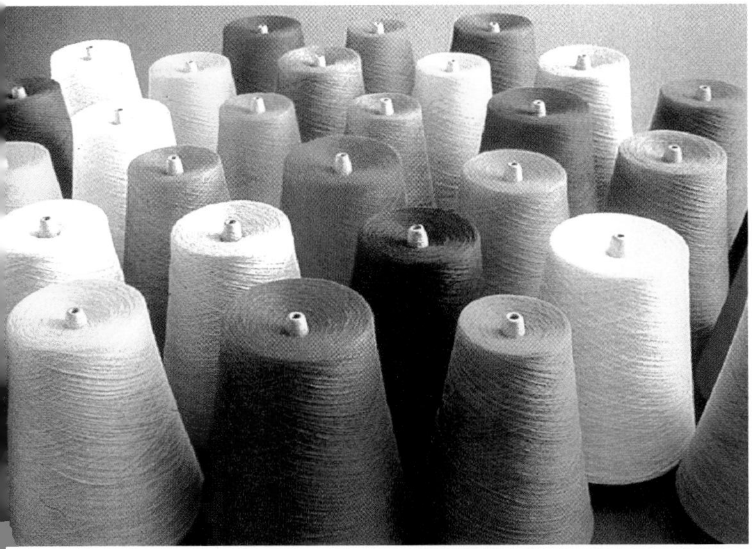

The National Cotton Council of America

10-13 Spools of same-colored yarn are dyed at one time in a large vat.

The National Cotton Council of America

10-14 Rolls of fabric are being piece dyed using popular colors.

The National Cotton Council of America

10-15 In roller printing, each engraved cylinder rolls over the fabric, imposing a multicolored design.

The National Cotton Council of America

10-16 A protective finish is being applied to this fabric using a high-speed, heat-activated process.

In **rotary screen printing**, dye is transferred to a fabric through a cylinder-shaped screen that rolls over the fabric, thus printing the design. A separate screen is required for each color. For many years, screen printing was done by hand. Now, it is one of the fastest printing processes.

Block printing is a method of hand-printing fabric by stamping a pattern with a dye-covered block. It is the oldest technique for decorating textiles. The process involves carving a design into a block and applying dye to the surface. Block printing is seldom done commercially because it is expensive and time-consuming.

Fabric Finishes

All fabrics receive one or more finishes during or after fabric construction, 10-16. Most finishes are applied to add certain characteristics to a fabric, such as increasing its wrinkle- or stain-resistance. Several fabric finishes are described in 10-17.

Textile Finishes	
Antistatic	Chemical treatment to prevent the buildup of static electricity
Beetling	Mechanical process for linen fabrics that improves luster, absorbency, and smoothness
Bleaching	Chemical treatment to whiten natural fibers
Brushing	Mechanical process to remove short fibers from a fabric's surface
Calendering	Mechanical process in which heat and pressure are applied to produce a smooth, polished surface
Crabbing	Process used to set wool fabrics
Crease-resistant	Chemical process to help fabrics resist wrinkles
Flame-retardant	Chemical finish to reduce the oxygen supply or to change the chemical makeup of fibers to reduce the chances of burning
Fulling	Process to improve the appearance and feel of wool fabrics
Mercerization	Chemical treatment for cotton and rayon fabrics that improves luster, strength, and absorbency
Moth-repellent	Chemical treatment for wool fabrics that repels moths
Mildew-resistant	Chemical treatment to prevent mildew from forming on fabrics
Napping	Process used to pull fiber ends from low-twist, spun yarns
Preshrunk	Process in which moisture and heat are used to shrink fabric before it is sold to the consumer
Sanforized™	A trademark referring to a fabric that has been processed to reduce shrinkage to no more than one percent
Scotchguard™	A trademark referring to a finish that resists water and oil stains
Shearing	Mechanical process to remove loose fiber or yarn ends from the surface of a fabric
Soil release	Chemical process to increase fabric absorbency so soil can be removed
Soil-resistant	Chemical process to make fibers less absorbent
Water-repellent	Chemical process that coats fabrics with wax, metals, or resins to resist water
Weighting	Chemical process that adds weight and crispness to silk fabrics

10-17 Textile finishes enhance the quality of fabrics. Specific finishes and their purposes are listed here.

Chapter Summary

Textile products are used throughout the home to add color, texture, and comfort. Typical products include: carpets, rugs, upholstery, and draperies.

Fiber is the basic element of most textiles. The type of fiber used determines a fabric's strength, elasticity, texture, shrinkage, warmth, absorbency, durability, and resistance to stains or mildew. Fibers are classified as natural and manufactured. Natural fibers come from naturally occurring plant, animal, or mineral sources. Manufactured fibers are chemically modified substances found in nature, such as wood pulp and petroleum. The two basic types of manufactured fibers are cellulosic and noncellulosic.

Yarns are made by twisting fibers together. Spun yarns are made from staple fibers. Silk and most manufactured fibers are made into multifilament yarns. Yarns may be classified as single, ply, or cord.

Weaving, knitting, and tufting yarns together are the most common types of fabric construction. Woven fabrics are made with warp and filling yarns interlaced in various patterns. Knitted fabrics are made by interlooping yarns in the weft- and warp-knitting methods. Tufting is a construction method used to make carpeting. By using other construction methods, fabrics are also made from felt, nonwovens, films, foams, and leather.

Dyeing and printing add color to fabric. In addition, all fabrics receive one or more finishes during or after fabric construction to add other desired characteristics.

Review Questions

1. What are some examples of the three basic substances from which natural fibers derive?
2. Is silk a good choice for sofa upholstery? Explain.
3. What are some examples of the two basic types of manufactured fibers?
4. What is the difference between spun and monofilament yarns?
5. What is the advantage of using blend or combination yarns?
6. How are the five major types of weaves formed?
7. Would you choose twill or tapestry weave for a family room sofa? Explain.
8. How is carpeting constructed through the tufting process?
9. What five types of fabric materials are *not* produced by weaving, knitting, or tufting?
10. In what stages can fabric be dyed? Which is the most expensive?
11. What are the three main methods of printing fabric and the steps involved?
12. What are four possible functions of different fabric finishes?

Suggested Activities

1. Collect as many samples of natural textile fibers as you can, identifying each. Label and mount the samples on illustration board for display.
2. Repeat the previous activity, this time focusing on carpet samples made of manufactured fibers.
3. Write a report on one of the following topics regarding manufactured fibers: historical milestones, recent scientific developments, or their significance to modern lifestyles.
4. Visit a local fabric store and ask a salesperson to show you the different types of woven fabrics. Collect samples of the five basic fabric weaves, if possible.
5. Write a short essay describing construction methods other than weaving, knitting, or tufting that are used to produce fabrics.
6. Look around your home for examples of household textiles or clothing garments made from printed fabric. Display at least one example to the class.
7. Examine the labels of five fabric/textile items in a local furniture, home improvement, or department store. Create a chart listing the five items, the fabric finishes applied, their brand names, and their functions.

Internet Resources

American Association of Textile Chemists and Colorists
aatcc.org

American Fiber Manufacturers Association/Fiber Economics Bureau, Inc.
fibersource.org

American Society for Testing and Materials
astm.org

American Society of Interior Designers
asid.org

Carpet and Rug Institute
carpet-rug.com

Institute for Business and Home Safety
ibhs.org

Insurance Information Institute
iii.org

U.S. Occupational Safety and Health Administration, “Safety and Health Topics: Textiles”
osha.gov/SLTC/textiles

Note: Web addresses may have changed since publication. For some entries, reaching the correct Web site may require keying *www.* into the address.

Part Four
Furniture

Chapter 11
Furniture Styles
Chapter 12
Furniture Construction and Selection

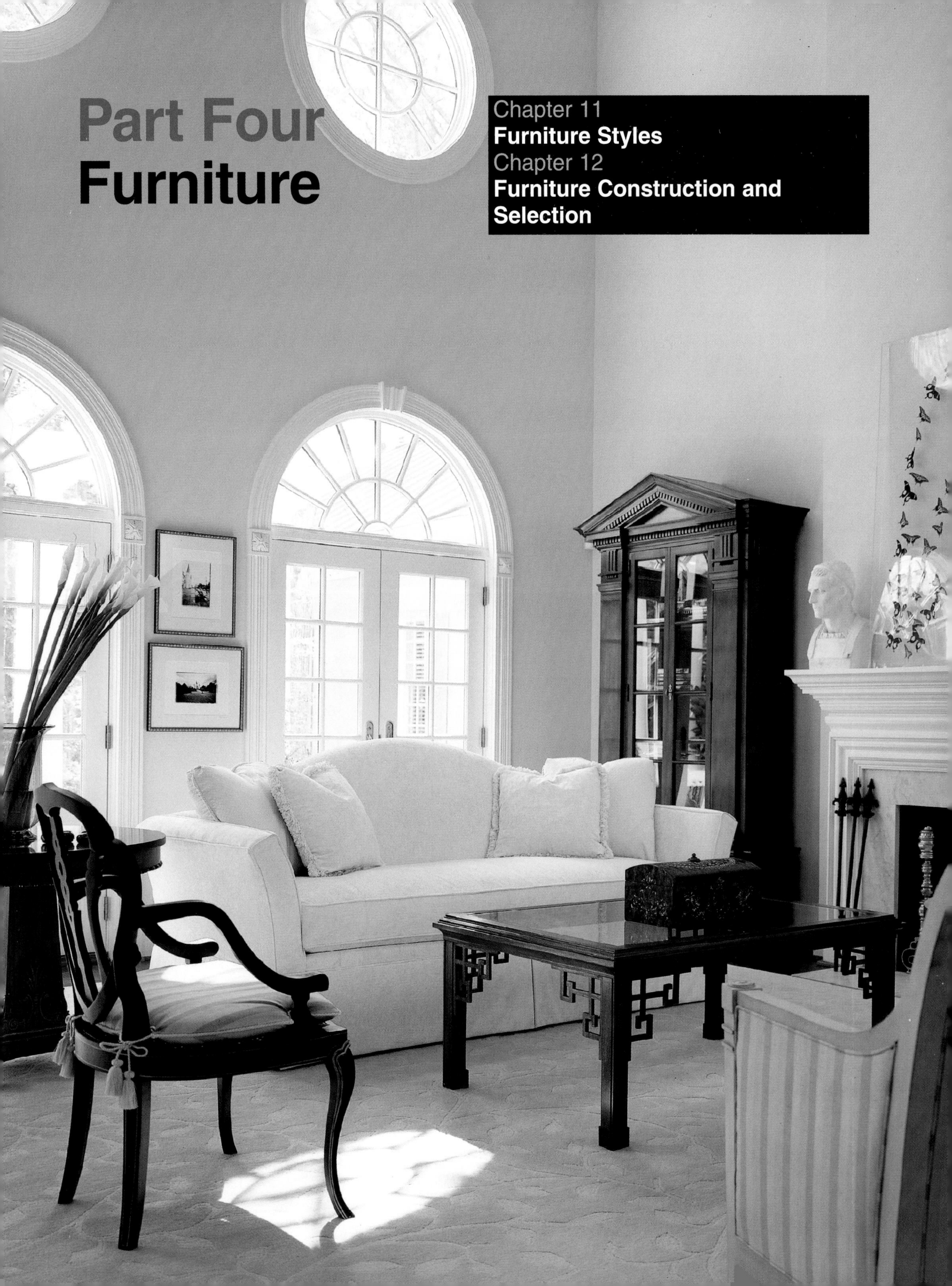

Chapter 11
Furniture Styles

Objectives

After studying this chapter, you will be able to
- list the distinguishing features of furniture from the Late Renaissance, Baroque, Regence, Rococo, Neoclassic, Directoire, and Empire periods in France.
- describe furniture of various styles from the Early, Middle, and Late Renaissance periods in England.
- cite the distinguishing features of the furniture of Chippendale, Hepplewhite, Sheraton, and the Adam brothers.
- differentiate the features of Early American, American Georgian, and Federal furniture styles.
- name and describe the regional styles of furniture found in early America.
- identify the main features of Twentieth-Century furniture styles.
- describe the features of Contemporary, Traditional, Casual, Country, and Eclectic furniture styles.

Key Terms

style
inlay
motif
cabriole leg
bulbous form
turned chair
wainscot chair
romayne work
split baluster
japanning
eclectic
chest
slatback chair
ladder-back chair
relief
highboy
lowboy
secretary
wicker furniture
rattan furniture

Furniture designs may be classified into the broad categories of Traditional, Twentieth-Century, and Twenty-First Century styles. Within these categories, there are several defined styles. The term **style** refers to a distinctive manner of design. The primary characteristics of several furniture styles are presented in this chapter. Several terms used in the description of these styles are listed in 11-1.

Furniture Terms	
Acanthus leaves	Large leaves used by the Greeks in decoration of architecture and artwork.
Arabesque	A scrolled leaf pattern, generally symmetrical in design.
Bible box	A small box used in colonial times to hold the family Bible.
Bun foot	A furniture support that is the shape of a flattened ball.
Flemish	Features that are characteristic of the region of Flanders. In medieval times, Flanders was a country bordered by France and Belgium.

11-1 Several terms are used in the description of furniture styles.

Furniture Terms	
Flemish foot	A furniture foot featuring a scroll design in an S or C shape.
Fluting	Parallel grooves used to ornament a surface. Fluting is commonly used on furniture supports and architectural columns.
Gothic	Term used to describe the arts of the Middle Ages. Cathedrals of this period, such as Notre Dame, are examples of this style. Gothic features are sometimes copied in furniture.
Gothic tracery	Lacelike patterns cut in stone on Gothic architecture.
Gilded bronze	Bronze that is worked into very thin sheets and used as decorative overlays on furniture.
Ionic capital	In ancient Greek and Roman architecture, a scroll-shaped decoration used at the top of a column.
Marquetry	Wooden inlays used to create patterns in furniture finishes. Special woods in interesting grain patterns or colors are often used. Marquetry is sometimes cut into shapes, such as flowers, or sometimes materials other than wood are used.
Ormolu	An alloy of copper and zinc with a goldlike appearance, used for furniture decoration.
Palmette	A furniture motif resembling a fan-shaped palm branch.
Ribband-back chair	A chair whose back has a pattern of interlaced ribbons.
Spade foot	A furniture foot with a squared-off, tapered shape. The spade foot is often set apart from the leg by a slight projection at the top of the foot.
Spooned-back splat	A vertical, spoon-shaped strip of carved wood used as a chair back. The contoured shape is considered more comfortable than the shape of a flat splat.
Thimble foot	A furniture foot with the same shape as a spade foot.
Trestle	A very plain table consisting of a wood slab for a top and a wood frame as a support.
Turning	An ornamentation used on furniture legs and other pieces made by rotating wood on a lathe and shaping it with cutting tools.

11-1 *Continued*

Traditional Styles

The Traditional styles of furniture discussed in this chapter originated during historical periods in France, England, and the United States. Rulers who commissioned cabinetmakers to produce pleasing designs inspired many European styles. For example, Napoleon inspired the French Empire style. Other furniture styles, like Queen Anne, were simply named after the reigning monarch. Still other furniture styles were named after the cabinetmakers who produced them. Chippendale and Hepplewhite are examples.

A chart of Traditional furniture styles, their timeframes, and their countries of origin appears in 11-2.

Traditional Furniture from France

Traditional furniture styles from France are often associated with the reigns of Louis XIII, XIV, XV, and XVI; the French Revolution; and the reign of Napoleon. However, the changes in furniture styles do not exactly correspond to the reigns of these rulers. The periods of French design are: Late Renaissance, Baroque, Regence, Rococo, Neoclassic, Directoire, and Empire.

Late Renaissance (1589-1643)

The Late Renaissance period spanned the reigns of Henry IV and Louis XIII. Under these monarchs, both Italian and Flemish influence could be seen in furniture styles. Furniture was large and upright. Walnut, oak, and ebony were the primary woods used, 11-3. Ornamentation consisted of tortoiseshell, gilded bronze, and marquetry, shown in 11-4. Marquetry is the result of a technique known as **inlay,** whereby pieces of wood, metal, ivory, or shell of contrasting color or texture are inserted in a background material to provide surface decoration.

Tall, slender columns and spiral *turnings* were used for supports and decoration. Bun feet and Flemish feet were typical of furniture during this period.

Baroque (1643-1700)

The Baroque period roughly corresponds to the reign of Louis XIV (1643-1715). The furniture of this period was massive, rectangular, and heavy in proportion to human size, 11-5. Marble tabletops were placed on elaborately carved, square legs.

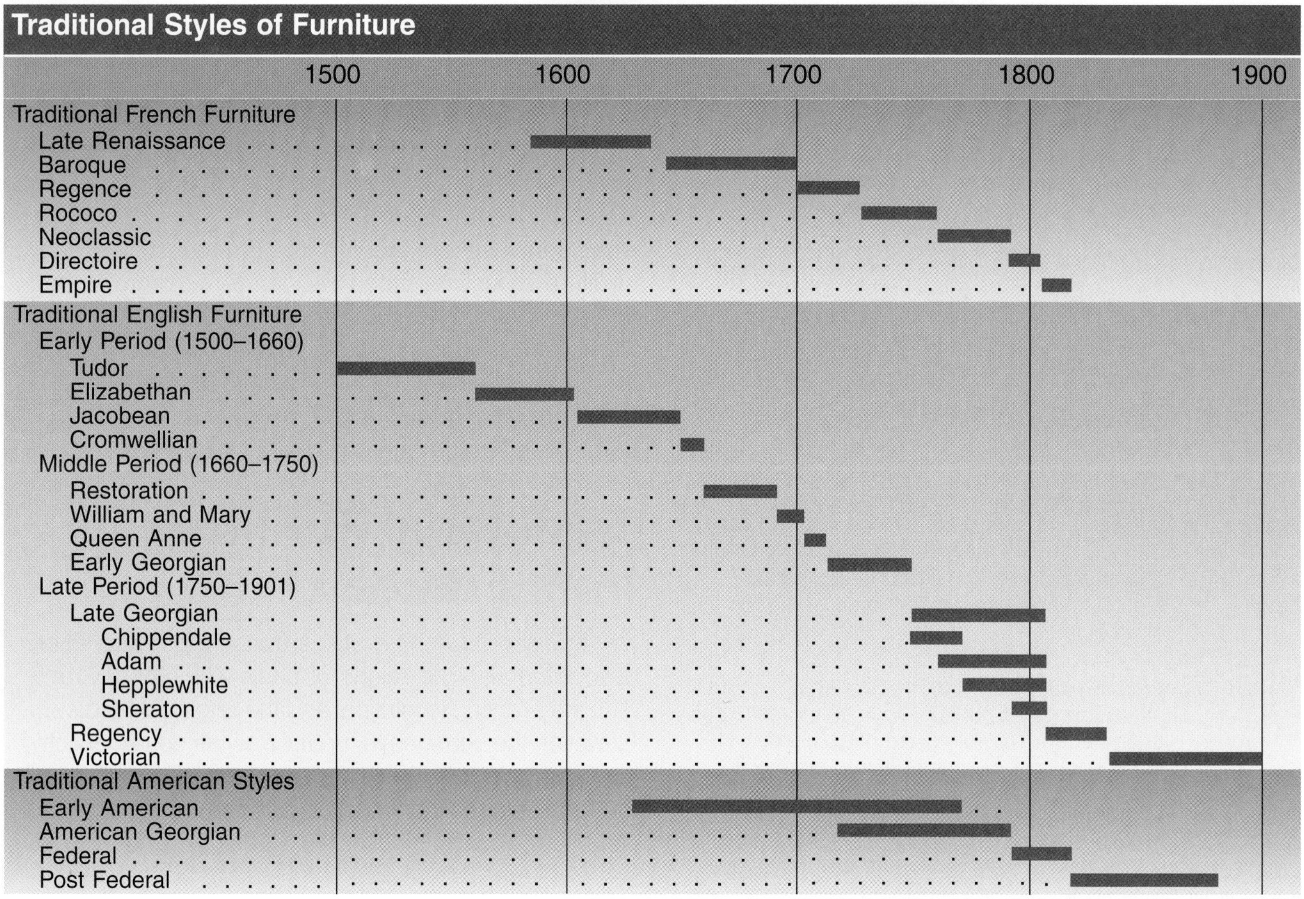

11-2 Periods of popularity for traditional furniture styles tend to overlap throughout history.

The Detroit Institute of Arts

11-3 This Louis XIII cabinet is made of ebony. Although it has heavy proportions, several slender columns are used for support. The cabinet rests on bun feet.

Upholstered chairs and sofas were covered in rich tapestries, brocades, and silks.

Moldings, carvings, and marquetry were also used, but new techniques to make more elaborate furniture were introduced by Andre-Charles Boulle. Boulle was master cabinetmaker to Louis XIV. He introduced the use of *ormolu*, an alloy of copper and zinc with the luster of gold, to use for ornamentation. He also created dazzling new inlays by using pewter, brass, and semitransparent tortoiseshell. This technique, known today as *boulle work*, was typical of Baroque furniture.

Regence (1700-1730)

The Regence period covered the later portion of the reign of Louis XIV. Furniture was still large, but it used more curves and lighter motifs, 11-6. A **motif** is a repeated figure or element in design or architecture. The **cabriole leg**, a curved furniture support in the shape of an animal leg, was introduced at this time, 11-7. Walnut and ebony began to be replaced by lighter woods. Regence was a transitional style between Baroque and Rococo.

The Detroit Institute of Arts

11-4 This Louis XIII cabinet has intricate marquetry on the doors and the inside chamber. Ormolu columns are used for decoration.

Baker Furniture Company

11-6 Furniture of the Regence period is large, but not as severely rectangular as Baroque furniture. This chair represents a transition between the Baroque and Rococo styles. It has curves, a serpentine crest rail, carved motifs, cabriole legs, and an upholstered seat and back.

 The Metropolitan Museum of Art

11-5 Baroque furniture was seldom in proportion to the people using it. This Louis XIV chair has massive proportions, square legs, and rich tapestry upholstery.

National Gallery of Art, Washington, DC

11-7 Cabriole legs and ormolu ornamentation grace this Regence table.

Rococo (1730-1760)

During the reign of Louis XV (1715-1774), intimacy and romanticism replaced the massive pomp of the Baroque style. Furniture was more scaled down to human proportions. Curves, flowing lines, and asymmetry replaced the rectangular Baroque shapes, 11-8. The cabriole leg, used in the Regence style, took on more elaborate form, and a scroll foot replaced the earlier goat's hoof.

Ornamentation was based on shapes of shells, foliage, shepherds' crooks, and musical instruments. Inlaying and marquetry of exotic woods were used, 11-9. Painted furniture in pale or neutral colors with contrasting molding became popular at this time.

Marble or leather tops were common on furniture pieces. Chairs were thickly cushioned and covered in patterned fabrics, 11-10. Fabric designs harmonized with the curved forms of the furniture.

The Rococo style was the first Traditional style that was truly French in origin. Italian influence of the Renaissance and Baroque styles was lost during this period. However, Chinese lacquer and Oriental motifs became popular components of Rococo furniture.

Neoclassic (1760-1789)

Neoclassic furniture was established in style just a few years before the reign of Louis XVI (1774-1789). Financial tension within France led to a trend toward simplicity among aristocrats. Sometimes called the Classic Revival style, the Neoclassic style

Baker Furniture Company

11-8 This Louis XV dining table has a veneered top in a butterfly wing pattern and an apron carved with floral motifs. The inlay is a result of the eighteenth-century technique of aligning bird's eye maple in a manner that allows the table's leaves to match the center when fully extended.

A

Hickory Chair Company

B

Hickory Chair Company

11-9 Continuous curves and carvings adorn this classic Louis XV open armchair. (A) Distinguishing features include a variety of hand-carved flowers and leaves, padded arm rests, gracefully shaped arm supports, and cabriole legs. This Louis XV armchair (B) has a high back, graceful seat rails, and cabriole legs with carved scroll or "escargot" feet.

kept the intimacy of Rococo, but returned to the straight lines of earlier styles.

Free curves and excessive ornamentation were replaced with straight lines, geometric curves, and symmetry, 11-11. Cabriole legs became less curved and eventually disappeared. Straight, tapered legs were emphasized with fluting and grooving, 11-12.

Simpler carvings and marquetry were the ornamentation. Motifs included roses, garlands, ribbons, and cupid's bows and darts. Some Greek and Roman influences were seen toward the end of the period.

Directoire (1789-1804)

The Directoire was the governmental body that ruled France for a short time after the French Revolution. The political upheaval disrupted the production of furniture. Those pieces that were built retained the graceful lines and proportions of the Neoclassic style associated with Louis XVI. However, symbols reminiscent of the French monarchy were rejected.

President Benjamin Harrison Memorial Home

11-10 Floral brocades were popular during the Rococo period, as this thickly cushioned Louis XV chair shows.

Hickory Chair Company

11-11 Neoclassic furniture kept the smaller proportions of Rococo styles, but returned to straight lines reminiscent of Louis XVI styling.

Hickory Chair Company

11-12 This Neoclassic end table demonstrates the style's characteristic tapered legs. It has cherry veneers, simplified lines, and hand-painted accents.

Motifs included military and agricultural forms, such as arrows, spears, drums, stars, and wheat. Furniture woods were mainly native fruitwood, walnut, and oak.

Greek and Egyptian forms were popular, 11-13. Chair backs that curved forward and sofa arms that curved out were borrowed from Greek styles. Furniture of this period is seen as a transition between the Neoclassic and Empire styles.

Empire (1804-1820)

Napoleon's political and military power inspired the Empire furniture style. He placed his mark on all aspects of the arts. Furniture became masculine with geometric shapes, absolute symmetry, and heavy, solid proportions, 11-14. Less carving and marquetry were used. Large surfaces featured plain, highly polished veneers, 11-15.

Ornamentation was mainly of bronze and ormolu. Motifs included military symbols; ancient Egyptian, Roman, and Greek symbols; and Napoleon's initial.

Styles were patterned after Greek and Roman designs, 11-16. These were chosen to emulate the power of Alexander and Caesar. Chairs and sofas of wood were designed to look like ancient stone and bronze ceremonial seats. Tabletops were made of thick marble. The most popular wood was mahogany, but elm and maple were also used.

Century Furniture Company

11-14 This majestic console captures the essence of the Empire style with its scalloped design and columnar legs that terminate with a shelf and feet shaped like a lion's paw.

Courtesy of the Art Institute of Chicago

11-13 Greek motifs like this charioteer were popular during the Directoire period.

Century Furniture Company

11-15 This Empire "X" stool borrows Greek and Roman forms. The shape became a classic in England, America, and France.

Toward the end of the Empire period, mass production began to take root in France. Factory techniques produced furniture that was inferior in quality, but relatively inexpensive. Thus, the Empire style was the last of the great French Traditional styles.

Traditional Furniture from England: Early Renaissance Period

The first of three main periods of traditional furniture from England is the Early Renaissance period (1500-1660). Early Renaissance furniture styles include: Tudor, Elizabethan, Jacobean, and Cromwellian. Each of these styles allowed a progressive transition from *Gothic* to Middle Renaissance furniture. This period is often called the age of oak.

Tudor (1500-1558)

The Tudor style spanned the reigns of Henry VII, Henry VIII, Edward VI, and Mary. Italian Renaissance influence was not as strong in England as it was in other European countries. Dutch and Flemish designs were much more influential.

While lighter woods were being used throughout Europe, native oak remained the primary wood for English furniture. Ornamentation included simple carvings and inlays. The Tudor rose and coat of arms, and *arabesques* were common motifs. Overall appearance was large and heavy, and structural forms were rectangular, as in the Gothic period.

Elizabethan (1558-1603)

The massive strength of the Tudor style remained during the reign of Elizabeth. Ornamentation was also similar, although a new type of decoration, called a **bulbous form**, was added to furniture supports. This melon shape was usually decorated with carvings or turnings.

Turned chairs and wainscot chairs were common during the Elizabethan period. A **turned chair** had a triangular seat with heavy, thick turnings for the back, arms, and legs. A **wainscot chair** had a rectangular, wooden seat with turned or column legs and a carved or inlaid wooden back.

Jacobean (1603-1649)

Jacobean furniture was produced during the reigns of James I and Charles I. During this time, furniture became slightly smaller, lighter, and less

The Saint Louis Art Museum

11-16 Greek motifs decorate these Empire chairs. Concave legs were typical of chairs from this period.

ornamented, 11-17. Bulbous forms became more slender, carving was less pronounced, and more emphasis was placed on turning and fluting.

Motifs of acanthus leaves, intertwined circles, palmettes, and ionic capitals were used. Caricatures of human heads, called **romayne work**, were also used for decoration. **Split balusters**, sometimes called split spindles, are short, turned pieces of wood split in half. They were often glued to surfaces. Upholstered chairs gained popularity, 11-18.

Cromwellian (1649-1660)

The Cromwellian period was a time of civil war, so furniture development was halted. Furniture was plain and undecorated, 11-19. None of the European Baroque influence was felt at this time in England.

Traditional Furniture from England: Middle Renaissance Period

The second of three main periods of Traditional furniture styles from England is the Middle Renaissance period (1660-1750). This period marked the close of the age of oak and the beginning of the age of walnut in England. Furniture styles include: Restoration, William and Mary, and Queen Anne.

Smithsonian Institution Photo No. 81-4979

11-18 This Jacobean side chair has a cushioned seat. Upholstered furniture became more popular during this period in England.

Smithsonian Institution Photo No. 42172

11-17 Jacobean furniture had little ornamentation. The slender bulbous forms on the legs are the only decorations in this Jacobean stool.

Restoration (1660-1689)

After the return of the monarchy, furniture became more extravagant. Under the reigns of Charles II and James II, European styles—especially Italian and French Baroque—influenced English furniture. Walnut became the popular wood.

Carvings and spiral turnings were still used, but marquetry and gilded metal gained popularity. Oriental lacquer was introduced at this time. Scrolls and floral patterns were common motifs. Caned chairs sported elaborate cushions with silk fringes.

William and Mary (1689-1702)

During the reign of William and Mary, furniture became simpler, more elegant, and less ornate, 11-20.

Museum of Fine Arts, Boston

11-19 This Cromwellian chair has little ornamentation compared to the Traditional English styles that preceded it.

Hickory Chair Company

11-20 This William and Mary armchair has polished wood construction with upholstered back and seat. The front legs incorporate bun feet and bell-and-cap turnings.

Woods were highly polished. Oriental lacquer gained popularity, and a new, less expensive technique, called **japanning**, was used to imitate the finish. Marquetry continued to be used.

Caned chairs became unfashionable and were replaced by wooden chairs with stuffed and upholstered backs and seats. Some leg forms were squared; others had mushroom, bell, or inverted cup turnings. Many legs ended in bun feet.

Queen Anne (1702-1714)

During the reign of Queen Anne, a strong Oriental influence was seen in furniture design. For the first time, gracefully curved lines dominated English furniture styles, 11-21. The cabriole leg, inspired by Oriental design, replaced the earlier, turned legs. Motifs included scalloped shells and Oriental designs, such as the lion mask. The claw-and-ball foot, adapted from a Chinese symbol, was used at the bottom of furniture legs. See 11-22. Spooned-back splats in curved shapes added comfort to chair backs.

Early Georgian (1714-1750)

Early Georgian styles evolved during the reign of George I. Styles of this period are so close to Queen Anne styles that they are often grouped as one style. Early Georgian furniture was heavier than Queen Anne furniture, and it further accented the curved line. See 11-23. Large veneered surfaces were featured. Spooned backs, cabriole legs, and claw-and-ball feet were still common features.

Traditional Furniture from England: Late Renaissance Period

The last of the three main periods of Traditional furniture styles from England is the Late Renaissance period (1750-1901). Styles of this period include: Late Georgian, Regency, and Victorian. The age of walnut and the age of satinwood occurred during the Late Renaissance period.

The Bartley Collection, Ltd.

11-21 This Queen Anne style highboy exhibits good proportions, sturdy construction, and functional design.

Thomasville Furniture Industries, Inc.

11-22 This table in the Queen Anne style features intricately carved leaf motifs on the legs with claw-and-ball feet.

Thomasville Furniture Industries, Inc.

11-23 Georgian furniture had more accented curves than Queen Anne furniture. Larger proportions were also used.

Late Georgian (1750-1810)

The late Georgian period spans parts of the reigns of George II and George III. New prosperity during this period called for more elaborate furniture.

Styles of this period were influenced by England's master cabinetmakers and prominent furniture designers: Thomas Chippendale, George Hepplewhite, Thomas Sheraton, and Robert and James Adam.

Thomas Chippendale

A London cabinetmaker, Thomas Chippendale produced refined, high quality furniture that capitalized on styles of the times, 11-24. In 1754, he published *The Gentlemen and Cabinetmaker's Director*, which illustrated his Queen Anne, French Rococo, Gothic, and Chinese styles. See 11-25.

Chairs were some of Chippendale's best and most characteristic pieces. They had elaborately carved backs in many styles, 11-26. Patterns were taken from Gothic tracery, Chinese latticework, and Rococo motifs. The *ribband-back* chair had an intricate design, which was credited to Chippendale. Earlier chairs had cabriole legs, but straight, square legs were later used.

A Diplomatic Reception Rooms, U.S. Department of State. Photography by Will Brown

B Baker Furniture Company

11-24 These Chippendale chairs (A) feature the upholstery and curved lines that were popular in the late Georgian period. Carvings imitating Gothic tracery are used on the front legs. The Chippendale dressing table and matching dressing stool (B) are from the same period.

11-25 These drawings are taken from Chippendale's book, *The Gentlemen and Cabinetmaker's Director.* They illustrate features typical of Chippendale's work.

Smithsonian Institution Photo No. 74-10579

11-26 This Chippendale chair features horizontal, knotted splats often called a pretzel back.

Chippendale worked almost exclusively in mahogany. Although Chippendale developed many styles, his Chinese furniture was distinctive. It is often called Chinese Chippendale, 11-27.

George Hepplewhite

In contrast to Chippendale's work, Hepplewhite featured slender lines and delicate proportions, 11-28. Subtle curves were incorporated. He used straight, tapered legs that were round or square. The legs ended in straight, spade, or thimble feet, 11-29. Chair backs were made in heart, oval, camel, wheel, and shield designs, 11-30. Hepplewhite popularized satinwood for its lighter quality; however, he used mahogany as well.

Little ornamentation was used on Hepplewhite furniture. Carvings included wheat, oval patterns, ribbons, and fluting. Painted motifs were an innovation of Hepplewhite's, and they included the three-feathered crest of the Prince of Wales and floral designs.

Thomas Sheraton

Thomas Sheraton designed furniture that other cabinetmakers constructed. He published *The*

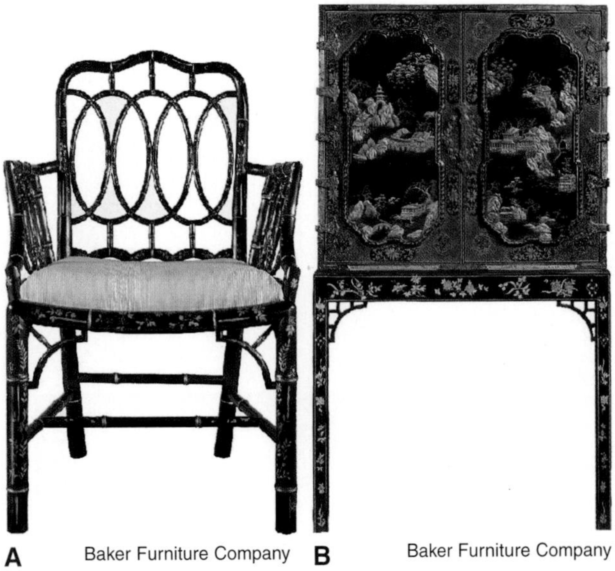

A Baker Furniture Company B Baker Furniture Company

11-27 These Chinese Chippendale pieces have a distinctive Oriental design. The chair (A) is carved to imitate bamboo. The cabinet (B) features an Oriental lacquer finish.

Baker Furniture Company

11-28 Hepplewhite designs were typically more slender than Chippendale designs. This rare Hepplewhite console table is inlaid with a delicate serpentine front.

Cabinetmaker and Upholsterer's Drawing Book in 1791. The book presented the furniture styles of 1791-1793. See 11-31. Like Chippendale, Sheraton became established as a leader in the cabinetmaking industry because of his book's success.

Sheraton's designs were dominated by straight lines, 11-32. He replaced Hepplewhite's flowing curves with segmented curves joined by straight lines. Although his chair legs were like Hepplewhite's, his chair backs were rectangular.

11-29 This drawing of a Hepplewhite couch features spade or thimble feet. The drawing is taken from *The Cabinetmaker and Upholsterer's Guide*, published by Hepplewhite's wife after his death.

Baker Furniture Company

11-30 This Hepplewhite chair features a back with a shield design.

A Baker Furniture Company

B Hickory Chair Company

11-31 This Sheraton style, double-pedestal dining table is crowned with an elegantly shaped top bordered by a wide mahogany band. The pedestal base is adorned with intricate acanthus leaves on urn and saber legs that curve outward to brass feet. (A) This Sheraton loveseat incorporates delicate spindlework on the front legs and arm rests. (B)

Diplomatic Reception Rooms, U.S. Department of State

11-32 This Sheraton chair has segmented curves joined by straight lines. The chair back is basically rectangular.

Motifs for Sheraton's pieces included urns, swags, and leaves. He was the first in England to decorate furniture with porcelain plaques. Sheraton designed pieces that incorporated such mechanical devices as disappearing drawers, folding tables, and secret compartments.

The Adam Brothers

Robert and James Adam were architects who employed cabinetmakers to build furniture that would complement their architecture. Their styles were symmetrical and were inspired by Greek and Pompeiian (Roman) designs, 11-33. The Adam brothers aided the transition from mahogany to satinwood as the preferred furniture wood.

11-33 These drawings are from *The Works of Architecture* of Robert and James Adam. Their Greek and Pompeiian designs were used in furniture as well as architecture.

Regency (1810-1837)

The Regency period marked the beginning of the decline of English furniture design. Cabinetmaking focused less on originality and more on reusing ancient Roman, Greek, and Egyptian designs for styles and motifs. See 11-34 and 11-35.

Victorian (1837-1901)

Under the reign of Queen Victoria, furniture designs were **eclectic**, or a mix of several different styles, 11-36. As industrialization began to take hold, motifs from earlier periods were combined, altered, and adapted to machine processes. Light and dark woods were contrasted, and elaborately

Baker Furniture Company

11-34 This English Regency chair features four delicately intertwined circles on the back. Below, a cane seat covered with a tasseled upholstered pad rests on saber legs with ring detailing.

Diplomatic Reception Rooms, U.S. Department of State. Photography by Will Brown

11-35 This Regency mirror features symmetrical leaf designs like those in Greek art.

A Smithsonian Institution Photo No. 76-9294 **B** Smithsonian Institution Photo No. 80-18054 **C** Smithsonian Institution Photo No. 79-7675

11-36 Victorian Furniture was heavily eclectic, borrowing from Renaissance, Rococo, Gothic, and other styles. Shown here are an upholstered chair (A), ebonized wood-and-metal desk (B), and an oak wash stand (C).

ornamented objects were easily mass produced, 11-37. Furniture became less expensive and was geared toward a middle-class market.

Traditional American Styles

Furniture of early America was a mixture of many styles from many lands. Colonists imported furniture and construction methods from their native homelands. Therefore, traditional American furniture styles are belated reflections of European styles.

Traditional American styles of furniture are classified into the following four categories: Early American, American Georgian, Federal, and Post Federal.

Early American (1630-1770)

Most Early American furniture was patterned after English Gothic and Jacobean styles. However, Early American styles were smaller and simpler. The American colonists were lower- and middle-class rural people who were not familiar with royal European furniture. They lacked proper tools, skills, and wood to copy the intricate designs of Europe. Homes were smaller, and survival, not furniture, was the main concern.

Home furnishings, for the most part, were few and very basic. The most standard item was the **chest**, a sturdy box with a lid and sometimes a lock that was used for storing and protecting items. It ranged from a small Bible box to a large trunk with drawers, 11-38. Chests, as well as other Early American furniture, often served dual functions. For instance, a slanted Bible box could be used as a lap desk. A low trunk doubled as a seat.

Tables were very plain; some were in the simple trestle style. To save space, drop-leaf and chair tables were often used. A chair table has a top that can be tilted back to reveal a chair underneath. See 11-39. Many homes had only one chair and several small stools or benches for seating.

Chairs were straight and upright, with flat or caned seats. Combining that feature with chair backs made of vertical posts created the **slatback chair**. This chair was quite uncomfortable. Later, slatbacks evolved into more comfortable ladder-back chairs, 11-40. A **ladder-back chair** had a back consisting of two upright posts connected by horizontal slats. Large cupboards were important pieces in kitchens. Four-poster beds, trundle beds, and wooden cradles were used in the bedrooms, 11-41.

Furniture decoration included split-spindles, turnings, and bun feet. Geometric or floral patterns were carved in low relief. A **relief** is a projecting detail, ornament, or figure. Pine, beech, and ash woods were used for furniture because they were

President Benjamin Harrison Memorial Home

11-37 This Victorian bed uses rosewood and satinwood for a contrasting design.

Smithsonian Institution Photo No. 54-484

11-38 This large chest has two drawers. Split spindles are glued on for decoration.

plentiful. Painted decoration was sometimes added or used in the place of carvings, 11-42.

By the end of the seventeenth century, colonists began to take greater interest in comfort and beauty. Styles began to change. Upholstered chairs and beds with curtains became more popular. Trained furniture makers had come to America, and they made furniture in the William and Mary style.

Smithsonian Institution Photo No. 72-4984

11-39 Chair tables were popular for tiny colonial houses because they saved space.

Smithsonian Institution Photo No. 30472

11-41 This plain cradle is typical of colonial style furniture.

A Hickory Chair Company B L. & J. G. Stickley, Inc. C Smithsonian Institution Photo No. 62.1760

11-40 This Early American country Queen Anne armchair (A) has a cane seat and splatback. It is a rather crude copy of a Queen Anne style chair. The vertical posts of slatback chairs (B) made sitting uncomfortable, but ladder-back chairs (C) provided slightly more comfort.

A Smithsonian Institution Photo No. 75-13602

B Smithsonian Institution Photo No. 75-689

11-42 Carved furniture was rare in early colonial days. Instead, paint was used for decoration, as shown in the floral designs of this Pennsylvania tulip-wood chest, circa 1760. (A) This late Colonial style, painted-wood miniature chest displays a scene. (B)

They used bun feet and turnings in mushrooms, bells, and inverted cups.

The pieces made by furniture craftsmen included highboys, lowboys, and chests, 11-43. A **highboy** is a tall chest on long legs with drawers generally divided to resemble a chest-on-chest. A **lowboy** is a low chest of drawers on short legs. Walnut and mahogany became more popular.

Smithsonian Institution Photo No. 46,936-E

11-43 With trained cabinetmakers in America, furniture became more refined. This simple but elegant chest features marquetry, brass handles, and bun feet.

American Georgian (1720-1790)

As the wealthy population grew in the colonies, people sought styles based on the English Georgian periods. Skilled American cabinetmakers, originally from England, began to reproduce English styles by copying from imported models and design books.

These cabinetmakers made some exact copies, but soon they varied the styles. American interpretations of English furniture are labeled with such names as American Queen Anne or American Chippendale. See 11-44. Interpretations varied from region to region. Boston, Newport, New York, and Philadelphia emerged as design centers with their own distinct furniture styles.

American chairs were contoured to fit the human form. Many were styled after Chippendale, Hepplewhite, and Sheraton designs. Couches and upholstered chairs, like the wing chair, became very popular.

By 1760, the Windsor chair from England became a standard in the colonies. American versions seldom had cabriole legs and ornamental back splats. Instead slender, turned legs that slanted outward were used, and banister backs in several distinctive shapes replaced English splats. A popular variation of the Windsor chair was a rocking chair that originated in Boston, 11-45.

A Smithsonian Institution Photo No. 81-4978

B Diplomatic Reception Rooms, U.S. Department of State

11-44 During the American Georgian period, American cabinetmakers developed their own variations of English styles, such as American Queen Anne, American Chippendale, and American Empire. Examples include the slant-front desk (A), walnut cabinet (B), and writing desk and chair (C).

C Diplomatic Reception Rooms, U.S. Department of State

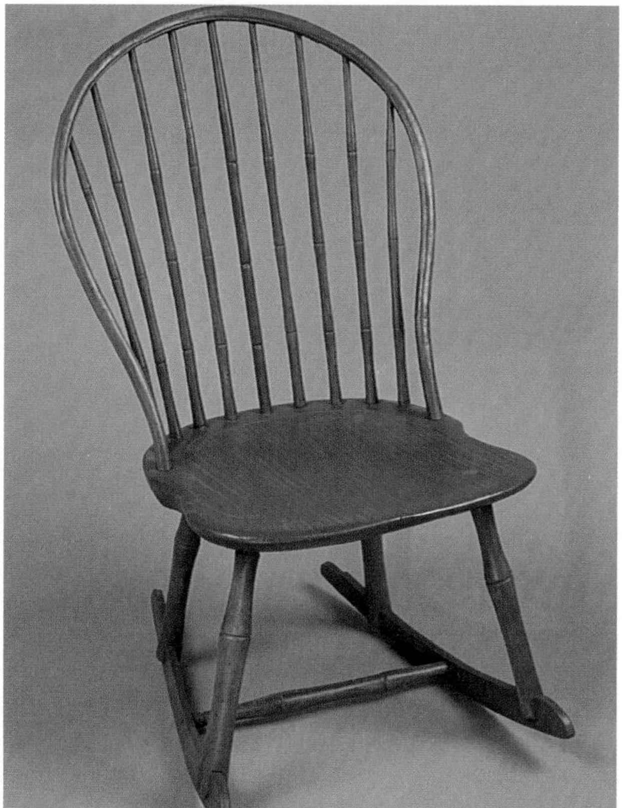

Smithsonian Institution Photo No. 76-1615

11-45 The Windsor rocker is an American version of the English Windsor chair.

One version of a chest, called a secretary, became popular during this period, 11-46. A **secretary** has drawers and a hinged writing surface. Highboys and lowboys became the most elegant storage pieces built in America. Philadelphia designs became the most popular; these had cabriole legs, simple lines, elaborate decoration, and brass hardware, 11-47.

Federal (1790-1820)

Little change in furniture designs occurred during the American Revolution. As normal relations with England resumed, English styles were again adopted by American cabinetmakers. Cabinetmakers had refined their techniques by this time, and pieces of excellent quality were produced. American furniture

Smithsonian Institution Photo No. 80-13975

11-46 The secretary has drawers, a hinged writing surface, and doors above the writing surface.

Smithsonian Institution Photo No. 46,936-A

11-47 This Philadelphia highboy features cabriole legs with claw-and-ball feet, intricate carving, and brass handles.

of this period was delicate and well proportioned, but not as elaborate as English styles, 11-48.

Federal style furniture was made from mahogany, satinwood, cherry, rosewood, maple, apple, and pear. Ornamentation was patriotic in nature. After the eagle was adopted as a national symbol, the motif was widely used to decorate furniture. Other symbols included cornucopias, fruit, flowers, and spiral turnings, 11-49.

In the late 1700's, the French Revolution brought an influx of aristocrats to America, and French-American bonds were strengthened. The American Directoire furniture style was inspired by this French influence. Chairs and sofas were modeled after Greek and Roman designs. Furniture legs were often concave, 11-50. Motifs include lion heads, acanthus leaves, lyres, swags, and festoons, 11-51.

Duncan Phyfe was considered the outstanding cabinetmaker of the Federal period. He designed his own interpretations of the Sheraton, Directoire,

Smithsonian Institution Photo No. 76-1982

11-49 Motifs of fruit and flowers are painted on this chair from the Federal period. Spiral turnings are used on the chair legs.

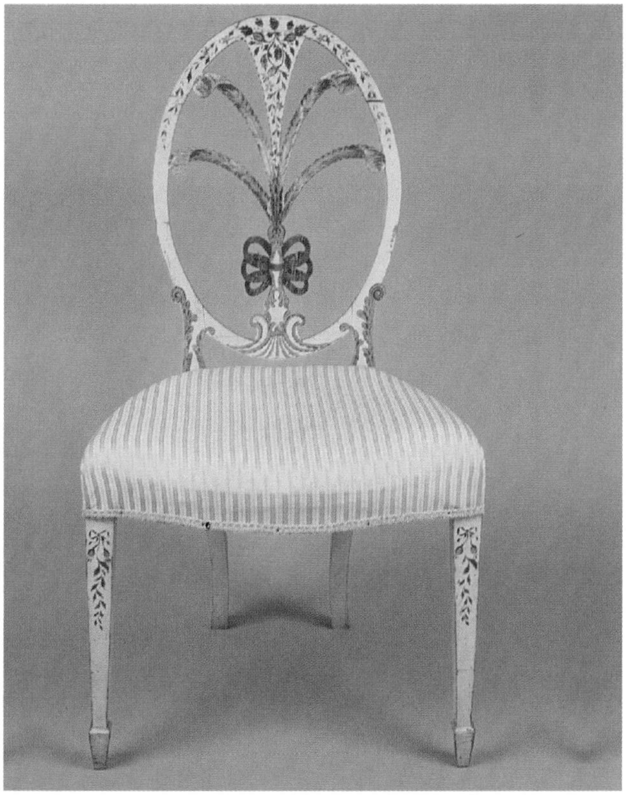

Smithsonian Institution Photo No. 76-1614

11-48 This Federal style chair is similar to Hepplewhite designs, but it is simpler. Fewer curves are used, and painted designs are used in place of intricate carvings.

Baker Furniture Company

11-50 This American Directoire chair features concave legs.

Baker Furniture Company

11-51 Influence of the French Empire style can be seen in this Federal side-leaf table with concave legs and a lyre motif.

A Diplomatic Reception Rooms, U.S. Department of State

B Baker Furniture Company

11-52 Duncan Phyfe patterned his work after Sheraton (A) and Federal (B) styles.

and Empire styles, 11-52. He worked primarily in mahogany and satinwood. Phyfe set the standards for other cabinetmakers of the time.

Regional Styles

Although common English and French styles dominated American design, various immigrant groups brought distinctive furniture styles to the New World. Their different furniture styles attracted attention and were eventually adopted on a wide scale.

The German Mennonites settled in Pennsylvania and used furniture that was simple and sturdy, but cheerful. They decorated their furniture with brightly painted or stenciled designs. The motifs included tulips, hearts, birds, and leaves in vibrant colors. These people and their furniture styles were mistakenly called Pennsylvania Dutch instead of Deutsch, which means German.

Scandinavians settled in the Midwest, mostly in Minnesota and Wisconsin. Their furniture styles were similar to those of the Pennsylvania Dutch, but they used animal and human motifs. The Scandinavian painted designs were more realistic than those of the Pennsylvania Dutch and did not have as much popular appeal.

The Shakers were a religious group from England who valued cleanliness, order, and functionalism. They were strict, hard-working people, and their thoughts about lifestyle influenced their furniture designs. Their furniture was lightweight, simple, easy to clean, and completely void of ornamentation, 11-53. Much of their furniture was built into the room, and many pieces served more than one function. The Shaker belief that every object should have a function is considered the forerunner of modern design concepts.

Post Federal (1820-1880)

During the Post Federal era, America began to develop a large class of wealthy industrialists. This group called for furniture that demonstrated their wealth, even if the furniture was not well designed.

From 1820 to 1840, the American Empire style was popular. This furniture had heavy proportions and cumbersome lines. Furniture from this period is considered to mark the decline of American furniture styles. Duncan Phyfe is said to have referred to his furniture from this period as butcher furniture.

From 1840 to 1880, American designs were patterned after English Victorian styles, 11-54. American Victorian, like its English counterpart, borrowed heavily from past designs. Often, several designs were mixed on one furniture piece, resulting in a cluttered look. As in England, American designs were adapted to mechanization. Early mechanization emphasized production quantity, not quality. Quality was lower, the look was awkward and poorly designed, and several styles were combined into one piece of furniture.

Shaker Workshops

11-53 Shaker furniture is simple and unadorned.

Twentieth-Century Furniture Styles

The cluttered Victorian styles of the late 1880s caused furniture designers to react with simpler lines and forms. Styles popularized in the twentieth

Century Furniture Company

11-54 This Post Federal bedroom set features details used in the English Victorian style. Pieces were made using mechanization.

century are sometimes called Modern styles. They include: Art Nouveau, Frank Lloyd Wright, Bauhaus, and Scandinavian.

Art Nouveau

The Art Nouveau style was based on a rebellion against the ornamentation of the Victorian style, 11-55. Almost no ornamentation was used, and inexpensive woods replaced mahogany and satinwood. The goal of Art Nouveau was to create beautiful furniture for its artistic merit, not its cost.

Smithsonian Institution Photo No. 79-7677

11-55 This Art Nouveau chair is much simpler than Victorian chairs of the time. Later Art Nouveau chairs are similar in shape, but backs and legs are much less ornamented.

Furniture was designed to work with mechanization, not against it. Furniture of this time was based on flowing, natural lines ending in a curve similar to the bud of a plant, 11-56. Art Nouveau furniture is still popular, and pieces may be seen in many restaurants, nightclubs, and cafes.

Frank Lloyd Wright

In the early 1900s, an American architect named Frank Lloyd Wright designed and built a series of homes called Prairie Style. His homes represented the beginning of modern home design and offered innovations in furniture design.

Wright's architecture emphasized nature and used simple lines and forms. Wright believed that a structure, its surroundings, and its furnishings should be parts of a whole. He tried to accomplish this by blending the structure into the surroundings and integrating the furniture into the structure wherever possible. Wright referred to this design relationship as *organic*.

The furniture was composed of geometric shapes, slats, and flat surfaces. See 11-57. Surfaces were usually natural and void of ornament. Prairie Style furniture is often regarded as architectural sculpture.

Bauhaus

Walter Gropius founded a school known as the Bauhaus in Germany in 1919. The school focused on the design of buildings, furniture, textiles, and

11-56 This metal insert in a rustic furniture piece exemplifies the gentle curves favored by Art Nouveau designers.

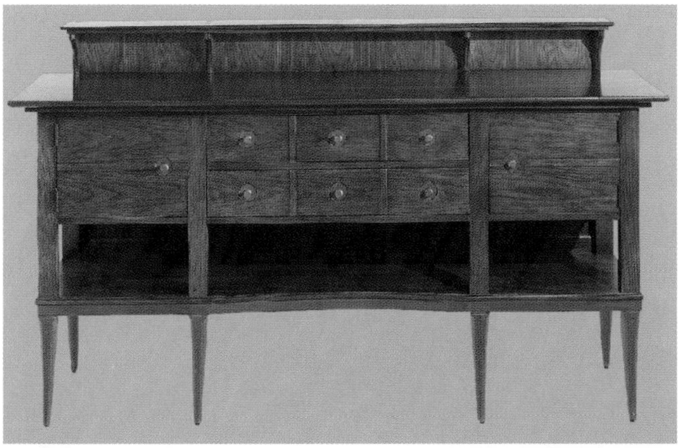

A Hickory Chair Company

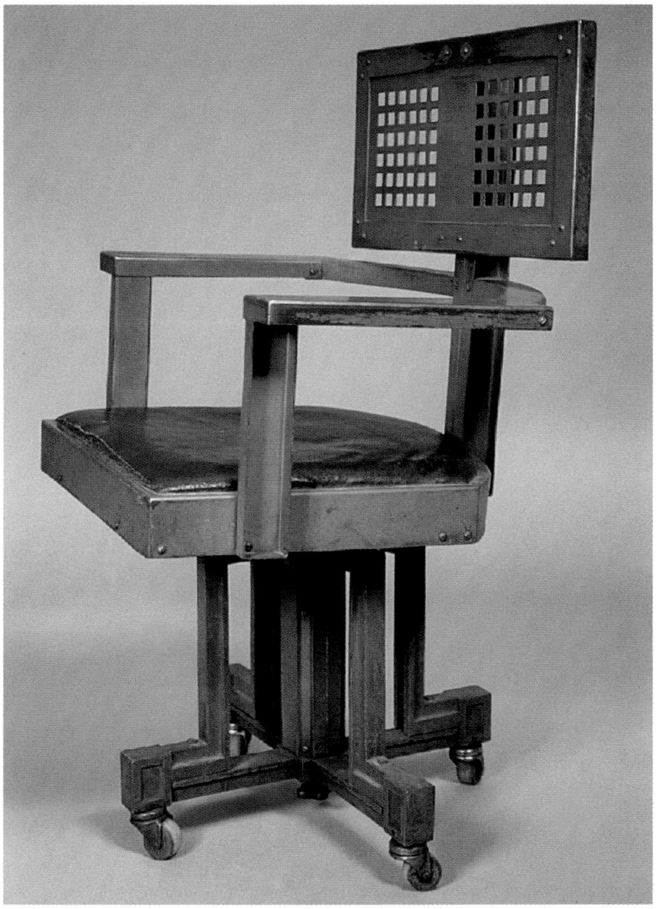

B Smithsonian Institution Photo No. 72-10527

11-57 This elegant sideboard (A) combines a splayed, open-leg base, gallery shelf, and center drawers flanked by doors—both with pulls and figured woods. Frank Lloyd Wright furniture (B) is rectangular and unornamented. The simple design gives emphasis to the wood's natural grain.

household articles that were made by machine. The guiding principle was to simplify the design of objects.

One of the first examples of Bauhaus furniture was a tubular steel chair, designed by Hungarian Marcel Breuer in 1925. The chair had canvas or leather straps stretched across metal tubes to form the seat, back, and armrests. There have been many adaptations of this well-known chair.

Mies Van der Rohe became director of the Bauhaus in 1930 and worked to spread the machine-oriented viewpoint in Europe and the United States. Styles were based on the philosophy that *form follows function*. Only those features that directly concerned function were included in Bauhaus design. See 11-58.

Scandinavian

Scandinavian design was influenced by traditional Nordic methods used to make molded skis. Wood was curved by applying heat or steam to many veneers of wood, 11-59. Scandinavian white birch, a light, highly resilient wood, was commonly used, 11-60. As mechanization reached Scandinavia, these techniques were applied to furniture production. The result was a sleek, clean-lined style of furniture that was both elegant and functional.

Herman Miller

11-58 The Bauhaus principle of simple design was used to make this Eames chair. Leather is stretched over a metal framework. Leather cushions are added for comfort.

Westnofa USA, Inc.

11-59 This unique Scandinavian dining set was made by curving the veneered wood pieces.

Chele Benjamin, ASID, Illinois Chapter

11-60 Birch, a popular wood for Scandinavian furniture, is used in the side chairs of this inviting living room.

La Rocco Galleries, Inc., Naples, Florida

11-61 This highly polished wood accent table represents the principles of Art Deco.

Art Deco

Art Deco in this country evolved from the Art Moderne style that originated in the 1920s. Art Deco was influenced by Art Nouveau, the Bauhaus, and cubism. One of its major goals was to adapt design to mass production. It was, in essence, a reaction against the exaggerated curves of Art Nouveau. Notables in the movement were Scottish designer Charles Rennie Mackintosh and Viennese architect-designer Josef Hoffmann.

Art Deco replaced the graceful curvilinear designs of the Nouveau style with geometric and rectilinear shapes, 11-61. Art Deco style in this country lasted into the 1940s. From the late 1940s to 1965, the style went out of fashion.

Twenty-First Century Furniture Styles

Furniture of the twenty-first century has not yet been categorized into distinct styles, but furniture manufacturers and students of furniture generally agree that five furniture styles dominate America today. They are: Contemporary, Traditional, Casual, Country, and Eclectic.

Contemporary

Contemporary furniture styles are the very latest designs and styles. They contain the new, the unclassified, and the experimental. No rules or guidelines apply to this furniture design, and it is impossible to know which Contemporary designs of today will become the classic styles of tomorrow, 11-62.

Often Contemporary designs incorporate one or more materials besides wood, such as canvas, leather, plastic, metal, wicker, rattan, bamboo, or glass. See 11-63. Furniture-design inspiration ranges from abstract art to everyday objects. Some designs are created simply for the artistic pleasure of the designer, but they usually cater to the mobile middle-class market. Most of today's furniture, therefore, must be affordable, lightweight, and adaptable to a wide range of uses and decorating treatments, 11-64.

Some relatively recent innovations include folding canvas chairs, waterbeds, and modular furniture units, 11-65.

Traditional

Traditional furniture includes styles and designs that have evolved from earlier French, English, and American styles, 11-66. Traditional furniture woods,

David Welter

11-62 This stylish china cabinet may very well be the forerunner of a new classic design.

June Sherman, ASID, Illinois Chapter

11-63 Wood, metal, and glass often are combined in modern furnishings, such as in this dining set for a sunny breakfast room.

11-64 This dining room set is affordable and lends itself to a variety of decorative schemes.

WCI Communities, Inc.

11-65 Modular furniture is a popular choice of many interior designers for contemporary settings.

Thomasville Furniture Industries, Inc.

11-66 This Traditional style dining room set is highly reminiscent of an earlier English furniture style.

finishes, and fabrics are generally used for this furniture. Traditional furniture is most easily recognized by its graceful lines, balance, and proportions. Hand-rubbed finishes, carvings, and darker tones are also characteristics of this style. Traditional furniture is usually considered elegant and formal.

Casual

Casual furniture is ideal for comfort and informality. Less-expensive woods or veneers such as pine, ash, oak, maple, or redwood are generally used, and finishes are production grade. Fabrics for Casual style furniture provide durability and color. Some Casual furniture is large with ample padding, while other pieces are more utilitarian in appearance, 11-67.

Durable, lightweight wicker, rattan, and bamboo furniture is used indoors as well as outdoors. **Wicker furniture** is made by weaving various natural or synthetic materials such as willow, reed, rattan, or spirally twisted paper around a frame. See 11-68. **Rattan furniture** is made from a vinelike, climbing form of palm, 11-69. More than any earlier furniture style, Casual furniture has evolved from lifestyle influences.

11-68 This wicker chair is not only comfortable, but also very durable.

11-67 A metal folding chair is casual and highly utilitarian.

11-69 Rattan furniture is sturdy and may be used as indoor or outdoor furniture.

Country

Country furniture is an outgrowth of the lifestyles and needs of rural folk. Most of this furniture was designed to meet practical needs rather than as a show of wealth or class. Country furniture has its roots in furniture from America, France, England, and Ireland. As a rule, this furniture is made from domestic woods that are painted or distressed. Like Casual style furniture, Country style furniture utilizes materials that can endure significant wear and use. The furniture is usually comfortable and sturdy, 11-70.

Thomasville Furniture Industries, Inc.

11-70 A trestle dining table and complementary chairs are the essence of Country style furniture.

Eclectic

Eclectic furniture is a mixture of styles, periods, or influences, 11-71. Some pieces may have elements of several recognized styles combined in a single piece, while others seem to have no obvious elements of previous styles. Each piece must be judged on its design characteristics and functionality for a particular use or room setting.

11-71 This eclectic room setting incorporates several furniture styles.

Chapter Summary

The broad categories of furniture design are Traditional (styles from France, England, and the United States), Twentieth-Century, and Twenty-First Century styles. Within these categories are many distinct furniture designs.

Traditional French furniture design (1589-1820) evolved into seven styles: Late Renaissance, Baroque, Regence, Rococo, Neoclassic, Directoire, and Empire. Important furniture developments during the period included marquetry, turnings, ormolu, and the cabriole leg.

Traditional furniture from England dates back to early, middle, and late Renaissance periods. The early Renaissance period (1500-1660) was the age of oak. It included Tudor, Elizabethan, Jacobean, and Cromwellian furniture styles. Important furniture developments were the bulbous form, turned and wainscot chairs, romayne work, and split balusters.

Middle Renaissance furniture from England (1660-1750) marked the close of the age of oak and the beginning of the age of walnut. Restoration, William and Mary, Queen Anne, and Early Georgian were the furniture styles of the period. Important furniture developments included Oriental lacquer, japanning, spooned-back splats, and claw-and-ball feet.

Late Renaissance furniture from England (1750-1901) marked the age of walnut and the age of satinwood. The period included Late Georgian styles, which were known for high quality because of renowned, master cabinetmakers and designers. The Regency and Victorian periods followed. Important furniture developments included the ribband-back chair, painted motifs, and mechanical components such as secret compartments.

A mixture of furniture designs from many lands was evident during the Traditional American period (1630-1880), which included Early American, American Georgian, Federal, and Post Federal styles. A master cabinetmaker and several immigrant groups influenced the high quality of Federal furniture design. Important furniture of the period included chests, slatback and ladder-back chairs, highboys, lowboys, the Windsor chair, and the secretary.

Twentieth-Century furniture used simpler styles and forms. The period included Art Nouveau, Frank Lloyd Wright, Bauhaus, Scandinavian, and Art Deco styles.

Today's furniture, called Twenty-First Century styles, is generally grouped into the following five categories: Contemporary, Traditional, Casual, Country, and Eclectic.

Review Questions

1. What metal was introduced during the Baroque period?
2. What types of ornamentation were popular for Baroque furniture?
3. What kind of furniture leg was introduced during the Regence period in France?
4. What were the main features of Rococo furniture? How did Rococo furniture differ from Baroque furniture?
5. How do the motifs of the Neoclassic and Directoire periods differ?
6. What earlier styles were copied in Empire furniture?
7. How did Jacobean furniture differ from Tudor and Elizabethan furniture?
8. What type of furniture finish became popular during the reign of William and Mary?
9. What features were typical of Queen Anne and Early Georgian furniture?
10. How did Chippendale furniture differ from Hepplewhite furniture? How did Hepplewhite furniture differ from Sheraton furniture?
11. In Early American homes, what were the most common furnishings? furniture decorations?
12. What furniture styles became popular during the American Georgian period?
13. What motifs were popular during the Federal period?
14. What features were typical of German, Scandinavian, and Shaker furniture?
15. How did mechanization affect furniture production in France, England, and America?
16. What features are most common in Twentieth-Century furniture styles?
17. Which category of Twenty-First Century includes the very latest styles and designs?
18. What furniture style's evolution was particularly influenced by lifestyles?

Suggested Activities

1. Chart the distinguishing features of furniture from the Late Renaissance, Baroque, Regence, Rococo, Neoclassic, Directoire, and Empire periods in France.
2. In a short essay, describe Thomas Chippendale furniture designs and how he popularized them.
3. List the characteristics of English furniture styles in the Late Renaissance period.
4. Compare and contrast Early American and Federal furniture in America.
5. Describe the following Twentieth-Century furniture styles: Art Nouveau, Frank Lloyd Wright, Bauhaus, Scandinavian, and Art Deco styles.
6. Create a display board of Twenty-First Century furniture styles by using a collage of pictures from magazines. Label each of the five styles.

Internet Resources

Antique Furniture Dealers
rubylane.com

Architectural Digest Magazine
archdigest.com

Architectural Record Magazine
architecturalrecord.com

Baker Furniture
kohlerinteriors.com

Bartley Collection Ltd.
bartleycollection.com

Broyhill Furniture Industries, Inc.
broyhillfurn.com

Fine Woodworking Magazine
finewoodworking.com

Hickory Chair Company
hickorychair.com

Interior Design Magazine
interiordesign.net

Lane Furniture Industries
lanefurniture.com

Thomasville Furniture Industries, Inc.
thomasville.com

Note: Web addresses may have changed since publication. For some entries, reaching the correct Web site may require keying *www.* into the address.

Acknowledgments

Figure 11-3. © The Detroit Institute of Arts, gift of friends of K. T. Keller in honor of his seventieth birthday, 55.458.

Figure 11-4. © The Detroit Institute of Arts, gift of friends of K. T. Keller in honor of his seventieth birthday, 55.458.

Figure 11-5. The Metropolitan Museum of Art, Fletcher Fund, 1929 (29.21).

Figure 11-13. French, Jacob Freres, cabinet, ca. 1796, thuyawood and ebony with ormolu mounts, 40½ in. by 45½ in. by 25½ in., purchased from the bequest of Cornelia Conger, 1974.251, © The Art Institute of Chicago. All rights reserved.

Figure 11-16. Pair of Klismos Side Chairs, ca. 1815-1820, The Saint Louis Art Museum, Funds given by the Decorative Arts Society in Honor of Charles E. Buckley, 217: 1975.1,.2.

Figure 11-19. Great chair, Boston, ca. 1660, maple, oak, and Russia leather, 38 in. by 23⅝ in. by 16⅜ in., Seth K. Sweetser fund, 1977.711, Museum of Fine Arts, Boston.

Chapter 12
Furniture Construction and Selection

Objectives

After studying this chapter, you will be able to

- list and describe the types of woods used in furniture construction.
- evaluate the type and quality of a furniture joint.
- describe the methods and materials used in the construction of upholstered furniture.
- list ways in which metals and plastics are used in furniture.
- evaluate the usability of furniture according to its quality, cost, style, size, fabric, ergonomics, and maintenance requirements.

Key Terms

case goods
pitch
check
veneer
patina
frame
seat base
serpentine spring
helical
coil spring
welting
innerspring mattress
gauge
pocketed
air chamber mattress
plating

Furniture is a major consideration in any housing unit. It is a chief factor in physical comfort and in the design of a home. Furniture increases the usefulness of an area and expresses the personality of household members. It can make you feel at ease or uncomfortable in your surroundings.

Furniture is expensive and should be chosen with much care and thought. Price and quality of furniture is affected by the materials and methods used in construction. This chapter provides background information in furniture construction. It also shows you how to use this and other information to evaluate and select appropriate furniture.

Materials and construction are critical factors in the quality of furniture. Well-built pieces from appropriate materials will provide years of useful service, but if either is shortchanged, the results will be less than satisfactory.

Wood, metals, plastics, and fabrics comprise the primary materials used to make furniture. Construction techniques are mainly concerned with methods of fastening pieces together to form a sturdy assembly that will hold its shape for a long time.

Wood Furniture

The most common material used in furniture is wood. Pieces of furniture that are made primarily of wood are called **case goods**. This category includes chests, dressers, tables, headboards, and desks, 12-1. Wood may also be used as a structural framework that is covered by other material, such as upholstery.

Hickory Chair Company

12-1 This elegant bedroom displays examples of case goods. The furniture exhibits good proportions, sturdy construction, and functional design.

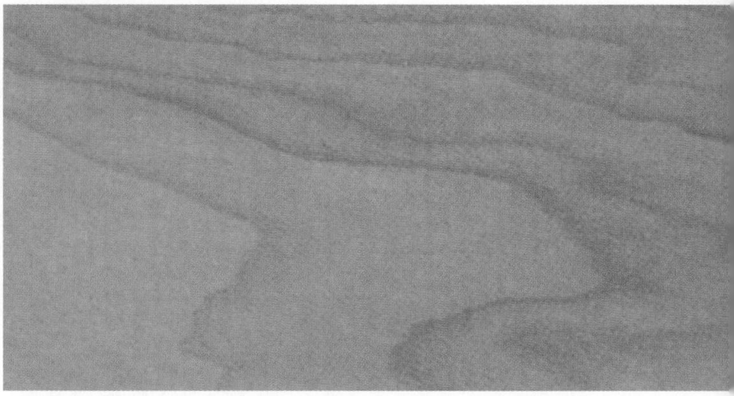

Black cherry. Fine grain, machines well, may be sanded to a smooth finish, moderately hard, heavy (36 lb./ft.^{3}), reddish-brown in color, beautiful grain pattern, and a fine furniture wood

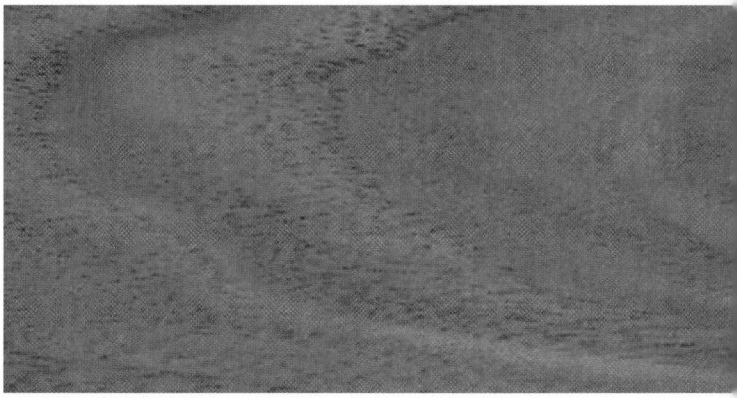

Black walnut. Strong in comparison to weight (38 lb./ft.^{3}), hard and dense, excellent machining properties, finely textured, beautiful grain pattern, chocolate brown heartwood, almost white sapwood, very popular, and a quality furniture wood

Pecan. Great strength and toughness, hard and heavy (50 lb./ft.^{3}), open grained, light brown in color, machines well, moderate gluing properties, and a popular furniture wood

12-2 These native hardwoods are used for fine furniture construction.

Wood Types

Various species of wood have different qualities that make them more suitable for certain uses. Solid woods, veneers, and processed woods may be used in furniture of different types and qualities. Wood finishes may also vary with the type and quality of a piece. Woods are classified as hardwoods or softwoods.

Hardwoods

Hardwoods are generally preferred over softwood for quality furniture because they have greater dimensional stability and more durability. Hardwoods also have less **pitch**, a natural resin common in softwoods that absorbs stains and other finishes differently from the wood fibers. Hardwoods are firmer than softwoods, so they hold nails and screws better and are less likely to dent. However, hardwoods are generally more expensive than softwoods.

The types of native hardwoods most commonly used for fine furniture are black cherry, black walnut, pecan, sugar maple, and white oak. See 12-2. More exotic, imported woods include cocobola, mahogany, rosewood, teak, and zebrawood, 12-3.

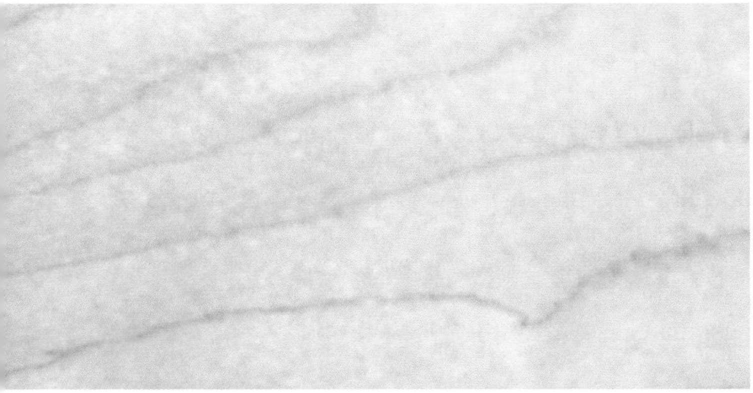

Sugar maple, also called hard maple. Hard, strong, heavy (44 lb./ft.^{3}), fine texture, nice grain pattern, light tan color, machines well, and a fine furniture wood

White oak. Very durable, strong and heavy (47 lb./ft.^{3}), grayish-brown heartwood, open grained, glues well, and a quality furniture wood

12-2 Native hardwoods *Continued*

Cocobola (Central America). Dense, hard, oily, dark red color, tightly interwoven grain, somewhat difficult to work, and used for fancy cabinetwork

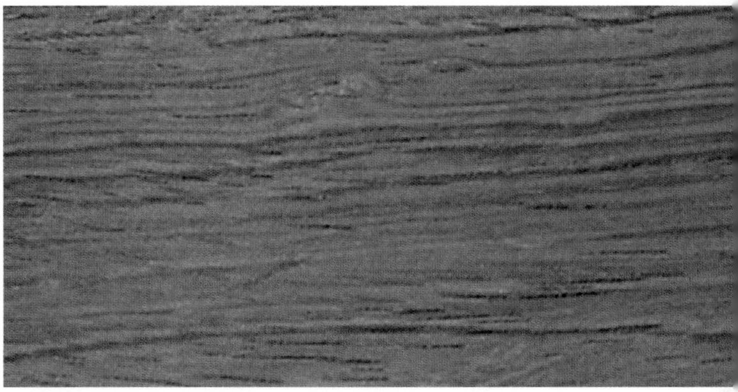

Rosewood (Brazil, Ceylon, Madagascar, and Central America). Very hard, large irregular pores, dark brown with black streaks, and a quality furniture material

Mahogany (Honduras). Medium hard and dense (32 lb./ft.^{3}), stable wood, even texture, open grain, beautiful grain pattern, excellent machining qualities, carves well, and used for high-quality furniture

Teak. (Burma, India, Thailand, and Java). Hard and strong, brown with a yellow cast, oily, and a fine furniture material

12-3 These imported hardwoods are used in more-exotic, quality furniture.

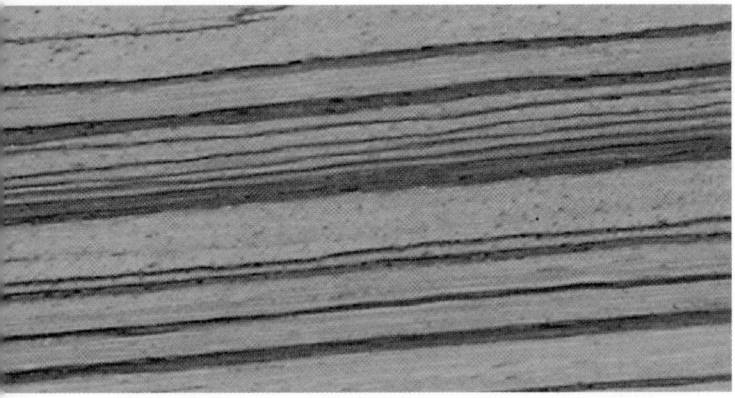

Zebrawood, also called Zebrano. (Central and West Africa). Hard, heavy, open grain, medium texture, light golden color with narrow streaks of brown, highly decorative, spectacular pattern when quarter-sawed, and an excellent furniture material

12-3 Imported hardwoods *Continued*

Softwoods

With changing moisture conditions, softwoods generally develop cracks and checks. A **check** is a small split that runs parallel to the grain of the wood. Softwoods also have less strength than hardwoods and are less expensive. Cost may outweigh other considerations depending on how the wood is used.

Softwoods are often used for back panels on case goods, since beauty and strength are not essential. They are also used to make processed woods.

Popular furniture softwoods include cypress, eastern red cedar, ponderosa pine, redwood, sugar pine, and white pine. Their qualities are listed in 12-4.

For rustic or outdoor pieces, softwoods are often preferred. Pine, for example, develops checks and cracks that are considered attractive for country

Cypress. Lightweight (32 lb./ft.^{3}), coarse texture, easily worked, durable, excellent exterior-furniture wood, and light yellow with brown streaks

Ponderosa pine. Lightweight (28 lb./ft.^{3}), uniform texture, easily worked, rather weak, little warpage, cream to reddish-brown in color, and used for rustic furniture

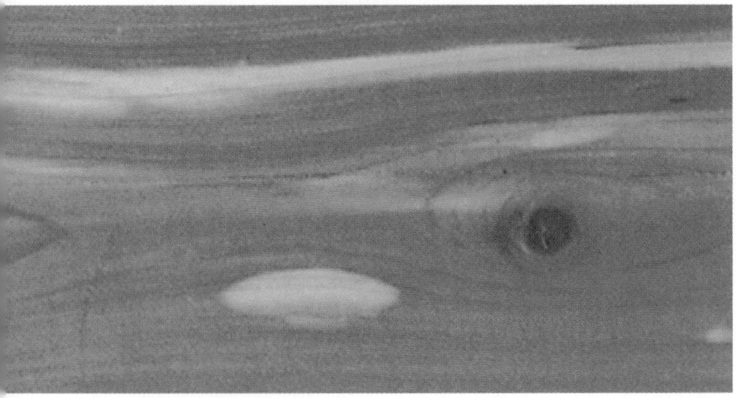

Eastern red cedar. Medium dense (34 lb./ft^3), close grain, durable, red heartwood, white sapwood, nice aroma, and used mainly for chests and closets

Redwood. Lightweight (28 lb./ft.^{3}), usually fine and even grain, reddish-brown in color, lighter sapwood, easy to work, durable, and used for outdoor furniture

12-4 These softwoods are commonly used for outdoor or less-expensive furniture.

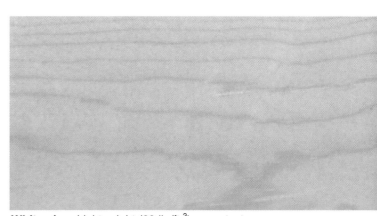

Sugar pine. Lightweight (26 lb./ft.^{3}), uniform texture, light brown in color with tiny resin canals, straight grain, warp resistant, easily worked, and used for rustic furniture

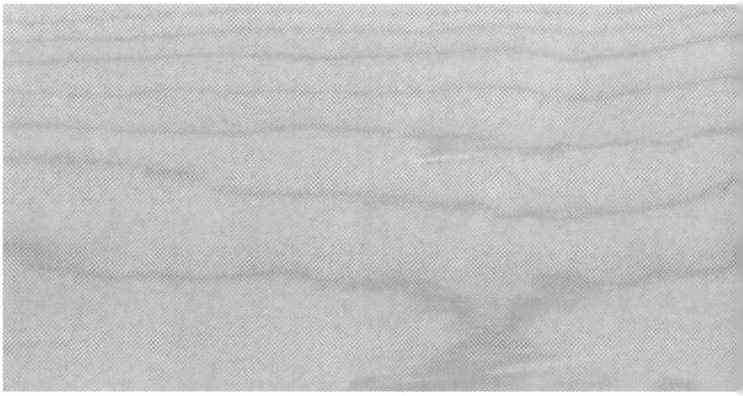

White pine. Lightweight (28 lb./ft.^{3}), even texture, cream colored, available in knotty pine grades, and used for rustic furniture

12-4 Softwoods *Continued*

furniture. Redwood is coarse and splintery, but it withstands weather very well and is popular for outdoor furniture.

Wood Veneers

Wood veneers permit the use of rare and expensive woods in furniture that would otherwise be too expensive or impractical. A **veneer** is a thin slice of wood cut from a log. Five basic methods of cutting veneers are used: rotary cut, flat slicing, quarter slicing, half-round slicing, and rift-cut, 12-5.

- For a *rotary cut*, the log is mounted in a lathe and thin layers of wood are pulled off as the log is turned, producing a bold, variegated, rippled figure pattern. Most softwood veneers are made in this way.
- *Flat slicing* produces a variegated, wavy figure by slicing parallel to a line through the center of the log.
- *Quarter slicing* produces a series of stripes by positioning the growth rings at a right angle to the knife.
- *Half-round slicing* has characteristics of both rotary cut and flat-sliced veneers. The cut is slightly across the annual growth rings of the log.
- *Rift-cut* veneer is used for oak and other woods that have ray cells radiating from the center of the log. The method emphasizes these cell patterns.

Veneer patterns are obtained by matching pieces of veneer in various ways. The most common patterns are: book match, slip match, and special match, 12-6.

- In a *book match*, every other sheet is turned over, like leaves of a book. Therefore, the back of one veneer sheet meets the front of the adjacent veneer. This produces a matching joint design with a mirrored-image look.

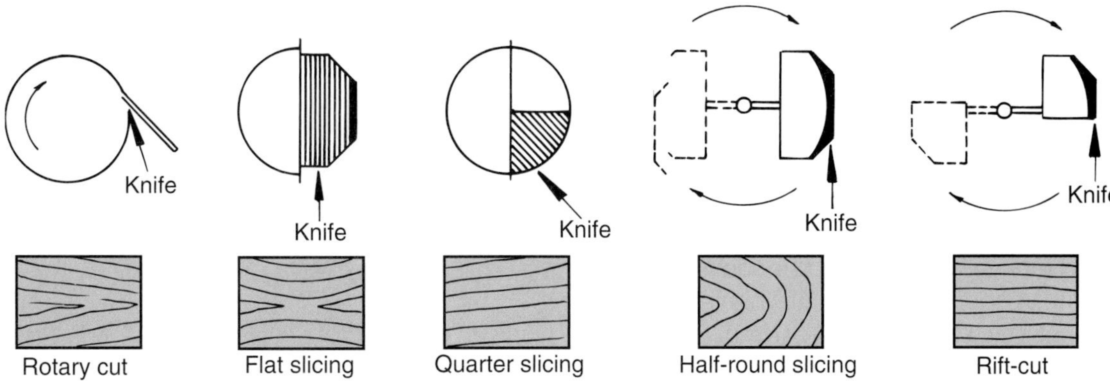

12-5 Different methods of cutting produce different visual characteristics in the veneer. The five basic cutting methods are shown with the grain patterns that typically result.

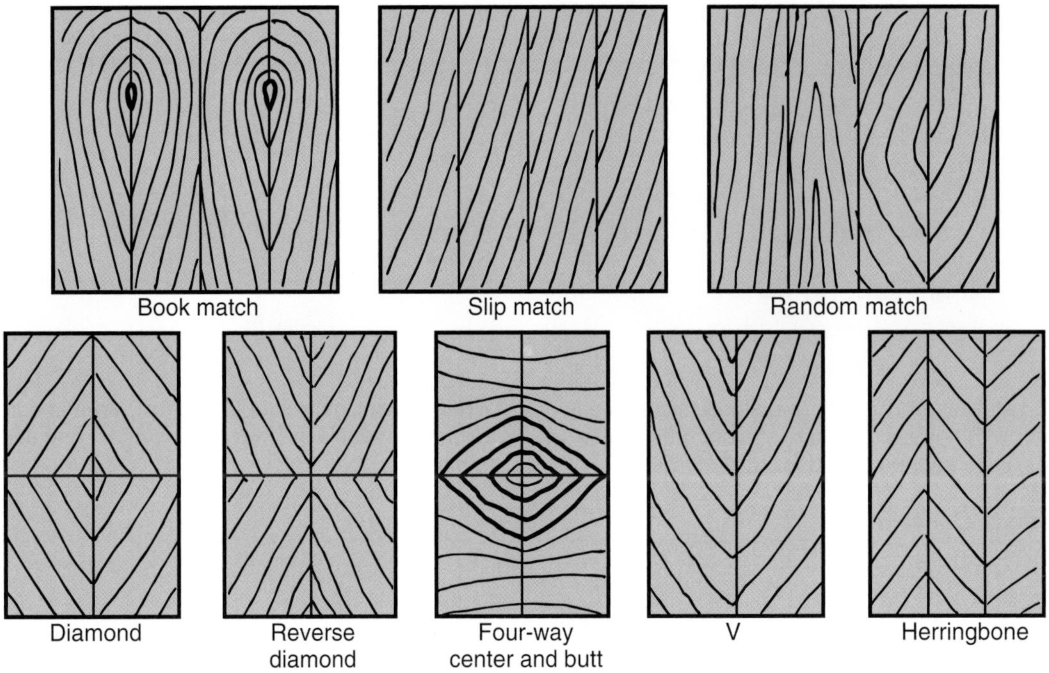

12-6 Various methods of matching veneer pieces produce different patterns.

- A *slip match* results when adjacent sheets are joined side by side, without turning, to repeat the same grain pattern.
- A *special match* may be used to produce a variety of patterns, such as diamond, reverse diamond, V, herringbone, checkerboard, and others. All of these patterns are used in furniture today.

Veneer figure patterns are greatly affected by the tree section that is used. Although most veneer is cut from the trunk of the tree, some of the more interesting and valuable patterns are cut from the crotch, burl, or stump, 12-7. Veneers cut from a crotch have plumelike designs. Burls produce veneers with a pattern of swirls, and stumps yield rippling patterns with sharp contrasts.

Veneered furniture is made by gluing together layers, or plies, of wood to make plywood. The outer layer is a better-quality veneer, while less expensive veneers or pressed wood are used as inner layers. Usually three, five, or seven layers are bonded together. The layers are placed so the grain of one layer is at right angles to the grain of the next.

Most fine case goods, especially cupboards, chests, and tables, have veneered wood for exterior construction. Veneers are practical when solid wood is too expensive, like rosewood, or too heavy, like ebony.

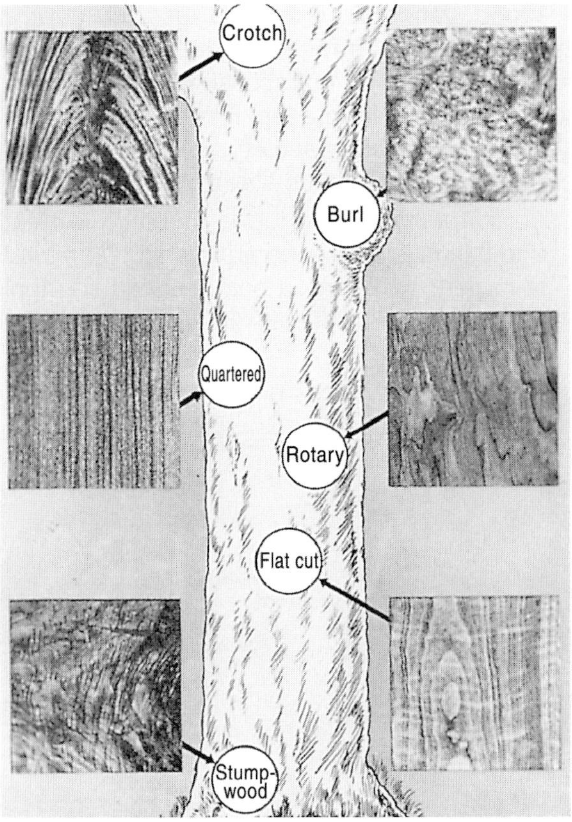

12-7 Wood cut from different parts of the tree produces different grain patterns.

Solid Wood

If a case good is made from solid wood, any exposed parts are made from the same wood. No veneer is used, but the unexposed parts of the piece may be made from different wood.

Solid wood has a greater tendency to crack, warp, and swell than a well-constructed veneered wood. It also is more expensive than veneer. For these reasons, solid woods are more often used for framework, while veneered wood is used for side, top, front, and back panels. Maple, pine, cherry, and birch are most commonly used for solid wood furniture.

Composite Board

Technology makes it possible to form wood boards from wood particles. These processed woods are less expensive and often more durable than solid woods or veneered plywood. For these reasons, composite board is becoming a common material in furniture.

The two main types of processed woods are hardboard and particleboard. Both are formed by combining wood particles, various resins, pressure, and heat.

Hardboard is made from wood fibers into all-wood panels. The fibers are extracted from wood chips by steam or chemical processes and compressed under heat. Hardboard is exceptionally strong and resistant to splits, cracks, splinters, abrasion, and moisture. Its surface can be smooth or textured to imitate the look of wood grain. However, surface designs cannot perfectly match the pattern of fine wood, so hardboard may not be suitable for some furniture uses. Hardboard is considered an excellent material for furniture door and drawer parts, tabletops, and the backs of bookcases, cabinets, and chests in less-expensive furniture.

Particleboard is made from wood shavings that are pressed together with heat and adhesive. Usually, several kinds of softwoods are used in the same piece of particleboard. Fir, poplar, pine, hemlock, and aspen are most commonly used. Like hardboard, particleboard is sturdy and versatile. Particleboard is often used as the core wood for cabinets and other furniture of low quality. The surface may be covered with laminated plastic or wood veneer. Uncovered surfaces of particleboard can be identified by an irregular, crystallized pattern.

Wood Finishes

Fine-quality wood furniture should be properly treated and finished. Added color should come from several layers of finishing materials that work with the natural grain of the wood. Polishing, sanding, and rubbing will produce a **patina,** a mellow glow with richness and depth of tone.

Stains, oils, waxes, glazes, or sealers may be used during the finishing process. Good finishes will produce a smooth surface and protect wood from heat, moisture, and scratches.

Poor-quality furniture is often finished with thick, stained varnish or one coat of varnish that dries quickly. Brush marks may be evident on the surface. The shine will be hard and glossy instead of mellow and rich. Such finishes do not last as long as fine finishes.

Wood Furniture Construction

Most furniture today is made using modern machinery, but no piece is entirely "machine-made." Assembly or some finishing details are still performed by hand on quality furniture. The techniques used to fasten the various pieces together are just as important as the materials used in the furniture.

A piece of furniture is no stronger than its joints. Quality joinery is expensive, time-consuming, and frequently hidden from view. Many different techniques and kinds of joints were developed over the years to produce quality furniture. Several types of joining methods are listed here.

- The *butt joint* is the simplest type of joint to construct. It is made by butting the end or edge of one board against another, 12-8. The joint is generally held together with glue, screws, or nails. Surfaces being joined should fit closely and be square with each other. The butt joint is a weak joint.
- A *rabbet joint* is formed by cutting a recess in one or both pieces to be joined. The recess is cut along an edge or on the end, 12-9. Rabbet joints are easy to make and generally used on the corners of boxes, cases, drawers, and back panels of case goods. Glue and screws or nails may be used. The rabbet joint is stronger than the butt joint.

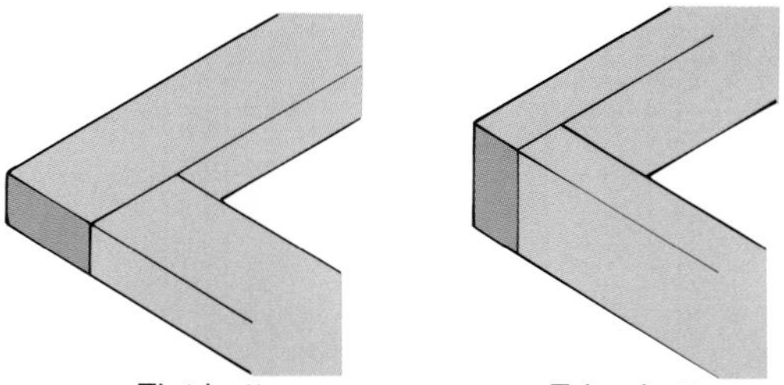

12-8 Butt joints are considered weak joints.

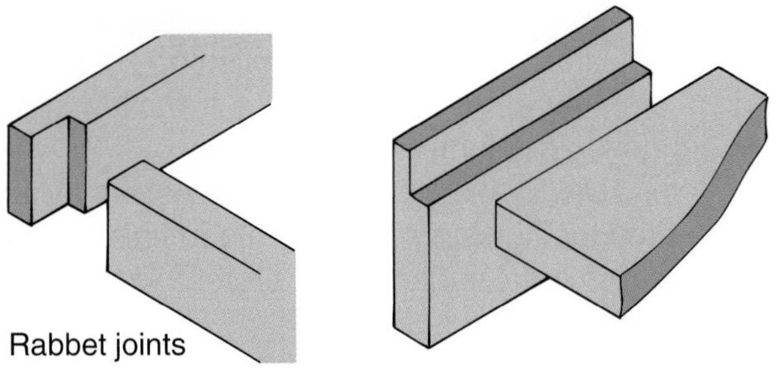

12-9 The cutting and fitting of a rabbet joint makes it stronger than a butt joint, but it is still relatively weak.

- A *dado* is a rectangular recess cut across the grain of the wood. The dado is cut to the width of the piece to be joined, which is fitted into the dado. These joints are used for installing shelves, frames, and partitions in cabinets. They form strong joints when properly glued and carefully fitted. See 12-10.
- Several types of *lap joints* are used in furniture construction. They include: end-lap, half-lap, cross-lap, and middle-lap. Lap joints are made by cutting away an equal amount of wood from each piece so their surfaces are flush when fitted together, 12-11. Lap joints are used to join corners of furniture frames and exterior pieces of wood that cross each other. Hidden glue and screws may be used to secure the joint for a strong connection.
- *Dowel joints* are used when extra strength is desired with another type of joint, such as the butt, rabbet, dado, or lap joint. Dowels are generally made of birch and range in ⅛ in. increments from ⅛ to 1 in. diameters. The length and diameter of the dowels used depend on the size of the pieces being joined. Glue is used to secure the dowels, 12-12.
- The *mortise-and-tenon joint* is a very strong type of joint. Three main forms are used: blind, open, and haunched. Their construction is shown in 12-13. Mortise-and-tenon joints are used to join legs or rails to tables, benches, and chairs.
- A *tongue-and-groove joint* is used along the common edge of two boards. The tongue is cut on one board, and the matching groove is formed on the edge of the other. The joint may be glued, but generally it is not when used in

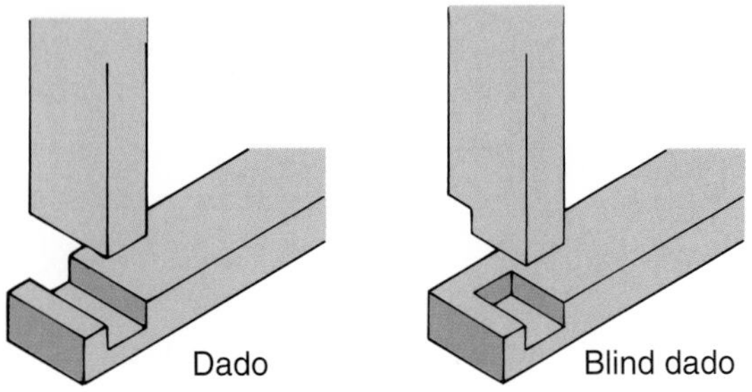

12-10 Dado joints are very strong when properly fitted and glued.

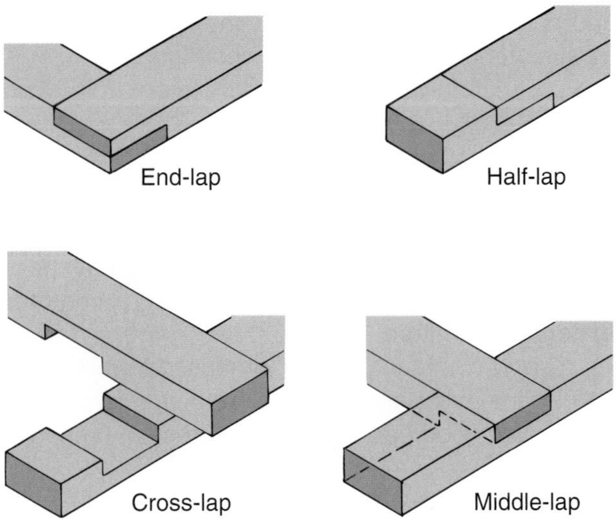

12-11 Lap joints are used widely in furniture construction for frames and crossed exterior pieces.

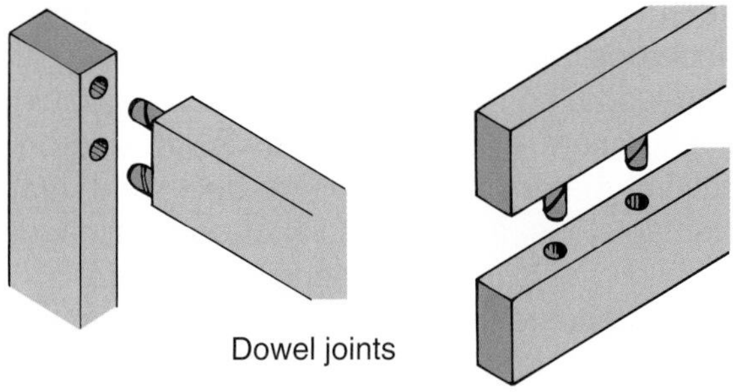

12-12 Dowels may be used with several types of joints to improve their strength.

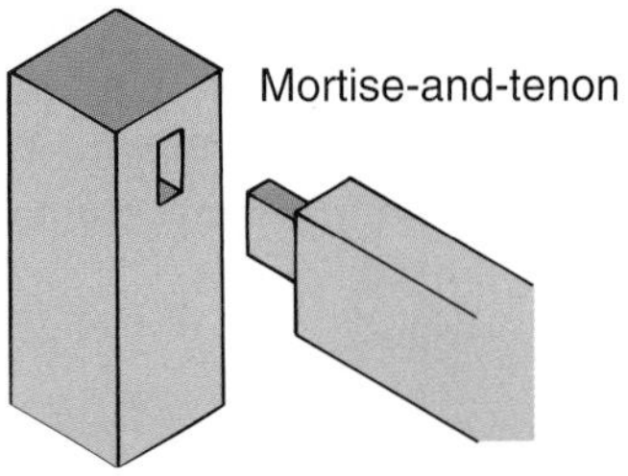

12-13 Mortise-and-tenon joints form very strong joints and are useful in attaching furniture legs and rails.

panel construction. More than one tongue-and-groove joint may be used on a thick piece of wood. This joint forms a solid connection between the pieces, 12-14.

- *Spline joints* are used along the edges or at the corner of two pieces. A spline joint is a simple butt joint with a thin piece of wood inserted in a groove to strengthen the joint. See 12-15. For greater strength, the grain of the spline should be perpendicular to the groove.
- *Dovetail joints* are used to fasten corner joints, especially those on drawers. A high degree of precision is necessary to make a tight-fitting dovetail joint, but it provides maximum strength. Several variations of the joint are possible, such as lap, through, and half-blind dovetails. The principle technique is similar, however, in all variations. A typical dovetail joint is shown in 12-16.
- *Blocking* consists of small pieces of wood attached between the adjacent sides of two pieces for added strength. It is used at inside corners, such as the area where a table leg is fastened to a rail under the tabletop. Blocking may be used in out-of-view areas where more strength is required. Blocks are usually glued and/or screwed in place, 12-17.

All the joints used in furniture construction may be glued. Modern glues develop tremendous strength and generally exceed the strength of the wood.

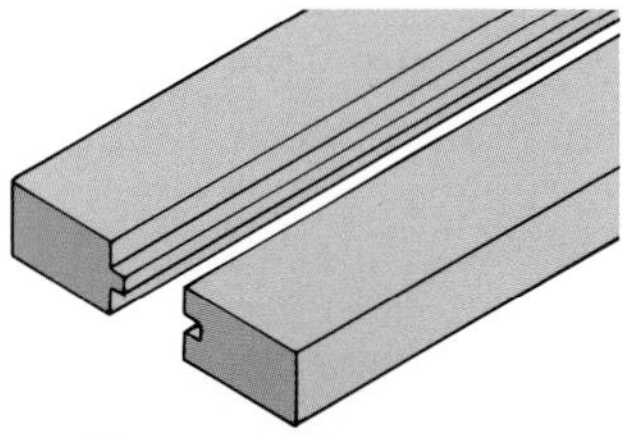

12-14 Tongue-and-groove joints are used along the common edge of two boards.

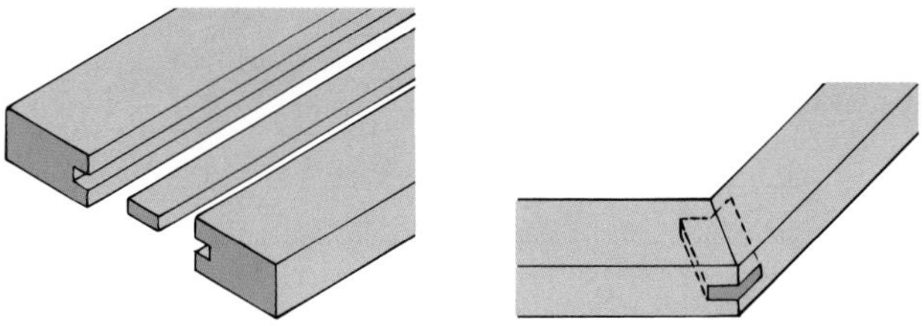

12-15 Spline joints are used to increase the strength of other joints.

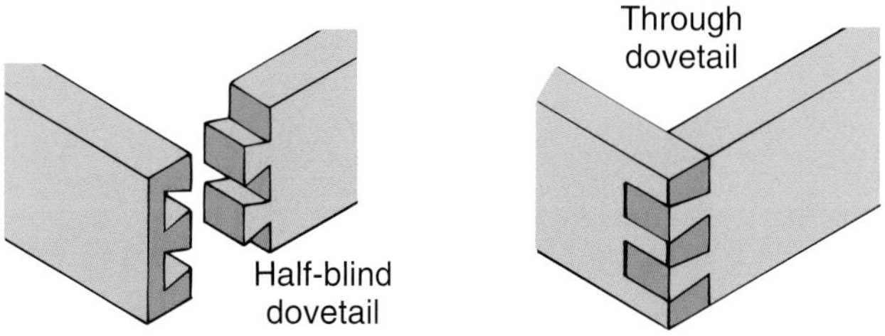

12-16 Dovetail joints are used on high-quality construction to provide maximum strength.

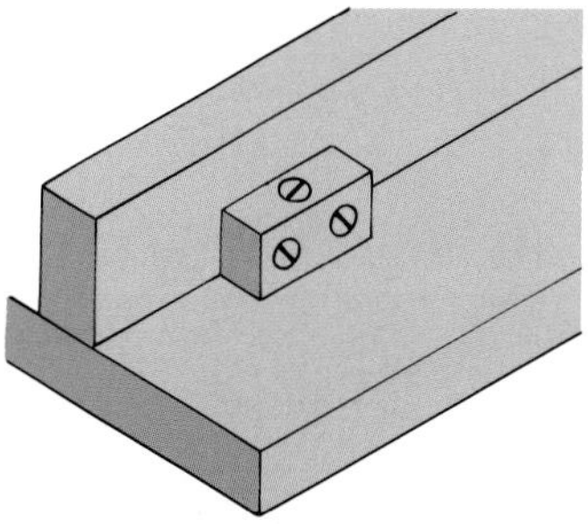

12-17 Blocking is used to reinforce other joints, but it should be located in areas that are not visible.

Upholstered Furniture

Upholstered furniture incorporates a frame, cushioning material, and covering, 12-18. Pieces such as sofas and chairs are frequently upholstered. This furniture must be carefully examined to accurately judge quality because so much of the construction is hidden.

Fabrics

Upholstery fabrics should be functional as well as attractive. How a piece of furniture will be used helps to determine what type of upholstery is most suitable. Overall, fabrics should be comfortable, durable, attractive, and soil resistant.

Plain or twill weaves are recommended for furniture that is used frequently. Pile-weave fabrics, such as velvet and corduroy, show wear much more quickly. Brocades and tapestry fabrics are beautiful, but their threads catch and snag easily. These fabrics may be more suitable for seldom-used living room furniture.

Both natural and synthetic fibers are used in upholstered furniture. While natural fibers are attractive, the addition of fabric finishes and synthetic fibers, such as polyester and nylon, increase a fabric's strength and stain resistance.

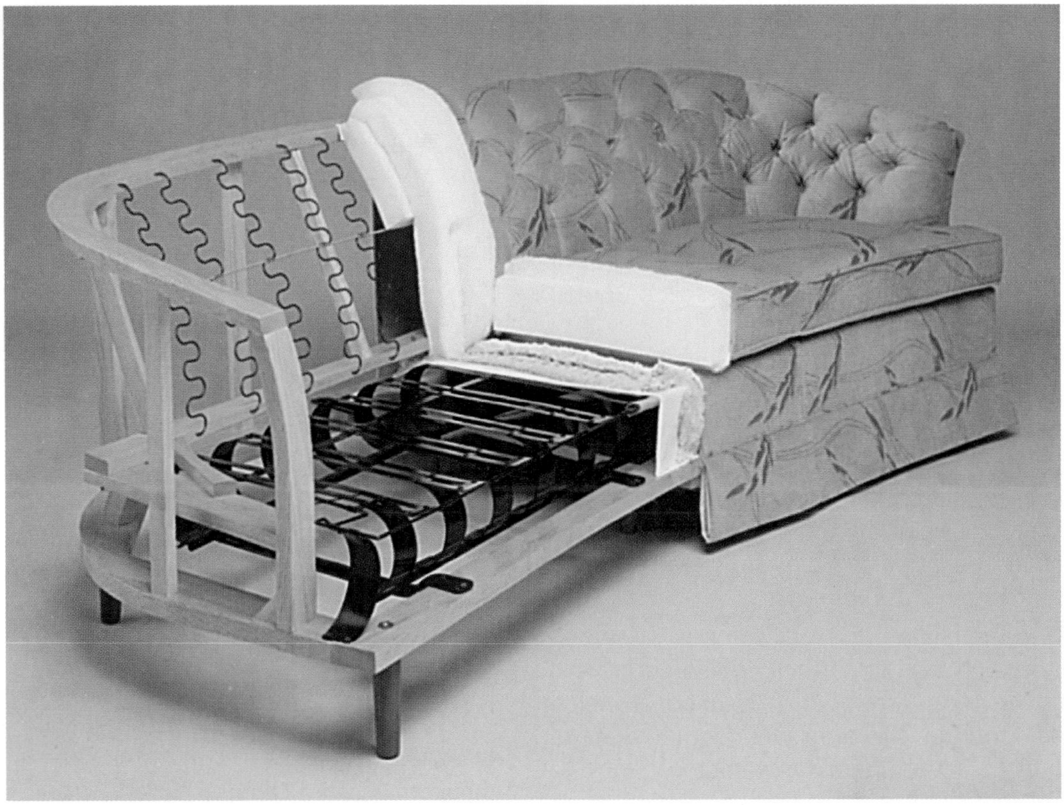

Flexsteel Industries, Inc.

12-18 Upholstered furniture consists of a wooden frame and spring supports covered with padding and upholstery. The main construction of an upholstered piece is hidden from the view.

Nonwoven fabrics such as leather and vinyl are also used for upholstery. They are sturdy and easily cleaned. Leather is durable and attractive, but very expensive. Less-expensive vinyl can be made to resemble leather.

Upholstered Furniture Construction

The frame of an upholstered piece is generally made of kiln-dried hardwood. On upholstered furniture, the **frame** is the wood support beneath the textile covering. Wood that is not properly dried is more likely to split and buckle. The joints should be strengthened with dowels and glue blocks. Padding on the frame is desirable at points exposed to wear. The manufacturer's tag or literature should provide useful information about the frame's construction. Remember, if the piece has a weak or poorly constructed frame, its durability may not be satisfactory.

The part of a chair or sofa that serves as the platform for cushioning materials is called the **seat base**. Several types of springs are used in seat bases. One type is the **serpentine spring**, which is a long spring that repeats the shape of an S. See 12-19. This flat spring is nailed, screwed, or stapled to the frame at equidistant points from other flat springs. Springs are linked together with tiny coiled springs called **helicals**. This type of construction produces a minimum amount of bulk.

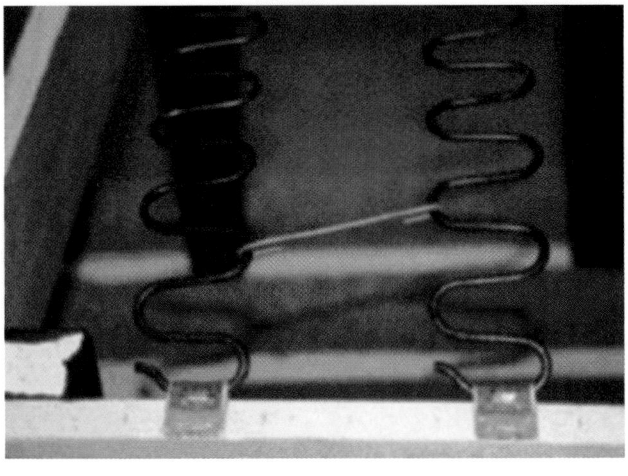

12-19 The S-type spring is used on seat bases when a minimum of bulk is desired.

Another type of frequently used, seat-base construction uses the **coil spring**, which has a three-dimensional spiral shape. See 12-20. Several coil springs are attached to webbing or steel bands. An average chair would generally have 9 to 12 springs per seat, with each tied as frequently as 8 times in quality pieces.

A thick layer of cushioning material should be applied directly over the springs and frame. Several materials are used, such as cellular foams, fiberfill, feathers, and down. The most expensive furniture has feathers or down, while the least expensive usually has some type of fiberfill. Polyurethane foam is used on most furniture today for cushioning.

The outer covering is the most visible part of an upholstered piece. The seams should be straight and tight with no loose threads. **Welting**, cording sewn into the seams, adds strength, See 12-21. Buttons and zippers should also be secure.

Bedding

An **innerspring mattress** contains a series of springs covered with padding. It is similar in construction to upholstered furniture, 12-22. The springs vary in number, size, placement, and wire thickness, called **gauge**. Coil springs may be individually **pocketed**, or covered with padding. A good-quality innerspring mattress should have the following:

- at least 300 heavy coils firmly anchored
- good padding and insulation over the coils
- a tightly woven cover that fits snugly

Foam mattresses are made of latex or polyurethane foam. They are lightweight and less expensive than innerspring mattresses. A good foam mattress is about 6 in. thick, with holes or cores that make the mattress more comfortable. People with allergies often use foam mattresses.

A water bed has a mattress that is a plastic bag filled with water supported by a frame and watertight liner. The liner is placed between the frame and mattress to protect against potential leaks. A heating device is used to warm the water. A water-filled mattress conforms exactly to body curves, but may result in a "hammock effect." Water beds range from full motion to waveless. The weight of a water bed may be a special concern since the standard size weighs about 1,600 pounds when filled.

Air chamber mattresses, the most recent innovation in mattress construction, provide support and comfort that is superior to metal-coil mattresses and water beds. The **air chamber mattresses** has a series of air chambers made from puncture-resistant flexible rubber. Mattress firmness can be controlled.

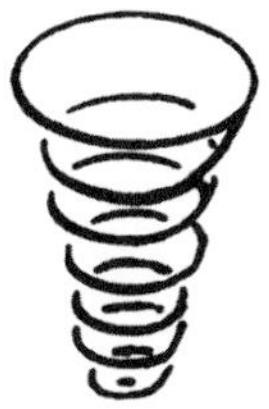

12-20 Coil springs of heavy weight that are properly anchored provide a comfortable, resilient seat base.

Brenton Bacari, ASID, Bacari Design, Washington DC

12-21 The welting on this chair is attractive, but it also adds strength to the seams.

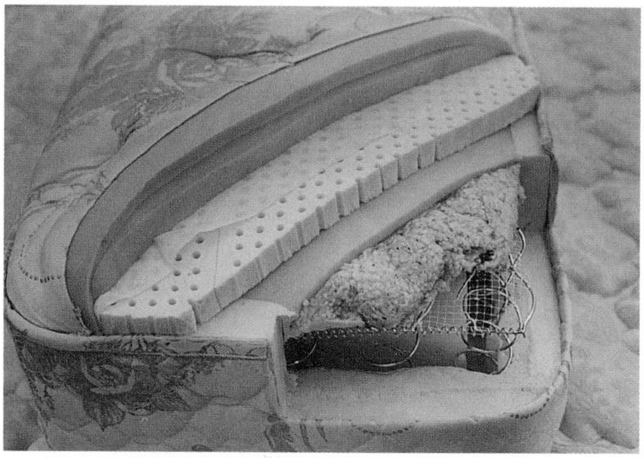

12-22 A good mattress consists of heavy-gauge coils that are firmly anchored.

The mattress contains a multicushion suspension design that contours to the body to provide comfort and support. Double-reinforced, I-beam construction results in durable holding power. See 12-23. The dual-density foam perimeter provides maximum structural support.

Metal Furniture

There are many types and styles of metal furniture available today. The majority of structural metals used are steel, iron, and aluminum, 12-24. Several metal coatings or platings are also popular.

Many modern furniture pieces are made from steel tubing. These pieces are strong, lightweight, and fairly inexpensive. They may be assembled with mechanical fasteners, or they may be welded.

Aluminum tubing is used frequently for lawn furniture. It is lighter in weight and less expensive than steel. However, it is not as strong and tends to bend and dent.

Wrought iron is used to make decorative outdoor furniture, 12-25. Cast iron, steel, and aluminum are more popular than wrought iron, however, and use forms in its shape. Since casting is more easily adapted to mass production, cast furniture is less expensive. Cast iron is heavy and brittle. Iron is usually coated or plated to protect it from rust. Cast metal is also used for furniture hardware.

Some metal-frame furniture is plated, 12-26. Chrome, brass, nickel, copper, and zinc are common plating materials. **Plating** is a thin coating of metal over another material for added protection or attractiveness. Often, a less expensive metal is plated with an attractive metal. Sometimes using a solid metal such as copper would produce a weak or heavy piece of furniture, so plating with the metal is more practical.

Brass and copper plating is costly but attractive. It has a tendency to tarnish and must be polished frequently. Some manufacturers place a protective coating of clear lacquer or enamel over these metals to help prevent tarnishing.

Baked enamel coatings have expanded the popularity of metal furniture, 12-27. A wide variety of

12-23 Air mattresses do not rely on support from springs or water. Instead, they support the body on a cushion of air. Generally, the firmness of each side of the bed can be adjusted using an air-pressure control system.

John Boucher, photographer. Courtesy of Herman Miller

12-24 Polished aluminum was used for the framework of these Eames lounge chairs and table with Lafonda base.

Gayla Pressner, ASID, Illinois Chapter

12-25 These chairs and table were fabricated using wrought iron rods formed into decorative shapes.

Spiegel, Inc.

12-26 This dinette set is made from steel tubing with chrome plating. The plating protects the steel tubing and provides a durable, decorative finish.

Brown Jordan

12-27 Baked enamel forms a durable coating for these outdoor pieces made from steel tubing.

colors are available in finishes that can be washed and are weather resistant. Kitchen cabinets, outdoor furniture, doors, and bathroom cabinets are examples of pieces made of enameled metal.

Plastic Furniture

Plastics possess an almost endless variety of characteristics. They can imitate almost any other material or display a unique character of their own. Plastic furniture is lightweight, durable, inexpensive, and easily cleaned, 12-28.

Some of the broad families of plastics that have been used in furniture include: vinyls, styrenes, polycarbonates, cellulosics, nylons, polyurethanes, polyesters, and acrylics.

The ability to manufacture plastics in rigid shapes or flexible foams opens many options for this versatile construction material. Transparent and translucent plastics have special qualities that enhance some furniture designs. Plastics will probably replace many traditional materials used in furniture production.

Smithsonian Institution Photo No. 76-5831

12-28 The tulip chair designed by Eero Saarienen is a modern piece of furniture that makes use of plastic's ability to easily accept molding.

Furniture Selection

When selecting furniture, personal taste should be a primary consideration, but information will help you make more satisfactory choices. Knowing the names of furniture pieces and their proper definitions will help you communicate properly when discussing furniture with a dealer. See 12-29.

Quality, cost, style, size, fabric, ergonomic design, and maintenance requirements are important points to consider. The guidelines discussed here will help you choose furniture that provides satisfaction for many years.

Quality and Cost

Furniture is expensive, so care must be taken to get the best quality possible for the price paid. Knowledge of furniture materials and construction will help you know what to examine when judging quality. Much of furniture construction is hidden, however, so it is important to buy from a dealer who stands by his or her products.

The Federal Trade Commission (FTC) has instituted Guides for the Household Furniture Industry. These rules prohibit furniture manufacturers and dealers from providing false or misleading information about their furniture. The dealer cannot remove a manufacturer's tags and labels with information about materials and construction.

These rules also require manufacturers to state what types of outer coverings and interior paddings are used on upholstered furniture. Leather and leather imitations must be marked as such. Manufacturers must indicate if vinyl, other plastics, or marble dust are used in an imitation of leather, wood, slate, or marble.

Descriptions of wood furniture follow strict guidelines. If a label states that a piece is made of one wood, any exposed parts must be made of that wood. Labels must state that a veneered piece is veneered. Specific terms used to describe wood must conform to meanings determined by the FTC.

- *Solid* means that all exposed wood is of the same solid wood through the entire thickness of the piece. No veneers are used.
- *Genuine* means that the exposed parts are of the same wood, but that they are veneered.
- If *veneered* wood is made from plywood, the layers will be placed with the grain at right angles to each other.
- *Laminated* wood refers to wood made of plys, with all layers having their grain in the same direction.
- *Combination* is a term used to describe furniture with more than one type of wood used in the exposed parts.
- *All-wood construction* means the wood exposed is the same throughout the entire thickness of the piece.

Labels are helpful in evaluating furniture, but they don't tell you everything. Before any piece of furniture is taken home, the buyer should examine it carefully.

With case furniture, rub your hand over the surface. It should be smooth with no rough spots, splinters, or protruding nails. Check the back and inside surfaces as well. Stains should be even in color throughout the piece. Construction should be solid. Tap the panels of the furniture. If you hear a

Furniture Names	
Armoire	Large wooden piece with doors, used in place of a closet for storing clothing or household linens.
Barcelona chair	Classic, contemporary chair design characterized by a stainless steel frame and upholstered leather back and seat.
Bentwood	Furniture pieces made from wood that is steam-bent into curved shapes.
Bergere	Upholstered armchair with closed, upholstered sides and visible wood frame.
Bombe chest	Regence or Louis XV commode with bulging sides, front, or both.
Breakfront	Wide, tall cabinet with wood doors and drawers on the bottom and glass doors above. This piece is similar to the modern china cabinet.
Camelback	Chair or sofa with a curved hump along the back.
Campaign furniture	Furnishings with metal corners and handles patterned after military chests.
Chesterfield	Overstuffed sofa with upholstered ends.
Club chair	Comfortable, heavily upholstered chair with a cushioned seat.
Coffee table	Long, low table often placed in front of a sofa to hold newspapers, magazines, and beverages.
Commode	Low chest of drawers generally placed against the wall.
Console	Versatile table used in many locations. It was originally a shelf attached to the wall.
Couch	Synonymous with sofa. Originally it referred to a sofa with a low back and one raised end.
Credenza (or sideboard)	Storage piece about chair-rail height with doors and drawers, usually designed for the dining room. May also be used in other rooms.
Davenport	Upholstered sofa that may be made into a bed.
Director's Chair	Folding wooden-frame chair with a canvas seat and back.
Divan	Generally a living room piece with a concealed mattress that pulls out from the seat. It offers dual-purpose seating and sleeping.
Etagere	Standing set of shelves with sides open or closed, depending on the design. Very versatile piece that may be used alone or in multiples. May be used to form modular wall units for living, dining, or bedroom.
Fauteuil	French open armchair with wooden arms and caned or upholstered seat and back.
Gateleg table	Space-saving table with hinged leaves and legs that swing out like a gate to support the leaves when raised.
Hutch	Chest or cabinet on legs with an open shelf above.
Lounge	Type of backless couch with one high end for reclining.
Lounge chair	Comfortable, roomy chair available in several styles.
Loveseat	Small sofa for two people.
Modulars	Uniform structural components that can be grouped together, used separately, or arranged in a variety of combinations. Usually three or four standard modules are used to form the system.
Morris chair	Large armchair with loose cushions and a movable back.
Occasional table	Small table, sometimes with shelves or drawers, usually placed at the end of a sofa. May serve as a lamp table, but generally is a little shorter.
Parsons table	Classic square or rectangular table with apron and legs of the same width.
Pedestal table	Any table supported by a single post rather than four legs.
Poster bed	Bed with four decorative posts.
Savonarola	Italian Renaissance chair with a carved wood back and a frame composed of interlacing curved shapes.
Sawbuck table	Any large table with two X-shaped supports.
Sectional	Piece of seating furniture composed of sections that can be arranged separately or together.
Semainier	Tall, narrow chest, originally French, with seven drawers. May be used in small bedrooms, dens, or guest rooms.
Settee	Lightweight, double-seat, upholstered piece with a back and sometimes arms.
Settles	Colonial piece similar to a settee, but made of wood.
Side chair	Armless dining chair.
Sofa	Broad, inclusive term that refers to a seat for two or more people.
Sofa bed	Sofa with a back that folds back flat to form a bed area. It requires less space than the divan.
Studio couch	Living room sleeper that has an upholstered mattress resting on an upholstered steel unit. Bolsters are used to form the back.
Studio lounge	Single sleeper of a slab construction with flat springs and foam rubber padding.
Trundle bed	Low bed on casters that rolls under a full-height bed.
Wing chair	Overstuffed chair that has projecting sides on the high, upholstered back.

12-29 Using the proper names of furniture pieces helps to accurately communicate furniture details.

dull thud, the construction is solid. Pieces that sound hollow are probably constructed from thin panels of wood attached to wooden frames.

All furniture should have a sturdy base. Place firm pressure on the top or side of a piece to see if it wobbles. Make sure that all working parts work. Doors should open and shut easily, and they should fit squarely into their frame. Hinges should be properly aligned and should not squeak.

Drawers should roll smoothly when opened and shut. Avoid drawers that jar, catch, or slide without rollers. Keep in mind what will be stored in the drawers. Dresser drawers must be free of surface flaws that might snag your clothing.

When pricing furniture, solid construction should be a primary consideration, 12-30. Intricate carvings, heavy shaped moldings, deep patinas, and curved construction all add to the beauty and price of a piece, but they are not essentials. When looking for inexpensive but durable furniture, it is wise to choose pieces without these features. Your dollars will be invested in solid construction.

The type of retailer selling the furniture also affects prices. The quality of some bargain-priced pieces may compare to more expensive furniture. However, service may be limited or sales may be final. Discontinued items often are good buys, but buying matching pieces later will not be possible. Often there are disadvantages, in quality or service, to buying furniture at lower prices. Make sure you know what the disadvantages are and whether you can accept them.

Style

There are no set rules for choosing a furniture style, but it is important for furniture to blend with a room's overall design and mood. When shopping for furniture, it is helpful to carry swatches of fabrics, paint chips, or other color samples to make sure the furniture will coordinate with the room's decor. Individual pieces do not need to match precisely, but they should blend visually with the other pieces in a room, 12-31.

In common rooms such as a living room, the tastes of all family members should be considered. Items that are particularly displeasing to any one member should be avoided since all family members will use the room. Bedrooms and other private rooms allow for a more individualized style choice.

Size

Furniture size is important from two aspects. First, the furniture must fit into your house or apartment. Doors, stairs, and halls may present problems.

Kreg Tool Co.

12-30 The construction techniques used in this case goods piece provide maximum strength and rigidity to the finished article.

WCI Communities, Inc.

12-31 Furniture may display materials and colors different from the surrounding items in a room, but it should enhance the room's basic style or mood.

The size of these openings should be measured before choosing furniture. An item of the proper color and style is useless to you if it will not fit through the front door.

Secondly, furniture should be the appropriate scale for its use and location. The seat of a chair or couch should be slightly lower than the back of your knee—around 15 to 18 in. high. If a seat is higher, your feet will not be able to rest on the floor comfortably. If it is lower, sitting and standing will be difficult.

Chairs used at tables or desks should be streamlined to fit well and allow free movement. A long sofa is needed to allow adults to stretch out comfortably, but it may be too long for an intimate conversation area.

Furniture should be proportional to the dimensions of the room, 12-32. There should be ample space for circulation after all furniture is arranged in a room. Putting too much furniture or very large pieces into a room detracts from the overall plan and hinders the use of space. A diagram of standard furniture sizes is provided in A-18 of the Appendix.

Spiegel, Inc.

12-32 A four-poster bed may look great in a furniture showroom, but it could be overpowering in a small bedroom. Check room measurements carefully to make sure there will be ample space for clearance and other furnishings. This bed with thin posts is scaled well for the small room and tall window.

Upholstery Fabric

The outer covering is the most visible part of an upholstered piece. The seams should be straight and tight with no loose threads. Welting or cording sewn into the seams should be smooth. Buttons and zippers should be secure.

When examining upholstered furniture, open and close all zippers to make sure they work smoothly. Also, see if upholstery fabric is underlined. Sit or lie on all chairs, sofas, and beds. Make sure that sitting and standing are not awkward or difficult tasks. You should not be able to feel individual springs through the cushioning material.

Overall, upholstery fabric should be comfortable, durable, attractive, and soil resistant. Fibers determine a fabric's qualities, including strength; shrinkage; warmth; durability; and resistance to stains, fire, sunlight, mildew, and abrasion. The construction of the fabric also affects the upholstery's strength, stability, warmth, durability, and suitability for its intended purpose. Information about the fibers and fabric construction most suitable for upholstery is covered in Chapter 10.

Ergonomics in Furniture Design

Providing comfort for the user is a key requirement of furniture. Because people vary in size and proportion, a single piece of furniture may not be comfortable for everyone. How effectively the human body is accommodated by an item directly relates to its comfort level. Furniture that is comfortable tends to incorporate ergonomic principles. The goal of ergonomic furniture design is to produce furnishings that are comfortable to use for their intended functions.

Furniture should be easy to use, operate, and clean. Pieces for seating should be scaled to human dimensions and provide good back support. Tables should be the proper height for the intended use. Storage should be convenient and accessible. Special furniture may be needed to meet the functional needs of those with physical disabilities.

Furniture for seating has been the primary focus of ergonomic design principles. Anthropometic data, which measures the size and proportion of the human body, suggests that maximum comfort results when weight and pressure are distributed and tension eased by furniture directly proportional to the human body.

Ideally, the height of a seat should be slightly shorter than the length of the sitter's lower legs so his or her feet can rest on the floor comfortably. To reduce pressure under the knee, the length of the seat should be slightly shorter than the person's upper legs. The seat should be wide enough to permit some movement, and its shape should be resilient so that pressure is not concentrated on the small, weight-bearing edge of the pelvis. The angle between the seat and back should be 95 degrees or more so the back is tilted at least 5 degrees beyond the vertical position to buttress the person's weight. Adjustable seating is more desirable and often more comfortable than fixed furniture.

Good furniture design applies ergonomic principles so the highest degree of function and comfort are attained.

Plain & Fancy Custom Cabinetry, Inc.

12-33 This beautiful cabinetry incorporates smooth surfaces that are easy to clean.

Maintenance

How much time and money must be spent in the upkeep of furniture is an important consideration. Fine wood furniture requires special cleaners and must be waxed regularly. Upholstered furniture may be vacuumed, but occasional steam cleaning may be necessary. Stain removal may be difficult if the upholstery fabric is not easily removable.

Features that aid in cleanability include smooth surfaces with very little carving or grooving, 12-33. Woods may be treated with special coatings to make them more resistant to stains and easier to clean. Removable slipcovers can be washed by machine and are easily replaced when they wear out. Treated fabrics resist stains. Plastic, metal, and vinyl furniture surfaces are resistant to stains and easy to clean.

Cleanability and maintenance requirements should be compatible with a family's lifestyle. A family with no children, for example, may choose furniture with plush upholstery, fine wood, and intricate carving, 12-34. A working couple with young children, on the other hand, should choose easy-to-maintain upholstered furniture and smooth case goods with protective coatings.

Thomasville Furniture Industries, Inc.

12-34 The white upholstery is a sure sign that this dining room set is not intended for everyday meals with young children.

Chapter Summary

Furniture increases the usefulness of an area and expresses the personality of household members. Price and quality of furniture is affected by the materials and methods used in construction. Wood, metals, plastics, and fabrics comprise the primary materials used to make furniture.

Wood, the most common material used in furniture, is frequently used as a structural framework that is covered by other material such as fabric. Solid woods, veneers, and processed woods are used in furniture construction. Hardwoods are generally preferred over softwoods for high-quality furniture. Softwoods are sometimes used for back panels on case goods or for rustic furniture. Wood veneers permit the use of rare and expensive woods for furniture. The joints used to fasten the various pieces of furniture together provide varying degrees of strength.

Upholstered furniture combines the frame, cushioning, and covering. Upholstery fabrics should be functional, attractive, comfortable, desirable, and soil resistant. Padding, a seat base, and springs are also needed for seating areas. An innerspring mattress is similar in construction to upholstered furniture since it is a series of springs covered with padding.

Steel, aluminum and iron account for the majority of structural metals used in furniture. Wrought iron is used to make outdoor furniture. Some type of coating is generally required for iron or steel furniture to protect it from the elements. Plastic furniture is lightweight, durable, inexpensive, and easily cleaned.

Since furniture is expensive, care must be taken to get the best quality possible for the cost. Read the labels, examine workmanship, and consider ergonomic qualities in addition to checking style, size, upholstery fabric, and maintenance requirements.

Review Questions

1. How do hardwoods differ from softwoods in furniture construction?
2. What are the five methods of cutting veneers? What kind of pattern does each produce?
3. How does veneered wood compare to solid wood in furniture construction?
4. How are processed woods used in furniture?
5. What types of joints are used to construct wood furniture? Briefly describe each.
6. Of the joints used in wood furniture, which is the weakest?
7. What type of fabric construction would you recommend for upholstered furniture used by a family with young children?
8. What construction factors are important to consider regarding the seating area of upholstered furniture pieces?
9. What metals are used in furniture production? What are the advantages and disadvantages of their use?
10. What requirements of the Federal Trade Commission help consumers with their furniture purchases?
11. Before shopping for furniture, what information and materials should the buyer take along?
12. What factors should be considered when selecting upholstery fabric?

Suggested Activities

1. List and describe five different woods used in furniture construction.
2. Prepare a short essay that describes how wood joints are used in furniture construction. Include the functions of the various joints in your descriptions as well as their names and degree of strength.
3. Describe the basic components of an upholstered piece of furniture and their respective functions.
4. Examine samples of product literature that describes various types of metal and plastic furniture. Compare the claims for each type of furniture.
5. Prepare a survey form identifying the factors consumers consider when selecting furniture. Survey five adults to determine their most important purchasing considerations for the last piece of furniture they bought. Have them rank, from 1 (most important) to 6 (least important), the following factors: quality/durability, cost, style/appearance, size, ergonomics/comfort, and low maintenance. Summarize your findings in a paragraph.
6. Select a piece of furniture in your home or in the classroom. Consider how well it incorporates ergonomic principles and recommend any adjustments that would cause improvement.

Internet Resources

Ball and Ball, manufacturer of antique brass furniture hardware
ballandball-us.com

Bartley Collection Ltd.
bartleycollection.com

Center for Furniture Craftsmanship
woodschool.org

Connecticut Valley School of Woodworking
schoolofwoodworking.com

Fine Woodworking Magazine
finewoodworking.com

Lie-Nielsen Toolworks, Inc.
lie-nielsen.com

Natuzzi, manufacturer of leather-upholstered furniture
natuzzi.com

Sauder Woodworking Company
sauder.com

Note: Web addresses may have changed since publication. For some entries, reaching the correct Web site may require keying *www.* into the address.

Part Five
Structural Systems

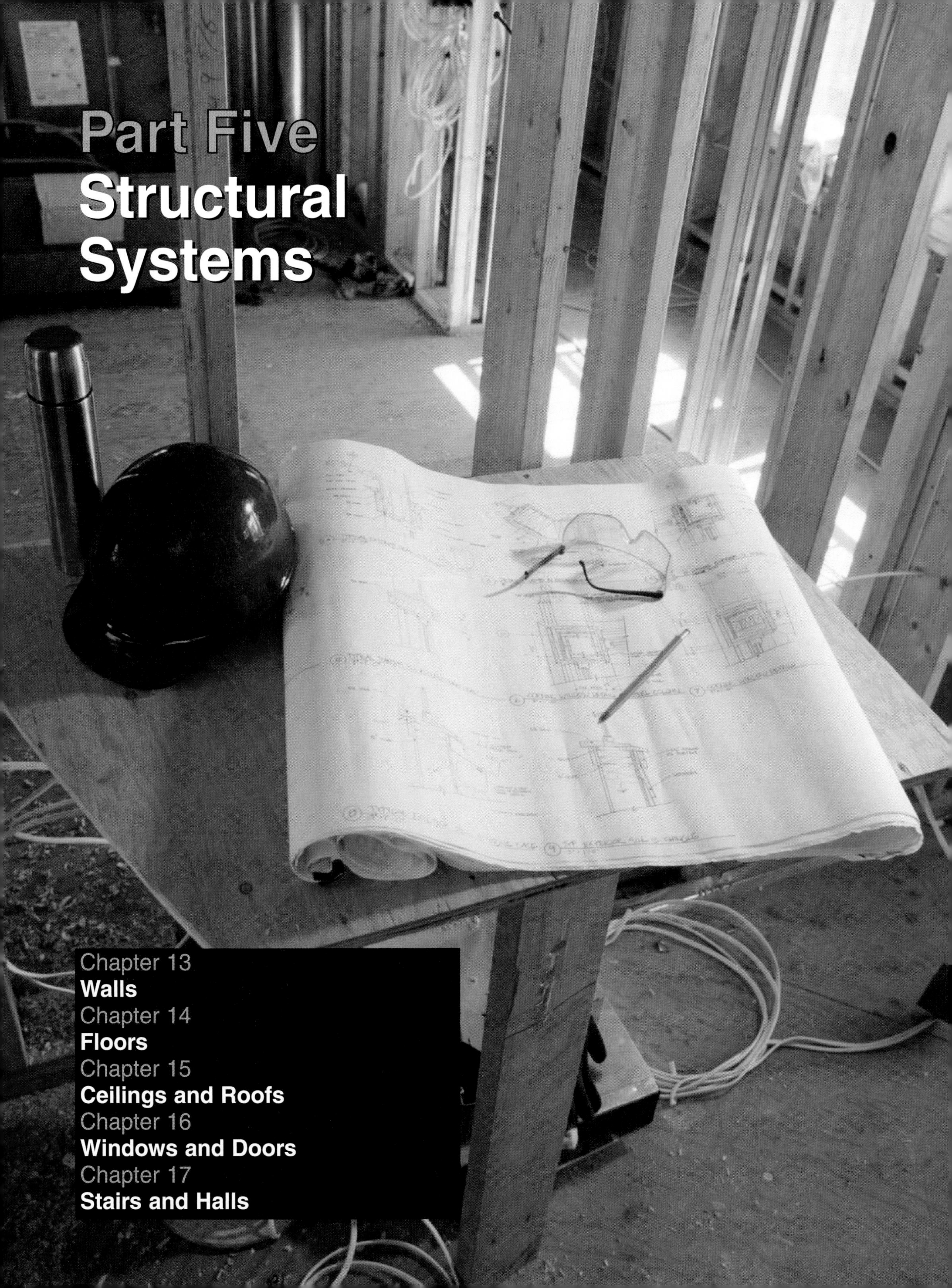

Chapter 13
Walls

Objectives

After studying this chapter, you will be able to

- describe the basic construction techniques used in building frame, masonry veneer, and masonry walls.
- evaluate the appropriateness of an exterior wall in relationship to its style, maintenance requirements, and ability to withstand weather conditions.
- list and describe various types of wall treatments.
- choose a wall treatment that is appropriate for both the function and design of a setting.

Key Terms

bearing wall	footing
nonbearing wall	pilasters
gypsum wallboard	stucco
drywall	latex
lintel	alkyd
veneer wall	cove molding
wood foundation	wainscot
header course	active wall
furring strip	passive wall
foundation wall	

Walls are one of three basic elements of any room—floors, ceilings, and walls. They serve both aesthetic and practical functions. They define space, assure privacy, provide protection, and form a barrier to the weather. The wall area of a home is so large that it plays an important role in determining the character of a home or room. Floors and ceilings are discussed in Chapters 14 and 15.

This chapter examines the types of walls found in housing structures and provides a basic understanding of their construction. The properties of several types of wall treatments are discussed, and guidelines for choosing a wall treatment are provided.

Wall Types

The main types of walls used in residential housing construction are frame walls and masonry walls. They each have characteristics that present advantages and disadvantages.

Walls may be described as bearing or nonbearing. A **bearing wall** supports some weight from the ceiling or roof of a structure. A **nonbearing wall** does not support any weight from the structure beyond its own weight.

Frame Walls

Frame walls may be used as interior or exterior walls, depending on the type of material that is used to cover them. Interior frame walls are called partitions to distinguish them from exterior walls. Exterior frame walls are usually bearing walls. While some main partitions also are bearing walls, most interior walls are nonbearing.

Frame wall construction consists of regularly spaced wood or metal studs attached to a sole plate at the bottom and a double plate at the top, 13-1. Most studs are 2 by 4 in. wood boards, but steel studs are also available, 13-2.

A typical frame wall is 8 ft. high from finished floor to finished ceiling, with studs placed 12, 16, or 24 in. apart. The 16 in. spacing is most common.

Frame walls are made from kiln-dried lumber with moisture content of 15 to 19 percent. The moisture

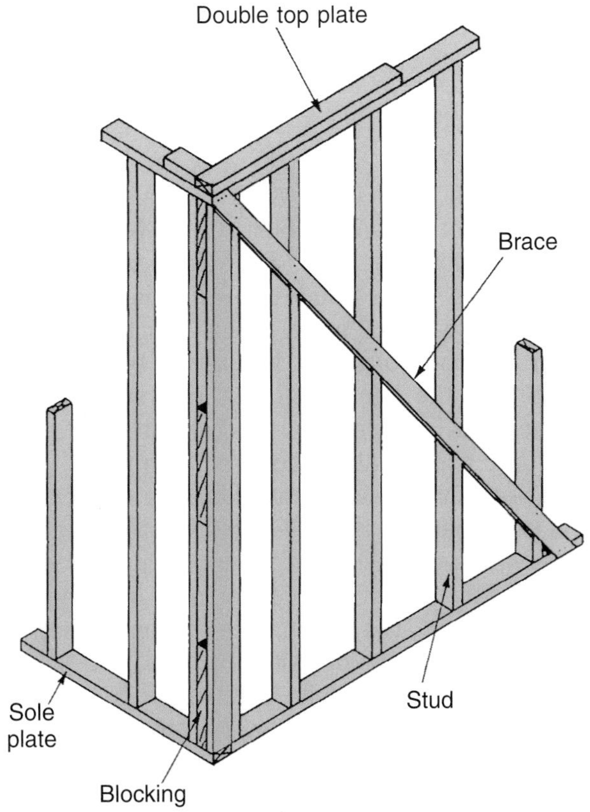

13-1 A frame wall consists of evenly spaced studs attached to a sole plate at the bottom and a plate at the top. Braces help make the wall more secure.

13-2 Steel studs are used to frame the exterior wall in this large, modern structure.

content should correspond to the atmospheric moisture level at the structure's location to reduce the chances of shrinking and warping. Construction grade lumber of Douglas fir, southern yellow pine, hemlock, spruce, and larch is generally used. The steel component, known as the structural C, is the predominant shape used for wall studs. Gauges from 12 to 22 are available.

A frame partition is composed of studs covered by some type of sheet product. The most frequently used material is **gypsum wallboard**, a sheet material used to cover wall studs made of a gypsum core covered with heavy paper surfaces. It is more commonly called **drywall**. The wallboard is available in 4 by 7 ft. to 4 by 14 ft. sheets. Thicknesses available include ¼, ⅜, ½, and ⅝ in. When a single thickness of drywall is used on a wall, ½ in. board is usually applied. A typical interior frame wall with drywall is 4½ in. thick—the thickness of the stud plus two thicknesses of ½ in. drywall. See 13-3.

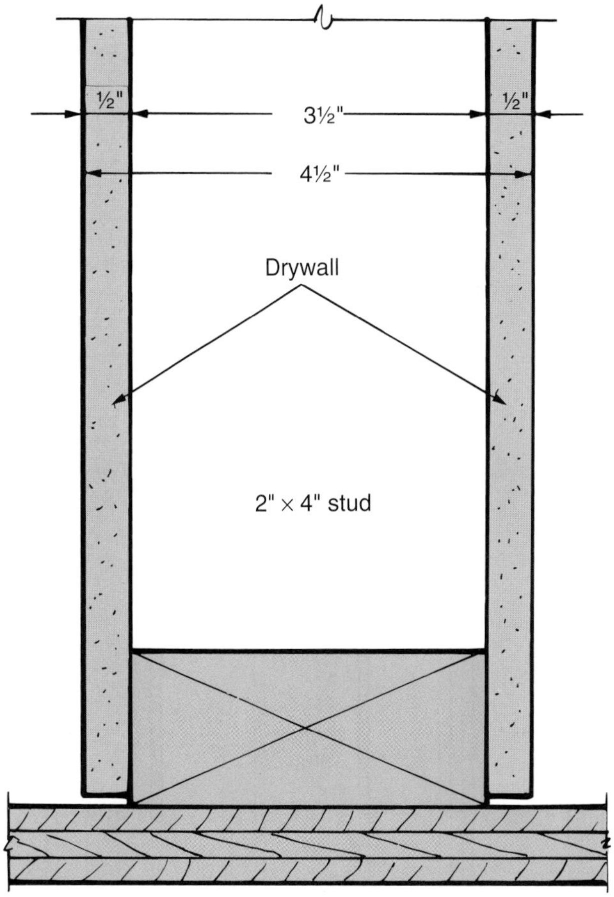

13-3 An interior frame wall covered with drywall is 4½ in. thick.

Openings in frame walls for windows and doors require special construction. An example of how openings are framed to provide extra strength is shown in 13-4. Each opening has a heavier member, called a **lintel**, over the opening to support the weight above. Construction is similar for interior and exterior openings.

Exterior frame walls are composed of the same type of studs as partitions. They are covered with drywall or paneling, but several other materials are also applied. Generally, 3½ in. of insulation is placed between the studs to reduce heat loss during cold weather and heat gain during warm weather. The outside face of the wall has a protective layer, or *sheathing*, nailed to the studs to help weatherproof the wall. However, in warmer climates or summer homes, sheathing is sometimes eliminated. Typical sheathing materials are: ½ in. plywood, ½ in. weatherboard, or ¾ in. rigid foam insulation. A layer of building felt is placed over the sheathing; then siding is applied.

Several types of exterior siding are available; they are discussed under "Wall Treatments" in this chapter. The thickness of siding seldom exceeds 1 in. The thickness of an exterior frame wall with rigid foam sheathing and 5/8 in. siding averages 5 3/8 in. See 13-5. The nominal size frequently used on construction drawings is 6 in.

Veneer Walls

Brick or other masonry may be used as a covering for a frame wall. When masonry is used in this way, a **veneer wall** is built, 13-6. Masonry on a veneer wall does not provide structural support. The veneer is tied to the frame wall with metal ties that are spaced so each 2 sq. ft. area of wall has one tie.

An air space of about 1 in. is left between the sheathing of the frame wall and the masonry. This air space provides insulation and allows moisture to collect and escape at the bottom of the wall.

Veneer units are generally about 4 in. thick, but stone is frequently 6 in. thick. The thickness of a brick veneer wall averages about 9¾ in. (½ in. of drywall, 3½ in. of stud, ¾ in. of rigid foam, 1 in. of air space, and 4 in. of brick). The nominal size generally used on a drawing for this type of wall is 10 in.

Masonry veneer walls are very popular and appear to be more expensive than they are. They provide the advantages of a solid masonry wall with few disadvantages. For example, the installation of

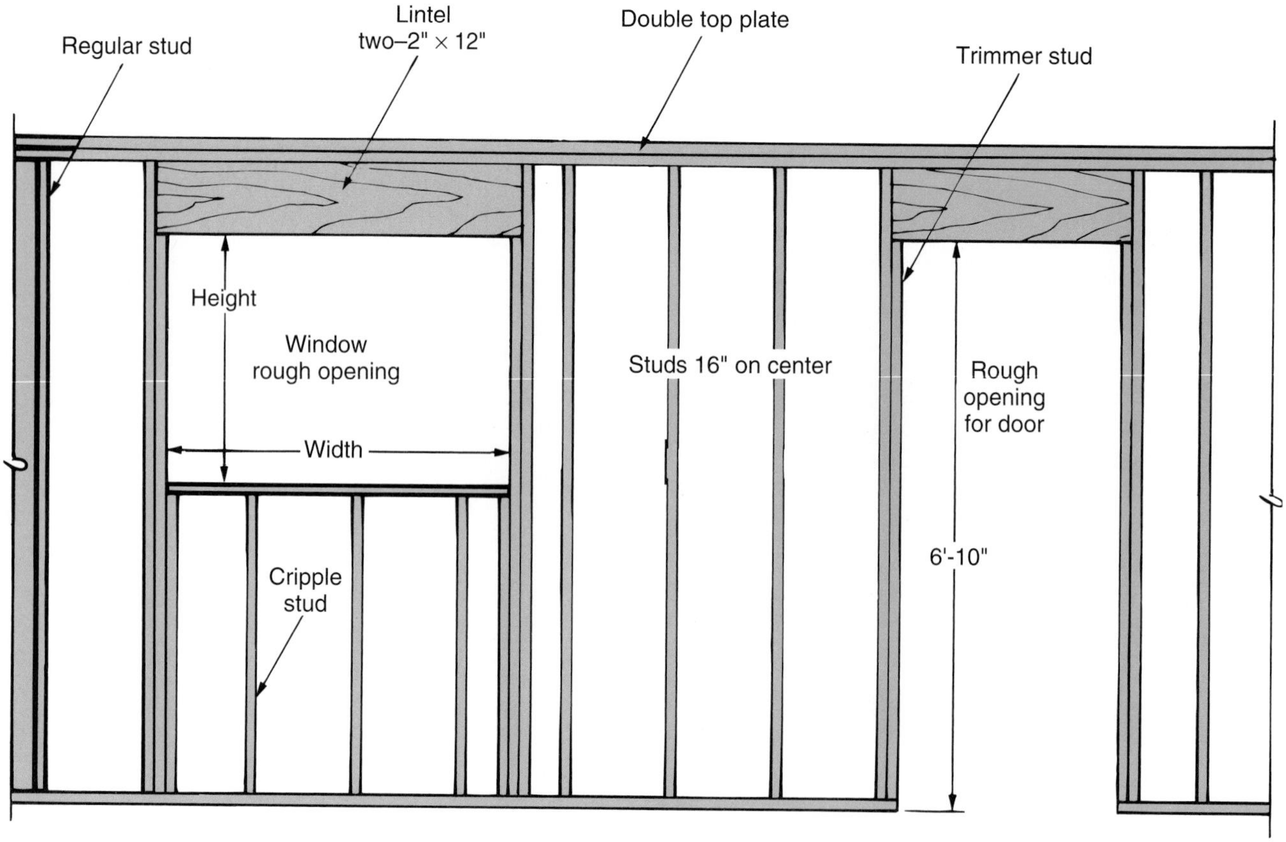

13-4 A lintel is required to support the weight above a window or door opening.

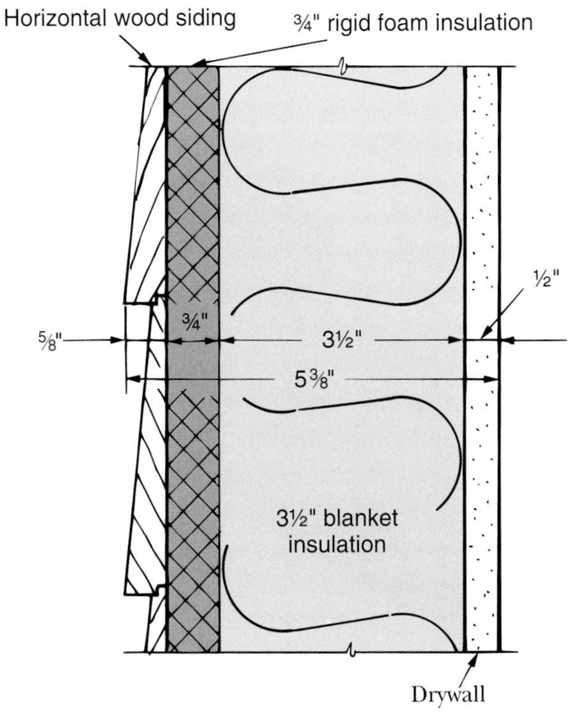

13-5 A 5⅜ in. thick exterior wall allows space for 3½ in. of blanket insulation and ¾ in. of rigid foam insulation. The blanket insulation usually has a vapor barrier on the inside surface to reduce moisture loss in the winter.

plumbing and electrical facilities is more difficult and costly in solid masonry than in masonry veneer.

Wood Foundations

Currently some basement walls are made of pressure treated lumber. This type of basement wall is called a **wood foundation**. Wood foundations are found most frequently in northern U.S. areas, where masonry building is halted during the winter months. Wood foundations are not yet approved by all local building codes.

Research has shown that lumber treated with preservatives can resist rot for many years. Therefore, pressure treated lumber should be quite serviceable as a foundation material. Wood foundations are much less expensive than traditional concrete foundations.

Masonry Walls

A true masonry wall is constructed entirely of brick, concrete block, stone, clay tile, or a combination of these materials. With the exception of basement walls, few exterior walls are constructed only of masonry materials. Most brick structures are made of

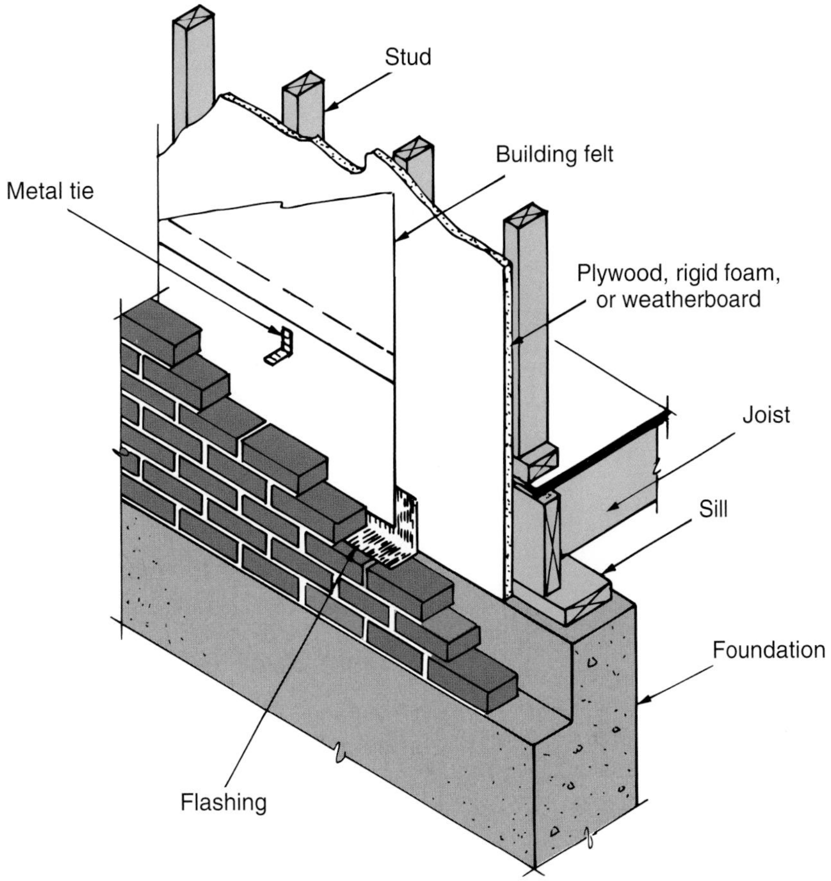

13-6 A brick veneer is attached to a frame wall using metal ties every 2 sq. ft.

veneer walls. Concrete block, however, is used as an exterior masonry wall in many sections of the country. A typical concrete block wall is shown in 13-7.

Masonry walls for residential construction are generally about 8 in. thick. Using two thicknesses of regular brick or one thickness of 8 in. wide concrete block can make a proper wall. Walls that require more than one thickness of masonry must be bonded together. They may be bonded by using corrugated metal ties placed between the mortar joints or by using a header course every 16 in. vertically. A **header course** is a row of bricks or blocks that are placed across two rows to hold them together. See 13-8.

If the interior of a masonry wall is to be covered, furring strips are required on the inside of the wall, 13-9. A **furring strip** is a strip of wood about the width of a stud used on concrete walls as a base for the attachment of another wall surface such as drywall or paneling. Insulation is frequently placed between the furring strips, and the covering is attached to the strips. If furring strips and a wall

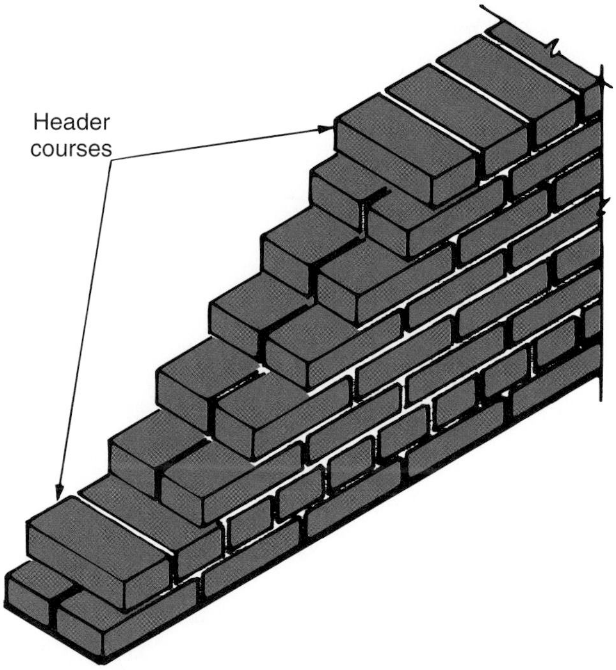

13-8 A header is a brick that is laid across a row. A course is a row of bricks. Placing a header course every sixth course will sufficiently bond an 8 in. thick wall.

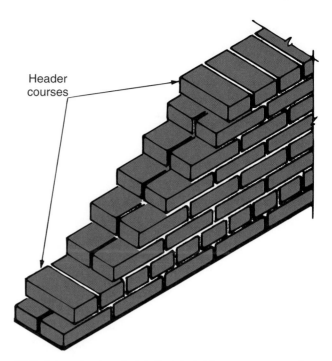

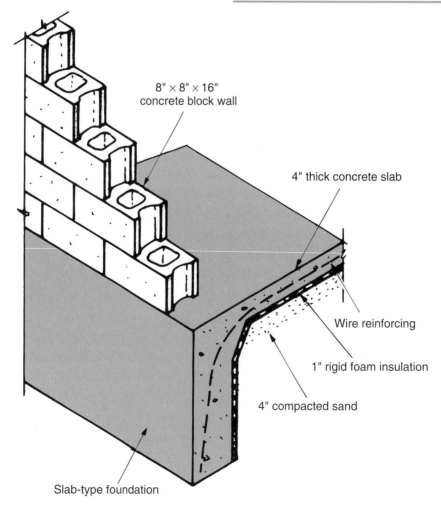

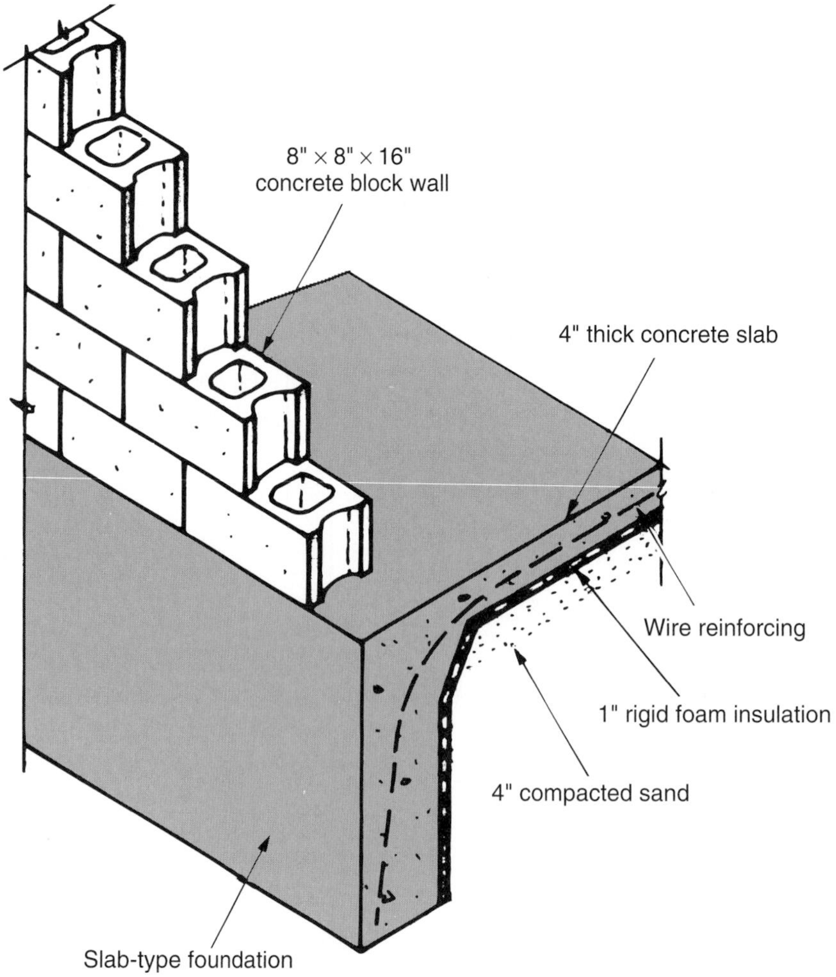

13-7 A slab-type foundation with concrete block walls is common for ranch-style homes with no basement.

Certain Teed Corporation

13-9 Furring strips must be attached to a masonry wall if paneling or drywall is installed. Insulation with a vapor barrier may be stapled to the furring strips before the surface material is installed.

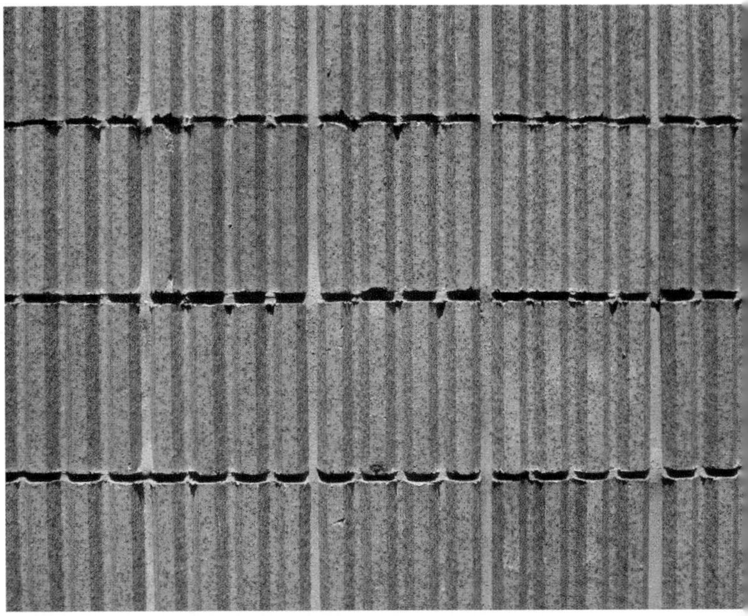

13-10 Fluted concrete blocks produce a highly textured wall with strong, vertical lines.

covering are not used, a masonry wall feels cold and damp. Many interesting colors, textures, and designs are possible with masonry materials, 13-10. These materials may be used for exterior or interior walls, but adequate foundation support must be provided because these materials are very heavy.

Concrete walls are used mainly for foundation walls, but they may be used for exterior walls above grade. A **foundation wall** is normally the part of the dwelling that extends from the first floor to the footing base, 13-11. A **footing** is a wide projection at the base of the foundation wall. It distributes the load of the wall's weight to a wider area.

Foundation walls are generally made from concrete cast in forms or from concrete blocks laid to form the wall. The thickness of a foundation wall is dependent on the following factors:

- type of structure to be built
- height of the wall
- ground pressures exerted against the wall

In general, however, a 10 in. thick foundation is used under a frame or concrete block structure. For a structure of brick veneer on a frame, a 12 in. thick foundation is commonly used. An 8 in. thick concrete block wall is acceptable for a one-story structure with a crawl space underneath it.

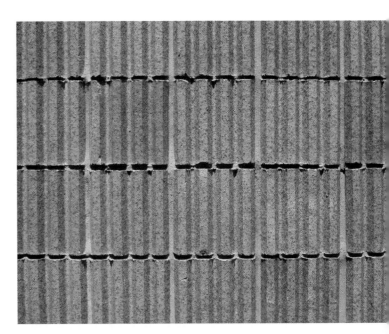

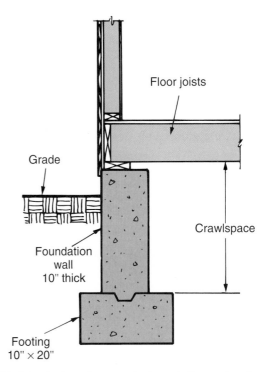

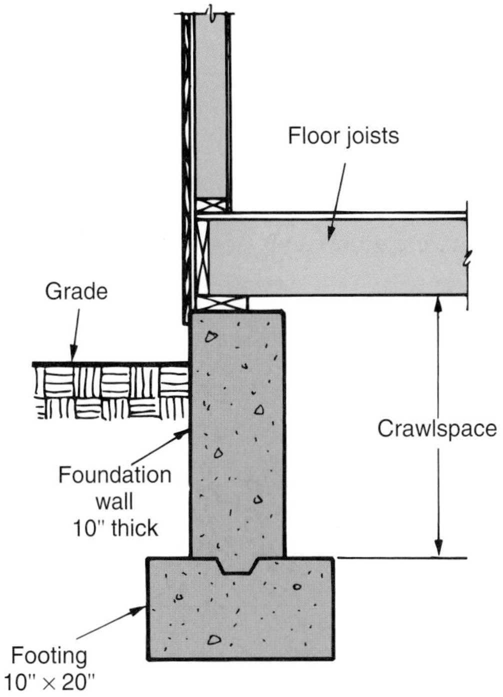

13-11 A typical cast concrete foundation extends from the underside of the floor joist to the concrete footing. If a crawlspace is under the structure rather than a basement, its minimum height is 18 in.

If a wall is unusually long or high, or if it will be expected to resist strong earth pressure, reinforcing steel is added to strengthen the wall. The same effect can be accomplished by making the wall thicker or by adding several pilasters along the wall. **Pilasters** are thickened sections built into the wall from the footing to the top of the wall. See 13-12.

Basement walls should be damp-proofed on the outside to prevent groundwater from seeping through the wall. Poured concrete walls are generally painted with a heavy coat of hot tar, two coats of cement-based paints, or a commercially prepared coating especially designed for that purpose. Concrete block walls frequently have a thick coat of cement mortar applied before coating them with one of the materials listed above. This is called *parging*.

These techniques are very helpful in reducing moisture, but good drainage at the base of the wall is essential. A drain tile surrounded by a bed of gravel is the typical method of providing drainage, 13-13.

Wall Treatments

Many types of wall treatments are available. Those used primarily for exterior surfaces include wood siding and manufactured siding of aluminum, vinyl, and fiberglass. Wall treatments used for either the interior or exterior include wood shingles, decorative masonry, stucco, plaster, and paint. Treatments used primarily for interior wall surfaces include wallpaper, fabric, paneling, tile, and mirrors.

Wood Siding

Wood siding is the most common exterior wall treatment. Horizontal wood siding consists of boards that overlap. Generally, boards are *beveled*, or narrower on one edge than the other. Beveled siding is usually 3/16 in. thick on one edge and 1/2 to 3/4 in. thick on the other. Beveling reduces the apparent thickness of an exterior wall.

Horizontal wood siding is considered attractive; many homeowners prefer the look of horizontal lines on their home, 13-14. It is relatively inexpensive, but requires much maintenance and upkeep compared to other exterior wall coverings. Wood is subject to rotting and shows wear from outdoor exposure more easily than other substances. It must be repainted or have some other protective finish applied every few years to shield it from weathering.

Other types of wood siding include vertical siding and plywood siding. Usually, these are not painted, but are treated with a protective finish. They may be stained for a rustic appearance. These types of wood siding are usually more expensive than standard wood siding, but require less maintenance.

Vertical siding may be used to set off entrances, but is also used as a main wall covering. It may be placed at an angle for added interest. To achieve the look of vertical siding, exterior plywood may be

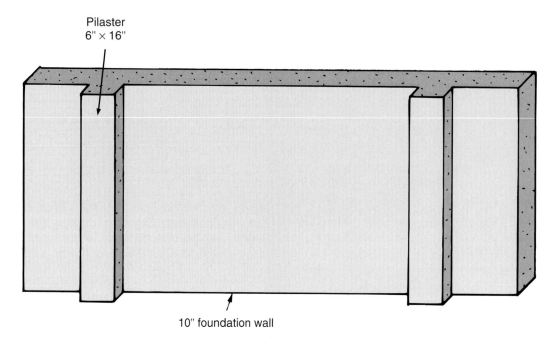

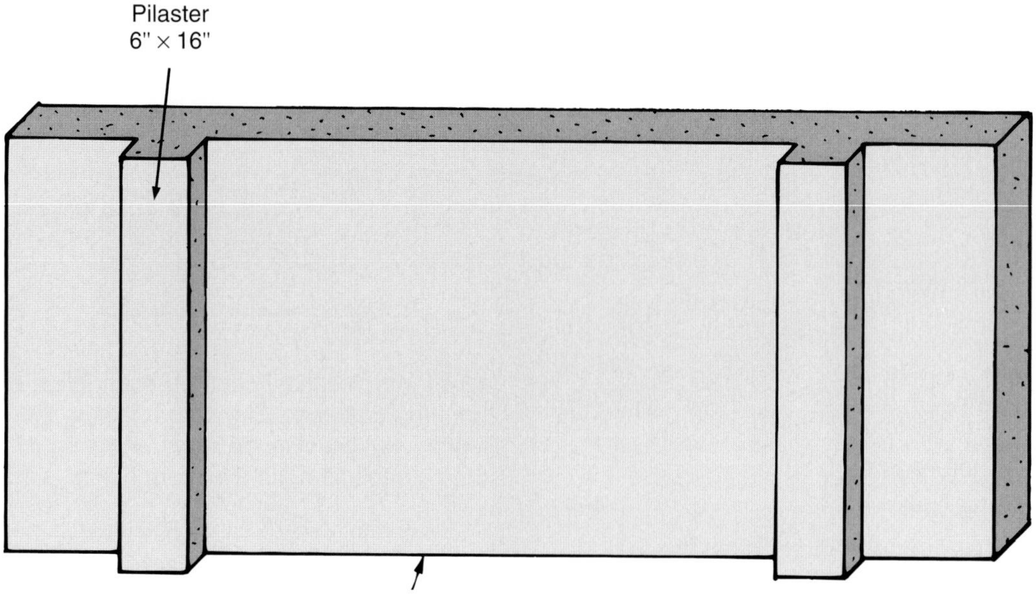

13-12 A long basement wall is strengthened to resist earth pressure by placing pilasters about every 12 ft.

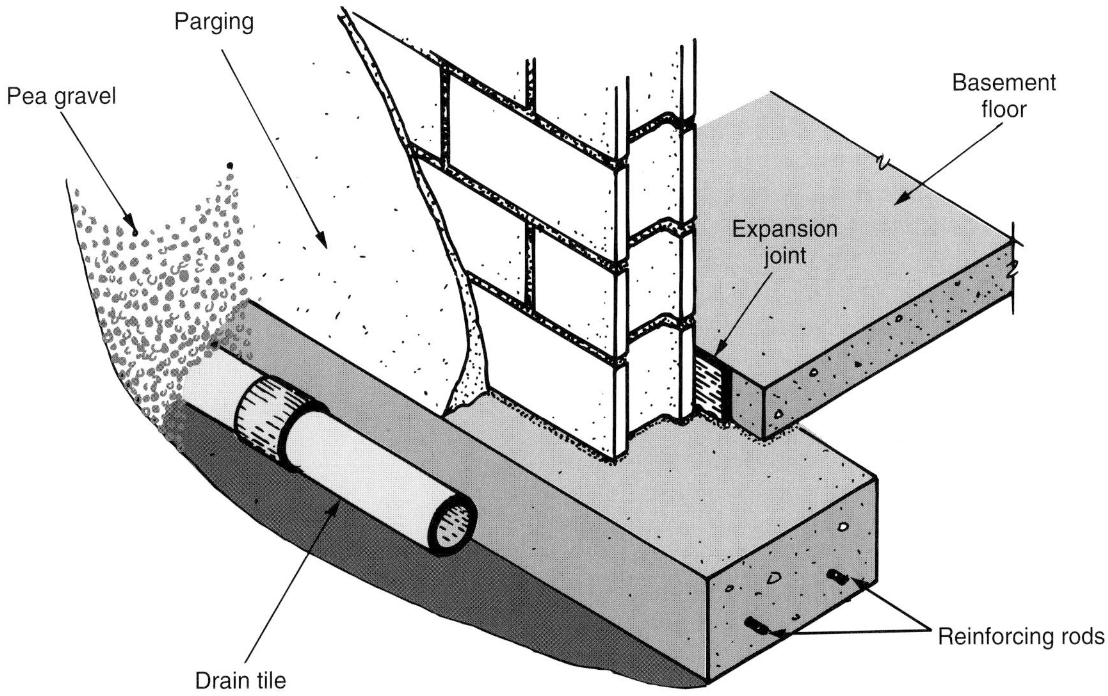

13-13 Drain tile should be placed as low as possible to remove groundwater around a basement wall.

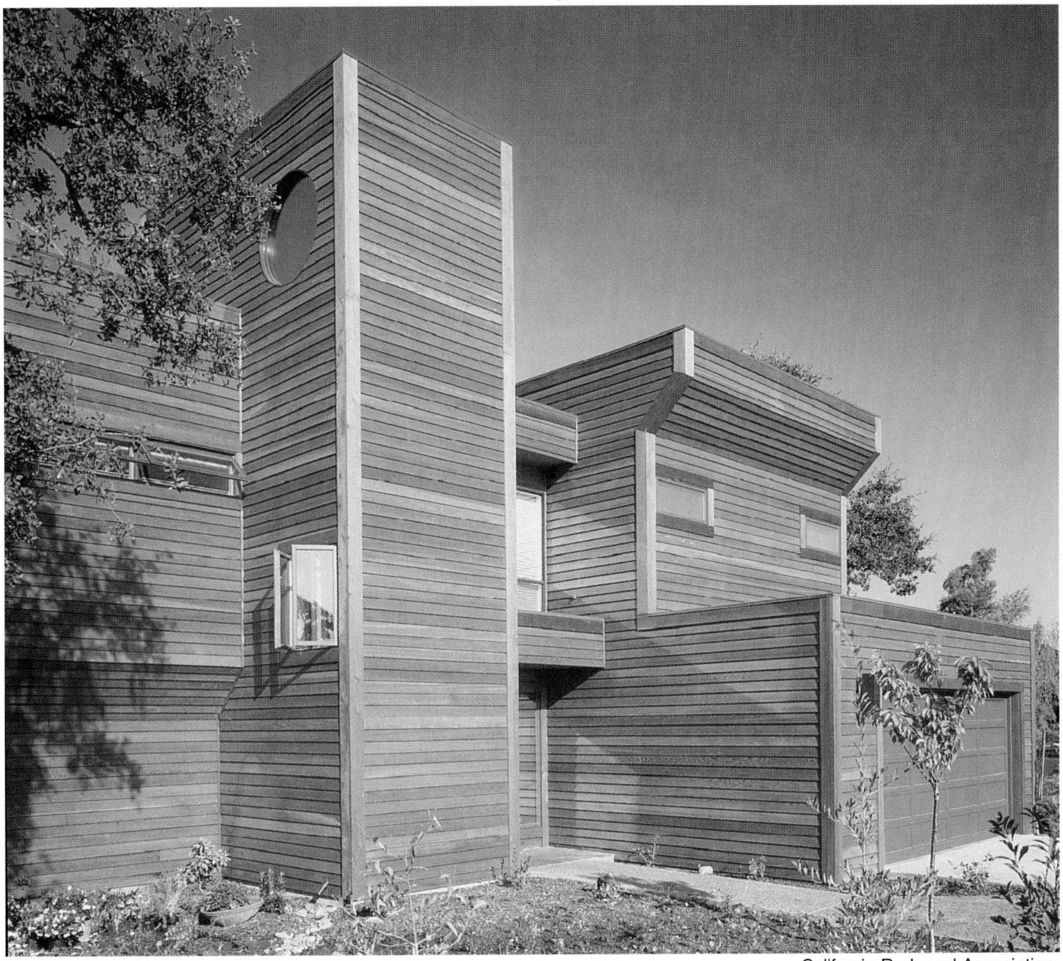

California Redwood Association

13-14 The horizontal siding on this modern home provides a dramatic effect.

used. It can be applied more quickly and easily because of its large panels.

Manufactured Siding

Manufactured materials such as aluminum, vinyl, and fiberglass are being used as alternatives to wood siding in some areas, especially those with cold, harsh climates. See 13-15. These materials imitate the look of wood, but offer low maintenance and high durability. Many also provide higher insulative value than wood.

Aluminum Siding

Aluminum siding is a popular product, mainly because of its low maintenance cost. Aluminum siding has a baked-on enamel finish and resembles painted wood siding. It can be used on new construction or over any existing exterior finish that is structurally sound.

A variety of horizontal and vertical panel styles in both smooth and textured designs are available. An insulated panel is also produced with a fiberboard material laminated to the back surface. Panels are fabricated with prepunched nail and vent holes and special interlocking design. Standard strips are easily attached around windows and doors to provide a weatherproof seal. Special corners and pieces of trim are often formed on the job site.

Aluminum siding should be grounded as a precaution against faulty electrical wiring. Recommended procedures for this operation are available from the Aluminum Siding Association.

Vinyl Siding

Vinyl siding is similar to aluminum siding in appearance, but it is less likely to dent and does not conduct electricity. Vinyl siding is made from a rigid polyvinyl chloride that is tough and durable. This material, commonly called vinyl, is extruded into horizontal or vertical siding units.

Vinyl siding is usually installed with backer board or insulation board behind each sheet. This backer adds rigidity and strength as well as insulation. Panels are designed with interlocking joints that are moisture proof. Since the siding must be allowed to expand and contract slightly with temperature changes, the nail holes are slotted to provide movement.

Fiberglass Siding

Fiberglass is used to make products that resemble natural wood shingles. They are long lasting and do not require painting or treating.

13-15 This vinyl siding looks like traditional wood siding, but it lasts longer, requires less maintenance, and provides more insulative value.

Mineral Fiber Shingles

Mineral fiber shingles are made from asbestos and concrete. Because of the concern over asbestos-containing products, these shingles are no longer available. Some older homes may still have mineral fiber shingles, but painting will help to seal exposed asbestos fibers. A professional who knows how to properly work with asbestos products should do any major repair work.

Wood Shingles

Wood shingles are made in a variety of styles. The most popular type of wood used is cedar. Shingles are nailed on individually or applied in remanufactured panels.

Red cedar shingles have long been a trusted exterior material. They last for over 50 years as a roofing material and indefinitely as an exterior siding. Shingles of red cedar also help to create superior interiors because of cedar's blend of beauty and character. They are rustic and casual. The dimensional structure of wood shingles adds depth to an otherwise flat wall. In addition to being beautiful, cedar shingles are practical, requiring little maintenance, 13-16.

Cedar shingles can be allowed to mellow naturally with age, or they can be painted or stained any color. A semitransparent stain will allow the wood's natural grain to show. Other finishes that can be used include: linseed oil, lacquer, varnish, stain, wax, and paint.

A very rustic appearance is possible using hand-split shakes. The texture of shakes is exceptional, but they are more costly and more difficult to install than shingles. Their rough texture lends itself best to larger areas.

Decorative Masonry

Most decorative masonry wall treatments generally must be chosen before the wall is completed, but some treatments are possible using very thin veneers for existing walls, 13-17. Projecting and recessing masonry units or using blocks with sculptured faces can accomplish wall texture with depth. See 13-18.

A wall may be formed by omitting some units. Form can also be achieved by using perforated units to construct a grill or screen over an existing wall or to build a wall by itself. The units may be typical brick or special block or tile designed for this purpose.

Pattern bonds are used to develop a series of interesting designs. These patterns may be used on exterior as well as interior walls or floors.

Mortar joints between masonry units may be used to add another dimension to a masonry wall. Joints may be tooled into different shapes, or they may be colored to complement the design scheme or accent the masonry units.

Stucco or Plaster

The term **stucco** has traditionally meant exterior plastering, but today it may refer to the final finished coat of the plastering process on an interior or exterior surface. Interior plaster generally uses a gypsum material, while exterior stucco is formed

13-16 Red cedar shingles add texture and interest to this exterior. Shingles may be used for interior walls.

13-17 Very thin brick veneer decorates this interior wall to give the appearance of solid brick.

13-18 These split-fluted concrete blocks create strong texture and visual interest.

13-19 This is a close-up view of a typical stucco pattern.

with a Portland cement material. Different materials are used because exterior stucco must be more durable to withstand outdoor weather conditions.

Stucco can be applied directly to concrete and masonry surfaces. It can also be applied to wood and metal framing that has been covered with a fine wire mesh or another material providing a good bond. It is fairly inexpensive, but has a tendency to crack and chip, especially when used for an exterior treatment. Stucco exteriors are most popular in dry, hot climates, such as southwestern U.S. areas. Stucco is also used to create a Mediterranean or Spanish style appearance for a house or room.

As a wall treatment, stucco refers to the finish coat that provides the texture and character of the wall, 13-19. The finish coat may be up to ¼ in. thick and applied in many designs. Following are some of the typical stucco textures that a plasterer can achieve:

- *Float finish*–forms surface with a piece of carpet or a rubber-faced float.
- *Wet dash finish*–applies coarse aggregate mix with a brush.
- *Dash-troweled finish*–smoothes the high spots of a dashed surface with a trowel.
- *Stipple-troweled finish*–flecks the surface with quick jabs of a broom and trowels high spots smooth.
- *Pebble-dash finish*–throws small, decorative stones against the wet surface to create an exposed aggregate finish.
- *Combed finish*–forms the surface with a notched template.
- *Smooth-troweled finish*–makes the surface very flat.
- *Sand finish*–creates the surface with a wooden float.
- *Acoustical finish*–machine sprays a very textured surface.
- *Swirl finish*–produces swirls with a brush, trowel, or other object.

The range of textures available with stucco is almost limitless, and a style compatible with almost any design scheme is possible. Color may be added to the stucco material itself, or the surface can be painted. Highly textured stucco on interior walls is gaining popularity.

Paint

Paint is the most popular wall treatment because it is inexpensive, quick to use, easy to apply, and available in a wide variety of colors, 13-20. Also, it can be easily changed later. Paint is easily coordinated

Gail Prauss, ASID, Illinois Chapter

13-20 Using a paint color not usually associated with a bedroom creates a unique, exciting look.

with the colors in furniture or accessories. Matching these colors is a fairly easy and relatively precise process.

Paints are categorized as **latex**, which is water based, or **alkyd**, which is oil based. Each is preferred for different kinds of applications, and each is produced in matte, gloss, and textured finishes. They are designed for exterior or interior use.

Exterior paints are usually called house paint. Oil-based paint is the most common type of house paint, but water-based paints are available as well. House paints are usually self-cleaning. This means the paint will develop a chalky surface at a controlled rate. This chalky surface will wash away with surface dirt when it rains, leaving the paint clean and fresh looking. Because of this chalking quality, house paint is not recommended for stairway rails or other surfaces that are touched frequently, since the chalk will rub onto other surfaces that come in contact with it.

Primer should be used before paint is applied to any new surface, interior or exterior, but it is especially important for exterior surfaces. Primer prepares a surface for paint and helps it to remain durable and retain its color.

Water-based paints are easy to apply with a roller and dry quickly. Uneven painting is less noticeable with water-based paint than with oil-based paint, and painting equipment is easily cleaned with water. One disadvantage, however, is that hiding power is less than that of an oil-based paint.

Oil-based paints stand up to heavy scrubbing and are logical choices for bathrooms and kitchens. These paints require a solvent thinner and take longer to dry. Also, they usually give off more fumes than water-based paints. Equipment used for painting is more difficult to clean.

High-gloss, semigloss, and flat finishes are choices for aesthetics as well as practicality. High-gloss enamels are attractive on woodwork because of the high reflectance, durability, and ease in cleaning, 13-21. They are also used on decorative walls where a lacquered look is desired. Semigloss finishes also resist stains and are easily cleaned. They can be used on walls or woodwork.

Flat finishes are porous and do not resist stains very well. They are very popular, however, as a wall paint because of their soft appearance. Flat paints are not recommended for woodwork.

Texture paints add another dimension in addition to color. They may be applied with a brush, roller, sponge, broom, or sprayer. This type of paint is very useful for hiding imperfections in a wall's surface. However, once a textured paint is applied, it is difficult to change or repaint the surface.

Wallpaper

Originally, wallpaper was used by the poor to copy the expensive textiles used by the rich, but

13-21 Three different types of paint are used in this room. Flat white is used on the walls, semigloss on the door, and enamel on the trim.

today it is used at all income levels to decorate walls. Wallpaper is economically practical and can be used in any room. It completely covers old wall treatments.

Many colors, patterns, and textures can be produced on wallpaper, 13-22. Wallpaper may even imitate other materials. Test samples are available to help you choose appropriate patterns for a room. Patterns should coordinate with the color and design of furnishings and accessories in a room. See 13-23. Many types of wallpapers have prepasted or self-adhesive backs and can be applied without the help of a professional.

When selecting wallpaper, be sure to consider the conditions it must endure in a proposed location. For example, flocked paper is not a good choice where grease or dust is present. A washable paper is better for these locations.

Wallpaper is ideal for disguising odd-shaped architectural details. A busy, random pattern is best for this purpose because it will blend the lines of a room together with the pattern.

Wallpaper has many advantages as a wall covering material. It:

- is available in a wide price range.
- can make a room appear formal or informal, larger or smaller, and quiet or vibrant.
- can be used as a foundation for period furnishings.
- is a quick, easy way to remodel or change a room's decor.
- provides continuity to a basic design theme.
- can be used to establish the scale of an interior space.

13-22 Stock wallpaper is available to coordinate with almost any color or design scheme.

Lis King

13-23 The two wallpaper patterns in this room coordinate with each other and blend well with the floral pattern of the couch. Use of the two patterns also helps make this alcove seem separate and more private.

Fabric

Fabrics provide unique texture to a wall and offer a wide range of colors and patterns. They may be attached to the wall with glue, tacks, or double-faced carpet tape, 13-24. Fabrics may also be fastened to a frame and mounted to the wall.

The best types of fabric for wall covering are thick enough to prevent glue from showing through. They should be resistant to staining, fading, mildew, and shrinking. Fabrics such as grass cloth and burlap are popular.

Coco Lee, ASID, & Greg Geidel, ASID, Illinois Chapter

13-24 Walls of velvet complement the black desk, red draperies, and stylish accessories in this elegant study.

Carpeting is sometimes used as a wall covering. It provides great texture and continuity between the wall and the floor. Carpeting on the wall also is functional as sound insulation.

Paneling and Boards

Wood paneling and boards are available in a wide range of colors, grains, and species. Few materials rival the beauty of wood. Whether it is used in the form of panels or narrower pieces called boards, wood has a character all its own. It is most frequently chosen for its aesthetic qualities, but paneling is also a practical wall treatment.

New processes make modern paneling very wear resistant, easy to clean, and colorful. Many types of plywood paneling designed for exterior applications are also effective when used as an interior wall treatment. Rough-sawn and brush-textured panels are popular. When finished with a transparent, colored stain, they produce a warm, inviting atmosphere.

Paneling or boards are practical for many reasons. For example, insulation is easily added to a wall that will be paneled. Furring strips can be nailed to the existing wall, and insulation can be placed between the strips. Paneling over insulation will produce a new wall and reduce noise and heat transfer.

Paneling is also practical for repairing a damaged wall or for building a new partition. Paneling is economical and can be installed by the homeowner with a few tools and moderate skill.

Paneling and boards are durable and require little maintenance. These qualities make paneling popular for family rooms, game rooms, and kitchens.

Several types of siding boards may be used on interior walls. They are installed vertically, at an angle, or horizontally, 13-25. Types of boards include beveled, channel, shiplapped, and tongue and grooved.

California Redwood Association

13-25 Clear grade redwood boards were used for this dramatic effect. A clear, protective finish was applied to emphasize the natural beauty of the wood.

Another type of paneling that is gaining greater acceptance is hardboard. Hardboard is a pressed fiber product manufactured in a broad range of face patterns and textures. Many types can be used in any room, including the bathroom or other high-moisture areas.

Plastic-laminate paneling is surfaced with a material similar to that used on countertops. It is especially practical in areas of constant use, such as kitchens and bathrooms. It is also available in simulated wood and in various patterns and colors. Plastic laminate paneling is very durable.

Ceramic Tile

Ceramic tile is used as an attractive, durable, and easily cleaned wall covering. It has wide appeal for bathrooms, kitchens, and other high-use areas. In recent years, the variety and beauty of these tiles brought them into all areas of the home. Their many colors and shapes are usable with a variety of design styles.

Glazed tile is the most practical type of tile for walls in kitchens and bathrooms, 13-26. It has a smooth, hard surface that is easily cleaned. Unglazed tile is porous and does not resist stains, but it provides a cool, earthy look suitable for some room decors. Ceramic tile is relatively expensive, but it is very long lasting and requires little maintenance.

Mirrors

Mirrors are often used to cover one wall in a room for accent and can make a small room appear large. A series of 12 in. squares or larger mirrors can be combined to cover a wall, or special-order mirrors can be purchased in wall-size dimensions. Distortion-free glass should be used for large mirrors.

Mirrors are expensive, but they produce a dramatic effect and are easy to maintain, 13-27. Several styles are available, including clear, smoked, and patterned.

Mirrored walls can be attractive, but they are not always appropriate, especially if the view reflected is undesirable. Mirrors should never be placed on a wall that is not truly vertical because the image reflected will be distorted. Placing strips of mirrors at eye level often is sufficient to produce the effect of making a room seem more spacious.

Selection of Wall Treatments

Walls account for more space than any other single element in a home. The selection of treatments for these walls deserves special consideration. The type of treatment used should vary according to the function and design of a home.

Function

Each type of wall treatment has qualities that may enhance or detract from a room's function. The formality level, amount of visual interest, texture, and light-absorbency level of a wall treatment are qualities that should coordinate with the function of a room.

The formality level of a room's wall coverings should fit the room's atmosphere and use. A formal living room or dining room requires formal walls. Formality is achieved through symmetrical balance and precise, stable forms. Wall treatments that set the stage for formal design include **cove molding**,

American Olean

13-26 Glazed ceramic tile is a practical wall covering for bathrooms because it is moisture resistant and easily cleaned.

Century Furniture Company

13-27 An attractive, well-placed mirror can complete the design of a space and become its focal point.

a continuous strip of decorative trim that usually borders a room, and wainscoting. A **wainscot** refers to the lower 3 or 4 ft. of a wall when it is finished differently from the rest of the wall, 13-28. Using texture or a symmetrical pattern can produce a formal appearance.

An informal wall might be used in a game room, a child's bedroom, or a casual living room. Random wallpaper patterns or graphic designs painted on the wall add to a less formal appearance.

The amount of a wall's visual interest is described by using the terms *active* and *passive.* A wall that suggests movement and attracts attention is an **active wall.** Attracting attention can be accomplished by the use of design, texture, or color. A brightly painted accent wall or a boldly patterned treatment produces an active wall, 13-29. A **passive wall** is used as a background element and does not attract attention. Off-white wall treatments and wallpaper with fine prints are passive.

Active versus passive wall treatments are more suitable for some rooms than others. For example, most people prefer bedrooms that look restful and quiet, and passive wall treatments can help accomplish this effect. Active walls are more suitable in a playroom.

Texture adds to functionality and helps to create an overall atmosphere for a room. Formal walls are more likely to be smooth while informal walls may be textured. A smooth, easily cleaned surface should be used in areas where dust or grease is stirred, such as a crafts room or kitchen. Textured

American Olean

13-28 Wainscoting plays a major role in creating a formal, stately decor in this entryway.

Linda Truckenmiller, ASID, Illinois Chapter

13-29 Staircases often are passive elements in a home, but this attractive, Mediterranean scene near the top of the stairs draws attention.

walls are more suitable for a music room because they absorb sound better.

Absorbent or reflective light qualities can add to or detract from the functionality of a room. Absorbent wall treatments that reduce the sun's glare should be selected for rooms that have a southern exposure or are mainly used in the daytime, 13-30. Reflective room treatments work better in artificially lighted rooms. A small room will seem larger if one wall is highly reflective.

Appearance

Using the principles of design helps create walls with a pleasing appearance. One important principle to consider is the scale of the wall. Color and patterns affect wall scale in the following ways:

- Large, bold patterns are overpowering on a small wall. If a room is very large, they will make the walls appear closer.

13-30 The flat white painted surface of these walls adds to the usefulness of this room during the day.

- Small-scale patterns in light colors make a wall appear larger.
- A tall wall appears lower if the color of the ceiling is extended to the molding on a wall. Vertical stripes will make a wall appear taller, an effect useful in rooms with low ceilings.
- Mirrors create an illusion of more space. Scenes in perspective lead the eye beyond the wall for the same affect, 13-31.

Anita Bayer, ASID, Illinois Chapter

13-31 The forest scene in this wall mural, complemented by tent-like window coverings, creates the illusion of space beyond the bedroom's walls.

The type of wall covering chosen should coordinate with the types of furnishings in a room. If furnishings are traditional, then wall coverings should reflect the style of that period. See 13-32.

Colors should coordinate with, but not overpower, furniture. Walls that exactly match the color or pattern of the furniture will make the furniture blend into the walls.

Choosing a dominant feature in a room will help determine what type of wall covering should be used, 13-33. If a room will contain several choice furniture pieces, then the walls should serve as a passive background. If the activity in the room is the focus instead of the furnishings, then a dominant wall treatment may be more effective.

An art wall or collection display can produce a dominant wall. Bright, abstract colors and shapes also form an accent.

13-32 Using wallpaper from the same period and style as the other pieces in the room helps to unify the room's overall design.

13-33 The use of a passive wallpaper design enhances the fireplace as a focal point.

Chapter Summary

The selection of wall treatments should receive special consideration because walls account for more space than any other single element in a home. The main types of walls used in residential housing construction are frame walls and masonry walls. Walls are also bearing or nonbearing.

Frame walls may be either interior or exterior walls, depending on the type of material used to cover them. Interior walls are called partitions. Frame-wall construction consists of regularly spaced studs that are attached to a bottom sole plate and a double top plate. Frame walls are made from kiln-dried lumber of Douglas fir, southern yellow pine, hemlock, spruce, and larch. Frame walls are also made from steel framing members. Openings in frame walls require special construction methods.

Exterior frame walls are covered with weather-resistant materials on the outside. Brick veneer is a typical covering used in the place of exterior siding. Foundation walls may be constructed from masonry, concrete, or pressure treated wood. Solid masonry walls must be furred on the inside to receive drywall, plaster, or paneling. Concrete or masonry foundation walls usually require a footing to spread the load over a wider area.

Several types of wall treatments are used for walls. Common exterior treatments include siding (wood, plastic, aluminum), shingles, decorative masonry, stucco, and paint. Common interior treatments include wallpaper, fabric, paneling, tile, painted drywall, and mirrors.

Factors to consider when selecting an interior wall treatment include the function of the room, the level of formality desired, and the appropriate amount of visual interest. The wall treatments and colors used greatly affect a room's scale and appearance.

Review Questions

1. When is a bearing wall used? a nonbearing wall?
2. How does the construction of an exterior frame wall differ from that of a partition?
3. What is the difference between a brick veneer wall and a masonry wall?
4. Which type of brick wall is most common today?
5. What is necessary for applying paneling or drywall to a masonry wall?
6. How is a basic concrete foundation constructed?
7. What techniques can be used to protect a foundation from water seepage?
8. How does manufactured siding differ from wood siding? To whom would you recommend each?
9. What types of wall treatments are available for adding texture to interior walls?
10. What are the two main categories of paint and the types of finishes in which they are available?
11. What does it mean when house paint is described as self-cleaning?
12. What are the advantages of wallpaper as a wall covering?
13. What four factors should be considered when determining whether a wall treatment is appropriate for a room?
14. What wall treatments can make a small room appear larger?

Suggested Activities

1. Visit a residence under construction to examine the exterior and interior walls. Make a sketch (section view) of each different wall, showing all of its components. Be sure to first gain permission to visit the construction site.
2. Write a short essay describing the components of an exterior veneer wall. Identify typical veneer materials used for this type of wall.
3. Explain the advantages and disadvantages of wood foundations versus traditional masonry or concrete foundations.
4. Collect samples of materials used for exterior walls including wood, vinyl, and aluminum siding. Display them to the class.
5. List interior wall finishes other than paint with a brief description of each. Explain how you might consider using each of them in your future home.
6. Prepare a chart listing the elements of design. For each, describe the related principles to remember when choosing interior wall treatments.

Internet Resources

American ConForm Industries, a producer of insulated, stay-in-place concrete forms
smartblock.com

Anchor Retaining Wall Systems
anchorwall.com

Boral Bricks Inc.
boralbricks.com

California Redwood Association
calredwood.org

Cultured Stone, a producer of manufactured stone veneers
culturedstone.com

Insulating Concrete Form Association
forms.org

Keystone Retaining Wall Systems
keystonewalls.com

Masonite International Corporation, a door manufacturer
masonite.com

Melton Classics, Inc., a producer of millwork
meltonclassics.com

National Precast Concrete Association
precast.org

Note: Web addresses may have changed since publication. For some entries, reaching the correct Web site may require keying *www.* into the address.

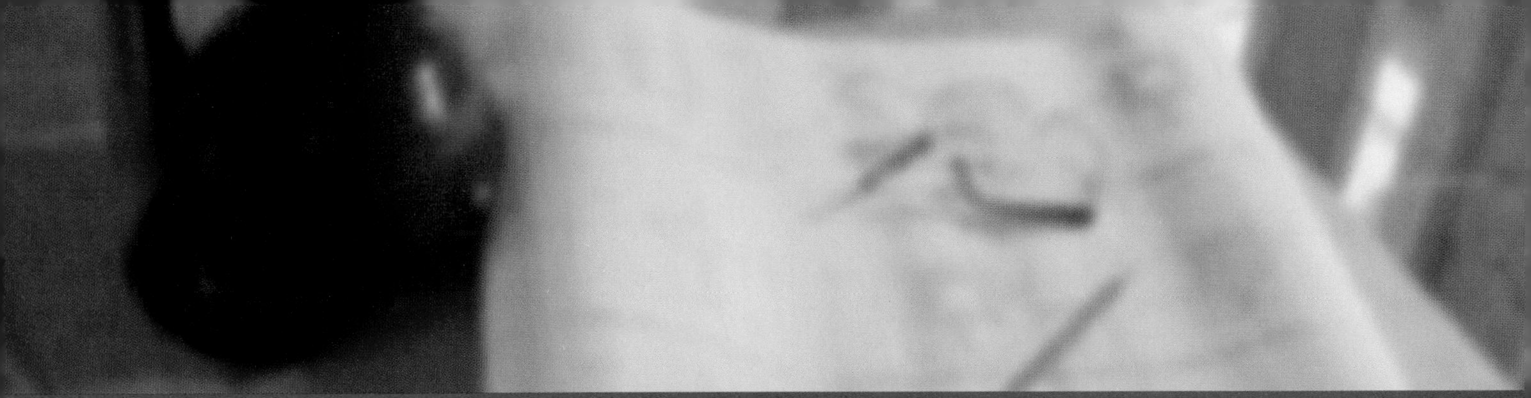

Chapter 14
Floors

Objectives

After studying this chapter, you will be able to

- differentiate the materials and construction methods used to make concrete floors and wood frame floors.
- describe the construction methods used in laying flooring materials and floor coverings.
- compare the appearance, texture, and maintenance requirements of various flooring materials and floor coverings.
- evaluate the appropriateness of a floor treatment for a room according to principles of function and design.

Key Terms

joist
truss
platform framing
balloon framing
live load
thickened edge-slab
floating slab
flooring materials
floor coverings
sleepers
mastic
floating floor
radiant floor
grout
terrazzo
resilient floor covering

Floors constitute an important element of every area of the home. They support a home's furnishings and occupants, provide decoration, and supply space for movement within the structure. The basic types of floor construction and typical floor treatments are discussed in this chapter.

Floor Systems

Floor systems for housing structures may be classified as wood floors or concrete floors. Most dwellings contain both. Methods of floor construction vary from one section of the country to another, but basic construction components are the same.

Wood Floor Construction

Wood floor systems are composed of several structural elements. These generally include support beams, joists or trusses, a subfloor, and a finished floor, 14-1. A **joist** is a construction board with a cross-section ranging from 2 by 8 in. to 2 by 12 in. A **truss** is an assembly of structural members designed to span longer distances than a common joist.

Wood floors are generally built over a crawlspace, basement, or lower main floor level. All floor systems are supported by a foundation wall, which may also be a basement wall.

Two types of floor framing are used. They are platform framing and balloon framing. With **platform framing**, the floor is placed on a sill that is connected to the top of the wall below it. The floor acts as a platform. The walls above the floor are constructed separately and placed on the platform.

With **balloon framing**, the wall is continuous from the sill to the top of the wall, and the floor joists are attached to the studs. Figure 14-2 shows how these framing techniques differ. Platform framing is used more widely today because of fire-safety concerns with balloon framing. Balloon framing is

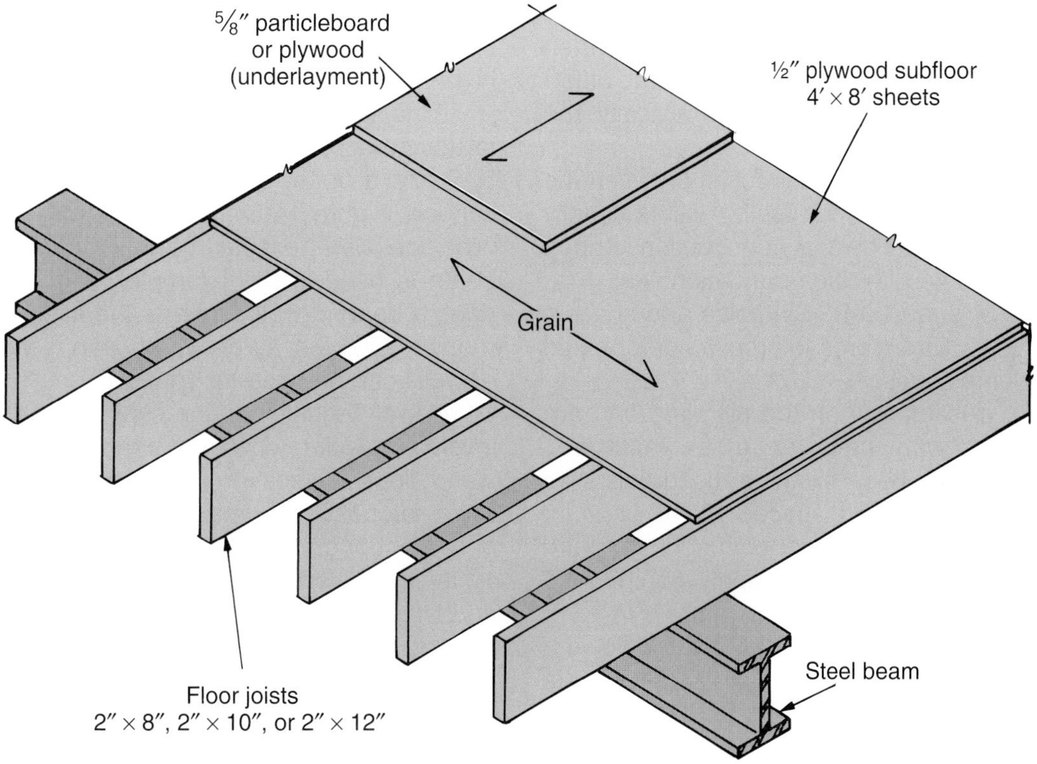

14-1 The typical components of a wood floor system are the supporting beam, floor joists, plywood subfloor, and underlayment.

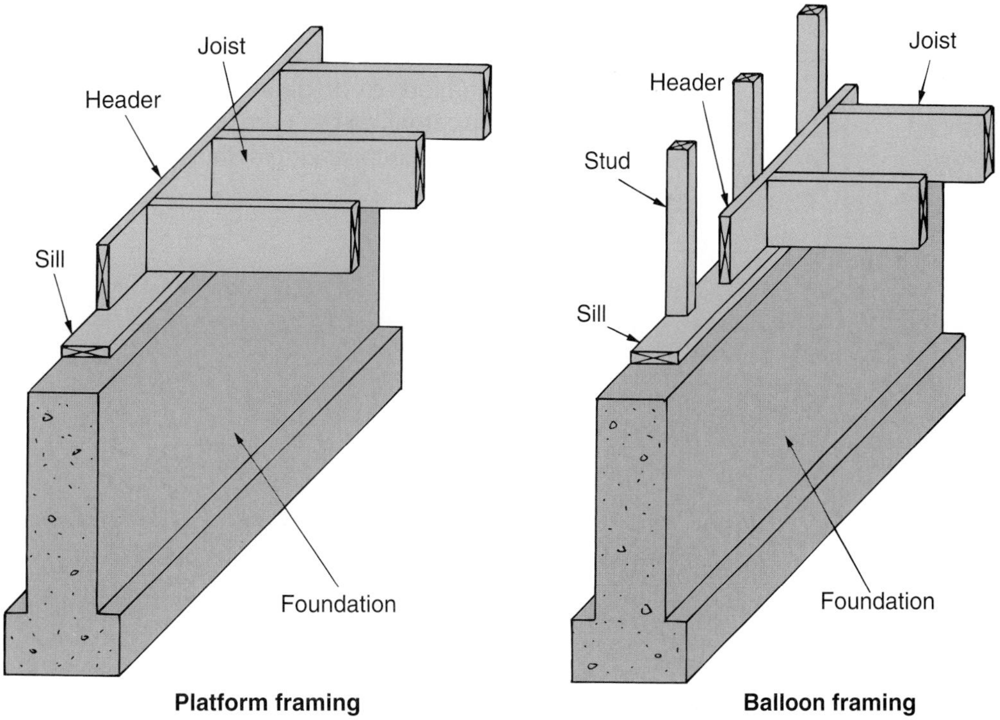

14-2 Frame floors are placed directly on the foundation in platform framing. In balloon framing, the floor frame is fitted into the wall.

an older technique that was used extensively in homes 100 years ago. It may be a concern when remodeling some older homes. Except for the differences mentioned, both frames are basically the same construction.

The sill plate forms the connection between the foundation wall and the floor itself. A sill is usually made of 2 by 6 in. or 2 by 8 in. construction lumber. It may be attached to the foundation wall with anchor bolts or straps, 14-3. The size and spacing requirements vary from area to area, as determined by local building codes.

Joists or trusses rest on the sill plate and are fastened to it with nails or other fasteners. Traditionally, wood floor systems used joists to support the floor. Joists are spaced 12, 16, or 24 in. apart, with 16 in. spacing most common. Size and spacing of joists is related to the span required and the load they will support.

A **live load**—the weight of furniture, people, and their household possessions—of 30 lb./ft.^{2} is considered standard for bedrooms and other light-loaded rooms. Kitchens, living rooms, and some other rooms are designed to support heavier loads. A design weight of 40 lb./ft.^{2} is used in these areas.

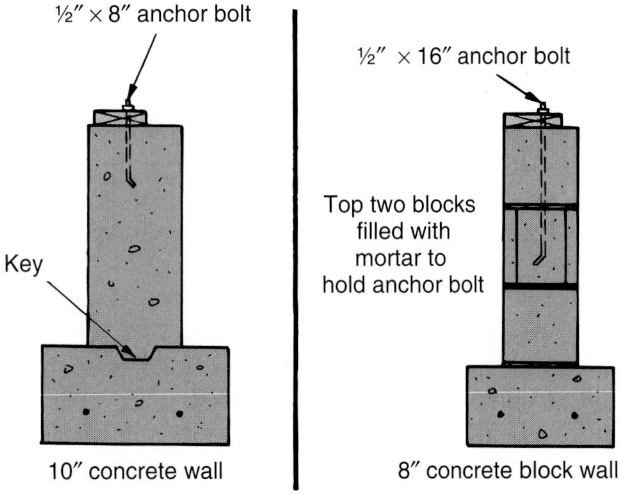

14-3 Sills may be anchored to either cast concrete or concrete-block foundation walls. Cast concrete walls require an 8 in. anchor bolt, while the anchor bolt for a concrete block wall should be 16 in. The longer bolt is needed to reach the second course of block for a secure anchor.

Spans that can be supported by various sizes of joists under live loads of 30 lb./ft.^{2} and 40 lb./ft.^{2} are listed in 14-4.

If the span required for a floor is greater than the joists can support, extra support must be provided. Typically, a beam or bearing wall is used for extra support. Figure 14-5 shows a basement that is too wide for joists to span without added support. A beam is used in the example on the left. On the right, a bearing wall supports the joists. If a floor is required to cover a very wide span, several beams or walls can be used for support.

Newer techniques for supporting wood floors involve replacing joists and beams with engineered wood floor trusses or I-joists. Both eliminate the need for posts, beams, and bearing walls in the basement or crawlspace, 14-6. For example, typical 12 in. floor trusses spaced 24 in. apart can support 40 lb./ft.^{2} over a span of 25 ft. They are produced in a large variety of sizes, usually from 2 by 4 in. pieces fastened together with metal plates. As large structural lumber becomes harder to find and prices continue to rise, more floor trusses and I-joists will be used in construction.

Once the joists or trusses are in place, the subfloor is attached. In the past, a covering of ½ in. plywood has been used to provide a large work area for people and equipment until the floor is finished. After the walls and roof are complete, an underlayment of ⅝ in. particleboard or plywood is nailed and glued over the subfloor. Another approach is to combine the subfloor and underlayment into a single thickness to save labor costs.

Joist Size	Maximum Length of Span to Support 30 lb./ft.^{2}	Maximum Length of Span to Support 40 lb./ft.^{2}
2 by 8	14′ 9″	13′ 6″
2 by 10	18′ 3″	16′ 9″
2 by 12	21′ 9″	19′ 11″

14-4 Joists listed here can support different spans of weight. Length of spans is based on joists spaced 16 in. apart.

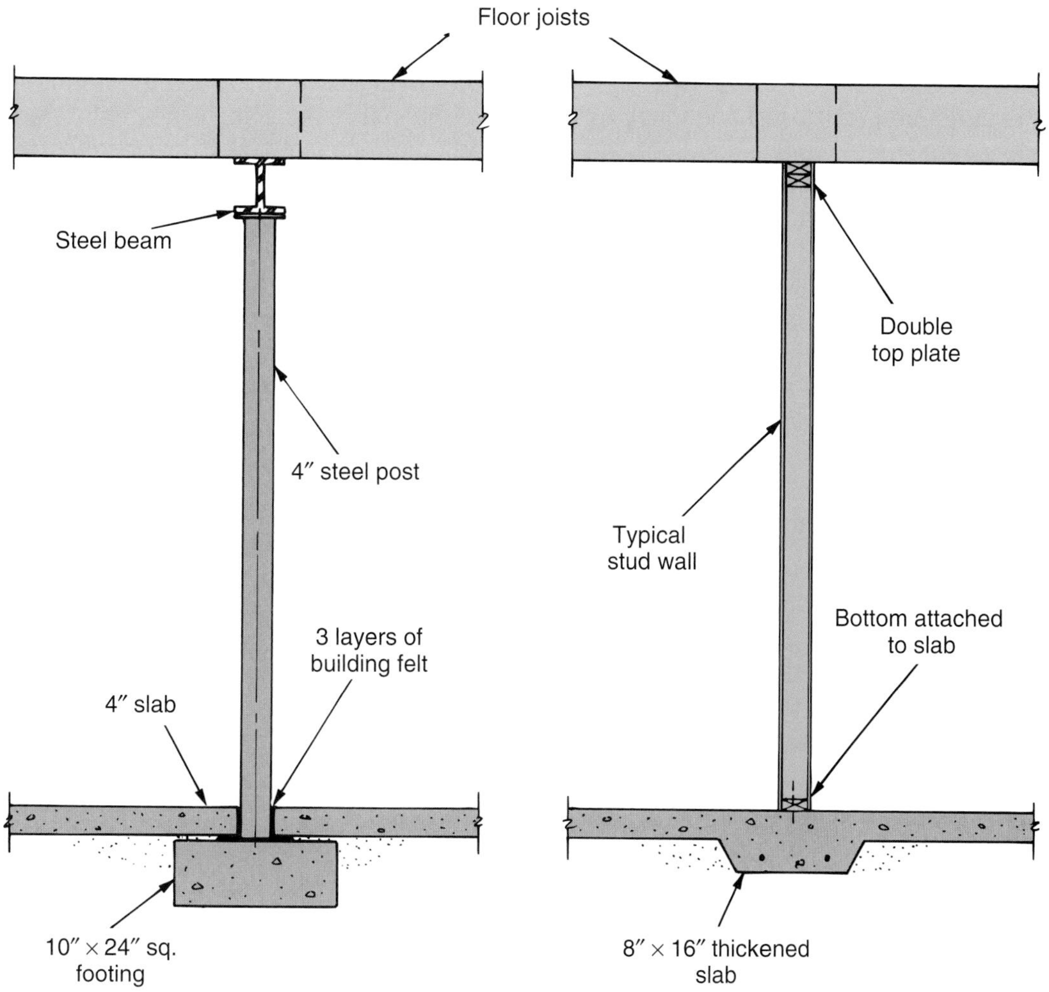

14-5 Either a beam or bearing partition may be used to support joists when the span is too great. Steel posts are used to support the beam if needed.

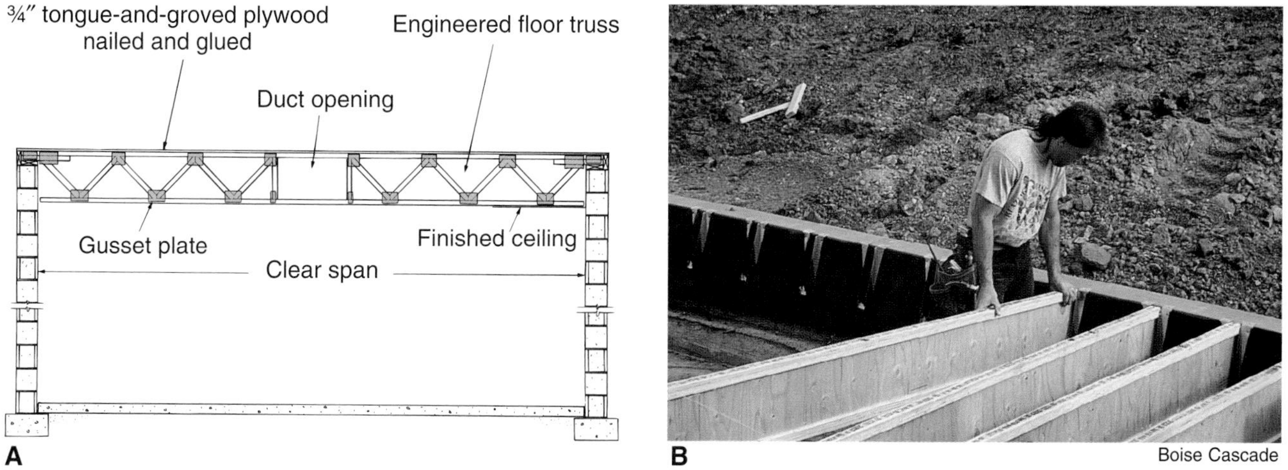

14-6 Floor trusses (A) and I-joists (B) are engineered to span long distances with support only at the ends. Plywood decking is glued and nailed at the top of the trusses or I-joists. Typical ceiling materials may be attached to the underside.

With this method, tongue-and-groove plywood of ¾ in. thickness, shown in 14-7, is nailed and glued to the joists or trusses. Both methods are acceptable.

Once the structure is enclosed and much of the interior work is completed, the finished floor can be put in place. Types of floor finishes are described later in this chapter under "Floor Treatments."

Concrete Floor Construction

The use of concrete slabs for floors in homes and garages is common throughout the United States. This type of construction is generally economical. It produces a satisfactory floor system if designed and built properly.

Two types of concrete floor systems are commonly used for residential structures. The first combines the slab and foundation into a single unit, called a **thickened-edge slab**. The second type is a **floating slab**, which is separate from the foundation wall. In both cases the slab rests on undisturbed earth or compacted fill. However, the thickened slab is supported along the edges. The floating slab is only supported by the soil below it. See 14-8.

Heating ducts, conduits, and water pipes are frequently cast into the floor of structures with a thickened-edge slab since this type of construction does not have a basement or crawlspace. The edge of the slab may be enlarged to accommodate heating ducts. See 14-9.

Electrical conduits and water pipes must be planned accurately so they will be in the right location once the floor is in place. A disadvantage of this type of floor is that these utilities are inaccessible.

Whether and how a concrete floor will be finished may affect preliminary construction. For example, nailing strips may be embedded in the slab during construction if the floor is to be carpeted, 14-10. Some treatments such as slate or flagstone require a mortar bed to compensate for materials of varying thicknesses. See 14-11. This process adds height to the floor, so extra height should be allowed in preliminary building. Planning the type of floor treatment before casting the slab helps to eliminate later problems.

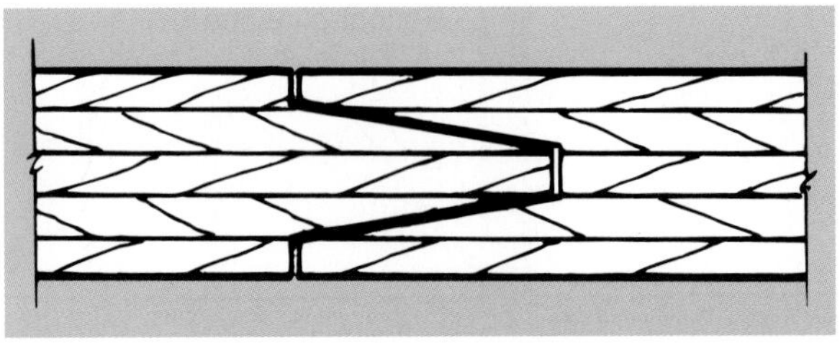

Boise Cascade

14-7 Plywood sheathing may be joined by using tongue-and-groove joints. These joints do not need to be centered over floor joists.

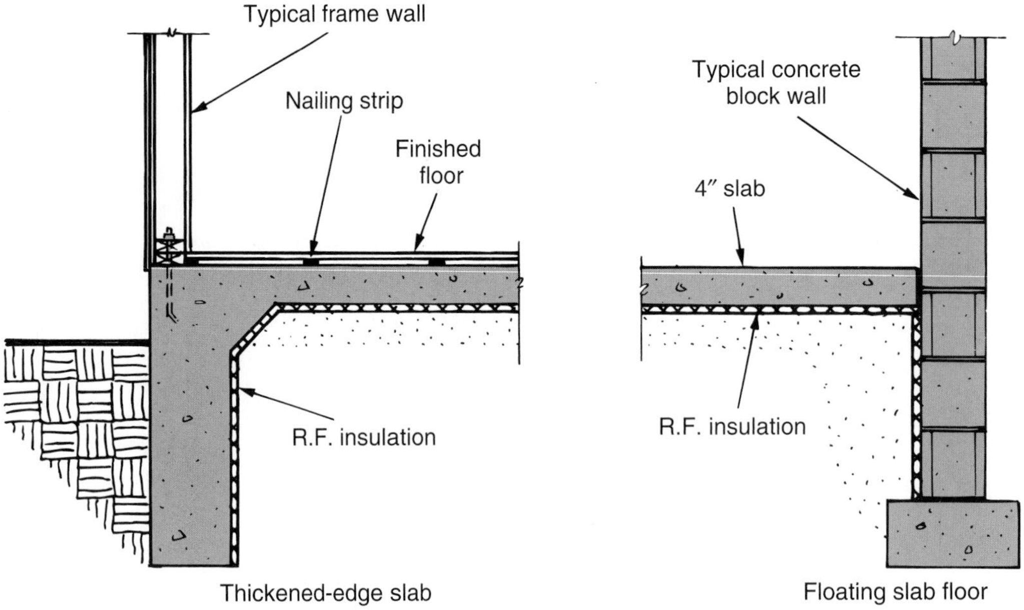

14-8 Concrete slabs may be supported along the edge, or they may rest on sand fill. Both types of construction are used in housing structures.

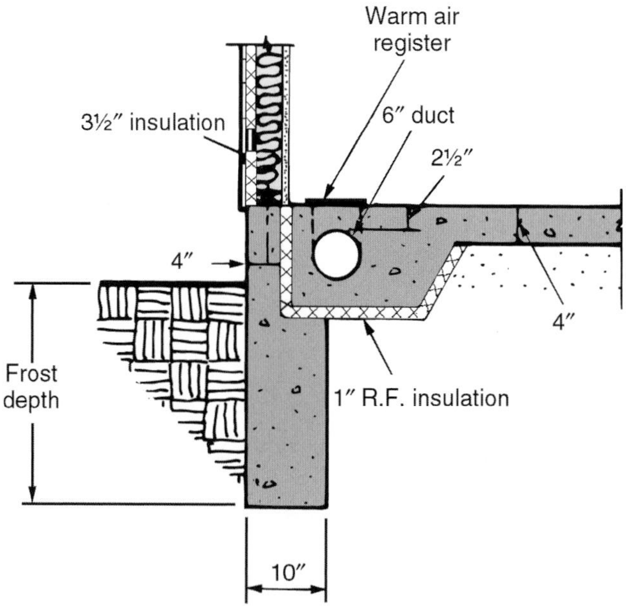

14-9 This type of insulated, thickened-edge slab has the heating duct cast in the slab. Rigid foam insulation is used to prevent heat loss through the concrete.

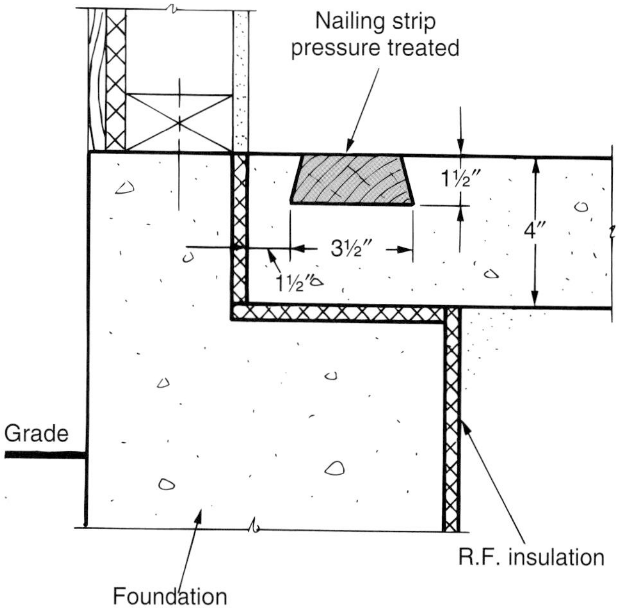

14-10 A nailing strip for carpet or other attachments is easily included when the concrete is poured. The beveled edges on the strip hold it tightly in the concrete.

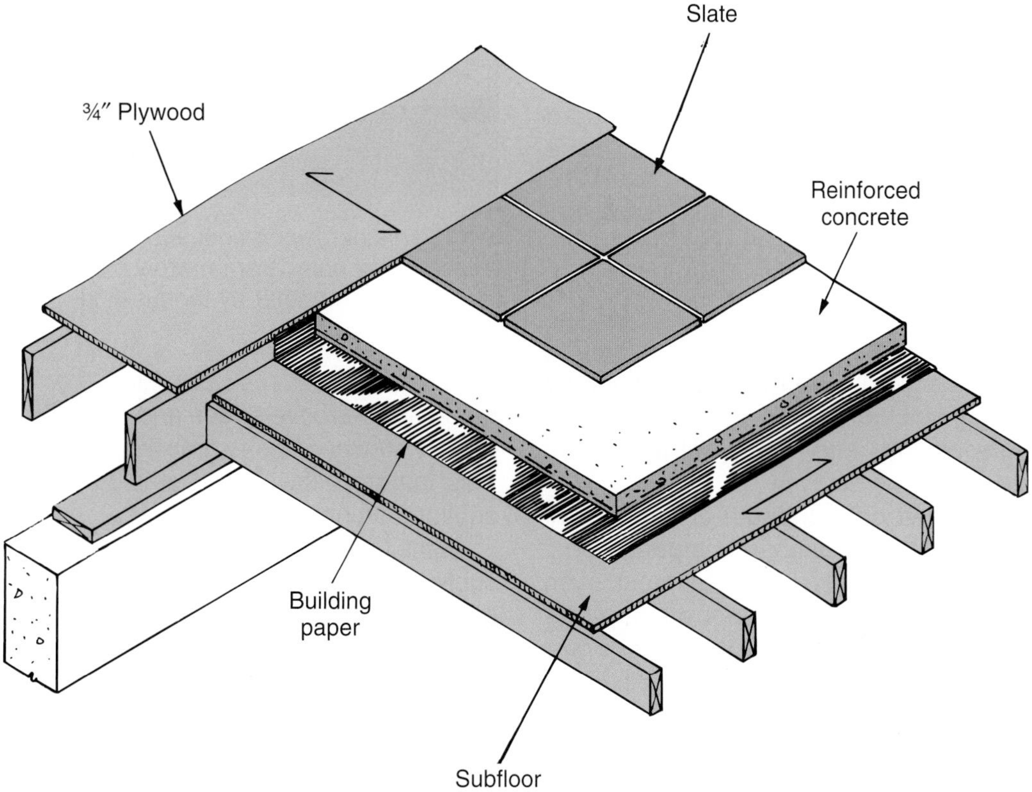

14-11 Masonry floors typically have reinforced concrete subfloors.

Floor Treatments

Floor treatments are categorized as flooring materials and floor coverings. **Flooring materials** refer to treatments that are structurally part of a floor and serve as its top surface. They are usually more permanent than floor coverings. **Floor coverings** are treatments attached to the floor's surface that are not a structural part of it.

Flooring Materials

The flooring materials commonly used in residential housing include: wood, ceramic tile, concrete, masonry, and terrazzo. Flooring materials do not include underlayment or subfloor, but the finish floor material may require special consideration of these elements.

Wood

Wood, especially hardwood, is a material commonly chosen for floors. It is beautiful, wear resistant, and readily available. Even though many new materials are now produced for floors, wood is still popular. Hardwood species that are frequently chosen include oak, birch, beech, and hard maple. Some softwood species are also used for flooring. They include fir, larch, hemlock, and southern pine. Softwoods are durable if quarter-sawed lumber is used because the edge grain is exposed. Standard flooring boards are available in most of these species.

The National Oak Flooring Manufacturers Association, Maple Flooring Manufacturing Association, National Bureau of Standards, and other organizations established standards for the quality of hardwood flooring. Softwood flooring strips are graded according to rules established by several groups, including the Western Wood Products Association and the Southern Pine Association.

Grading is based on the length of the pieces, their appearance, and the number of imperfections. The highest grades usually have the most even coloring and contain few knotholes or other imperfections. They are more expensive than lower grades of wood. Lower grades generally have a rustic appearance.

There are three main types of wood flooring used in housing structures: strip flooring, wood planks, and parquet. Strip flooring consists of pieces cut into narrow strips of varied lengths, 14-12. It is available in widths from 1½ to 3¼ in. and in thicknesses of ⅜, ½, and 25⁄32 in. Most strip flooring has tongue-and-groove edges and ends. Strip flooring is usually concave or has grooves cut on the backside. This feature allows each strip to lie flat when the subfloor is uneven.

WCI Communities, Inc.

14-12 This hardwood floor is an example of strip flooring. The boards are narrow pieces of various lengths held together by tongue-and-groove joints.

Strip flooring may be applied over a wood subfloor or concrete slab. The strips are generally nailed into the subfloor. If the application is over concrete, then strips are nailed to **sleepers**, which are furring strips embedded in a concrete slab so a floor treatment can be fastened to it. See 14-13. It is a good idea to use a vapor barrier between the concrete and flooring because concrete may become damp. Some expansion space should be allowed between hardwood strips because they swell with moisture changes. The strips may buckle or move a partition wall if expansion space is not allowed.

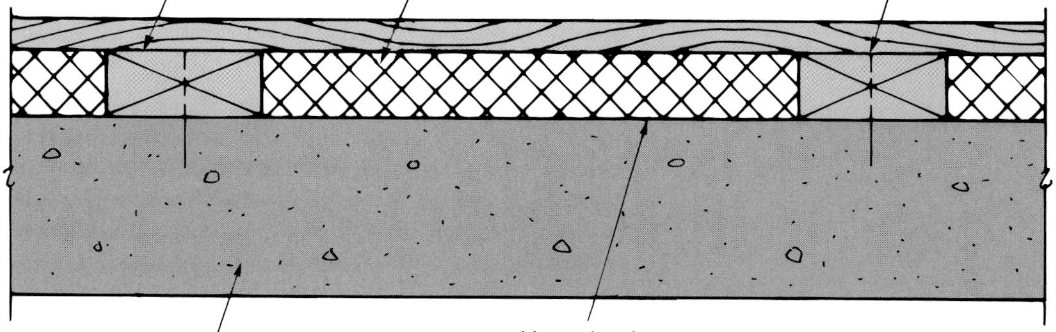

14-13 When wood flooring is used over a concrete slab, the furring strips should be treated to prevent decay.

Floorboards wider than 3½ in. are called planks. Planks are usually 25⁄32 in. thick, but they are also available in a 33⁄32 in. thickness. Widths range from 4 to 8 in. and lengths range from 4 to 16 ft. Floorboards are generally attached to a wood subfloor with screws covered with wood plugs. They can also be attached to concrete with **mastic**, a thick type of adhesive. Planks are designed to simulate colonial flooring. See 14-14.

Some types of strip-and-plank flooring can be installed as a **floating floor**. Floorboards are fastened together using a unique clip system hidden under the boards. The clips add resiliency, while allowing for the slight expansion that occurs with any solid wood flooring. This system is especially designed for installations over concrete or radiant floors. A **radiant floor** has imbedded heating elements, such as electrical resistance wires or copper tubing.

Wood block flooring, more commonly called *parquet*, is produced in three different types: unit, laminated, and slat blocks. Unit blocks and laminated blocks are factory-joined pieces that are usually 6, 8, 9, or 12 in. squares. Unit blocks are made from several short lengths of ¾ in. thick strip flooring, 14-15. This type of parquet is often called solid parquet. Laminated blocks are made from three or five thin plies of parquet block to form a block ⅜ or ½ in. thick block. See 14-16. Parquet blocks are available with a wood or foam backing. Foam backing insulates, provides a moisture barrier, deadens sound, and is resilient.

Slat block is a third type of parquet that comes as individual slats of hardwood, ranging from ¾ to 3 in. wide

Broyhill Furniture Industries, Inc.

14-14 Wood planks are wider than strip flooring and generally appear more rustic than other types of flooring material.

Bruce Hardwood Floors

14-15 Each square of this wood-block floor is made of several short strips of wood that have been glued together. Tongue-and-groove edges hold the blocks together securely.

Bruce Hardwood Floors

14-16 This type of flooring is made from blocks that are combined in a construction similar to plywood. Each square is butted against the adjacent square.

and 4 to 7 in. long. These pieces are square-edged and may be laid in several different patterns, 14-17. All types of parquet flooring can be attached to wood or concrete floor with mastic.

Floor systems are available that enable the designer to create an unlimited number of flooring designs. Boards are available in modular lengths of 9, 18, 27, and 36 in. This system allows for a wide variety of patterns, ranging from typical strip or plank applications to herringbone or parquet patterns.

Most types of wood flooring have a factory-applied finish. This type of finish is considered superior to on-the-site applications because the conditions are more accurately controlled. Polyurethane finishes range from low to high gloss, while urethane finishes provide a highly polished look. Acrylic-impregnated, finished wood flooring has a low-gloss appearance. All three finishes are water-resistant and may be used in kitchens as well as other areas of the home. Wax-and-oil-finished wood flooring provides a natural look and may be used in high traffic areas. Wood flooring should not, however, be placed in areas subject to food and liquid spills. Installing finished flooring requires considerable care since hammer marks will damage the finish.

Wood floors offer design flexibility because wood is an ageless material. It complements any decor and lifestyle and adds warmth and character to any room.

Wood floors do require special care. All types of finished flooring should be swept, vacuumed, or

Bruce Hardwood Floor

14-17 The herringbone pattern is one design that can be made with slat block flooring. Each piece of wood in the floor is individually laid.

Plain & Fancy Custom Cabinetry, Inc.

14-18 The wood flooring boards show through the gray-and-white-checkered pattern of this painted kitchen floor for an interesting effect.

dusted regularly, and spills should be cleaned with a damp cloth. Polyurethane, urethane, and acrylic-impregnated wood flooring should not be waxed. Some manufacturers recommend specific wood care products for their hardwood floors.

Wood floors are long lasting, and most may be refinished to coordinate with different styles of décor. Color can be added by staining stripped wood or painting unattractive wood flooring. The use of two or more colors can result in a variety of pleasing patterns. See 14-18.

Ceramic Tile

Ceramic tile is a popular flooring material because it lasts indefinitely and requires little maintenance. However, tile is expensive to install and cool to the touch. The three main types of tile—glazed, ceramic mosaic, and quarry and paver tile—are discussed in Chapter 9.

Glazed tile is available in a variety of colors and patterns. Although some types cannot take heavy abuse, newer styles are double- or triple-glazed for extra durability. Glazed tile does not require waxing or special care to maintain its shine. Used in dining rooms, living rooms, and other areas of the home, glazed tile is especially popular for bathroom and kitchen floors, 14-19.

Ceramic mosaic tile is very popular for kitchen and bathroom floors, 14-20. However, ceramic tile is also used in other areas of the house, 14-21. Mosaic tile for floors is generally back- or face-mounted to squares of paper or some other material. These larger units can be installed more quickly and easily.

Paver and quarry tile are designed for traffic areas. Since their color permeates the tile, wear from heavy traffic does not show. These tiles also are frostproof, so they can be used outdoors. Their color and texture are suitable for informal décor, 14-22.

Grout is a substance used to fill the joints between tiles. It may be cementitious, resinous, or a combination of both. The type of grout used depends upon the requirements of the tile and its applications.

Cementitious grouts consist of Portland cement modified to provide qualities such as whiteness, uniformity, hardness, flexibility, and water retention. Resinous grouts, or epoxies, possess special properties such as

Formica Corporation

14-19 Glazed tile is a popular choice of flooring material for kitchens. It is attractive, easy to maintain, and resistant to wear from heavy traffic.

14-20 Ceramic floor tile provides an attractive bathroom floor that is easily maintained.

Trade Commission of Spain

14-21 Ceramic mosaic tile is frequently used for borders.

14-22 Quarry tile was chosen for this high-traffic area. The earthy color is attractive, yet the tile is practical.

high bond strength and resistance to chemicals. However, resinous grouts are harder to apply and more expensive.

Concrete and Masonry

Concrete and masonry floors have a high resistance to abrasion and may incorporate unlimited pattern, texture, and color combinations. They are suitable for both indoor and outdoor floors. Indoor floors may be waxed for a warmer, more polished look. The basic types of concrete and masonry floors used in housing structures include: concrete, brick, slate, and flagstone.

Concrete floors can have a smooth or textured surface, and color can be added, 14-23. The most common treatment of concrete as a floor material is to trowel it smooth. The surface produced is serviceable for garage, porch, and patio floors. This type of floor is functional rather than decorative.

In traditional as well as contemporary homes, indoor and outdoor brick floors are popular, 14-24.

Portland Cement Association

14-23 This concrete patio has exposed aggregate and a decorative color design to add interest.

Many patterns are possible and color combinations are almost endless. Regular brick or special pavers may be used to form a brick floor using regular mortar joints. Brick pavers are thinner than conventional brick. Some are glazed, but most are not. The common size of pavers is 1¼ by 3⅝ by 7⅝ in. Brick floors are more practical if installed over a concrete slab rather than a wood-floor base.

Slate floors add a touch of class to a room. Slate is expensive, but is durable and luxurious looking, 14-25. It may be used anywhere a tile or brick floor is desirable. Slate frequently is a blue-gray color, but is also available in green, red, brown, or black. The same type of bed is required for slate as for ceramic tile. With the thin-set method, which uses no mortar bed, slate pieces of equal thickness are needed. A variable-thickness, flooring material may be used with the thick-bed method, where mortar is used to level the slate floor. Slate may be cut to form regular patterns of rectangular shapes, or it may be used in random shapes and patterns, 14-26. A thin mortar joint of ¼ in. is best with slate and should remain consistent throughout the floor area.

Flagstone floors are very popular for patios and other exterior applications, but they produce a practical and serviceable interior floor as well. Random shapes and colors best describe a flagstone floor, 14-27. Native stone is selected and split for use in these floors. Usually, sedimentary stone is used because it can be split into large, flat pieces. These are ideal for paving a floor.

Flagstone floors may be left rough and highly textured or ground smooth. They are expensive but

14-24 The driveway is made from brick pavers to complement the contemporary design of this home.

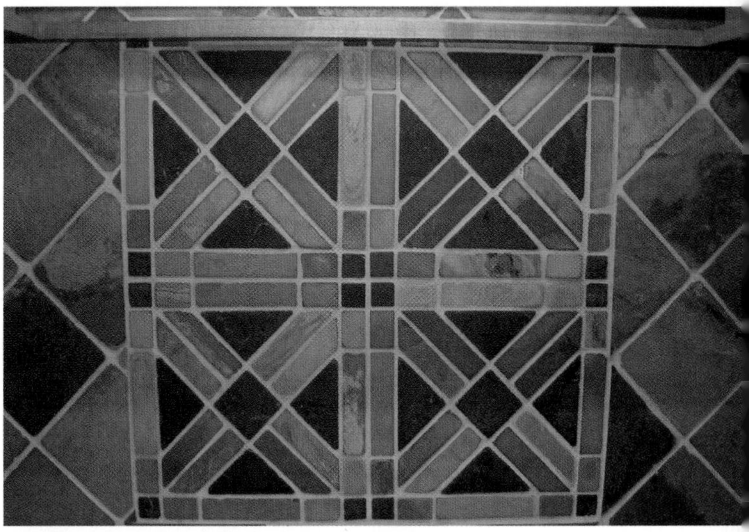

14-25 This slate floor is composed primarily of 6 x 6 in. tumbled slate squares with a decorative insert of other shapes and sizes.

Bill Whetstone, Landscape Designer

14-26 This attractive, formal patio is surfaced with slate of various shapes and sizes.

Photograph by John Fulker

14-27 Native stone of varied colors is used to create flagstone floors.

attractive. This floor material may be used in any room or area of the house. It is easy to maintain and lasts indefinitely. Cleaning with a damp mop is all a stone floor requires to maintain its beauty.

Masonry floors are usually more expensive than other floors, but they are highly durable and always in style. As new masonry materials are developed, the range of choices increases and applications are broadened. Concrete and masonry are materials of permanence; they should be chosen with care because they cannot be changed easily.

Terrazzo

The term *terrazzo* is an Italian word that means "terrace on the roof." Originally, decorative chips from mosaic work were saved and used to make colorful and durable indoor and outdoor floors. **Terrazzo** is a type of floor surface made of marble chips bound together with Portland cement. When the cement hardens, the surface is ground smooth and polished. Rustic terrazzo is also popular. It may contain gravel or marble chips, and its finish is left rough, 14-28.

Terrazzo floors are hard, smooth, and easy to maintain: damp mopping restores their luster. They may, however, be waxed for a more polished surface. They last indefinitely and are popular in heavy traffic areas. A wide range of colors and chip sizes is available. Terrazzo is a permanent floor material that is expensive, due to high labor costs for installation. These floors require a solid base of concrete with a minimum terrazzo topping of ¼ in. Divider strips of brass or other noncorrosive material are used to

14-28 Rustic terrazzo is generally made from smooth stones. It is not ground to a polish like indoor terrazzo floors.

control shrinkage and cracks and form designs in the finished floor. Terrazzo is an old flooring material, but it is still popular today because of its beauty, durability, and low-maintenance requirements.

Floor Coverings

Floor coverings play a large and important role in the total design of a room or area. Although they may be changed more frequently than flooring materials, they last several years and require a substantial investment. Therefore, floor coverings should be chosen with care. The main types of floor coverings used in residential housing include soft floor coverings and resilient products.

Soft Floor Coverings

Soft floor coverings include carpeting and rugs. Carpeting is fastened directly to the floor and usually covers it from wall to wall. It is sold by the roll in standard widths ranging from 27 in. to 18 ft. Rugs are not fastened to the floor and usually do not cover it completely.

A soft floor covering's characteristics are determined by its fibers, construction, texture, and density. The type of padding used with carpeting also affects its characteristics.

About 90 percent of the carpets and rugs produced today are made from four manufactured fibers: nylon, acrylic, polyester, and olefin. Wool is still used, but it has been replaced extensively by manufactured fibers. No single fiber is perfect for all types of carpeting. Durability, resilience, ability to maintain color, and ease of cleaning are factors to consider when choosing a soft floor covering.

Wool produces a highly durable, luxurious carpet. It has good resistance to abrasion and excellent resiliency. It has superior resistance to soil and fading so it retains its original appearance for years. Static buildup is not a problem with wool fibers. Wool is the most expensive of the popular carpet fibers.

Nylon has a reputation for tough, long-lasting wear. It is highly resistant to crushing and matting, but it may pill. Nylon fiber conducts static electricity unless an antistatic finish is applied. It is easy to clean, but its color will fade under prolonged exposure to light.

Of the synthetic fibers used in carpets, acrylic fiber looks and feels the most like wool. It accepts dye well and has color retention similar to wool. It is soft to the touch and has good elasticity, but it does not resist crushing as well as wool. Acrylic accumulates very little static buildup.

Polyester has a feel somewhat similar to wool. It resists wear but does not resist crushing as well as other fibers. However, it is economical for use in heavy-duty carpets. Of the manufactured fibers, polyester generates the least amount of static electricity.

Olefin is very tough and a good fiber for carpets used in high traffic areas. It is highly water resistant, very resistant to fading and staining, and ideal for indoor/outdoor carpeting. On the other hand, olefin is difficult to dye and not very resilient. Because it reduces static electricity, olefin is commonly used in computer rooms and similar areas.

The method of construction used in making a rug or carpet is a factor in appearance, wearability, quality, and price. One method is not necessarily better than another; there are various grades within each method. The five basic construction techniques used to make soft-floor coverings are: tufting, weaving, knitting, needle-punching, and flocking. The characteristics of each of these methods are outlined in 14-29.

The pile of the yarns produces the texture of soft floor coverings. The yarns may be cut, uncut, set in different lengths, twisted, or untwisted. The five basic types of carpet texture are: cut, level-loop, multi-level loop, cut and loop, and shag pile. Their characteristics are outlined in 14-30.

The density of a soft floor covering's pile is a key factor in determining the quality of a carpet. Finding the number of tufts per sq. in. of surface area can help you compare carpet density. Denser carpets will probably wear longer, 14-31. The type of fiber, construction, and backing are other factors to consider when determining quality. For example, a tight-loop construction of a good, abrasion-resistant fiber will wear longer than a plush construction of the same fiber. The strength of the backing is important because no matter how wear-resistant a fiber is, if the backing deteriorates, the life of the carpet will be reduced.

A carpet padding or cushion protects a carpet and provides more comfort for the user. It also improves the carpet's appearance and length of life. The main purpose of padding is to prevent the pile from being crushed by traffic. It also smoothes any irregularities that may be in the subfloor. The five main types of padding are: hair or felt, rubberized felt, sponge rubber, polymeric foam, and attached lining.

Hair or felt padding gives long wear and firm support. However, it may stretch and shed and is not mildew resistant. This type of carpet backing is not usually recommended by the carpet industry, especially in damp climates. Rubberized felt has the same advantages as hair or felt, but it has a layer of rubber attached to reduce stretching.

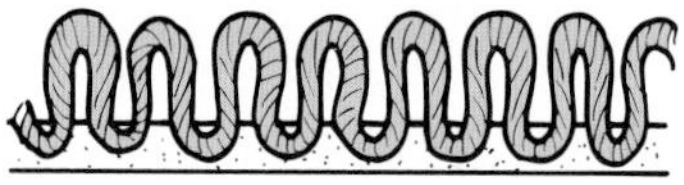

Tufted Carpet

Tufting. Pile tufts are inserted by needles threaded with yarn into a prefabricated backing material. Tufts are locked into place with latex adhesive. Yarns may be looped, cut, or both. A second layer of backing is used for dimensional stability. Tufting is used for over 90 percent of the total production of carpets.

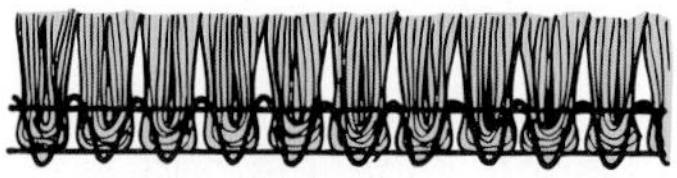

Woven Carpet

Weaving. Backing yarns (warp and weft) and surface yarns (pile) are interlocked simultaneously, creating a single fabric. There are three main types of woven carpets. A Wilton weave produces many patterns and colors in cut or loop pile. The Axminster weave is produced in cut pile only, with each individually set. This permits a great variety of patterns. A velvet or plush weave is generally monochromatic with all pile cut to the same length.

Knitted Carpet

Knitting. The backing, stitching, and pile yarns are looped together with three sets of needles. Knitting produces an uncut, loop pile. A latex backing is applied for added body.

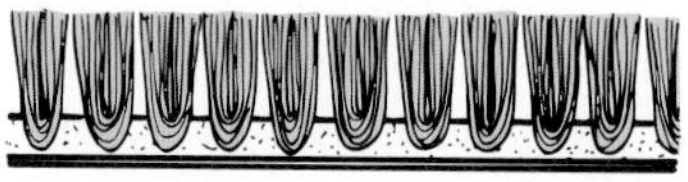

Needle-Punched Carpet

Needle-Punching. A web of fibers is interlocked through the use of felting needles. They have a felted or flat-textured construction. A latex backing is added for strength. This type of construction is used mainly for indoor/outdoor carpeting.

Flocked Carpet

Flocking. Short, chopped fibers are attached to adhesive-backed fabric by an electric charge. Fibers are embedded vertically to produce a single-level, cut-pile surface similar to velour. Colored patterns may be printed on flocked carpet.

14-29 The construction technique used to make soft floor coverings affects their appearance and durability.

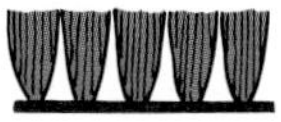

Velvet Plush

Saxony Plush

Frieze

Cut Pile

Cut Pile. The pile loops are cut, leaving two individual yarns in place of each yarn loop. There are three basic types. Velvet plush has very little twist in the yarns for an elegant, level sweep of color. Saxony plush has two or more yarns twisted together so each tuft is distinguishable from the surface. Freize is made of tightly twisted, well-defined yarns, producing a pebbly effect.

Level Loop Pile

Level Loop Pile. All pile loops are left uncut and equal in height. The pattern produced is smooth, level, and long wearing.

Multi-Level Loop Pile

Multi-Level Loop Pile. Loops are left uncut, but at different heights. Usually, there are two or three different heights in one carpet for a sculptured look.

Cut and Loop Pile

Cut and Loop Pile. Cut pile and loop pile are combined in the same carpet. Many patterns of surface textures are possible.

Shag

Shag. Cut pile is very long. Different lengths are available. Shags produce a casual, highly textured effect.

14-30 Using different construction techniques produces various pile textures.

Sponge rubber, the most popular carpet padding, is produced in flat or bubble forms. It resists mildew, is mothproof, and comes in several thicknesses. Polymeric foam is a cellular type of structure that resists mildew, fungus, and moths. Rubber backing may be used in any location.

An attached lining is usually made of foam rubber. It is less expensive than other types of padding. A carpet with an attached lining may be placed directly on concrete or other subfloor material.

Quality padding can increase the life of a carpet by 100 percent over the same carpet using a low-quality

14-31 One characteristic used to judge the quality of a carpet is the density of pile. The carpet sample on top has fewer tufts than the sample below.

or improper pad. Padding is especially important for carpets because they are usually more permanent and more expensive than rugs.

Rugs are constructed similarly to carpets, but are manufactured in different sizes. Common sizes may be categorized into three types: room-size rugs, area rugs, and scatter rugs.

A room-size rug leaves a border of the floor's perimeter exposed. This frames the floor area and defines the space. Room-size rugs are available in standard sizes, such as 9 by 12 ft., 12 by 12 ft., and 12 by 15 ft. Room-size rugs do not require special installation and are relatively easy to remove and send out for cleaning. They sometimes can be turned to equalize the exposure of various areas to traffic and wear. Room-size rugs can be moved to a new room or location more easily than wall-to-wall carpeting.

Area rugs are available in a wide variety of colors, textures, sizes, and shapes. They are not designed to cover the entire floor, but to emphasize or define areas of the room. They can also emphasize separate functions in a dual-purpose room. Area rugs are often used to unify a furniture grouping, 14-32. They may also serve as a focal point in a room's design. Area rugs can be used in almost any room of the home, especially to make a large room seem smaller or a small room feel cozy.

Scatter rugs are generally smaller and less formal than area rugs. They are used to reduce wear in the underlying floor from heavy traffic or to provide accents of color, 14-33. Scatter rugs are good covers for permanent surfaces that are prone to dirt or spills because they are easily machine washed.

The Oshkosh, WI, private residence of Chancellor Richard H. Wells and family, formerly the Alberta Kimball Home

14-32 The area rug in this room is used to unify the furniture grouping.

Manufactured Housing Institute

14-33 Scatter rugs are often used to add color to a room. On smooth floors, they may also provide a slip-proof area for standing.

Resilient Floor Covering

A **resilient floor covering** is a smooth, hard material in sheet or tile form that returns to its original shape. The main types of resilient floor coverings are: asphalt, cork, rubber, vinyl, and poured seamless floors.

Tiles in 9 or 12 in. squares are usually cemented or taped to the floor, but sheet materials may be laid loose or attached. Installing tile usually involves less waste than installing sheet materials. Worn areas, too, can be replaced easily in tile floors without replacing the entire floor covering. However, the newer tiles are generally brighter in color than the rest of the floor.

Sheet floor covering comes in rolls with standard widths of 6, 9, and 12 ft. It has the advantage of being seamless. Therefore, it is favored for areas where spills may seep into the cracks between tiles. It may also be extended a few inches up the wall to eliminate common dirt traps where walls meet floors.

Asphalt tile is durable and moisture resistant, but it may be damaged by grease. Also, it does not recover well from indentation. It is a good floor covering for below-grade, concrete floors. Asphalt tile is the least expensive of all permanent, smooth floor coverings. Tiles are plain or marbleized and come in a full range of lighter hues. The surface is slippery when wet and moderately hard.

Cork tile is rather expensive and a luxury floor covering for light-traffic areas. It is quiet and comfortable, but it damages easily. It is not resistant to grease or stains, and it requires careful wax maintenance. Its pattern ranges from fine to coarse, and color ranges from light to dark brown.

Vinyl cork tile results from sealing cork under a clear, plastic covering. It is more resistant to dents and dirt than cork tile, and it is easier to maintain. However, it is not strong enough to hold up well under heavy traffic. Vinyl cork tile may be used at any grade level.

Rubber tile is more common in commercial use than residential use, but it may be used in a home. It is quiet, comfortable, and very resilient. It has good resistance to denting and staining, although some types are not resistant to grease. Rubber tile requires a moderate amount of maintenance. It is available in bright, clear colors that may be plain or marbleized.

Vinyl tile is made of solid vinyl, 14-34. It resists damage from alcohol, petroleum products, ammonia,

Armstrong World Industries, Inc.

14-34 Solid vinyl tile is a good choice for a dining area because of its low maintenance and wear resistance.

bleach, household cleaners, stains, and grease. It is very durable and suitable for most home traffic. Vinyl tile requires a fair amount of care, but with no-wax finishes, they are relatively easy to maintain. Vinyl tile is moderately expensive. Its wide range of styles, patterns, colors, and high level of durability make it one of the most popular resilient floor coverings for residential use.

Printing a pattern on a vinyl sheet and covering the sheet with a layer of clear vinyl produces rotovinyl. This resilient flooring is suitable for light-traffic areas. It is also available with a cushion backing for extra wear and comfort, 14-35.

The surface design of an inlaid vinyl sheet penetrates its entire depth. Consequently, the original color and pattern will remain as long as the flooring does. Inlaid vinyl sheets are available with or without a cushioned back.

Sheet vinyl is available with a no-wax finish. This floor covering has a special, clear urethane coating that provides high shine without waxing. The surface resists scuffs and can be cleaned with a damp mop. Vinyl no-wax floors are very durable. Sheet vinyl with a no-wax finish is the most popular resilient floor covering material for today's homes.

Poured seamless floors consist of an epoxy base and a hard urethane finish. They can be used over many surfaces such as concrete, wood, vinyl, rubber, or asphalt tiles. They are stain resistant as well as dent and scratch resistant. The surface is easy to maintain with a damp mop, and applying a new coat of clear finish can restore gloss.

Armstrong World Industries, Inc.

14-35 Cushioned, printed vinyl floor covering has good durability, but it is more comfortable and warmer than other hard-floor coverings and materials.

Selection of Floor Treatments

Floors are no longer treated as bland spaces with no design interest. In recent years, floors have received as much fashion consideration as any other part of the home. Their importance in making living spaces functional and comfortable also makes them key considerations in planning any type of housing.

Function

Floors have an important functional role in a living space. They make it possible for us to move from one area of the structure to another. They also define space, support the furnishings, and shield the occupants from the earth below. These are important factors to keep in mind when considering various design treatments. For example, a beautiful white carpet is not practical for families with children and pets. Floors receive the most wear and dirt of any surface in the home. The challenge is to select floor treatments that are practical and attractive so the floors can make a positive contribution to the overall beauty and function of the home.

There are several strengths and weaknesses to consider when selecting a floor treatment for a specific application. For example, halls, foyers, baths, and kitchens are heavy-traffic areas where dirt and moisture are prevalent. The most practical choice for such areas is a durable, smooth treatment, such as resilient floor covering or ceramic tile, 14-36.

Another factor to consider is the amount of time needed to maintain a floor treatment. Many people prefer the beauty of all-wood floors, but they do not want to spend time waxing and polishing their floors. Some floor materials have special coatings or treatments that make them easier to maintain. Colors can hide or emphasize dirt. Light-colored floor treatments show dirt more easily than dark-colored floors. Multicolored or patterned floors, such as a tweed carpet, act as a camouflage to dirt, 14-37.

Cost is a major consideration in selecting floor treatments. It is important, however, to consider the durability and maintenance ease of a floor treatment in relationship to its cost. For example, wood and ceramic are more expensive than vinyl tile or carpeting, but they also last longer.

Florida Tile

14-36 Tile floors are becoming popular for living and family rooms because they are attractive and easily cleaned.

14-37 A tweed carpet does not show dirt or lint as much as solid-colored carpets do. A tweed carpet is a good choice for high-activity areas of a home.

The degree of hardness or softness of a floor is another consideration when choosing a floor treatment. Soft flooring usually feels warmer and is more comfortable than hard flooring. However, hard flooring is usually more durable and easier to clean.

Appearance

Different types of floor coverings convey different moods. Each type blends better with some styles of décor than with others. The floor unifies the room's components and should blend with the color, style, and formality of the furnishings.

A floor can dominate the room's design when intense colors or bold patterns are used, 14-38. Such floors can become focal points in rooms with few or simple furnishings. Simple floor patterns and light or neutral colors are more suitable for rooms with dominant furnishings or accessories.

The intensity of a color increases with size. Therefore, a small sample of a floor treatment will appear much lighter than an entire floor of that treatment.

The type of floor covering used can convey a warm or cool feeling. Generally, smooth treatments generate a cool atmosphere, while more textured treatments such as carpeting convey a feeling of warmth. Warm colors can make a room seem cozy, whereas cool colors have a calming affect.

Floor coverings can affect the apparent size of a room. Dark colors can pull elements together and make the room look smaller. Conversely, light colors produce a more spacious effect, 14-39. Using just one floor treatment in a room also promotes a more spacious feeling because of the large, unbroken expanse forming the background.

American Olean

14-38 Bold-blue sheet vinyl was selected for this neutral décor to emphasize the outdoor lake view.

14-39 The light carpet in this room helps to give an open, airy impression.

Chapter Summary

Floors support furnishings and occupants, provide decoration, and facilitate movement within the structure. Floor systems in most dwellings are either wood or concrete.

Wood floor systems consist of support beams, joists or trusses, subfloor, and finished floor. Wood floors are usually built over a crawlspace, basement, or lower main floor level. All floor systems are supported by a foundation or basement wall. Two types of floor framing are used—platform and balloon framing. The sill plate forms the connection between the foundation wall and the floor. Joists or trusses rest on the sill plate. Joist size and spacing are related to the live load to be supported and the distance spanned.

Concrete slabs are also used for floors. The thickened-edge slab usually includes perimeter heating/cooling ducts, but the floating slab is separate from the foundation wall. Almost any floor treatment can be used with a slab-floor system.

Floor treatments are usually categorized as flooring materials and floor coverings. Flooring materials are a part of the floor structure. For both wood frame and concrete floors, wood flooring is popular and available in strip flooring, wood planks, and parquet. Ceramic tile is also popular, especially for concrete floors. The three main types of tile are: glazed, ceramic mosaic, and quarry and paver tiles. Concrete and masonry floors are used inside or outside a home in unlimited patterns, textures, and color combinations. Terrazzo floors, made from stone chips and cement binder, are an expensive, but high-quality floor.

Floor coverings used in a dwelling are generally carpeting, rugs, and resilient products. Most soft floor coverings today contain nylon, acrylic, polyester, and olefin. Resilient floor coverings are smooth, hard materials that return to their original shape. The main types include asphalt, cork, rubber, vinyl, and poured seamless floors.

Floors receive as much fashion consideration as any other part of the house. Cost, maintenance, décor, and traffic patterns must be taken into account when selecting a floor treatment suited for a particular application.

Review Questions

1. How is a platform-frame floor constructed?
2. When comparing concrete floors, what is the difference between a thickened-edge slab and a floating slab?
3. How is strip flooring installed?
4. What are some advantages and disadvantages of ceramic tile as a flooring material?
5. For what rooms is ceramic tile recommended?
6. What types of masonry materials may be used as flooring materials?
7. What type of floor construction is recommended for masonry floors?
8. What are the outstanding features of the four fibers most commonly used in carpet production?
9. What factors affect the strength of a carpet?
10. How are room-size, area, and scatter rugs commonly used in a home?
11. Which type of resilient floor covering is the easiest to maintain? the most difficult to maintain?
12. How can floor treatments affect a room's appearance and make it look smaller? larger? warmer? cooler?

Suggested Activities

1. Discuss the similarities and differences between platform framing and balloon framing. Use sketches to clarify your discussion.
2. Lead a class discussion on the basic construction of a concrete floor and its advantages and disadvantages when compared to a wood frame floor.
3. Make sketches of common wood-flooring materials. Draw each using the same scale.
4. Visit a home improvement center or tile outlet store to research the types, sizes, and prices of ceramic floor tile available. Record your findings in a chart.
5. Using the library, Internet, or other source, research terrazzo. Write a descriptive essay about using it as a flooring material and identify your sources.
6. Visit a carpet outlet store to examine the following types of carpet construction: tufting, weaving, knitting, needle-punching, and flocking. If necessary, ask a salesperson for help in finding samples. Record your observations regarding appearance, price, and fiber content.
7. Select a type of resilient floor covering and research the steps required for installing the material. Be prepared to make a brief report in class.
8. List important factors that should be considered when planning a floor treatment.
9. Examine the floors in your home and determine the floor treatment(s) used in each. Make a chart listing each room and the floor treatments it contains.

Internet Resources

American Iron and Steel Institute
steel.org

Armstrong World Industries, Inc.
armstrong.com

Boise Cascade Engineered Wood Products
bcewp.com

Congoleum Corporation, a supplier of flooring products
congoleum.com

Hartco Flooring, an Armstrong Company
hartcoflooring.com

Portland Cement Association
concretehomes.com

Southern Pine Council
southernpine.com

The Engineered Wood Association
apawood.org

Trex Company, a manufacturer of nonwood decking
trex.com

U. S. Forest Products Laboratory
fpl.fs.fed.us

Western Wood Products Association
wwpa.org

Note: Web addresses may have changed since publication. For some entries, reaching the correct Web site may require keying *www.* into the address.

Chapter 15
Ceilings and Roofs

Objectives

After studying this chapter, you will be able to

- describe the construction methods and materials used to build a roof.
- evaluate ceiling-surface materials according to their ease of placement, cost, and treatment requirements.
- explain how a roof is constructed and identify its major parts.
- identify common roof styles.
- list and describe various types of roofing materials.

Key Terms

cathedral ceiling
lath
scratch coat
brown coat
suspended ceiling
ridge
rise
span
run
cornice
soffit
gable end
flashing

Ceilings and roofs help to confine the space within a house. A ceiling defines the height of a room, provides support for lighting fixtures, and adds to the decor of the space. A roof protects the home from heat, cold, rain, snow, wind, and other elements. It also serves as an integral part of the exterior style of a home. This chapter outlines the construction and treatment of ceilings and roofs.

Ceilings

Like walls and floors, ceilings help to define the limits of a room. Standard ceiling heights of modern homes are much lower than those of older homes. Homes built in the late 1700s have ceilings as high as 12 to 14 ft. Homes of the early 1900s may have 9 ft. high ceilings. Today, the standard ceiling height in first- and second-floor areas is 8 ft., however, ceiling heights are beginning to rise again. Finished basement ceilings are often 7 ft. high because space is needed to enclose heating ducts, beams, and plumbing. The lower ceiling heights save on construction costs. They also make heating the home less expensive.

Ceiling Construction

Most residential ceilings have a frame construction similar to that of floors, 15-1. A ceiling, however, uses lighter joists because it does not need to support much weight. Rafters above the joists support the roof.

When there is another room or attic above, the floor of that space serves as the ceiling for the room below. A ceiling cover can be attached directly to the floor joists.

If a ceiling spans a very long distance, a beam may be needed for extra support. Roof trusses may also be used as a ceiling frame. Like floor trusses, roof trusses use small pieces of lumber fastened together with metal plates, 15-2. They eliminate the need for a separate ceiling frame. Also, they can span greater distances than traditional ceiling joists.

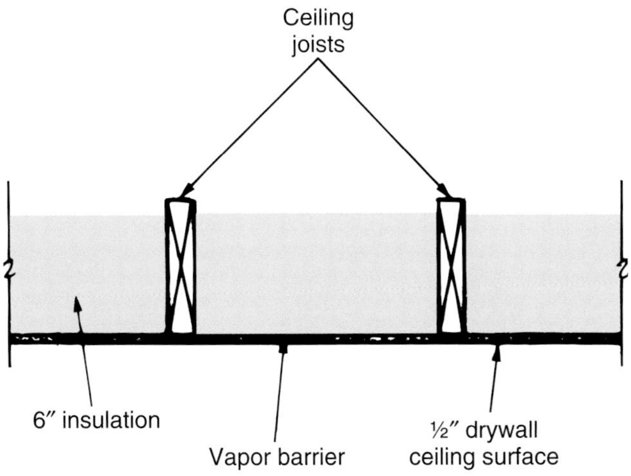

15-1 Like floors, ceilings are constructed of joists. The ceiling-surface material is attached to the ceiling frame.

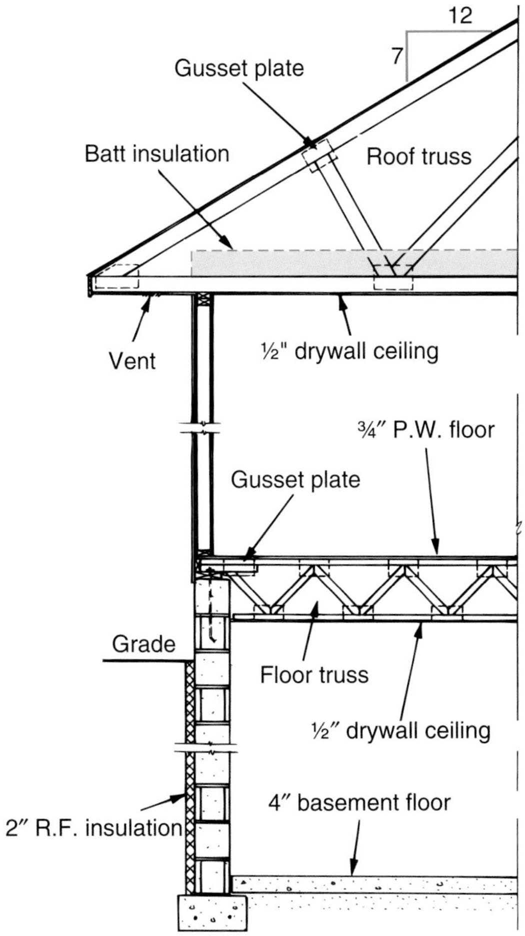

15-2 Ceiling-surface materials can be applied to roof trusses without adding a joist frame.

Ceiling-joist spacing is typically 16 in. on center, but spacings of 12 and 24 in. are also used. Trusses are generally spaced 24 in. apart.

Another choice for residential housing is the **cathedral ceiling.** This type of ceiling has exposed beams and a surface covering that is attached to the rafters. See 15-3. Since no surface covering is placed below the support beams, ceiling joists are not needed.

Ceiling-Surface Materials

Several different materials are commonly used to form the ceiling surface. The most typical are gypsum board, plaster, wood boards, and suspended ceiling materials. See 15-4. All of these result in surfaces that can be covered with a ceiling treatment or left untreated.

Gypsum Board Ceilings

Gypsum board is used for ceiling surfaces as well as for walls, 15-5. It has replaced plaster as the most-used ceiling material in housing structures. It

Cultured Stone by Stucco Stone Products, Inc.

15-3 A cathedral ceiling has exposed beams, so joists are not necessary.

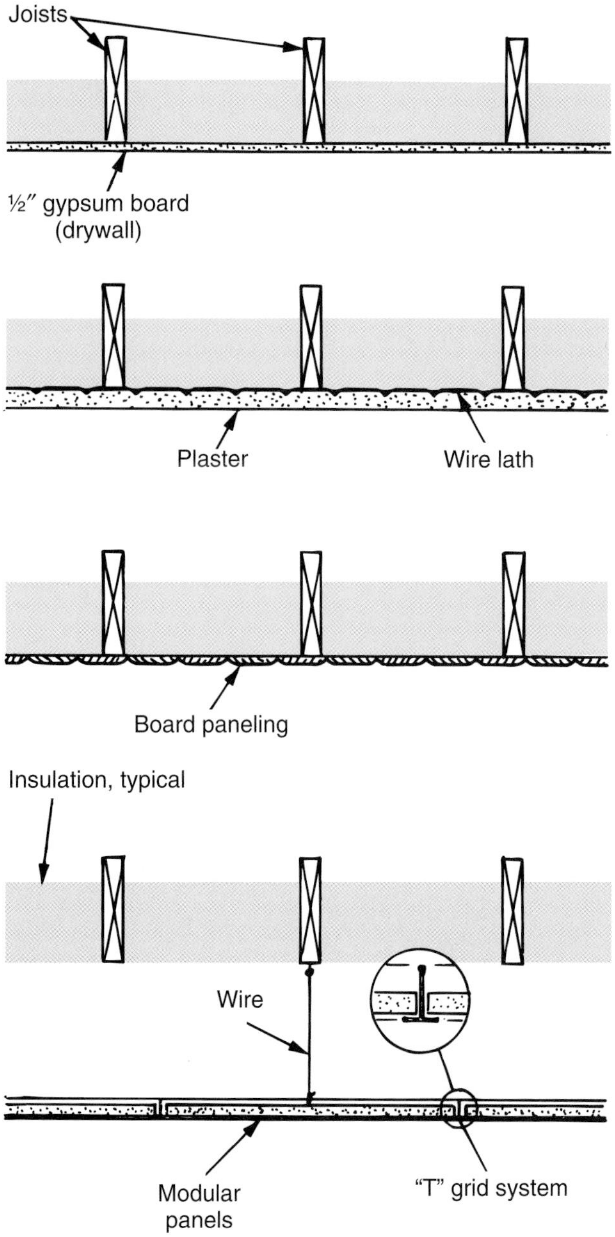

15-4 The most common ceiling-surface materials are gypsum board, plaster, wood panels, and suspended ceiling materials.

15-5 Gypsum provides a smooth ceiling surface that can be painted. It is a good choice for any room in the house.

is less expensive than plaster and installed more quickly. Gypsum board can be finished with several types of treatments. It is also fire resistant.

When used as a ceiling surface, gypsum board is attached to joists or trusses using nails and adhesive. The adjoining edges are covered with a perforated tape and gypsum compound. This procedure forms a smooth surface suitable for painting or other treatment. Two thicknesses of drywall can be used to form a ceiling of superior quality. This type of construction is less likely to show cracks from shrinkage and loose nails as the ceiling ages.

Plaster Ceilings

Gypsum plaster is a traditional ceiling material. It is durable, economical, fire resistant, and structurally rigid. It is also a good sound insulator. Plaster can be applied to curved as well as flat surfaces and can be molded into shapes, 15-6.

Some sort of base must be attached to the ceiling before plaster can be applied. The base material is called a **lath**. Commonly used laths are of gypsum, perforated gypsum, insulating fireboard, and expanded metal. Two or three coats of plaster are applied over the lath. The first coat of plaster finish applied directly to the lath is called the **scratch coat**. When it has hardened somewhat, it is *raked*, or scratched, to provide a good bond for the next coat. When three coats are used, the second coat, called the **brown coat**, forms a base for the finish coat of plaster. The finish coat may be troweled smooth or given a textured finish, 15-7.

A NMC/Focal Point

B NMC/Focal Point

15-6 Plaster can be molded into decorative ceiling coves and used as a ceiling-surface material (A). Rosettes and other decorative moldings can be made from plaster (B).

The total thickness of plaster on a ceiling should be at least ½ in. Plaster on a masonry surface or a metal lath is usually thicker. Plaster may be applied by hand or with a plastering machine. Paint is often used as a treatment for plaster ceilings.

Paneled Ceilings

Wood boards or sheet products can be used as a ceiling-surface material, 15-8. Solid wood-paneling boards are available in several designs ideal for ceilings. They range in widths from 4 to 12 in. and are usually ¾ in. thick, but thinner styles are available. Boards are nailed directly to joists or trusses. They may be stained, painted, sealed with a clear finish, or left untreated.

Plywood paneling can be nailed directly to joists or trusses, too. Many types are prefinished and

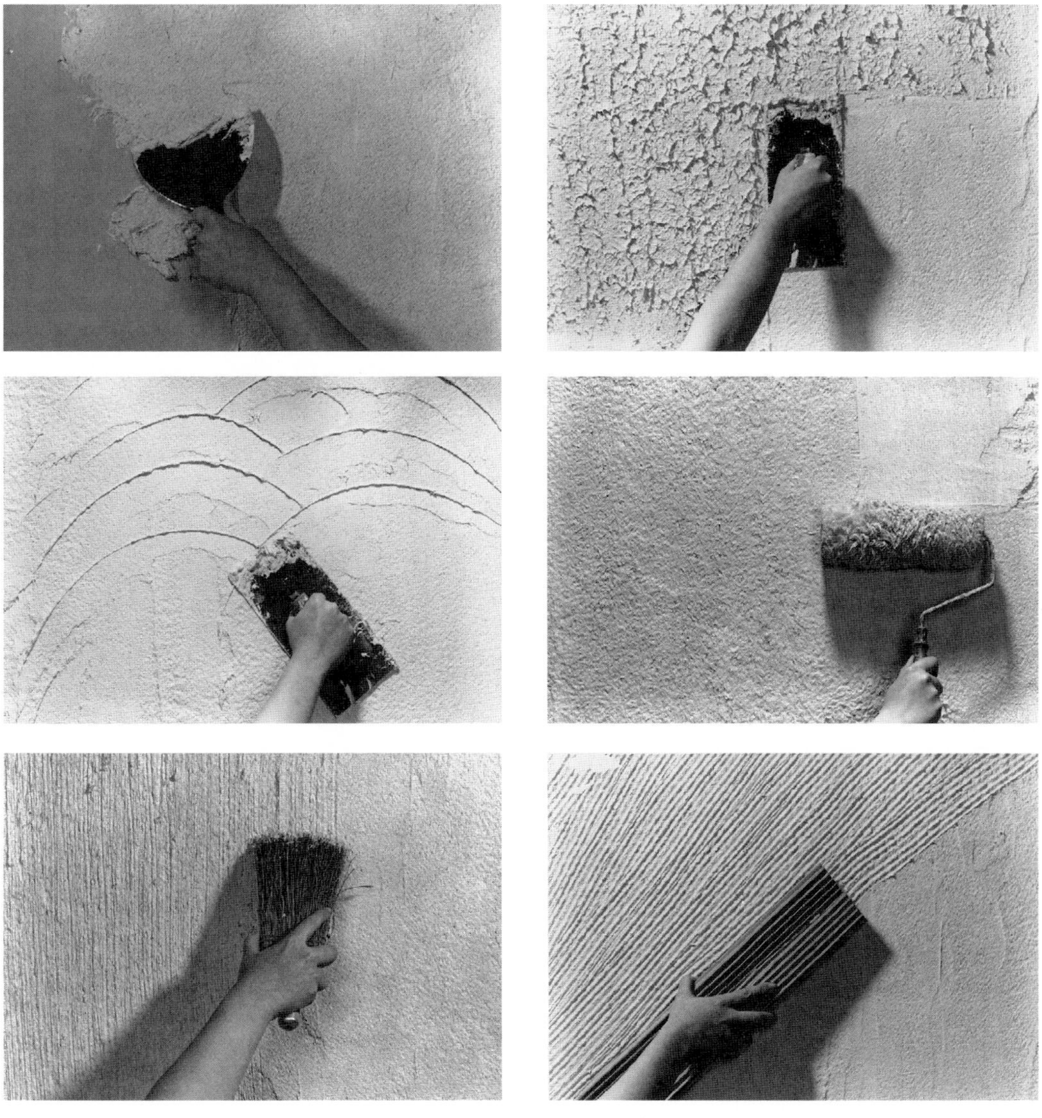

15-7 Several methods can be used to produce textured patterns in plaster.

A Arcways, Inc. B The Oshkosh, WI, private residence of Chancellor Richard H. Wells and family, formerly the Alberta Kimball Home

15-8 Individual boards form the sloped ceiling in this modern home (A). The ceiling panels in this room are made from a prefinished plywood product (B).

require no further treatment. Paneled ceilings are durable and need little maintenance.

Suspended Ceilings

A **suspended ceiling** is popular for kitchens, bathrooms, and basements, but it may be used in any location of the home. Suspended ceilings use a metal framework designed to support ceiling panels. The supports form a grid pattern that commonly holds either 2 by 2 ft. or 2 by 4 ft. ceiling panels, 15-9. The grid is suspended from joists or trusses by wires.

Standard, prefinished panels for suspended ceilings are available in a wide variety of styles, 15-10. Translucent panels are used to form luminous ceilings, popular for bathrooms and recreation rooms. Fluorescent lighting is placed above the ceiling panels.

15-9 Suspended ceilings consist of a metal grid that supports ceiling panels. Clear panels can be used for an illuminated ceiling.

Ceiling Treatments

Many ceiling surface materials are prefinished and require no further treatment. Gypsum board and plaster, however, require some form of ceiling treatment, which usually consists of paint or ceiling tiles.

Paint

Paint, a popular ceiling treatment, is easy to apply and provides a passive background for a room. White and light colors are most common because they help reflect diffused light. They also

western red cedar, give a house a rustic appearance, 15-25. Wood-roofing materials are more expensive than asphalt materials.

Tile, Slate, and Concrete Materials

These materials are expensive, but they can enhance the architectural style of a home. They are heavy and require special roof construction to support the weight. Concrete materials have an appearance similar to tile and slate, but weigh and cost less, 15-26. These materials are very durable and will last for the life of the structure.

Photo Courtesy of James Hardie® Siding Products

15-24 Asphalt shingles are the most popular roofing material.

15-25 Wood shakes provide a rustic appearance.

Metal

The most popular metal used for roofing is copper. It is seldom used to cover an entire roof because it is very expensive. However, copper roofing can be used in smaller quantities to accent the style of the house, 15-27. Copper is the most durable of all roofing materials.

15-26 Concrete roof tiles are made to resemble terra cotta tile.

15-27 Copper is an elegant but expensive roofing material.

Chapter Summary

Ceilings and roofs confine the space in a dwelling and protect the interior space from the elements. The roof serves as an integral part of the exterior design, while the ceiling is part of the interior design.

Ceilings help define the limits of a room. Ceiling heights are a function of architectural style and location in the structure. Most residential ceilings have a frame construction similar to that of floors. Others may use roof trusses for support. Gypsum board, plaster, wood boards, and suspended ceiling materials are used to form the ceiling surface. Ceiling treatments may be added to the ceiling surface materials as paint or ceiling tiles, or installed as prefinished materials.

Roofs are part of the basic house structure. Roof framing consists of rafters and ceiling joists or roof trusses. Important concepts related to roofs include: span, slope, rise, and run; cornice design; flashing; and roof styles. Common roofing materials include asphalt roofing, wood shingles and shakes, tile, slate, concrete materials, and metal. The type of roofing material chosen will have an important impact on the overall appearance of the exterior of the dwelling.

Review Questions

1. How do ceiling joists compare to floor joists?
2. Would gypsum board or plaster be more practical for a flat, rectangular ceiling? for a curved ceiling?
3. How is a suspended ceiling constructed?
4. For what rooms is a suspended ceiling popular?
5. What is the most common ceiling treatment?
6. How is the ridge of a roof formed?
7. How is the slope of a roof determined?
8. Where is flashing normally located?
9. Which roof style does the best job of preventing water and snow buildup?
10. How do the roofing materials for flat and shed roofs differ from the materials used for other styles of roofs?
11. What roofing material is least expensive? most durable?

Suggested Activities

1. Write a short essay describing how a ceiling is constructed in frame construction.
2. List several ceiling-surface materials and discuss each in terms of appearance and construction considerations.
3. Describe the construction methods and materials used to build a roof.
4. Collect photos from magazines or take your own photos of different cornice designs. Identify each type and display them to the class.
5. Pick a popular roof style in your community. Describe its features, overall appearance, and relative cost to build. Also identify the types of roofing materials generally used in your area on this style of roof.

Internet Resources

American Iron and Steel Institute
steel.org

Architectural Ornament, Inc., manufacturers of polyurethane architectural molding
architectural-ornament.com

ATAS International, Inc., a manufacturer of metal roofing
atas.com

Cor-A-Vent, Inc., a manufacturer of roof vents
cor-a-vent.com

Elk Corporation of America, a manufacturer of premium roofing materials
elkcorp.com

Georgia Pacific Corporation, supplier of building products
gp.com/build

International Zinc Association
iza.com

James Hardie® Building Products, Inc.
jameshardie.com

Knauf Fiber Glass, manufacturer of thermal and acoustical fiberglass insulation
knauffiberglass.com

Reynolds Building Products
reynoldsbp.com

Note: Web addresses may have changed since publication. For some entries, reaching the correct Web site may require keying *www.* into the address.

Chapter 16
Windows and Doors

Objectives

After studying this chapter, you will be able to
- list standard types of windows available for residential use and cite their advantages and disadvantages.
- evaluate the quality of a window's construction in terms of appearance, function, and insulative value.
- select and place windows in a home so that optimum lighting, ventilation, privacy, and appearance are achieved.
- list and describe various types of window treatments.
- distinguish among various types of doors by their appearance and method of operation.
- describe the construction of a door.
- list possible treatments for interior and exterior doors.

Key Terms

sash	ruffled curtains
muntins	cafe curtains
cornice	window shades
valance	hollow-core flush door
lambrequin	solid-core flush door
shirred curtains	door jamb

Windows and doors influence the interior and exterior appearance of the home. They provide both a physical and visual connection between two areas. They shield an opening from the elements and provide privacy while allowing light, ventilation, and a broadened view. Windows and doors should be planned to provide their optimum contribution to the function and design of a structure.

Windows

Windows serve many functions. They provide natural light, ventilation, and privacy. They also contribute to the atmosphere of a room, add detail to a decorative scheme, and give balance and design to the exterior of a structure, 16-1.

16-1 Windows play an important role in the exterior design of this home. The basic architectural theme is repeated at each window to provide continuity.

Window Types

Sliding windows, swinging windows, and fixed windows are the three basic types of windows used in housing construction. Combination windows and overhead windows are also used. The kind selected depends on the functions to be performed, architectural style of the structure, construction considerations, building codes, costs, and personal taste.

Sliding Windows

The most common type of sliding window is the *double-hung window*. See 16-2. It is a classic design that has remained popular since colonial times. The main glass area is called a **sash**. The window opens vertically from the bottom, the top, or both. Two sashes are held in the window frame. When slid up or down, each sash is held in place by friction, springs, or weights. Double-hung windows are usually tall rather than wide, with both sashes the same size.

Several advantages are associated with double-hung windows. They are readily available and produced in a wide variety of sizes. They are easy to install and rarely warp or stick. They do not project inside or outside to interfere with draperies or traffic. The horizontal lines of double-hung windows are considered more attractive and less distracting than the lines of other types of windows. See 16-3.

Double-hung windows are difficult to clean on the outside. However, many newer types of sashes are easy to remove or pivot inward for cleaning. No protection from the rain is provided by open double-hung windows. They are sometimes difficult to open and close when furniture is placed in front of the window.

Horizontal sliding windows move on tracks at the bottom and top of the windows. They generally contain two movable sashes, but only half of the window area can be opened at one time, 16-4. Screens are mounted from the outside. A wide range of standard sizes is available.

16-2 Double-hung windows are the most popular window used in residential housing.

Caradco Wood Windows and Patio Doors

16-3 Double-hung windows are often paired with special-shaped windows to create a dramatic look.

Photo courtesy of Hurd Windows and Patio Doors

16-4 Horizontal siding windows are available in a wide variety of sizes and generally contain two movable sashes.

Swinging Windows

Types of swinging windows include: casement, awning, hopper, and jalousie windows. Casement windows usually have two sashes hinged at the side to swing outward. Cranks are generally used to open and close casements, but push bars or handles may be used.

Casement windows are great ventilators, 16-5. Because the sash swings out, air that would otherwise pass the opening is directed inward. Casements are opened easily with a crank, even when they are located above a kitchen counter or behind furniture. Screens and storm sashes are easy to install and remove because they are located inside.

Casement windows have several disadvantages. They project outward and may be bumped into easily, so they should not be used near walks or play areas. They collect dirt easily because of their construction and do not keep out rain when open. Some may consider the vertical lines of these windows distracting.

Andersen Corporation

16-5 Casement windows provide a good view and swing out for ventilation.

Awning windows are hinged at the top and swing outward, 16-6. They are manufactured as single or multiple units stacked in a single frame. The sashes are opened with a crank or push bar and provide good ventilation and rain protection. Screens, which are located inside, can easily be removed for window cleaning.

Awning windows, like casements, should not be located where they might interfere with pedestrian traffic, such as between the house and carport. They also collect dirt when open.

Hopper windows are hinged at the bottom and swing into a room. A lock handle positioned at the top of each unit opens them. Designed for low placement on a wall, hopper windows improve air movement and do not interfere much with draperies. They are frequently used as basement windows as well.

Hopper windows are usually manufactured as one unit. They are easy to clean, but they interfere with inside room space near the window. Screens must be removed from the outside.

Jalousie windows consist of a series of narrow horizontal slats, 3 to 8 in. wide, that are held by a metal frame. The slats operate in unison, similar to venetian blinds. They open outward, but produce little interference due to their narrow slats. The amount of ventilation is adjusted by using a crank. Screens and storm windows are located inside when used with jalousie windows.

Andersen Corporation

16-6 Awning windows may be stacked to provide maximum ventilation and view.

Jalousies are used where ventilation is a major concern. They do not seal well and allow substantial air infiltration when closed. They are difficult to wash because of the small glass sections. Jalousie windows are produced in a variety of sizes, with increasing widths of 2 in. increments and lengths of 2½ in. increments.

Fixed and Special-Shaped Windows

The purpose of fixed windows is to admit light and provide a view, 16-7A. They do not permit ventilation. Picture windows, a type of fixed window, are generally oriented to an exterior setting that enhances a room in the living area. Fixed windows are usually custom made rather than a standard size.

Special-shaped windows, such as triangles, trapezoids, octagons, and circle-top windows, are generally used as an architectural design element. See 16-7B. They permit daylight, but are rarely designed to open and provide ventilation. The glass in these windows is set in one of the following: a fixed sash mounted in a frame that will match the regular ventilating windows or a special frame formed in the wall opening. Since fixed and special-shaped windows do not open, weather stripping, hardware, and screens are not required.

Combination Windows

Fixed windows may be used as units with sliding and swinging windows. Such units are called combination windows. For example, hopper windows are often combined with an upper, fixed window. A three-section window may have fixed glass in the center and casements on both sides. Awning windows may be placed above or below a fixed window. Combination windows allow an unobstructed view and ventilation.

Bay and bow windows are combination windows with their sections at angles so the window projects out from the structure. Bay windows generally use two double-hung windows with a fixed window in the center, 16-8. The side windows are normally placed at 45° angles to the exterior wall.

Bow windows are usually constructed with casement and fixed windows. Standard combinations of four to seven units are common. These window units form an arc that extends beyond the outside wall, 16-9.

A Pozzi Wood Windows

B Andersen Corporation

16-7 Fixed windows (A) are used in areas where view or lighting is more important than ventilation. Special-shaped windows (B) can be used with any movable window unit.

16-8 A bay window has a projected area of fixed glass with double-hung windows on both sides.

Caradco Windows and Doors

16-9 A bow window provides a panoramic view and adds interest to the exterior design of a house.

Skylights and Clerestory Windows

Skylights and clerestory windows are used to admit light into areas of a structure that have little or no natural light. Skylights are usually located on the roof or ceiling; clerestory windows are placed high on a wall. Their use can achieve dramatic lighting effects in a room. Some skylights and clerestory windows may open for ventilation.

Skylights are available in several basic shapes and sizes as well as unlimited custom designs. Clerestory windows may be a series of standard windows or custom-made, fixed windows, 16-10.

Window Construction

Windows consist of a frame, one or more sashes, and any necessary weather stripping or hardware. Sashes may have **muntins**. These are small vertical and horizontal bars that separate the total glass area into smaller units. Frame materials include: wood, metal, vinyl, and metal- or vinyl-clad wood.

Wood as a window framing material is a good insulator. It is considered attractive and blends well with most interiors. However, wood expands and contracts with different moisture conditions. This may cause gaps and sticking at different times of

A Velux-America, Inc.

B Marvin Windows and Doors

16-10 Skylights (A) and clerestory windows (B) give a room an airy appearance.

the year. Also, wood needs a protective coating of paint or vinyl that must be properly maintained.

Metal window frames are usually made from aluminum, although steel, brass, and bronze windows are also made. Aluminum windows are less expensive than wood and require less maintenance. Aluminum is very strong, allowing a thinner, lighter frame than is possible with wood. It is usually coated for an attractive, maintenance-free finish. It can be left plain if desired because it naturally forms an oxide coating that needs no other treatment. Aluminum is not a good insulator, however, and condensation may form on it when interior temperatures differ greatly from exterior temperatures. Vinyl frames are similar to metal frames, but they are better insulators.

Metal-clad wood frames are covered with aluminum on the exterior or both exterior and interior sides. This type of window offers the low maintenance of aluminum and the insulating value of wood. Windows covered only on the exterior side also allow an interior wood finish.

Each style of window is constructed differently, and construction will vary with different manufacturers. Details of construction can be obtained from the window manufacturer.

Heat Loss

As the cost of home heating rises, heat loss around windows and through glass becomes a major concern. Proper sealing and weather stripping helps prevent drafts that cause heat loss or gain.

Heat loss or gain through glass can be minimized in several ways, 16-11. A single-pane glass window is not a good insulator, but its insulation value can be nearly doubled by adding a storm window. Dead air space between storm windows and regular windows acts as an insulator.

Insulating glass works on the same concept of using a pocket of air as an insulator. The window consists of two panes of glass, called *double glazing*, with a space between them of ¼ to ⅝ in. that contains air or some other gas. Insulated glass panes are produced as sealed units with metal or welded glass edges. The air between the panes is dehydrated to prevent condensation. New types of dry gas provide even better insulative value. Some manufacturers add a third pane to insulated glass,

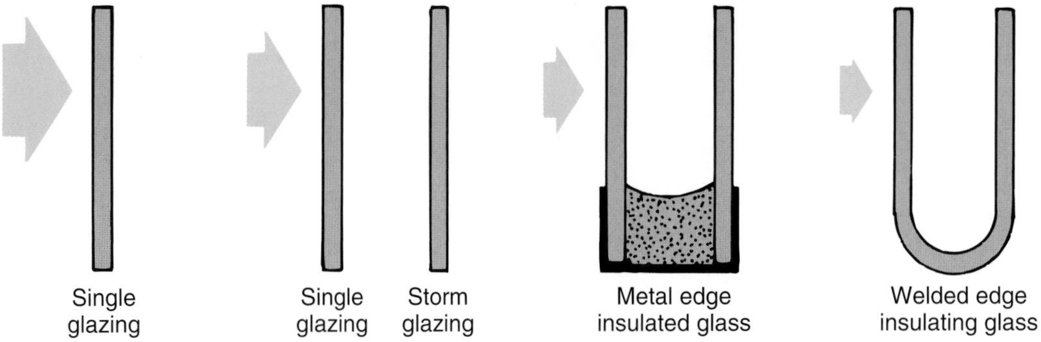

16-11 The type of glazing used in a window affects how much heat is lost through it. The size of the arrows represents the relative amount of heat lost through various types of windows.

which is called *triple glazing.* Insulated glass may be used in combination with storm windows to reduce heat loss or gain.

Reflective coatings on glass can reduce heat loss or gain. The glass manufacturer usually applies them, but the window manufacturer may add special films to cover the glass. The coatings may be transparent or tinted.

In the winter, when the sun is low and shining directly into a window, quality windows can transmit sunlight into a home and trap its heat. Solar gain may even exceed heat loss through glass if the window has a southern exposure. A proper roof overhang will shade the higher, summer sunlight from entering a window, and a properly insulated window will reduce unwanted heat gain in the home. See 16-12.

Window Symbols

Standard window symbols are used on construction drawings to communicate the type and location of windows in the structure. Figure 16-13 shows some of these symbols with an elevation view. The sill below the window is shown where one is used. There is generally no sill on basement windows and some modern picture-frame type windows used in frame construction.

Window Selection and Placement

Uniform lighting is desirable in a room, and proper window placement and selection helps eliminate very dark or bright areas. Generally, when the

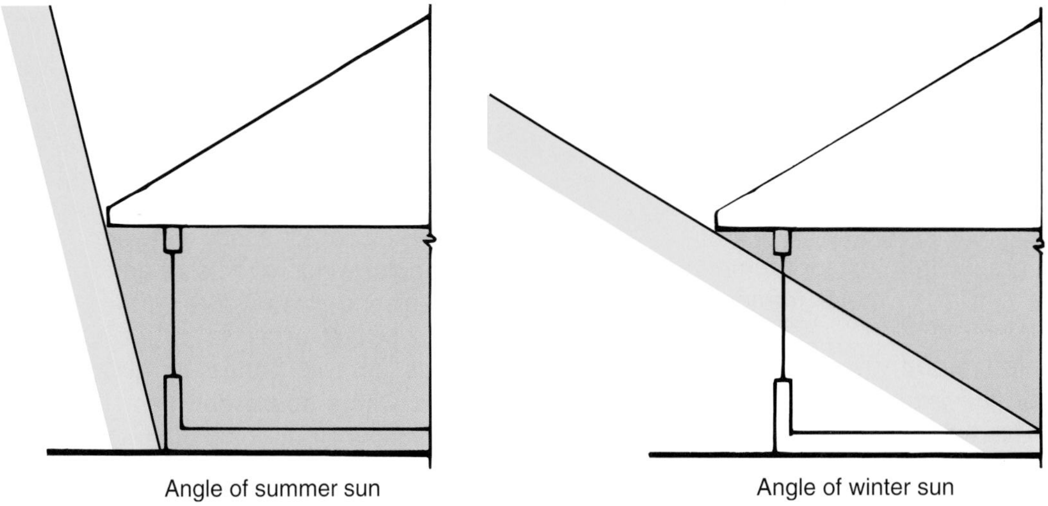

16-12 When an overhang is properly designed, the sun is shaded from a room in the summer, but enters it in the winter.

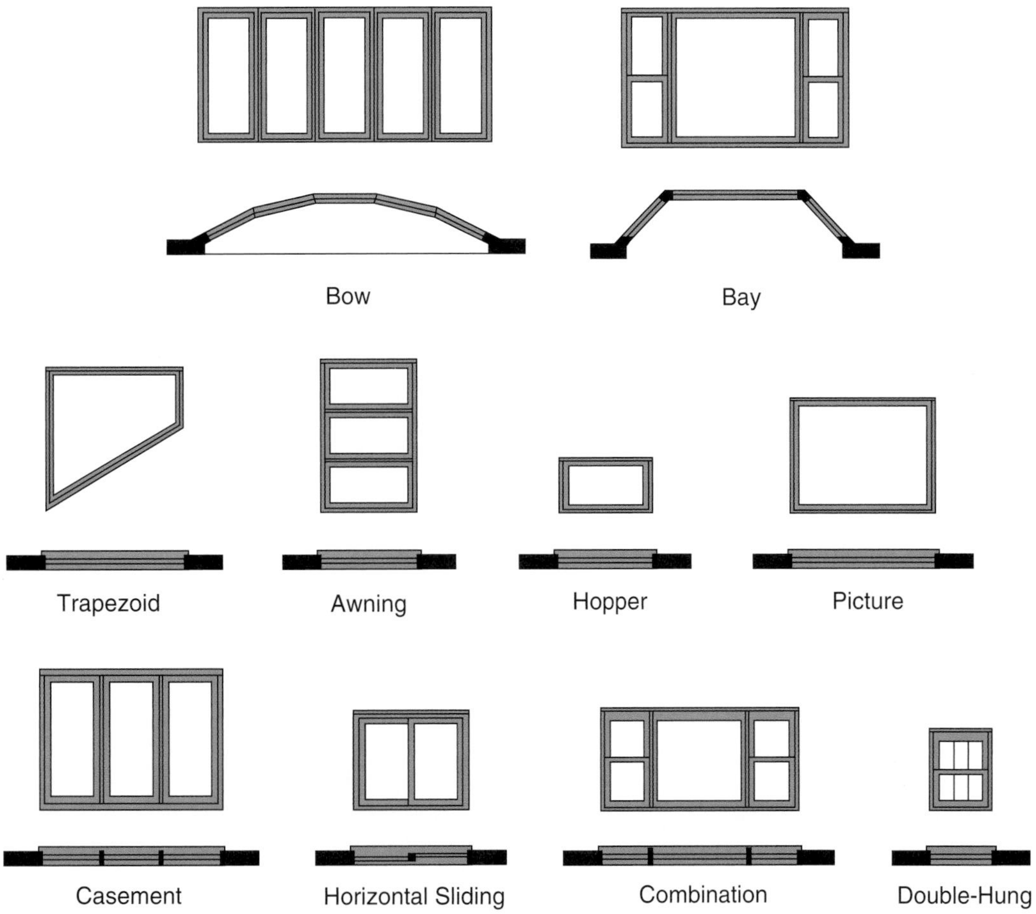

16-13 Various symbols are used to represent windows on construction drawings.

glass area is 20 percent of a room's floor area, adequate natural light is provided even on cloudy days. Draperies or blinds can be used to shield light on extremely sunny days.

Windows that face south provide more light than windows facing other directions. One large window provides more even lighting than several smaller ones. Windows on more than one wall distribute light better than windows on a single wall. Windows placed high on a wall allow more light to enter a room than low windows.

Natural ventilation in a living space is necessary throughout the year. Windows are a prime source of ventilation, especially during warm weather. Adequate ventilation is provided if openings equal about 10 percent of the home's floor area and take advantage of breezes. The types of ventilation provided by different window placements are shown in 16-14.

Privacy is a concern with window placement, and different types of windows provide varying amounts of sound privacy. Closed windows provide a barrier that helps keep exterior noise out and interior noise in. For louder surroundings, insulated glass windows can provide sound reduction while still providing natural light.

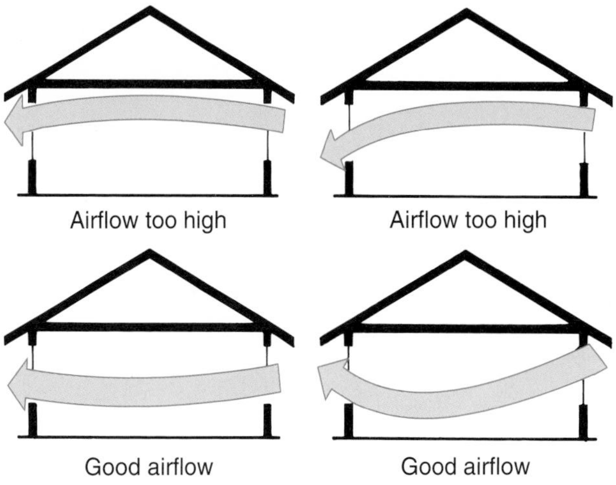

16-14 Window placement affects airflow through a living space.

For sight privacy, window glass that is textured, colored, or higher than eye level is effective in bedrooms, bathrooms, or other private areas. Outdoor shrubbery and fences can help obstruct the view into a window from public areas. The use of window treatments easily changes a room's level of privacy.

Windows can help create an atmosphere by framing an attractive view that enhances the room's overall appearance. Vertical windows accent a narrow view, while horizontal windows allow a panoramic view. Windows also promote a feeling of open space by extending the line of vision past the wall. When a window is used for aesthetic value and is not required for ventilation, fixed glass is appropriate.

Windows have a dominant effect on the exterior appearance of a structure, 16-15. Exteriors are becoming simpler through elimination of costly, unnecessary decoration. As this happens, windows become more important to the architectural character of the structure. Although windows should first meet interior requirements, adjustments may be desirable to create a more acceptable exterior. A properly designed exterior should provide continuity between wall and window areas, 16-16.

For more information about window styles and sizes, see Figures A-19 through A-23 in the Appendix.

Window Treatments

The purpose of window treatments is twofold. First, they function to control light, air, and privacy. Secondly, they complement the design scheme and, therefore, help beautify the interior. Frequently,

Las Vegas Smart House

16-16 This house has windows that blend well with its architectural style.

16-15 Windows are the dominant architectural feature of this modern home.

one purpose will have higher priority than the other for each room or specific window.

Before selecting a window treatment for a room, consider the style of living intended for the area—informal, formal, or a mixture. Also consider the role the window will play in the total design scheme. For example, will the window be the focal point or a background element? A large window with an impressive view should be a focal point, but a window without a nice view may serve as a background for other room elements.

Window treatments can be chosen to correct cases of poor design. If windows are out of proportion to the rest of the room—too narrow, short, or irregular in size—the proper window treatment can change the home's appearance.

Another consideration when selecting window treatments is the direction the window faces. North windows receive no direct sunlight; they usually require a different treatment than south or west windows that receive much direct light.

Finally, window treatments must be able to withstand moisture, strong sunlight, frequent use, and the other conditions to which they will be subjected. Only materials that will retain their original quality under these conditions should be used.

Century Furniture Company

16-17 Draperies can be distinguished from curtains by their heavy, pleated panels. These draperies are hung on a decorative rod.

Interior Window Treatments

Several basic interior window treatments are possible, including: draperies, curtains, shades, blinds, shutters, panels, and other treatments. One or more of these treatments generally coordinate with most design schemes.

Draperies

Draperies are generally defined as pleated panels that can cover the glass area or be pulled to one or both sides for decorative purposes, 16-17. Center draw draperies open and close at the center of the window, while one-way draw draperies pull as one unit across the entire window area. Stationary panel draperies stay positioned at the sides of a window to frame the view. These are used when privacy is not essential.

Tier draperies utilize several tiers of short draperies. Each tier may be controlled individually, providing great variability in the level of natural light in a room.

Sheer casement draperies are see-through draperies. They provide some privacy and filter sunlight, but not to the extent of typical heavier fabrics, 16-18. Often they are hung close to the glass, while heavier, more opaque draperies are

WCI Communities, Inc.

16-18 These double-draw sheer draperies provide some privacy, but allow light to enter the room.

positioned further from the wall. They provide filtered light when the heavier draperies are open and maximum privacy when they are closed. This pairing of draperies is called double-draw draperies.

Draperies are frequently topped with cornices, valances, or lambrequins. A **cornice** is a horizontal decorative treatment across the top of the window generally made of wood that is padded and covered with fabric, 16-19. A **valance** is a horizontal, decorative, fabric treatment across the top of draperies to provide a finished appearance and hide hardware and cords. A **lambrequin** is a cornice that extends down the sides of the window.

Curtains

Curtains are usually considered less formal than draperies. They add to the casual charm of any room. Popular types of curtains include: shirred, ruffled, and cafe curtains.

Shirred curtains are gathered directly on rods. Some curtain panels can be placed on rods at the top and bottom, and then stretched tightly for a somewhat formal look, 16-20.

Ruffled curtains are edged with ruffles on the hem and sometimes the sides. They are frequently finished with ruffled valances and tiebacks, 16-21. A tieback is a cord or fabric strip used to hold back a curtain panel to the side of the window. Priscilla-type curtains cross at the top and are generally made of sheer or semisheer fabrics that are ruffled on three sides.

Cafe curtains are straight curtains hung from rings that slide along a rod. They may be used in tiers to cover an entire window, or they may cover the window bottom with or without a matching valance at the top, 16-22. The curtain tops may be looped, scalloped, or pinch pleated. Cafe curtains are considered the most informal of the curtain types.

Century Furniture Company

16-19 A cornice accents the formality of a room.

Spiegel, Inc.

16-20 When made of a lightweight fabric, shirred curtains allow light to filter into a room.

Shades

The second most common window treatment is **window shades**. These are screens of fabric or other material that filter or block light. Many people use shades in combination with decorative curtains to protect the curtains from fading and block light without closing the curtains. Shades are also effective in reducing heat loss in winter and heat gain in summer.

The main types of shades include: roller, Roman, Austrian, and pleated shades. *Roller shades* are composed of a strip of material hung on a roller from the top of a window, 16-23. The strip is pulled down to close the shade, and it rolls up by a spring mechanism. Roller shades are available in translucent and opaque styles. They are produced in regular and reversed roller types. Reversed roller shades roll toward the window.

Roman shades do not roll up; cords pull them up. They are made from decorative fabric and are generally used alone as a window covering. Roman shades hang flat when closed, but fold into horizontal pleats when raised, 16-24.

Austrian shades are designed to operate the same as Roman shades. However, they have scallops

Manufactured Housing Institute

16-22 Cafe curtains are the most informal type of curtain. They may be used in tiers or with blinds.

Country Curtains

16-21 Ruffled curtains help create a pleasant, informal atmosphere in a room.

B&W Manufacturing, Inc.

16-23 Roller shades may be used alone or with another window treatment.

Smith + Noble Windoware

16-24 Roman shades are raised by cords to compress into a stack of folds.

Hunter Douglas

16-25 Although translucent, most pleated shades are good insulators.

of sheer fabric between the vertical cords. They are often used in formal rooms where they provide an elegant accent.

Pleated fabric shades are available in two types: accordion and honeycomb. Accordion pleated shades generally have a single layer of polyester web, mesh, or solid fabric that is folded into thin, horizontal pleats. They are raised or lowered using cords. These shades are manufactured in a wide range of colors and finishes and some are insulated. Fabrics vary from translucent to opaque and can be plain or patterned.

Honeycomb shades have smaller pleats and usually a heavier polyester fabric. They operate on the same principle as the single-pleated shade except two pleated shades are bonded together. This results in a honeycomb cross-section. Consequently, air pockets are formed that increase energy efficiency. The exterior side of the shade is usually white to reflect the sun's rays, but the inside may be any color or pattern, 16-25.

Blinds

Horizontal blinds are popular window treatments that are available with three basic choices of slat widths: 2 in. *venetian blinds,* 1 in. *miniblinds*, and ½ in. *microblinds*. Venetian blinds incorporate a series of slats supported by tapes and operated by cords. The slats are wood, metal, or plastic.

The contemporary version of the venetian blind is the miniblind. The narrow slats are held by thin cords that create almost no interference with the view, 16-26. They are lightweight, can be mounted on the inside or outside of the casing, and create a trim look. Miniblinds are available in a wide range of colors and, when used alone, they can add sophistication to the most formal interiors. Miniblinds can also be used with a wide variety of draw or side draperies. These blinds are difficult to dust and clean, but some windows enclose the blinds between two panes of glass to reduce dust problems, 16-27.

The newest version of the venetian blind is the microblind. The very narrow slats are smooth when closed and nearly invisible when open. Microblinds are also made in a wide variety of colors and have characteristics similar to miniblinds, but are not as durable.

The special advantages of horizontal blinds include nearly complete control of light and the direction of airflow. They can be completely hidden behind a valance or other treatment if desired. They are relatively durable, inexpensive, and aesthetically pleasing. New materials, patterns, and colors have made these blinds a versatile decorating tool.

Smith + Noble Windoware

16-26 The narrow slats of these modern wooden blinds are both functional and attractive.

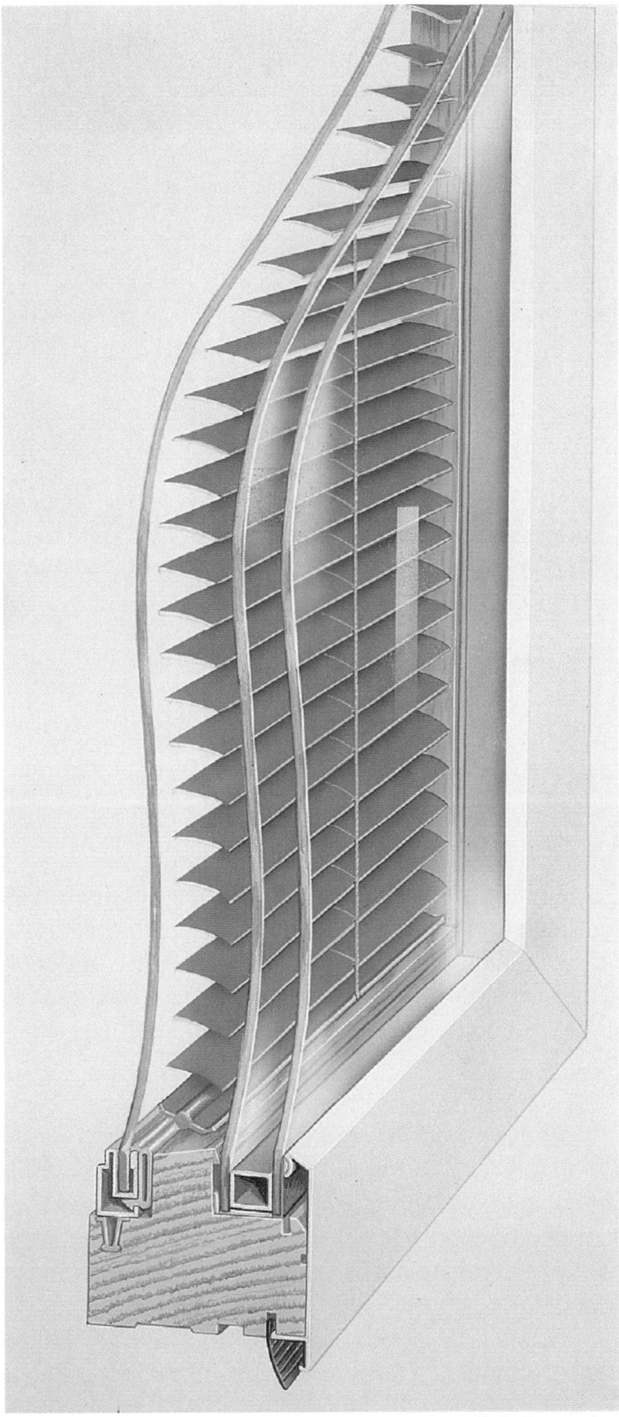

Pella Corporation

16-27 Miniblinds are placed between two panels of glass in some windows. This eliminates the need to clean the blinds.

Vertical blinds consist of a series of vertical slats that hang from an upper track, 16-28. Slats made of metal, fabric-covered plastic, or wood may be joined by a chain at the bottom. Some can accommodate inserts of coordinating fabric or wallpaper. Vertical blinds can be angled from side to side to control the sunlight or completely shut to conserve energy. They provide a view only in the direction of the opened slats and block all other views. They create a feeling of height in the room and do not collect dust as quickly as horizontal blinds. One disadvantage of vertical blinds is children and pets can easily damage them.

Shutters

Shutters are available in both traditional and contemporary styles. Traditional shutters have louvered or fixed slats. Contemporary shutters utilize fretwork inserts combined with a backing of fabric or some other opaque material. Shutters are attached with hinges so they can be opened to admit light and more ventilation. One or more units may be connected to cover several windows or a single, wide window.

Photo of Kirsch LouverDrape Verticals courtesy of Levolor Kirsch Window Fashions

16-28 Vertical slat blinds are elegant and practical, and they help make a window appear taller.

Drexel Heritage Furnishings, Inc.

16-29 The screen covering these windows diffuses the light, obscures the outside view, and creates the peaceful mood associated with Oriental settings.

Shutters may be used in combination with curtains and blinds or other window treatments. They can be painted to match any color scheme or decor. They provide privacy and ventilation, which makes them good choices for bedrooms and bathrooms.

Sliding Panels and Screens

Sliding panels and screens can provide dramatic window treatments and a spectacular room focus. Wood panels may have latticework or carving backed with translucent or opaque material. They may be stained or painted to match the room's decor.

Stretching fabric over a wooden frame makes fabric panels. These may be manufactured or custom made with fabrics that match or complement other pieces in the room. Some panels have painted scenes that serve as a focal point.

Sliding screens may be used in place of draperies or curtains. See 16-29. They frequently cover sliding glass doors and windows and may be used with casement windows that swing outward. These screens require a series of tracks at the top and bottom as well as space beside the door or window if they are to be fully opened.

Other Treatments

Privacy and shade from sun is not always necessary for all types of windows. Stained glass or etched glass windows are highly decorative by themselves and need no other treatment, 16-30. Decorative wood frames may be used to accent a window. Houseplants on window shelves or in nearby hanging planters provide partial coverage and a refreshing appearance.

Exterior Window Treatments

Exterior window treatments have two advantages. First and most obviously, they enhance the exterior appearance of the house. Secondly, they can affect the interior in a positive way without interfering with interior wall space or furniture. Some of the more popular exterior window treatments include: awnings, shutters, trellises, and grilles.

Awnings

Awnings are available in weather-resistant fabrics or metal. They protect the window from rain and wind and produce soft lighting inside the home. Some awnings are stationary, 16-31, while others

16-30 Stained glass is highly decorative and requires no further window treatment.

16-31 An awning shades a room from direct sunlight and adds detail to the architecture.

Photo Courtesy of James Hardie® Siding Products

16-32 Decorative shutters provide a pleasing addition to this dwelling.

can roll up. The selection of awnings should be coordinated with other exterior elements to avoid an added-on look.

Shutters

Functional shutters are not used nearly as often today as they were in the past. Most shutters today are purely decorative; they are fixed in place and simply frame the window, 16-32. When they are designed to cover a window, they provide excellent protection against bad weather.

Trellises

Trellises are popular for providing shade and can be designed to complement the architectural style of any house. Sometimes climbing plants are incorporated with the trellis to enhance the window's appearance.

Grilles

Grilles are usually considered stationary window coverings. They are made from wood, plastic, metal, or masonry. Grilles are effective for providing privacy, shade, and ventilation.

Selection of Window Treatments

Windows provide an excellent opportunity to add design interest to any room decor with one or more of the many types of curtains, draperies, shades, blinds, shutters, or panels and screens available. Exterior window treatments, using awnings, shutters, trellises, or grilles, can be used effectively to enhance the outside of a home.

Function and Decoration

Windows serve several important functions in a living space. They provide natural light and ventilation, contribute to the atmosphere of a room, and add detail to the decorative scheme. On the exterior, they give balance and design to the overall structure. These are important considerations to remember when selecting window treatments.

In addition, various window treatments have their own strengths and weaknesses to take into account before making choices for your home. Consider the following:

- A brightly colored drapery will call attention to the window, whereas unpatterned fabrics similar to the wall color will act as a gradual transition between the wall and glass.
- Rooms with low ceilings look higher if draperies extend from floor to ceiling.
- Draw curtains and draperies provide flexible control of light and privacy.
- Heavy draperies can be used to absorb noise in proportion to the thickness of the fabric, the depth of the folds, and the area covered.
- The use of drapery lining prevents draperies from fading, protects them from sun deterioration, and reduces any dust or drafts coming through a window. The lining also provides extra insulation, adds fullness to the drapery, and provides a uniform exterior appearance.
- Small rooms look larger if curtains and draperies blend and extend the length of the walls.
- Sheer curtains and draperies can be used to treat several small windows in close proximity as a single window, thereby reducing a choppy appearance.
- Pastel sheers can be used to tint the whole room when light filters through. For daytime use, sheers diffuse the light and provide some privacy.
- Color value is generally the most noticeable quality of a window treatment.
- A dreary room will seem brighter when cheerful colors or interesting patterns are used on windows.
- Styles of valances can help establish the character of various historical periods, 16-33.
- Formal treatments such as lambrequins, cornices, and valances lend themselves to rooms with a more formal atmosphere or period furnishings.
- Cornices can increase energy efficiency of the window treatment because they are closed at the top, stopping the airflow above the window.
- Decorative rods can contribute to the total window design, 16-34.
- Shades reduce light and increase privacy in relation to their thickness or opaqueness.
- Roller shades are easy to maintain, insulate against heat and cold, and can filter light or darken a room.
- When privacy is a consideration, blinds, shades, or heavy draperies are usually the best choices.
- Exterior window treatments, such as awnings or shutters, provide effective climate control without taking wall space within the room. Awnings can reduce interior heat gain by as much as 75 percent
- Exterior shutters increase security and protect windows during bad weather, 16-35.

President Benjamin Harrison Home, Indianapolis, IN

16-33 The valance and drapery in this period home help to provide unity to the decor.

Smith + Noble Windoware

16-34 Black curtain rods shaped to resemble wrought iron are an attractive window accent for these simple, white sheers.

- Grilles can provide added security against home invaders when fastened to the window frame.

Doors

Doors are necessary for connecting one area to another while providing protection and privacy. They also contribute to the atmosphere of a room and give balance and design to the exterior of a structure. Some also add detail to the decorative scheme.

Door Types

The main types of doors used in residential construction are: flush, stile-and-rail, swinging, sliding, folding, and garage doors. The kind selected depends on the architectural style of the structure, construction considerations, building codes, costs, and personal taste.

16-35 The motorized storm shutters on this home protect it during inclement weather and while occupants are away.

Flush Doors

Flush doors are the most commonly used doors in current construction. They are manufactured in woods such as birch, mahogany, and oak as well as metal and vinyl. These materials are used as panel coverings for flush doors, resulting in a flat, plain surface, 16-36A.

A **hollow-core flush door** has a framework core covered with a wood, metal, or vinyl veneer. Regardless of the covering, the core is usually made of wood. Hollow-core doors are lightweight and relatively inexpensive. Their strength and insulation value are low, however, so they are used almost exclusively as interior doors.

A **solid-core flush door** consists of solid particleboard or tightly fitted blocks of wood covered with a veneer. These doors are heavy and strong. They also are good insulators. Solid-core doors are more expensive than hollow-core doors so are usually used as exterior doors.

Standard interior flush doors are 1⅜ in. thick and 6 ft. 8 in., or 80 in., high. Widths range in increments of 2 in. from 2 to 3 ft. Wider or narrower doors can be made to fit special needs. Exterior flush doors are produced in widths from 2½ to 3½ ft. in 2 in. increments. Heights include: 6 ft. 6 in., 6 ft. 8 in., 7 ft., 7 ft. 6 in., and 8 ft. Standard exterior doors are 1¾ in. thick, but larger doors are usually 2¼ in. thick.

Stile-and-Rail Doors

Stile-and-rail doors are constructed with a strong, heavy frame around the perimeter of the

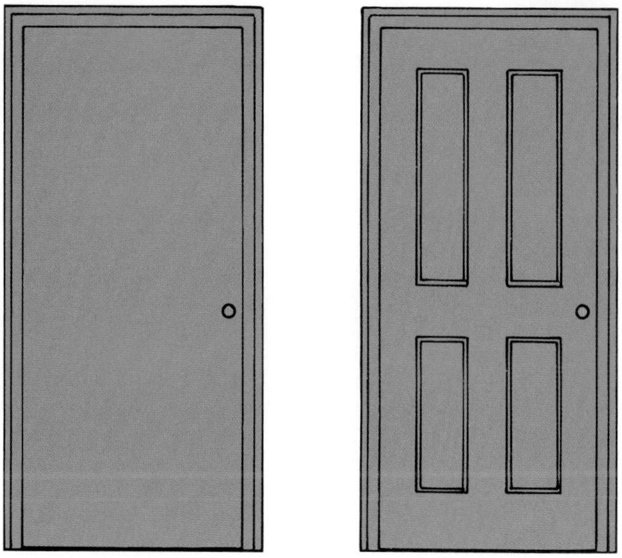

16-36 A flush door (A) has a smooth surface with a hollow or solid core. In a stile-and-rail door (B), various styles are possible with different geometric arrangements of the panels.

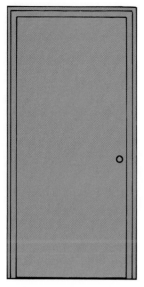

16-37 French doors are stile-and-rail doors with all-glass panels.

door, 16-36B. Vertical frame members, called stiles, and horizontal members, called rails, provide support across the center of the door. The space between the stiles and rails is filled with thinner panels that are set into the framework. These panels are most commonly made of glass or wood. Many different styles are possible by altering the size, shape, and arrangement of the panels.

Panel doors are stile-and-rail doors that use thinner wood panels within the framework. They are solid and provide complete sight privacy and good sound privacy when closed. Sash doors are nearly the same as panel doors, but one or more of the panels are glass. French doors are sash doors with all-glass panels, 16-37. Sash doors provide privacy, but they also allow light and a view.

Louver doors have a series of wooden slats set between the stiles and rails. These doors are not solid, so they are not practical for exterior use. They are appropriate where good ventilation is desirable or where privacy is not important. Louver doors are commonly used for closets, laundry rooms, or space divisions.

Swinging Doors

If a door is placed on hinges so it swings out from the wall, it is called a swinging door. Swinging doors are the most convenient to operate for passage from room to room; they are also the most secure. Ample space must be allowed for the door to swing fully open.

Most swinging doors only open in one direction, but special hinges may be used so the door opens both ways, sweeping a full 180° arc. This type of door is called a *double-action door*. See 16-38A. It has a spring in the hinge that returns the door to its closed position.

Double-action doors are used between rooms with frequent cross traffic that require a closed door most of the time. Space must be allowed on both sides of these doors so that the door can swing freely. Sometimes two of these doors are paired to create swinging double doors.

A *Dutch door* is a swinging door with independently moving upper and lower halves, 16-38B. The top half may be open for free movement of air, while the bottom half provides a closure for small children and pets.

Sliding Doors

Sliding doors are set on a track and are opened or closed by gliding along the track. Glides on the floor keep the doors from swinging. They are useful because they do not require extra clearance space for opening. The three main types of sliding doors are: bypass, pocket, and surface-sliding doors.

Bypass doors are the most commonly used type of sliding door. They are popular for closets and other large openings. The doors are set on adjacent, parallel tracks so each can move past the other. Door handles are recessed to avoid interfering with passage. The most common sets of bypass doors have two doors, but more can be used to cover a larger opening, 16-38C. One disadvantage of this type of door is: the total opening is obscured by the width of one door even when fully opened.

These doors may be purchased in standard 2 to 3 ft. widths, 6 ft. 8 in. and 8 ft. heights, and a 1 3/8 in. thickness. They may be flush or stile and have a rail of wood or metal construction.

Glass sliding doors are a type of bypass door popular for exterior use. See 16-39. Usually two glass panels are used; in some cases, only one moves. Glass sliding doors allow a broad, unobstructed view and serve as a convenient passageway between the interior and exterior of a house. They may have a bronze, aluminum, wood, or steel frame. Standard sizes of glass sliding doors are shown in Figure A-24 in the Appendix. Sliding screen doors may be used with the doors. The door units are constructed of insulating glass or a single thickness of glass.

16-39 Sliding glass doors permit access to the outside while providing a broad view.

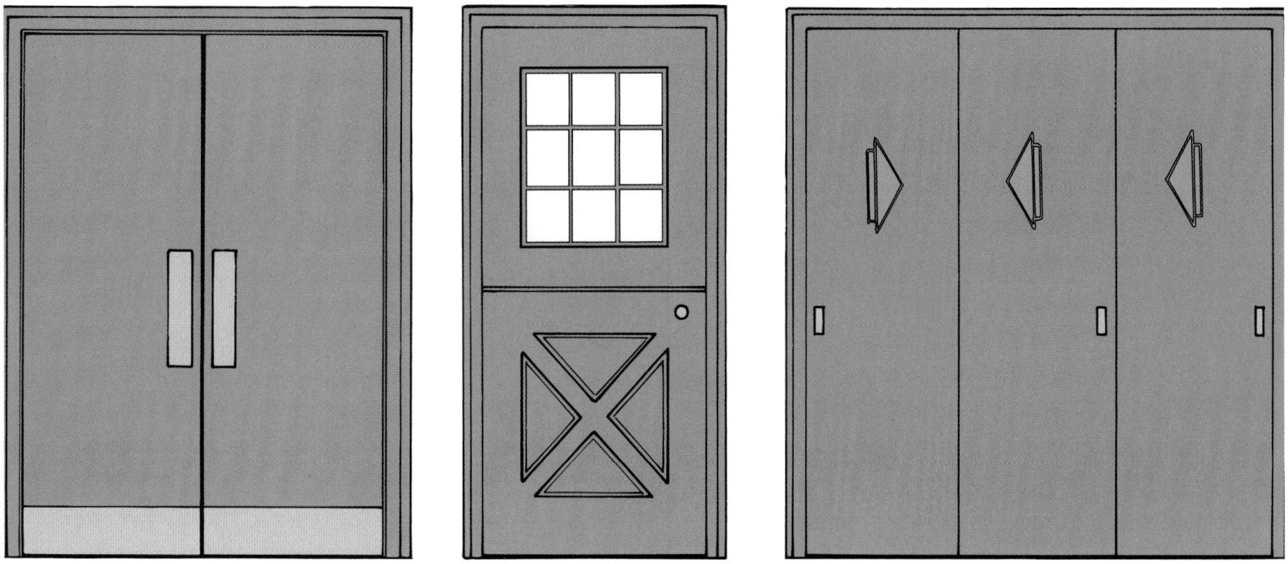

A B C

16-38 Double-action doors (A) open easily and swing shut automatically. Dutch doors (B) are swinging doors with independently moving top and bottom halves. Sliding doors (C) are on parallel tracks so they can slide past each other.

Pocket doors are sliding doors that fit within the wall when open. See 16-40A. They are useful where space is not available for a swinging door. They are more difficult to operate than swinging doors, and they require hollow wall space beside them. Consequently, it is difficult to use this space for mounting objects, such as wall cabinets and telephones.

Surface-sliding doors run on a track that extends onto the wall beside the doorway. This type of door requires free wall space for opening the door.

Folding Doors

The most common types of folding doors are: bifold, multifold, and accordion doors. They are hung on overhead tracks with nylon rollers or glides, like sliding doors. Folding doors fold back into a stack when open.

Bifolding doors are made of two units joined with hinges, 16-40B. The construction is either flush or stile and rail. The doors are usually installed in pairs that open from the center. If more than two units are joined, a *multifolding door* is made.

Bifolding and multifolding doors may be slightly thinner than typical flush or panel doors. Wood doors are 1⅛ in. thick, and metal doors are 1 in. thick. They may be purchased in either 6 ft. 8 in. or 8 ft. heights. The most common use of these doors is for closets. They require less operating space than a typical flush or panel door. However, the panels swing out from the wall so some clearance space is needed.

Accordion doors are generally used to close large openings where other types of doors would be impractical. They consist of very narrow panels that fold back and require very little space when open, 16-41. They are made of wood slats, plastic, or other sturdy, flexible materials. They are available in sizes to fit almost any opening.

Garage Doors

There are two basic types of doors that account for most garage doors used today: the overhead sectional and the one-piece overhead. See 16-42. These doors are produced in wood, metal, and fiberglass.

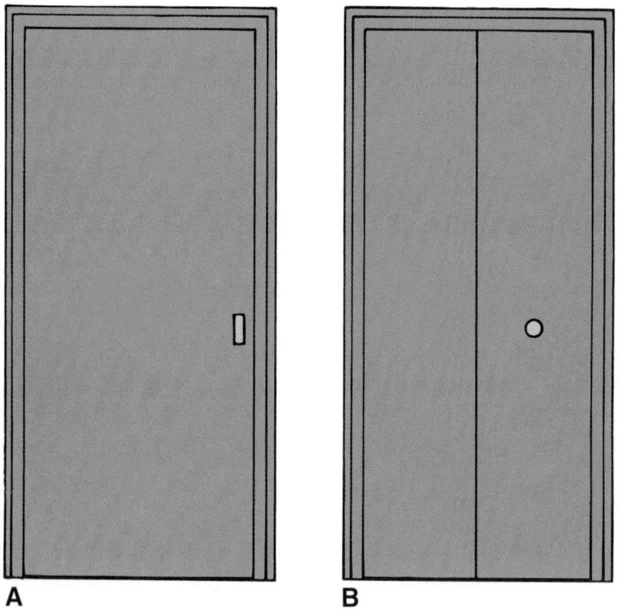

16-40 Pocket doors (A) recess into the wall and require no clearance space in a room. Each unit of a bifold door (B) contains two panels that are hinged together and fold back when open.

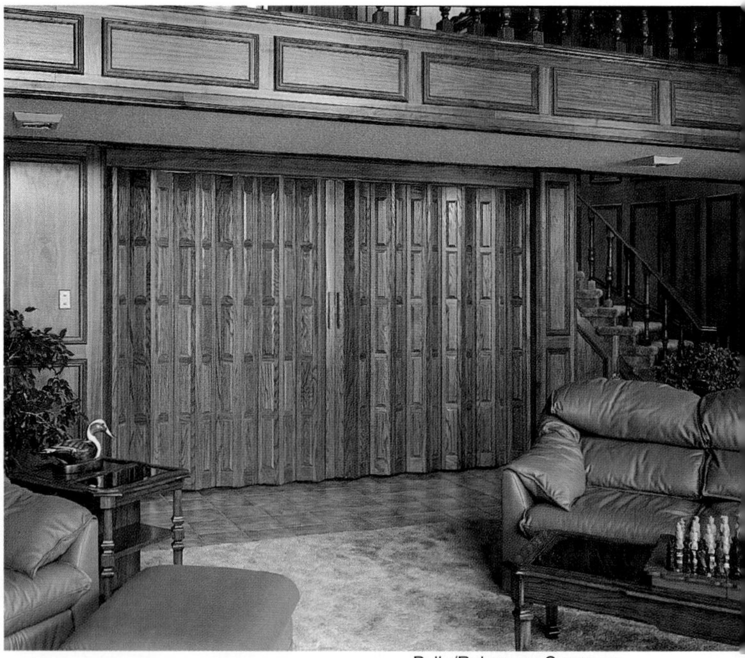

Pella/Rolscreen Company

16-41 Accordion doors are useful for closing large openings where little clearance space is available.

Garage door sizes are keyed to single-car and double-car garage openings. Typical door widths are 8, 9, and 10 ft. for single-car garages, and 16, 17, and 18 ft. for double-car garages. Standard heights are 6 ft. 6 in. and 7 ft. Commercial garage-door sizes are available to accommodate larger vehicles, such as motor homes and travel trailers.

Manville Building Materials Corp.

16-42 Overhead sectional garage doors (A) have several panels hinged together so the door can follow a curved track when opening. The one-piece overhead door (B) is a single unit that swings up and out when opened.

If an automatic garage door opener is installed, proper space and wiring must be provided. Adequate headroom is necessary to mount the motor drive on the ceiling above the door when it is open. Also, an electrical outlet is required to operate the motor.

Door Construction

A door is typically mounted in a **door jamb**. This is a door frame that fits inside the rough opening in a wall, allowing the door to fit and close securely into the wall. Door jambs are constructed of wood in most residential homes, although metal may be used.

Door jambs consist of two side jambs and a head jamb across the top, 16-43. Most exterior doors require a sill at the bottom to prevent drafts and leaks. Garage doors are an exception. Doorsills may be made of wood, brick, stone, or concrete. Many ready-made styles and types are available, but they are frequently custom made on the job.

Exterior door jambs are usually $1\frac{1}{8}$ in. thick while interior jambs are $\frac{3}{4}$ in. thick. The doorstop is rabbeted into an exterior jamb, but it is nailed to the face of an interior jamb. The doorstop is a strip, usually of wood, around the door jamb that prevents the door from swinging through the opening to the other side.

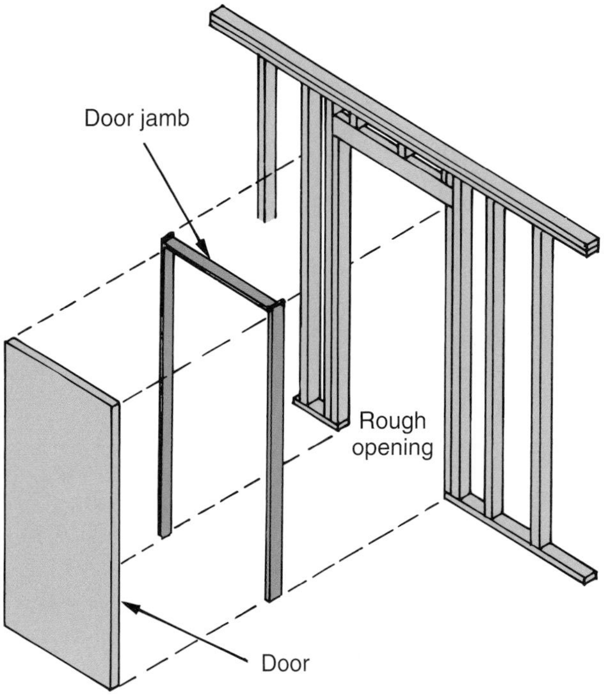

16-43 A door jamb is fitted into the rough opening of a wall. It provides a secure fit for a closed door.

Door jambs for interior and exterior doors are available as preassembled units with the door already hung and ready for installation. These units are called prehung doors. Rough openings must be sized properly to these units since little adjustment is possible.

Door Symbols

Standard door symbols are used on construction drawings to communicate the type and locations of doors in a structure. Some of the accepted symbols are shown in 16-44 with an elevation view to help clarify the type of door shown. Sills are on all exterior doors except garage doors.

Door Treatments

Doors sometimes receive little attention in the total planning and decorating scheme of a home. However, their treatment should be given careful consideration. A main entry door may be the focal

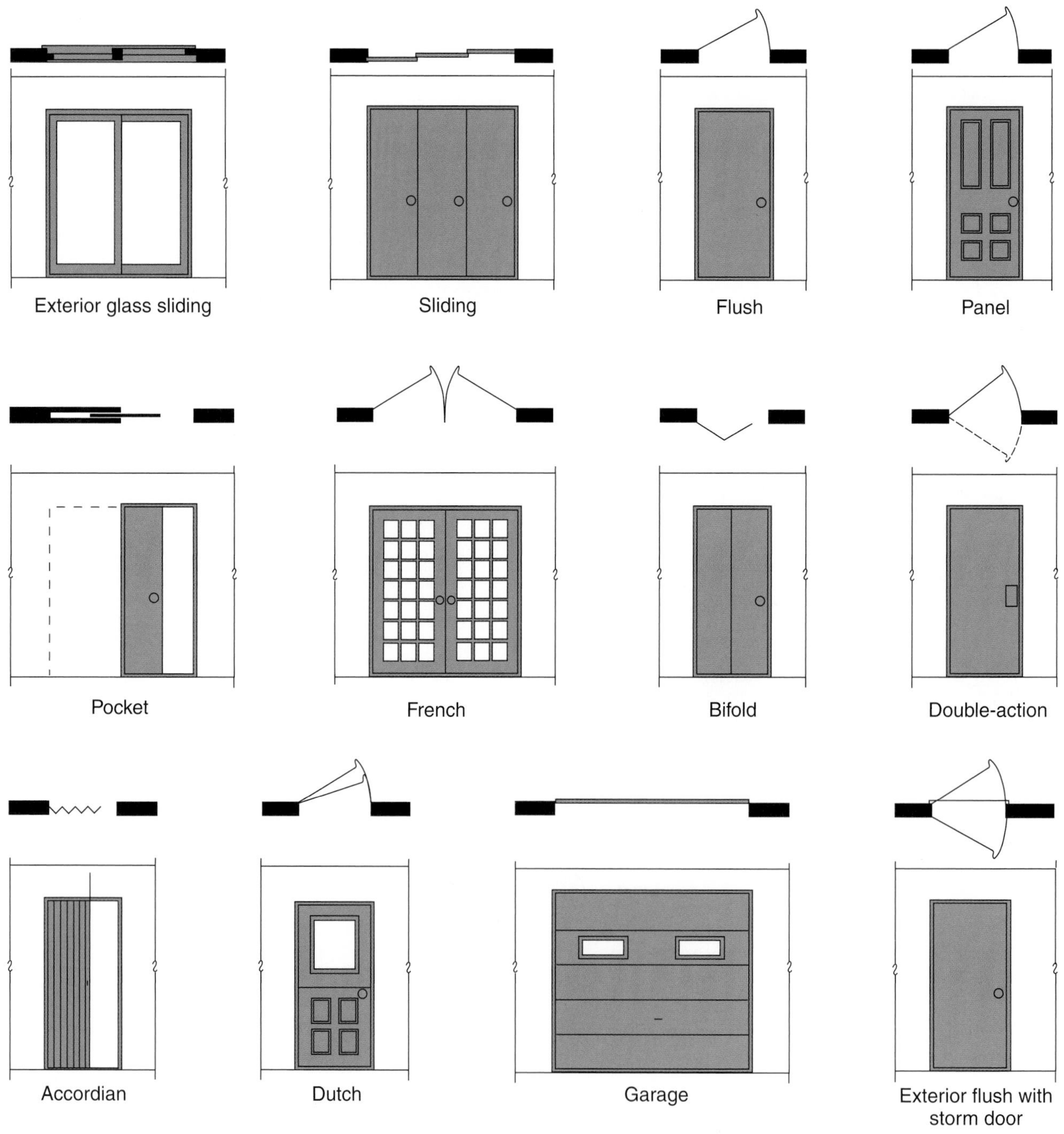

16-44 Various symbols are used to represent doors on construction drawings.

point of a home's exterior, 16-45. Interior doors may serve as an accent to a room's decor.

Main entry doors should be attractive on both the outside and the inside. Many treatments may be applied to the exterior of a plain, flush door. These include accent painting, molding, or decorative hardware. Manufactured or custom-made doors may have decorative carvings or stained or leaded glass inserts. Panel doors are attractive when painted in two colors to accent the panels.

Although many interior doors are of stained wood, other treatments are possible. A door can be decorated to complement a room's design, but first consider whether the door will be opened or closed all the time.

Covering a door with the same treatment used on the walls may soften its effect. Wallpaper, paint, or fabric are common wall treatments that can be used on doors. Panel doors may have coordinating fabric or wallpaper inserts. Some older homes may have too many doors to make furniture arrangement practical. A door may be temporarily closed off with fabric, screens, or wall units.

A Chamberlain Group

B Therma-Tru Corporation

16-45 Decorative panels (A) on an entrance door add interest to a plain surface. Leaded glass (B) accents the interior of the home as well as the exterior.

Chapter Summary

Windows provide natural light, ventilation, and privacy as well as contribute to the atmosphere of a room. There are three basic types of windows—sliding, swinging, and fixed windows. The most common type of sliding window is the double-hung window. Several kinds of swinging windows are produced, with casement being the most popular. Most windows provide ventilation, but fixed and special-shaped windows do not. Bay, bow, and other combination windows are made from two or more styles fastened together into a single window unit. Skylights and clerestory windows admit light into areas of the structure that have little or no natural light.

Windows generally consist of a frame, one or more sashes, weather stripping, and hardware. Window frames are made from wood, plastics, and metals. Modern windows are designed to reduce heat loss or heat gain.

Window treatments control light, air, and privacy and complement the design scheme. The window treatments selected should consider the intended style of living and design scheme. Interior window treatments include: draperies, curtains, shades, blinds, sliding panels and screens, or other treatments such as stained or etched glass. Exterior window treatments include: awnings, shutters, trellises, or grilles. Several important principles must be considered to choose good window treatments.

The main types of doors used in a residence are: flush, stile-and-rail, swinging, sliding, folding, and garage doors. A door is usually mounted in a door jamb made of wood, but metal jambs are available. Door treatments are important to the overall design scheme, but especially for an entry door intended to be the focal point of the exterior design.

Review Questions

1. Identify several important functions that windows provide in a living space.
2. What important function do windows provide to the exterior of a structure?
3. What are the main advantages and disadvantages of sliding, fixed, and swinging windows?
4. What types of units are available as combination windows? For what uses are combination windows appropriate?
5. What are the advantages and disadvantages of wood and metal window frames?
6. To decrease the tendency of heat to escape through windows, what can manufacturers do?
7. What is the difference between curtains and draperies?
8. Why are draperies lined?
9. What types of window treatments are best for completely blocking sunlight from a room? for providing filtered sunlight?
10. What are two reasons for using exterior shutters?
11. What types of exterior window treatments are available for residential use?
12. How does the construction of a flush door differ from the construction of a stile-and-rail door?
13. How are interior doors constructed differently from exterior doors?
14. What type of door is recommended for a doorway that has no clearance space for a swinging door? Why?
15. Other than staining, what are some treatments that can be used to decorate doors?

Suggested Activities

1. Research the Web site of a national window manufacturer and report the types of window products made by the company.
2. Survey each room in your home to identify the number and types of windows present. Record your findings.
3. Sketch several common shapes of special-shaped windows.
4. Write an essay about heat loss (or heat gain) as it relates to windows in a residence.
5. Create a poster board showing the many choices in window treatments and label each type displayed. Use sketches, Internet print-outs, and/or clippings from magazines and sales brochures.
6. Select a window in your room or home and describe the window treatment you would choose to update it. Describe he window's appearance now versus the final "look" you envision. Explain the advantages of the new look versus the old.
7. Prepare a list of the types of doors that are available for use in a residential structure. Describe the characteristics of each type.
8. Describe an entry-door treatment in your community that impresses you and write an essay explaining why. Identify the principles of good design that are evident and summarize your thoughts in a paragraph.

Internet Resources

Caradco, a manufacturer of wood windows and patio doors
caradco.com

Hurd Windows and Patio Doors
hurd.com

Marvin Windows and Doors
marvin.com

MI Home Products, a manufacturer of windows and doors
mihomeproducts.com

Pease Entry Systems, a manufacturer of entry doors
peasedoors.com

Pella Corporation, a manufacturer of windows and doors
pella.com

Pozzi Wood Windows
pozzi.com

Raynor Garage Doors
raynor.com

Velux-America, Inc. supplier of roof windows and skylights
velux.com

Windsor Windows and Doors
windsorwindows.com

Note: Web addresses may have changed since publication. For some entries, reaching the correct Web site may require keying *www.* into the address.

Chapter 17
Stairs and Halls

Objectives

After studying this chapter, you will be able to
- describe the seven basic design shapes used for stairways and evaluate their appropriateness for various applications.
- evaluate a stairway in terms of comfort and safety.
- identify stairway requirements for individuals with special needs.
- apply basic design principles to the choice of stairway treatments.
- evaluate a hallway in terms of function, durability, and decoration.

Key Terms

landing
main stairway
service stairway
straight-run stairs
L stairs
double-L stairs
U stairs
winder stairs
spiral stairs
circular stairs

Stairs and halls are designed to provide access to various living areas of a structure. They make it possible for a person to pass from one room to another without interfering with activities in those rooms. Hallways provide passage between rooms on one level of a structure. Stairs are used to connect different levels.

Stairways

A stairway is a series of steps that leads from one level to another in a structure. Landings are also considered part of the stairway. A **landing** is a flat floor area that may be placed at any point along a staircase. Steps and landings may be combined into a variety of designs to fit different structural, functional, and decorative needs. A list of terms used to describe stairways appears in 17-1.

Housing units with a first and second floor have a **main stairway** between those levels. Dwellings with two levels of the split-foyer design have a main stairway between the upper level and the foyer and another between the lower level and the foyer. Structures with basements have a **service stairway** from the basement to the first level, generally leading to a service area on the first floor. Main and service stairways are usually constructed differently and do not have the same degree of visibility in a home.

Main stairways are generally assembled with prefabricated parts produced in a mill or cabinet shop. The finest types are made from hardwoods or other wear-resistant materials such as terrazzo, stone, or tile. The main stairway is commonly used as a focal point in a decorating scheme, 17-2. Therefore, decoration as well as safety and convenience are concerns.

Service stairways are generally not visible to guests and, as a result, receive less design emphasis than main stairs. These stairways are usually constructed

Stairway Terms	
Balusters	Vertical members that support the handrail on open stairs.
Enclosed stairs	Stairs that have a wall on both sides. Also known as closed, housed, or boxed stairs.
Headroom	The shortest, clear vertical distance measured between the nosing of the treads and the ceiling.
Landing	A flat floor area at either end of the stairs and possibly at some midway point. They are commonly used in L and U stairs.
Nosing	The projection, usually rounded, of a stair tread that extends past the face of the riser below.
Open stairs	Stairs that have no wall on one or both sides.
Rise	The distance from the top surface of one tread to the top surface of the next.
Riser	The vertical face of a step.
Run	The horizontal distance from the face of one riser to the face of the next.
Stairwell	The opening in which a set of stairs is constructed.
Stringer	A structural member that supports the treads and risers. Housed stringers are routed or grooved to receive the treads and risers. Plain stringers are cut or notched to fit the profile of the stairs.
Total rise	The total floor-to-floor vertical height of the stairs.
Total run	The total horizontal length of the stairs.
Tread	The horizontal member of each step.

17-1 To understand a discussion of stairways, it is helpful to know the definitions of these terms.

Denise Arjmano, ASID, Illinois Chapter

17-2 A main stairway is usually visible from public rooms in a home, so it should be attractively designed.

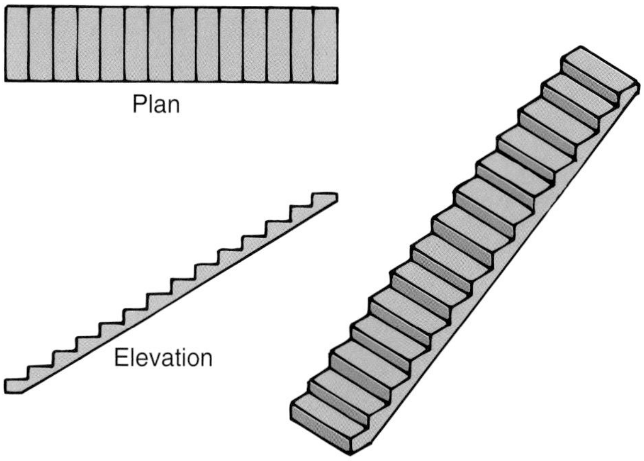

17-3 Straight-run stairs connect two levels without a turn or landing between the stairs.

on site from typical construction materials, usually softwoods. The main concerns when constructing service stairways are safety and convenience.

Stair Designs

Seven basic design shapes are used for stairways: straight-run, L, double-L, U, winder, spiral, and circular stairs.

Straight-run stairs have no turns or landings between the ends. See 17-3. Generally, they are the simplest and the most economical of all designs to build. Straight-run stairs are used more frequently than any other type.

L stairs have one landing at some point along the flight of stairs and change direction at that point, 17-4. If the landing is near the top or bottom of the stairs, the term *long L* is used to describe the design. The L-stair design is used when the space needed for a straight-run stairway is not available or when a change in direction is desired.

Double-L stairs have two landings along the flight, each with a 90° turn. This design type is used when neither the straight-run nor the L stairs can be used, 17-5. They are much more expensive to build and, as a result, are not frequently used.

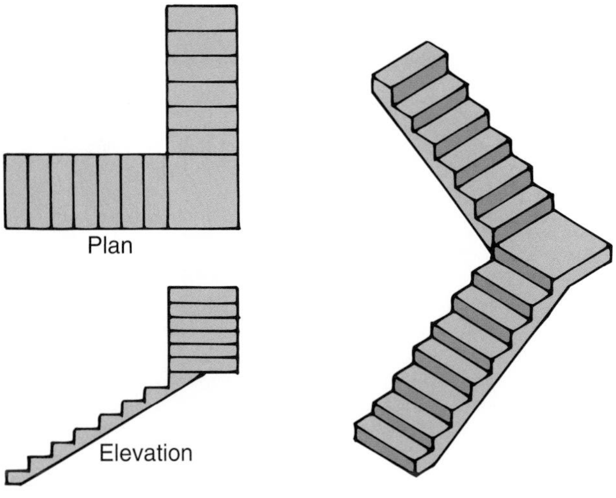

17-4 L stairs may be used where sufficient length is not available to construct straight-run stairs.

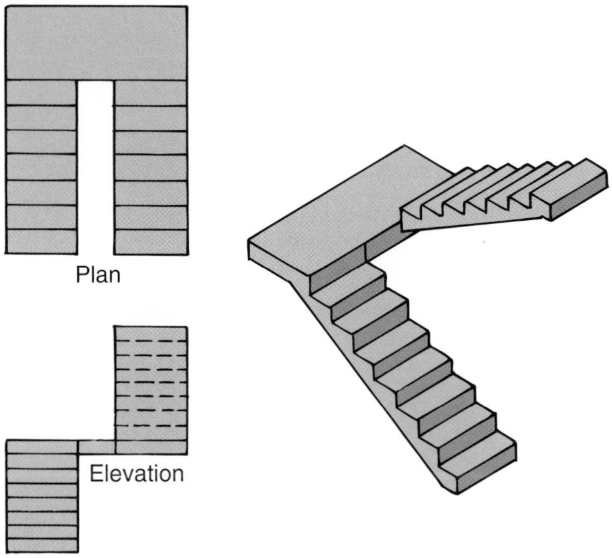

17-6 Wide-U stairs have a well hole between the two flights of steps. They require more space to construct than other designs.

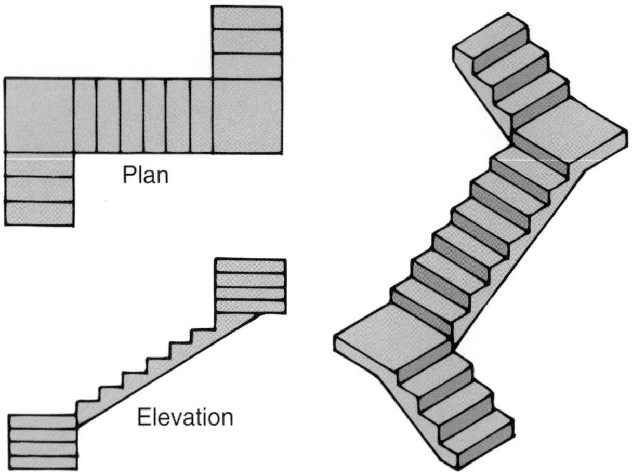

17-5 Double-L stairs have two turns. They are not used frequently because of excessive cost.

U stairs have two flights of steps parallel to each other with one landing between them. Two types of U stairs are possible, *wide U* and *narrow U*. Wide-U stairs have a well hole between the two sets of steps, 17-6. Narrow-U stairs are more compact, with little or no space between the flights, 17-7.

Winder stairs have wedge-shaped steps that are substituted for a landing, 17-8. Winder stairs are unsafe because of the varied and narrow tread width at the winding area. This design should be avoided whenever possible.

Spiral stairs consist of a number of wedge-shaped steps that may be fastened together to form a cylindrical stairway. They take up very little floor space, but they are more difficult to use than straight stairs. Manufactured kits have made this design popular. See 17-9.

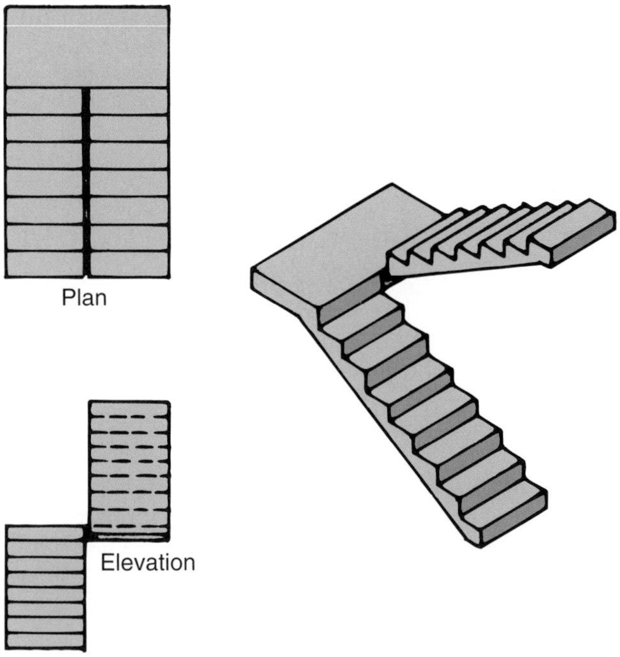

17-7 Narrow-U stairs are similar in design to wide-U stairs, but have less space between the flights.

Circular stairs are a custom-built, curved stairway made of trapezoid-shaped steps. The basic shape of the stairs is an arc or irregular curve. These stairways are impressive in very large homes. See 17-10.

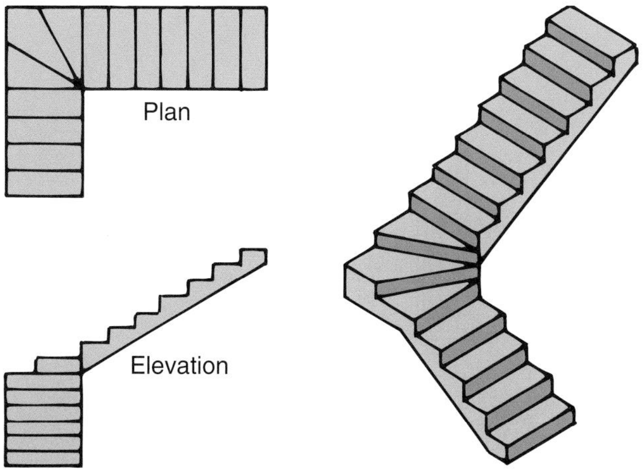

17-8 Winder stairs have wedge-shaped treads instead of a landing. They are generally considered unsafe because of the varied tread width.

Arcways, Inc.

17-9 Spiral stairs are useful where limited space is a major concern.

Stairway Comfort and Safety

A safe and comfortable stairway is based on the stride of an average person stepping up the height of a riser and forward the depth of a tread. Based on this guideline, the ideal stair should have a riser height of 7¼ in. and a run of 10½ in. These dimensions produce a stair-slope angle of about 34°. See 17-11. Some variation, however, is permitted. Generally, a riser height between 7 and 7⅝ in. and

Arcways, Inc.

17-10 Circular stairs may be the main focal point of a large, formal entryway.

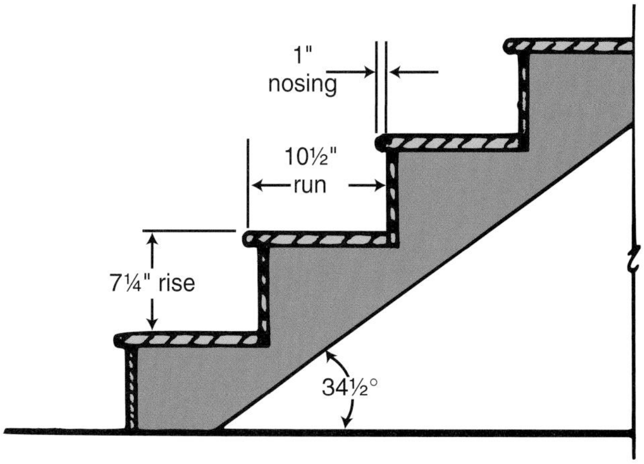

17-11 For safe use, stair dimensions should fit the stride of the average adult.

a run between 10 and 11 in. is acceptable if the angle of stairs is between 30° and 35°.

Each riser height and tread width should be the same for every step of the stairway. Uniform steps help prevent tripping or stumbling.

Stair width is another factor to consider. The minimum acceptable width of the main and service stairways is 36 in., but widths of 38 to 42 in. are preferred. Frequently, main stairs are slightly wider than service stairs, but both need to be wide enough to carry large furniture pieces from one level to another and to allow passage along the stairway. Stairways with turns should be wider than straight stairways to provide the same degree of accessibility.

Safety is also dependent on good lighting, adequate handrails, nonskid treads, and plenty of headroom. All stairways should have at least one lighting fixture located so that each step is clearly visible. Switches at both ends of the stairs are necessary to use the light each time it is needed.

Handrails are required on at least one side. They should continue the entire length of the stairs including landings. The recommended height of handrails along the stairs is 30 in. above the nosing of each step and 34 in. above the floor on landings. Rails may be attached to one or both sides of the stairs as desired. Railings are very important around open stairwells. They should be strong enough to support body weight.

A nonskid covering on each tread is a desirable feature. Carpeting is safe on properly designed stairways with a moderate slope angle and wide treads. Using carpeting on narrow treads of steep stairs, however, can make the stairway slippery and unsafe.

A vertical distance of 6½ ft. is the accepted minimum headroom for a safe stairway. It is measured from the nosing line of each step to the ceiling, 17-12. Headroom is not a problem when one stairway is located directly above another as in a two-story building with a basement. This arrangement also saves floor space, 17-13.

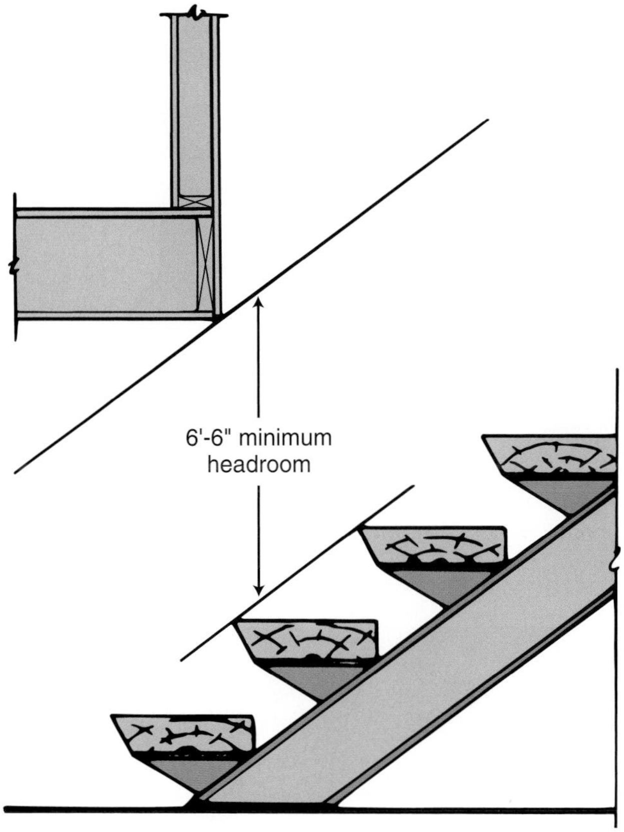

17-12 A safe minimum headroom for residential stairways is 6 ft. 6 in.

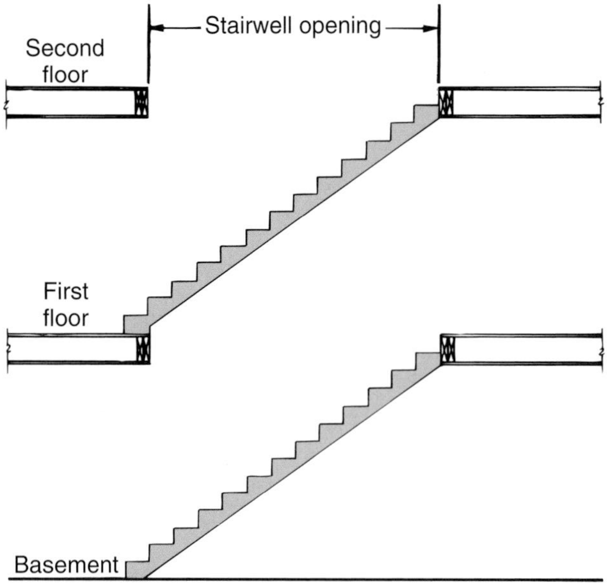

17-13 Stairways placed over one another in a two-story house save floor space and eliminate the problem of allowing extra space for headroom.

Adaptations for Special Needs

Sometimes stairs can be adapted for individuals who have difficulty walking by simply installing sturdy handrails on both sides of the stairway. The treads should be covered with a nonskid surface and open risers should be closed. Ideally, risers should be lowered and the treads should be widened, which would require rebuilding the stairway.

Installing a stairlift is a consideration for people who cannot climb stairs. One type of stairlift carries a person up and down on a special seat built into a fixture installed on the wall. Another type lifts a person seated in a wheelchair. Installing an elevator, perhaps in a space formerly occupied by a closet, is yet another alternative.

Ramps

Ramps installed at entries can enable people who find walking difficult or impossible to enter a structure. The recommended slope is 1 ft. rise for every 12 ft. of distance or a ratio of 1:12. In other words, to access a height of 3 ft., a ramp 36 ft. long should be planned. If a more gradual slope is required, a 60 ft. ramp should be planned to access a height of 3 ft. The recommended ramp width is 48 in., but 32 in. is minimum and 36 in. is required for using a wheelchair.

The maximum length of a ramp is 30 ft. Ramps longer than 30 ft. should be built in two or more sections with each section separated by a landing at least 5 ft. square. Landings are necessary rest stops for individuals who have difficulty moving uphill. An entry platform should extend 18 in. beyond the handle side of the door to allow a wheelchair user to open the door easily.

For safety, handrails should be placed on both sides of the ramp, usually 3 ft. high. Wheelchair users, however, can pull themselves up a ramp more easily when handrails are 30 in. high. If curbs are used, they should be placed on both sides of the ramp at least 2 in. high. Ramps should have nonslip surfaces and, if possible, protection from rain, snow, and ice.

Stairway Treatments

Stairways should be decorated to add interest and enjoyment to the living space. Generally, the decor of the room nearest the stairway determines the decor of the stairs, 17-14. For example, if the main stairway begins in the foyer, then identical or coordinating color schemes and carpeting may be

Armstrong World Industries, Inc.

17-14 Continuing the wall color up the stairway and painting its woodwork to match the wood trim used in the room helps visually tie the two areas together.

continued up the stairs. Hints of the scheme of the upper floor may be added.

Sometimes a stairway is unique in design or workmanship, 17-15. A unique stairway should become a focal point, with wall treatments and other decor accenting the stairway.

Stair coverings must be skidproof and durable. Carpeting with short, tight pile is best. Padding should not be too thick to prevent a firm footing. If steps have a good wood finish, but carpeting is still desired, exposing wood on both sides of the carpet will echo the wood handrails and enhance the design scheme. Nonskid strips or finish are available for exposed wood stairs.

When stone, terrazzo, tile, or other special materials are chosen for stairways, they usually are a continuation of the same materials used in a connecting room. See 17-16. These materials may function as structural members as well as decoration.

Halls

Hallways are necessary elements of most homes. They provide main avenues for traffic circulation and access to various parts of the living space. Each

Gerri Wiley, ASID, Illinois Chapter, and Kristie Geggie

17-15 This L stairway is a focal point for the room because of its unique design.

Western Pennsylvania Conservancy

17-16 Stone stairs are used in this home to accent the design of the stone walls.

member of the household passes through the halls many times each day, so halls should be pleasant and functional.

Standard residential hallways range in width from 36 to 42 in. Proper width is dependent on the length, shape, and expected use of a hall. Only very short halls should be 36 in. wide. Long halls no wider than 36 in. appear too narrow. Halls with right-angle turns need to be wider than 36 in. to provide room for moving furniture. If a hall is used frequently, space should be provided so people can pass each other comfortably. Hallways used less frequently can be narrower.

The floor covering for hallways is important. It should be durable since halls have frequent traffic in a concentrated space. See 17-17. Coverings such as cork tile, low-quality carpeting, and less durable types of vinyl tile are not recommended for hallways.

Walls along hallways also experience heavy wear. Washable wallpaper, paint, or other treatments are appropriate, especially if small children are in the home. Patterns that do not show dirt, and handprints help to keep the hallway looking clean.

The color of the hallway should coordinate with the rooms that open into it. Often, the wall and floor coverings used in a main room are continued through the hallway.

17-17 A ceramic tile floor is both attractive and practical for a frequently used entryway. Wear does not show and the floor is easily maintained.

Chapter Summary

Stairs and halls are designed to provide access to various living areas of a structure. A stairway is a series of steps that connect one level of the home with another. A landing is a flat area that may be placed at any point along a staircase.

A main stairway is required when a housing unit has a first and second floor. It connects these levels together. Houses may also have service stairs that connect the first floor to the basement. Main and service stairways follow seven basic designs. Comfort and safety should be the main concerns when designing and building stairs.

Stairs may be adapted to accommodate people with special needs. Covering treads with nonskid surface materials, making treads wider and risers lower, and providing a stairlift are some ways to make stairs more accessible. Providing ramps on the outside of the structure aids in accessibility.

Stairways should be decorated to add interest and enjoyment to the living space. A unique stairway may become the focal point in the decorating scheme. As a rule, the decor of the stairway should be a continuation of the room closest to it. Hallways should be pleasant and functional. Adequate width and a functional floor covering are important factors.

Review Questions

1. How do main stairways differ from service stairways?
2. What are the seven basic design shapes used for stairways?
3. Of the seven basic stairway designs, which two would use the least amount of floor space in a two-story home?
4. What points of construction should be considered when making sure a stairway is safe?
5. How do stairs designed for individuals with special needs differ from typical stairs?
6. What is the recommended slope of a ramp?
7. What factors should be considered when determining how wide a hall should be?

Suggested Activities

1. Describe the seven basic design shapes used for stairways and evaluate their appropriateness for various applications.
2. List all the factors necessary for stair comfort and safety.
3. Draw a plan view and elevation view of a ramp designed for wheelchair accessibility. Show dimensions, slope, and all other important features.
4. Prepare a survey of hall recommendations to ensure good design. Use the survey to evaluate a hallway in your home. Summarize your findings in a paragraph.
5. Tour one or more model homes in your community. Observe typical treatments for halls and stairways.

Internet Resources

Acorn Stairlifts
acornstairlifts.com

Architectural Digest Magazine
archdigest.com

Arcways, Inc., a manufacturer of custom stairways
arcways.com

Institute for Business and Home Safety
ibhs.org

Insurance Information Institute
iii.org

Louisiana-Pacific Corporation, a manufacturer of building materials
lpcorp.com

National Hardwood Lumber Association
natlhardwood.org

The McGraw-Hill Companies, Inc. construction products marketplace
sweets.com

Note: Web addresses may have changed since publication. For some entries, reaching the correct Web site may require keying *www.* into the address.

Part Six
House Systems

Chapter 18
Lighting

Objectives

After studying this chapter, you will be able to

- explain how natural light can be used to enhance the decor of a home.
- list the advantages and disadvantages of incandescent, halogen, and fluorescent lights.
- explain the difference between general, task, and accent lighting, and list types of fixtures that can be used to create each type of lighting.
- evaluate the appropriateness of lighting sources for the activities of a room.

Key Terms

natural light
artificial light
incandescent light
halogen bulbs
fluorescent light
general lighting
direct lighting
indirect lighting
task lighting
accent lighting
footcandle
structural fixtures
portable fixtures
luminous ceiling
recessed lights
track lighting
strip lighting

Lighting affects the beauty and efficiency of a home. Proper home lighting allows a person to perform tasks safely and efficiently without eyestrain. Well-planned lighting also enhances the mood and decorative scheme of a home. To utilize light sources fully, a person should understand how different forms and arrangements of light affect the surroundings. Both natural and artificial light should be considered when planning a residential lighting scheme.

Natural Light

Natural light is provided by the sun. Along with making colors seem sharper and brighter, sunlight generates a feeling of well-being. The amount of natural light that enters a room is controlled by the following factors: size, number, and arrangement of windows; type of window treatments; and placement of rooms.

Natural light gives objects warm, flattering tones, 18-1, but strong sunlight may produce harsh shadows and reflections. Smooth or shiny surfaces in rooms that receive many hours of full sunlight can cause considerable glare and eyestrain. Window treatments, however, can be used as filters to reduce the intensity of sunlight.

Exterior foliage is also useful for filtering light, 18-2. Deciduous trees, which have leaves only in summer, are especially effective in front of windows with a southern exposure. They temper light from the hot summer sun but shed their leaves in winter, allowing sunlight to penetrate the home when its warmth is most needed.

Ideally, a home should take advantage of natural light. A kitchen or breakfast area used every morning, for example, would benefit from an eastern exposure. The location of rooms should also reflect the lighting preferences of the homeowners. Early-risers may likewise prefer an eastern exposure for their bedrooms. Since southern exposures provide

Hickory Chair Company

18-1 Sunlight brings out warm, flattering tones in objects. It also emphasizes textures by creating sharp, contrasting shadows.

18-2 Trees help filter hot summer sunlight.

steady sunlight throughout the day, many kitchens and family rooms occupy this part of the house.

In some rooms, natural light is unnecessary and may even be a hindrance. Many people prefer their bedrooms with subdued lighting, which is achieved when rooms face north. A northern exposure is also useful for rooms that require even lighting, such as an art studio.

Sunlight as a light source is not always dependable. Therefore, rooms utilizing natural light need artificial light as well, 18-3. Artificial light, however, usually changes the appearance of colors and textures. The appearance of a room in both types of light should be considered when planning a room's decor.

18-3 This living area successfully blends natural and artificial light in a stylish decor.

Artificial Light

Artificial light is both predictable and controllable. **Artificial light** is produced by incandescent, halogen, and fluorescent bulbs. These provide different quantities and qualities of light that, in turn, produce different effects.

Incandescent Sources

Incandescent light is produced when electricity passes through a fine tungsten filament in a vacuum bulb. This causes the wire to heat and glow. The light from incandescent sources is yellow-white, the color of light that most flatters skin tones. There are two basic types of incandescent light sources: general-service and reflectorized bulbs, 18-4.

General-service bulbs are available in a wide variety of shapes and wattages, generally ranging from 25 to 150 watts. Larger bulbs are available for situations where very bright light is needed. Three-way bulbs contain two filaments that are operated simultaneously or independently to offer three different levels of light. Small, low-wattage bulbs are commonly used for decorative purposes or as nightlights.

The most common incandescent bulb is the pear-shaped, general-service bulb. Other shapes include globes and decorative bulbs in flame and teardrop shapes. Clear bulbs allow light to shine at full strength but produce glare, making them unsuitable for many uses unless they are covered. However, small, clear bulbs used in chandeliers or for other decorative purposes produce a brilliant sparkle. Frosted bulbs disperse light more evenly, decrease glare, soften shadows, and remain cooler.

The other category of incandescent bulb is the reflectorized bulb, which is a cone-shaped bulb used for floodlights and spotlights. These bulbs have an opaque silver coating inside to direct light forward and provide better beam control. Floodlights spread light, while spotlights concentrate it into a beam.

The manufacture of several incandescent bulbs in the reflectorized family was discontinued October 31, 1995, as a result of the Energy Policy Act of 1992. However, inventory supplies of bulbs made before that date may still be available for sale. These bulbs include most common reflector lamps used for spotlighting: R lamps, also called reflector bulbs, and nonhalogen PAR lamps, also known as parabolic aluminized reflectors. The exceptions are 65-watt, R-30, and PAR lamps that use halogen or krypton gas to increase energy efficiency.

Incandescent lights are inexpensive to install and easy to replace. They do not hum, flicker, or interfere with other electrical devices.

Halogen Sources

A **halogen bulb** is a type of lighting with tungsten filaments that produces bright white light, matching the quality of pure daylight. These bulbs make colors look their best. To accommodate a wide range of uses, they are available in a variety of sizes and shapes, 18-5. Halogen bulbs are available in both line-voltage (120 volts) and low-voltage varieties. Low-voltage types require a transformer to step down the voltage.

Halogen bulbs have a longer life and use less energy than incandescent bulbs, but are more expensive initially. Compared with light from typical incandescent bulbs, halogen light is much brighter. For example, a 90-watt halogen floodlight creates the same amount of light as a 150-watt incandescent

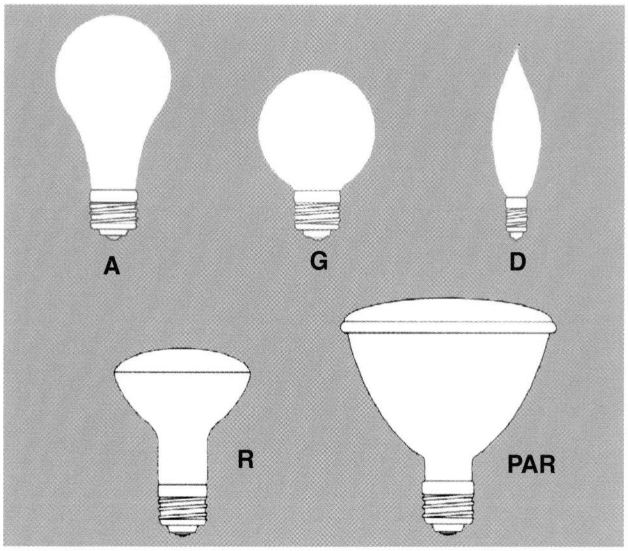

American Lighting Association

18-4 Incandescent bulbs come in a variety of shapes to fit different functions.

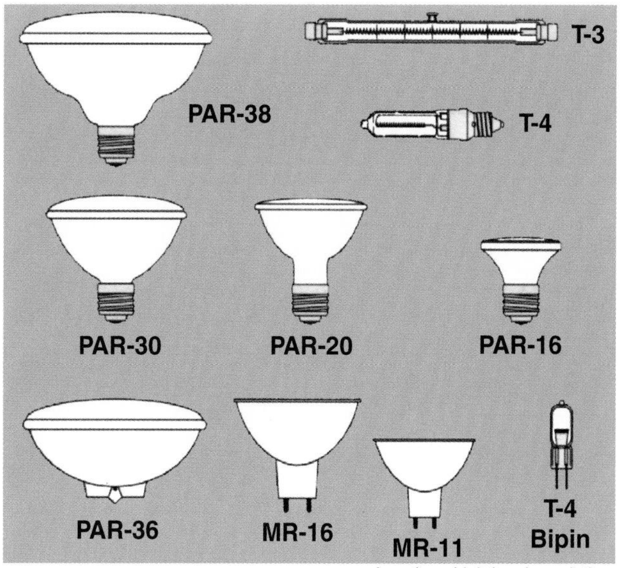

American Lighting Association

18-5 Halogen lights represent the newest category of lighting on the market.

floodlight, thus producing an energy savings of 40 percent. They also last three times longer than typical incandescent bulbs. Halogen bulbs fit a standard socket, are available for interior and exterior use, and come in compact bulbs for special lamps.

Fluorescent Sources

Fluorescent light is produced in a glass tube by releasing electricity through a mercury vapor to make invisible ultraviolet rays. A coating of fluorescent chemicals on the inside of the glass tube transforms the rays into visible, white light.

Fluorescent lamps are available as tubes, screw-in bulbs, and compact fluorescents, 18-6. Straight tubes range in length from 12 in. to 48 in. and in power usage from 13 to 40 watts. The manufacture of the familiar 40-watt, 4-ft. tube was discontinued on October 31, 1995. Compact fluorescents are rapidly becoming the lamp of choice. They produce approximately the same amount of light as ordinary incandescent bulbs, but use almost 75 percent less electricity. They fit a standard lightbulb socket; produce an attractive soft, white light; and last approximately 10 to 20 times longer than an ordinary bulb.

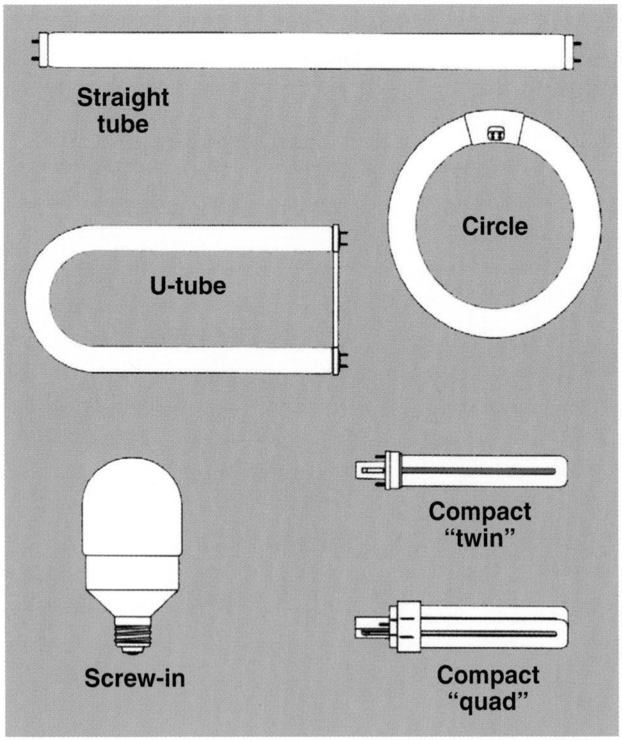

American Lighting Association

18-6 The two most common shapes of fluorescent tubes are straight and circuline tubes, but bulb-like shapes are also available.

Manufacturers of fluorescent lamps have made significant efforts to improve the quality of their products. They introduced bulbs with greater energy efficiencies and pleasing warm-white light. These improvements produced a product that is a departure from the old fluorescent bulbs known for a cold, bluish light.

Fluorescent lights disperse light over a larger area than incandescent lights and cause less glare. They require less energy to operate and produce almost no heat. However, fluorescent lamps have some disadvantages. They are available in a limited variety of interchangeable styles. They are more expensive than incandescent bulbs to install and replace, and they are more likely to interfere with other electrical devices. With most fluorescent bulbs, there is a slight delay between turning on the light fixture and seeing light.

Applications of Lighting

There are three basic types of lighting: general, task, and accent lighting. A good lighting plan incorporates all three types.

General lighting provides a comfortable, even level of brightness throughout a room. It allows individuals to see and walk around safely and is fundamental to any lighting plan. With this type of lighting, each aspect of a room is given equal emphasis.

General lighting can be direct or indirect. **Direct lighting** produces strong illumination because it travels directly from the light source to the object being lit. It creates sharp contrasts between light and darkness and can cause eyestrain when used as the only lighting source.

Indirect lighting is diffused light produced by directing the light toward an intermediate surface that reflects the light into the room. Indirect light is usually focused onto the ceiling or walls, 18-7. It is more diffused than direct light, resulting in less contrast and softer shadows.

Task lighting provides strong light to a small area. It helps individuals perform specific tasks, such as sewing, reading, preparing food, and shaving, 18-8. It should be free of distracting glare and bright enough for handling the task. For example, more light is needed for doing fine needlework than for playing table games.

Accent lighting uses a highly concentrated beam to highlight an area or object. See 18-9. It may be used to spotlight household plants and prized possessions or to illuminate an interesting room or outdoor feature. To be effective, accent lighting needs at least three times as much light on the focal point as the surrounding light level.

American Lighting Association

18-7 The chandelier provides direct lighting while the other light fixtures in this room provide indirect lighting.

18-8 Task lighting is needed to illuminate this bathroom vanity.

For a good balance of lighting in a room, a combination of general and task lighting is needed. Light treatments used as accents take the lighting one step further and add drama.

The amount of illumination produced by a room's light sources is measured in footcandles. A **footcandle** is defined as the amount of illumination produced by a standard plumber's candle at a distance of one foot. Light meters can be used to measure the number of footcandles produced by a light. Recommended amounts of light in footcandles for specific activities are listed in 18-10.

Generally, as the wattage of a light source increases, the intensity of light produced also increases. However, halogen and fluorescent light sources provide more light per watt of electricity than regular incandescent bulbs.

American Lighting Association

18-9 Mini-spotlights in display cases create a background of interesting accent lighting in this family room.

Footcandle Requirements	
Activity	**Footcandles**
Sewing dark-colored fabrics	100-200
Crafts requiring fine detail	100-200
Concentrated studying or reading	50-100
Sewing medium-colored fabrics	50-100
Workshop tasks	50-100
Kitchen, preparing food	50-100
Laundry, pretreating stains	50-100
Ironing	50-100
Kitchen and laundry, general tasks	20-50
Casual reading	20-50
Grooming	20-50
Dining	10-20
Conversation	10-20

18-10 Lighting needs vary with different activities.

The amount of light reflected and absorbed within a room also affects the intensity of the light level. Light is reflected from smooth surfaces and light colors, but absorbed by textured surfaces and dark colors. As more of the room's light is absorbed, the intensity of the light level decreases. Likewise, light is more intense in a highly reflective room. The percentage of light reflected by various colors is shown in A-25 of the Appendix.

Colored light is less intense than white light, but it can produce interesting effects. Colored lights intensify objects of the same color range and decrease the intensity of their complement. For instance, a bulb with a yellow light will intensify yellow and orange objects, but it will subdue colors in the blue and violet range.

Warm-colored light, such as red or yellow, will make a room appear cozy and brighter. Cool-colored lights, such as blue or blue-green, make a room seem cool and open. White light shows a room at its truest color values and produces the most illumination.

Selection and Placement

The atmosphere and appearance of a room is affected by the selection and placement of artificial lighting. Different types of fixtures can be used to meet decorative and functional needs. Each area of the house has special lighting concerns. When planning lighting, the specific needs of each room should be considered separately.

Lighting Fixtures

Fixtures for the home should provide adequate light for activities and blend with decor. The size and scale of fixtures should be proportionate to other items in a room and the room itself. A fixture should be easy to clean, and the lightbulb or tube should be easy to replace.

Different types of fixtures are designed to meet specific lighting needs. Lighting fixtures used throughout the home are structural or portable. **Structural fixtures** are permanently built into the home. **Portable fixtures** are not a part of the home's architectural structure; they can be placed and removed with relative ease.

Structural Fixtures

Several types of structural lighting can be used to meet specific lighting needs.

Luminous ceilings are made of transparent or translucent ceiling panels lighted from above, 18-11. Fluorescent tubes are used to provide even light. An entire ceiling may be illuminated or just selected panels. Luminous ceilings provide good general lighting for tasks and group activities.

Recessed lights are small, circular lights that are installed in the ceiling, 18-12. They can be flush with the ceiling or projecting slightly. This quality makes them especially useful in rooms with low ceilings.

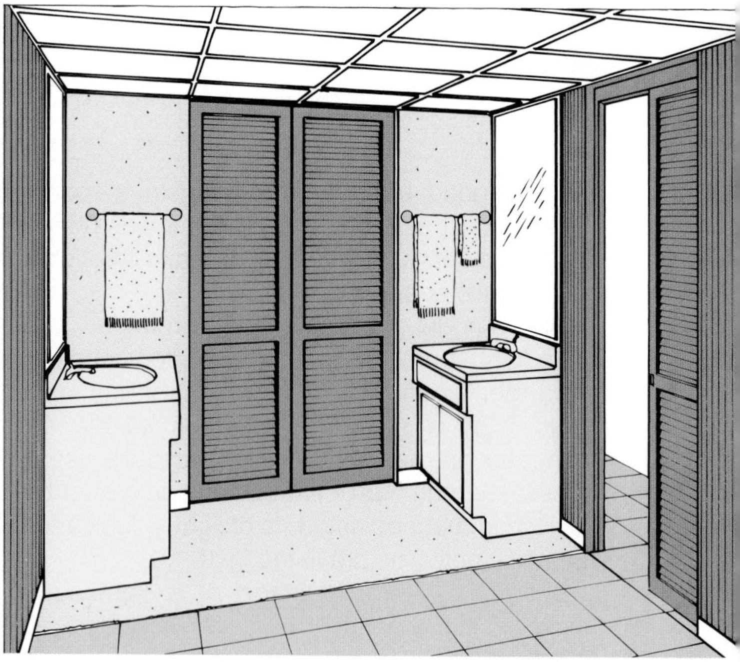

18-11 Luminous ceilings are used in bathrooms and other areas that require bright, even general lighting.

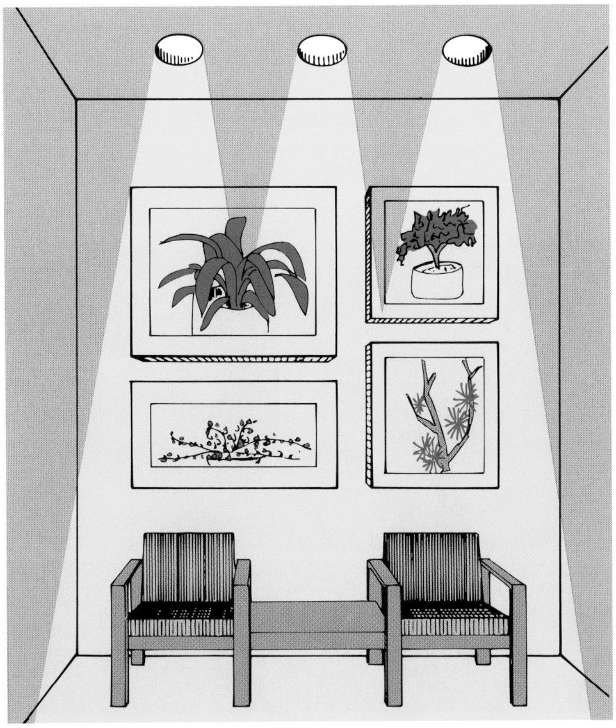

18-12 Recessed lights provide effective accent lighting.

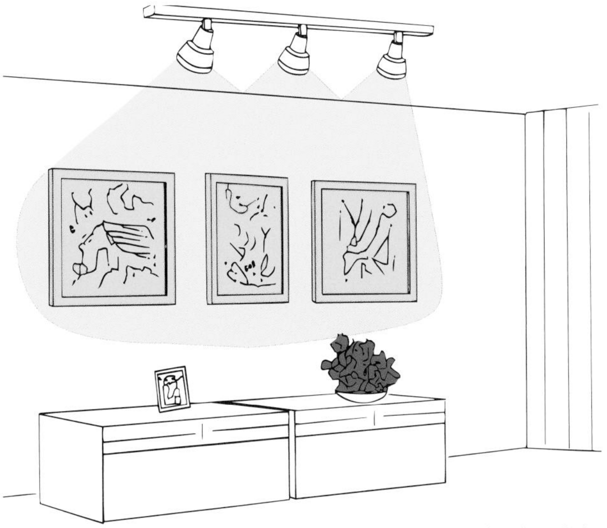

American Lighting Association

18-13 Track lighting can be adjusted to meet specific lighting needs.

Light from these fixtures may spotlight one area, flood a wall with light, or provide diffused general lighting.

Track lighting is mounted in a metal strip that allows fixtures to be placed anywhere along the strip. See 18-13. The fixtures may be swiveled or rotated to shine light in any direction. As a result, the room's lighting can be changed as needed. This type of lighting is usually considered for accent lighting, but can also provide general and task lighting. Track lights should be at least 4 ft. apart to avoid a cluttered look.

Strip lighting consists of a strip of receptacles to hold a series of incandescent bulbs or fluorescent tubes. It is very useful in work areas and around mirrors, 18-14. Strip lighting is a good source of task lighting, particularly in bathrooms and dressing areas.

Portable Fixtures

Portable fixtures, such as the common table lamp, are not a structural part of the house. A single lamp is usually used to provide task or accent lighting, but two or more lamps can provide general lighting. Table and floor lamps come in various heights and styles intended for different uses.

Lamps should be chosen to fit the function they will serve. They should have heavy, stable bases that will not tip easily. If task lighting is desired, an opaque shade with white lining is most effective

American Lighting Association

18-14 Strip lighting is often used around mirrors to provide good task lighting.

because the light stays concentrated within a small circular area.

Proper height is an important consideration. For reading and other tasks, the bottom edge of the lampshade should be at eye level for a seated person. A distance of 40 to 42 in. from the floor to the bottom of the shade is ideal, 18-15.

Lampshades affect the intensity and direction of light from a lamp. Translucent shades allow some light to pass through the shade and provide more general lighting than opaque shades. Opaque shades confine light to a small area. Tall, steep shades create a smaller, more concentrated circle of light. Low, wide, or angled shades disperse light into a larger circle.

Standard wall and ceiling fixtures are also considered portable, even though the wiring required for these fixtures is a part of the structure, 18-16. These fixtures may be placed and removed with relative ease compared to structural lighting fixtures.

Standard wall and ceiling fixtures come in a wide variety of styles and colors. Combining two or more in a room provides good general lighting. Chandeliers may provide general lighting but are generally designed for accent lighting or for task lighting over a dining area. Chandeliers, *pendants*, and other types of hanging lights placed over a dining area should be 30 in. above the table in an 8 ft. high room, 18-17. For each additional foot of room height, 3 in. should be added.

Undercabinet and undershelf fixtures provide task and accent lighting. When used in kitchens, laundry areas, and workshops, undercabinet fixtures are usually fluorescent. They light countertops well and provide generous, glare-free light at

American Lighting Association

18-16 All wall and ceiling lights in this room are considered portable fixtures.

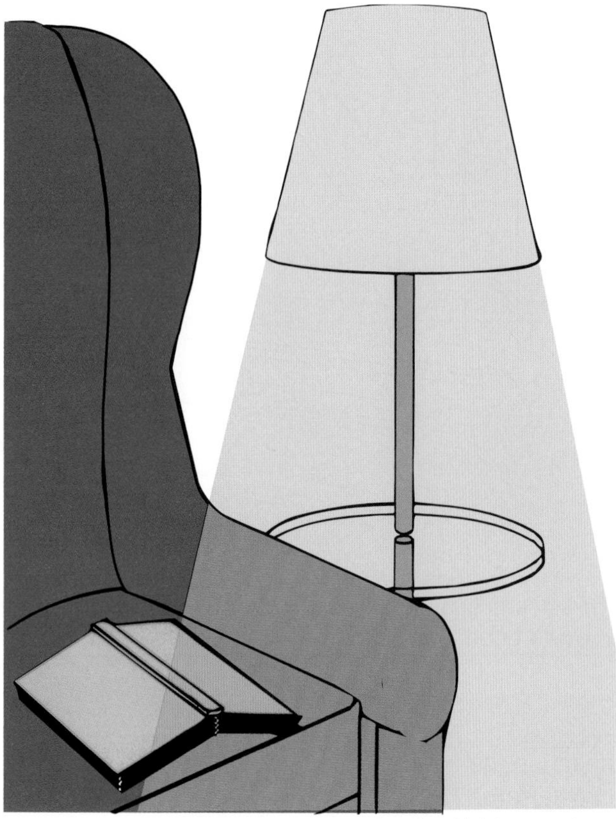

American Lighting Association

18-15 Lamps should be placed so the bottom edge of the shade is eye level for a seated person.

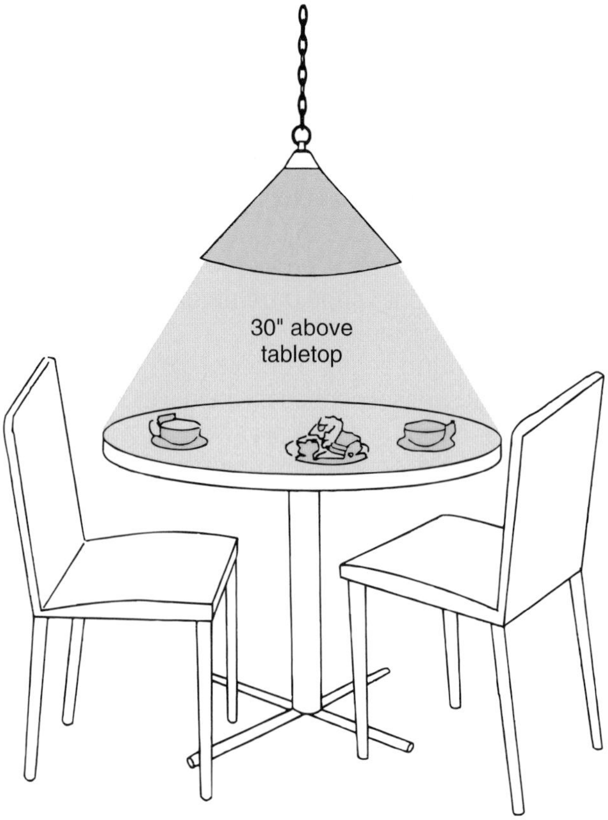

American Lighting Association

18-17 Light fixtures hung over eating areas should allow a 30-inch vertical clearance above the tabletop.

task level. See 18-18. Undershelf accent lighting uses low-voltage incandescent lighting, such as minilights and miniature track lights.

Lighting Areas of the Home

The first step in planning lighting for an area is to decide how the area will be used. The function of each area should be designated on a room floor plan. Each room may have several areas with specific lighting needs. After needs are identified, the basic types of lighting required—general, task, or accent—can be determined. Only then can the most functional lighting fixtures for each area be chosen.

Entryways and Foyers

Lighting in the entryway and foyer should be sufficient for circulation and safety. The exterior entry should be well lighted so a person can locate the lockset, identify the house number, and clearly see a guest. Light should be directed outward and downward, 18-19. A lighted doorbell button is also helpful.

Interior lighting should be soft enough to make a smooth transition from darkness to light, 18-20. Diffused, general light will enable guests to greet their hosts, use the coat closet, and walk comfortably to the next room. Decorative accent lighting is also a good choice for this area.

Living Rooms

General lighting for living rooms should be provided by several sources. Recessed or track lights can either wash entire areas with light to highlight interesting textures or focus a beam on accented items, 18-21. Task lighting for reading or conversation

American Lighting Association

18-19 A well-lighted front entrance adds an inviting look to a home and increases safety.

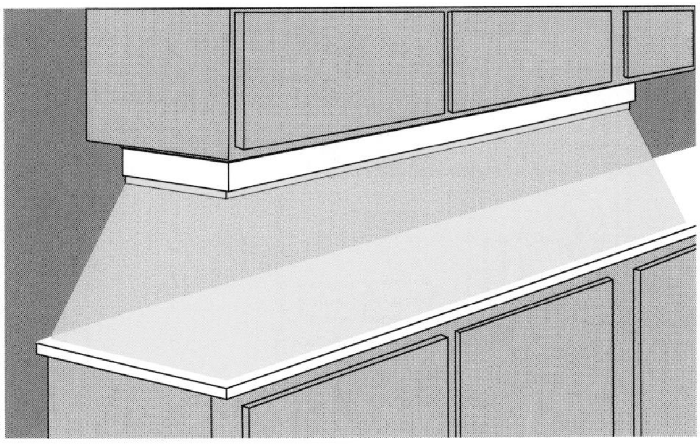

American Lighting Association

18-18 Undercabinet fixtures flood countertops with light.

American Lighting Association

18-20 Usually ceiling fixtures are installed in entryways to provide generous lighting.

American Lighting Association

18-21 This living room is lighted by table lamps, recessed fixtures, and accent lighting over the picture.

should be provided. Fireplaces, family portraits, and prized possessions in the room provide ample opportunities for accent lighting. Decorative lamps or hanging lights may also be used.

Family and Recreation Rooms

The variety of activities that take place in family rooms requires flexible lighting. Lamps with three-way bulbs provide different light levels to complement the many different activities that take place individually or in groups. Soft light is best for quiet activities such as listening to music and viewing television, 18-22. Good general lighting is also needed.

Dining Rooms

Local lighting over the dining table is the main source of light in the dining room. Chandeliers and hanging lights are popular for this area, but light should not shine directly into the diners' eyes, 18-23. Bright light is needed for family meals and other activities that use the dinner table, such as playing games, doing homework, and paying bills. Low light may be desired for evening dining, which can be accomplished by adjusting a dimmer control.

American Lighting Association

18-22 Miniature track lighting and minilights can provide both general and accent lighting in the home entertainment area.

Century Furniture Company

18-23 This pendant is hung at the correct height to provide comfortable task lighting during meals and general lighting afterward.

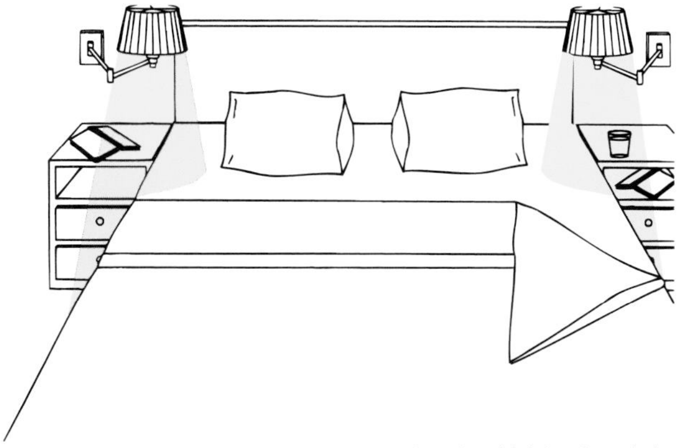

American Lighting Association

18-24 Small specialty lamps address specific lighting needs, such as this handy task light that serves primarily as a reading light.

American Lighting Association

18-25 A home office needs general and task lighting, but can also include accent lighting.

Task lighting is useful for the serving area or buffet, and several types of accent lighting are possible. Accent light strips may be used in cabinets to light china displays, while ceiling track or recessed lights can provide dramatic lighting.

Bedrooms

Diffused general lighting is most suitable for bedrooms, but task lighting is needed for a desk or computer area. Lighting near the closet and chest should be bright enough to see colors accurately and coordinate clothing pieces. Also, bright lights are needed for grooming areas. At least one light should be near the bed for reading and getting up safely at night. See 18-24. Children's rooms may also need small nightlights to allow safer circulation at night.

Home Offices

The room should be free of harsh contrasts and distracting glares. Home offices need well-diffused, general lighting to create a comfortable environment, but good task lighting is most important. Accent lighting may also be used to highlight valued possessions, such as hobby displays, trophies, and honors, 18-25.

Bathrooms

Bathrooms need good general lighting and warm-white task lighting for grooming. The area in front of the mirror should have even lighting that does not cast shadows, 18-26. Some of the specialized lighting fixtures in bathrooms include: lighted magnifying mirrors, ventilator lights, and recessed infrared heat lamps.

Kitchens

Safety and efficiency are major concerns in kitchens, so ample bright light is essential, especially under countertops, 18-27. Kitchens with a snack bar or dining area may also have a chandelier, pendant, or other chain-hung ceiling light. Various types of accent lighting can enhance a kitchen's appearance, such as minilights placed above or below cabinets, or inside open cabinets.

Utility Areas

Bright, diffused general lighting is needed in utility areas, such as basements and laundry rooms, 18-28. Luminous ceilings are often used in these areas as well as generous task lighting.

Special-Purpose Rooms

Lighting for special-purpose rooms should fit the tasks to be performed. For instance, a hobby room requires strong, direct light, while an art studio needs even, indirect lighting. As with kitchen lighting, workshops require good general lighting and task lighting.

American Lighting Association

18-27 There are no dark corners or countertops in this brightly lighted kitchen.

18-26 The fixture over the mirror is a warm-white light, which flatters skin tones.

American Lighting Association

18-28 A large ceiling fixture with fluorescent tubes provides plenty of well-diffused general lighting for laundry tasks.

Stairs and Halls

When choosing stairway lighting, safety should be the foremost goal. Lighting should be bright enough to clearly illuminate each step. Good lighting at the top and bottom landings is essential. See 18-29. Switches should be located at both the top and bottom of stairways so lights can be turned on from both locations.

Good general lighting throughout hallways is just as important. Recessed lights or ceiling fixtures are commonly used, but hanging lights are an alternative for high ceilings. See 18-30. Interesting wall fixtures, table lamps, and accent lighting on walls or portraits are other considerations.

Exteriors

Exterior lighting can enhance the architectural features of the house and emphasize the landscape while providing safety benefits, 18-31. Landscape lighting also illuminates the views through windows at night and makes the home's outdoor areas more usable.

Floodlights and spotlights can highlight trees, decorative gardens, and other landscape features. Decorative pools may be accented with spotlights or underwater lights installed in the sides. Focusing lights upward through trees can create interesting shadows on exterior walls. Decorative lampposts in the front yard of a home create a welcoming effect and illuminate the path to the house.

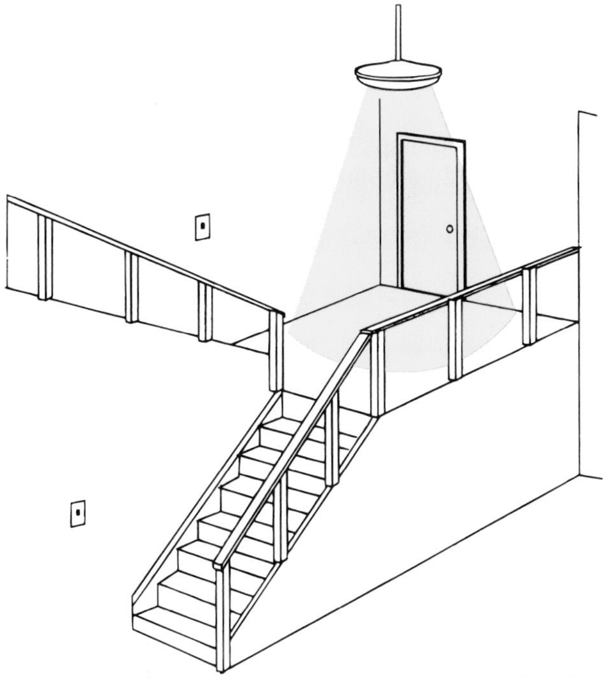

American Lighting Association

18-29 Stairs and landings should be well lighted to prevent accidents.

Century Furniture Company

18-30 Attractive lighting fixtures brighten this hallway.

California Redwood Association

18-31 Exterior lighting gives plantings and walkways an enchanting appearance.

Patios, terraces, and swimming pool areas require light for evening use. General lighting from a source above eye level should be provided. See 18-32. When more than one source is used, evenly spaced lights minimize dark spots. Pathways and steps deserve special attention and should be well lighted with a spotlight overhead or several recessed lights at walking level.

Lighting Controls

Lighting controls should be an integral part of a lighting design because they make different uses and decorative effects possible from the same fixtures. With a mere touch of a pad or twist of a dial, lighting intensity can be adjusted to match any activity or need. Making some lights dimmer and others brighter alters the mood of the room. Lighting controls also help to lower light levels to conserve energy and increase bulb life.

Sophisticated devices are available today that manage all home lighting from master controls, telephones, or home computers. Master controls provide convenient on/off switching and dimming throughout the home. Status controls indicate which preset scenes, pathways, or modes are active and which lights are on. With the flick of a button, lights inside or outside the home can be turned on or off at a predetermined time, no matter where the occupants are.

These integrated lighting control systems can also link to a security system to turn on or flash lights to increase the safety of the home. While occupants are away, these integrated systems can perform the following tasks: turn on whole-house functions, arm the security system, adjust lights, set heating and air conditioning units to energy-saving modes, close motorized shades, and simulate the occupied appearance of the home. These systems are used in new construction or for retrofitting existing homes.

American Lighting Association

18-32 Beaming a spotlight from branches of a tree is one way to light a frequently used outdoor area.

Chapter Summary

Lighting is an essential element in any dwelling. The amount of natural light in a room is unpredictable, but too much light can be controlled. Artificial light is both predictable and controllable. It is available from incandescent, halogen, and fluorescent sources. The color of light is yellow-white from incandescent sources, bright white from halogen bulbs, and white from fluorescent bulbs.

General lighting provides a comfortable, even level of brightness throughout a room. This type of lighting can be either direct or indirect. Individuals perform specific tasks, such as reading, using the computer, and preparing food with task lighting. Accent lighting uses a highly concentrated beam of light to highlight an area or object.

The type and location of artificial lighting sources affect the atmosphere and appearance of a room. Lighting fixtures should provide adequate light for activities and blend with the decor. Structural fixtures include luminous ceilings, recessed lights, track lighting, and strip lighting. Portable lighting includes table and floor lamps as well as fixtures mounted on wall and ceiling surfaces.

The first step in planning lighting for an area is to decide how the area will be used. Then, the basic types of lighting required can be determined. Special considerations for specific areas of the home's interior and exterior help determine the most appropriate lighting choices for each area. Lighting controls should also be considered when planning a lighting system for a home.

Review Questions

1. How can the amount of natural light entering a room be controlled?
2. How does incandescent light differ from fluorescent light?
3. What are the advantages and disadvantages of incandescent and fluorescent lamps?
4. What are the advantages of a halogen-tungsten lamp?
5. How does the light of today's fluorescent lamps differ from that of earlier types?
6. What are the three main applications of lighting?
7. What increases the intensity of light in a room?
8. What types of general-lighting fixtures are used to provide indirect lighting? direct lighting?
9. What types of fixtures can be used to provide accent lighting?
10. What considerations are important when choosing a reading lamp?
11. What points should be considered when planning lighting for a room?
12. How does kitchen lighting differ from lighting in a living room?
13. How can lighting enhance the exterior of a home?

Suggested Activities

1. Write an essay explaining how natural light can be used to enhance the decor of a home. (You may refer to window styles discussed in Chapter 16.)
2. Tour a home improvement center to observe the incandescent, halogen, and fluorescent lights available. Select one of each type to use together in a well-planned lighting scheme for a specific room. Describe and explain your choices.
3. Interview a lighting specialist or research the information on the American Lighting Association's Web site for guidelines on conserving energy with lighting. Summarize your findings.
4. Explain the difference between general, task, and accent lighting, and list the types of fixtures that can be used to create each.
5. Select a picture of a dining room, living room, or bedroom from a magazine. Then, identify ways to enhance the lighting design.
6. Describe why lighting controls are an integral part of a lighting design.

Internet Resources

American Lighting Association
americanlightingassoc.com

Brass Light Gallery
brasslight.com

Cooper Wiring Devices
eagle-electric.com

General Electric, home lighting products
ge.com/product/home/lighting.htm

Hunter Fan Company
hunterfan.com

Leviton, a manufacturer of electrical and electronic products
leviton.com

Lightolier® Controls, a manufacturer of lighting controls
lolcontrols.com

Lutron, a manufacturer of lighting control products
lutron.com

Progress Lighting
progresslighting.com

Sea Gull Lighting Products, Inc.
seagulllighting.com

The Siemon Company, a manufacturer of home cabling systems
homecabling.com

Note: Web addresses may have changed since publication. For some entries, reaching the correct Web site may require keying *www.* into the address.

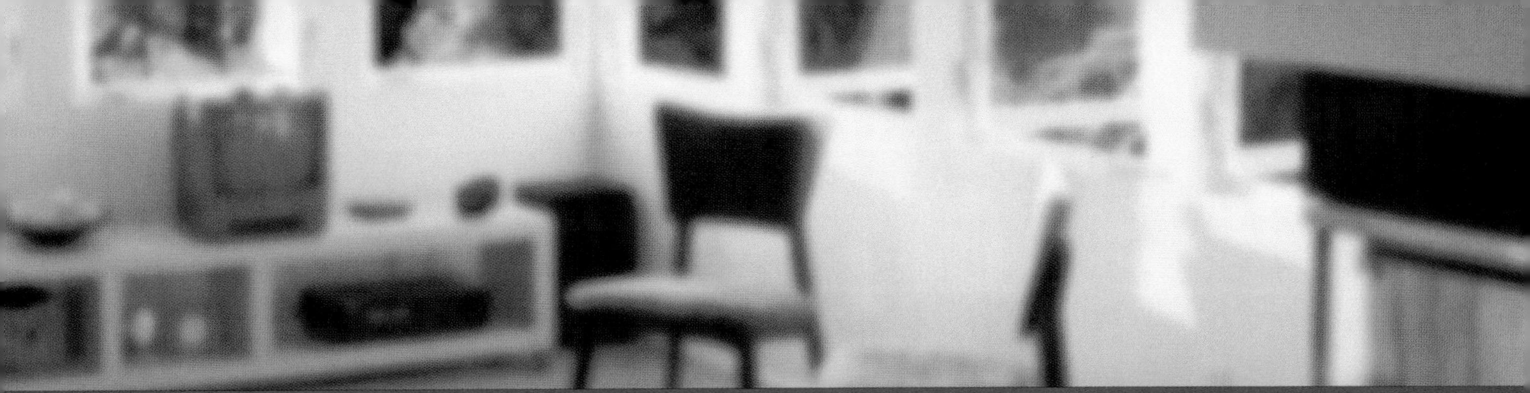

Chapter 19
Electrical and Plumbing Systems

Objectives

After studying this chapter, you will be able to

- list the three main components of the wiring system and explain how they operate.
- evaluate the adequacy of a wiring system in relation to a household's needs.
- trace the flow of the water-supply system into and out of the house, explaining the functions of its various components.
- evaluate a house's plumbing system according to basic guidelines for planning a system.

Key Terms

service-entrance panel
overcurrent devices
branch circuits
general-purpose circuits
small-appliance circuits
individual-appliance circuits
water-supply system
wastewater-removal system
soil stack
trap

The electrical and plumbing systems affect the efficiency, comfort, and design of a home. A well-designed home utilizes these systems so it can be functional as well as beautiful. This chapter provides an overview of the operation of the electrical and plumbing systems. Planning guidelines are also presented.

The Electrical System

A well-planned electrical system is needed for a safe, efficient home. Inadequate systems can lead to electrical overloading, loss of power, and in extreme cases, electrical fires. Planning for an electrical system requires an understanding of the system components. This information, plus knowledge of a housing unit's electrical requirements, can be used to design an efficient system.

Electrical-System Components

The main components of an electrical system are the service-entrance panel, branch circuits, receptacles, and switches. To understand the function and operation of these components, knowledge of terms used in their description is useful, 19-1.

Service-Entrance Panel

The **service-entrance panel** is the main distribution box that receives the electricity and distributes it to various points in the house through branch circuits. It serves as a monitor for a housing unit's electrical system, 19-2. The panel receives power from the power company and distributes the power throughout the house. It contains several **overcurrent devices**, which prevent excessive flow of current in a circuit such as fuses or breakers. Each of these supplies power to a branch circuit. The service-entrance panel also has a main disconnect switch to shut down a home's entire electrical system.

Electrical Terms	
Ampere	The unit of current used to measure the amount of electricity flowing through a wire during a certain amount of time.
Circuit	A path through which electricity flows from a source to one or more outlets and back to the source.
Circuit breaker	A device designed to open (turn off) and close (turn on) a circuit by nonautomatic means. It will also open the circuit automatically when the circuit is overloaded.
Conductor	A material that permits the flow of electricity. In wiring, the term usually refers to a wire.
Convenience outlet	A device attached to a circuit to allow electricity to be drawn for small appliances or lighting.
Fuse	A safety device that opens the circuit when it is overloaded by melting a fusible link.
Lighting outlet	An outlet intended for the use of a lighting fixture.
Receptacle	A contact device installed at an outlet for the connection of an attachment plug and flexible cord.
Service entrance	The fittings and conductors that bring electricity into the building.
Voltage	A measure of the pressure that forces current through a wire.
Watt	A measure of electrical power. The number of amperes in a circuit multiplied by the number of volts equals the number of watts the circuit provides. Most appliances and lighting devices are rated for power usage in watts.

19-1 Knowledge of general electrical terms will help in understanding electrical systems.

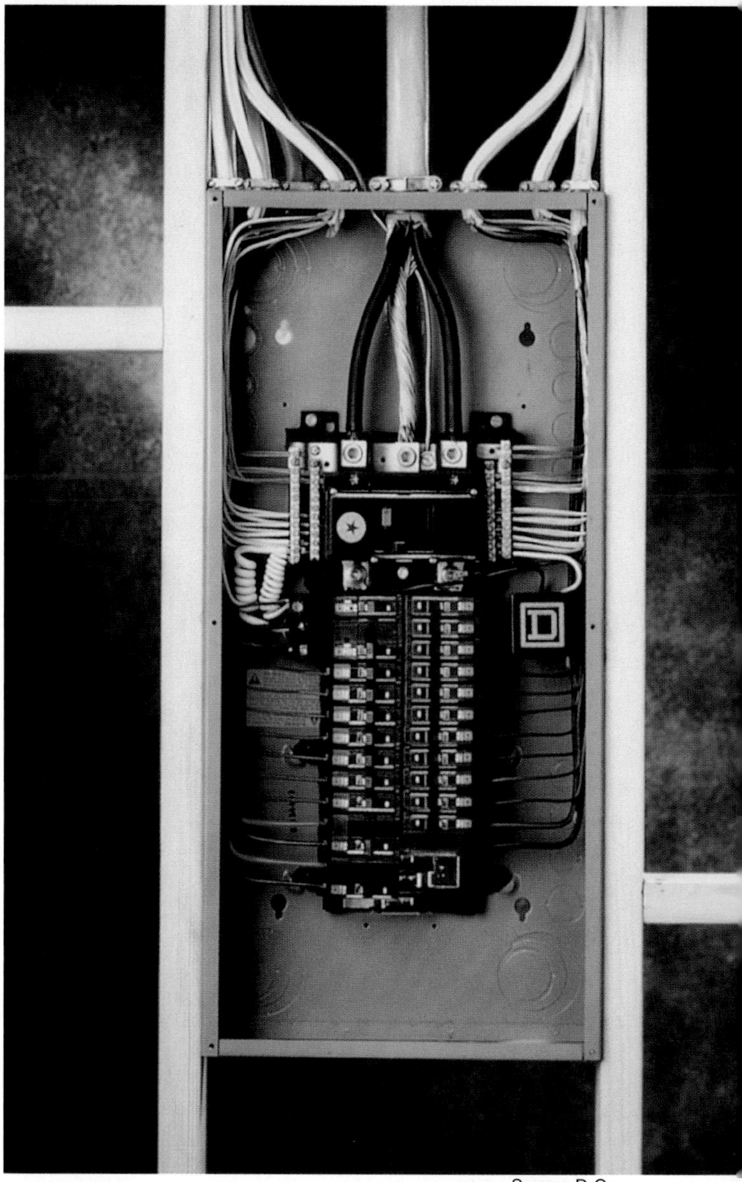

Square D Co.

19-2 This service-entrance panel receives power from the two large black wires and the large bare wire at the top of the panel. The power is distributed throughout the house using individual circuits.

The capacity of the service-entrance panel determines the total circuit capacity of a home. Therefore, future electrical needs should be considered when determining the total capacity of a service-entrance panel. Both 120- and 240-volt service are available for residential use. If two power lines run into a service-entrance panel, 120-volt service is available. Three lines indicate 240-volt service.

Branch Circuits

Once the electricity passes the main disconnect switch, it is routed to several **branch circuits**. These are individual electrical circuits from the service-entrance panel. Branch circuits provide overcurrent protection from overloads and wire shorts. Branch circuits make it possible to use smaller, less expensive wire. Each circuit has an automatic circuit breaker or fuse that stops the current when the circuit becomes overloaded, 19-3.

The National Electrical Code requires that enough branch circuits be supplied so circuit loads are distributed evenly. To comply, three general classes of circuits are commonly used: general-purpose, small-appliance, and individual-appliance circuits.

General-purpose circuits supply power to permanently installed lighting fixtures and to receptacle outlets for devices that use little wattage in

Square D Co.

19-3 A circuit breaker will automatically break the current if there is an overload on the circuit. The current must be switched on manually.

operation. These include such items as lamps, clocks, and radios, but not most kitchen appliances. A 120-volt circuit is used to supply power for these items.

Each circuit may have a capacity of either 15 or 20 amperes, using #14 wire and #12 wire, respectively. The total number of watts provided by a circuit equals the number of volts multiplied by the number of amperes in a circuit. Therefore, a 15-ampere circuit will supply 1,800 watts, and a 20-ampere circuit will supply 2,400 watts.

Small-appliance circuits power appliances that require a moderate amount of current, such as electric frypans and blenders. They are common in kitchens, but may also be used in dining areas, laundry rooms, workshops, or garages.

Small-appliance circuits are powered by a 120-volt circuit with a 20-ampere capacity. A circuit may supply power to several convenience outlets. However, no lighting fixtures are connected to the circuit. The National Electrical Code requires a minimum of two separate small-appliance circuits in each kitchen.

Individual-appliance circuits serve permanently installed appliances that use large amounts of electricity or have an automatic starting motor. These appliances include electric ranges, refrigerators, dishwashers, water heaters, washers, dryers, furnaces, and water pumps. An individual circuit should be used with any permanent, motor-driven appliance that requires over 1,440 watts for operation. The electrical requirements for several typical appliances are shown in 19-4.

Receptacles

The most common type of receptacle is the duplex receptacle, which accommodates two plugs, 19-5. Variations are the simplex (one plug), triplex (three plugs), and quad receptacles (four plugs). These types of receptacles generally have grounding terminals to accommodate three-prong plugs.

Appliances that require 240-volt circuits, such as electric ranges and clothes dryers, must have 240-volt receptacles. These receptacles are usually larger in size with openings specifically arranged for three-prong plugs. The special arrangement of the openings makes it impossible to plug an appliance requiring 240 volts into a 120-volt circuit.

A ground-fault circuit interrupter (GFCI) is a safety device that continually monitors the amount of current going to the load and returning, and opens the circuit if less returns. GFCIs are used for receptacles in bathrooms, kitchens, and around pools, 19-6. These outlets protect against electric shock if there is a short in an appliance.

Other special-purpose receptacles include weatherproof, clock, and television receptacles. Weatherproof receptacles have waterproof covers. They are intended for outdoor use. Clock receptacles are recessed so a plugged-in clock will hang flush with the wall. Television receptacles frequently provide power for the appliance as well as antenna or cable connections.

Switches

Switches are used to control permanently installed lighting fixtures and some appliances. They may also control some convenience outlets, making it possible to switch on a lamp before entering a room.

There are several types of residential switches, including single-pole, three-way, four-way, dimmer, and pull-chain switches.

- The single-pole switch is the most common. The switch has two positions, *on* and *off*. It may control one or more fixtures from one location only.
- Three-way switches are used to control one or more fixtures from two locations. They use two controls that do not have *on* and *off* identified on the switch.
- To control fixtures from three locations, a four-way switch is used in combination with two three-way switches.

Typical Electrical Requirements				
Appliance or Equipment	Typical Watts	Usual Voltage	Wire Size	Recommended Fuse Size
Air conditioner (20,000 Btu)	1,200	120/240	12	20 amp
Automatic dryer (electric)	5,000	120/240	10	30 amp
Automatic washer	700	120	12	20 amp
Band saw	300	120	12	20 amp
Bathroom heater	2,000	120/240	12	20 amp
Dehumidifier	350	120	12	20 amp
Dishwasher	1,200	120/240	12	20 amp
Freezer	350	120	12	20 amp
Furnace (gas)	800	120	12	20 amp
Iron	1,100	120	12	20 amp
Microwave oven	1,450	120	12	20 amp
Range (electric, with oven)	12,000	240	6	50 amp
Range oven (separate)	5,000	120/240	10	30 amp
Range top (separate)	5,000	120/240	10	30 amp
Refrigerator	300	120	12	20 amp
Roaster	1,400	120	12	20 amp
Rotisserie	1,400	120	12	20 amp
Table saw	1,000	120/240	12	20 amp
Television	300	120	12	20 amp
Toaster	1,000	120	12	20 amp
Waffle iron	1,000	120	12	20 amp
Waste disposer	300	120	12	20 amp
Water heater (electric)	5,000	120/240	10	30 amp

19-4 Appliances have different electrical requirements that should be met by the proper type of circuit.

Leviton Manufacturing Co., Inc.

19-5 This duplex receptacle has a grounding terminal, as is indicated by the third slot in each plug receptacle.

Leviton Manufacturing Co., Inc.

19-6 This duplex outlet is protected by a ground-fault circuit interrupter (GFCI).

- A dimmer switch may be used with any incandescent lighting fixture to vary its intensity, 19-7. Besides *on* and *off* positions, it has a control that varies the light's intensity from bright to dim.
- Pull-chain switches are turned *on* and *off* by pulling a chain directly attached to the fixture. They are generally used for inexpensive fixtures in closets, attics, or other infrequently used areas.

Switches are made in a variety of designs. The handle-type switch is the most common in residential use. See 19-8. A spring inside the handle moves it to the next position in a rapid motion, causing a snapping sound. Newer variations operate more quietly because mercury is used instead of a spring to open and close the circuit.

There are push-button switches and flat switches that use a rocker-type mechanism for operation, 19-9. Several types of switches contain safety lights. Other special switches include weatherproof switches and key-operated switches.

Low-voltage switching is a new type of switch system that is being used more often. In this system, switches are connected to relays using small, doorbell-type wire. The relay operates a line-voltage switch to control a fixture. Such a system is less expensive than conventional wiring because smaller wire is used. This system can be expanded so all electrical devices may be operated from one or more master panels or a home computer.

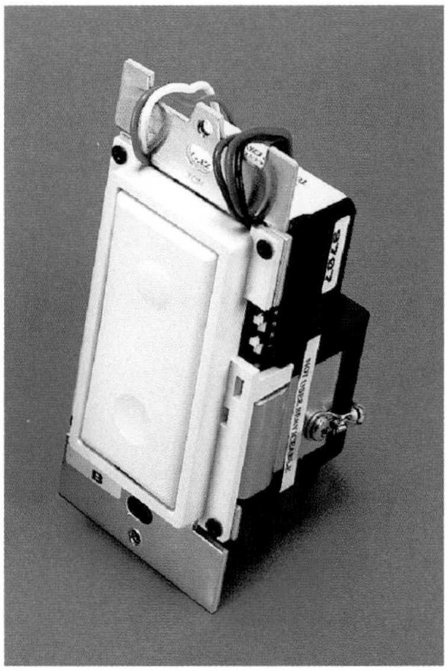

OnQ Technologies, Inc.

19-7 A dimmer switch allows variation in the intensity of a light.

Planning the Electrical System

Since it is expensive and time-consuming to expand an electrical system, present and future needs should be considered in the planning stages. The number of electrical devices used in the home has increased dramatically in recent years, and this trend is expected to continue. Often, new appliances are added without consideration of whether a house's wiring system can handle the extra load. Therefore, the electrical capacity of a house should be large enough so new devices can be added safely in future years.

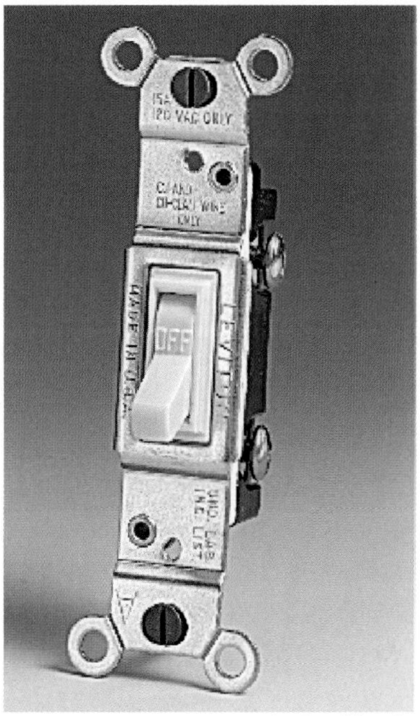

Leviton Manufacturing Co., Inc.

19-8 A handle-type switch contains mercury or a spring to connect and break the circuit.

Leviton Manufacturing Co., Inc.

19-9 Modern rocker-type switches are available with or without a built-in safety light.

Circuitry Requirements

The required number and type of circuits can be estimated by examining the electrical requirements and placement of regularly used equipment. For instance, small-appliance circuits will be needed anywhere that food may be prepared, 19-10. This could include the dining room or basement as well as the kitchen.

For lighting, the National Electrical Code requires a minimum of three watts of lighting capacity per sq. ft of floor space. Therefore, one circuit could provide lighting for 800 sq. ft. However, this is a minimum allowance, and one general-purpose circuit per 500 sq. ft. is a safer and more practical guideline for modern homes.

Future modifications to the home are important to consider when planning the location and number of individual circuits. For example, if a second oven may be added to a home later or if the laundry area may be moved in the future, allowances should be made.

After estimating total current and future electrical needs, the number and types of circuits to include in the service-entrance panel can be determined. Extra capacity—for new circuits or extra loads on present circuits—should be allowed for future needs.

Receptacles and Switches

There should be an adequate number of receptacles and switches for convenience and safety. All should be installed where they are easy to reach.

Switches for lights should be located at each frequently used entrance of a room so that it is not necessary to walk across a dark room to turn on a light, 19-11. In rooms with more than one entrance, three-way and four-way switches can be used.

A well-planned receptacle layout requires no extension cords. For living areas, the National Electrical Code specifies at least three outlets per room, with no point along a wall more than 6 ft. from a receptacle. Receptacles placed about 8 ft. apart provide a more convenient arrangement, 19-12. More outlets may be placed in areas where use of many electrical items is anticipated. Receptacles should also be planned for halls, closets, and other areas of the home that require the use of vacuum cleaners, nightlights, and other electrical equipment.

Placement of receptacles may be adjusted so furniture arrangement will not interfere with the use of receptacles. Large pieces of furniture frequently hide outlets and make them difficult to reach. One solution is to locate outlets closer to corners than to midway along walls, where furniture is normally placed.

Receptacles are usually located 12 to 18 in. above the floor, but some are more suitable at 36 in. from the floor. For instance, a 36 in. high receptacle would be convenient in a dining area for hot plates and other appliances used at table level. Higher receptacles should be planned for easy access to appliances such as refrigerators and clothes washers.

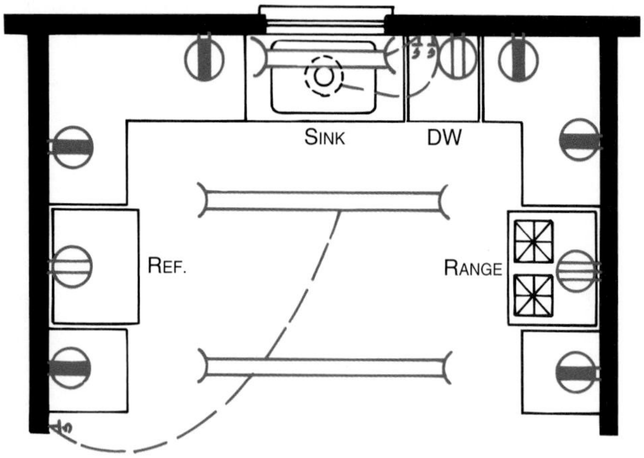

19-10 Small-appliance outlets should be located throughout the kitchen for convenience. Individual-appliance outlets should be available for such appliances as the range, dishwasher, and refrigerator. A general-purpose circuit is needed for lighting fixtures.

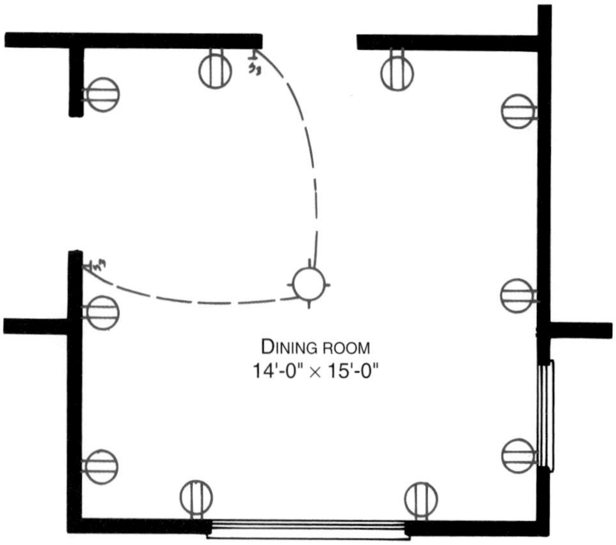

19-11 Rooms should have light switches at all entrances so walking across a dark room to get to the switch is not necessary.

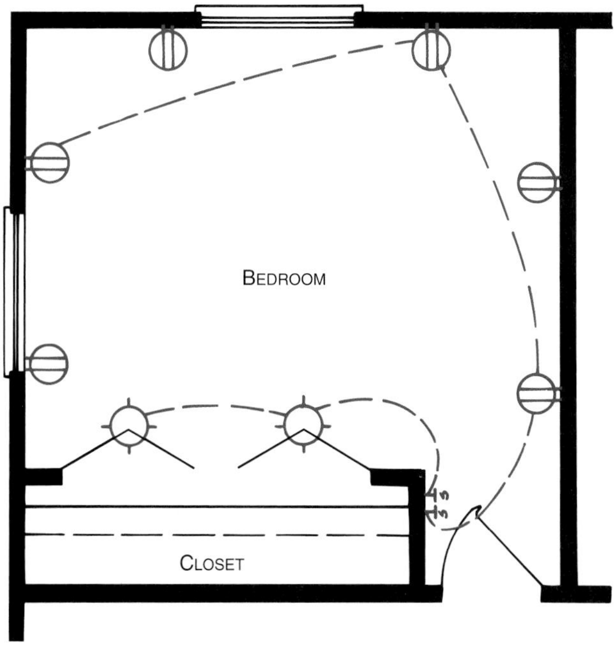

19-12 Receptacles should be placed about 8 ft. apart for easy access.

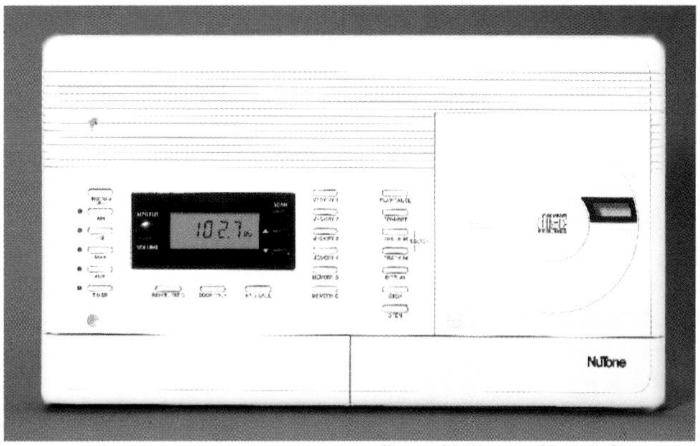

Broan-NuTone, a Nortek Company

19-13 This radio-intercom unit has a built-in CD player. The home communication system provides up to 20 stations plus door speakers, one-button intercom operation, and function display.

Signal and Communication Systems

Advances in technology are making signal and communication systems affordable to homeowners. These systems "sense" visitors, allow family members to communicate within the home, and permit the monitoring of systems in the dwelling and on the property.

A popular signal and communication system is the doorbell, which can sound like a simple buzzer or sophisticated chimes. Doorbells, buzzers, chimes, and similar signal systems may incorporate different tones for different entrances to the home.

Signaling circuits supply the electrical power to buzzers, doorbells, chimes, signal lights, or warning devices. Remote-control, low-voltage circuits are also included in this category.

An audio or visual system consists of a master station, 19-13, and numerous intercom stations located throughout the house and at entrances. Some larger systems include a radio and recorder.

Security systems are equipped with detection devices and alarms to alert the resident of fires and unwanted intruders. Detection devices include heat sensors, which can be set for normal temperatures in sleeping, living, and service areas, and higher temperatures for the attic and furnace room. The security system also includes intrusion detectors that signal when someone has entered the property or home. Security systems may be equipped with an automatic telephone-dialing machine that plays a taped emergency message to local authorities. Cables can be installed during construction or remodeling of the home to connect security systems as well as a television antenna, cable or satellite service, and telephone lines.

The Plumbing System

The residential plumbing system provides an adequate supply of water for household use in desired locations. It also removes the wastewater through a sanitary sewer or private septic system. There are three primary parts to a residential plumbing system—the water-supply system, the wastewater removal system, and the plumbing fixtures.

Water Supply

The residential **water-supply system** is the source and provider of water to residences, such as a city water main or private well. The pipe that enters the structure from the supply system is called the building main, 19-14. Once it enters a building, it branches into the cold water main and the hot water main. The water may pass through a water softener, filter, or other treatment device before dividing into hot and cold water mains.

The cold water main is routed to areas of the home where fixtures are located. A cold water branch line is run from the cold water main to each fixture. A shutoff valve is installed in the building main, the cold water main, and each branch line.

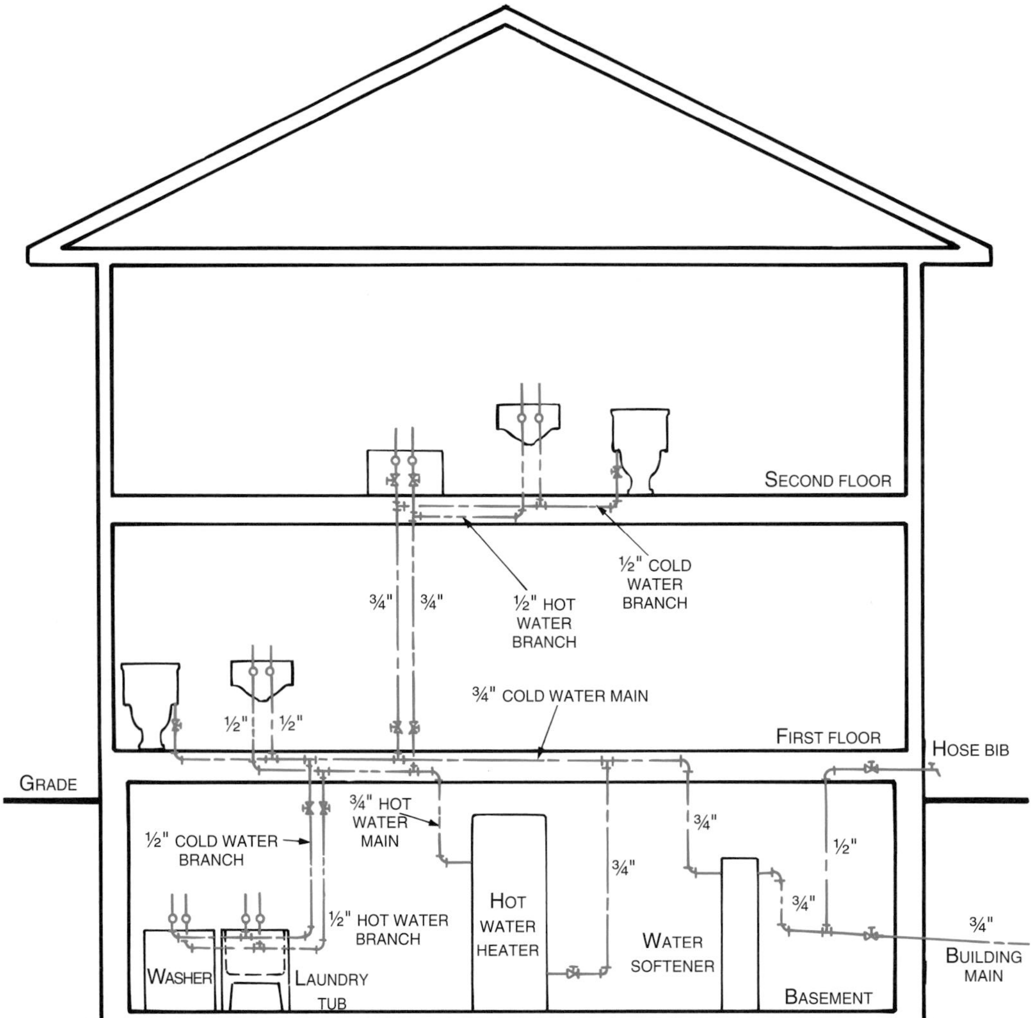

19-14 The water-supply system provides both hot and cold water to fixtures in the home.

These valves make it possible to work on one part of the plumbing system without shutting down the entire system.

The hot water main begins at the water heater. It generally travels through the house parallel to the cold water main. Shutoff valves are installed in hot water lines just as they are in cold water lines.

Piping for the water-supply system may be located in the floor, walls, or ceiling of a home. Pipes usually have a diameter of ½ to ¾ in. Materials used for piping include copper tubing, plastic pipe, and galvanized steel pipe. Local code requirements sometimes restrict the use of plastic pipe.

Wastewater Removal

Wastewater is carried to the sanitary sewer or private septic tank through the **wastewater-removal system**, 19-15. These pipes are separate from the water-supply system. Wastewater lines are also much larger than water-supply lines to accommodate waste materials. Provisions must also be made so pipes are accessible if they become clogged.

The wastewater-removal system, unlike the water-supply system, is not pressurized. It depends on gravity to carry the used water and waste to the sewer. Gases created by the wastewater must also be removed. Soil stacks are used so water and waste drain down and gases vent out above the roof. A **soil stack** is a tall, vertical drainpipe that collects waste from fixtures on all floors of the house. The stack extends above the roof to let gases escape.

Every housing unit must have at least one soil stack for each water closet. Additional stacks are required for other fixtures in isolated locations. Local

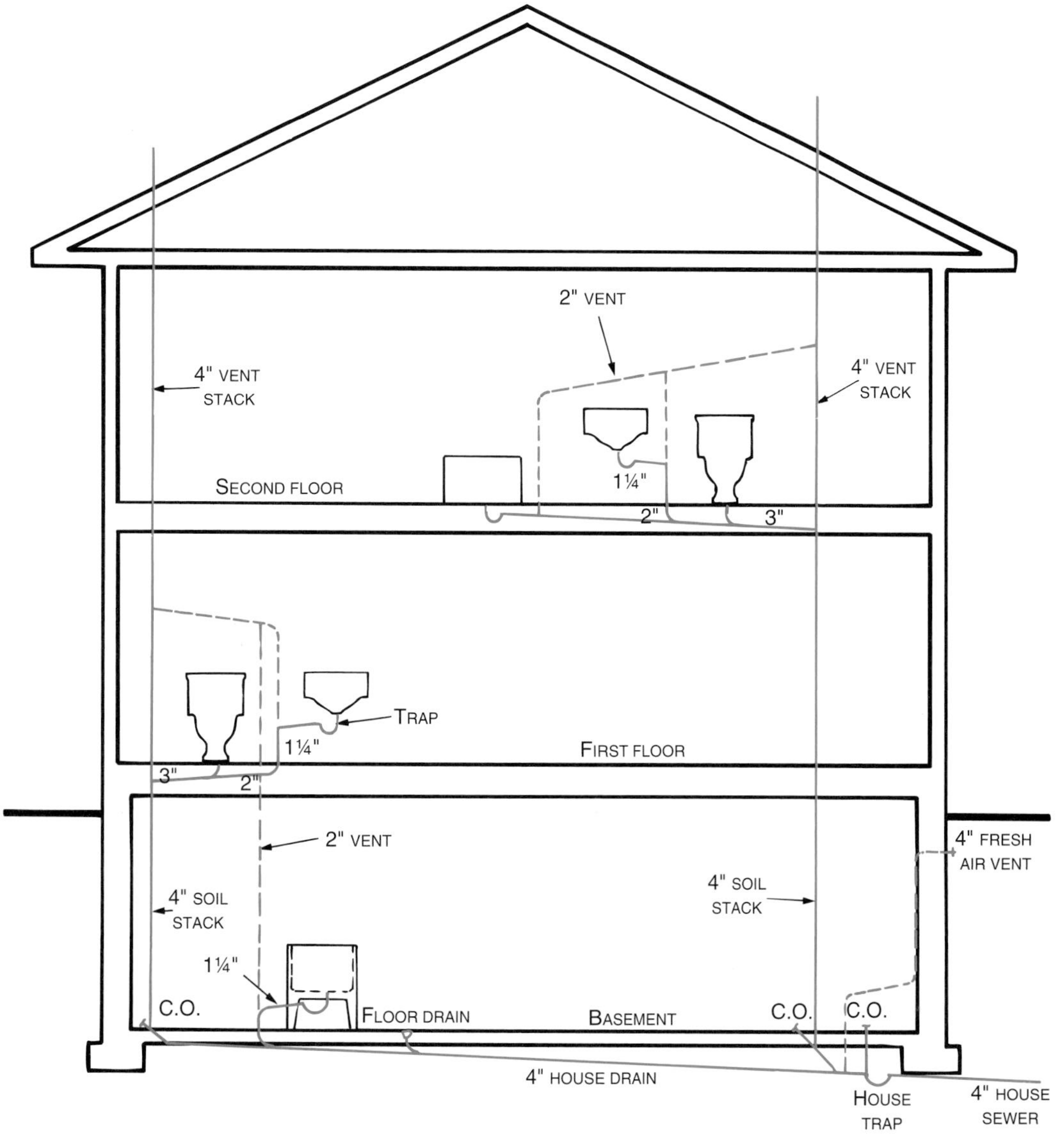

19-15 The wastewater-removal system depends on gravity to function, so horizontal pipes must slope toward the drain.

plumbing codes should be consulted. Below all plumbing fixtures except water closets, a trap is installed. A **trap** is a U-curved pipe that holds water to prevent sewer gases from backing into the living space. See 19-16. Water closets do not need a trap installed because they have a built-in trap.

Several types of pipes are used for wastewater systems, but those made of cast iron, copper and brass alloy, or plastic are most common. Their diameters are usually 3 or 4 in. Again, local codes may specify the type of pipe required in the area.

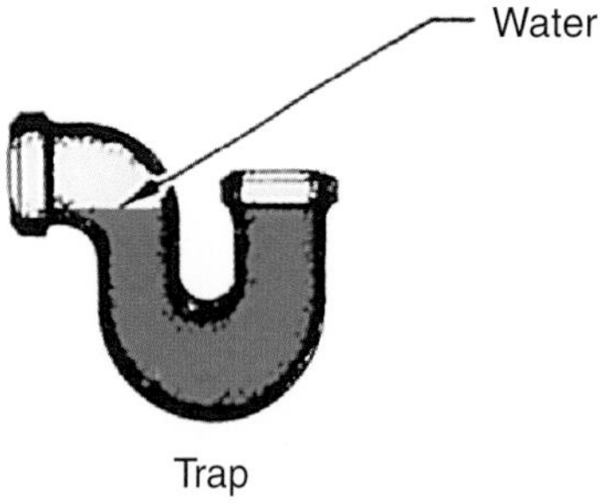

Insinkerator

19-16 The loop in this pipe is a trap that prevents wastewater gases from entering the house.

Fixtures

A plumbing fixture is any water-using appliance such as a dishwasher and clothes washer plus other items connected to the plumbing system, such as a sink, shower stall, and water closet. Several factors should be considered when planning for plumbing fixtures. They include style, size, fixture material, support for the fixture, and supply and drain requirements.

Style has implications for installation as well as décor. For example, lavatories are available in many styles, such as flattop with no back, shelf or ledge back, countertop, and corner. They may be freestanding, wall hung, or mounted in a vanity, 19-17. Specific fixture styles are shown in Chapters 3, 4, and 5. Each type must be installed in a different manner.

Plumbing fixtures are available in a wide range of sizes. A good example is bathtubs. Some of the standard sizes include widths from 30 to 32 in. and lengths from 4½ to 6 ft. A fixture should fit properly into the space provided.

The material from which a fixture is made affects the price and durability of the product. For example, sinks are available in enameled cast iron, enameled steel, stainless steel, and some plastics. Each type of material has qualities that make it more suitable for some uses and locations than others. Manufacturers have recommendations related to these factors for their products.

Plumbing features are frequently heavy so they may require special structural support. Water closets are one example. Adequate floor support is necessary for a typical floor-mounted model. Special blocking and wall reinforcement should be built into the original structure, if possible, for wall-mounted models. Reinforcement may be added during remodeling as well.

Since each plumbing fixture will be connected to the water supply and wastewater systems, specific water supply and drain requirements must be considered. Water-supply lines to most fixtures may be ½ in. in diameter. Drain lines vary greatly in size. Showers generally require 2 in. drains, while sinks, lavatories, bathtubs, and dishwashers frequently use 1½ in. drains. Water closets need either 3 or 4 in. drains, depending on local codes.

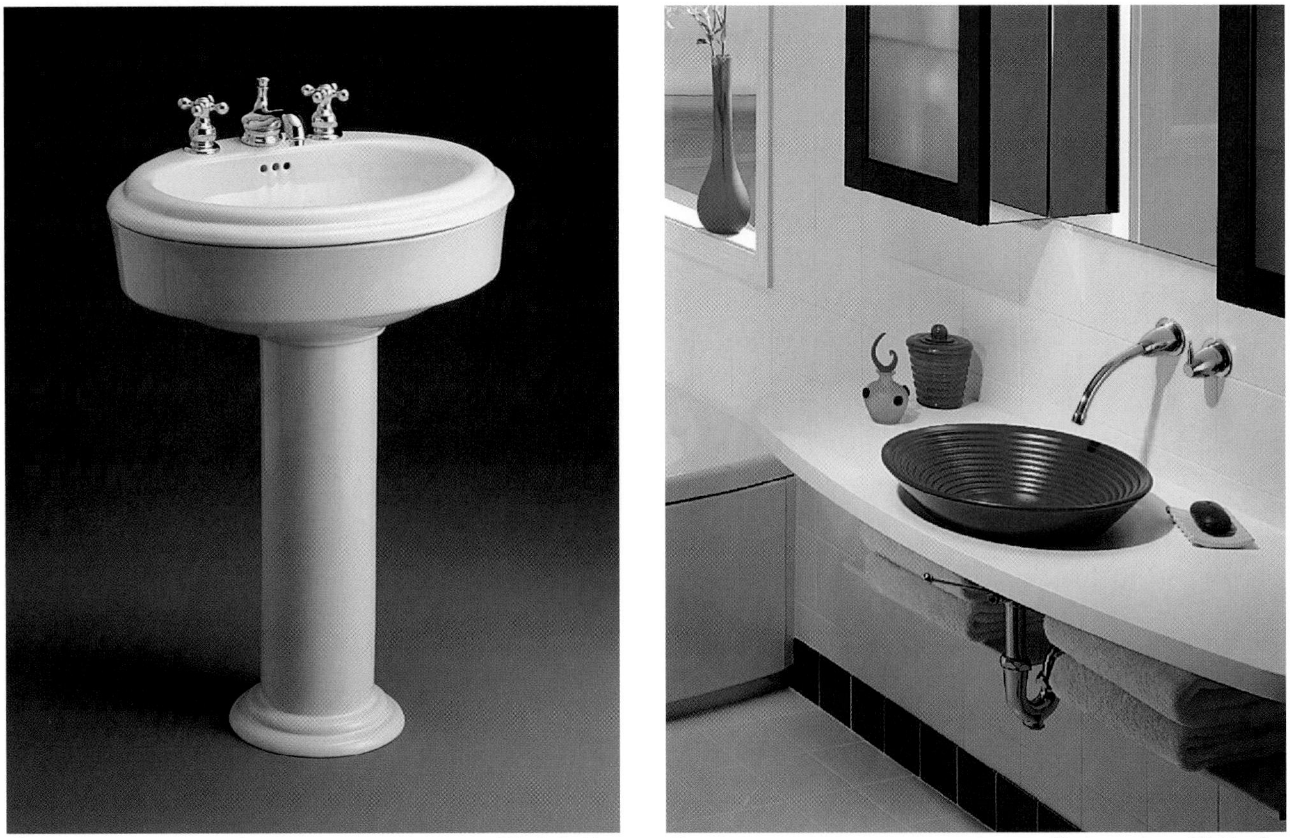

A Eljer Industries B Photo courtesy of Kohler Co.

19-17 Lavatories may be freestanding models (A) or they may be enclosed in a vanity or ledge (B).

Planning the Plumbing System

The specific details of the plumbing system are best handled by an expert. However, a basic knowledge of guidelines and options is useful to the beginning housing student.

A plumbing system is more efficient and less expensive if areas that require plumbing are kept as close to each other as possible. This way, water mains and stacks can be shorter and less complex.

The most efficient arrangement is placing rooms that require plumbing adjacent to each other on the same floor. Fixtures would be placed on an adjoining wall so water mains and main stacks are easily shared. For example, with a bathroom next to the kitchen, the kitchen sink, shower, and bathroom sink can be placed on the adjoining wall. This arrangement is not always practical, however, from a lifestyle standpoint.

Another efficient arrangement is locating a room requiring plumbing directly over another. For instance, laundry rooms are often placed in the basement directly below the kitchen. Bathrooms on different floors are usually aligned so plumbing mains can easily be shared.

Another decision when planning the home plumbing system is deciding what size of water heater to install. The capacity of the water heater determines how much hot water can be used at one time before running out. A guideline for appropriate capacities is shown in 19-18.

New trends in residential appliance use require special plumbing considerations. In some baths, for example, extra sinks are installed for convenience. Kitchens may have a secondary sink for food preparation in addition to the main sink. Clothes washers, dishwashers, and refrigerators with ice makers require their own water hookups. Whirlpool baths and in-ground swimming pools are gaining popularity as a part of the residential house, 19-19. These options should be considered early in the planning stages of any construction or remodeling project so the plumbing system can accommodate them.

Water Heating Needs

Hot Water Uses	Water Heater Capacity
Minimum hot water needed for two people with one bath and a clothes washer	30 gallons
Each additional person	add 3.5 gallons
Each additional bathroom	add 3.5 gallons
Automatic dishwasher	add 5.0 gallons

19-18 The proper size of a water heater for a household can be estimated with the use of this chart.

19-19 Outdoor plumbing lines are needed if a hot tub is installed.

Chapter Summary

The main components of an electrical system are the service-entrance panel, branch circuits, receptacles, and switches. The service-entrance panel serves as a monitor for the system. Branch circuits provide overcurrent protection and use smaller wires to each termination point. Receptacles provide a connection point for appliances or other users of electricity. Switches control the devices that use electricity.

It is important to follow the recommendations of the National Electrical Code to develop a system that is both safe and efficient. In addition, care should be taken to plan an electrical system that will accommodate future needs.

Signal and communication systems use electricity to control doorbells, chimes, security systems, and fire detection devices.

The plumbing system of a dwelling provides an adequate supply of water for household use in desired locations. It also removes wastewater through a sanitary sewer or private septic system. There are three primary parts to a residential plumbing system—a water-supply system, wastewater-removal system, and plumbing fixtures. The water-supply system includes the separate branch lines carrying hot and cold water plus the water conditioning equipment. The wastewater-removal system carries wastewater to the sanitary sewer or private septic system. Residential plumbing fixtures include: sinks, shower stalls, water closets, dishwashers, clothes washers, and tubs. Plumbing fixtures are available in a wide variety of styles. A plumbing expert is most qualified to handle specific details of a plumbing system.

Review Questions

1. What is a service-entrance panel?
2. How can a branch circuit protect a wiring system?
3. How many and what type of circuits should a kitchen have when it contains an electric range, refrigerator, dishwasher, and other smaller appliances?
4. What points should be considered when placing receptacles and switches in a house?
5. How does the water-supply system differ from the wastewater-removal system?
6. What factors should be considered when planning for plumbing fixtures?
7. What size of water heater is the minimum that should be considered for a household with three family members, two baths, one clothes washer, and one dishwasher?
8. What three functions does a home signal and communication system perform?

Suggested Activities

1. Observe the service-entrance panel of your home with the supervision of a knowledgeable adult. Draw a sketch to display to the class.
2. Describe to a classmate how low-voltage switching works.
3. What are the functions of signal and communication systems? Identify such systems at your school.
4. Trace the flow of the water-supply system into your home. Sketch the system in an illustration similar to Fig. 19-14.
5. Investigate why some wastewater-removal systems malfunction after heavy rains. Summarize your findings in a paragraph.
6. List guidelines for planning a residential plumbing system. In an essay, explain how well your home's plumbing follows the guidelines.

Internet Resources

A.O. Smith Water Products Company
hotwater.com

B.F. Goodrich's FlowGuard Gold home page
flowguardgold.com

Cooper Wiring Devices
eagle-electric.com

Geist Manufacturing, Inc., manufacturer of cord and cable covers
flexiduct.com

Kohler Company, a manufacturer of plumbing products
kohler.com

Leviton, a manufacturer of electrical and electronic products
leviton.com

Moen, Inc., a manufacturer of plumbing products
moen.com

Price Pfister, a manufacturer of plumbing products
pricepfister.com

Sterling Plumbing, a Kohler Company
sterlingplumbing.com

Vanguard Piping Systems, Inc.
vanguardpipe.com

Whirlpool Corporation
whirlpool.com

Note: Web addresses may have changed since publication. For some entries, reaching the correct Web site may require keying *www.* into the address.

Chapter 20
Climate Control, Fireplaces, and Stoves

Objectives

After studying this chapter, you will be able to
- evaluate the level of climate control in a house by determining the number and type of climate-control devices in the house.
- describe the operations of various heating and cooling systems.
- list the components and structural considerations involved in using solar heating systems.
- describe the construction of fireplaces and stoves and explain how they heat a room.

Key Terms

solar collector
compressor-cycle system
independent evaporator unit
insulation
draft
single-face fireplace
two-face opposite fireplace
two-face adjacent fireplace
three-face fireplace
radiant heat
circulating stove

Living spaces are more comfortable today than ever before because of climate-control systems. A total climate-control system involves temperature control, humidity control, air circulation, and air cleaning. Most modern homes have at least some kind of temperature-control system. Total climate control within a home is becoming more common.

Climate Control

Using heating and cooling systems controls the temperature of a home. Insulation is used to help temperature-control systems work more efficiently. Most homes in areas that have cold weather at least part of the year use some form of heating system. Cooling systems are most common in hot, humid areas, but they are also used in northern areas for the summer season.

Conventional Heating Systems

A home can be heated by using one of several systems. The most commonly used types are: forced warm air, hydronic systems, electric radiant heat, and heat-pump systems. Because these systems use different methods to heat the air, they have different advantages and disadvantages. These are listed in 20-1.

Forced Warm-Air Systems

A forced warm-air system uses a furnace, blower, and duct system to heat a house. Air is first heated in the furnace. See 20-2. Furnaces commonly use natural gas or electricity for fuel. Some use oil, coal, and wood, but they are not as common. As the fuel is expended, heat is produced and transmitted to the air.

The blower moves the heated air into the ducts and brings in cold air from the space being heated. The ducts carry the air from the furnace to each

Heating Systems

1. Forced Warm-Air System

Advantages

Is relatively inexpensive to install.
Provides heat quickly.
Can use heating ducts for air cooling.
Simplifies humidification.
Accommodates air cleaners.

Disadvantages

Uses large ducts, which are sometimes difficult to route throughout the dwelling.
Is noisy.
Moves air rapidly, which is objectionable to some people.
Cannot move air properly when furniture blocks registers.
Permits only one zone of heating per furnace.

2. Hydronic System

Advantages

Runs quietly.
Provides even heat with no drafts.
Is clean.
Is efficient.
Permits different heating zones.

Disadvantages

Has a slow reaction time.
Cannot accommodate air cooling.
Cannot accommodate air filtration.
Cannot accommodate humidification.

3. Electric Radiant

Advantages

System is clean and quiet.
It produces a constant level of heat.
System components can be hidden.
It permits different heating zones.
No chimney is required.
It is dependable and free of maintenance.

Disadvantages

There is no provision for humidification.
There is no provision for air filtration.
There is no provision for cooling.
It has a slow reaction time.
It is expensive to operate in some areas of the country.

4. Central Heat Pump

Advantages

Is clean and needs no chimney.
Uses little inside space because the main unit is located outdoors.
Provides both heating and cooling in the same unit.
Simplifies air cleaning and humidification.
Is highly efficient in mild climates.

Disadvantages

Heats inefficiently when the temperature outdoors is below 30° F.
Requires a duct system with a blower to move air.
Costs more than most systems to install.
May not provide adequate heat in very cold climates.

5. Active Solar Heat System

Advantages

Is clean, nonpolluting, and environmentally attractive.
Is very safe.
Provides free energy.
Operates inexpensively.

Disadvantages

Is affected by the weather and, therefore, is not dependable.
Will not work in all areas of the country.
Is expensive to install.
Requires considerable maintenance.
May freeze and ruin collectors if the pump fails (in some water systems).
Generally requires a backup heating system.

20-1 Because heating systems operate differently, they have different advantages and disadvantages.

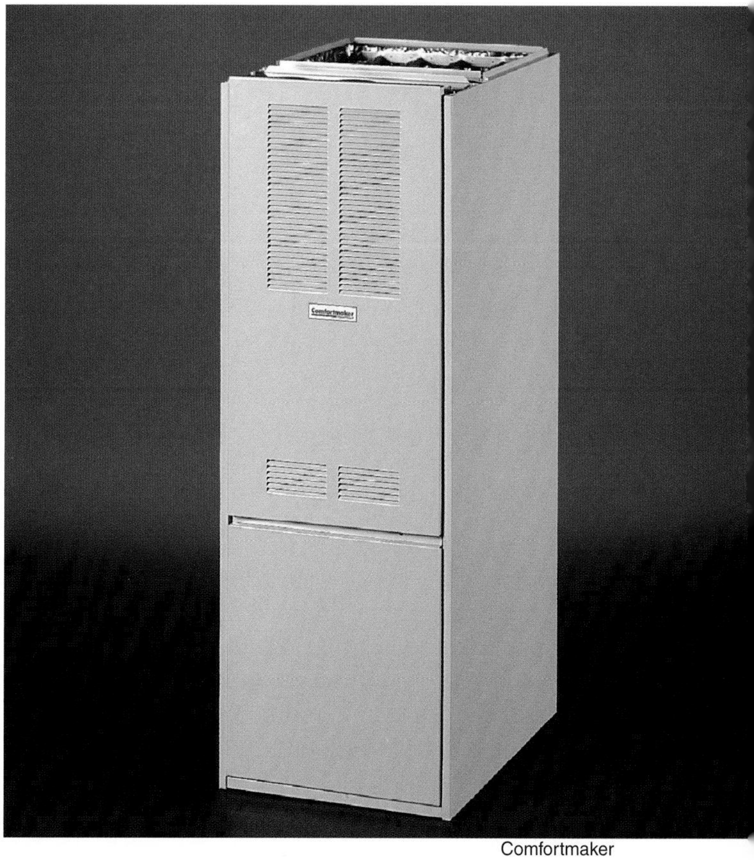

Comfortmaker

20-2 This furnace represents the latest technology in forced warm air furnaces. The blower is located in the lower compartment of the furnace.

room, 20-3. One set of ducts is used to carry warm air to each room. Another set, called the cold air return, carries cold air from each room back to the furnace. This cycle is repeated until the desired temperature is reached in the heated area. A thermostat in the living space controls the amount of heat delivered.

20-3 The duct system carries heat to every room in the house.

Registers are generally located close to the floor along the outside walls of the home. This eliminates cold floors and provides more even heating. The number of registers in a room depends on the size, expected heat loss, and desired temperature of the room.

Hydronic Systems

A hydronic system uses hot water to heat a home. The system consists of a boiler, pump, water pipes, and radiators or radiant panels. Water is heated in the boiler using natural gas or fuel oil, 20-4. Electricity, wood, and coal may also be used. When the water is sufficiently hot, it is pumped through pipes to the radiators located throughout the living space. They are usually located on outside walls to increase comfort and reduce cold air drafts. See 20-5. As the heat is removed from the water in the radiators, the water is pumped back to the boiler to be reheated.

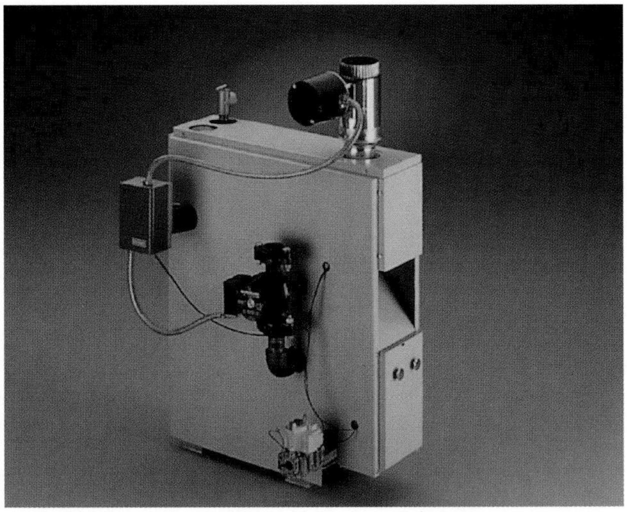

United Technologies Carrier

20-4 A hydronic furnace has a large chamber to heat water.

Another type of hydronic heating system uses copper tubing embedded in a concrete floor or plastered ceiling to heat a home. This system is usually limited to mild climates where the temperature is not likely to drop rapidly in a short time. It may also be used as an auxiliary heating system for a section of the home.

Electric Radiant Systems

Electric radiant systems use resistance wiring to produce heat in the wire. No pumps, blowers, registers, furnace, or chimney are required for this type of system. The wire is embedded in the ceiling or floor, or mounted in baseboard convectors. See 20-6. If the wire is located in the ceiling or floor, the entire system is hidden.

Central Heat-Pump Systems

The central heat-pump system uses an electric refrigeration unit to heat and cool a living space. The

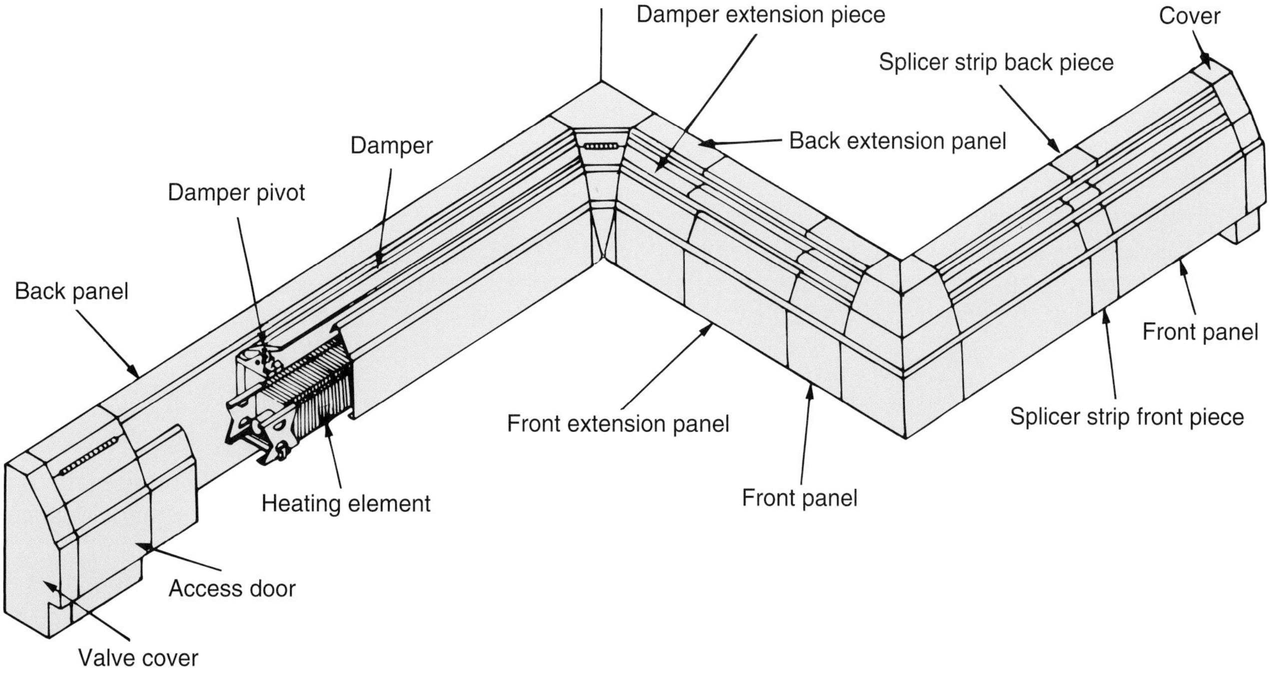

20-5 Hydronic radiant panels are located along the baseboard of a room to provide even heat.

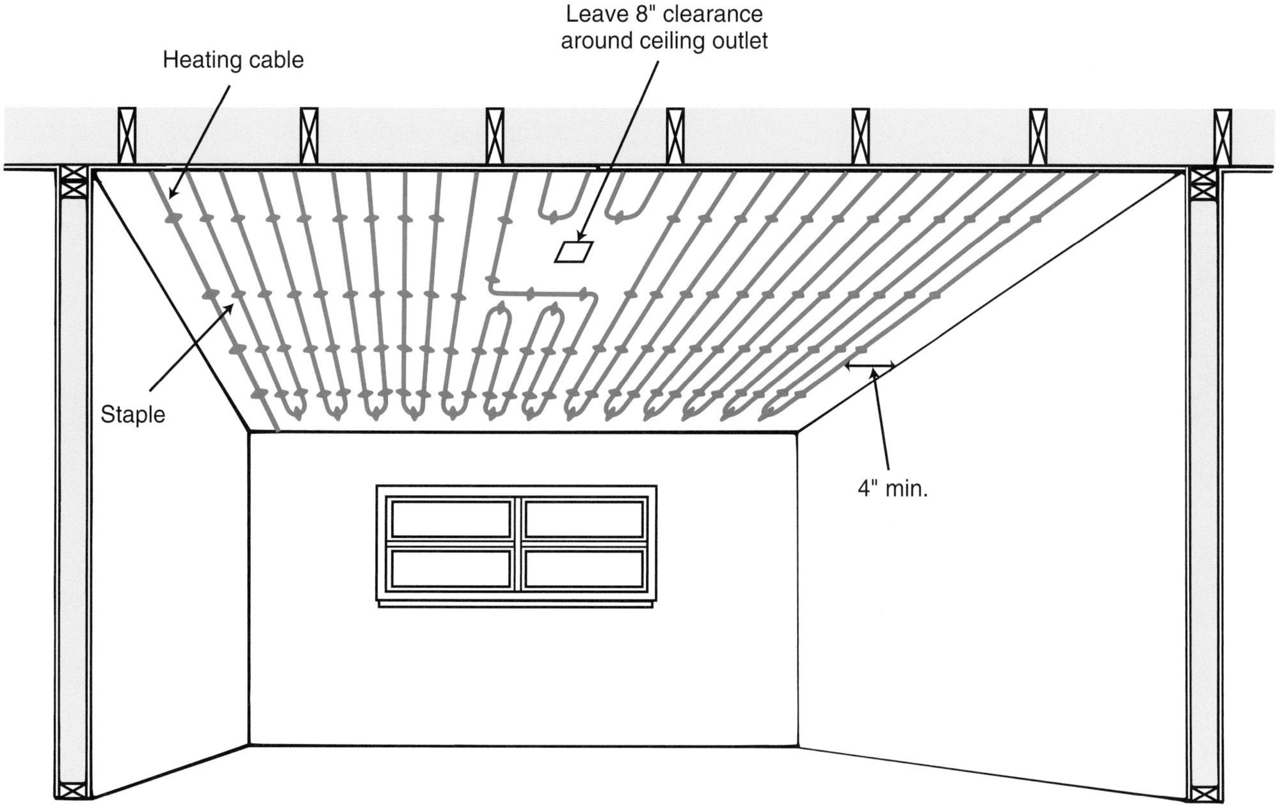

20-6 Resistance wiring for electric radiant systems can be embedded in the ceiling.

refrigeration unit contains a compressor, circulating fluid (refrigerant), and two heat exchangers. See 20-7. It operates by removing heat from air or water.

In cold weather, heat is removed from outside air and pumped into the house. In warm weather, heat is removed from air in the house and pumped outside. Some heat pumps are connected to a water well. Well water facilitates more efficient operation than outside air because it is warmer than exterior air in cold weather and cooler in hot weather. Heat pumps may also be connected to solar collectors that provide some heat, even on cloudy days.

Solar Heating Systems

Solar heating systems use energy from the sun to heat a home. They are fairly new types of heating systems, but they are gaining popularity as fuel costs rise. Although solar heating is fairly reliable, it is usually used in combination with another fuel-powered, backup system for emergency use. The two main types of solar heating systems are active systems and passive systems.

Active Solar Heating

Active systems involve collecting, storing, and distributing heat energy within a living space. A typical solar system contains a bank of collectors, a heat storage area, and a distribution system with controls for operating the system, 20-8. The distribution system may operate with warm air and ducts, similar to a forced warm-air system, or it may use warm water and pipes, similar to a hydronic system. Warm-air systems are more popular for home heating.

20-7 This heat-pump compressor/condenser unit is designed for outside installation.

A **solar collector** is part of an active solar heating system designed to absorb heat from the sun. It is usually placed on the roof of a house to get maximum exposure to sunlight. See 20-9. Several sizes and types are available, ranging in efficiency from 15 to 65 percent. Some have built-in insulation. Collectors may have single, double, or triple glazing. The amount of insulation and type of glazing affects the efficiency of the collector, especially in cold climates.

A solar collector contains an absorber plate that is heated by the sun's rays. There are many designs and styles. Copper is the most efficient and expensive material used for absorber plates. Aluminum is commonly used and fairly efficient as well. Absorber plates are generally covered with a flat black coating to absorb as much energy as possible.

After heat energy is collected, it is transferred to a storage area. Warm-air systems generally use a large box or crawl space area filled with stones to collect heat. Warm-water systems use a large tank to store heat in water. Either type of storage must be well insulated to prevent loss of heat.

The size of storage needed is related to the amount of solar energy available, the size and type of collector, efficiency of the storage media, heat loss in the storage area, and household needs. The storage should be large enough to store the heat required for three days of cloudy weather. Longer storage would require an area too large and expensive to be practical. Average storage size for warm-air systems usually ranges from ½ to 1 cu. ft. of stone for each sq. ft. of collector area. A warm-water storage tank requires half the space to store the same amount of heat.

A blower for air systems or a pump for water systems distributes heat from the collectors and storage to the living space. The blower or pump is activated by a complex set of controls that respond to temperature sensors located in the collectors, storage area, and living space.

Passive Solar Heating

Passive solar heating is used in homes as a supplement to heating systems. It uses the structure of the house as both the collector and storage for heat. Specially built walls use concrete block as heat collectors with glass panels to contain heat in the structure, 20-10. Passive walls do not have a distribution system to move warm air throughout the house.

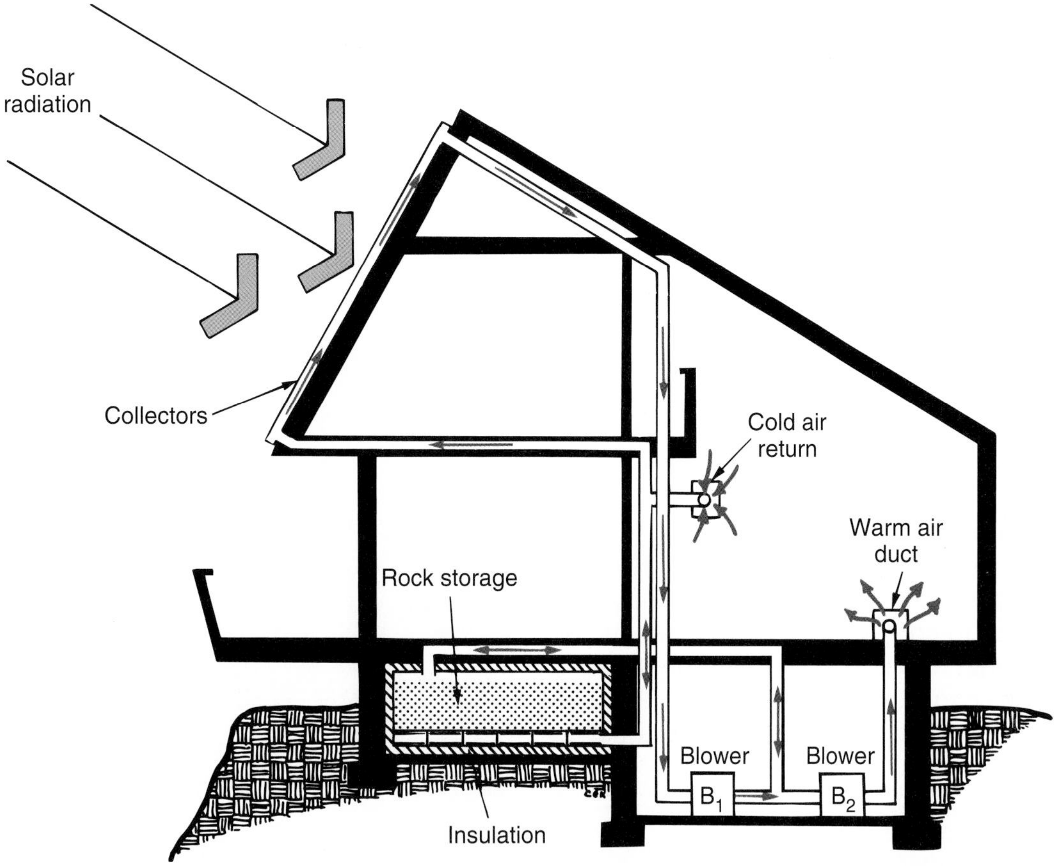

20-8 An active solar heating system collects heat using solar panels. Heat is then transferred to storage. A duct system similar to the type used with a forced warm-air system is used to circulate heat throughout the house.

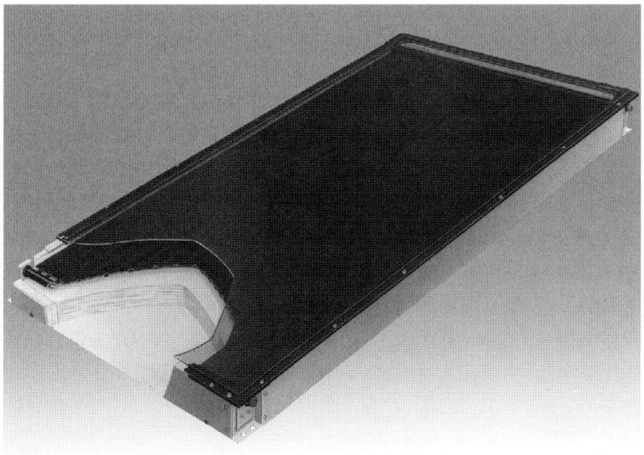

20-9 This solar panel has single glazing, an absorber plate, and insulation.

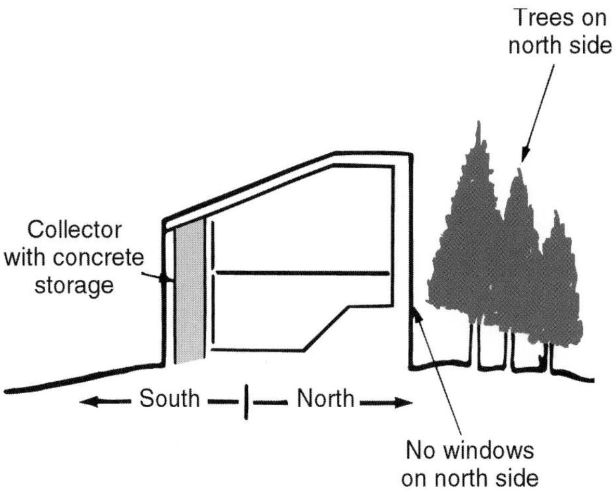

20-10 Passive solar heating is built directly into the walls of the home. It is more effective when used on walls with a southern exposure in homes without north-facing windows.

Passive heating requires special construction, so it is not a practical option unless a new home is built. A home using passive panels will be most efficient if its north side is windowless and the panels have a southern exposure.

Cooling Systems

Cooling systems remove heat from a building and provide cool, clean, dehumidified air. This allows a home to be comfortable in warm, humid weather. Also, since windows are closed, infiltration of dirt, pollen, and dust is reduced. Central air conditioners are the most efficient types of residential cooling systems. Room air conditioners are not cooling systems, but they are used in some homes and many apartments for local cooling.

The most common residential cooling system is the compressor-cycle system. Heat pumps are frequently used to cool homes as well. The operation of heat pumps is discussed in the heating section of this chapter.

The **compressor-cycle system** uses a highly compressed, chemical refrigerant to cool air. The refrigerant passes through the compressor where it is pressurized and becomes a hot gas. It is then pumped to the condenser and cooled to condense into a liquid state. The liquid is pumped to the evaporator cooling coil where it removes heat from the air in the home as it evaporates into a gas again.

As room air is cooled, moisture in the air condenses on the fins of the condenser and is drained away. This process dehumidifies the air and increases the comfort level. The cooled air is moved to various parts of the living space through a system of ducts. If a forced warm-air system heats the home, its ducts are also used to carry cooled air propelled by the furnace blower.

Compressor-cycle units normally have two separate components. The cooling coils are mounted on the furnace to allow the furnace blower to circulate the cooled air. The second part of the unit containing the compressor and condenser are located outside the home, 20-11. When a cooling system operates independently of the furnace, the compressor/condenser unit is used with an **independent evaporator unit**. This unit consists of a blower, cooling coils, and filter. It may use a separate duct system or existing ducts.

Room air-conditioning units contain a compressor, condenser, cooling coil, and fan all in one unit, 20-12. They are usually installed in a window or wall opening designed for the unit. These systems should be well covered during cool weather because cold air will enter the room through the unit.

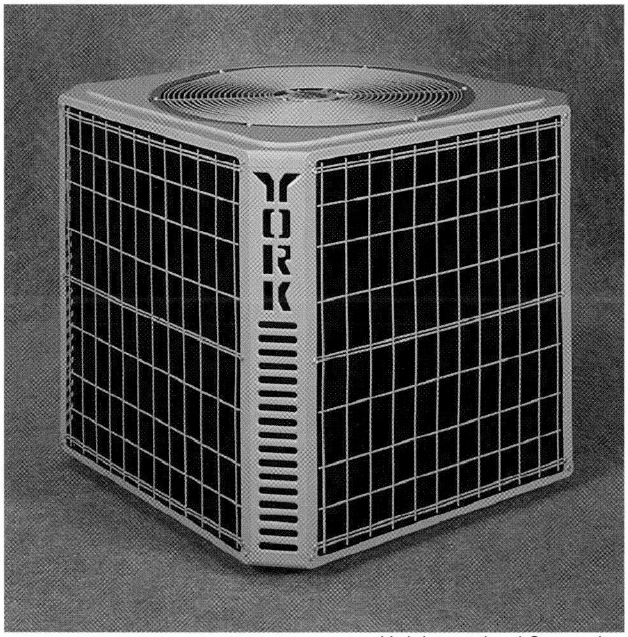

York International Corporation

20-11 The compressor/condenser unit for a central air conditioner is located outside the home.

General Electric Company

20-12 Room air conditioners contain the compressor/condenser unit, cooling coil, and fan. Most are placed in windows, but some are installed in an exterior wall.

Insulation

The function of insulation in a structure is to prevent excessive heat loss in cold weather and heat gain in warm weather. **Insulation** is a material that efficiently resists the flow of heat through it. Common examples of insulation include glass fiber, foamed glass, foamed plastics, and expanded minerals such as vermiculite. These materials are very efficient in resisting the flow of heat.

When comparing the efficiency of various insulators, the level of resistance to heat is designated as the R-value. R-values are higher for products with higher insulative efficiency. R-values for common materials of the same thickness are listed in 20-13. The total resistance of a wall is determined by adding the R-values of each material in the wall. See 20-14.

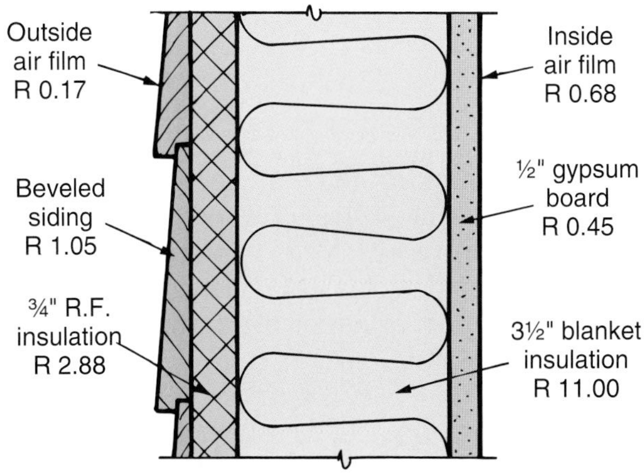

20-14 To find the R-value of a wall, the R-values of each wall component are added. This wall has an R-value of 16.23.

Other Factors

Although temperature is the most obvious factor in climate control, other conditions affect the comfort level of a house. Humidity control, fresh air circulation, and air cleaning also affect climate. Systems that accommodate these factors allow total climate control of a house.

Humidity Control

Humidity is the amount of moisture in the air. A humidity level of about 50 percent is comfortable when the temperature is 75°F. Humidity in the home drops to low levels in the winter because of the heating process. Low humidity in the home can cause throat and skin irritation and cracks in the furniture. A humidifier can be used to add moisture back to dry air.

Insulation Value Comparisons

The higher the R-value is, the better the insulating properties of the material.

Material (1 in. Thickness)	R-Value
Expanded polystyrene	3.85
Mineral batt insulation	3.50
Glass fiber insulation	3.50
Plywood	1.30
Glass	0.88
Sand plaster	0.30
Common brick	0.20
Concrete	0.08

20-13 If a product has a high R-value, it is a good insulator.

A humidifier may be a freestanding unit, or it may be attached directly to a forced warm-air furnace. Humidifiers may add as many as 15 gallons or more of water to indoor air each day. Most have automatic controls that may be set to provide the desired amount of humidity.

In warm weather, air in the home has too much humidity. Humid air feels sticky and uncomfortable. Excessive humidity causes wood doors, windows, and drawers to swell and stick. Condensation may occur as well, causing wood to warp. A dehumidifier may be installed to remove excess water from the air. It removes the evaporated water in the air by condensing the water on cold coils, thus reducing the humidity level.

Dehumidifiers are frequently individual, portable units. They have a removable container, which must be emptied periodically, that collects the water removed from the air. Dehumidification occurs automatically when an air conditioner is used.

Air Circulation

Modern living spaces are almost airtight to reduce heat loss in winter and heat gain in summer. As a result, little fresh air leaks in. If the same air is continuously circulated in a home without adding a fresh supply, the air becomes stale.

A circulation system that operates even when air is at the proper temperature helps to keep air fresh. Fans, either built into the central heating system or added in the attic, help to circulate air. A circulation system eliminates high concentrations of moisture, smoke, or fumes.

Air Cleaning

An air-cleaning device removes dust and foreign materials from the air. Some furnaces have built-in filters, and others have electronic air-cleaning grids, 20-15. Grids remove about 95 percent of the dust particles in the air. The grid works by placing an electrical charge on each airborne contaminant and attaching these particles to a metal plate. The accumulated dust and dirt is removed when the filter is changed or cleaned.

Fireplaces and Stoves

Fireplaces and stoves have received renewed interest in recent years as fuel prices have risen. They may be used as a heat source as well as a focal point. New developments make fireplaces and stoves efficient devices for heating an area.

Fireplaces

Several types of fireplaces are found in homes today. Traditional fireplaces are of solid masonry, while newer types are constructed of metal. The metal fireplaces may be covered with brick to look like solid masonry fireplaces. Many of these burn wood, but some are gas fired or electric, giving the appearance of a wood fire.

A fireplace generally consists of a firebox, damper, and flue, 20-16. The firebox and inner hearth (the floor of the firebox) are made of fireproof material to withstand damage from the burning fire. A special brick, called firebrick, is often used. The top of the firebox is covered with a damper that controls the burning rate and prevents downdrafts of cold air.

A flue is necessary to carry smoke to the outside of the house and facilitate a good draft for the fire. A **draft** is the upward flow of air that draws

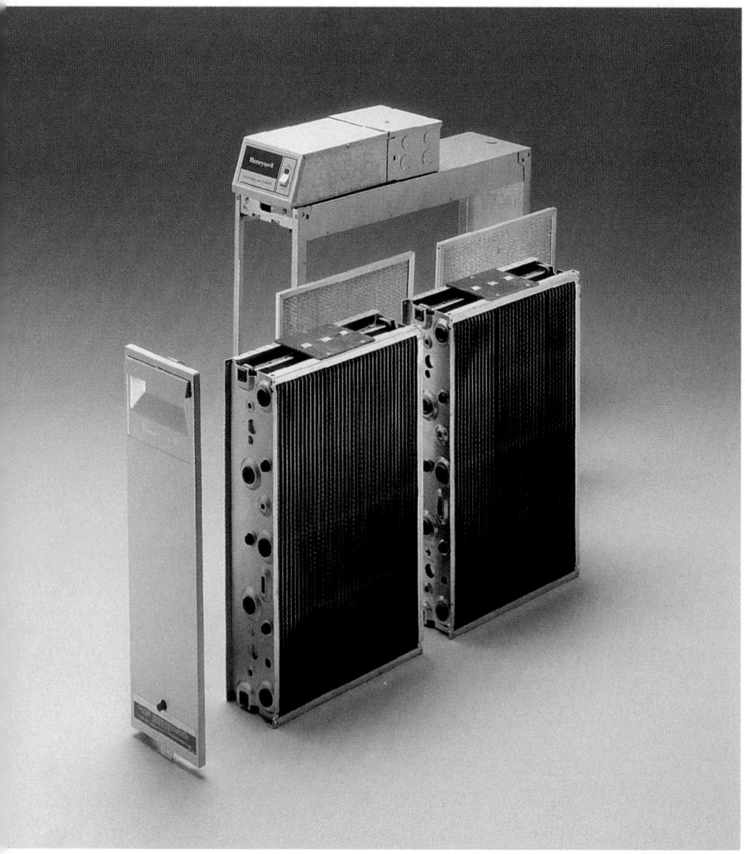

Honeywell, Inc.

20-15 Electronic air cleaners remove dust, dirt, pollen, tobacco, and cooking odors from the home.

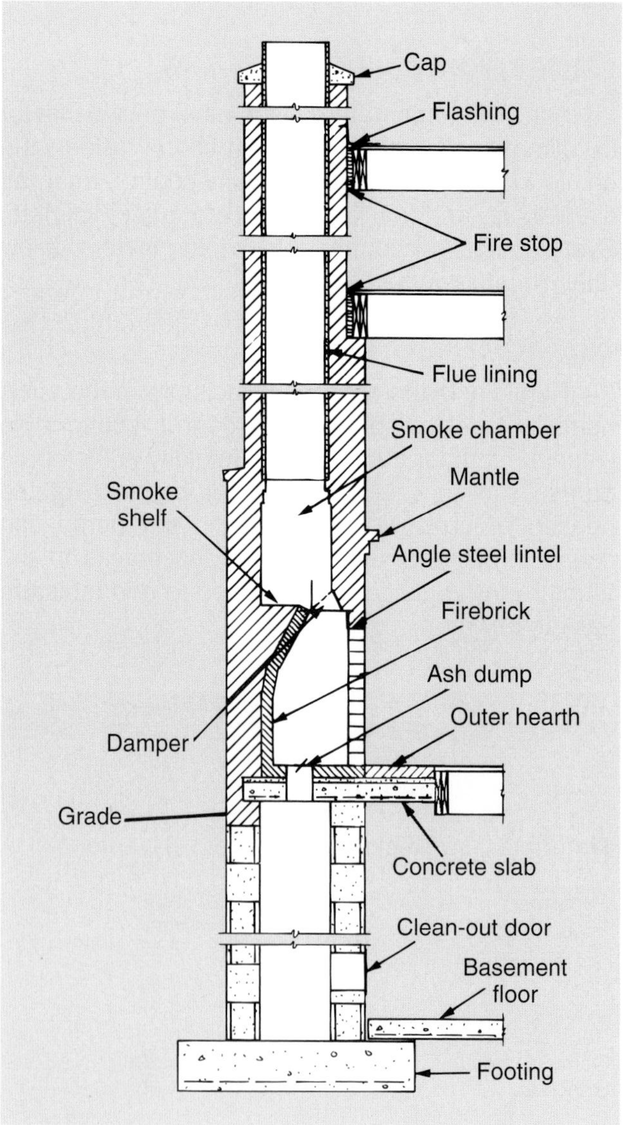

20-16 A fireplace is designed to facilitate efficient burning of wood and to remove smoke from the house.

in sufficient oxygen for a fire to burn well. Draft is increased as the height and area of the flue are increased. A wider area just above the firebox, called the smoke chamber, helps to increase the draft by causing the air to move in a swirling motion.

A masonry fireplace has a firebox and inner hearth lined with firebrick. The flue is generally lined with clay tile. Masonry fireplaces may be single-face, two-face opposite, two-face adjacent, or three-face in design.

- The **single-face fireplace** has one opening in the firebox. It is the most common type of fireplace built, 20-17. It burns more efficiently than the other designs because it has a good oxygen flow into the fireplace. The most popular size is 36 in. wide, but sizes may vary from 24 to 96 in.
- A **two-face opposite fireplace** is open on the front and back sides, 20-18. With this design, care must be taken to prevent a draft from one side to the other. The draft may cause smoke to enter the house. The opening width of this design ranges from 28 to 48 in.
- A **two-face adjacent fireplace** is open on the front and one adjacent side, 20-19. It is also known as a projecting corner fireplace. Opening sizes range from 28 to 60 in.

20-18 The two-face opposite fireplace enables a view from two rooms.

20-17 A single-face fireplace has the most efficient design.

20-19 A two-face adjacent design is usually used for a corner fireplace.

- A **three-face fireplace** is open on three sides, 20-20. Because the opening is so large, a draft for this type of fireplace is not always sufficient for a good fire. Three-face fireplaces are made in the same sizes as two-face opposite designs.

Prefabricated metal fireplaces are more efficient for producing heat than traditional fireplaces. Wall-mounted and freestanding models are usually metal on the outside. They are complete from the factory; only the flue must be added.

Prefabricated heat-circulating fireplaces require framing or masonry enclosures, 20-21. They may have brick-lined fireboxes to look identical to traditional masonry fireplaces. These units are very efficient because the sides and back consist of a double-wall passageway used to heat air. Cool air in a room is drawn into the chamber, heated, and returned to the room through registers above the chamber.

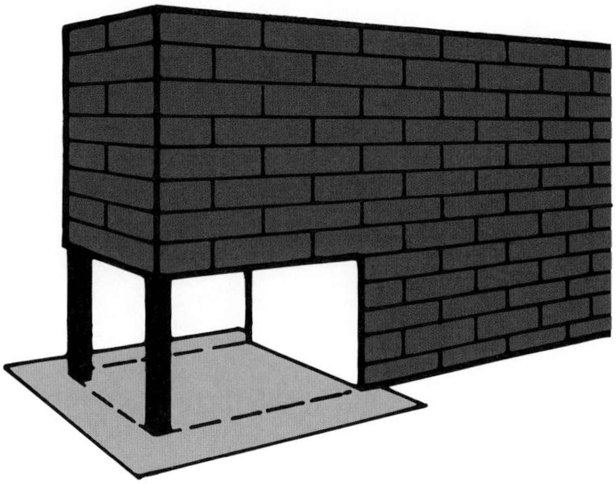

20-20 The three-face fireplace has the least efficient design.

Air for combustion is piped into the sealed firebox from the outside. Glass doors on the firebox prevent the loss of warm room air up the chimney. This design also reduces the fireplace's tendency to pull cold air into a room through cracks around doors and windows. Some models use a small electric fan to increase airflow.

Safety is a major concern with fireplaces because sparks may ignite objects within a room. Placing a fire screen in front of a fireplace opening will help prevent sparks from flying into the room. Glass doors that fit tightly over the fireplace opening provide maximum protection against sparks, 20-22. They also reduce heat loss when the fireplace is not in operation. Nonflammable materials should be used on the floor directly in front of the fireplace. Combustible materials, such as carpeting, draperies, paneling, and wood or upholstered furniture, should be kept at a safe distance from the fireplace.

Stoves

Stoves generally produce more usable heat than fireplaces. They also provide a cozy, decorative addition to a room, 20-23. Stoves used for heat are usually fueled by coal or wood. They are generally used as local sources of heat in homes with central

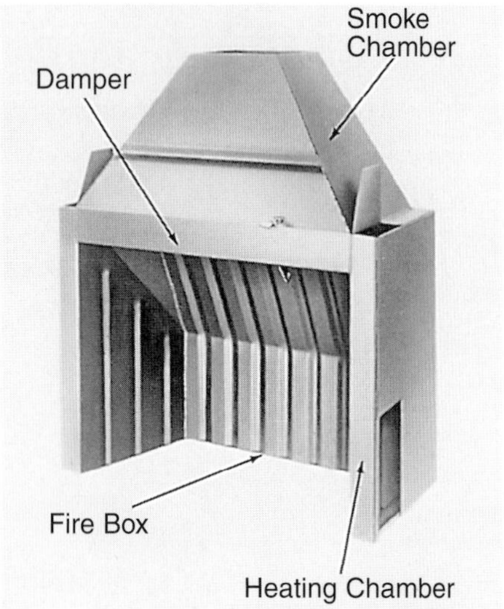

A Whittier Steel & Mfg., Inc.

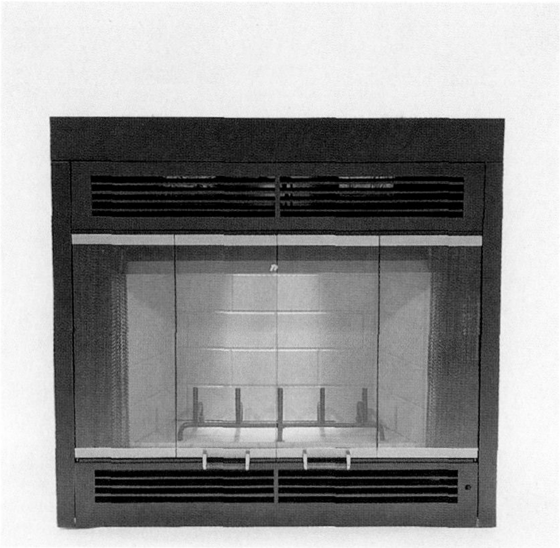

B Superior Fireplace Company

20-21 A heat-circulating fireplace increases a fire's heating efficiency by drawing room air into the heating chamber and returning heated air to the room (A). When installed, the heat-circulating fireplace looks just like a traditional masonry fireplace (B).

Manufactured Housing Institute

20-22 Screens help prevent sparks from escaping the fireplace and possibly igniting flammable items.

heating systems. Models vary according to their level of efficiency, and these levels should be checked before purchasing a stove.

The two main types of stoves are radiant and circulating stoves. Both types of stoves produce **radiant heat**, which passes through the air with no assistance from airflow. However, circulating stoves use airflow as well as radiation to distribute heat throughout a room.

A **circulating stove** is a radiant stove surrounded by an outer jacket. The jacket has openings at the bottom and top so air can flow between the stove and jacket, 20-24. Either natural airflow or small fans move the air around the stove. The airflow enables a room to be heated more evenly and efficiently than is possible with radiant heat alone.

Circulating stoves are safer for home use than radiant stoves because the exposed surfaces are not as hot. Serious burns may result from touching a radiant stove. Circulating stoves may be placed closer to combustible materials than radiant stoves

HearthStone

20-23 Stoves are more efficient heating devices than fireplaces. They can have a cozy appearance.

Vermont Castings, Inc.

20-24 A circulating stove allows air to flow around the fire to assure steady, even heat in a room.

because of their lower surface temperatures. This allows more flexibility in placing a stove.

Stoves are sometimes classified according to their heating efficiency. Low-efficiency stoves, which are generally 20 to 30 percent efficient, generally have the simplest construction. They route primary-combustion air in a straight path through or across the flame. No provision is made for secondary combustion of gases produced during burning. Examples include simple box stoves, Franklin stoves, potbelly stoves, and some parlor stoves.

Medium-efficiency stoves operate in the range of 35 to 50 percent efficiency. Their design has better control of the amount of primary and secondary air used for combustion. Most of these stoves have less air leakage into the stove. In addition to these features, they generally have some type of thermostat or temperature controlling device to ensure a constant burning rate.

High-efficiency stoves are over 50 percent efficient. They regulate airflow as the medium-efficiency stoves do, but also use baffles, long smoke paths, and heat-exchange devices to increase heat output. These stoves are more expensive to purchase, but deliver more heat per unit of fuel. Increased efficiency frequently offsets a higher initial cost if the stove is operated regularly.

The location of the stove can influence its efficient distribution of heat. Improved heat distribution can be accomplished in several ways. First, a stove placed in a large area between two rooms can heat both rooms more efficiently than if located in one of the rooms. If this is not possible, then a large opening between the two rooms will improve heat distribution. The opening should extend to the ceiling since warm air rises to the ceiling. Another approach is to install large registers at the top and bottom of the wall between rooms to be heated. The registers will allow heated air to move more easily between the rooms.

Stairways provide excellent passageways for heated air to reach spaces above. They also serve as return routes for cool air. If an open stairway does not exist, registers may be installed in the ceiling of the room with the stove so warmed air can rise to the rooms above. A cold-air return should be considered if there is no natural route for cool air to flow back to the stove.

Small, inexpensive fans, like those used to cool computers, may be installed at strategic locations to bring warm air into an area. These fans are inexpensive to operate and increase air circulation very efficiently.

Locating a stove along an exterior wall will result in greater heat loss through that wall, but this is the most common location since the flue is frequently located on an outside wall. If an interior wall location is used, the wall should be properly insulated to prevent heat drain to unheated areas, such as a garage or unused attic.

A stove is frequently located inside or in front of an existing fireplace. This is logical because the flue is already in place, but locating the stove inside the fireplace will most likely reduce its efficiency. The fireplace materials will absorb large amounts of heat and hinder circulation of warm air from the stove. When the stove is positioned in front of a fireplace, the opening of the fireplace should be covered with sheet metal to reflect the heat back into the room.

Fire is a source of warmth and comfort, but it can cause considerable destruction and even death when not monitored and controlled. Refer to Chapter 23, "Designing for Health and Safety," for information about carbon monoxide and smoke detectors.

Chapter Summary

A total climate-control system involves managing temperature, humidity, air circulation, and air cleaning. All affect the comfort level in a home.

Temperature control requires heating and cooling systems. Forced warm air, hydronic, electric radiant, and central heat pump are the four types of conventional heating systems available. Each type has advantages and disadvantages that must be weighed for a particular installation. Solar heating systems are also used. Active solar systems collect, store, and distribute heat energy within a living space. Passive solar systems, which use the structure of the dwelling as both heat collector and storage, supplement other heating systems.

Cooling systems remove heat from a building and provide cool, clean, dehumidified air. Central air conditioners are the most efficient residential cooling systems. The most common type of cooling system is the compressor-cycle air conditioner, but heat pumps are also used.

Insulation is an important part of any structure that is heated or cooled because it prevents excessive heat loss or gain. Insulation is any material that efficiently resists heat flow. Examples include: glass fiber, foamed glass, foamed plastics, and expanded minerals such as vermiculite.

Four styles of masonry fireplaces are used in residences: single-face, two-face opposite, two-face adjacent, and three-face fireplaces. Prefabricated metal fireplaces are popular and more efficient.

Stoves, usually fueled by wood or coal, often produce more usable heat than fireplaces. Two main types of stoves are common: radiant and circulating stoves. Highly efficient stoves are over 50 percent efficient.

Review Questions

1. What are the advantages and disadvantages of the four main types of heating systems used in residential housing?
2. How does an active solar heating system heat a house?
3. What building features are important for effective passive solar heating?
4. How does a compressor-cycle, air-conditioning system function?
5. Among compressor-cycle systems, what types of air conditioners are available?
6. What is an R-value?
7. How are R-values used to choose insulation?
8. How does a humidifier function?
9. How does a dehumidifier function?
10. How do the components of a fireplace facilitate efficient heating?
11. How does a circulating stove differ from a radiant stove?
12. Is a circulating stove or radiant stove the more efficient source of heat for a room?

Suggested Activities

1. Contact people in your neighborhood who have forced warm-air, hydronic, or electric radiant heating systems. Survey their opinions of each system's dependability, advantages, disadvantages, economy, and serviceability. Report their reactions.
2. Visit a local heating and air-conditioning equipment supplier. Request catalogs and other literature showing choices of residential heating and cooling equipment. Present them to the class.
3. Write an essay comparing the similarities and differences of active and passive solar heating systems.
4. Describe to a classmate how a compressor-cycle cooling system works.
5. Investigate the Web site of a room air conditioner manufacturer to learn how to determine the best size for a room. Then, determine the size range that is best for your bedroom. In a written report, describe the steps you took to make your decision.
6. Collect literature and materials commonly used in modern fireplaces and bring them to class. Display the literature and materials and describe them in class.
7. Visit your community's building department and obtain a copy of local code restrictions for installing wood burning stoves. Summarize the main points in a written report.

Internet Resources

Carrier Corporation, a manufacturer of heating and cooling equipment
carrier.com

Ventamatic, Ltd., a supplier of attic ventilators
bvc.com

Honeywell International Inc., a provider of automation and control solutions
honeywell.com

Invensys Climate Controls
invensysclimate.com

Lennox Industries Inc., a manufacturer of indoor comfort and air-quality products
lennox.com

Martin Industries, Inc., a manufacturer of fireplaces
martinindustries.com

Melton Classics, Inc., a producer of millwork
meltonclassics.com

Napoleon, a manufacturer of fireplaces, stoves, and inserts
napoleon.on.ca

The McGraw-Hill Companies, Inc. construction products marketplace
sweets.com

The Trane Company
trane.com

Whirlpool Corporation
whirlpool.com

Note: Web addresses may have changed since publication. For some entries, reaching the correct Web site may require keying *www.* into the address.

Chapter 21
Communication, Security, and Home Automation

Objectives

After studying this chapter, you will be able to
- determine the features related to information, communication, and security that should be considered when designing a new home or remodeling.
- define common terms associated with information, communication, security, and home automation.
- list the components of a security system designed to protect residential property.
- identify the components of a home-automation system.
- describe the elements of a low-voltage switching system.

Key Terms

monitoring functions
switching functions
activating functions
programming functions
communication/recording functions
alarm functions
cable pair
signaling circuits
structured wiring
wiring closet
perimeter system
motion detectors
panic button
network
open standard
hard-wired systems
power line technology
structured wiring systems
bundled cable
combination systems
relays

Many new technologies that provide security systems, home automation, and information and communication capabilities via voice and data lines have recently emerged. Some of these technologies, such as sound systems, cable television, and telephone wiring, are familiar to nearly all homebuilders. However, the cabling and devices used to manage home automation and security systems are not as well-known to most builders. Consequently, successful incorporation of these systems into a home usually requires an expert's advice.

The best time to consider installing such systems is when planning and designing a new home. The cost is less and system integration is more efficient when components are installed as the home is constructed. However, an existing house can be retrofitted with these systems in some cases.

Types of System Functions

Modern technology features that should be considered when designing a new home involve five general areas. These areas are based on the basic function each feature provides. The five basic types of system functions are: monitoring, switching/activating, programming, communication/recording, and alarm functions.

Monitoring Functions

Devices that perform **monitoring functions** examine certain aspects of the house to determine the status of each. The device then reports that information either to the homeowner or to another device that reacts to it. Some examples of conditions that may be monitored include the following:

- movement within the house
- sound within the house
- window and door status, such as open or closed
- intruder actions and movements
- heating, cooling, and humidity levels
- smoke and carbon monoxide gas levels

Switching Functions

Devices that perform **switching functions** initiate an action based on data input. Switching functions are also called **activating functions**. For example, when the temperature drops below a certain level, the furnace is switched on, based on a signal from the thermostat. Some actions that switching devices may initiate include the following:

- turning lights on or off
- turning appliances on or off
- activating an audio system
- activating various functions of an entertainment center
- opening or closing draperies, shades, and skylights
- locking or unlocking doors, windows, and vents

Lutron Electronics, Inc.

21-1 This programmable lighting controller can set 10 separate lighting scenes from multiple locations.

Programming Functions

Devices that perform **programming functions** can control a sequence of planned events. For example, a timer on a lamp is a simple device that performs a programming function. At predetermined times programmed into the device, the timer turns the light on and later turns it off, 21-1. Devices that perform programming functions can be used to create a timed sequence for operating the following:

- lighting
- entertainment systems
- climate control

Communication and Recording Functions

Devices that perform **communication/recording functions** can record, play back, and/or allow live voice, video, or data communication. Examples of these devices include intercoms, voice or videophones, and closed-circuit video cameras. Pieces of equipment that receive commands remotely by phone or the Internet to relay to another device also are communication devices.

Alarm Functions

Devices that perform **alarm functions** alert the homeowner or a home security agency to potential dangers based on a signal from a monitoring device. For example, a motion detector may signal an "intruder alert" that, in turn, warns the homeowner and alerts a home security agency, 21-2. Other alarm devices may alert the homeowner to unsafe health conditions from gases and smoke or warn of a malfunctioning appliance.

Information and Communication Systems

A new home in today's society should have a minimum of two standard telephone lines. These lines provide the wiring for information transfer and communication. One line, the traditional phone line,

21-2 This motion sensor detects movement inside the house, which may be caused by an intruder, and will alert the occupants and/or the security command center.

is generally dedicated to voice communication. The other telephone line is used for data transmission, such as for Internet access.

The telephone lines are two wires called a **cable pair**. The wires are powered at the telephone company with a direct current to operate the telephone equipment. The cable pair from the telephone company terminates in a cable termination box on the outside of the house. From there, the cable pair enters the building and usually connects to a terminal block (42A block) or network interface device inside the building. The terminal block is the point of connection for all the telephones in the home. Single telephone service on a single circuit can be used by one or more telephones or modems.

Signal and Communication Systems

Advances in technology are making signal and communication systems affordable to homeowners. These systems "sense" visitors, allow people to communicate within the home, and permit the monitoring of the many systems in the dwelling and on the property.

A popular signal and communication system is the doorbell, which can sound like a simple buzzer or sophisticated chimes. Doorbells, buzzers, chimes, and similar signal systems may incorporate different tones for different entrances to the home.

Signaling circuits supply the electrical power to buzzers, doorbells, chimes, signal lights, or warning devices. Remote control, low-voltage circuits are also included in this category.

Structured Wiring

Structured wiring is an organized arrangement of high-quality cables and connections that distribute services throughout the home. Older homes most likely have a minimal wiring structure with one line for a telephone and one line for cable TV, although many older homes are not wired for cable TV. This arrangement does not permit optimal high-speed lines for computers or fax machines. The lines were designed for voice only, not data or video communication.

Newer homes wired for the latest technology have Category 5 cable, which is capable of carrying information at high speeds, 21-3. Category 5 cable permits high-speed Internet access. High-quality video cable provides access to digital TV services

21-3 Category 5 cable is the most popular cable for computer and data networks. Notice the twisted pairs.

such as digital cable or satellite, which offer greater channel selection and sharper picture quality. The cable used for high-quality video is Radio Grade 6 cable, also called RG-6 cable and RG-6 quad shield. See 21-4. Furthermore, structured wiring efficiently distributes incoming video services to the rooms where they are desired.

The central hub of a structured wiring installation is the **wiring closet**. Sometimes it is called a *wiring cabinet.* All devices are connected to the wiring closet with Category 5 cable or Radio Grade 6 cable, depending on the requirements of the device. Wiring closets may be mounted between the studs or on the wall. The wiring closet should be located where it will be most efficient. For example, it should not be located close to the house electrical service panel, as this will cause electrical interference. Also, the wiring closet should be located so cable lengths do not exceed 285 ft. since longer lengths can reduce signal quality.

Security Systems

Security systems are important for safeguarding homes and their occupants from intruders and fire. The following statistics from the Federal Bureau of Investigation and the Consumer Product Safety Commission indicate why such protection is necessary:

- Two-thirds of all burglaries are residential.
- Two-thirds of burglaries involve forcible entry, with over half of these occurring during daylight hours.

21-4 Radio Grade 6 cable is used for cable TV, digital cable, digital satellite, cable modems, and other video applications.

- More than half a million residential fires serious enough to be reported to fire departments occur annually.
- Over 4,000 people die each year in home fires.

Home security systems are very inexpensive compared to the value of the lives and property they protect. Even when such tragedies do not affect your home, these security systems provide peace of mind.

Systems to Protect Property

To protect your home while it is unoccupied, a minimal system may be suitable. Since the earliest warning is not necessary for personal protection, it will probably be acceptable to detect an intruder after they are already inside the home.

For property protection, frequently, only the doors are protected and then motion detectors are relied upon for cost effectiveness. For example, if you wish to safeguard a one-story house and your only concern is burglar and fire protection when you are away, a system with the following components may be adequate:

- Control panel—is the brains of the system.
- Touch pad—provides a method of telling the system what to do.
- Siren—provides a warning sound and/or frightens intruders.
- Door sensors—detect entry.
- Passive infrared (PIR) or motion sensors—detect the body heat or movement of an intruder.
- Smoke detectors—sense the presence of smoke. They should be on every level of the home.

This system, while adequate for some homeowners, provides limited protection. It would not be effective if items of special value were present, such as artwork, jewelry, or firearms.

Systems to Protect Occupants and Property

The first line of defense in a security system designed to protect the occupants as well as the property is a **perimeter system**. In a perimeter system, all doors and windows are wired with magnetic switches inside the frame. An alarm is activated when a switch is disturbed as a door or window is opened. Every point of entry—main entry doors, service doors, basement doors, sliding glass doors, and all windows—must be wired for the perimeter to be secure. These security systems are controlled through a keypad, 21-5.

21-5 The security system keypad, located inside this enclosure, enables the control of all system functions. This keypad also features a built-in audio alarm that will sound when there is trouble.

Exterior lighting should be controlled by the security system, too. The sudden onset of lights will alert neighbors and help frighten away an intruder.

The magnetic switches of the perimeter system, which are located in door and window frames, detect an intruder only when a window or door is opened. They will not detect entry through broken glass. Consequently, the ideal perimeter system should also include glass-break detection. High-tech, glass-break detectors contain a small microphone connected to a sound processor. The microphone is tuned to the frequency of breaking glass, and the processor measures the sound against a preset characteristic pattern. In addition, a shock sensor detects the tiny shock wave that passes through the home when the glass is broken. Only when there is the sound of breaking glass and a resulting shock wave will the alarm be activated.

A well-secured home still needs interior protection even though all entry points and glass areas are wired and monitored. An intruder might gain entry in some other way, such as cutting a hole in the roof or removing an attic vent. **Motion detectors** sense an intruder who has bypassed the perimeter system and gained entry to the home. They provide the final line of defense for home security systems.

An added level of interior protection is necessary because the intruder may know how to disarm the system or, like any device, a switch may fail. In this event, a method to manually sound an alarm is needed. Most security-system consoles have a **panic button** that sets off an audible siren or sends an "alarm" message silently to a monitoring station.

Finally, fire protection should be a part of every home security system. Smoke detectors provide the earliest warning of fire, 21-6. Most deaths from nighttime fire are the result of smoke inhalation, not fire, because the victim does not wake up.

The fire system remains active even when the burglar alarm is turned off. Check with your local building department to determine the location and number of smoke detectors you need. Generally, they should be placed in every bedroom, hall, and level of the house.

When a fire or intruder is detected, the residents must be alerted to the emergency. This is usually accomplished with audible signals located for everyone in the home to hear. In addition, a loud (120 decibels at 10 ft.) electronic siren should be located outside the home.

Even though these alarms, sirens, and detectors will greatly increase the chances of surviving a fire or intruder, central-station monitoring is a sure way to call others for help. Central-station monitoring is provided by private home-security agencies. There are several national chains as well as many local

21-6 This smoke detector is wired to the home security system and remains active even when the burglar alarm is turned off.

agencies. Consult your local yellow pages or police or fire departments for recommendations.

Home Automation

Consider the scenario described in 21-7. Such a scenario is possible today with "smart" products that have the ability to "talk" and "listen" to one another—to **network**. A network can be as small as two appliances interacting or as comprehensive as all the electronic products in a home doing so. In complex systems, a central controller is needed to manage communication and actions between all systems based on the homeowner's instructions, 21-8.

Developing a network standard is a project that has been underway for several years. In the U.S., four home-network efforts are leading the work: Consumer Electronic Bus (CEBus), Smart House®, Echelon®, and Integrated Networks. Each approach is quite different in scope, business structure, and intended market. The CEBus is supported by the Electronic Industries Association and consumer electronics manufacturers such as Home Controls, Incorporated. Other companies, like Carrier and Eaton, are original supporters of Smart House® for new construction and retrofit. Still other companies are supporting Echelon® or Integrated Networks.

CEBus is the only North American effort that meets the definition of an open standard. An **open standard** is a system that is free for all interested parties to implement and use. The CEBus program is a committee effort with volunteer participation and is open to all companies. Manufacturers can send their messages on any media found in the home—electric wire, telephone wire, radio frequency, infrared (line of sight), coaxial cable, and optical fiber.

The Smart House Limited Partnership (SHLP) is a for-profit consortium funded by the National Association of Home Builders and private homebuilder investors. Smart House® uses a totally new system of wiring throughout the home. It uses three types of multiconductor cable as well as gas plumbing. Cable must be installed at the time of construction. A central controller manages the system.

Echelon Corporation offers a third philosophy of creating a network. While CEBus and Smart House® focus on fully integrating products and systems within the home, Echelon's network is intended for any environment in which electronic products need to communicate. Echelon has created LONWorks®, a computer software program that includes all the features needed for building an automated network. LON is the abbreviation for "local operating network." To use the network, manufacturers must develop products in harmony with Echelon technology. Echelon is licensing its technology to chipmakers and will receive royalties.

The Leviton Integrated Networks™ (LIN) is a product of Leviton Manufacturing Company. It is a structured wiring system that is gaining popularity. Leviton offers a simple solution to today's technology-wired home. It supports high-speed Internet and computer networking, whole-house audio, multiroom video, family video monitoring, and home-security capabilities.

It is too early to know which, if any, home-automation approach will ultimately win the marketplace. However, the potential for this market is very large. As the home-automation market expands over the next several years, new players will inevitably bring new products to the marketplace.

Living in a "Smart" Home

Before returning home from a winter vacation, you call your home and tell it to warm up. A central controller activates the furnace, and the inside temperature is comfortable when you arrive.

Then, before going to bed, you use your phone to tell the house "good night." One command sets the thermostat to a lower temperature, adjusts the house lighting to "nighttime," arms the security system, and checks the home's electronic locks.

If you get up during the night for a cold drink of juice from the refrigerator, the house gently brightens the lights in front of you and dims them after you pass. The security system keeps track of you so it knows not to call the police as you pass the sensors. Any new presence, such as a potential burglar, would trigger an alarm and tell you which room had been entered.

At 6:00 a.m., a "good morning" sequence turns up the thermostat, turns off the outside lighting at dawn, turns on a light in the master bath, and wakes you up at 7:00 a.m. with your favorite radio station.

Your washing machine, which you loaded with clothes from the trip, will begin its work midmorning after the solar water heater indicates there is enough warm water for washing.

21-7 A computer network can make home equipment seem "smart," but they are merely following the owner's programmed commands.

Types of Home Automation Systems

For discussion purposes, home automation systems may be grouped into four basic approaches: hard-wired systems, power line technology, structured

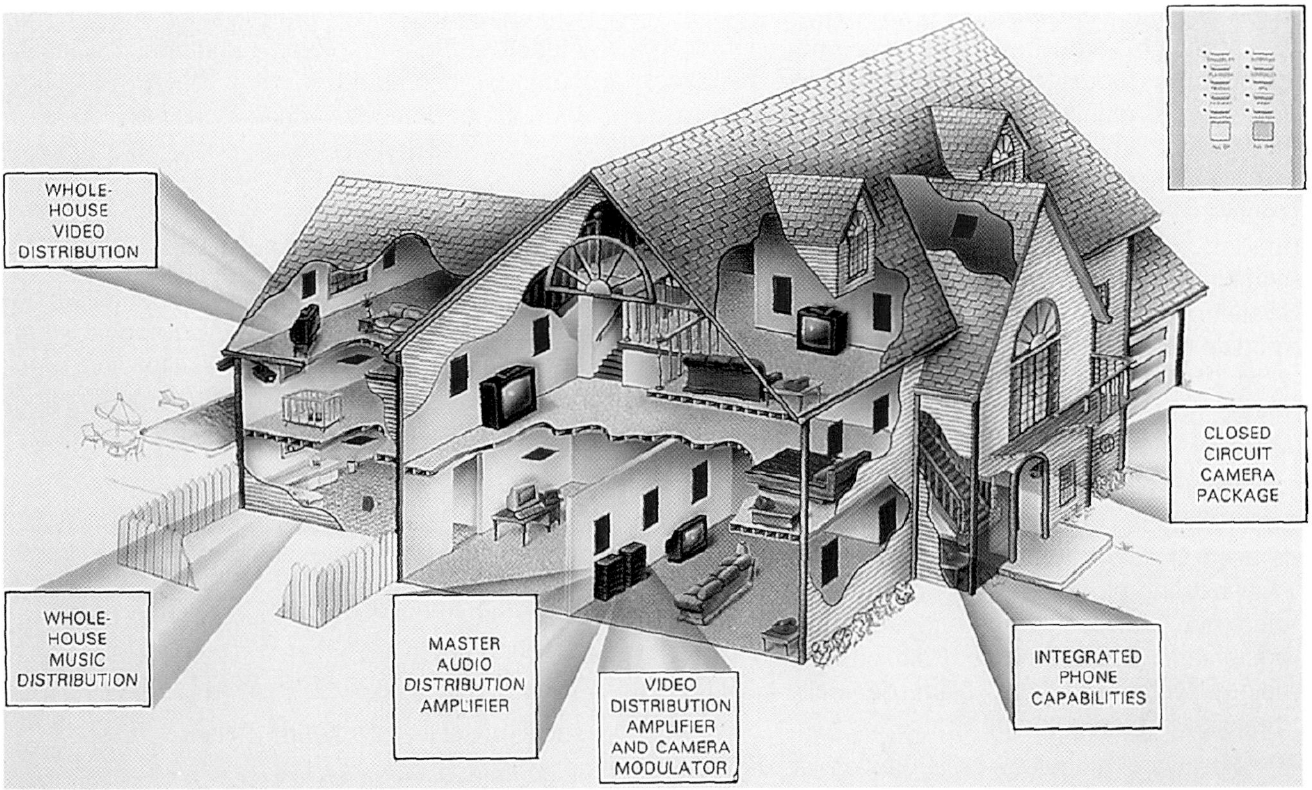

Square D Company

21-8 This home automation system networks the TV, video recorder, phone, and stereo so they can work together based on the homeowner's instructions.

wiring systems, and combination systems. These approaches generally focus on the hardware and, in some cases, the software. There are advocates for each type of system and a need for each. However, factors such as cost, convenience, complexity, and available features will likely drive the decision to choose a particular system.

Hard-Wired Systems

Hard-wired systems are dedicated (stand-alone) systems that are self-contained and part of the infrastructure of the building. They are commonly found in commercial or industrial applications. The primary reasons for their infrequent use in residential structures is their complexity, cost, and need for highly skilled professionals to design, install, and maintain the system.

Hard-wired systems are used in security and surveillance applications because of their high level of reliability. They are also used in heating, ventilation, and air-conditioning applications in large buildings where constant monitoring is necessary. Another common application is the sophisticated lighting control found in theaters, schools, and high-end homes, 21-9. Hard-wired systems are seldom

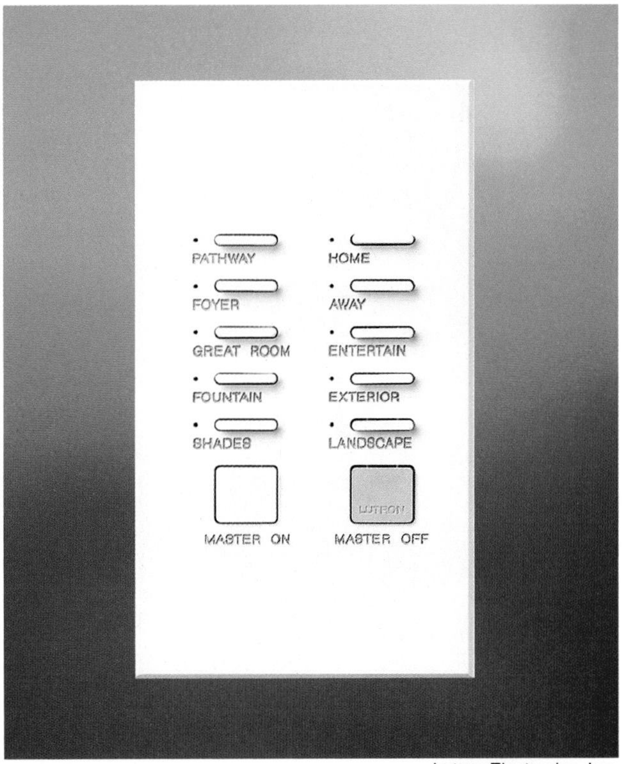

Lutron Electronics, Inc.

21-9 This programmable lighting controller can set 10 separate lighting scenes for multiple locations.

used for computer networks or video applications. Even though hard-wired systems are not used for computer networks, devices such as control panels for sound or lighting can be programmed using a connected computer.

Hard-wired systems, in some instances, can be controlled remotely through hand-held controllers or the Internet. In addition, progress is being made to combine hard-wired systems with structured wiring systems. For example, 21-10 shows a security module that works with a structured wiring enclosure, 21-11.

Power Line Technology

More than 20 years ago, a protocol called X10 was developed to automate the home. This protocol is used in **power line technology** to send signals over existing electrical wiring to control almost any electrical device—lamps, appliances, or other equipment. See 21-12. A basic power line technology system, or X10 system, generally includes the following three components:

- Hardware modules—switch on/off appliances, lamps, or other electrical equipment. Most anything plugged into a regular convenience outlet can be switched on and off with a module.
- Computer interface—send commands to the modules. This is often an interface with a personal computer via the serial port, the Internet, or home network connection.
- Software program—controls the interfaced hardware.

Power line technology is popular in the remodeling market because no new cabling is needed. X10 systems are inexpensive, but do not provide as many features as other systems. Also, the fact that existing wiring is used severely limits what can become part of the home security or automation system.

Structured Wiring Systems

Structured wiring systems provide for complete home security and home automation in one package. Functions may include the following:

- telephone network
- computer network
- satellite, cable, or antenna TV service
- telecommunication service
- broadband technology
- video distribution

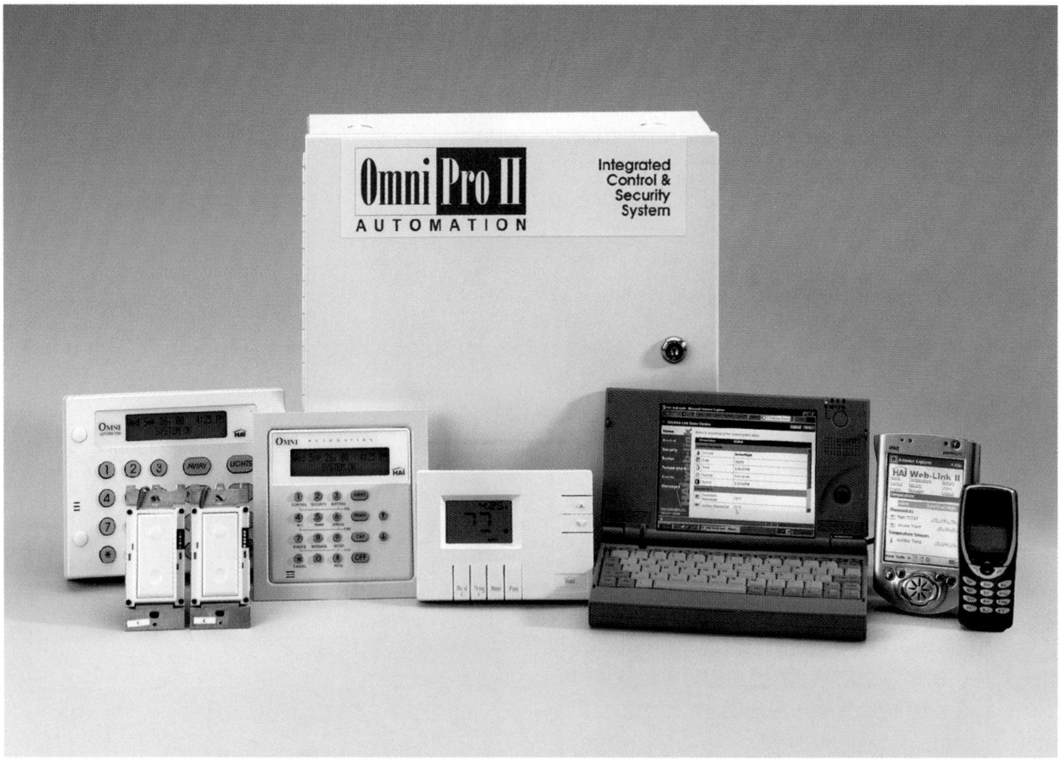

Home Automation, Inc.

21-10 This security and automation package accepts standard sensors for fire, lighting, heating/cooling systems, appliances, and intruders.

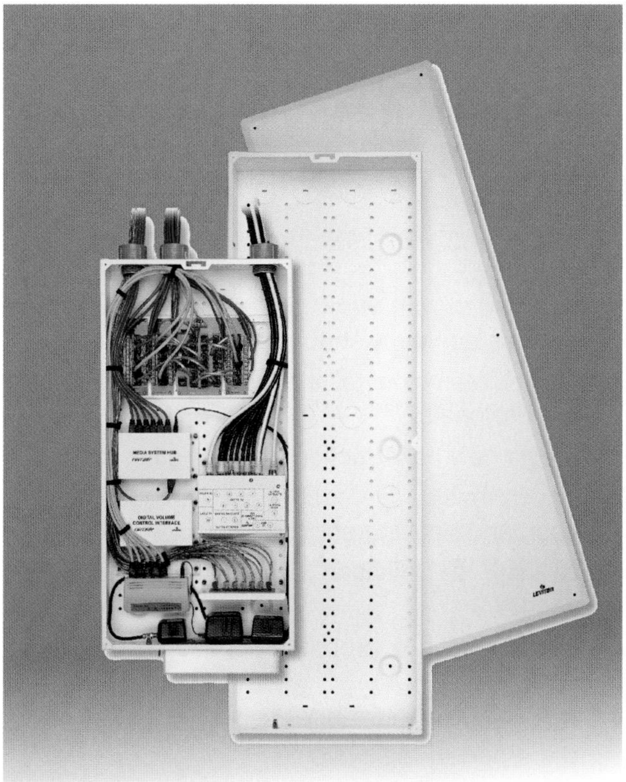

Leviton Manufacturing Co., Inc.

21-11 This is a typical wiring enclosure used in hard-wired systems.

Leviton Manufacturing Co., Inc.

21-12 This system package provides everything needed for both programmed and manual control of lighting and appliances using a home's existing wiring.

- in-home cameras
- links to a security system
- provision for future technology

All of these separate systems are joined in one network connection center within a wiring closet, 21-13.

The wiring in a structured wiring system generally consists of Category 5 cable from the wiring closet to all locations within the home for security, entertainment, phone, computer and Internet devices. Radio Grade 6 quad shield cable is also installed for cable TV, digital cable, digital satellite, cable modems, and in-home cameras. Manufacturers of speakers, motor controls, or other unique applications that are a part of the structured wiring system will specify the proper cable for their devices. As with other systems, a computer interface is possible with most systems for programming and control functions.

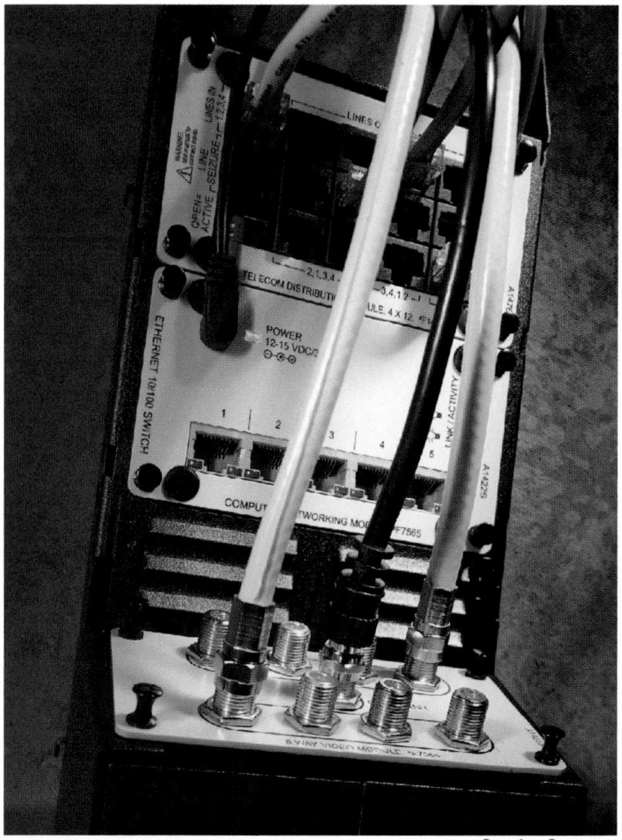

Greyfox Systems

21-13 This wiring enclosure is for a structured wiring system. Notice the patch cables used to connect the devices.

You have the option of running individual cables or bundled cables to each location. **Bundled cable** has several conductors inside one PVC jacket, 21-14. Installing individual cables typically saves several feet of cable compared to using bundled cable. Almost any combination of cables is available to meet the needs of each location in the home.

In structured wiring, all hardware—cable, plugs, jacks, and faceplates—must be compatible and have the same rating. Numerous products on the market can work together to build the structured wiring system, 21-15.

The structured wiring system seems to be the preferred system for new construction. However, it is very difficult to install such a system in an existing home. If remodeling is in progress and walls are stripped to the studs, structured wiring may be an option.

Combination Systems

Combination systems pick and choose from hard-wired systems, power line technology, and structured wiring systems. Therefore, the opportunity exists to design a very high-tech, customized system. A combination system is the best approach when cost is not a limiting factor and a customized installation meets the owner's special needs or desires. See 21-16.

What is now very complicated might evolve into simpler solutions in the future that use fewer types of cabling, wiring closets, plugs, jacks, and so forth. For example, consider using a single type of cable for everything, such as Category 5E, the enhanced version of Category 5 cable. Several companies are turning their attention to combination systems in anticipation of an expanding market.

Home Automation Questions

The following list of questions may be helpful in planning a home automation/security system. The answers may eliminate or lead you toward a certain system.

- What do you want to accomplish? Which devices do you wish to monitor or control?
- Do you plan to install the system yourself or hire professionals?
- Is this new construction or an existing home?
- Which basic approach best fits your needs, cost, and housing structure?
- Is there a packaged product that meets your needs?
- Do you have a proposed location for a wiring closet?
- Have you planned the location of devices that are a part of the system?
- Have you decided on the style of jacks, plugs, and faceplates? See 21-17.
- Will an intercom/music system be part of your system? See 21-18.
- Will your system provide for future developments and new technology?
- Do you have enough information to proceed?

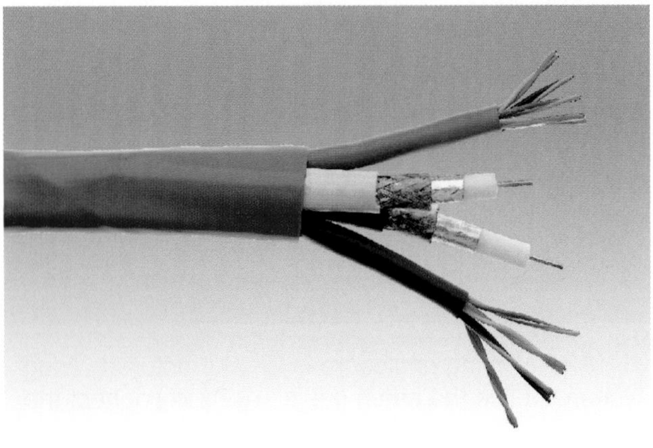

Belden Electronics Division

21-14 This is a structured wiring bundled cable that contains two Category 5E cables and two quad-shield coax.

OnQ Technologies, Inc.

21-15 A modular jack and faceplate system allows custom configured terminations.

A Home Automation, Inc.

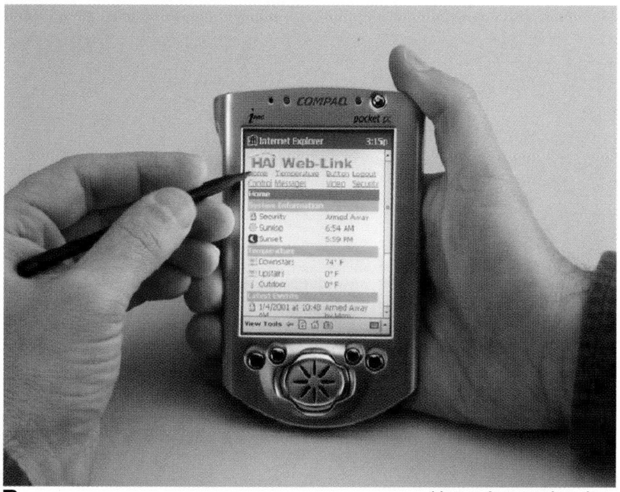

B Home Automation, Inc.

21-16 This custom combination system allows the homeowner to access and control the system over the Internet (A). A hand-held personal organizer enables a homeowner to monitor the system from a remote location via the Internet (B).

A

B Leviton Manufacturing Co., Inc.

21-17 A variety of wall plates are used with home automation systems.

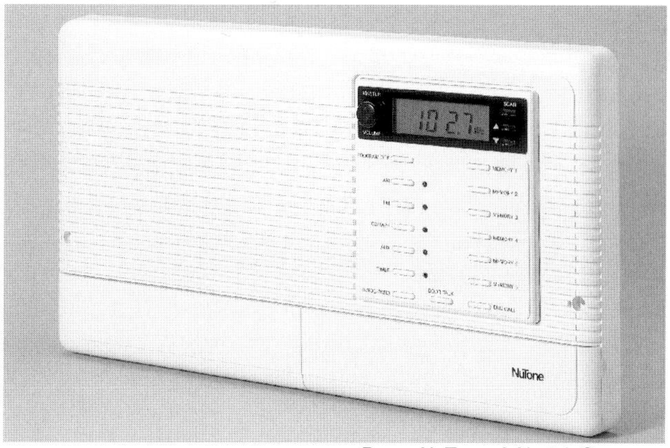

Broan-NuTone, A Nortek Company

21-18 This voice/music intercom master control station facilitates communication and monitoring at numerous locations.

Low-Voltage Switching

In using low-voltage switching, convenience outlets are wired in the conventional way with #12 or #14 conductors. Switches, on the other hand, are wired to relays using conductors similar to those used for wiring doorbells and chimes. These conductors carry only 24 volts provided by a transformer that supplies current for the relays. **Relays** are electrically operated switches. The switches do not require boxes.

Low-voltage switching, or remote control wiring as it is sometimes called, has possibilities for unique installations. Remote control systems (low-voltage switching) provide a simplified way of controlling lights in all parts of the home from one or more locations. For example, it is possible to operate fixtures located at various points in the house from the master bedroom. This is one of the advantages of low-voltage switching.

Chapter Summary

Many new technologies have emerged in the past few years that provide for security systems, home automation, and information and communication via voice and data lines. This new technology can be divided into five basic areas based on function—monitoring, switching (activating), programming, communication/recording, and alarm functions. Monitoring functions examine certain aspects of the house to determine their status. Devices that perform switching functions initiate an action based on an input. Programming functions control a sequence of events. Devices that perform communication/recording functions allow or record voice, video, or data communication. Alarm functions alert the homeowner or a security agency to potential dangers based on a signal from a monitoring device.

A new home should have a minimum of two standard telephone lines—one for voice and one for data. Structured wiring should be considered when planning a new home or major renovation. Structured wiring provides for an organized approach to the distribution of services to the rooms where they are needed. The wiring closet is the control hub in a structured wiring installation.

There are two basic approaches to providing home security—systems to protect property versus systems to protect occupants and property.

Home automation is a reality today and many companies and groups are involved. In this country, four protocols are leading the home network efforts; only one is based on an open standard. It is too early to know which approach will ultimately win the marketplace.

There are four basic approaches to home automation systems, with each one having advantages and disadvantages for any specific application. Factors such as cost, complexity, dependability, and convenience will drive consumer decisions involved in choosing a system.

Low-voltage switching or remote control wiring has possibilities for unique applications. For example, it can be used to operate fixtures from a central location such as the master bedroom.

Review Questions

1. What basic type of system function does each of the following reflect?
   A. signaling the presence of smoke
   B. turning various lights on and off at specific times
   C. turning the furnace on and off
   D. playing back voice messages
   E. checking the in-home humidity level
2. What three functions does a signal and communication system perform in the home?
3. For reliable performance, what maximum length of Category 5 cable should be used?
   A. 125 feet
   B. 285 feet
   C. 580 feet
   D. 825 feet
4. For property protection in which motion detectors are relied upon for cost effectiveness, what is the only part of the structure that is protected?
5. Why should a perimeter system include glass-break detection?
6. What is the key to a functional home automation system?
7. What are the four leading efforts to create a network standard?
8. Which home automation system meets the definition of an open standard?
9. What are the four basic types of home automation systems?
10. In low-voltage switching, how many volts of current are provided by a transformer?

Suggested Activities

1. Search the Internet to find information about data and video conductors. Prepare a report on your findings. Identify your sources.
2. Go to your local home-improvement center. Make a list of the hardware and software items offered there for a home automation system. Identify the functions that each performs.
3. Create new CADD symbols for use in construction drawings that signify the following: home automation, security wiring, video data, signaling circuits, and information and communication wiring. Label the drawings and present them to the class.
4. Select a floor plan that you like that does not include home automation features. Using CADD, design a home automation system. Include a security system as part of the home automation system. Place symbols for the home automation system on a separate layer.

Internet Resources

Archtek Telecom Corp., manufacturer of broadband access equipment
archtek.com

Consumer Electronics Association TechHome Division
techhome.org

Echelon Corporation, supplier of infrastructure hardware and software to the device networking market
echelon.com

ELAN Home Systems, supplier of whole-house entertainment, communication, and control systems.
elanhomesystems.com

ELK Products, Inc., supplier of home security and automation products
elkproducts.com

Leviton, a manufacturer of electrical and electronic products
leviton.com

Lightolier® Controls, a manufacturer of lighting controls
lolcontrols.com

M&S Systems, a manufacturer of music and communication systems
mssystems.com

Smarthome™, Inc., a supplier of home automation equipment
smarthome.com

X10 Home Solutions, a supplier of home automation products
x10.com

Note: Web addresses may have changed since publication. For some entries, reaching the correct Web site may require keying *www.* into the address.

Chapter 22
Energy and Water Conservation

Objectives

After studying this chapter, you will be able to

- evaluate the energy efficiency of a home according to its orientation, insulation, construction, and site.
- identify the efficiency of an appliance by using EnergyGuide and Energy Star labels and by checking for energy-saving features.
- list the advantages and disadvantages of using solar or wind energy for a home energy supply.
- list ways to use computers to decrease home energy consumption.
- list the residential water-saving measures required by law.
- explain how green building promotes conservation.

Key Terms

orientation
blanket insulation
insulation boards
loose-fill insulation
earth berm
EnergyGuide
Energy Star label
balance point
horizontal axis washer
green building

Homes can use as much as 20 percent of a nation's energy consumption. Rising energy costs and the growing concern over dwindling energy reserves have focused attention on conserving energy. Conservation may involve special architectural and site considerations for a house. It also involves the use of energy-saving appliances and alternative energy sources.

Architectural and Site Considerations

Many structural factors can decrease a home's energy use. Some must be added as the structure is built or remodeled. Others may be applied to an existing home. Architectural considerations include the home's orientation, its insulation, the placement and construction of windows and doors, roof and wall construction, and placement of heating and plumbing systems. Site considerations include landscaping techniques that can help to conserve energy.

Orientation

Orientation is the placement or alignment of an object. To improve the energy efficiency of a home, its orientation to the environment should work with sunlight and winds. Orientation refers to the placement of rooms within the structure as well as the placement of the structure on a site.

Orientation can be used to maximize or minimize the effect of the sun upon a structure. Generally, the west and south sides of a house are warmer than the north and east sides. The south side is exposed almost constantly to the sun while the north side is shaded and cooler.

In cool climates, the living areas of the home should be placed on the south side. See 22-1. The

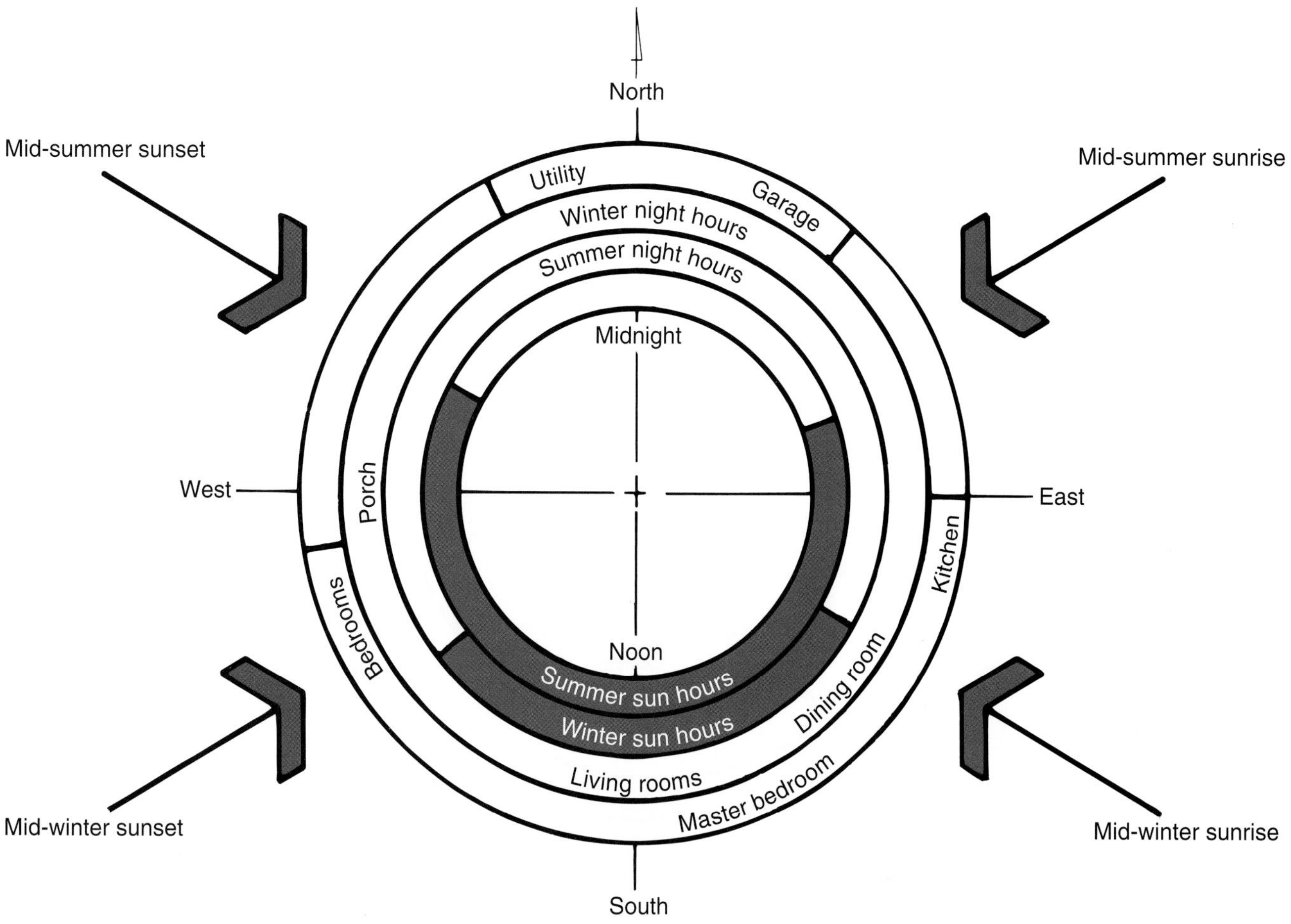

22-1 Living areas for homes in cold climates should have a southern exposure.

garage and utility room are often placed on the north side. In warmer climates, the living areas are placed on the north side of the home because there is less sunlight and heat, 22-2. Devices to shade the south side are also desirable.

The east side of a house receives full sun in the morning. This helps to warm a room after a cool evening. Rooms that are used in the morning, such as the kitchen and dining room, often face east. Rooms facing west are heated by the sun in the afternoon. Awnings, trees, or other methods of shading are needed to keep the west side of the house cool.

Wind also affects the amount of energy required to heat or cool a home. The direction of prevailing winds varies from one section of the country to another. Local weather bureaus can supply information about prevailing wind directions in specific areas.

Orientation to minimize the effect of wind is important in areas where heating is a major concern. Cold winds should be blocked to reduce heat loss. The garage and utility rooms may be placed as buffers to winter storms. Porches with windscreens may also act as buffers. A vestibule can be used to prevent outdoor air from entering the living areas of the home. It should be designed so the outside door must be closed before the inside door can be opened.

In pleasant weather, comfortable breezes should be allowed to blow through the living and sleeping areas of a home. If breezes are blocked, it is likely that cooling devices will be needed more often for these areas.

Insulation

The object of insulating a home is to surround the living space with a “thermal blanket” to keep the home warm in cold weather and cool in warm weather. Local utility companies provide recommendations for the amount of insulation needed in the

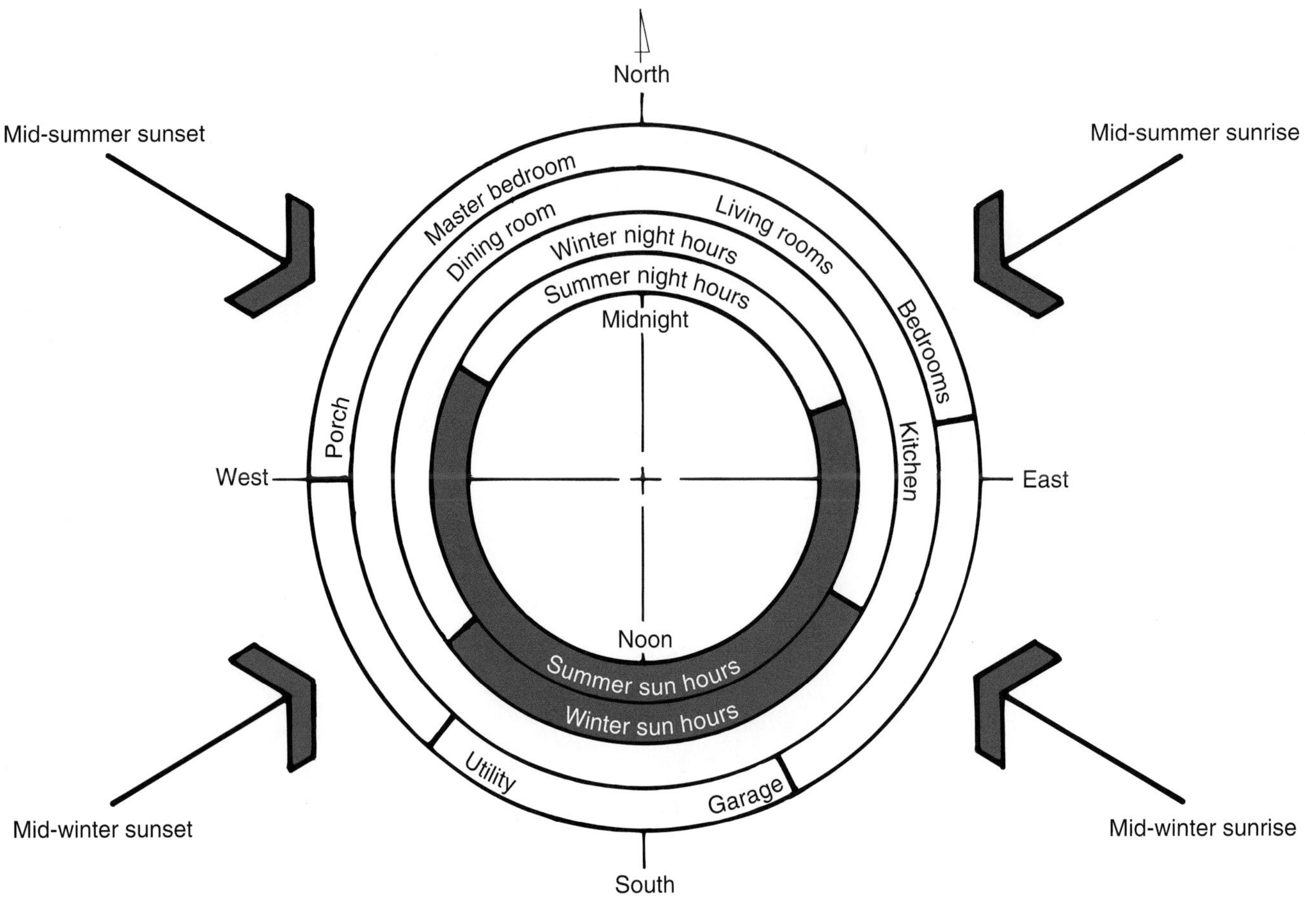

22-2 In warm climates, living areas should have a northern exposure to keep rooms cool.

area. Because different insulating materials of the same thickness have different levels of thermal resistance, R-values are used to indicate the amount of insulation needed.

Insulation may be made from different materials that vary in efficiency, quality, and safety level. It is available in three forms: blankets, boards, and loose fill. They are designed for areas of different shapes and reachability.

Blanket insulation is thick, flexible, and made from mineral wool. See 22-3. The composition of blanket insulation is most commonly rock wool or fiberglass. It can be cut or curved to fit the space. Blanket insulation is produced in rolls or batts cut into 4 or 8 ft. lengths. Different thicknesses and R-values are available to fit specific needs.

Blanket insulation may be purchased with or without an attached vapor barrier. It is commonly used in attics, floors, walls, and around pipes and ducts.

Insulation boards are rigid panels made of foamed plastics. They are available in ½ to 4 in. thicknesses, 2 to 4 ft. widths, and an 8 ft. length.

Manville Building Materials Corp.

22-3 Blanket insulation with a vapor barrier is usually installed between wall studs and ceiling joists.

Their R-value is higher than most forms of insulation of the same thickness, but they tend to be more expensive. Insulation boards are usually made of polyurethane or polystyrene. See 22-4. This type of insulation is approved for use between concrete basement walls and earth. However, some local fire codes do not allow board insulation above ground because it is considered a fire hazard. Local fire codes should be consulted before installing this type of insulation.

Because the boards are inflexible, they are generally added during construction. They may be used around foundations, between studs in side-walls, and between studs and siding as sheathing. Board insulation is available with or without a vapor barrier.

Loose-fill insulation has the form of small pieces of mineral fiber, cellulose fiber, or expanded materials such as perlite and vermiculite. Expanded materials are usually more expensive than other forms of loose fill. Loose-fill insulation is ideal for inaccessible spaces where blankets or boards cannot be installed. It may be used in attic floors, inside frame walls, in cores of concrete blocks, and as filler between batts and rolls, 22-5.

Insulating Power of Various Materials

This shows the thickness of various materials required to equal the insulation value of 1″ of rigid polyurethane insulation per sq. ft. of surface area.

Material	R-Value/Inch	Thickness
Expanded polyurethane (rigid insulation)	5.88	1.00″
Wood fiber insulation	4.00	1.47″
Expanded polystyrene (rigid insulation)	3.85	1.53″
Mineral wool from rock, slag, or glass	3.12	1.88″
Expanded perlite	2.78	2.12″
Cellular glass (foamed)	2.44	2.41″
Expanded vermiculite	2.18	2.70″
Hardwoods (maple, oak)	0.91	6.46″
Concrete blocks, rectangular, 2 core	0.13	45.23″
Brick (face)	0.11	53.45″
Stone (sandstone or limestone)	0.08	73.50″

22-4 To achieve the same R-value as rigid insulation per square foot of surface area, much thicker forms of other materials must be used.

Manville Building Materials Corp.

22-5 This attic has several inches of loose-fill insulation. Additional blanket insulation is being added to reduce heat loss.

All ceilings, exterior walls, and floors above cold spaces should be well insulated. In most homes the greatest amount of heat loss or gain is between the ceiling and roof. This area should be heavily insulated. Walls and floors also require adequate insulation. Some new homes have board insulation around basement walls. This insulates the basement area and helps to keep rooms above the basement insulated as well. Local R-value recommendations should be used as a guideline for insulating a new home or adding insulation to an older home.

To reduce heating or cooling losses, insulation should fit snugly in ceilings, floors, and walls. Attic insulation should not block air circulation vents in the eaves of the house. Air movement in the attic prevents moisture and condensation from accumulating in cold weather. In warm weather, moving air lessens heat buildup in the attic.

A vapor barrier should be placed between the interior and the insulation so the exposed side of the insulation is facing outward. If the vapor barrier faces outward, vapor will be trapped inside the insulation material. Unfaced insulation, insulation without a vapor barrier, should be used when placing new insulation over the old.

Windows and Doors

Windows should be placed in coordination with sunlight and breezes for the most comfort and energy efficiency. Homes in colder climates should have more window area on the south side of the home to receive heat from the sun in the winter. The window area on the north side of the home should be kept to a minimum to prevent heat loss. In warm areas fewer windows should be placed on the south side, and more windows may be placed on the north side of the house.

In cold climates, large areas of windows should be avoided on the side of the home that receives strong winds. For warm weather, windows should be located to take advantage of prevailing breezes. Windows placed away from exterior corners allow the best movement of air. Air should flow across the room at a medium height.

Using insulating windows or storm windows helps reduce unwanted heat loss or gain. Insulating glass windows should be considered when planning a new home or replacing windows in an existing home. Using insulating or storm windows can result in monetary savings up to 15 percent in poorly insulated homes. (For more information about the insulative value of windows, refer to Chapter 16, "Windows and Doors.")

Approximately 13 percent of air infiltration occurs around exterior window frames. Caulking and weather stripping prevent air leaks from lowering the efficiency of heating or cooling systems.

Poorly insulated exterior doors can be sites of heat loss or heat gain. Steel doors with an insulating plastic foam core are good insulators. Magnetic or interlocking vinyl weather stripping reduces air infiltration around doors. Storm doors, like storm windows, increase the insulative value of a door. Storm doors may have screen replacements to provide ventilation in warm weather.

Roofs and Walls

The construction of roofs and walls affects the energy efficiency of a home. Proper roof color can increase the efficiency of heating and cooling systems. Light colored roofs reflect heat, while dark colored roofs absorb heat. Homes in cold climates should have dark colored roofs to help keep the house warm. Homes in warm climates will stay cooler if they have a light colored roof.

A roof overhang of proper length helps to control the effect of sunlight on a home. The angle of sunlight is higher in the summer and lower in the winter, 22-6. A proper overhang shades south windows from higher, summer sun but allows lower, winter sun to enter the windows.

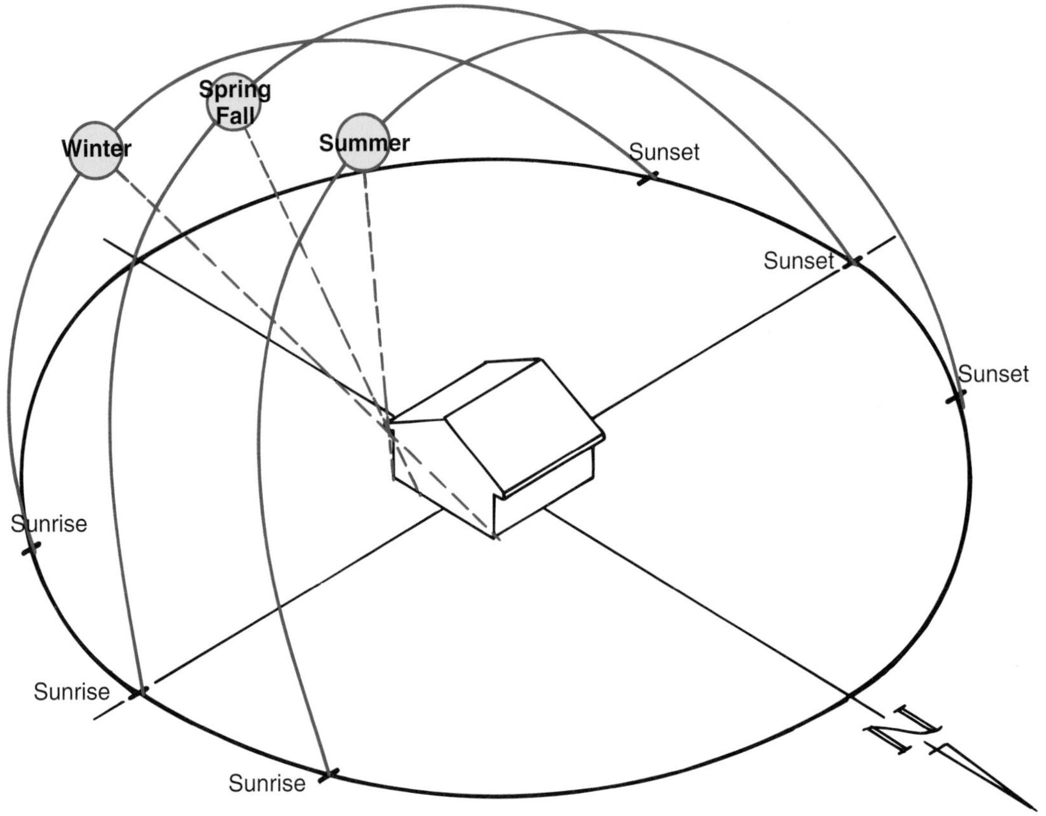

22-6 As the angle of the sun changes from season to season, the amount of sun entering the house also changes. A proper roof overhang takes advantage of the angle of the sun for heating and cooling.

The bottom edge of the roof should be constructed so the soffit (eave) is level with the tops of exterior walls, 22-7. This design allows the extension of ceiling insulation over the exterior wall without blocking ventilation space.

To allow space for more wall insulation, an exterior wall may be double framed, 22-8. The two frames are placed side by side and spaced with 7¼ in. of space between the back of the interior finish and the back of the sheathing. Wall studs are spaced 24 in. apart and alternated between the two frames. Alternating studs leaves an open space between the stud and wall surface on one side. In this way, insulation can cover the studs, reducing thermal loss through framing.

Any gaps in construction should be filled to prevent air infiltration. Exterior sheathing should extend from the top of the foundation to the top of the wall at the soffit, 22-9. Joints of plywood siding should be sealed. Insulating sill sealer should be used between the house sill and the top of the foundation wall.

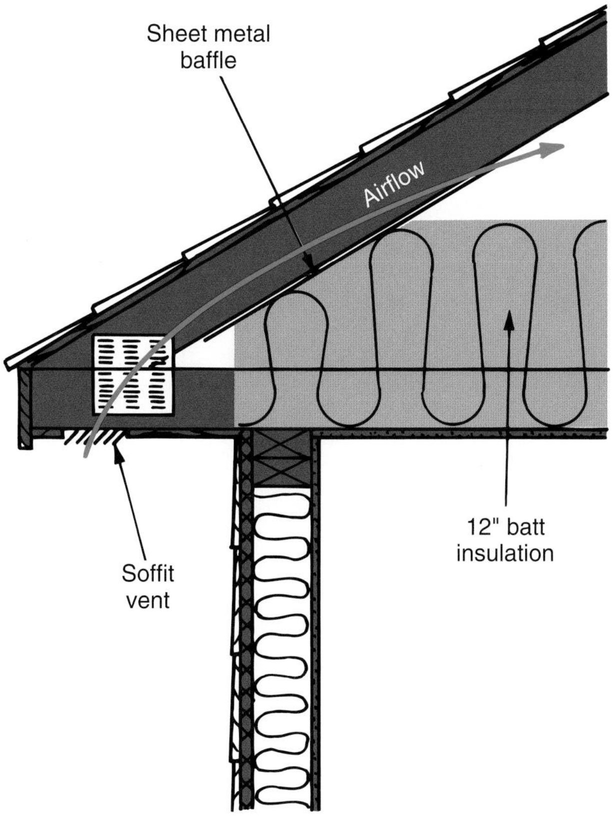

22-7 When the soffit is level with the ceiling, insulation can be extended to the outside of the exterior wall without interfering with attic ventilation.

Heating and Plumbing Systems

The heating system is one of the largest energy users in the home and, therefore, should be as efficient as possible. Warm-air ducts in unheated spaces should be insulated. Ducts should be located around the perimeter of the home, and

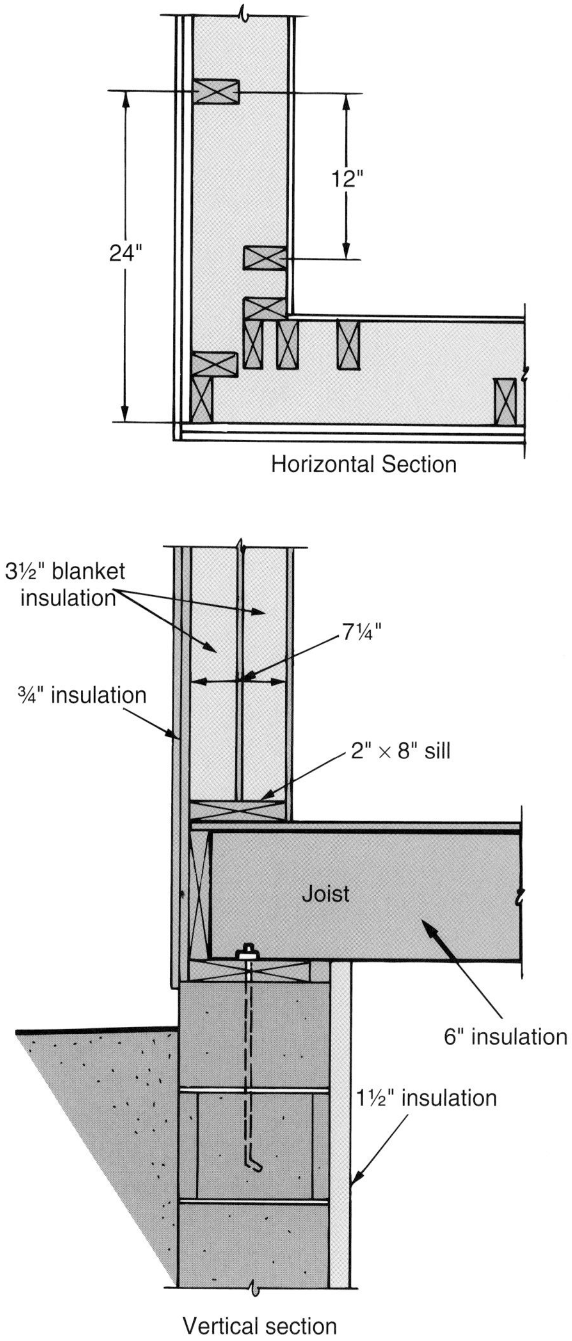

22-8 A double-framed wall allows more room for insulation.

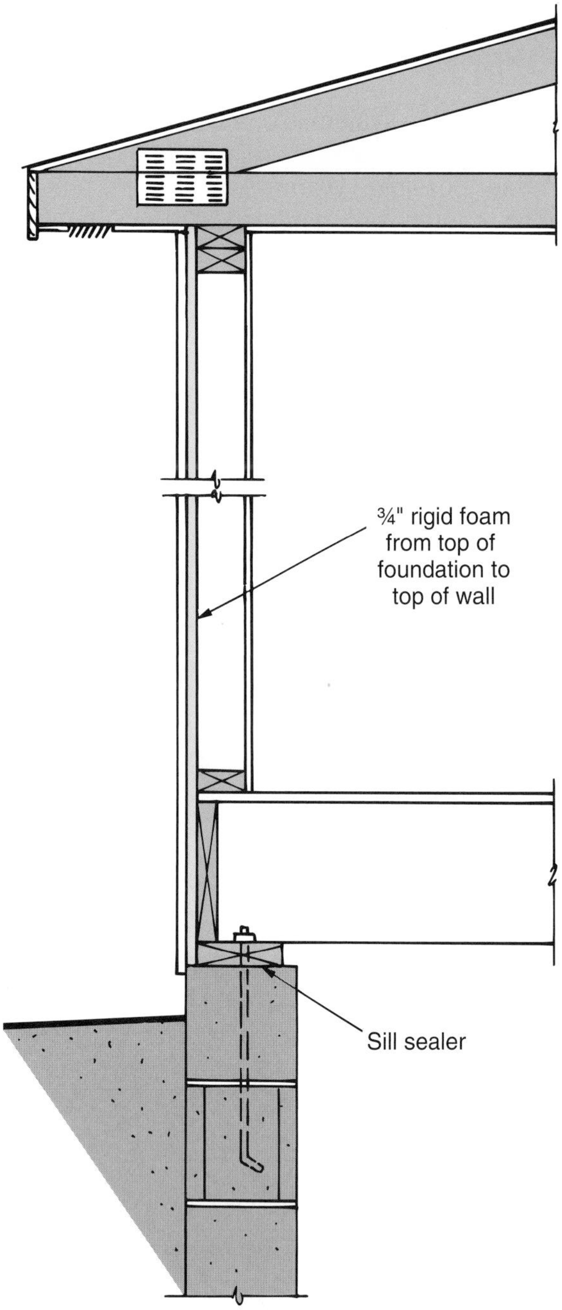

22-9 When wall sheathing covers the joist area, less air infiltration occurs between the floor and joists.

WCI Communities, Inc.

22-10 A ceiling fan uses little energy as it recirculates heated (or cooled) air back into the living space to increase comfort.

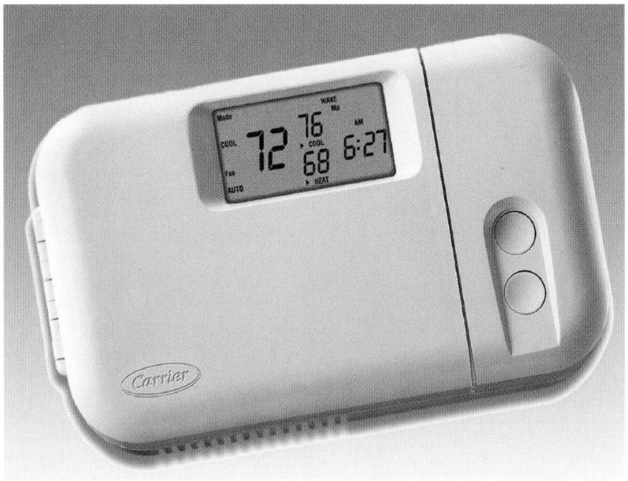

Copyright Carrier Corporation

22-11 A programmable thermostat can be used to maximize energy savings.

warm-air registers should be placed near large glass areas to replace heat loss. Placing ductwork directly under floor panels allows heat loss from ducts to radiate up into the home. Installing dampers in ducts enables the heating system to be shut off in rooms that do not need to be heated.

Ceiling fans help recirculate heated air during cold weather, 22-10. They also recirculate cool air in warm weather. A programmable thermostat, 22-11, saves energy by automatically lowering temperatures at night or when everyone is away and by raising temperatures during active times.

The cost of heating water accounts for 10 to 15 percent of the average household energy bill. Therefore, one way to conserve energy in the home is to increase the efficiency of the home plumbing system.

Plumbing mains should be centrally located to reduce the number and length of hot water lines. This will lower the chance of heat loss caused by running hot water long distances from the water heater. Hot water pipes that are very long or that run through unheated areas should be insulated. Water heaters in unheated areas should also be insulated. Flow restrictors to regulate the flow of hot water may be placed in faucets and showerheads.

Site Considerations

Outside the home, trees can be used to help conserve energy. Evergreens can be grown along the north wall of a home to block the winter winds. Deciduous trees planted along the south or west wall provide shade in the summer and allow sunlight to enter the house in the winter.

Tree species should be chosen to fit the purpose intended. For areas of general shade, wide-spreading trees such as walnuts, maples, and oaks should be used. Other trees can be used for small areas of local shade, such as persimmons, goldenrains, and red horsechestnuts. Sweet gums, poplars, and pine trees are used for vertical screening. They help to filter wind. Shrubs and vines can also be used to provide shade and block wind.

Earth berms can be used to protect the north side of a home from wind. An **earth berm** is a ledge or mound of earth that helps direct prevailing winds up and over the house. This protects the home from heat loss due to blasts of cold air on the structure's exterior.

Energy-Saving Appliances

Energy-saving models are built to perform all the same appliance functions, but with less energy. A highly energy-efficient appliance is generally more expensive, but the energy saved over the life of the appliance usually pays for the higher purchase price.

An **EnergyGuide** is a yellow label required on certain new major appliances to identify the energy used and how it compares to that used by similar models. See 22-12. Labels for most appliances display yearly operating cost estimates based on average national electric and gas rates. These appear on refrigerators, freezers, dishwashers, clothes washers, and water heaters. A lower operating cost means greater appliance efficiency.

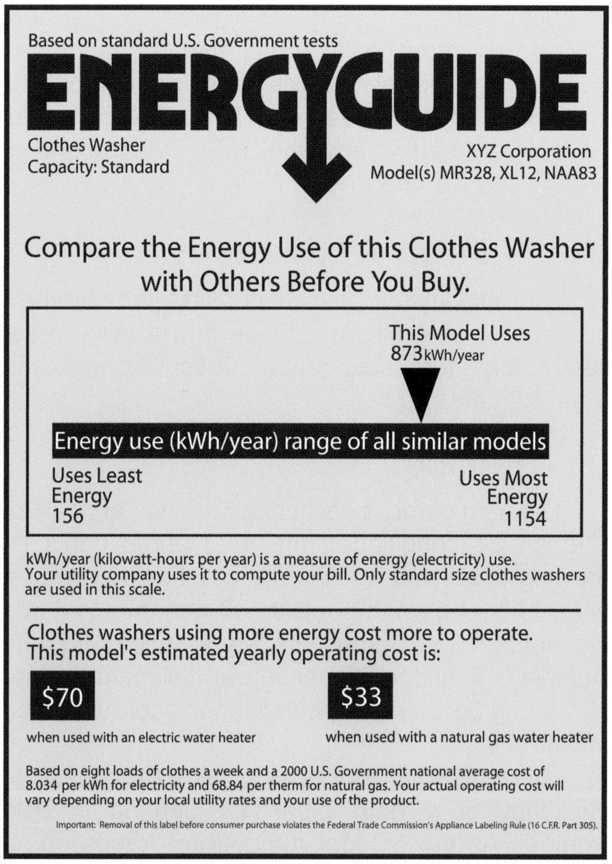

22-12 An EnergyGuide label shows how an appliance compares in energy consumption to comparable models on the market. For appliances that use water, operating cost depends on whether the water heater uses gas or electricity.

For furnaces, air conditioners, and heat pumps, the energy label displays energy-efficiency ratings. A higher rating means greater appliance efficiency.

Ranges, ovens, clothes dryers, humidifiers, dehumidifiers, and portable space heaters are not required to have EnergyGuides because there is little variation in energy use from one model to another. Instead, frequency of use determines their operating costs. When replacing older appliances or selecting new appliances for a home, energy-saving models should be considered. The U.S. Federal Trade Commission operates the EnergyGuide labeling program.

In addition to the EnergyGuide label, another label identifies energy-efficient appliances. The **Energy Star label** indicates that a product is at least 10 percent more energy efficient than competing products. See 22-13. Besides appliances, the label appears on products in more than 30 categories including lighting, electronics, windows, computers, and even new homes. The U.S. Environmental Protection Agency and the U.S. Department of Energy sponsor the Energy Star program.

Utility Area Appliances

The appliances most responsible for a home's gas and electric bills are those in the utility area: heat pumps, furnaces, central air conditioners, and water heaters.

Heat Pumps

The heat pump is efficient for heating or cooling. Like an air conditioner, the heat pump cools by drawing heat out of the home. For heating, it extracts heat from the outside air and pumps it into the home. Heat pumps are equal in cooling efficiency to an air conditioner. In warm climates, either a heat pump or an air conditioner could be used effectively.

The temperature of outdoor air determines the efficiency of a heat pump for heating in cold weather. As the outdoor temperature drops, more energy is required by the pump to heat the house. When the outdoor temperature drops low enough so the heat pump uses as much energy as it produces, a gas or electric heater is more efficient for indoor heating. This temperature, called the **balance point**, is usually around 30°F. After the outdoor temperature drops below that point, an auxiliary heating system should be used.

Furnaces

New heating systems are technologically improved and up to 25 percent more efficient than earlier models. Gas-fired furnaces use electronic igniters instead of continuously burning pilots. Electronic ignitions can be installed on older gas furnaces missing this feature. Automatic flue dampers may be added to furnaces to reduce heat loss when the furnace is off. See 22-14.

Central Air Conditioners

The more efficient central air conditioners have higher SEERs. These models produce the most cooling for the energy used. Many new models have energy-saving settings to provide partial cooling in unoccupied rooms.

Water Heaters

Having two or more inches of insulation around a water heater keeps water warm longer and lessens the need for frequent reheating. As a result, less energy is used. For areas of the home that do not need continuously heated water, small water heaters provide hot water on demand, 22-15. These heaters are usually installed under bathroom and kitchen sinks.

A newer method of heating water involves using the heat generated from an operating air conditioner or heat pump. A hot water bank, heat-recovery unit harnesses the waste heat, 22-16. The unit uses two concentric pipes to heat water. The inner pipe circulates water from the home's water heater, while the outer pipe circulates refrigerant gas that has been heated from the waste heat of an air conditioner or a heat pump. This method can heat up to 46 gallons of water per hour and can also be adapted for use in cold weather. The home's water heater is used as a backup system.

Service Area Appliances

After the utility area, the service area accounts for the next greatest energy use in the home. The

22-13 This label assures consumers that the product is one of the most energy efficient on the market.

Honeywell, Inc.

22-14 An automatic flue damper closes the flue opening when the furnace is not in operation. This reduces heating costs.

A.O. Smith Water Products Company

22-15 This under-sink unit produces instant hot water. Only a cold water line is connected to the unit, and an electric heating element provides the heat.

appliances in the service area include refrigerators, freezers, cooking equipment, dishwashers, laundry equipment, and room air conditioners.

Refrigerators and Freezers

The efficiency of refrigerators has improved dramatically in the last 20 years because of better insulation, more efficient cooling units, and improved airflow systems. Compressor units in new refrigerators are smaller and require less energy than those in older models, but they run for longer periods.

Freezers, too, have better insulation and more efficient cooling units. Chest freezers are generally the most energy-efficient models because they do not have the self-defrost feature. Manual-defrost freezers require less energy than self-defrosting models if frost is not allowed to accumulate more than ¼ in. A frost buildup causes the freezer to run longer and work harder.

Ranges and Ovens

Electric and gas ranges and ovens are already about as energy efficient as possible. More insulation

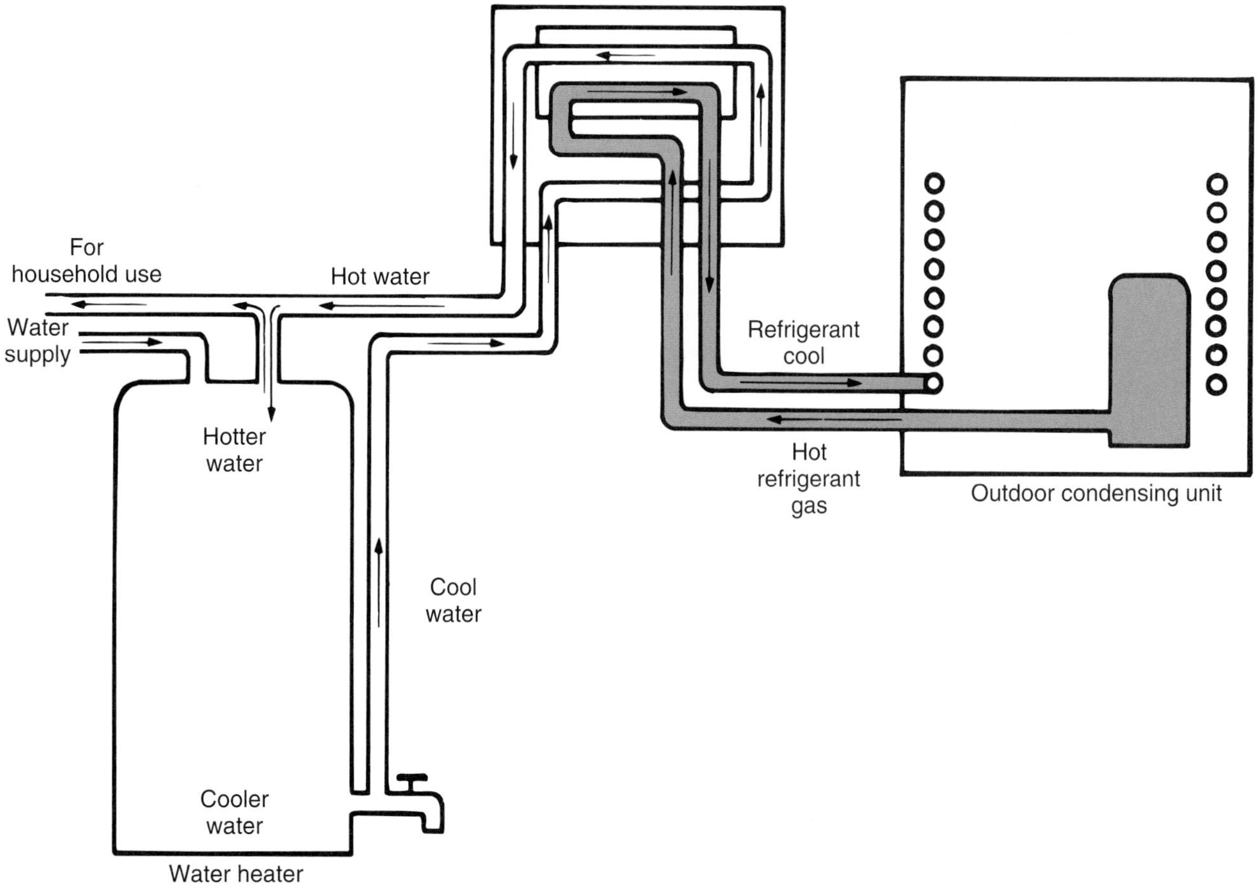

22-16 A hot water, bank-recovery unit uses waste heat from an air conditioner or heat pump to heat household water.

and snugger door gaskets result in less heat loss. Gas ranges eliminated continuous burning pilots and added electronic igniter systems to reduce gas usage. These appliances do not have EnergyGuide labels because personal use habits account for most variations in their energy consumption.

Convection ovens use circulation fans to increase the cooking efficiency of conventional ovens. They use less energy because cooking time is reduced and greater quantities of food can bake at the same time on several shelves.

Microwave ovens cook food without heating the oven or the kitchen, so they do not tax the air conditioning, 22-17. They are far more efficient than conventional ovens for heating liquids and cooking small quantities of food.

General Electric Company

22-17 Microwave ovens cook most foods using a fraction of the energy used by conventional methods.

Dishwashers

EnergyGuide labels give a general indication of a dishwasher's efficiency. Almost 85 percent of the dishwasher's energy use is for heated water from the home water heater. The air-drying option, short-wash cycles for lightly soiled loads, and other energy-saving features help decrease operating costs.

Some models also have a delay-start feature that programs the dishwasher to run during the night or at off-peak times when demand for electricity is low. In some areas, reduced rates apply during off-peak periods. Dishwashers are energy savers if consumers simply scrape table scraps from soiled dishes rather than prewashing them before loading them into the dishwasher.

Washers and Dryers

Less than 10 percent of the energy used by a washer is used for operating the washer's motor and other parts. The remaining 90 percent is used for heating the water. Consequently, the best way to save energy with laundry appliances is to avoid wasting water and use less. New models have water-level controls to allow users to match the water level to the load size.

The **horizontal-axis washer**, a redesign of the traditional washer, goes one step further to reduce water use. The washer tub opens in front, like a dryer, and agitates the load on its side, 22-18. Instead of submerging the laundry in wash water as upright washers do, the horizontal-axis model gently lifts and drops the clothes in water no higher than the door opening. This washer style uses considerably less water and energy than an upright washer, 22-19.

The most energy-saving dryers have moisture- or temperature-sensors that turn the appliance off automatically when clothes are dry. This prevents overdrying and wrinkling the clothes and wasting energy.

Room Air Conditioners

The more efficient models have higher EERs. Air conditioning units should be located where they will be shaded to help increase their efficiency.

Energy Alternatives

While traditional energy resources are being conserved, alternate sources are being developed for residential use. The sun and the wind can be used as private sources of energy. Many homeowners have adapted solar energy for heating and others have adapted wind energy to generate electricity.

Maytag Appliances

22-18 This horizontal-axis washer is the first on the U.S. market. It reduces water use by 40 percent, energy use by 65 percent, and utility bills by $100 per year.

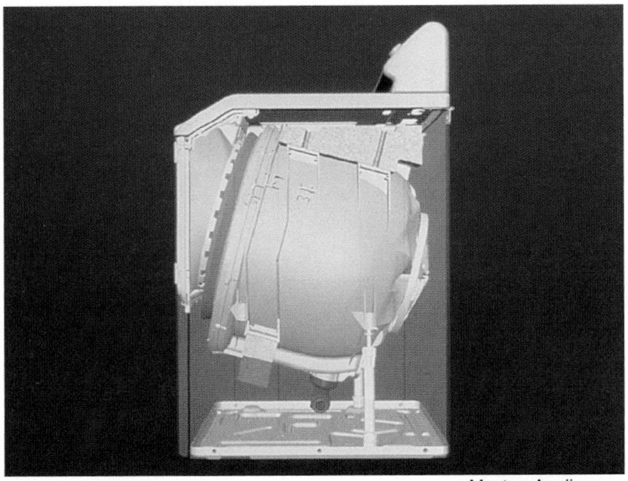

Maytag Appliances

22-19 This revolutionary washer design features a washtub tilted at a 15-degree angle for improved visibility and reach.

Solar Energy

Solar energy can provide all the heat needed in a home in moderately cold weather. During very cold winter months, solar heating can be used to reduce the amount of heat supplied by a conventional system. Many homeowners successfully use solar energy for active and passive heating. (For more information about active and passive solar heating, refer to Chapter 20, "Climate Control, Fireplaces, and Stoves.")

Solar heating systems use a resource that is inexhaustible and freely available. Using renewable energy sources helps conserve nonrenewable fuels. However, initial costs for installing solar heating systems are high. Some type of heat storage or auxiliary heating system must be available for use when there is no sunlight.

Experiments in producing electricity by harnessing solar energy are underway. The University of Delaware has designed a solar electrical system using a metal grid to activate current by sunlight. This system is still too inefficient and expensive for widespread use, but further research may produce systems that are practical for residential use.

Wind Energy

Wind can be harnessed to produce electricity by using a windmill. The Public Utilities Regulatory Policy Act of 1978 supports the private use of windmills as an option for homeowners. This act requires power companies to supply auxiliary power to homes with windmill generators and to buy any oversupply that is generated. Consequently, homeowners have an auxiliary power source during long periods when winds are calm and a way to preserve extra power produced during periods of strong winds.

Depending on the area's wind source, which involves both wind speed and consistency, a good windmill can easily supply the electrical needs of an average home. However, the windmill must be large enough to meet those needs. Cost is preventing the widespread use of windmills, although up-front costs can be recouped in 5 to 15 years. The average installed windmill costs $2,000 per-kilowatt for capacities up to 10 kilowatts and less for units with larger turbines. Prices will probably decrease with technological improvements and mass production.

Energy Management with Computers

Computer systems can be used in the home to keep energy costs as low as possible. Already, computer chips in appliances turn them off automatically when not in use. Computer-controlled thermostats are also available. These can be programmed to automatically lower and raise the home's temperature as needed.

Computer systems can be used for total energy management. Software programs are available to design the most energy-efficient homes. These programs help the homeowner determine the optimum site orientation, window placement, and other factors to increase energy efficiency.

Within the home, a total energy management system can automatically roll shades up and down to admit sun or block out cold. The computer automatically turns lights on and off as people enter and leave rooms. Heating and cooling systems are adjusted to outdoor weather conditions for the most efficient use of heating and cooling appliances. A total energy management system can activate water heaters when needed and also provide a burglar alarm system for the home.

It is possible for computer systems to cut energy use by as much as 30 to 50 percent. However, to obtain greater energy savings, the home must be designed with energy efficiency in mind. Most computer-monitored homes use solar energy for heating and have special design features to increase the insulation level of the walls. Computer home-management systems are still very expensive. They are not widely used, but their use is expected to increase in the future.

Water Conservation

Until 1975, when pressurized toilet tanks were introduced, almost all residential toilets used gravity and five to six gallons of water to rinse the bowl and wash the waste down the drain. During the 1980s, however, the limitations of our water supply became a concern. Demand for fresh water increased significantly, and in some areas, water conservation laws were passed.

Toilet manufacturers responded by developing low-flow models that used 3.5 gallons per flush (gpf). A severe water shortage in California in the late 1980s prompted the state legislature to make 1.6 gpf toilets mandatory in all new, residential construction. Other states followed California's lead.

Finally, the U.S. Congress passed a national standard, the National Energy Policy Act, which addressed energy use as well as water conservation. It stipulated that new toilets manufactured in the United States or imported for residential use after January 1, 1994, must not exceed 1.6 gpf. Although the law permits manufacturers to continue making 3.5 gpf toilets for commercial installations, California, New York, Massachusetts, Texas, and other states require 1.6 gpf designs for commercial jobs as well.

After January 1, 1994, the legal flow rate was slowed to 2.5 gallons per minute at a line pressure of 80 lbs. per sq. in. for showerheads and lavatory and kitchen faucets, 22-20. These limitations save millions of gallons of potable water each year and help preserve our fresh water supply.

Green Building

What is "green building"? What does it mean to be "green"? **Green building** is a way for builders to minimize the environmental impact of their construction projects. The term refers to both a design/building process and the resulting structure. Green buildings use key resources such as land, energy, water, wood, and other materials much more efficiently. The buildings create healthier environments for living and working and less waste to tax local disposal facilities.

For example, reusing sites and materials, building with engineered lumber, using high-efficiency boilers, and separating construction wastes are examples of green awareness. Generally, green building focuses on five categories that affect how buildings are designed, built and maintained: site and ecosystems, energy use, water use, resources and materials, and indoor environment.

Photo courtesy of Kohler Co.

22-20 Because too much water was being wasted in many kitchens and bathrooms, a Federal law was enacted to limit the water-flow rate of faucets and showerheads.

Marvin Windows and Doors

22-21 This home meets most requirements for green building. It uses engineered lumber, insulated glass windows, and large areas of south-facing glass to admit light. In addition, environmentally friendly materials were used in the construction and décor.

To qualify as green, a project must generally meet four goals: reduce energy and water use, use clean energy, provide a healthy indoor environment, and use environmentally friendly materials.

Reduce energy and water use. Green buildings are designed to save energy through use of a well-insulated building "shell" and efficient appliances that use less electricity and/or water. This also includes using natural lighting and thermally efficient windows, 22-21. Also, building smaller dwellings having less wasted space reduces energy use.

Use clean energy. Whenever possible, green buildings use solar energy to heat living space and water. This option may not be possible in some areas of the country. Coal, oil, and gas are considered nongreen sources.

Provide a healthy indoor environment. Products and finishes that emit harmful chemicals are avoided in green buildings. Good ventilation is used to maintain good air quality.

Use environmentally friendly materials. Green buildings use materials that are considered environmentally friendly. To meet this requirement, a material must satisfy at least one of the following conditions:

- is made from recycled material
- can easily be recycled at the end of its useful life
- is made from sustainable harvested wood
- has a long and useful life with minimal maintenance
- requires little energy to manufacture and deliver
- uses no dangerous materials in the manufacturing process

Green building is regarded as much more expensive than conventional construction, but studies prove otherwise when lifetime costs are considered. A green building costs about two percent more in up-front expenses. These expenses are generally due to increased architectural and engineering design time needed to integrate the resource-saving processes and materials into a project. Over the life of the building, however, the savings in maintenance and operating expenses are 10 times greater than the initial added expense.

Chapter Summary

Many structural factors can be used to decrease a home's energy use. Orientation can maximize or minimize the effect of sun and wind on the structure. Insulation keeps a home warm in winter and cool in summer. Windows and doors allow sunlight and breezes to enter for maximum comfort. Insulated or storm windows help reduce heat loss or gain and prevent unwanted air leaks when caulked and weather-stripped. Wall and roof construction affects the energy efficiency of a home, as does roof color and length of overhang.

The heating system, one of the largest users of energy in the home, should be as efficient as possible. Installing insulated ducts, dampers in ducts, and ceiling fans can improve efficiency. Insulating hot water pipes and water heaters will help reduce the average household's energy bill.

Selecting energy-saving appliances can reduce energy waste in the home. Check for EnergyGuide and Energy Star labels. System appliances such as heat pumps, furnaces, central air conditioners, water heaters, refrigerators, freezers, ranges, ovens, dishwashers, washers, dryers, and room air conditioners have improved their energy efficiency significantly in recent years. Compare the energy efficiency rating of products before purchasing.

Consider alternative energy sources such as solar and wind energy. Energy management with computers can also reduce energy use. These options will not work for everyone, but may be the right choice for specific installations. Water conservation has improved as a result of installing toilets, faucets, and showerheads with reduced flow rates.

Review Questions

1. How should a home in a northern state be oriented for maximum energy efficiency?
2. What kind of insulation has the best R-value?
3. Why would large windows be placed on the south side of a home?
4. What methods can be used to build roofs and walls that increase the energy efficiency of a home?
5. How can the energy efficiency of heating systems be increased?
6. How can the energy efficiency of plumbing systems be increased?
7. How can landscaping be used to increase the energy efficiency of a home?
8. How is an EnergyGuide used to determine the efficiency of an appliance?
9. What are the advantages and disadvantages of using solar energy for heat?
10. What are the advantages and disadvantages of using wind power for generating electricity?
11. How can computers be used to increase the energy efficiency of a home?
12. What is the flow-rate limit for toilets manufactured today?
13. What is the flow-rate limit for new showerheads and kitchen and lavatory faucets?
14. Name the four criteria that a project must meet to qualify as "green."

Suggested Activities

1. Summarize the structural factors of a house that can decrease energy use. Describe the role of each.
2. Prepare a list of actions to take to reduce the energy of the heating and plumbing system of a residence.
3. List the advantages and disadvantages of using solar or wind energy for a home energy supply.
4. List several ways that computers can be used to decrease home energy consumption.
5. Prepare a list of the residential water-saving measures recognized by law.

Internet Resources

Air Conditioning and Refrigeration Institute
ari.org

American Solar Energy Society
ases.org

Earthship Biotecture, a source of information and building services for thermal-mass housing
earthship.org

EnergyGuide Program
ftc.gov/bcp/conline/edcams/appliances/eg.htm

Energy Star Program
energystar.gov

Heliodyne, Inc., a manufacturer of solar heating products
heliodyne.com

Renewable Energy Policy Project
crest.org

The Reinforced Earth Company, a design/supply retaining-wall firm
recousa.com

U.S. Department of Energy, National Renewable Energy Laboratory
nrel.gov

U.S. Department of Energy, Office of Energy Efficiency and Renewable Energy
eren.doe.gov

U.S. Green Building Council, a nonprofit coalition of building industry members
usgbc.org

Note: Web addresses may have changed since publication. For some entries, reaching the correct Web site may require keying *www.* into the address.

Chapter 23
Designing for Health and Safety

Objectives

After studying this chapter you will be able to:

- identify fire hazards around the home and explain preventive measures.
- explain the hazards associated with carbon monoxide and ways to prevent them.
- explain the hazards associated with radon in residential housing and identify preventive measures.
- point out problems in residential structures associated with excess moisture.
- describe the dangers associated with weather- and nature-related events such as earthquakes, floods, tornadoes, and hurricanes.
- list steps that can be taken to lessen the damage and destruction of weather- and nature-related events.

Key Terms

smoke detector	seismic
combustion	flash flood
carbon monoxide (CO)	floodplain
radon	tornado
water vapor	tornado watch
condensation	tornado warning
ventilation	safe room
molds	hurricane
Stachybotrys atra	storm surge
earthquake zone	hurricane codes

Contrary to what you may think, the home can be a very unsafe place. Experts say more injuries occur in the home than anywhere else. Therefore, every effort should be made to keep dwellings as safe as possible. While model building codes focus on creating a safe structure, this chapter highlights safety considerations within the homeowner's control. They include: smoke and fire detection, carbon monoxide (CO) detection, radon detection and reduction, moisture and mold problems, weather- and nature-related safety, and general home safety.

Smoke and Fire Detection

Structural fires are a significant danger to every home. According to recent national fire statistics, a fire department responds to a fire every 15 seconds, and a person is killed every two hours. More than $900,000 in property is lost to fire every hour. Eighty percent of all fire deaths occur in the home. Home fires are one of the most serious hazards, usually affecting small children and the elderly. The leading causes of deadly fires include the following:

- falling asleep while smoking
- improperly using flammable materials to start a fire
- operating unsafe electrical or heating equipment
- placing flammable materials too close to a potential source of ignition

Fire Prevention

Several commonsense rules can help prevent a fire in your home. Here are some of the most obvious.

- Keep an operable fire extinguisher in an obvious location. It will not prevent a fire, but may allow you to extinguish a small fire before it gets out of control.
- Do not overload electrical circuits, 23-1. Overloaded circuits generate excess heat that may ignite nearby materials.
- Have your heating system inspected yearly. A dirty or improperly operating heating system can ignite a fire.
- Keep matches and lighters away from children.
- Store flammable liquids in approved containers.
- Dispose the trash regularly. Accumulated trash can fuel a fire.
- Select upholstered furniture that is resistant to smoldering cigarettes.
- Use seasoned wood in wood-burning stoves and fireplaces. Green wood creates creosote buildup, which can lead to a chimney fire.
- Have fireplaces and wood-burning stoves cleaned on a regular basis to remove any creosote buildup.

Smoke Detectors

A **smoke detector** is a small appliance that signals the presence of smoke. Detectors for the hearing impaired set off an ultrabright strobe light, while common models make a loud warning signal, 23-2. There are two basic types of smoke detectors—ionization and photoelectric. The ionization type responds more rapidly to fires with visible flames, but the photoelectric detector senses a smoldering or slow-burning fire quicker. Both types provide early fire warning.

Make sure your home has an adequate number of detection devices to provide real protection. Less than one-third of all homes have sufficient smoke alarms. For best coverage, according to the U.S. Consumer Product Safety Commission, you need at least one smoke detector on each floor of the house, including the basement and finished attic.

23-1 The electrical outlet is overloaded, which is a definite fire hazard.

23-2 This a typical residential smoke alarm. This model is battery powered.

On the first floor, the living room or family room is often a good central location for a smoke detector. Another central spot is the top of the stairwell between the first and second floors. In this location, a detector will detect the first signs of fire on either floor and sound an early warning. If bedrooms are far apart—on different floors or separated by a long hallway—consider installing a detector outside each bedroom. For detailed instructions on where to install detectors, be sure to refer to the model's use-and-care guide.

Some smoke alarms are powered by batteries or household current with a battery backup. A chirping detector alerts you to replace the battery. New lithium batteries last about 10 years, making once-a-year battery replacement a thing of the past. However, you must still check each device at least once a year to make sure it is working properly. Your life may depend on it.

Fire Safety Code Requirements

The model building codes specify minimum requirements for fire safety. The following list identifies the requirements often cited by codes that can be readily enforced by law.

- Every occupied room in a residence must have at least two exits, one of which must be a doorway. Also, bedrooms that are below grade (in basements) must be directly accessible to the outside.
- The only access to an occupied room may not be folding stairs, a ladder, or trapdoor.
- Every bedroom must have a window that can be easily opened by hand from the inside, unless the room has two interior exits or a direct exterior exit. The window must have a clear 5 sq. ft. or larger opening with no less than 22 in. in any direction. The bottom of the window must be no higher than 48 in. from the floor.
- Paths from bedrooms to exits must be at least 3 ft. wide.
- Exit paths from any room must not pass through a room controlled by another family or through a space subject to locking.
- All exit doors must be at least 24 in. wide.
- All stairs must be at least 36 in. wide with risers no higher than 8 in. and treads wider than 9 in.
- Quick-opening devices must be on all storm windows, screens, and burglar guards.
- Inside quick-release catches must be used as door-locking devices for easy exit.
- Bathroom door locks must allow opening from the outside without a special key. See 23-3.
- Children must be able to easily open closet doors from the inside.
- Smoke detectors should be installed outside each sleeping area and on every level of the house used for occupancy.
- Exit paths must not be blocked in the event of a malfunctioning combustion heater or stove.

Combustion refers to the process of burning. Combustion appliances and equipment include those that burn natural or propane gas, oil, wood, or coal.

More information on fire safety requirement is available in the National Fire Codes. Also, check your local code for additional requirements. Many areas, such as large metropolitan areas, may have codes that exceed these requirements.

Fire Extinguishers

Every residence should have a functioning fire extinguisher located where it can be easily found, 23-4. Fire extinguishers are classified according to the type of burning material they handle effectively. The Class A extinguisher handles fires involving paper, wood, fabric, and other ordinary combustible materials. Class B extinguishers control fires from burning liquids, such as a grease fire. Class C extinguishers are used on electrical fires. Many fire extinguishers are labeled ABC and can handle all types of fires.

23-3 This bathroom door lock set can be opened from the outside with any slender probe or "key."

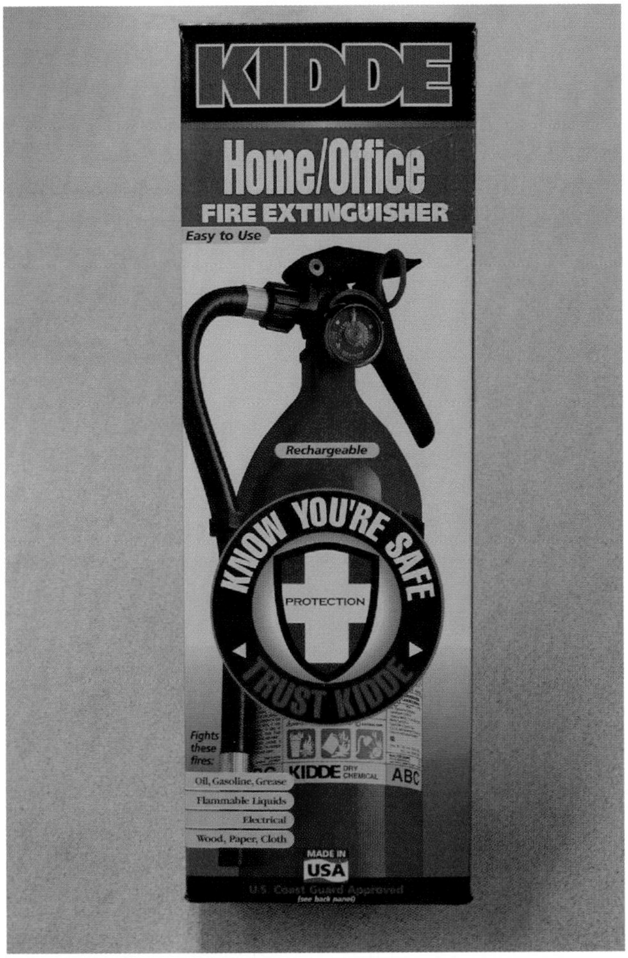

23-4 A typical dry-chemical ABC fire extinguisher may be used on fires involving oil, gasoline, grease, flammable liquids, wood, paper, cloth, and electricity.

Carbon Monoxide Detection

Carbon monoxide (CO) is a colorless, odorless, potentially deadly gas that forms when carbon in fuel is not burned completely. Dangerous CO concentrations may be produced by wood stoves, gas or oil furnaces, fireplaces, gas ranges, clothes dryers, water heaters, space heaters, charcoal grills, or even cars in attached garages.

The risk posed by properly installed and functioning appliances is minimal. However, sloppy installation, damaged equipment, or improper construction practices can allow CO to enter the living space in harmful concentrations. Today's more energy-efficient, airtight home designs can compound the problem by trapping CO-polluted air.

Carbon Monoxide Poisoning

Carbon monoxide is absorbed into the body through the lungs and binds to the hemoglobin in red blood cells. This reduces the blood's ability to transport oxygen. Eventually, CO displaces enough oxygen to result in suffocation. The result of this suffocation is brain damage or death. One-third of all survivors of CO poisoning have lasting memory disorders or personality changes. In addition, heart attacks have been associated with high CO levels.

Air-borne CO concentrations are measured in parts per million (ppm). The percentage of CO in the blood is called COHb. It is a function of the CO concentration in the air and the length of time a person is exposed to the CO. Even though CO concentrations of 15,000 ppm can kill a person in minutes, longer exposures to small concentrations are also dangerous. A longer exposure allows CO to accumulate in the bloodstream, resulting in a lethal COHb.

Symptoms of low-level CO poisoning are similar to those of the flu. Symptoms include headaches, drowsiness, fatigue, nausea, and vomiting. These symptoms can result from exposure to concentrations of 350 ppm for an hour. After four hours, the exposure can cause brain damage or death.

Since the symptoms of CO poisoning are easily mistaken for the flu, some health experts believe as many as one-third of all cases go undetected. According to the Mayo Clinic, accidental exposure to CO in the home contributes to approximately 1,500 deaths annually. In addition, an estimated 10,000 people in this country seek medical attention or lose at least one day of normal activities because of CO inhalation.

Carbon Monoxide Detectors

When combustion appliances are used in the home, a CO detector is inexpensive insurance against unnecessary health risks, 23-5. A properly working detector can provide an early warning to occupants before gas concentrations reach a dangerous level. If a home has even one combustion appliance, it should have a CO detector.

An appropriate CO detector should have a label indicating that it meets or exceeds Underwriters Laboratories Standard 2034. To meet this standard, a detector must sound the alarm when CO concentrations register 100 ppm for 90 minutes, 200 ppm for 35 minutes, and 400 ppm for 15 minutes. Detectors are available that will detect CO concentrations as low as 5 ppm.

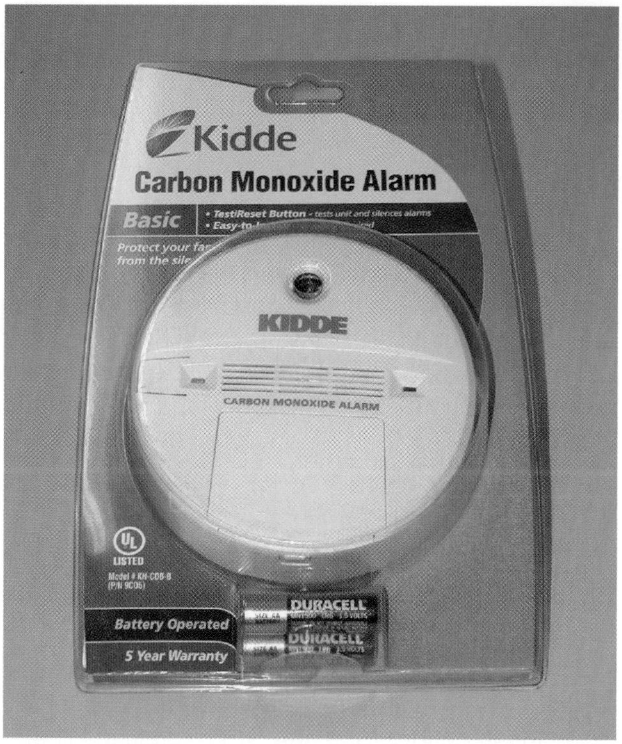

23-5 This residential carbon monoxide detector is battery operated.

Like smoke alarms, CO detectors should be mounted on the hallway ceiling outside the bedrooms. For additional safety, a CO detector should be placed in the furnace room and near any combustion equipment. Models currently on the market are powered either by 115-volt household current or batteries. See 23-6 for possible sources of CO gas and the recommended location of CO detectors.

Radon Detection

Radon is an invisible, odorless, radioactive gas. It comes from the natural decay of uranium found in soil, rock, and water. Radon rises from the ground into the home. It is found across the country and in any type of building. However, homes with radon are likely to cause the greatest exposure since that is where people spend most of their time. Radon can be dangerous in high concentrations.

The Environmental Protection Agency (EPA) estimates that one of every 15 U.S. homes has elevated radon levels. According to the surgeon general, radon is the second leading cause of lung

Potential Carbon Monoxide Sources in the Home

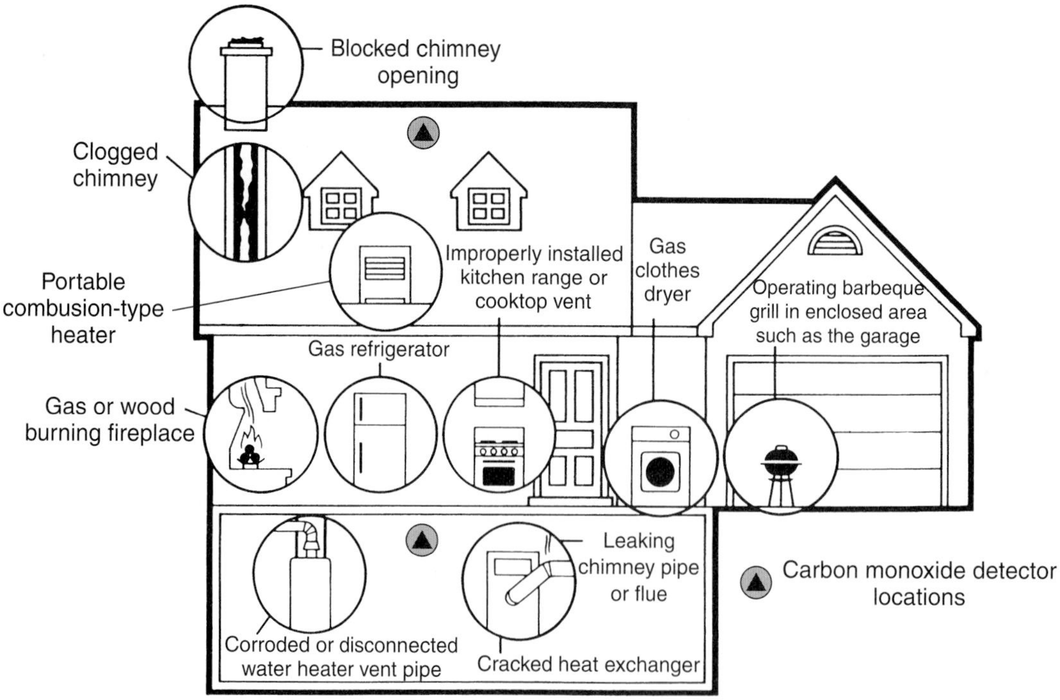

Provided by First Alert®

23-6 This drawing identifies potential carbon monoxide sources in the home and ideal locations for carbon monoxide detectors.

cancer in the country. In 1988 Congress passed the *Indoor Radon Abatement Act,* setting EPA's goal for reducing indoor radon levels to those of outdoor air—0.2 to 0.5 picocuries per liter of air (pCi/L). Radon level is sometimes expressed in working levels (WL).

Radon in the Home

Any home, whether old or new, can be subject to high levels of radon. Radon enters the home through cracks in solid floors, gaps in suspended floors, construction joints, wall cracks or cavities, gaps around service pipes, and the water supply. Typically, radon levels from water are not as great as from soil. The rate at which radon enters a home depends on the amount of radon in the soil, number of escape routes from the soil into the home, and ventilation in the home.

Fresh air dilutes radon. When homes are closed for winter heating or summer air conditioning, the radon levels start to build. Unoccupied homes trap and accumulate higher levels than homes that are occupied. Natural air movement tends to draw a greater concentration of the soil gas inside the house.

Radon Testing

The EPA recommends that radon levels be checked in any structure having one or two floors. The test is very simple and requires only a few minutes to administer. There are several kinds of testing devices available, 23-7. The two general types of testing devices are short-term and long-term. When selecting a test kit, look for the statement *Meets EPA Requirements* on the package.

Short-term testing requires 2 to 90 days, depending on the device. Passive devices include charcoal canisters, alpha track detectors, electret ion chambers, continuous monitors, and charcoal liquid scintillation devices. An advantage of using a short-term device is the quickness of getting test results. A disadvantage of this type of testing device is learning the current radon level but not the average level year-round. Radon levels vary from day to day and season to season.

Long-term testing devices take more than 90 days. Passive devices include alpha track and electret detectors. Active devices require power to function and include continuous radon monitors and continuous working level monitors. Active devices continuously measure and record the amount of radon or its decay products in the air of the home. The advantage of using a long-term device is learning the year-round average of radon levels in the home. The disadvantage is the longer time it takes to obtain the test results.

PRO-LAB, Inc.

23-7 This radon gas test kit provides two calibrated short-term radon gas detectors. This allows two tests to run at the same time and in the same location to get the most accurate results.

Radon testing should occur when the house is occupied. Doors and windows should be kept closed as much as possible. The detector should be placed in the lowest level, such as the basement or first floor. Keep the detector 20 in. above the floor and away from drafts, high heat, high humidity, and exterior walls.

At the completion of the test, the testing device is sent to a laboratory for analysis. If the reading on a short-term test is 4 pCi/L (0.02 WL) or higher, a second test is recommended. If the second test or a long-term test gives that or a higher result, the EPA recommends having the home fixed. Of course, high levels indicate a greater urgency. Readings below 4 pCi/L may provide some risk and future testing is suggested. The EPA recommends testing for radon every few years to determine if radon levels are increasing.

Radon Mitigation

Reducing the radon level indoors is called radon mitigation, and several methods are available. The radon level, costs of installation and system operation, house size, and foundation types are all factors that affect the method to use.

If a contractor will do the work, use one that is state certified or has completed EPA's Radon Contractor Proficiency Program. If you plan to do the repairs yourself, help is available from your state or the EPA. Basements and slab-on-grade construction require the following three-step process:

1. Soil-gas entry should be minimized by sealing joints, cracks, and other openings in slabs, below-grade walls, and floors, including openings for the sump pump. In addition, gas-retarding barriers—polyethylene membranes under floors and parging on outside walls—should be installed.
2. Install an active, fan-driven radon-removal vent-pipe system, 23-8. A passive system may also be installed that can be activated later by adding a fan, usually in the attic.
3. Reduce the "stack" or "chimney" effect in basements, which can draw soil gas into the home. This can be done by closing air passages between floors and providing fresh air from outside for combustion devices and exhaust fans.

Crawl spaces require the diversion of radon before it reaches the living space. The crawl space should be adequately vented to outside air. To prevent radon gas from seeping into the structure, the soil should be covered with a polyethylene membrane or concrete and the tops of block foundation walls should be sealed. Seal openings in floors and ductwork with caulks, foams, and tapes.

Moisture and Mold Problems

The occurrence of moisture and mold problems in residential structures has increased significantly in recent years. One reason is new buildings are constructed to have less air infiltration and heat loss/gain. In fact, EPA studies show that many new

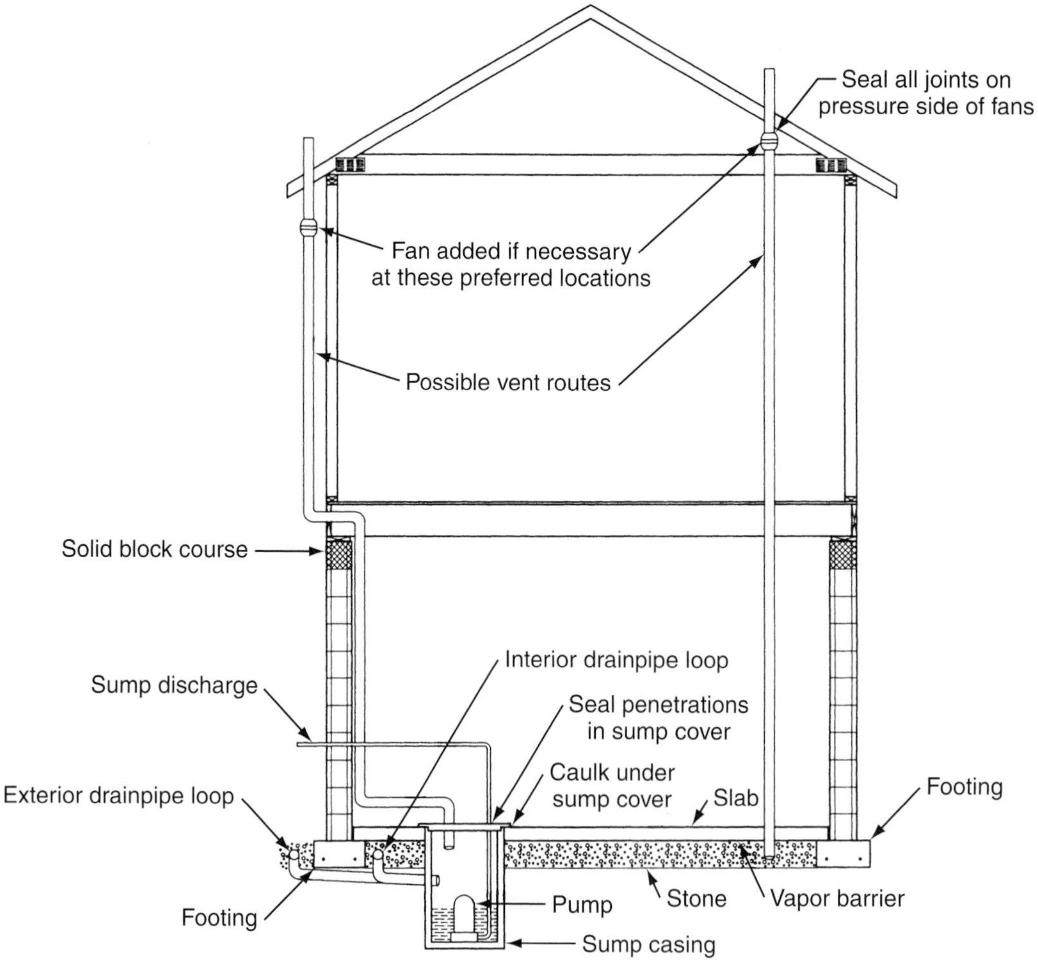

23-8 This diagram shows an active, fan-driven radon-removal, vent-pipe system.

homes have poorer air quality compared to outdoor levels. This condition has resulted in the term *sick house syndrome.*

In many instances, the root problem is excessive moisture within the structure. This is frequently due to unwanted moisture entering the building from one or more locations. When this moisture remains over time, the growth of unhealthy mold sets in, 23-9. Gradual deterioration of the building materials accompanies mold growth. Once this cycle begins, the space inside the dwelling may rapidly reach a point where it is not healthy for occupants.

Migration of Water Vapor

All air contains some invisible moisture called **water vapor**. *Relative humidity* is a measure of water vapor in the air. Warm air can hold more moisture than cold air. When water vapor comes in contact with a cold surface, condensation forms. **Condensation** is water vapor that has returned to a liquid state. If the surface is 32°F or lower, frost forms. The most common visual example of condensation in the home is the formation of water or frost on a window during cold weather.

The temperature at which water vapor condenses varies in relation to the surface temperature and the amount of water vapor in the air. Condensation becomes a serious problem in the home when it occurs on or within the walls, floors, and ceilings. Evidence of condensation may appear in one or more of the following forms:

- damp spots on ceilings and the room side of exterior walls
- water and frost on inside surfaces of windows
- moisture on basement sidewalls and floors
- water-filled blisters on outside paint surfaces
- marbles of ice on attic floors resulting from condensation of water on points of nails protruding through roof sheathing

The amount of vapor pressure depends on the amount of vapor in the air. This pressure forces moisture to dryer, lower-pressure areas. Thus, excessive moisture in a warm house is forced to the outside in cold weather and condensation on the inner surfaces or within the walls may occur. By controlling the amount of water vapor, condensation can be prevented.

Since water vapor is not visible or easily detected until it condenses, occupants are generally not aware of a problem. As a result, little thought is generally given to controlling water vapor until condensation problems arise.

Sources of Water Vapor

Everyday household activities produce considerable moisture inside the dwelling. Some of the most obvious sources include people, bathing facilities, cooking processes, laundry, and open gas flames. Sources of water vapor in the structure itself may include wet plaster, seepage in basements, unexcavated basements, and foundation leaks. Water vapor will always be present inside the home from routine activities, but with proper ventilation the moisture is not excessive or harmful, 23-10.

23-9 The bathroom is a prime location for the growth of mold, as this sink edge shows. Frequent cleaning and additional ventilation will reduce its occurrence.

Broan-NuTone, a Nortek Company

23-10 A typical bathroom ventilation fan removes water vapor from inside the house and thus reduces the chance of mold growth.

Problems such as foundation leaks and basement seepage, however, should be corrected.

Water condensation is not only a cold-weather problem, but a summertime problem as well. For example, what happens if warm, moist air from the outside on muggy days enters the cool basement air? Condensation occurs when the warm air comes in contact with cool basement walls, floors, and cold water pipes. This scenario is similar to the condensation on a cold glass of ice water. Also, houses having a first floor made of concrete laid on the ground exhibit condensation problems in the summertime.

Preventive Measures

The control of excessive water vapor, and thus condensation, varies with the type of structure and the parts of a house. There are three principal cures to reduce condensation problems. These can be used individually or in combination.

- Reduce interior humidity by controlling water vapor at the source, ventilating, and eliminating deliberately added moisture.
- Use vapor barriers—membranes or paints—to stop the flow of moisture through building materials.
- Raise inner surface temperatures by insulating.

To avoid condensation in a house built over a crawl space, the crawl space must be kept dry. The following points should be addressed.

- Grade the lot correctly for good drainage.
- Use gutters and downspouts and/or wide overhangs to eliminate rain seepage.
- Lay a moistureproof cover on the ground of the crawl space to prevent the rise of moisture. Generally, a polyethylene film 4 to 6 milliliters (ml) thick will serve this purpose.
- Provide foundation vents to allow escape of moisture from the crawl space.
- Where floor insulation is used, install a vapor barrier either directly above it or between the subfloor and the finish flooring.

To avoid condensation in a slab-floor construction, follow these recommendations:

- Insulate by using gravel, cinders, crushed rock, or other insulating material underneath the floor.
- Provide good drainage.
- Install insulation at the edges of the slab and a vapor barrier under the slab to prevent ground moisture from entering the building. See 23-11.

Ventilation

Ventilation is the circulation of fresh air. It can be used to reduce excessive humidity that cannot be controlled at its source, 23-12. The model building codes generally specify the number and size of vents to use in a given structure. However, there are so many variables that minimum recommendations may not suffice in every case.

23-11 A polyethylene film placed under a concrete slab will reduce moisture penetration through the slab.

Broan-NuTone, a Nortek Company

23-12 This fan-powered roof vent is capable of cooling an attic up to 1,800 sq. ft.

It is more satisfactory to provide controlled (powered) ventilation than to depend on uncontrolled vents and cracks, such as around windows and doors. If a home is heated by a combustion furnace, an outside air intake can be added to the system. The same is true for a combustion-type water heater and fireplace. Proper ventilation may be the solution to most moisture vapor problems in the home.

Health Hazards Associated with Mold

Molds can be found almost anywhere moisture is present. Therefore, the moisture control within a house is an important part of mold prevention. Certain molds present health hazards. To help reduce these hazards, it is important to reduce the chances of mold growth.

Molds are a type of fungus that reproduces through the production of spores. These spores are always present in the air indoors and outside. When mold spores settle on organic materials in the presence of moisture, they may begin to grow. For example, molds live in the soil and break down plant material through digestion. In this instance, molds play a positive role by helping to reduce dead vegetation.

Some molds can grow on wood, paper, carpet, and foods, 23-13. Mold growth will generally occur indoors when excessive moisture accumulates. It is virtually impossible to eliminate mold spores inside the home, but the best way to reduce mold growth is to control moisture.

23-13 This wood has mold growing on it. During the construction process, lumber should be protected from excessive moisture to reduce the chance of mold growth.

Types of Molds

According to the EPA, there are approximately 100 common types of mold found in homes that may cause health problems. Molds that are commonly found in indoor air include the *Cladosporium, Pencillum,* and *Alternaria* species. More serious molds, however, are the pathogenic species of fungi that are sometimes present in indoor air. These may include *Aspergillus flavus, Aspergillus fumigatus, Aspergillus niger,* and *Stachybotrys atra.*

Stachybotrys atra is a potentially dangerous greenish-black mold that grows on materials with high-cellulose and low-nitrogen content. It is commonly called black mold. Materials in the home that support its growth include wood, fiberboard, gypsum board, paper, ceiling tiles, and cardboard, 23-14. *Stachybotrys atra* is linked to a number of deaths, particularly infant deaths. However, not all black mold is *Stachybotrys atra.*

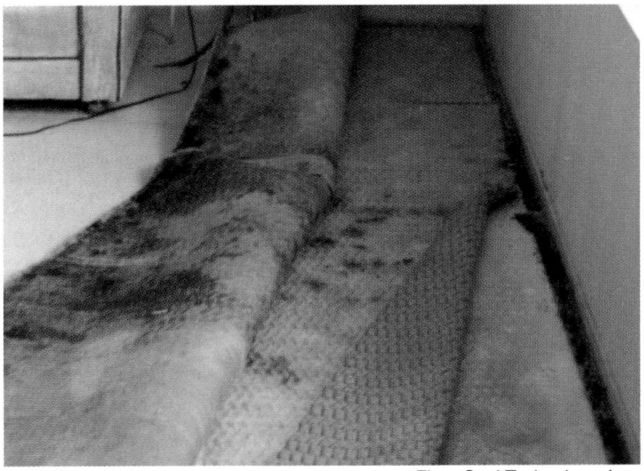

Floor Seal Technology, Inc.

23-14 Black mold (*Stachybotrys atra*) can grow on wood, fiberboard, gypsum board, paper, ceiling tiles, and cardboard. The carpet and padding shown here are contaminated.

Health Problems

Exposure to mold has been identified as a potential cause of many health problems such as asthma, sinusitis, nosebleeds, chest congestion, allergic responses, and infection-type diseases. Allergic responses include allergic rhinitis (hay fever), skin and upper respiratory tract irritation, and hypersensitivity Pneumonitis. Infection-type diseases include athlete's foot, yeast infections, histoplasmosis, and aspergillosis.

Health officials report that the most common health problems caused by indoor molds produce allergy-type symptoms. However, other more serious health problems can occur. In general, exposure to mold results in the following types of ailments.

- upper respiratory infections
- breathing difficulties
- coughing
- sore throat
- nasal and sinus congestion
- skin and eye irritation

Mold Prevention and Removal

If you discover a mold problem in your home, you should remove it and take steps to eliminate the excess moisture encouraging its growth. Follow these steps:

- Remove any visible mold from hard surfaces and allow them to dry. Carpet, ceiling tiles, and other soft materials that contain mold should be replaced.
- Eliminate unwanted water from leaky faucets or other sources.
- Clean and dry any appliance drip pans on a regular basis.
- Vent clothes dryers to the outdoors.
- When bathing, cooking, or using the clothes washer, turn on an exhaust fan or open a window.
- Take steps to reduce indoor humidity to between 30 and 50 percent relative humidity.

Surfaces with mold should be cleaned with a household bleach and water mixture. Be sure the area is ventilated and apply the bleach-water mixture with a sponge. Allow the mixture to work for 15 minutes; then dry the surface. Be sure to wear an approved mask and rubber gloves. When in doubt, consult a professional.

Weather- and Nature-Related Safety

Every area of the country is faced with one or more destructive forces of nature such as flooding, hurricanes, tornadoes, and earthquakes. Flooding, for example, is responsible for more property damage and deaths than hurricanes, tornadoes, and earthquakes combined. All residential structures should be designed and built to reasonably resist nature's destructive forces.

Earthquakes

An **earthquake zone** is an area that is prone to earthquakes. Most people think of California when earthquakes are mentioned, but anywhere west or just east of the Rocky Mountains is an earthquake zone. In addition, the area along the Mississippi River from Arkansas through Tennessee to Illinois is in the New Madrid earthquake zone, site of the most severe U.S. earthquake on record. Other earthquake zones include the southern Appalachians, the northeastern states, and Alaska.

As indicated on the seismic zone map in 23-15, there is some chance of earthquake damage in all regions of the country. **Seismic** refers to earth vibrations. Areas that have a very low chance of damage include the southern halves of Florida and Texas, a portion of the Gulf Coast, and the islands of Hawaii.

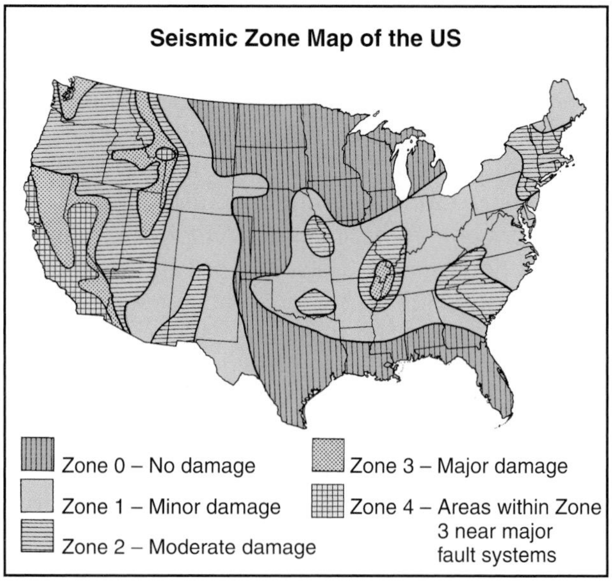

Provided by the International Conference of Building Officials

23-15 This seismic zone map shows areas most likely to experience earthquakes.

Reducing Earthquake Damage to Dwellings

Five basic areas need to be addressed to reduce the hazards of earthquakes—siting considerations, soil and foundation types, building shapes and mass, structural details, and drainage. A thorough analysis of any existing or proposed structure should take all of these factors into account.

The notion that a structure can be earthquake proof is misleading because it is impossible to build a structure that can withstand any earthquake. However, the goal of reducing a dwelling's risk of serious structural failure is important. See 23-16 for an example of the destructive force that an earthquake can inflict on residential structures.

Four kinds of structural elements need careful consideration to determine what strengthening strategies are practical. The structural elements to consider are as follows:

- the foundation that supports the building
- horizontal members, such as floors
- columns, posts, and other vertical members that transfer the weight of the structure to the foundation
- all points of connection

These elements are covered in detail in Chapter 23 of the *1988 Uniform Building Code*. Also, check with your local building department for specific recommendations.

Interior Space

You can reduce damage inside your home by doing the following before an earthquake strikes.

- Attach pictures and mirrors securely to the wall.
- Anchor bookcases, shelving units, and filing cabinets to the wall.
- Cover windows and glass doors with safety film.
- Add a ledge to shelves to prevent spilling. Place heavier items on the bottom shelves.
- Install latches on drawers and cabinets to prevent their contents from spilling.
- Secure hanging items to the permanent structure of your house.
- Connect computers, TVs, and other small appliances to their support bases.
- Use straps or cables to secure large appliances and water heaters to the wall.
- Fit all gas appliances with flexible connections and/or breakaway gas shut-off devices. Check your local code to see what is approved.

House Structure

The following summary describes ways to reduce structural damage to a dwelling from an earthquake:

- Bolt the sill plate to the foundation with anchor bolts spaced no farther than 4 ft. apart. See 23-17.

A FEMA News Photo

B FEMA News Photo

23-16 These residences were damaged on January 17, 1994, in the Northridge, California, earthquake. The disaster caused 72 deaths and about $25 billion in damages to approximately 114,000 residential and commercial buildings.

23-17 The sill plate should be bolted to the foundation with anchor bolts spaced no farther than 4 ft. apart.

23-18 Thick metal straps have been added to the connections between the posts and beam in this structure to resist lateral forces.

- Reinforce cripple walls (short walls) with a plywood shear wall that connects the sill plate, cripple studs, and wall plates. Generally, ½ in. CDX plywood is used for one-story homes, ⅝ in. plywood for two-story houses, and ¾ in. plywood for three-story structures.
- Install blocking at the midspan and ends of floor joists. Long spans may require additional blocking. Use angle steel or metal angle clips to attach the joists ends to the rim joists and between the rim joist and sill plate.
- Add metal clips, T-straps, or steel brackets at all connections between posts and beams, See 23-18. Beams should be securely attached to piers with heavy metal straps and anchor bolts.
- Hurricane ties should be installed between the top plates or bond beams and the rafters and ceiling joists. See 23-19.
- Chimneys are particularly vulnerable to earthquake damage. A large reinforced footing, structural steel bracing, ties to framing, and reduced weight above the roof line can reduce the potential for damage.

23-19 Hurricane ties should be placed between the concrete bond beam and each roof truss to resist uplift forces.

Floods

Communities located in low-lying areas, near a body of water, or downstream from a dam have the highest flood risk. A **flash flood** is especially dangerous because it consists of a high volume of fast-moving water that develops suddenly. Consider the following facts:

- The force of 6 in. of swiftly moving water can cause you to lose your footing.
- Flash-flood waters can move boulders, uproot trees, demolish buildings, and wash out bridges.
- Only 2 ft. of moving water can sweep away an automobile.

Floods are at the top of the list of the most common and devastating of all natural disasters, 23-20. Flooding occurs after heavy thunderstorms,

FEMA News Photo, Photographer Andrea Booher

23-20 This aerial photograph shows flooded homes in LeClaire, Iowa, along the Mississippi River in 2001.

23-21 To exceed the highest point of the area's 100-year flood, the finished floor of this house is 14 ft. above the mean sea level.

frequent spring rains, and rapid snow thaws. Some of the worst flooding was caused by dam failures that quickly release large volumes of water, thus causing a flash flood.

Floodplain Risk

Historically, people have built their homes next to rivers, lakes, and the ocean for an obvious reason—water was the main mode of transportation. Building next to a body of water has benefits, but there are drawbacks as well. New rules and requirements have resulted from the experience of building in flood-prone areas, and flood mitigation has become very important to everyone.

Natural **floodplains** have been identified throughout the United States according to the average number of years between flooding, such as a 100-year or 500-year floodplain. Floodplain maps are examined by local building departments when issuing building permits. Generally, new buildings are prohibited in areas that flood frequently. A new structure may be permitted if its elevation is located significantly above the floodplain, 23-21.

Flood Mitigation

Examples of flood mitigation include the following:

- relocating homes out of the floodplain
- elevating homes above the base floodplain (usually the 100-year floodplain)
- minimizing the dwelling's vulnerability to flood damage through both structural and nonstructural means

Check your local model building code for information regarding building in flood-prone areas before selecting a site for a new home or purchasing an existing home. The result of building in a floodplain without taking proper precautions is shown in 23-22.

FEMA News Photo, Photographer Dave Gatley

23-22 These flooded homes are located along the Wapsipinicon River in Littleton, Iowa.

Tornadoes

A **tornado** is a swirling column of air extending from a thunderstorm cloud to the ground. Most tornadoes generally form when warm, humid air along the ground is pushed up rapidly by cooler air. This movement of air then develops into a spinning vortex, or funnel, and can become a tornado. A tornado may also be a byproduct of a hurricane. The average tornado is about 200 yards wide and several miles high. Winds typically swirl in a cyclonic direction, counter-clockwise in the northern hemisphere.

Tornado alley is a term describing the area from north Texas through eastern Nebraska to northeast Indiana. The area is known for the number and severity of tornadoes. However, you are still vulnerable to tornadoes even if you live outside this area. Texas, Oklahoma, and Kansas often have more tornadoes than other states, but other parts of the country have tornadoes on a regular basis.

Homes that are built strictly to current model building codes for high-wind regions have a much better chance of surviving violent windstorms than homes that do not meet these requirements. In spite of what some may think, wind speeds in most tornadoes are at or below the design speeds that most typical building codes address. Records show that about 85 percent of all reported tornadoes have wind speeds of 112 mph or less. In other words, a house built to code will resist the majority of tornadoes.

Tornado Season

Tornadoes can form at almost any time of the year. The peak season varies by location. In general, tornadoes in this country are most prevalent in April, May, and June, 23-23. This is the time of year when cold northerly winds collide with warm, humid air from the Gulf of Mexico. This seasonal clash of warm and cold air masses fits the model required for tornado formation.

Tornadoes can occur at any time of day or night. However, approximately 80 percent form between noon and midnight. An average year will produce 800 to 1,000 tornadoes in the United States.

Building to Resist Tornadoes

No aboveground structure is completely tornado proof, but taking certain steps can give a house a better chance of surviving a tornado. The following recommendations are intended to aid the design and building processes.

FEMA News Photo, Photographer Dave Saville

23-23 More than 400 homes in Hoisington, Kansas, were damaged or destroyed by a tornado that struck the town on April 21, 2001.

Windows

Install impact-resistant windows. These windows are specially designed to resist high winds and are commonly available in hurricane-prone areas.

Entry Doors

Exterior doors should have at least three hinges and a 1 in. long deadbolt security lock. Anchoring the door frames securely to the wall framing is very important.

Sliding Glass Doors

These doors are more vulnerable to wind damage than most other doors because of their large glass exposure. Install impact-resistant door systems made of laminated glass, plastic glazing, or a combination.

Garage Doors

Garage doors are highly susceptible to wind damage because of their size and construction. Have a qualified inspector determine if both the door and frame will resist high winds. If purchasing a new door, check the wind rating and select a door that will withstand at least 110 mph winds.

Roofs

Be sure the roof covering and sheathing will resist high winds. All roofing materials are not equal in this respect. If you are replacing an existing roof, a qualified roofing contractor can take the following steps to increase the stability of the roof.

1. Remove the existing roofing materials down to the sheathing.
2. Inspect the rafters or trusses to be sure they are securely connected to the walls.
3. Cut out and replace any damaged sheathing. Be sure it is nailed according to the recommended schedule required by the local code.
4. Install a roof covering that is designed for high-wind areas. Attachment must follow manufacturer's specifications.

Gables

Gable end walls must be braced properly to resist high winds. For guidance, check the current model building code for high-wind regions, or consult your local building department.

Connections

Connections between the foundation and walls, floor and walls, and roof structure and walls are critical points, 23-24. Appropriate connectors must be used and attached properly if the total structure is to resist high winds.

Anchors

The exterior walls must be properly anchored to the foundation. Approved anchor bolts and/or straps and fasteners can be used for this purpose.

23-24 Joists hangers were used in this structure to increase its strength and resist damaging winds.

Upper Stories

If the house has more than one story, be sure the wall framing of the upper stories is properly connected to the lower wall framing. Use approved straps and fasteners.

Roof Framing

Anchor the roof framing to the exterior walls with approved straps, clips, and fasteners. Consult the model building code for specifications or get help from your local building department.

Tornado Warnings

No dwelling is tornado proof, so you should take steps to protect yourself and your family when a tornado threatens. A **tornado watch** is a warning issued when conditions are favorable for tornado formation. A **tornado warning** is an alert issued when a tornado has been sighted or detected on radar.

Most communities have a severe-weather warning system. Be familiar with it. Make sure every member of your family knows what to do when a tornado watch or warning is sounded. During the "watch" phase of the storm, remove anything in your yard that can become flying debris in high winds. Do *not* attempt this after the warning is sounded.

When a tornado warning is sounded, seek shelter immediately. Decide ahead of time where you will seek shelter. It could be a local community shelter or your own underground storm cellar. Some newer homes have a **safe room** within the house that is constructed to withstand tornado-force winds. Stay away from windows, preferably under something sturdy like a workbench or staircase. Seek the center and lowest section of the structure.

Develop a family plan for protection and escape, and a meeting place to reunite if members become separated. Assemble an emergency kit that includes the following:

- emergency cooking equipment and a three-day supply of food and drinking water
- flashlight, portable lantern, and fresh batteries
- prescription medications, eyeglasses, and first aid supplies
- clothing and blankets
- a portable weather radio that plays National Weather Service broadcasts from the National Oceanic and Atmospheric Administration (NOAA)
- basic tools and work gloves
- credit cards, cash, important documents such as insurance policies, and extra keys

For safety reasons, there are several situations to avoid during a tornado. Never open windows as this only increases interior water and wind damage to a home. Do not stay in a trailer, mobile home, or manufactured home since they are too light to resist tornado-force winds even if tied down. Do not attempt to ride out the storm in an automobile since a strong tornado can lift, throw, and destroy a vehicle.

Hurricanes

A **hurricane** is a tropical storm with winds at a sustained speed of 74 mph (64 knots) or more. Hurricane winds blow in a large spiral around a relatively calm center, called the eye. The eye is usually 20 to 30 miles across, but the storm may extend out to 400 miles or more. The U.S. regions most vulnerable to hurricanes include the Atlantic and Gulf coasts from Texas to Maine. Other areas prone to hurricanes are the Caribbean territories and tropical areas of the western Pacific that include Hawaii, Guam, American Samoa, and Saipan. August and September are the peak months of the hurricane season, which lasts from June 1 through November 30.

When a hurricane approaches land, it usually brings torrential rains, high winds, and storm surges. Of these three events, the storm surge is generally the most dangerous. A **storm surge** is a dome of ocean water fueled by the hurricane that can be 20 ft. at its highest point and up to 100 miles wide. The power of the surge can demolish communities along the coast as it sweeps ashore. Statistics show that 90 percent of hurricane fatalities can be attributed to drowning in a storm surge.

The greatest hurricane damage occurs when the storm hits land. Damaging forces include strong winds, storm surge, flooding, tornadoes, and rip tides. Together, these forces can demolish almost every structure in their path.

Hurricanes have different names throughout the world. For example, in the western North Pacific and Philippines, these systems are referred to as typhoons. In the Indian and South Pacific Oceans, these strong storms are called tropical cyclones. Systems that develop over the Atlantic or the eastern Pacific Oceans are called hurricanes.

On average, 10 tropical storms develop each year in the North Atlantic Ocean. Of these, six usually reach hurricane strength and two may strike the U.S. coast. The deadliest hurricane in U.S. history was the 1990 Galveston, Texas, hurricane, which took 6,000 lives.

In 1992, two major hurricanes hit the United States in less than four weeks. First, Hurricane Andrew pounded Florida and Louisiana, killing over 50 people. It was the most expensive natural disaster in U.S. history, 23-25. Damage estimates ranged from $15 billion to $30 billion. Three weeks later, Hurricane Iniki swept across three Hawaiian islands causing over $1 billion in damage, mostly in Kauai.

Hurricane Mitigation Through Codes

Many states and local governments in coastal areas of the U.S. have enacted **hurricane codes**. These are building restrictions designed to reduce damage to property during a hurricane. For example, Florida has instituted the Coastal Construction Control Line (CCCL). This defines the extent of a zone from the coastline inland that is subject to flooding, erosion, and other impacts during a 100-year storm. Properties located between the coast and the CCCL are subject to state-enforced elevation and construction requirements.

The CCCL foundation and elevation requirements in this area are even more stringent than National Flood Insurance Program (NFIP) coastal (V-Zone) requirements. Likewise, the CCCL wind-load requirements for properties between the ocean and the CCCL are more stringent than those of the model building codes.

There is proof that more stringent codes and enforcement work. Consider, for example, the experience gained from Hurricane Opal. On October 4, 1995,

FEMA News Photo

23-25 Many homes and businesses suffered extensive damage from Hurricane Andrew on August 24, 1992. One million people were evacuated and 54 died in this hurricane.

it struck a portion of the Florida Coastline as a Category 3 hurricane with 110 to 115 mph winds. However, none of the 576 major habitable structures located seaward of the CCCL and permitted by the state under then-current codes sustained substantial damage. See 23-26. Most of the damage was caused by coastal flooding that included storm surge, wind-generated waves, and flood-induced erosion. Some floodborne debris also contributed to damage.

By contrast, 768 of the 1,366 major habitable structures in the area that were not permitted by the state or were constructed prior to state-permitting requirements sustained extensive structural damage during the storm. It is very clear that more stringent requirements and stricter enforcement can safeguard lives and property.

Building to Resist Hurricanes

The following recommendations are intended to provide broad guidance in the design and building of a dwelling that will more likely resist the forces of a hurricane. However, local and state codes should always be consulted.

Windows

Install impact-resistant window systems. As an alternative, install impact-resistant shutters or panels that cover window openings and protect glass from being broken by flying debris, 23-27.

Entry Doors

Install at least three hinges on exterior doors that are 6 ft. 8 in. high. Four hinges should be installed on exterior doors that are 8 ft. high. Install a dead bolt security lock with a bolt at least 1 in. long. Be sure door frames and hinges are securely anchored to the wall framing. Doors should be solid-core or steel doors.

Sliding Glass Doors

Reduce the vulnerability of sliding glass doors to wind damage by installing an impact-resistant door system made with laminated glass, plastic glazing, or a combination of plastic and glass. Another option is installing hurricane panels that completely cover the doors entirely.

23-26 This coastal home meets the current hurricane codes. It has no living area on the ground level.

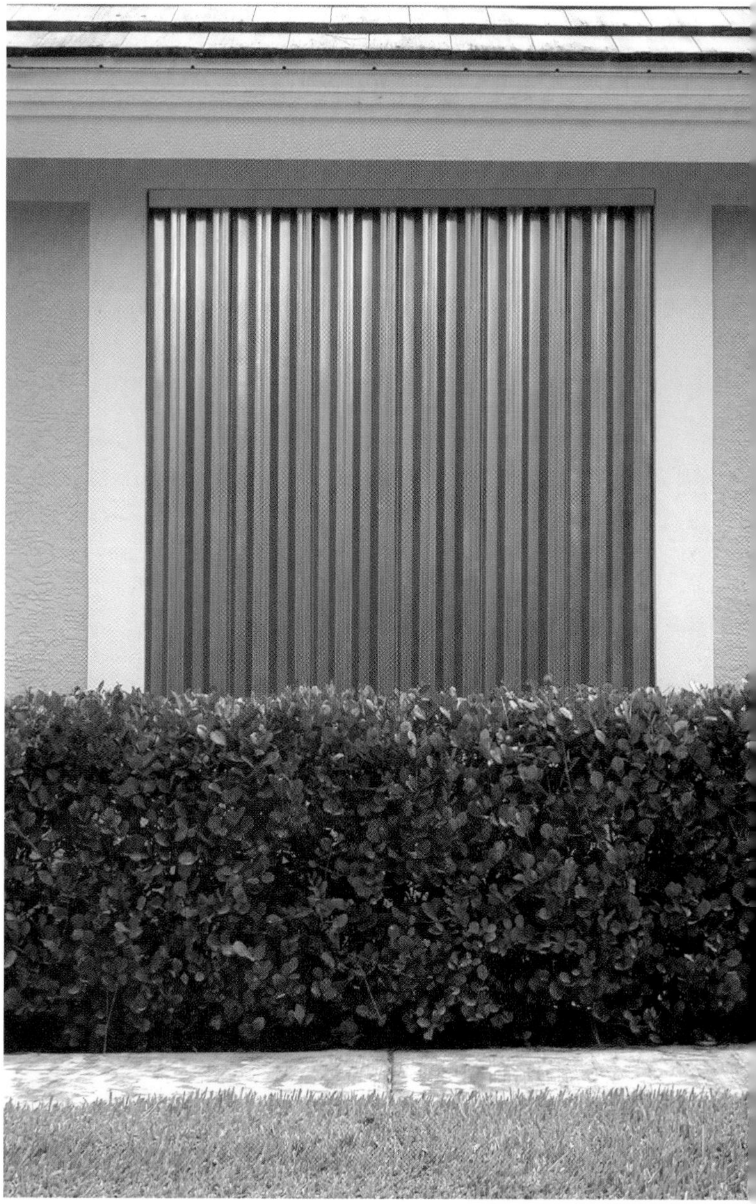

23-27 Hurricane storm panels have been custom made to fit each exterior opening in this building. They will resist damage from 120 mph winds.

Garage Doors

Since the large area of garage doors is highly susceptible to wind damage, purchase a door certified to withstand at least 110 mph winds. Be sure the track system has the same rating and is solidly anchored to the wall with bolts or screws. Doors wider than 8 ft. must have metal stiffeners to resist hurricane-level winds, 23-28.

Landscaping

Use shredded bark as a landscaping material instead of gravel or rock. Remove weak branches and trees that could fall on the house during a storm.

Roofs

The roof structure and covering are areas of significant concern during very high winds. Select a roofing material that is designed to resist high winds, 23-29. Be sure to follow recommended installation procedures. Roof sheathing should be fastened as prescribed by the code in your area. This may include the use of construction adhesive, as well as nails. Every truss or rafter must be secured to the exterior wall with clips and/or straps. Proper nailing is very important to the quality of the installation. In addition, the roof structure must be braced inside to produce a rigid structure able to resist hurricane winds.

Gables

The end walls of a gable roof are particularly vulnerable to high wind damage. Make certain they are braced properly. Check with your local building department or truss manufacturer.

23-29 The roofing material on this home is concrete tile. When attached properly, it will resist typical hurricane-strength winds.

Connections

Reinforce the points where the roof and the foundation meet the exterior walls of the structure. This is generally accomplished through the use of anchors, straps, or clips. Walls are usually anchored to the foundation using anchor bolts or straps placed around the perimeter of the foundation at about 4 ft. intervals. See 23-30. Second-story framing must be securely fastened to the lower level through the use of straps that bridge the floor joist area.

23-28 The strength of garage doors can be increased greatly by adding metal stiffeners to each panel of the door. This door will resist 120 mph winds.

23-30 Anchor bolts are used in this slab-type foundation to connect the exterior walls to the foundation.

Hurricane Warnings

Prepare an escape plan for when a hurricane threatens. Most communities have a disaster preparedness plan and you should be familiar with it. Create a family plan as well. Identify escape routes and select an emergency meeting place for your family to gather if you become separated. Contact relatives to relieve their concern.

Also, prepare your home for the storm before it arrives. Hurricanes usually take several days to develop and that provides time to get ready. Develop an emergency kit like the one recommended earlier in this chapter for tornado alerts.

Remove items outside the home that might be blown away or into your home during the storm. Follow news reports about the weather so you know what to expect. Shut off the water and gas supply. Disconnect all electrical appliances except food storage. Wrap outside electric motors with plastic to prevent water damage. Be sure to fill the fuel tanks in your vehicles because fuel may not be available for evacuation or for several days following the storm. Finally, obey evacuation orders from local authorities.

General Home Safety

Most people believe their homes are safe, but survey evidence shows that most homes are not. So, what can be done to improve the safety of a home? First, consider some of the U.S. statistics related to home safety.

- According to the National Safety Council, most of the 28,400 accidental deaths that occur in homes each year (about one-third) are from falls.
- About 200,000 people older than 65 are hospitalized annually with a broken hip suffered in a fall. Many of these occur in the home.
- Nearly half of all home fires and 60 percent of fire-related deaths occur in residences without smoke detectors.
- The major causes of accidents in the home are falls, burns, electrical shock, and poisonings.
- Most electrical shocks in the home result from misusing household appliances.

The first step in preventing accidents and injuries in the home is making sure the home meets the model building code in your area. The major purpose of the code is to improve safety. To be certain that newly constructed homes conform to the requirements, they must pass an inspection before an occupancy permit is issued. Many older or poorly maintained homes would probably fail the inspection.

Secondly, many commonsense actions that relate to everyday living can improve home safety, such as the following:

- Keep stairs free of toys and other items.
- Remove trip hazards from traffic circulation patterns.
- Keep the area around a fireplace or heater free of combustible materials.
- Secure flammable and toxic liquids.
- Limit the use of extension cords.
- Keep electrical and mechanical appliances and devices in good repair.
- Choose rugs with nonskid backing.
- Provide adequate lighting in hazard-prone areas. See 23-31.
- Make your home childproof when youngsters are around.
- Follow good housekeeping practices.

Finally, it is a good idea to prepare a complete description of your personal belongings in case a disaster destroys some or all of your personal property. Videotaping your home and its contents can serve as a record. Store this tape and/or a list of your possessions in a safe place.

WCI Communities, Inc.

23-31 The exterior lighting at the main entry of this home will reduce the chance of tripping accidents on the entry steps.

Chapter Summary

Experts say that more injuries occur in the home than anywhere else. Structural fires are a significant danger to every home, and commonsense rules can prevent them. Smoke detectors should be placed in every home in locations specified by the experts. Fire safety code requirements should be followed. Fire extinguishers are classified according to the type of burning material on which they are to be used.

Protection against carbon monoxide (CO) poisoning is provided by placing detectors close to where combustion occurs. CO is an odorless, invisible gas that is potentially deadly. Radon also has these characteristics, but is radioactive, too. Radon detection and mitigation should be considered in every residence as large concentrations can harm health.

High water vapor needs to be controlled to prevent mold growth in the home. Ventilation can be used to reduce excessive humidity that cannot be controlled at its source. Molds are a type of fungus and can live on wood, fiberboard, gypsum board, paper, ceiling tiles, and carpeting. Molds can cause a variety of health problems ranging from mild to severe.

Dwellings are subject to damage and destruction from weather-and nature-related forces. These include earthquakes, floods, tornadoes, and hurricanes. The forces cannot be prevented, but many steps can be taken to lessen their impact on residential structures. Building dwellings according to model codes is a critical first step. Knowing which forces of nature are likely to impact your area and how to prepare for them is the next step. All households should prepare themselves for possible emergencies and follow the advice of local authorities when a catastrophe does hit their area.

For too many people, the home is the site of falls, burns, electric shock and poisonings. Commonsense actions should be taken to reduce the potential for accidents in the home.

Review Questions

1. Which of the following steps can help prevent a home fire?
   A. Have the heating system inspected yearly.
   B. Store flammable liquids in approved containers.
   C. Do not overload electrical circuits.
   D. All of the above.
2. Where in the home should a smoke detector be installed?
3. For fire safety, how many means of exit must every occupied room have?
4. Which type of fire extinguisher can stop a grease fire?
5. What potentially deadly gas is produced by incomplete combustion?
6. What health risk is linked to high radon levels in the home?
7. How can radon accumulation be reduced in basements and slab-on-grade construction?
8. Other than mold growth, what are four conditions that indicate excessive moisture in the home?
9. Which of the following is generally *not* a source of water vapor in the structure?
   A. wet plaster
   B. wet basement
   C. roof leak
   D. drippy outside hose bib
10. What is the best way to control indoor mold growth?
11. What are the most common health problems caused by indoor mold?
12. Which mold, commonly known as black mold, can cause serious health problems?
13. What destructive force of nature causes the most property damage and deaths?
14. What earthquake zone lies along the Mississippi River from Arkansas through Tennessee to Illinois?
15. What are the peak months of the U.S. tornado season?
16. At what sustained wind speed does a tropical storm become classified as a hurricane?
17. What are the peak months of the U.S. hurricane season?
18. Which of the following accounts for the greatest number of accidental deaths in U.S. homes?
    A. Drownings.
    B. Falls.
    C. Fires.
    D. Electrocution.

Suggested Activities

1. Examine your home for fire hazards and note their locations. Then, prepare a plan to eliminate the hazards.
2. Visit a local home improvement center or hardware store to examine the carbon monoxide detectors that are available. Identify the model you most prefer and, in a brief presentation to the class, describe the features that prompted your decision.
3. Research the topic of radon gas. Determine sections of the country where the radon hazard is most prevalent. Prepare a report identifying common methods of radon mitigation in those areas.
4. Prepare a report on one of the major weather-related hazards common in your area. Be sure to include such facts as areas of the country most vulnerable to the hazard, its frequency in your area, the average cost of the hazard in U.S. dollars and lives, and preventive measures. Record your sources.

Internet Resources

Building Systems Councils of National Association of Home Builders
buildingsystems.org

Centers for Disease Control and Prevention
cdc.gov

Federal Emergency Management Agency
fema.gov

Institute for Business and Home Safety
ibhs.org

Insurance Information Institute
iii.org

National Oceanic and Atmospheric Administration, source of the National Weather Service
noaa.gov

National Radon Safety Board
nrsb.org

National Safety Council
nsc.org

Portland Cement Association
concretehomes.com

The McGraw-Hill Companies, Inc. construction products marketplace
sweets.com

The Weather Channel
weather.com

U.S. Environmental Protection Agency
epa.gov

Note: Web addresses may have changed since publication. For some entries, reaching the correct Web site may require keying *www.* into the address.

Part Seven
Designing Exteriors and Remodeling

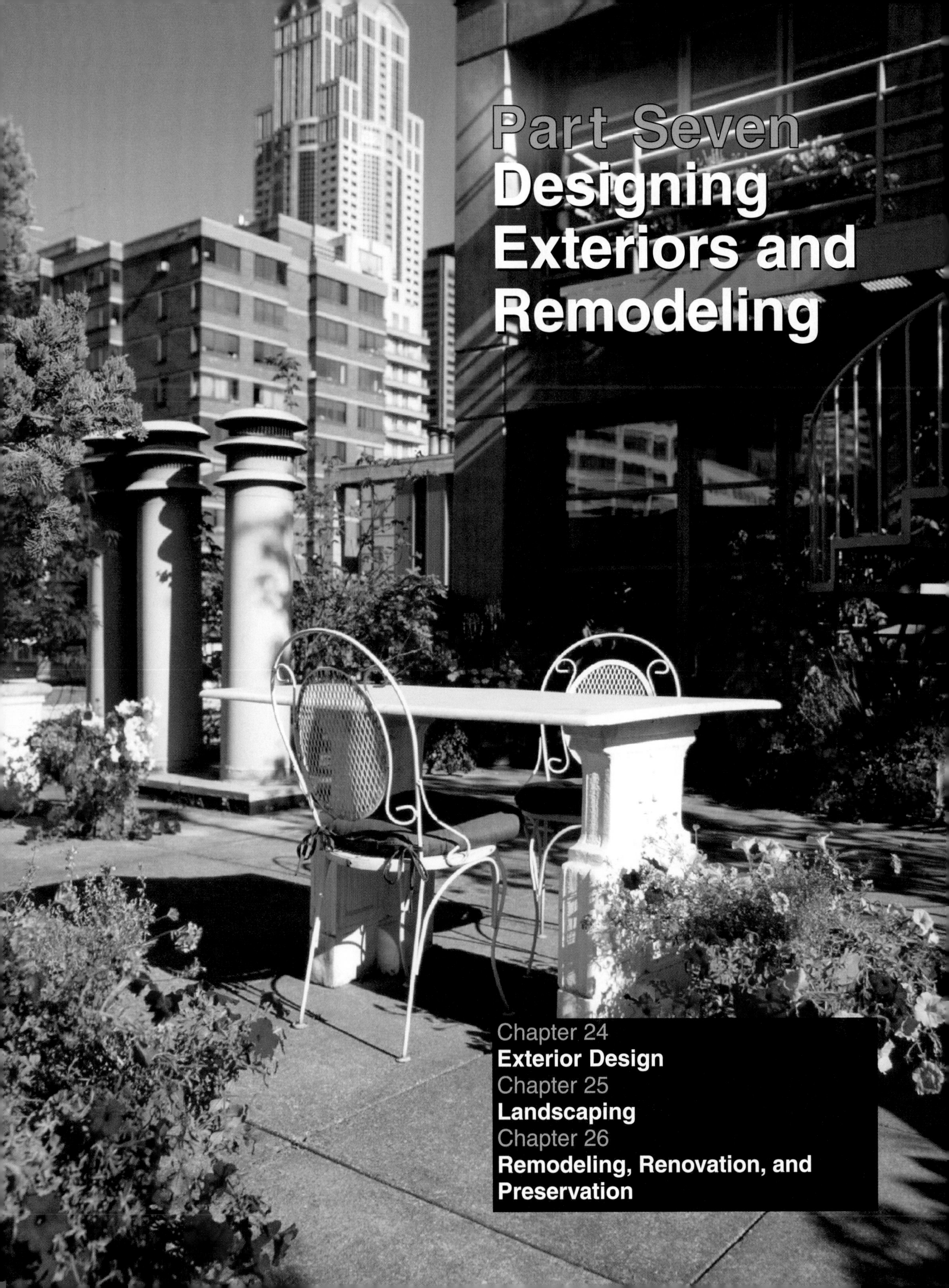

Chapter 24
Exterior Design

Objectives

After studying this chapter, you will be able to
- identify distinguishing features of traditional styles of homes.
- describe the designs of ranch and split-level homes, and list their advantages and disadvantages.
- determine the main purpose of a contemporary design, and list its design features, advantages, and disadvantages.

Key Terms

adobe
Dutch Colonial
dormer
Pennsylvania Dutch Colonial
pent roofs
French Normandy
half-timber
French doors
Louisiana French
Elizabethan
Cotswold cottage
half-house
double house
hillside ranch
raised ranch
geodesic dome
topography

A well-designed home is attractive on the outside as well as the inside. Exterior design determines the style and mood that a home conveys from the outside. It also determines the basic layout and design of the home's interior. Architects and homeowners may choose a traditional, modern, or contemporary style for the exterior of their home. Today's residential homes may be exact replicas of one style, or they may contain elements from two or more styles.

Traditional Styles

Over the years many different home styles have developed, usually in response to family needs, available natural resources, and climactic conditions. Some of these historical styles have become so popular that they continue to influence residential housing design today.

Native American

Native Americans built the first homes in America. Each Native American Indian tribe used materials and a building style to fit the environment of the region. Some settlers who came to America patterned their new homes after native dwellings. The Navajos of the southwest lived in eight-sided hogans made of logs and mud. The Seminole Indians of Florida lived in wood frame structures. The settlers borrowed these and other styles.

Probably the most lasting adaptation of an Indian-style home is the adobe home of New Mexico. An **adobe** is a building that has exterior walls of adobe brick, which are made of soil and straw and baked in the sun. The Pueblo Indians still live in adobe buildings built as early as the fifteenth century. These structures are characterized by thick, smooth adobe walls, flat roofs, deep-set windows, and rough pole beams projecting through the walls. See 24-1. The adobe homes are designed to stay cool in hot, dry weather.

The adobe style was adapted by early southwest settlers. Many adobe homes are still used in the New Mexico area. Modern homes in the southwest are often designed to look like adobe homes, although modern building materials are used.

Spanish

Spanish-style homes have existed in the southern part of North America since the late 1500s. They are characterized by white or tinted stucco walls and low-pitched tile roofs. See 24-1. Mexican barrel tile and red mission tile are most commonly used for the roof. For shade, roofs have broad overhangs. Colorful tile often paves the floors and surrounds doors and windows. Windows, doors, and colonnades are arched and accented with wrought iron railings and grilles.

The Spanish style is also characterized by its exposed roof beams, balconies, and wide porches. Many homes are built to surround an inner patio or courtyard. These homes are most suited to a warm, dry climate, such as that in the southwestern states.

Swedish

Swedish immigrants brought the log cabin to America. It became a popular home for the early pioneers who settled the Midwest. The original log cabins were small, rectangular one-story homes with shingle-covered gable roofs. (For pictures of roof styles, refer to Chapter 15, "Ceilings and Roofs.") Traditional windows were made of thin, oiled skins.

Today log homes are available in a wide variety of price ranges and floor plans from numerous companies across the country specializing in manufactured log houses. Log cabins may be built with round or squared-off logs. The squared-off logs produce a smoother wall.

Dutch

Dutch Colonial homes are most common in northern states such as New York and Delaware. See 24-1. Dutch homes are usually constructed of fieldstone or brick, but they may be constructed of wood. The most notable feature of the Dutch home is the gambrel roof that flares out at the bottom and extends to cover an open porch. This flared eave is known as the *Dutch kick.*

Dutch Colonial homes are also characterized by a central entrance, a chimney that is not centered, windows with small panes, and dormers in the second story. A **dormer** is a window set in a small projection from a slanted roof. Some very early Dutch homes have high gable roofs with an extended roof covering a porch. The extended roof and porch area surrounds the house.

Adobe

Spanish

Dutch Colonial

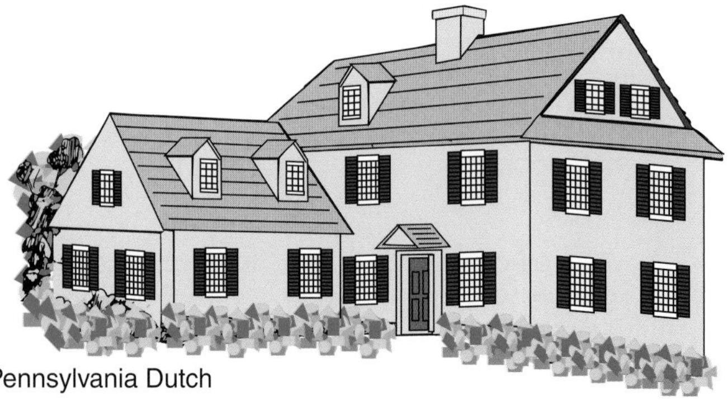

Pennsylvania Dutch

24-1 Early housing styles reflected the diverse preferences of the different cultures of people that settled the land.

German

The first German American homes, built in Pennsylvania, are called **Pennsylvania Dutch Colonial** homes, 24-1. They were built of thick, fieldstone walls for warmth and easy maintenance. Many German homes have small roof ledges between the first and second floor, called **pent roofs**. The pent roof and unsupported hood over the front entrance are distinguishing features of the Pennsylvania Dutch style.

French

The French influenced many American architectural styles. The earliest is the **French Normandy** style, brought by the Huguenots in the seventeenth century. Many Norman cottages are rectangular with hip roofs, but others have gable roofs and a central turret, 24-2. The turret was originally used for grain storage. Eventually, the turret was used to house a staircase. French Normandy homes are usually 1½ to 2½ stories high with brick, stone, or stucco walls. Often, portions of the walls are **half-timber** for decoration. Half-timber walls have large, rough wood support beams with a plaster or masonry filling between beams.

The French plantation house is similar in style to the rectangular Norman cottage, but the hip roof is extended into a very broad roof to cover a porch surrounding the house. Many **French doors**, which have large areas of paned glass, lead to the patio from all sides of the house. Later styles have the porch on the second floor supported by posts or pillars. See 24-2. The French plantation house is most common in southern states.

The **Louisiana French** style originated in New Orleans. One of its most outstanding features is a raised brick or stone basement to protect the house from floods. Balconies with lacy ironwork railings and white stucco walls are typical of the Louisiana French style, 24-2. Hip roofs with two chimneys are also typical.

The French manor is a stately home more common in northern states, 24-2. Its most distinguishing feature is a roof designed by a French architect named Mansard, called the Mansard roof. (See Figure 15-23 in Chapter 15.) The manors are rectangular and symmetrical with a wing on each

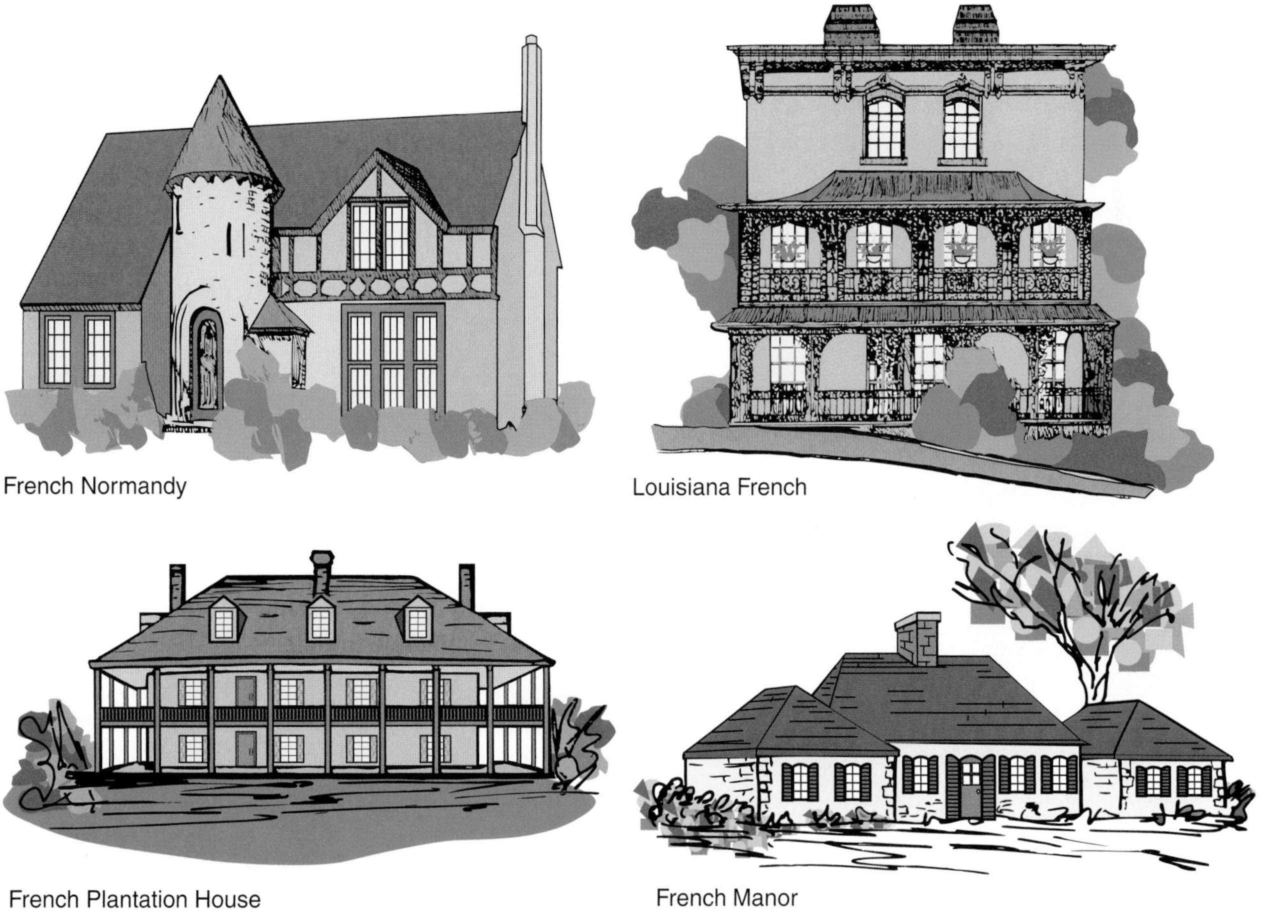

French Normandy

Louisiana French

French Plantation House

French Manor

24-2 The French influenced housing styles as early as the mid-seventeenth century.

side. The wings have dovecote roofs, while the main house has a Mansard roof with dormers. Walls are usually painted brick. Other French-style homes include the one-story French cottage and the French city house. The French city house, called French Provincial, is notable for its second-story windows that break the roofline, 24-3.

English

In the late 1500s, the Tudor-style home was predominant in England, 24-3. Tudor homes are of half-timber construction. They are usually two to three stories tall with an overhanging second story. Distinctive features include several gables on the roof and chimneys with many columns and decorative masonry. Many modern homes are patterned after Tudor manors, although modern building materials are used.

The **Elizabethan**-style manor has both Gothic and Dutch influence, 24-3. Elizabethan manors are usually of stone, brick, or half-timber construction. They are usually two or three stories high, in an E-shape or other irregular shape. Bay windows, recessed doorways in an arched frame, and decorative end gables are also typical.

The **Cotswold cottage** is another sixteenth century English style that gained popularity in twentieth century America. See 24-3. The name is derived

French Provincial

Elizabethan

Tudor

Cotswold Cottage

24-3 Accomplished tradesmen who built homes in Europe's cities copied their housing styles when they arrived here.

from "cot" or *cottage* and "wold" or *wood*, meaning "cottage in the wood." The style is distinguished by a compact size with a very steep gable roof. The design necessitates small, irregularly shaped rooms, and it is usually necessary to walk through one room to get to another. Casement windows and recessed, arched doorways are common. Walls may be brick, stone, wood, half-timber, or a combination.

English/Colonial

The earliest colonial homes were simple in design, sturdy, and fairly small. The **half-house** had only one main-floor room with a tiny entrance and a steep stairway leading to an attic. See 24-4. A fireplace and chimney were placed on a sidewall. Later two-room houses, also called **double houses**, were built with two rooms on the main floor, 24-5. In these homes, the fireplace was centrally located.

The architectural styles of early homes were adaptations of styles the colonists remembered from England. Typically borrowed features were steep, shingled roofs and brick or stone walls. Wood was used as a building material because it was so abundant.

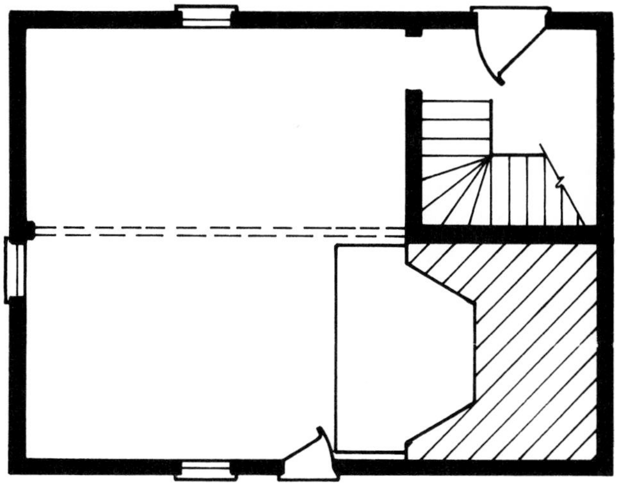

24-4 The half-house has one room on the main floor.

The Saltbox

The saltbox style evolved by adding a lean-to structure to half-houses and double houses, 24-6. The addition allowed extra space and protection from bitter winds common to New England winters. The home has a long roofline that slopes gently from the ridge to the eaves. The style is called saltbox because the house is shaped like the boxes colonists used for storing salt.

The Garrison

The garrison style is noted for its overhanging second story, 24-6, borrowed from medieval English architecture. Corners of the overhang are decorated with hand-carved brackets. Like other colonial homes, the garrison has a steep gable roof and a central fireplace. The walls are of narrow wood siding.

The overhanging second story can be seen in many modern adaptations of the garrison style. This feature has two main advantages. First, because there are separate corner posts for each floor, shorter, stronger posts can be used. Second, extra space may be added to the second level at little extra expense.

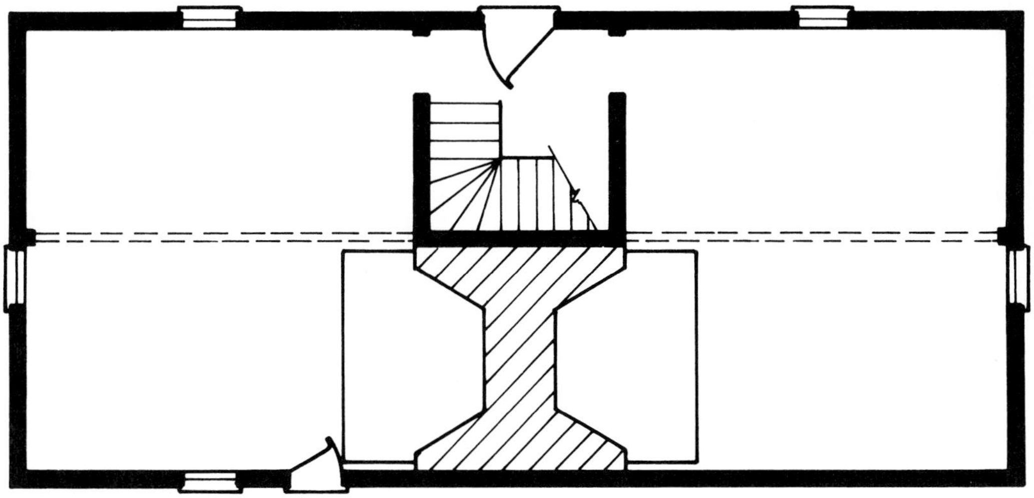

24-5 The double house has a second room added to double the size of the half-house's main floor.

The Cape Cod

The Cape Cod is one of the best-known examples of the traditional colonial styles. It is an outgrowth of the half-house and the double house. The Cape Cod home is a small cottage with a steep gable roof that has little overhang, 24-6. It usually has 1 or 1½ stories with a central chimney. The walls may have narrow wood siding or split shingles. A central doorway and small paned windows are common. Later Cape Cod homes have dormers on the second floor. They also have shutters on all the windows. A variation of the Cape Cod, called the Cape Ann, features a larger central chimney and a gambrel roof. See 24-6.

Georgian

As the colonies prospered, more lavish homes were built. Architects and architectural plans from England became available in the colonies. Many homes during this time were built in the Georgian style. The Georgian house is symmetrical with simple exterior lines, 24-7. It is large and formal looking, with symmetrically placed windows. Georgian homes are usually 2½ or 3 stories high, and a band of stone is often seen between stories.

Georgian homes usually have a high hip or gable roof with dormers. Some roofs have a flat area on top surrounded by an ornate railing, called a *balustrade*. The main door, centrally located, has pilasters on both sides and a pediment above the door. Pediments may be scrolled, triangular, broken, or segmental. A large chimney is located at each end of the roof. Brick or wood siding is most common.

Later Georgian homes have side wings added to the main house, 24-7. A projecting section, or pavilion, topped by a large triangular pediment is added to the front of the home as well. The pavilion may be enclosed, or it may be an open patio area supported by columns.

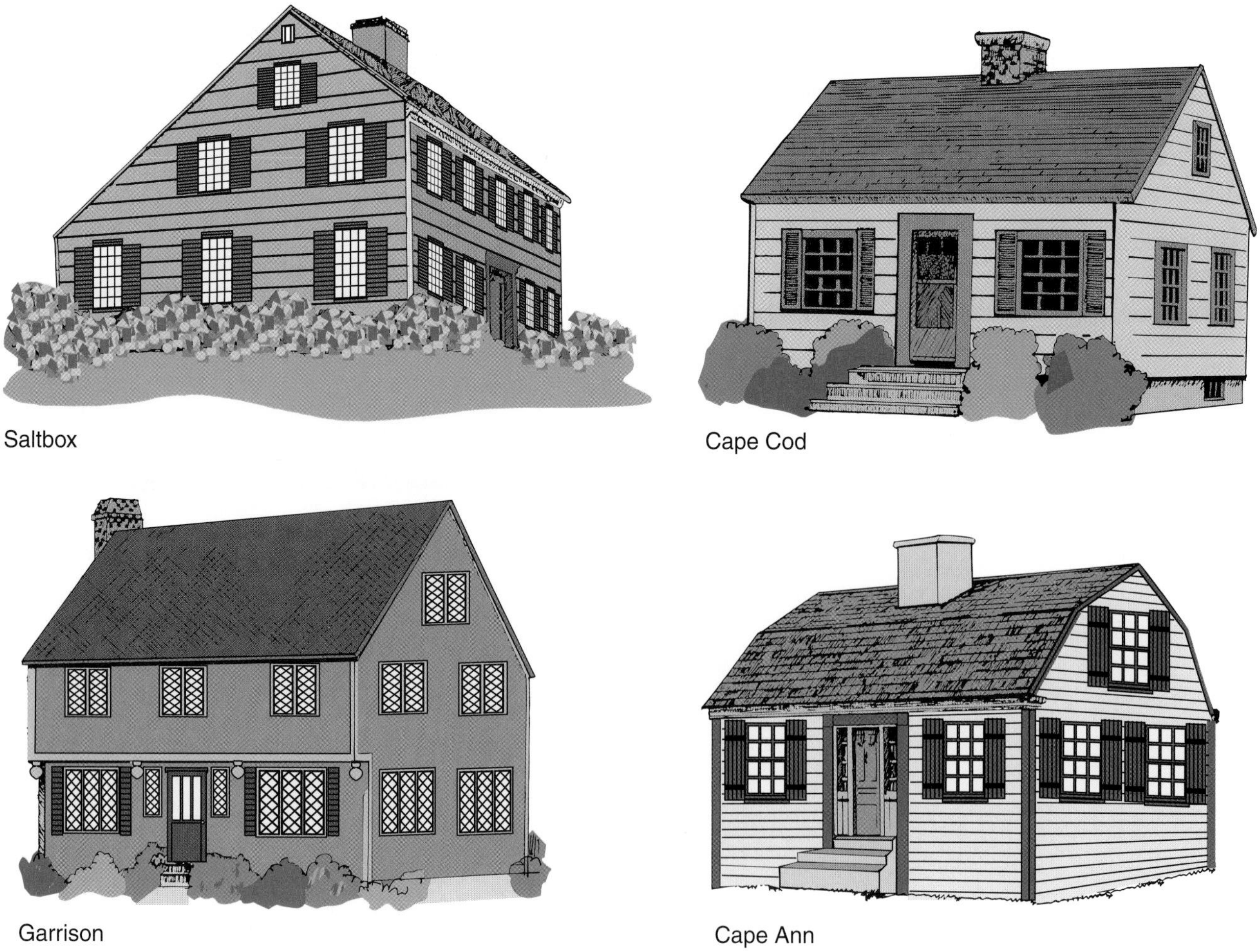

24-6 These simple styles represent some of the earliest homes built by colonists.

Federal

The Federal style of architecture is a departure from English styles of the same period, 24-7. As a newly formed country, America wanted an official architectural style. Thomas Jefferson, an architect as well as a statesman, drew upon the classic forms of Greek and Roman architecture for a new style.

The Federal style added Greek and Roman features to the basic Georgian home. Typical features include Greek columns and a portico in front of the main entrance. Windows and doors often have pediments above them. Circular and semicircular fanlights above the main entrance are also common. Roofs are fairly flat, with balustrades along the entire roof edge.

Greek Revival

During the Greek revival period, homes took on the classic proportions and ornamentation of Greek architecture, 24-7. Greek-style homes are usually large and rectangular. The main design feature is a two-story portico supported by Greek columns. The moderately sloped gable roof is placed so that the gable end faces forward, forming a triangular top. Construction may be of wood, brick, or stone, but the Greek-style home is usually painted white.

Many government buildings in America are patterned after this style. The style is also popular in modern residential structures. Often, smaller Greek-style homes do not have a portico, but pilasters are placed at the front corners of the house.

Southern Colonial

An outgrowth of the Greek revival style, the Southern Colonial style reflects the warmth, charm, and hospitality of the Old South. See 24-8. The outstanding architectural features of the style are the front colonnade and giant two-story portico. The extended portico shelters the front of the house from the hot sun. These homes are usually very large with upper and lower balconies.

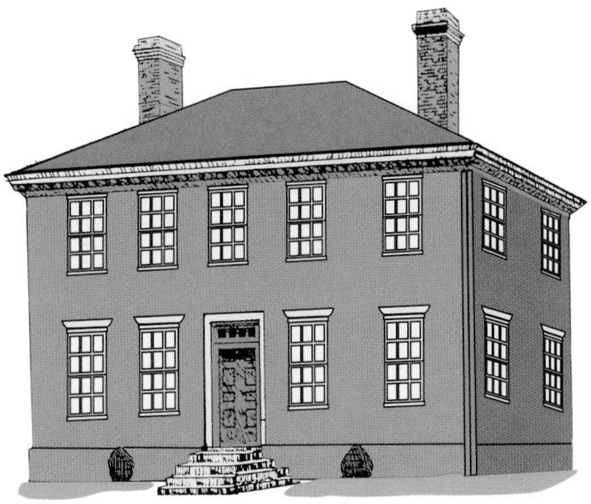

Early Georgian

Federal

Later Georgian

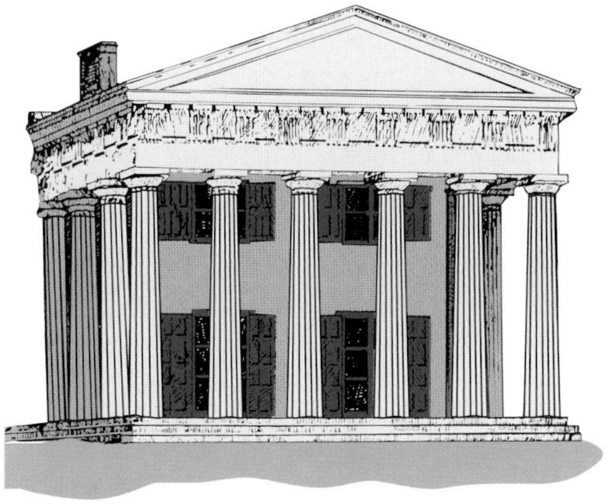

Greek Revival

24-7 These home styles have more decorative features than earlier housing styles.

Other features include three-story chimneys for bedroom fireplaces, a hip or gable roof, ornate woodwork, and wrought iron trim. A roof is often placed over the driveway to protect those entering at a side entrance.

Italianate

The Italianate style became popular in America in the 1830s. Borrowed from styles seen in Italian villas, the most outstanding feature of the style is a square tower at the top of the home, 24-8. The Italianate house has an upright appearance with tall, thin windows. A wide roof overhang with decorative brackets underneath is also typical. The city brownstone house was adapted from this style.

Victorian

After the Civil War, English influence returned to American architecture. The eclectic Victorian-style home, named for Queen Victoria, became prevalent, 24-8. This style is marked by an overabundance of decorative trim, high porches, steep gabled roofs, tall windows, and towers. Scrolls and other decorative trim, called *gingerbread*, surround eaves, windows, and doors. Many Victorian houses are still in use today.

Modern Designs

While modern-day housing borrows features and design elements from traditional styles, most of today's new housing is a variation of one of these basic styles: the ranch and the split-level designs. Both designs are conducive to today's lifestyle.

The Ranch House

The ranch style structure is a long, low, one-story building inspired by the ranchers' homes in the southwest, 24-9. The housing design was ideal for that region because of the informal lifestyle, open land areas, and warm climate. It has been successfully adapted to other climates as well.

Basic features of the ranch include a one-story design with no stairs, a low-pitched gable roof, and long, overhanging eaves. It is normally built on a concrete slab, but it may have a crawlspace or basement. The structure may be rectangular or in an irregular shape such as L, T, U, or H. Modern ranch homes have large areas of windows and sliding glass patio doors.

Variations of the ranch include the hillside ranch and the raised ranch. The **hillside ranch** is built on a hill so part of the basement is exposed. The

Southern Colonial

Italianate

Victorian

24-8 These home styles reflect the use of classical elements and unique blends.

Manufactured Housing Institute

24-9 The ranch home is on one level.

24-11 A split-level home can help maintain the natural setting of a sloping site.

exposed area may be used for a garage or a living area with a panoramic view. The **raised ranch**, also called the *split-entry ranch*, has part of the basement above ground, 24-10. This allows windows to be placed in basement walls.

The ranch style is ideal for indoor/outdoor living. The homes are comfortable and easily expanded. Outside maintenance tasks, such as painting, cleaning gutters, and replacing window screens, are not as difficult as with other home styles. However, ranch homes are more expensive to build per square foot of living space than two-story homes.

The Split-Level House

The split-level house is designed for a sloping or hilly site. The design takes advantage of what might otherwise prove to be a problem in elevation, 24-11.

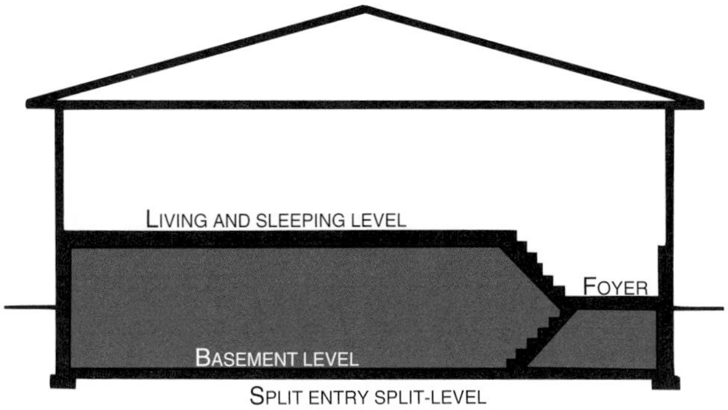

24-10 Part of the basement is above the ground in a split-entry or raised ranch.

Most split-level houses should not be built on flat lots, although some designs are occasionally used on flat land.

Efficient use of space is natural in the split-level design. The general arrangement places the sleeping, living, and recreation areas of the house on different levels. Very little hall space is needed with the split-level design.

The lowest level, called the basement level, generally serves as a basement, housing heating and cooling equipment, storage, and possibly a bath or work area. If a basement is not desired, a crawlspace area for maintenance and ventilation may be used. The basement level usually takes up 40 to 60 percent of the total space occupied by the house.

The second level of the house is the intermediate level. This area is at ground level, so the garage, recreation area, and foyer are usually placed here. The intermediate level may have a patio or terrace attached to it.

Slightly higher than the intermediate level is the living level. Due to the sloping site, this area is also at ground level. The kitchen, dining room, living room, and full- or half-bath are normally located on this level. The main entry and foyer may also be placed here, depending on the site and layout of the house. Patios, porches, and other outside living areas may also be an extension of this level.

At the highest elevation is the sleeping level, housing the bedrooms and bath. Because the sleeping level is separated from the living level, it is private and quiet. This area of a split-level house is similar to the second story of a two-story house.

There are three main variations of the split-level design: the side-to-side, the front-to-back, and the back-to-front, 24-12. Sites sloping from the left or right are best suited for the side-to-side design. Sites that are high in front and low in back are best for the front-to-back style. This house appears as a ranch from the front and as a two-story house from the back. A lot that is low in front and high in back requires a back-to-front design. In this style, the living area is at the rear of the house.

Split-level houses are natural solutions to building on hilly sites. They provide separation of functions within the house and require little hall space. However, they are frequently more expensive to build than two-story or ranch homes because of the complicated construction. Even heating may be difficult because of the different levels. The use of zoned heating, with separate thermostats for different areas of the house, can help maintain more even temperatures.

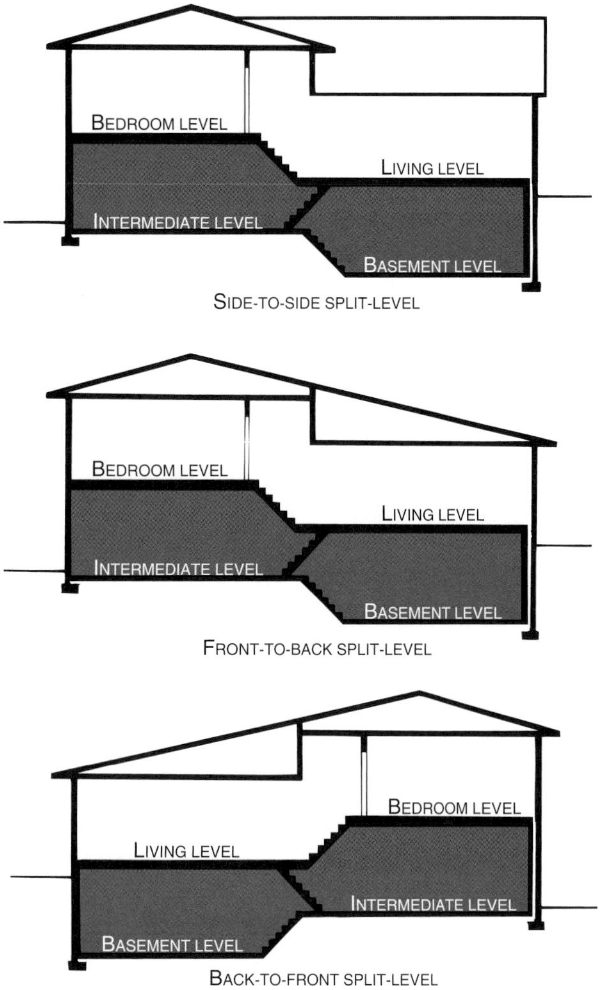

24-12 The three main types of split-level designs are side-to-side, front-to-back, and back-to-front.

Contemporary Designs

Contemporary designs are a departure from traditional housing styles and materials, 24-13. They are often experiments in solving modern housing challenges. Many need refinement because they are too individualistic or too narrowly conceived to be successful on a large scale. The trend is toward homes that complement the site and provide a feeling of openness while retaining privacy, 24-14. More attention is being focused on the natural

24-13 Nontraditional forms are used for contemporary designs.

24-14 Many contemporary homes are designed to harmonize with their surroundings.

elements—especially the natural resources used to construct and maintain a home and the natural forces impacting it.

Frank Lloyd Wright built some of the earliest contemporary homes. His homes, built around the 1940s, departed from traditional styles to fit the changes that were taking place in family lifestyles. Frank Lloyd Wright homes are designed to blend well with their natural surroundings. Often, trees and other natural features of a site are incorporated into the design. Building materials are usually wood or stone, but other materials that blend with the site may also be used. Wright homes are designed for efficiency, economy, and comfort.

Other contemporary homes are built with the effect of environmental conditions in mind. These include domes, solar homes, and underground structures.

Geodesic Domes

The **geodesic dome** is an engineered system of triangular frames that create self-reinforcing roof and wall units based on mathematically precise divisions of a sphere. The style was created by R. Buckminster Fuller. See 24-15. The triangular frames are generally factory assembled and then bolted together on site to form the finished structure. This design has been described as the most efficient system of structuring yet developed for housing.

Compared to conventional structures, the dome design reduces the quantity of building materials needed per square foot of usable area by about 30 percent. Heat loss is also reduced because of the home's reduced amount of exposed surface.

No interior or exterior support systems, such as walls or beams, are needed because a dome structure is self-supporting, 24-16. This feature provides great flexibility for interior floor plan designs. Other advantages include flexible interior decoration, structural superiority, low cost, and reduced energy needs. Manufactured domes are produced in one-story and two-story structures, with or without basements, 24-17. Conventional roofing materials such as asphalt shingles or cedar shakes are used to weatherproof the exterior.

Foam Domes

Another type of dome is built from polyurethane foam. The foam house not only uses new materials, but new concepts for building and design as well. A foam house can be built in weeks at about half the cost per sq. ft. of conventional homes. Foam homes are 40 to 60 percent more energy efficient than conventional homes.

Foam domes are built by spraying the walls of an inflated polyurethane balloon with polyurethane foam. After a few hours, the walls are dry and the balloon is peeled away, leaving a dome structure. A series of domes with the same or varying diameters may be built and joined to form a house.

Cathedralite Domes

24-15 The geodesic dome is constructed of several triangular wall pieces.

Hexadome of America, Inc., Nikkie Architecture

24-16 Because of the special construction of the geodesic dome, no support beams or support walls are needed.

A Linda Lindeman

B Monterey Domes

24-17 There is a wide variety of floor plans for Geodesic domes. For example, the first home (A) has a full basement, while the second home (B) has a double dome.

Trex Co.

24-18 Solar panels may be placed on solar or regular homes for active solar heating.

Solar Homes

Although both active and passive solar energy may be used to heat any kind of home, a true solar home has special design features for maximum energy efficiency. The homes may use an active solar heating system, 24-18, but passive solar heating is a predominant feature. The orientation and construction of the home are planned so weather conditions can be used to the home's advantage.

The most noticeable feature of a solar home is the large area of glass on the south side of the house, 24-19. Often greenhouses are placed on one or more sides. Insulating glass is used for window areas, and shutters are often installed to preserve indoor heat at night.

Many areas inside the solar home may be designed to collect and store heat for times when sunshine is not available, 24-20. Masonry floors and walls serve as collectors. Large barrels of water may also be used. Insulated earth beneath the home also stores heat.

Spaces for air infiltration are kept to a minimum in solar homes. A double-wall construction with an air space between the walls is used. This forms an envelope that acts as a natural heating and cooling system. Air between the walls is circulated throughout the house. Vestibules are placed in front of frequently used doors so outside air cannot enter when doors are opened. On the north side of the home, closets are located against exterior walls. Earth berms are usually placed along the sides of the home that receive the most wind.

Individual heating zones are planned so energy-powered heat is used only where it is necessary. Solar homes often have their own hot water system, heated by solar power. An active solar heater may be used for additional space- and water-heating.

The solar home design is most effective in areas that receive frequent sunshine. Proper orientation of the structure on the site must be possible as well. Data on the effectiveness of solar homes are available from the U.S. Department of Energy.

Larry Campbell

24-19 A passive solar home has large areas of glass on the south side of the home.

Rutt

24-20 Masonry floors are often used in solar homes to collect warmth from the sun.

Earth-Sheltered Homes

One of the newest contemporary designs is the earth-sheltered home, 24-21. Architects, builders, and designers know that earth, or soil, can provide a large thermal mass and act as an insulator. Earth can be used to shield structures from cold winter winds, noise, and undesirable views. Increased heating costs, improved and innovative building materials, new building technology, and the desire to find new solutions to old problems have sparked a new interest in this subject. The earth is now considered a major element in the basic design of housing.

Most earth-sheltered homes are built into the side of a hill so the south wall of the home is exposed. This wall generally has large areas of glass for solar heating. The tops of other walls are usually exposed enough to allow windows for natural lighting in most rooms, 24-22. The top of the home is covered with a layer of earth.

Several factors should be considered when designing and building an earth-sheltered home. They include site considerations such as orientation to sun and wind, soil type, and groundwater level. In addition, the load-bearing elements of the structure must be specifically designed to withstand tremendous earth pressure as well as heavy roof loads (approximately 100 to 120 lbs. per sq. ft. of roof for each foot of earth above).

Orientation on the Site

Proper orientation of the structure with respect to the sun and wind will provide energy savings as well as impact the quality of life inside the dwelling. Orientation to the sun is one of the most important considerations in the design of energy efficient dwellings. Radiant energy from the sun can help heat the interior space through active and/or passive heating.

Wind also is an important consideration for the orientation of an earth-sheltered dwelling. Heat loss increases dramatically when a building is exposed to cold winter winds. An orientation that minimizes the effect of wind will reduce heat loss. Earth sheltering provides a unique opportunity to shield the structure from winter winds and, at the same time, provide for ventilation in the summer.

Outdoor views may also be an orientation concern when planning for an earth-sheltered dwelling. Various basic designs allow for maximization of the view or just the opposite when the view is undesirable. As in planning any dwelling, the site should be selected first so the building design and site will complement each other.

Topography

Topography is the configuration of the land's surface with all its features, such as trees, streams, rocks, and manufactured structures. The design of

Terry Furst, Naturewood Homes and Domes

24-21 Earth-sheltered homes are usually built so the northern wall is in the side of a hill and the southern wall is exposed.

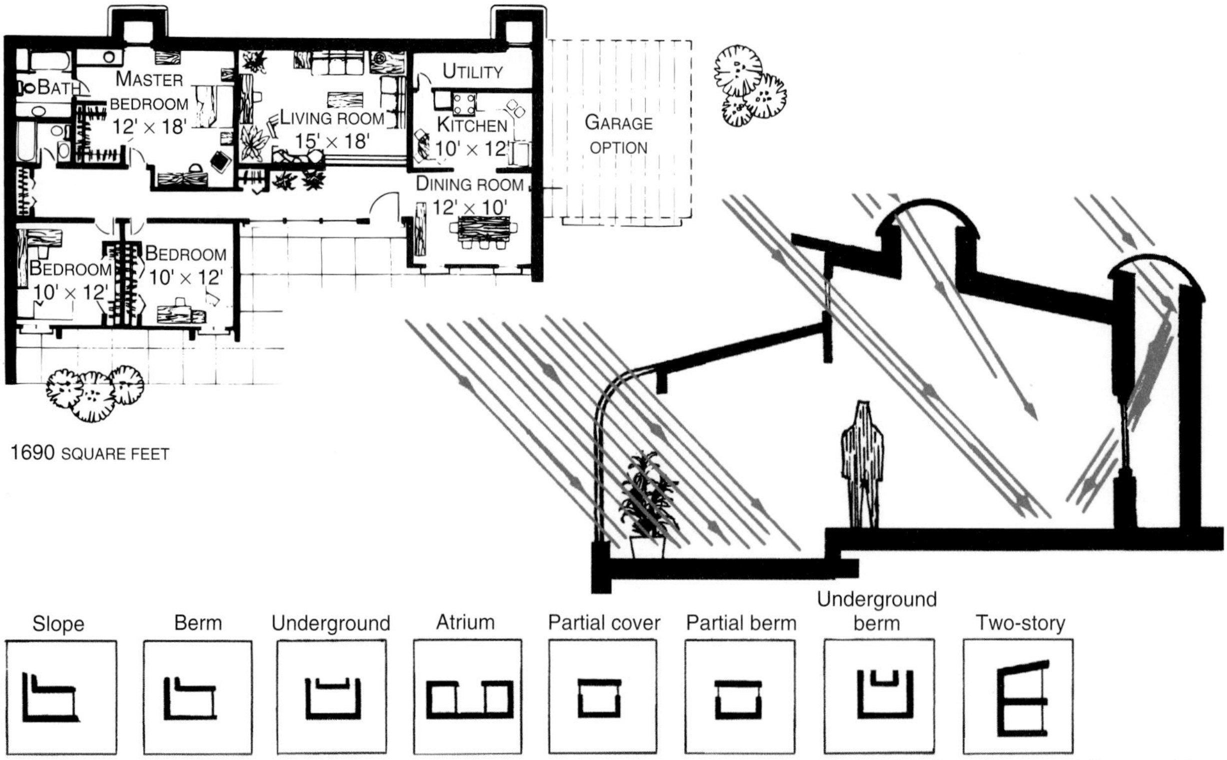

Terry Furst, Naturewood Homes and Domes

24-22 The interior of an earth-sheltered home can receive natural light through skylights or windows on an exposed upper portion of a wall.

an earth-sheltered dwelling may be affected in several ways by the site topography, 24-23. For example, wind patterns and temperature around the structure may be affected by changes in the terrain. Site contours also determine patterns of water runoff. However, the most important impact of topography on design is whether the site is sloped or flat. Sloping sites provide many more opportunities in design than flat sites for earth-sheltered structures.

Vegetation on the site is desirable for beautification as well as for reduction of erosion and noise. Deciduous trees provide shade in the summer and allow sun penetration in winter. Evergreens, when located properly, shield the building from winter winds.

Soil and Groundwater

Earth-sheltered structures usually require special evaluation of soils and groundwater conditions on the site. Some sites are not suitable choices for earth-sheltered dwellings because of the type of soil or groundwater conditions.

Two important soil characteristics to evaluate are its bearing capacity and tendency to expand when wet. An amateur should not attempt these calculations. The soil to avoid is expansive clay. It swells when wet and produces very high pressure that can cause damage to the structure. Groundwater around the structures causes extra loads on the building and adds waterproofing problems. Sites with a high water table or poor drainage are not good for an earth-sheltered dwelling. See 24-24.

Energy Conservation

Generally, the primary reason for building an earth-sheltered dwelling is the potential energy savings. Heat loss in a building is a function of the amount of surface through which heat can escape. Earth-sheltered dwellings are designed to have a smaller surface area exposed for heat loss. Earth placed against the walls and on the roof reduces that loss.

Structural Systems

The structural system is an important factor in any dwelling design. This is particularly true in an earth-sheltered home because of heavy roof loads. Two basic systems are used to support the load: conventional, flat-roof systems and somewhat unconventional systems with vault or dome shapes. Conventional roof systems use cast-in-place concrete slabs, concrete planks, and wood or steel post-and-beam systems.

Advantages of Earth-Sheltered Homes

Heating and cooling costs are greatly reduced. The site remains more natural, and there is more room for landscaping, gardening, and activities in the yard. Little exterior maintenance is required. The concrete structure is safer than traditional homes from fire, tornadoes, and burglars. Also, the interior of the home is quiet and private.

24-23 The topography of this site has been utilized in the placement and orientation of this earth-sheltered home.

24-24 This sloping site is ideal for an earth-sheltered home.

Chapter Summary

Over the years, many different exterior home styles developed and continue to influence residential housing designs today. Some early American homes were patterned after styles of the Native American Indian, such as the adobe. Spanish-style homes existed in the southern part of the continent from the late 1500s. The log-cabin style came to America with Swedish immigrants. Dutch Colonial homes were prevalent in New York and Delaware. Pennsylvania Dutch homes were the first German American homes built in Pennsylvania. The French influence was expressed through the French Normandy style, and later, the French plantation house and Louisiana French-style house.

English styles included the Tudor house as well as the Elizabethan manor that had both Gothic and Dutch influence. Another English-type house built in America was the Cotswold cottage. The earliest colonial houses were simple in design, sturdy, and fairly small. The half house was the most common, evolving into the saltbox style. The garrison style was borrowed from medieval English architecture. The Cape Cod, an outgrowth of the half-house, is one of the best-known examples of the traditional colonial styles. The Georgian-style house was more lavish.

The Federal style of architecture departed from English influence and represented an official American style. The Greek revival-style houses took on classic proportions and ornamentation of Greek architecture. Southern Colonials grew out of the Greek Revival style. The Italianate style became popular in America in the 1830s. After the Civil War, English influence once again returned in the form of Victorian architecture.

Modern designs are largely a variation of the ranch and split-level designs. The ranch style structure is a long, low one-story building inspired by the rancher's homes in the southwest. The split-level house, designed for a sloping site, offers three basic variations: side-to-side, front-to-back, and back-to-front designs.

Contemporary housing designs depart from traditional styles and materials. Most are experiments in solving modern housing challenges, such as geodesic domes, foam domes, solar houses, and earth-sheltered dwellings. Earth-sheltered dwellings have very specific site requirements and involve unique construction techniques to resist tremendous earth pressures.

Review Questions

1. What are some distinguishing architectural features of a Spanish-style home?
2. How does a Dutch house differ from a Pennsylvania Dutch house?
3. On what housing style did French doors originate?
4. What is the difference between the half-house, double house, and saltbox house?
5. What is the most outstanding feature of the garrison house?
6. What are the main architectural features of the Cape Cod home?
7. How does a Cape Ann home differ from a Cape Cod home?
8. What are the main features of the Georgian-style house?
9. How does the Georgian style compare to the Federal, Greek Revival, and Southern Colonial styles?
10. What is the most outstanding feature of the Italianate style?
11. What are the advantages and disadvantages of a ranch home?
12. What are the advantages and disadvantages of the split-level home?
13. How is a geodesic dome constructed?
14. What are the advantages of geodesic domes?
15. How is a foam dome constructed?
16. What are the major construction features of a solar home?
17. What are the advantages of an earth-sheltered structure?

Suggested Activities

1. Select and research one of the traditional home styles discussed in the text. Report how its design and building materials addressed the needs of the dwellers who popularized the style.
2. Investigate the oldest homes in your area and identify the basic housing style(s) they display. Identify the home features that led to your conclusion.
3. Tour a small area of your community to find out what percentage of homes are ranch, split-level, or multistory. In a report to the class, identify your tour route and your findings. If one style predominates, try to determine the reason(s).
4. Using popular magazines, search for pictures of contemporary residential designs. Prepare a poster that labels the various home styles.
5. Find out whether your area is conducive to building an earth-sheltered home. In an essay, explain why it is or is not.

Internet Resources

Alside, Inc., a manufacturer of low-maintenance siding
alside.com

Anchor Retaining Wall Systems
anchorwall.com

ATAS International, Inc., a manufacturer of metal roofing
atas.com

Builder Online, site of *BUILDER* and *BIG BUILDER Magazines*
builderonline.com

Cemplank, a manufacturer of fiber-cement building products
cemplank.com

HB&G, a manufacturer of columns and molding
hbgcolumns.com

Studer Residential Designs
studerdesigns.com

The Sater Design Collection, Inc.
saterdesign.com

Note: Web addresses may have changed since publication. For some entries, reaching the correct Web site may require keying *www.* into the address.

Chapter 25
Landscaping

Objectives

After studying this chapter, you will be able to

- describe physical factors outside the house that affect housing choices.
- list the main characteristics and functions of grass, ground covers, trees, shrubs, and vines.
- name and describe manufactured elements in a landscape and explain why they might be used.
- list the activities required to plan a landscape.
- evaluate the quality of a landscape according to the elements and principles of design.

Key Terms

indigenous
grasses
ground covers
trees
deciduous
ornamental
evergreens
broad conical
narrow conical
columnar
shrubs
vines

The purpose of landscaping is to create a personal, pleasant, and functional environment. It is more than merely selecting and arranging plants. A good landscape provides privacy, comfort, beauty, and ease of maintenance, 25-1. Elements such as paths, fences, walls, and architectural structures may be used in the landscape. Good landscaping requires thoughtful planning so the elements create a pleasant, usable environment.

Landscape Plants

Plants in the landscape are as important to the exterior design scheme as any piece of furniture or artwork is to interior design. Plants are decorative, but they have functional purposes as well. They provide protection from winds and reduce glare from the sun. They help to shield street noise and provide privacy. Plants act as natural air filters by absorbing pollutants and providing oxygen. They also provide a habitat for birds and animals.

A plant must be suited to the environment to grow well. Plants may be **indigenous**, or native to the area, or they may be imported. In planning a landscape, it is important to know the care requirements of plants chosen. Popular landscape plants may be

25-1 A good landscape is attractive, functional, and easy to maintain.

classified according to how they are used in a landscape. The main categories are grasses, ground covers, trees, shrubs, and vines.

Grasses

Both the leaves and stems of **grasses** grow from the bottom up. This makes them well suited to lawns because they can be cut repeatedly without dying. Although there are over 5,000 members of the grass family, only a few are suitable for lawns. Some types have been improved to resist disease and traffic, 25-2.

The most important factor in choosing a lawn grass is tolerance for a given climate. There are three main categories of grasses used in North America: warm-climate, cool-climate, and dryland grasses. See 25-3 for a list of the most popular varieties for each climate region.

25-2 This lawn grass, called St. Augustine carpet grass, is a warm-climate grass that grows well in full sun to heavy shade.

Ground Covers

Ground covers are defined as low, thick foliage used in place of grass. They vary in texture and color, 25-4. Some types are evergreen while others are deciduous. Many types grow where grass may not grow well, such as in dense shade, rocky patches, or gullies. Ground covers do not require much maintenance. They help to prevent erosion, control weeds, and reduce soil temperatures and loss of ground moisture during periods of extreme heat.

Ground covers are frequently used in shady areas or in spots where mowing would be difficult. This includes odd shaped or narrow spots and steep banks. Beneath evergreens, ground covers act as mulches. Ground covers can also be used as a foreground for a shrubbery border.

Ground covers should be chosen to fit the area where they will be used. Their height and spreading ability should be suitable for the location. Some types need full sun or full shade to survive; others will grow under any lighting conditions. Moisture and richness of soil are other factors to consider. Some of the most popular ground-cover plants and their important characteristics are identified in 25-5.

Lawn Grasses		
Warm-Climate Grasses		
Common Name	**Sun Conditions**	**Propagation**
Bermuda grass	Full sun	Sprigs or plugs
Carpet grass	Full sun to light shade	Plugs or seed
Centipede grass	Full sun to light shade	Sprigs or seed
St. Augustine grass	Full sun to heavy shade	Sprigs
Zoysia grass	Full sun to dense shade	Sprigs or plugs
Cool-Climate Grasses		
Kentucky bluegrass	Full sun	Seeds
Perennial rye grass	Full sun to partial shade	Seeds
Red fescue	Full sun to shade	Seeds
Redtop grass	Full sun to light shade	Seeds
Tall fescue	Full sun to shade	Seeds
Dryland Grasses		
Buffalo grass	Full sun	Plugs
Colonial bent grass	Full sun	Seeds

25-3 Various types of grasses are available to grow well in any environment.

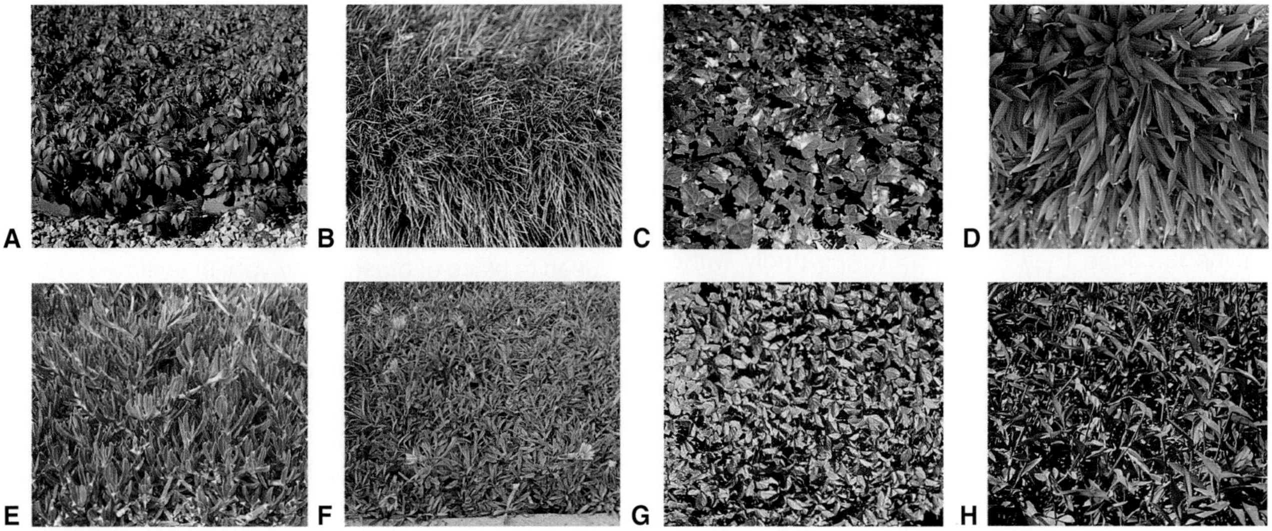

25-4 Ground covers are available in a variety of textures. Shown are some common ground covers: pachysandra (A), mondo grass (B), English ivy (C), creeping lily turf (D), hottentot fig (E), trailing gazinia (F), ajuga (G), and Moses-in-the-cradle (H).

Ground Cover Plants

Name	Lighting Requirements	Type and Use
Baby's tears	Shade	Perennial, base of trees
Bearberry	Sun to partial shade	Evergreen, banks
Blue leadwort	Shade	Perennial, under trees
Blue phlox	Partial shade	Perennial, under trees
Candytuft	Sun	Evergreen, banks and foreground
Carpet bugle	Sun to shade	Perennial, banks and borders
Crown vetch	Sun	Perennial, banks
Dichondra	Sun to shade	Perennial, between stones
English ivy	Shade	Evergreen vine, under trees
Forget-me-not	Partial shade	Perennial, moist areas
Ground morning glory	Sun	Perennial vine, slopes and beds
Lemon thyme	Sun	Perennial, among rocks
Lily-of-the-valley	Shade	Perennial, border
Pachysandra	Partial shade	Evergreen, under trees
Periwinkle or myrtle	Shade	Evergreen vine, under trees
Prostrate juniper	Sun	Evergreen, banks and edges
Rosea ice plant	Sun	Perennial, steep banks
Snow-in-summer	Sun to light shade	Perennial, edge of beds
Stone crops	Sun or partial shade	Perennial succulent, beds
Strawberry geranium	Shade	Evergreen, small areas
Sweet fern	Sun	Perennial, banks
Waukegan juniper	Sun	Evergreen, banks and edges

25-5 Many ground covers can be used in areas where grass does not grow well. They also add interest and texture to a landscape.

Trees

Trees are tall woody plants with single trunks. They fulfill several purposes such as providing beautiful form, foliage, or flowers. They may provide shade or shelter from the wind. Some trees provide fruit. Most trees give height to the appearance of the landscape.

As a landscape element, trees are used in several ways. For example, groups of trees may provide contrast to a large, open area. A dense grouping of trees may form a background for a home. Individual trees serve as focal points, 25-6.

Trees vary in their shape, form, and texture. They may be categorized into five main groups: native deciduous, flowering or ornamental, narrow-leaved evergreen, broad-leaved evergreen, and palm trees.

Native Deciduous Trees

These deciduous trees are species that grow naturally in a given area. **Deciduous** trees are plants that shed or lose their foliage at the end of the growing season. Native deciduous trees are some of the most suitable trees for the climate and soil conditions in their area. Some of the most popular types are shown in 25-7 along with their adult size and growing locations. Many deciduous trees have spectacular foliage in the fall, 25-8.

25-6 The tree in the center of the circular drive serves as a focal point for the front of this residence.

Ornamental Trees

An **ornamental** is a plant grown for its beauty. Ornamental trees have various outstanding characteristics that make them focal points in a landscape. They may have a special shape, leaf color, or blossom, 25-9. Flowering trees usually bear blossoms for several days or weeks each year.

Some ornamental trees are native while others are imported. Care should be taken to select a tree compatible with the climate and soil conditions of the landscape. Some popular flowering trees are listed in 25-10.

Narrow-Leaved Evergreen Trees

An **evergreen** is a plant with foliage that remains green all year. Narrow-leaved evergreens have needles rather than leaves. They furnish color

Native Deciduous Trees

Name	Height (ft.)	Spread (ft.)	Geographic Location
American elm	150	100	North central
Bald cypress	150	50	Maryland to Louisiana
Basswood	90	60	All except Gulf coast
Black walnut	100	75	Midwest
English maple	40	50	Northeast and Northwest
Hickory	100	75	Eastern half of the country
Honey locust	75	50	Most of the country
Northern red oak	75	50	All except Gulf coast
Sourwood	40	25	Northeast and Northwest
Sugar maple	125	75	Northern Midwest
Sweet gum	75	30	Southeast and West
Sycamore	100	75	All except Northeast

25-7 Each geographic location of the United States has native deciduous trees.

25-8 This deciduous maple tree brings flamboyant color to late summer and fall.

25-9 The flowering quince bears bright blossoms in early spring, making it a popular ornamental tree.

Ornamental Trees			
Name	**Height (ft.)**	**Spread (ft.)**	**Outstanding Characteristics**
Bloodleaf Japanese maple	15	15	Star-shaped red leaves
Crab apple	30	25	Bright blooms and colorful fruit
Crape myrtle	20	15	White, pink, red, lavender flowers
Eastern redbud	30	25	Pink-to-white flowers in spring
Flowering cherry	35	25	Profuse blooms in spring
Flowering dogwood	30	25	White or pink flowers
Hardy silk tree	35	35	Fluffy pink blossoms
Mountain ash	35	20	Clusters of red berries
Saucer magnolia	25	20	5 to 10 in. cup-shaped blooms
Star magnolia	20	15	3 to 4 in. white, fragrant blooms

25-10 An ornamental tree may have an attractive shape, leaf, or flower.

and mass all year long. Species include fir, hemlock, spruce, cedar, and pine. Northern climates have a broad variety of native narrow-leaved evergreens.

Although narrow-leaved evergreens are available in several heights, they usually have one of three main shapes, 25-11. The **broad conical** shape tapers gradually from a wide base to a single erect stem. This is the shape of the traditional Christmas tree. Broad conical trees are best displayed as individual plants, so they need plenty of space to develop.

Some evergreens have a **narrow conical** shape that tapers sharply from the base to the tip. They are compact and will fit into small areas. Narrow conical trees are usually placed in small groups.

Other evergreens have a **columnar** shape, meaning they have nearly vertical branches. They taper only slightly from the base to the top. These are useful for lining a drive or defining a boundary. Varieties of narrow-leaved evergreens are shown in 25-12.

A B C

25-11 The three main shapes of narrow-leaved evergreen trees are broad conical (A), narrow conical (B), and columnar (C).

Narrow-Leaved Evergreen Trees		
Name	**Basic Shape**	**Mature Height (ft.)**
Blue atlas cedar	Broad conical	60
Canada hemlock	Broad conical	50
Colorado spruce	Broad conical	40
Eastern white pine	Broad conical	60
Norfolk island pine	Broad conical	50
White fir	Broad conical	50
Carolina hemlock	Narrow conical	25
Douglas arborvitae	Narrow conical	30
Incense cedar	Narrow conical	50
California incense cedar	Columnar	50
Italian cypress	Columnar	50
Irish yew	Columnar	12
Yew podocarpus	Columnar	20

25-12 A wide variety of narrow-leaved evergreens are native to northern states.

Broad-Leaved Evergreen Trees

These trees have leaves that, at a distance, resemble those of deciduous trees. They grow in many shapes. Some are noted for their fragrant blossoms while others produce colorful berries, 25-13. Most broad-leaved evergreens are not hardy in colder climates. They are confined to warmer areas of the country.

A
B

25-13 Many types of broad-leaved evergreen trees may be used as accent plants in a landscape. Two examples are citrus (A) and sea grape (B).

These evergreens serve various purposes in the landscape. Some larger trees, like the southern magnolia, provide good shade and accent color when they blossom. Others, like the weeping bottlebrush, are pleasant along a driveway or property border. Citrus trees provide fruit. They are also used as accent or background plants. Popular broad-leaved evergreens are listed in 25-14.

Palms

Palms can be dramatic elements of a landscape, 25-15. They are generally found throughout

Broad-Leaved Evergreen Trees

Name	Mature Height (ft.)	Outstanding Characteristics
American holly	60	Bright red berries in the fall
Brazilian pepper tree	30	Fragrant berries
Camphor tree	50	Dense foliage
Citrus (orange, lemon, etc.)	25	Fragrant blossoms and edible fruit
Common olive	25	Silvery, green willowlike leaves
Eucalyptus	75	Fragrant leaves and attractive bark
Live oak	60	Great size and breadth
Southern magnolia	90	Fragrant blossoms up to 12 in. across
Sweet bay	50	Fragrant white blossoms
Weeping bottlebrush	25	Bright red blossoms in summer

25-14 Broad-leaved evergreens are native to southern states.

A

B

25-15 The blossom clusters of the queen palm (A) give the tree a unique appearance. The coconut palm (B) is more familiar in appearance.

Hawaii, most of California, parts of the Southwest, and in the Gulf Coast states including Florida. Most palms have a single trunk that is straight or slightly curved, but some grow in clumps. Leaf shapes vary from broad fans to feather-like fronds. Some popular palms are identified in 25-16.

Palms		
Name	**Height (ft.)**	**Outstanding Characteristics**
Butterfly palm	30	Many stems and fragrant flowers
Date palm	30	Grows in clumps
Lady palm	5	Reedy stems with broad leaves
Queen palm	40	Straight trunk with broad crown

25-16 Palms are generally found in southern coastal states.

A

B

25-17 Shrubs can be used as hedges (A and B) to provide privacy.

Shrubs

A **shrub** is a multistem, woody plant of relatively low height. Shrubs form the intermediate plantings between trees and grasses or ground covers. They are available in a wide range of shapes, types of foliage, and colors of blossoms and berries. They may be planted in hedges to function as a wall or fence, 25-17. Some are used as singular focal points, group plantings, or background plants. Few plant groups are as versatile as shrubs. Shrubs fall into three broad categories: deciduous, narrow-leaved evergreen, and broad-leaved evergreen.

Deciduous Shrubs

Like deciduous trees, deciduous shrubs lose their leaves in the winter. Some turn bright colors in the fall. Examples are the dwarf burning bush and the smoke bush. However, the main attraction of most deciduous shrubs is their spectacular spring and summer blossoms, 25-18. These include

A

B

25-18 The azalea (A) and the spreading cotoneaster (B) are examples of two flowering deciduous shrubs.

varieties such as the forsythia, rose of Sharon, flowering quince, and lilac. Popular deciduous shrubs are listed in 25-19.

Narrow-Leaved Evergreen Shrubs

These shrubs have needles instead of leaves. The three most common shapes are: upright, spreading, and creeping, 25-20. Upright evergreens have closely spaced stems that form a curved outline without pruning. Various types may reach heights from 3 to 10 ft. Spreading evergreens grow out as well as up, broadening at the top. Both upright and spreading shrubs are frequently used as foundation plants around a home.

Creeping evergreen shrubs spread horizontally. They are low to the ground and may be used as taller ground covers. They may also be grown individually as low bushes lining paths or in front of homes. Types of narrow-leaved evergreen shrubs are listed in 25-21.

Deciduous Shrubs

Name	Height (ft.)	Outstanding Characteristics
Azalea	10	Colorful blossoms
Bridalwreath spirea	5	Clusters of small flowers
Cranberry cotoneaster	3	Prostrate branches
Dwarf burning bush	3	Bright red leaves in fall
Flowering quince	5	Spectacular early blossoms
Forsythia	8	Bright yellow flowers in spring
Hydrangea	5	Large flower clusters
Lilac	15	Fragrant flower clusters
Privet	15	Hedge plant with bright green leaves
Rhododendron	4	Brilliant blossoms
Rose of Sharon	10	Flowers late in fall
Smokebush	15	Plumelike, redish purple blossoms
Tree peony	5	Large colorful flowers
Viburnum	8	Fragrant blossoms

25-19 Many deciduous shrubs flower or turn colors seasonally.

A B C

25-20 The three common forms of narrow-leaved shrubs are upright, spreading, and creeping. Shown here are the mugo pine (A), the spreading juniper (B), and the wilton carpet juniper (C).

Narrow-Leaved Evergreen Shrubs		
Name	**Basic Shape**	**Mature Height (ft.)**
Globe aborvitae	Upright	3
Japanese plum yew	Upright	8
Mugo pine	Upright	10
Sargent's weeping hemlock	Upright	15
Tanyosho pine	Upright	10
Chinese juniper	Spreading	4
Hick's yew	Spreading	16
Pfitzer juniper	Spreading	6
Salvin juniper	Spreading	6
Japanese garden juniper	Creeping	2
Wilton carpet juniper	Creeping	1

25-21 Several varieties of narrow-leaved evergreen shrubs are grown in the United States.

Broad-Leaved Evergreen Shrubs

These shrubs bear leaves, not needles, and do not lose their leaves seasonally. A wide variety of shrubs are in this group, 25-22. Some species are grown primarily for their flowers, such as the camellia, rhododendron, azalea, and Japanese andromeda. Others have brightly colored leaves, such as the gold dust tree, croton, and Chinese sacred bamboo.

Because broad-leaved evergreen shrubs are generally ornamental, they are usually planted individually or with ample spacing for visual impact. Several common broad-leaved evergreen shrubs are listed in 25-23.

Vines

Vines are plants having a flexible stem supported by climbing, twining, or creeping along a surface. They are decorative and functional in a landscape design, 25-24. Many vines have large clusters of flowers that attract attention. Others have leaves with interesting shapes. Vines can grow on a trellis and reduce the monotony of a large expanse of wall. They can dress up a plain fence or provide

25-22 A wide variety of shrubs are categorized as broad-leaved evergreens. Some examples are: camellia (A), croton (B), yellow-flowering hibiscus (C), pink-flowering hibiscus (D), flaming ixora (E), natal plum (F), and plumeria (G).

Broad-Leaved Evergreen Shrubs		
Name	**Height (ft.)**	**Outstanding Characteristics**
Camellia	10	Beautiful flowers
Chinese sacred bamboo	4	Colorful foliage
Croton	6	Great diversity in leaf shape and color
Elizabeth azalea	4	Abundant flowers
Everestianum catawba rododendron	6	Impressive floral display
Gardenia	5	Fragrant blossoms
Gold-dust tree	10	Green and yellow foliage
Hibiscus	6	Large colorful flowers
Ixora, flaming	6	Clusters of bright blossoms (red, white, pink, orange)
Japanese andromeda	5	Abundant flowers
Japanese fatsia	6	Glossy fan-shaped leaves
Japanese pittosporum	10	Leathery green leaves
Lemon bottlebrush	10	Many stamened red flowers
Loquat	15	Clusters of flowers and edible fruit
Mountain laurel	6	Large clusters of pink and white flowers
Natal plum	6	Shiny green leaves with fragrant white flowers
Oleander	12	Fragrant flowers
Sweet viburnum	8	Fragrant white blossoms

25-23 Broad-leaved evergreen shrubs are frequently used as focal points in a landscape.

A

B

C

25-24 Shown are three different types of vines: star jasmine (A), bougainvillea (B), and eleagnus(C).

shade in an arbor. Some vines used in landscaping are listed in 25-25.

Other Landscape Elements

Items other than plants are used to make a landscape more unified and functional. A good landscape plan is organized so several areas are

Vines		
Name	**Length (ft.)**	**Outstanding Characteristics**
Bougainvillea	15-25	Clusters of bright flowers
Carolina jasmine	25-30	Fragrant, tubelike yellow flowers
Chinese wisteria	to 40	Fragrant clusters of purple flowers
Clematis	6-15	Massive display of single or multicolored flowers
Climbing hydrangea	to 75	Spectacular white flowers
Honeysuckle	15-20	Fragrant flowers
Trumpet vine	25-30	Clusters of orange to red flowers

25-25 Several varieties of vines are available for landscaping.

provided for different functions. These spaces may be connected with garden paths, walks, and steps. Areas may be separated with banks, walls, and fences. Patios, decks, or paved game areas may be a part of the landscape. A decorative pool or fountain may serve as a focal point.

Paths, Walks, and Steps

A garden path can be an effective landscaping tool. Its obvious purpose is to connect one area with another to provide a walking area within a garden. However, it also provides a natural break in the landscape. If a path borders flower beds or a lawn, it adds interest to the design of the landscape, 25-26. Curved paths may be used to break the straight lines of a rectangular site.

A path should be at least 3 ft. wide to allow room for work tools. Informal materials, such as loose stone, wood chips, or laid flagstones separated by grass, are commonly used for paths, 25-27.

25-26 A path can act as a garden border and add interest to the landscape design.

25-27 Large, flat flagstone can be used to give a garden path an interesting pattern and texture.

Walks are more formal and permanent than paths, but they fulfill the same function. A walk should be at least 4½ ft. wide so two people can walk side by side comfortably. Materials used for walks include concrete, asphalt, masonry paving, or planks, 25-28. These materials are more expensive and more difficult to lay than materials used for paths. Masonry walks are the most expensive, followed in price by concrete and then asphalt. Walks made from wood vary in cost depending on the type of construction and wood used.

Steps are used in paths and walks when the elevation changes too rapidly to use an incline. They

25-28 Walks are more formal and permanent than paths; masonry is a common construction material for walks.

25-29 Steps are generally made of the same material as the walk or path. This walk is constructed from patterned concrete designed to simulate brick.

are usually constructed of the same material used for the path or walk, 25-29. The steps should be safe, with materials secured and lighting provided at night.

Texture, appearance, and maintenance are considerations when choosing materials for paths, walks, or steps. Rough textures produce an interesting, but less formal look than smooth textures. Rugged surfaces should be avoided, however, if small children will use the walk or path frequently for play. The appearance of materials—their patterns and colors—should blend with the rest of the landscape and the home's exterior design. Materials that will maintain their appearance over time should be chosen. Some materials may show wear or dirt more easily and thereby require more maintenance. Grass or weeds may grow between or through the materials and need removal.

Banks, Walls, and Fences

These elements separate areas of the landscape. Gently sloping banks form a natural separation between two levels. These are generally covered with lawn grass. Steeper banks are used for more pronounced changes in elevation. A ground cover, stones, wood beams, or retaining wall are used to maintain the bank and prevent erosion, 25-30. Plants may be used on the bank to add interest.

25-30 Plants covering steep banks add interest and help prevent erosion.

Walls are strong, permanent structures that serve as boundaries, enclose an area, and provide privacy. Low, wide walls can divide an area and provide seating. High walls are used for privacy. Walls may be solid or open. An example of an open wall is one made of pierced concrete block. Open walls, also called screens, allow a light breeze to pass through, but form a definite boundary.

Landscape walls can be built from a variety of materials. Concrete, masonry, and wood are common. See 25-31. Solid masonry and concrete walls are rigid and require a foundation. Wood walls are supported on posts so no foundation is needed. In some areas, movement associated with freezing and thawing of the ground can destroy rigid walls. Durable walls that are also considered "flexible" are built from cross-ties, pieces of broken concrete, or large, flat stones.

Appearance, durability, and cost are factors to consider when choosing wall materials. Materials should blend well with other elements of the site and be durable. Concrete and masonry are very durable materials, and pressure treated wood lasts many years. Any material chosen should be able to withstand local conditions. Cost should also be considered when choosing materials. Walls with poured foundations are more expensive to build than other types of walls.

Fences are generally less formal, less expensive, and less permanent than walls. Like walls, they may be used to define boundaries, provide protection and privacy, and block sun and wind. Fences help to contain children or pets within a yard. In many communities, fences are required around swimming pools to protect children and nonswimmers. The design of a fence may be limited depending on its function. Fences used simply for definition of boundaries may be very decorative. Fences for safety are generally less decorative, but variation is possible, 25-32.

25-31 Broken concrete (A) and native stone (B) are common materials for walls.

25-32 Stone (A), wood (B), and other interesting materials may be used for functional fences.

Patios, Decks, and Game Areas

Patios and decks are often used for relaxation or entertainment areas. Patios are usually constructed of concrete or masonry, 25-33. They are level with the ground, while decks are placed above ground. Decks are usually constructed of pressure treated wood, 25-34. A deck is useful on hilly areas to provide an even surface.

Patios and decks should be large enough for comfortable spacing of patio furniture. If a patio or deck area will be used frequently for entertaining, it should be large enough for guests to move freely.

Depending on the size of a landscape, a permanent area for games may be desired. A spacious, level lawn with no trees or plants provides an informal game area.

A dirt or sand area may suffice for such games as volleyball or horseshoes. Formal courts for tennis, basketball, or other sports are usually built of concrete or asphalt. When planning a game area, clearance space around the court should be included to prevent injuries or interference with the game. Suggested footage to allow for various games are listed in 25-35.

California Redwood Association

25-34 Decks are often used on hilly sites to provide a level area for patio furniture.

25-33 A patio is generally made of masonry set into the ground.

Pools and Fountains

Sparkling water has an almost universal appeal as do pools and fountains. They may be designed as a central feature of a garden or as a singular focal point. Pools may be used for swimming, but even these can be creatively designed, 25-36. A pool or fountain can also house fish and water-loving plants, 25-37. A fountain may be part of a pool, or it may be freestanding. Fountains require a power source to pump the circulating water.

The size, shape, and construction of an ornamental pool or fountain should be consistent with the climate and landscape design. Large, formal pools are not recommended for small, informal settings. Cost depends on the size of the pool and the type of construction used. The most expensive pools have poured concrete bases. However, an attractive, less-expensive pool can be built using a plastic liner held down with wood beams or stones.

Recommended Space for Game Areas

Game	Total Court and Clearance Areas (ft.)
Badminton	44 by 20
Basketball (half court)	37 by 42
Croquet	38 by 85
Horseshoes	50 by 10
Shuffleboard	52 by 6
Tennis	108 by 48
Tetherball	20 ft. circle
Volleyball	60 by 30

25-35 A space large enough for a game court should have ample clearance room.

California Redwood Association

25-36 The pool is the central feature in this outdoor living area.

A

B

25-37 Many ponds and ornamental pools (A) contain water-loving plants such as water lilies (B).

Planning the Landscape

A good landscape is carefully planned. The best method is to consider a lot's landscape possibilities before the house is sited. Planning should begin with an evaluation of the lot.

First, the weak and strong points of the yard should be considered. A rough plan of the present yard can be used. Every yard has some good features that can be kept. These should be marked, and features to be removed should be crossed out.

Next, the impact of the elements should be determined. Direction of prevailing winds, spots where water collects after rains, dry areas, soil quality, exposure to sun, and other conditions should be noted on the landscape plan. Any city zoning restrictions should be noted as well. This information is vital when planning the arrangement of a landscape. It will help in deciding what kinds of plants will do best in an area. It will also help to determine where an element might be needed for providing shade or blocking wind. If an area has very poor growing conditions, it might be more suited for a manufactured element, such as a pool or path.

When evaluating the lot, the view from the house and location of doors should also be considered. The view from a picture window or a sliding glass door should be attractive. Some people place a small, private garden outside a back door. One option is to add an exterior door to a bedroom for direct access to a private garden or patio.

After the present yard is evaluated, planning of the new landscape can begin. There are three main zones to consider in planning: the public, private, and service zone. The front yard is generally considered the public zone. It is usually designed for beauty and not activities. The service zone is usually at the side of the home connected to the service entrance. Its view should be screened from the public and private areas. The backyard is considered the private zone. It may contain both aesthetic and functional areas.

The private zone is usually divided into areas for different purposes. Areas may include a garden, pool, patio or entertaining area, and game area. How much space is devoted to each area will depend on lifestyle and preferences. Space allowed for each area should provide room for needed equipment, such as patio furniture or garden tools, and room for comfortable use of the area.

Once the areas are determined, placement of the landscape elements can begin. Keeping in mind the conditions already evaluated, areas for plants, patios, and other elements can be drawn on the plan, 25-38. Specific types of plants and materials can be chosen later.

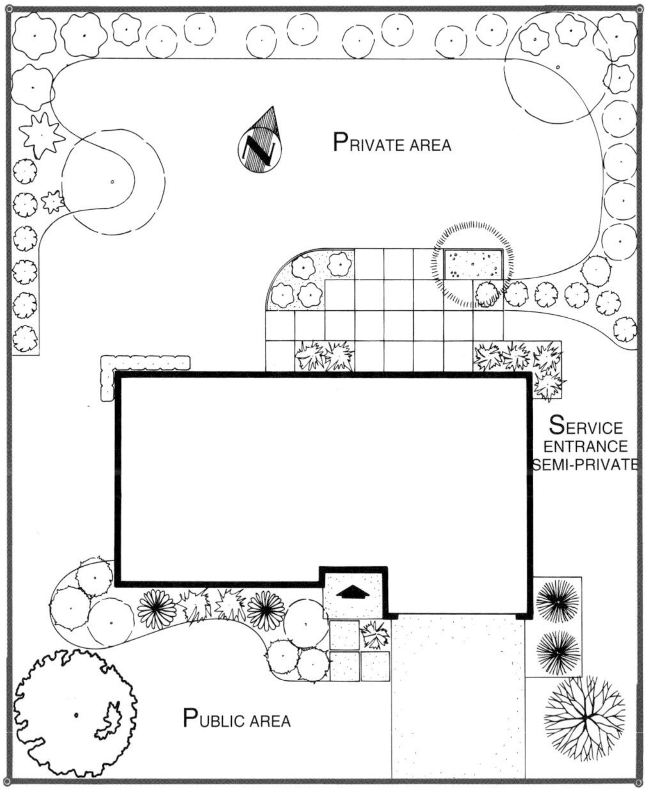

25-38 Landscape elements can be drawn into a plan after evaluation of the site.

Landscape elements may be placed to screen unpleasant views and provide privacy from neighbors. Trees or a special element may be desired in an open lawn area, but it is best to leave a wide expanse of lawn area open, 25-39. Scattering elements throughout the lawn area reduces the apparent size of the lawn and makes maintenance more difficult.

Once the rough plan is finished, actual choice and placement of plants and materials can begin. Shorter plants should be placed in front of taller plants for good visibility. A landscape will be more interesting all year long if plants are chosen to take advantage of seasonal color variations in their leaves and blossoms. Evergreens keep a fall or winter landscape from looking lifeless, 25-40.

Landscape Design

Design principles are as important to the landscape as they are to any interior room. However, the shapes, functions, and boundaries of a landscape are different from those of an interior. Therefore, application of the principles and elements of design to the landscape deserve special consideration.

Space

Space in the residential landscape can be thought of as one or more outdoor rooms, each with a particular purpose. Care should be taken in the design process to choose plants and other landscape elements that help define space. Smaller divisions within the total space are defined through the use of hedges, groupings of plants, walks, fences, or natural site features. See 25-41. Very large groupings should generally not be planned for small spaces, nor very small arrangements used in large spaces.

25-39 A yard appears more spacious and is easier to maintain if most elements are placed around the edges of the site.

Shouldice

25-40 A landscape with only deciduous plants appears barren in late fall and winter months. The addition of evergreens helps to enliven the landscape after other plants are bare.

Line

Line is used to create patterns in the landscape. Lines formed by plants or other elements direct the viewer's attention to a focal point. Straight lines, such as lot boundaries, fences, and patios, suggest uninterrupted movement. Curved lines are considered more pleasing and interesting than straight lines, 25-42. Some groups of plants should be planted in a curved or irregular pattern to avoid too many straight lines. If a landscape is well planned, the lines of the design will convey an overall theme.

Shape

Shape, although not a primary concern in a three-dimensional landscape, does apply to landscape elements such as paved areas and pool surfaces, 25-43. Shape also applies to formal plantings in geometric patterns—circles, squares, and rectangles—frequently used to define areas compatible with the overall landscape design. Irregular geometric shapes may be used to create interest in the design. However, they should not be used extensively because they tend to destroy the unity of the plan.

25-41 The drive leading up to this contemporary home divides the lawn space into two separate areas.

Form

The forms chosen for landscape elements may be aesthetic or functional. A widespreading tree can provide a shady area. Paths and walks lead from one area to another. The forms of plants can convey a vertical or horizontal appearance. Tall, thin plants give a feeling of height, while low, spreading plants have horizontal forms. Natural plant forms are less structured than the boxy, manufactured forms of the interior, 25-44. They give the landscape a refreshing appearance.

25-42 A curved path can add interest and break the monotony of a landscape with too many straight lines.

Texture

All landscape materials have texture. Lawn grass is finely textured, but ground covers have more depth. Some trees have smooth, shiny leaves and trunks, while others are coarse and rough. A garden path of pea gravel has a fine texture compared to a coarse wall of large, natural stone. A variety of texture in the landscape adds interest and reduces monotony, 25-45.

Color

Green is the prevailing color of the landscape where plants predominate. It is refreshing, and a variety of shades and hues can be combined for interest. Adding other colors creates variety and surprise in the landscape, 25-46. They may be used in one or two areas to create a focal point, but colors should not clash with or overpower the natural landscape.

25-43 The shape of this pool surface provides interest and is an integral part of the overall landscape design.

25-44 The natural forms of plants are limitless and unlike the boxy forms commonly used in interiors.

25-45 A variety of textures adds interest to a landscape.

25-46 Used effectively, colors other than green can become the focal point of a landscape.

Proportion

Good proportion is sometimes difficult to achieve in a landscape because there are no walls or ceilings to set boundaries as there are in a room. Exterior boundaries are much larger. The sky offers an unlimited space and adjacent lots act as visual extensions of the yard's boundaries. This larger frame of reference requires elements of larger proportions.

Generous spacing is necessary so objects do not seem cramped. Objects close together should be proportional to each other. A 5:3 ratio is considered pleasing to the eye. When considering the proportions of landscape elements, plan for the full-grown size of plants. Often, young trees or shrubs are planted too close together, then overpower a space when they mature. Ground covers or flowers can help fill space until larger plants are full grown.

Scale

In a properly designed landscape, the scale should harmonize with the size of the space people need for their activities. In a large-scale space, the point of emphasis may be a spectacular deck or a large mass of plants. In a small-scale design, greater detail in individual plants or landscape features can be observed at close range, 25-47. Plants that are too large for the space appear overpowering. Groupings of plants should be in proper scale with one another to provide unity in design.

Photo Courtesy of James Hardie® Siding Products

25-47 The scale of plantings around this home complements the size of the home and the space provided for plantings.

Balance

The architectural style of a home will often determine whether formal or informal balance is most appropriate, 25-48. For instance, the front yard of a formal Georgian manor would look best with a symmetrical arrangement of shrubbery and a central walk lined by trees. For a small, rambling cottage, however, an informal arrangement of evergreens and flowering shrubs are more suitable.

Emphasis

A good landscape plan has at least one focal point. A unique plant or structural feature may be the object of emphasis. The area surrounding a focal point should not detract from the object. For instance, a brightly colored shrub would not be placed next to an ornamental flowering tree. Such an arrangement would prevent either object from attracting full attention.

25-48 The off-center main entrance of this home is complemented by the informal balance of the landscape plants.

Rhythm

Rhythm or repetition reduces confusion within a landscape. It introduces a feeling of order into the design. Rhythm can be achieved by using a similar grouping of plants throughout the landscape.

Although rhythm helps to create a sense of unity, too much rhythm can be monotonous. For example, a composition that contains only pines—even of many varieties—can be monotonous if texture, shape, and color are uniform. Variety creates interest, and achieving a balance between variety and repetition is most pleasing, 25-49.

25-49 A balance of rhythm and variety is important in a landscape.

Chapter Summary

The purpose of landscaping is to create a personal, pleasant, and functional environment. A good landscape that provides privacy, comfort, beauty, and ease of maintenance requires thoughtful planning.

Plants in the landscape have both functional and decorative functions. Various grasses and ground covers serve to form the landscape's floor.

Trees provide beautiful form, foliage, or flowers and also give shade and/or shelter from the wind. Some provide fruit. Native deciduous trees require the least amount of maintenance. Ornamental trees serve as focal points in a landscape, while narrow-leaved evergreen trees provide color and mass all year long. Broad-leaved evergreen trees are not cold-hardy and tend to be tropical as a group. Palms are mostly tropical and generally have a single trunk, but some grow in clumps.

Shrubs are the intermediate plantings between trees and grasses or ground covers. They are available as deciduous shrubs, narrow-leaved evergreen shrubs, and broad-leaved evergreen shrubs. They contribute a wide range of shapes, types of foliage, and colors of blossoms and berries.

Vines are decorative and functional in the landscape. Many vines are selected for their large clusters of flowers while others have interesting shaped leaves.

Manufactured landscape elements provide variety and make the landscape more unified and functional. Paths, walks, and steps connect different areas within the landscape, while banks, walls, and fences separate them, sometimes to provide privacy. Paved areas such as patios, decks, and game areas are generally used for relaxation or entertainment. The sparkling water of pools and fountains provides almost universal appeal. Texture, appearance, and maintenance are important considerations when choosing materials for these landscape elements.

A good landscape is carefully planned—for best results, before the structure is sited. Weak and strong points of the site and the impact of various elements must be considered. The three main zones in the landscape—public, private, and service—must be determined before landscape elements can be placed for greatest impact and function. The basic design principles of space, line, shape, form, texture, color, proportion, scale, balance, emphasis, and rhythm help achieve landscaping-design goals.

Review Questions

1. What functions can plants serve within a landscape?
2. What is the difference between a grass and ground cover?
3. What are the five main types of trees and their identifying features?
4. How can shrubs be used within a landscape?
5. What is the difference between a walk and a path?
6. What kinds of materials can be used for walks and paths?
7. How are walls and fences used within a landscape?
8. How does the function of a wall or fence affect the type of material used?
9. Before planning a landscape, what should be known about the property?
10. How can a landscape be planned for an attractive appearance all year long?
11. How do the elements of space, line, shape, form, texture, and color apply to the landscape?
12. What is the ideal proportion to use for positioning objects that are close together in a landscape?
13. Why would a landscape consisting only of shrubs be considered a poor design?

Suggested Activities

1. Write an essay describing the purpose and value of landscaping for a home.
2. Research one tree native to your area. Report your findings regarding its growing habits and general appearance.
3. Using local sources, identify several plants in each of the following categories that grow in your area: grasses, ground covers, native deciduous trees, ornamental trees, narrow-leaved evergreens, and broad-leaved evergreens.
4. Discuss the function and design of paths, walks, and steps as they relate to the three zones in a residential landscape.
5. Imagine that a distant corner of the school's property were being converted to a home site with a dwelling similar to that found in the community. Develop a plan for a good landscape design.
6. Select a landscape design in your neighborhood and evaluate it according to the elements and principles of design presented in the text.

Internet Resources

American Society of Landscape Architects
asla.org

Asphalt Institute
asphaltinstitute.org

Better Homes and Gardens Magazine
bhg.com

California Redwood Association
calredwood.org

Cast Stone Institute
caststone.org

House and Garden Magazine
http://houseandgarden.com

Landscape Architecture Magazine
asla.org/nonmembers/lam.cfm

Note: Web addresses may have changed since publication. For some entries, reaching the correct Web site may require keying *www.* into the address.

Chapter 26
Remodeling, Renovation, and Preservation

Objectives

After studying this chapter, you will be able to

- list the reasons that people remodel and the factors they should consider before beginning a remodeling project.
- compare the five main types of remodeling according to cost, complexity, and time required.
- evaluate the remodeling needs of a family and select an appropriate type of remodeling.
- explain renovation.
- identify three types of historical preservation.
- explain the role of the family, interior designer, architect, and contractor in remodeling, renovation, or preservation projects.

Key Terms

remodeling
moisture barrier
dehumidifying system
attic
addition
renovation
historical preservation
restoration
adaptive reuse

Making structural changes to a home transforms the living space. The changes can be a wise investment that will increase the value of a home. Changing the dwelling can provide a larger or more comfortable home for the family. It may be a way to update part or all of a home's appearance. On the other hand, the changes may be undertaken to return the home to its original condition.

No matter what type of structural changes are planned, all family members can be involved. Family members may plan and gather information on their own or they may consult architects, contractors, and interior designers. The decisions made will affect the family for many years, so they should be made carefully.

Choosing to Remodel

Remodeling is changing an existing space into a new form. The least complex type of remodeling involves changing a space that is already part of the dwelling. Perhaps the family wants to change a room that is already used or convert unused space so it can be used as a living area. Adding more livable space to a dwelling generally requires more complex changes.

A family may decide to remodel for several reasons. As a family grows, its needs and living patterns may change.

- New family members may need their own bedrooms.
- Entertaining may become more common, requiring more adequate kitchen and living space, 26-1.
- Increases in income may spur the desire for updated styles and appliances.
- As the work schedules of family members become busier, a more efficient home may be needed.
- Older homes may need newer equipment or better insulation to keep up with higher fuel prices, 26-2.

26-1 As families grow and change, their housing needs change. This remodeled kitchen is up-to-date and efficient, making activities quicker and more pleasant.

Norandex/Reynolds Building Products

26-2 This older house is a prime candidate for remodeling to improve the heating/cooling, plumbing, and electrical systems.

When the housing cannot meet family needs, it is time to explore alternatives. Perhaps some families will move, but this is not a desirable alternative for all. Families may have close ties with neighbors, schools, and community organizations. The home may hold sentimental attachment. If much time and money has been spent on landscaping, moving may not be worthwhile, 26-3. The high cost of building or buying a new home may make remodeling a more practical alternative.

A desire or need for change is only one factor to consider when deciding whether or not to remodel. Other factors may affect the type of remodeling chosen, or they may persuade a family not to remodel at all. For instance, if a family plans to move within a year or two, remodeling is probably not a worthwhile investment. Some homeowners remodel, anticipating the desires of prospective homebuyers. Although remodeling can increase property value, most homebuyers prefer to make their own changes to a home. This makes remodeling a waste of time and money for the homeowner.

Local building ordinances and property taxes are also considerations when making remodeling choices. Remodeling may require several building permits, and many changes must comply with local codes. If remodeling increases the value of a home, it may also increase the cost of property taxes on the home. Usually, adding room additions and remodeling the exterior are more likely to require building permits and increase taxes. Remodeling of unused spaces within the home may be a better choice if complying with building ordinances or paying higher taxes is a problem.

The costs, time, and effort required to remodel must also be considered before starting a project. All three factors are affected by the size and complexity of the remodeling project. An accurate estimate of all costs of remodeling, including all building materials, utility additions, and labor, should be obtained before starting any remodeling project. Larger projects can be very expensive and may require financing. Costs can be spread over months or even years by remodeling a little at a time. Stretching the inconvenience of a remodeling project over a long period, however, might not be desirable for all families.

A remodeling project can vary in cost depending on the amount of time and effort spent by family members. If all work is contracted to professionals, the job will finish quickly with little effort from family members. However, contracted work is usually expensive, and good communication and supervision by a family member is needed to assure that work is done as desired.

At the other extreme, family members may do all the remodeling work. This method can save a great deal of money in labor costs. The finished work may also be more personalized than would have been possible with some contractors. However, the project will probably require much

California Redwood Association

26-3 Remodeling may be preferable to moving if much time and effort has been spent on landscaping the present lot.

more time, and unless the homeowner is very familiar with the type of work involved, serious remodeling errors may occur.

Many families choose to do some remodeling on their own and contract professionals for the most difficult jobs, 26-4. For instance, paneling and painting may be done by family members, while complex wiring changes are handled by an electrician. Splitting the work between family members and professionals can achieve good results at a low cost. It also assures safe construction and eliminates frustration with jobs that are too difficult for the amateur.

Remodeling is not just an option used by homeowners who do not want to move. It also offers choices to homebuyers who cannot afford custom-built housing. Many buy less expensive tract housing and remodel to meet their own needs. Others use remodeling to return old homes to their former glory.

26-4 Professional subcontractors may be hired to do complex jobs like building walls or a roof structure.

Types of Remodeling

Remodeling projects can be categorized into the following five main types:

- changing lived-in areas
- making unused space livable
- adding on
- buying to remodel
- preserving a historic home

Each category varies in the level of change and the complexity, cost, and time required for remodeling. Many remodeling projects may include more than one type of remodeling. Each type of remodeling should be considered so family needs can be met in the simplest, most satisfactory way.

Changing Lived-In Areas

Used or "lived-in" rooms are generally remodeled to update equipment, improve traffic patterns, or give the room a new appearance, 26-5. Kitchens are most commonly changed, and they are generally the most expensive room to remodel. Bathrooms, bedrooms, and other rooms may be changed as well.

Remodeling a lived-in room usually does not require major changes, such as tearing down a bearing wall or rewiring. Occasionally, a window or door may be enlarged or moved. Kitchen or bathroom remodeling may require relocation of some plumbing and wiring receptacles. However, changes are usually less complex than the changes required in other types of remodeling.

26-5 The screen porch has been enclosed and a ceramic tile floor added to provide a comfortable eating area.

Kitchens

Kitchens are usually remodeled when the homeowner wants to update or add appliances. While updating appliances, the homeowner may also want to improve the use of space, traffic patterns, availability of storage, and the efficiency of the work triangle. Information on kitchen planning in Chapter 5 can help in evaluating the present kitchen and planning the new one.

Many changes can be made to increase the efficiency of a kitchen. The circulation path can be improved by moving doors so traffic patterns do not interfere with the work triangle. An appliance may be moved to make a more efficient work triangle. General and local lighting may be enhanced. Counter space may be added to make room for preparing food or storing and using countertop appliances. Many new appliances can be mounted under wall cabinets to allow easy access and uncluttered counter space. Storage space may be added or improved for greater efficiency. For instance, a corner cabinet having space that is difficult to reach may be replaced with a lazy Susan. Pullout storage may also be used to improve access to items in cabinets.

If several new appliances are added or major appliances are moved, rewiring will be necessary. Additional circuits may also be needed. Changes in plumbing lines will be needed if the sink is moved, if a refrigerator with an automatic ice maker is added, or if a built-in dishwasher is moved or added. New ventilation must be installed when the range is moved or a gas grill is added.

Bathrooms

Like kitchens, bathrooms are often remodeled to update old fixtures. They can be costly to remodel if changes in plumbing lines are needed. Lines must be checked to make sure they are the correct size for new plumbing installations. Locating new fixtures in the same positions as old ones can reduce remodeling costs.

Other common bathroom improvements include moving a wall to enlarge the room, adding storage space, or installing a skylight for natural lighting and ventilation. Ceramic tile or other types of new floor and wall treatments may be added for easier maintenance.

Other Rooms

Relatively minor remodeling projects can dramatically change the appearance of rooms that do not house major appliances—bedrooms, living rooms, dining rooms, and others. Usually floor, wall, and ceiling treatments are updated, 26-6. New lighting fixtures may also be added. Partial walls or built-in storage may be added, too. Often these projects are simple enough for family members to do on their own.

More complicated changes may include moving or widening a doorway to improve circulation. Windows may also be added or enlarged to improve the view and increase ventilation. A wall may be removed so two small rooms are made into one. These changes are more complicated and should be done by someone with experience. The changes may affect the structural support of the house, and wiring and insulation may need to be altered.

Making Unused Space Livable

Many homes have areas that are not used as living space. These areas include garages, porches, attics, and basements. They have sound roofs, walls, and floors, but substantial changes are needed to make the areas suitable for living. It may be less expensive to remodel these areas than to add more space to a home. Also, remodeling unused space is often quicker and more convenient than adding new living space.

26-6 New carpeting, paint, and window treatments have been added to this remodeled bedroom.

Garages and Porches

Garages and porches are often converted into bedrooms, baths, dining rooms, family rooms, sunrooms, or studies, 26-7. These areas are remodeled because they are conveniently located in relation to other rooms in the house. For instance, a porch adjoining a kitchen would make a convenient breakfast room.

The foundations under these areas must be checked to make sure they are deep enough to comply with local building codes. Foundation requirements for garages and porches may be

A

B

26-7 This is a garage before remodeling (A) and the successful conversion of that garage to a library/solarium (B).

different than for living areas. A **moisture barrier** should be placed between the foundation and flooring materials. This is a membrane that retards the flow of moisture vapor and reduces condensation. Insulation should be added to meet the R-value recommended for living spaces. Additional wiring for lighting and outlets is usually needed.

Windows and doors are often changed or added when remodeling garages and porches. Insulated glass windows or storm windows may replace the original windows, 26-8. The garage door may be replaced with a sliding glass door or with a window. Doors that adjoin a garage or porch to the house may be changed for more logical access. Sliding glass doors, panel doors, or open doorways may be used to connect the area to the home.

Some type of heating supply is needed in remodeled porches and garages. If the room is open to an original room in the house, heating from the original room may be enough for both areas. However, if the room is separate, it will need its own heat supply. Heating ducts and vents may be extended into the room from the home heating system. A fireplace, stove, electric heating unit, or small furnace may also be used to heat the room. To insure proper heating, cooling, and ventilation of the remodeled area, it is wise to consult a heating/cooling professional for this aspect of the project.

Unfinished Basements

Unfinished basements are often remodeled for use as family rooms, recreation areas, hobby areas, and workshops, 26-9. Bedrooms may also be placed in basements if sufficient lighting and an outside entrance are provided. Bathrooms and a small kitchen area may be desired if the basement will be used for entertaining.

Basement areas are often damp, so vapor barriers and a dehumidifying system should be added for comfort. A **dehumidifying system** removes moisture vapor from the air to reduce the relative humidity in the space. If flooding or seepage is common, a sump pump should be added. Also, any leaks in the walls or floors should be repaired before installing wall and floor materials. If the foundation is sound, flooring materials can be applied directly to the surface. Paneling and drywall should be applied to furring strips to allow space for wiring and insulation.

Basements can be gloomy without sufficient natural and artificial light. Window wells and windows may be enlarged to increase natural light. Illuminated ceilings and recessed lighting are popular for basements. Additional wiring for light fixtures and outlets will be needed.

Additional plumbing lines are necessary if a bath or kitchen area is added to the basement. New

Pozzi Wood Windows

26-8 This remodeled deck has new decking and new-style patio doors.

Georgia Pacific Corporation

26-9 Dreary basements are often converted into usable family rooms.

fixtures should be placed as close as possible to existing plumbing lines to reduce cost.

Stairways and entrances may be moved or added when remodeling a basement to use space more efficiently. The original stairway may interfere with the desired floor plan for the basement. Original basement entrances are usually in a service area. If the remodeled basement is a living area, an entrance from an upstairs living area may be desired. A second stairway may be added for this purpose, 26-10. Once a basement is converted into a living area, a direct exit to the outdoors may be required. Check local fire protection codes and laws to be sure the remodeling project meets regulations.

Attics

An **attic** is the space between the ceiling and roof of a structure. In some house styles such as a Cape Cod, the attic is frequently converted to a bedroom, hobby room, or conversation area, 26-11. If a bedroom is placed in this area, a bathroom should also be added.

Logan Co.

26-10 A new stairway can be added to connect the basement with the living room.

A Georgia Pacific Corporation

B Georgia Pacific Corporation

26-11 This is an unfinished attic before (A) and after restoration. (B)

Before converting an attic, ceiling joists should be checked to determine if they are strong enough to serve as floor joists and support the load of the new room. Adequate headroom and usable floor space should also be available. At least 7 ft. of height should be allowed between the floor and the finished ceiling. The ceiling may slope from 7 ft. to 5 ft. high at one or opposite sides of the room, but these areas will be limited in use. If the floor is not strong enough or if adequate space is not available, remodeling may become complex and expensive.

Windows and skylights can be added to an attic for natural lighting. Dormers allow natural light and increase the amount of usable space in an attic by adding headroom. However, they are more costly to add than skylights and regular windows because they require modifications to the roof structure.

Adequate insulation for a living area must be added to the attic ceiling and walls. Proper ventilation is especially important since warm air tends to get trapped in attics. Ceiling fans and vents may be helpful. Additional wiring may be required, and if a bathroom is added, plumbing lines will be needed.

Adding On

Converting existing unused spaces may not be possible or practical. In these situations, the family may choose to build additional space onto a home. This new space is called an **addition**, and the process is called "adding on." Any type of space, such as a bedroom, bathroom, den, or garage, may be added to a home, 26-12. Additions may also be used to enlarge an existing room, such as a living room or kitchen.

When a room is built onto a home, the floor plan can be designed to meet the specific needs of the family. The new addition should harmonize with other rooms in the house. (Guidelines for planning rooms are covered in earlier chapters in this text, primarily Chapter 3 through Chapter 9.)

Building permits and inspections are almost always necessary when adding space to a home. Timing is important because weather conditions can hamper much of the work involved in building an addition. Local zoning laws may restrict the types

26-12 A main floor addition requires a new foundation and framework.

of additions allowed on a home. Usually, the exterior walls of a home must be kept a minimum distance from lot lines.

Ground-Level Additions

Adding on is usually more complex than changing areas within the original structure. Adding space involves changing a home's basic structure. A new area is created from the foundation to the roof, which alters the exterior appearance of the home. A ground-level addition may have a crawlspace or basement below and a second floor and/or attic above.

Adding space to a home usually involves the removal of all or part of an exterior wall. Most exterior walls are bearing walls, except for end walls of one-story dwellings with a gable roof. Temporary support, called *shoring*, must be used when such a wall is removed. Then, some type of permanent load-bearing support must be in place before the remodeling is finished, 26-13.

Walls that are removed are likely to contain wiring and plumbing. Rerouting of these lines may be necessary. Underground plumbing mains and cables should be checked before digging for an addition's foundation. In most states, the law requires checking utility lines before digging to prevent accidents.

Any planned addition should blend well with the architectural style of the existing home. The size, shape, and placement of the addition should not appear out-of-place or overpowering. The exterior design should be of the same style as the original house, 26-14. Placement, size, and style of windows and doors in the addition should also blend with the original structure. Landscaping elements can be used to blend the new addition into the original house.

The type of space to be added, location of rooms in the original home, and availability of space should be considered when deciding where to add a room. For instance, a game room or party room should not be next to the sleeping area. Instead, this would be a good location for another bedroom. Lot boundaries may not allow enough space for an addition on one or two sides of the home.

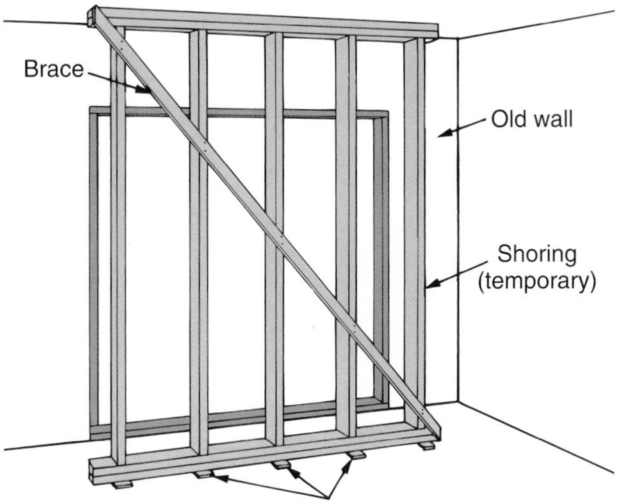

26-13 Temporary support must be used when a bearing wall is removed.

A

B

26-14 The entry before remodeling was uninteresting (A) so a raised-entry module was added (B). It blends seamlessly with the existing structure.

Second-Story Additions

Some homes may not have enough yard space for a ground-level addition. For example, in some areas, especially metropolitan areas, homes are on small lots. Often these homes are already at the permitted boundary limit. In addition, many areas have green-space requirements that dictate a certain ratio of yard area to house area. For these homes, the addition of a second story may be considered, 26-15. A second-story addition is usually much more expensive and complex than a ground-level addition. The roof must be removed and replaced to make room for the second story. The foundation and first-floor walls must be strong enough to support the weight of a second story. Stairways connecting the first and second floors must be built.

In addition to green-space requirements, some areas also have height restrictions. In these cases, if the house does not have a basement, one can be added. Adding a basement is very expensive and requires professional planning and construction. Generally, adding a basement should only be considered when all other options have been eliminated.

Buying to Remodel

Many homebuyers would like a custom-built home, but cannot afford one. Often, these people buy less expensive housing and remodel to meet their own needs and tastes. For example, most subdivisions contain a limited number of house styles. Yet, with additions and exterior and interior changes, the houses can be customized to suit various lifestyles and preferences. Therefore, when looking for a house to buy, also visualize what can be done with the structure and land.

Renovation

Another option for homebuyers that is gaining popularity is renovation of an older home, 26-16.

26-15 Second-story additions are complex and expensive.

A Norandex/Reynolds Building Products

B Norandex/Reynolds Building Products

26-16 This old home was in very poor condition (A), but renovation made it a spacious, modern place to live (B).

Renovation is returning a home to a previous condition, not necessarily its original condition, without changing the space. However, current styles, new materials, and updated appliances may be used in the renovation. Often, renovation is called "rehab." Renovation is an alternative to building from scratch. However, renovation is not restoration or preservation.

Often older homes can be purchased at reasonable cost because they are not suitable for living, although their basic structure is sound. Over the years, they have suffered from neglect because owners could not or would not pay the cost of repairs. Through renovation, however, these dwellings can return to their original condition and again become desirable places to live. Also, the renovated buildings can be much more valuable than the cost of the renovation. See 26-17. Many metropolitan areas support building rehab programs to encourage renovation of deteriorating homes in declining areas.

26-17 Many cities have old houses that may be purchased inexpensively and remodeled. The finished product is often more valuable than the cost of building a new structure.

Renovation is a major project requiring much time, money, and careful planning. Preliminary planning is especially important. Building codes must be strictly followed. The finished home may require many lengthy and expensive projects to achieve completion. See 26-18. Many of these projects will require contracted work.

Some homebuyers include the cost of remodeling in the amount of their house mortgage. Others obtain a mortgage for the cost of the house only and pay for the remodeling without financing. Another option is to refinance the house after all work is completed and use the equity from the increase in value to pay off the renovation expenses.

Careful inspection of a home is important when buying to renovate. Some homes may be very inexpensive, but renovating them would cost more than building a new home. A sound foundation and floor substructure are essential. Wood should be checked for insects and dry rot. If support beams are unsound, renovation will probably be too expensive to be worthwhile. Other areas to check are wiring, heating, roofing, walls, and insulation. Renovation can be expensive if major changes in these areas are needed.

The types of changes that will be needed and their estimated costs should be considered before purchasing a house for renovation. Often, it may be better to purchase a home that is a few thousand dollars more, but has sound wiring, plumbing, and structural members. The lower-priced house may ultimately cost more to renovate than the more expensive, but structurally sound house.

A Norandex/Reynolds Building Products

B Norandex/Reynolds Building Products

26-18 Remodeling an old house (A) usually requires considerable work on both the interior and exterior (B).

Historical Preservation

Historical preservation involves returning a building to its original condition while maintaining traditional styles, materials, and in some cases furnishings. In recent years there has been a renewed interest in historic preservation. Motivation has come from several areas:

- special groups who wish to preserve buildings of historical significance
- preservationists who believe these buildings should be saved for future generations
- architects, designers, and historians who wish to preserve our architectural heritage
- environmentalists who believe that preservation is one method of slowing the depletion of the earth's natural resources
- governmental agencies responsible for improving the quality of life in a community by creating uses for abandoned or neglected buildings
- developers and landlords who see an opportunity to make profits from virtually worthless, old buildings
- individuals who see opportunities in developing desirable living spaces in structures that are uninhabitable or designed for other purposes

Terms such as restoration, remodeling, and adaptive reuse describe the various types of historic preservation.

Restoration

Restoration involves returning a structure to its original condition. See 26-19. Many historic homes of an earlier period are painstakingly restored in every detail. Authentic materials, designs, and colors are researched to ensure accuracy. Furnishings of the period are collected for use in the structure, 26-20. In short, an intensive effort is exerted to return its appearance to a previous era.

Preservation Through Remodeling

Remodeling, by definition, involves changing the structure to meet new needs, use new technology, or comply with new code requirements. However, altering the structure may often be counter to its preservation. Generally, the remodeling of residential structures undergoing historical preservation only modifies slightly the intended use of the dwellings.

The most common remodeling projects for historical preservation include changing room layouts, adding space, or upgrading plumbing or wiring systems. It is possible to maintain the original restored exterior appearance while remodeling the interior to meet new needs. Without remodeling, the building would be unable to meet everyday living needs and possibly be demolished.

Adaptive Reuse

Adaptive reuse is the process of changing the function of a building. One example is changing an old factory building or warehouse into housing units.

26-19 This Victorian home in Newnan, Georgia, has been restored to its original splendor.

President Benjamin Harrison Memorial Home

26-20 These authentic furnishings are in the upstairs sitting room of the President Benjamin Harrison Home in Indianapolis, Indiana.

Sometimes buildings sit idle because they need extensive repairs or are no longer needed for their original purpose. They become eyesores and locations for crime and mischief. As a result, there is significant pressure from community groups and individuals to reclaim these buildings as useful structures. Through adaptive reuse, they can once again be functional assets to the community, 26-21.

Preparing Remodeling, Renovation, and Preservation Plans

A good remodeling, renovation, or preservation job is carefully planned before any work begins. Planning involves appraising the original house, determining the desired and needed changes, and drawing plans. An interior designer, architect, and/or contractor may be consulted in the planning stages.

The first step of planning involves determining the weak and strong points of the present home. Limited space and storage, inefficient appliances, and poor natural lighting are examples of items that may need changing. However, walls, molding, and flooring materials may be worth saving.

Photo Courtesy of James Hardie® Siding Products

26-21 Once a row of old, unused warehouses, these buildings were converted to restaurants, shops, and condominiums. This is an example of adaptive reuse.

The second step is to evaluate existing plumbing, heating, cooling, wiring, and insulation. If updating or repairs will be needed within a few years, it may be less expensive and more convenient to make changes during the current project. Replacing windows, doors, and appliances to increase a home's energy efficiency may also be considered.

After the area needing work has been evaluated, the next step in the project is creating a rough sketch of the original space. The sketch should include any architectural details such as windows, doors, steps, and fireplaces. Desired changes can be drawn, evaluated, and altered until a finished plan results, which is the final step in planning the project. (Guidelines for planning rooms are covered in earlier chapters in this text, primarily Chapter 3 through Chapter 9.)

The finished plan should be used when consulting contractors, ordering materials, and applying for building permits. Professionally drawn floor plans and elevations or rough plans with specified dimensions may be used. However, if contractors or subcontractors will do any work, professional symbols are essential, 26-22.

The Interior Designer

An interior designer may be consulted in the planning stages of remodeling. Some decorating, department, and home improvement stores offer the free services of a designer if products are purchased from their store. A freelance designer or a design firm are other choices for professional design advice.

The designer can translate the needs and desires of a family into concrete plans. They can help select materials that will be functional, tasteful, and within budget. Designers can coordinate fabrics, paints, floor and wall treatments, furnishings, accessories, and other items for the new interior. While helping a family evaluate a new floor plan, they make suggestions for improving the efficiency of circulation and the overall use of the space. The interior designer can be consulted separately or with an architect.

The Architect

When major projects are planned, an architect will probably be consulted. An architect can make suggestions to improve a remodeling plan and make sure the overall style of the home's exterior will remain well designed. The architect can also help determine whether remodeling plans comply with building, plumbing, and electrical codes.

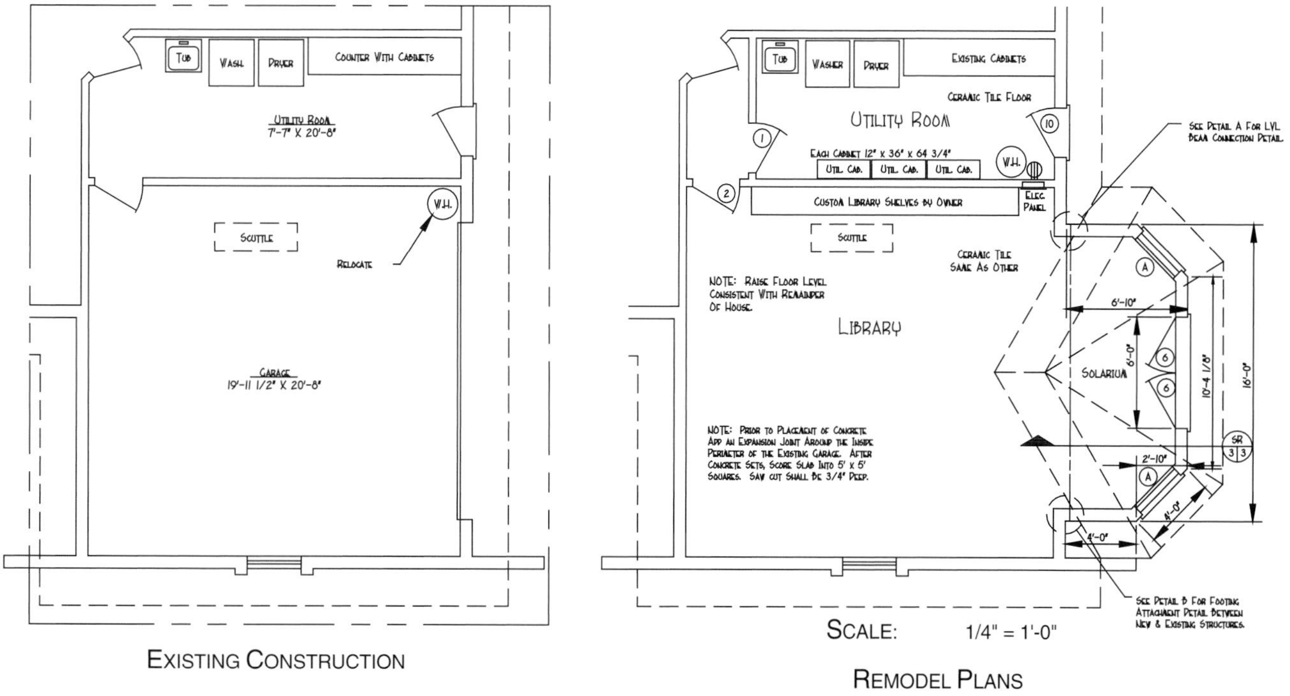

26-22 These are the working drawings for the conversion of a two-car garage into a library/solarium.

The architect can make final drawings of the proposed plan and write specifications for materials. The family may consult an architect only to evaluate and draw plans, or they may use the architect to contact a contractor and supervise the remodeling work to completion.

The Contractor

After planning is finished, a contractor may be hired to do the remodeling work. Many contractors specialize in remodeling. The contractor will obtain any necessary building permits and schedule the work of any subcontractors needed for the project. Subcontractors may include carpenters, plumbers, electricians, masons, and painters.

When contractors are hired for projects, they usually charge one fee for materials and labor. This helps eliminate the chance of unexpected expenses. If family members plan to do some of the work, a contractor may not be used. A family member may choose to serve as the contractor and hire any specific subcontractors needed. When a contractor is not used, an interior designer or architect can help estimate costs, or the family can make its own estimates. However, some unpredicted expenses would probably occur.

Chapter Summary

Remodeling changes an existing space into a new form. Choosing to remodel should be based on an analysis that determines whether remodeling is the best course of action, based on the cost, time, and effort required.

Changing lived-in areas, usually kitchens, replaces equipment, improves traffic patterns, or gives a room a new appearance. Making unused space livable involves converting the garage, porch, attic, or unfinished basement into living space. New additions to a home, whether ground level or a second-story add-on, should harmonize with the original house. Building permits and inspections are almost always required when adding on. Families sometimes buy an older home to remodel.

Renovation of an older home returns the structure to its condition in an earlier time. It is a major project that requires much time, money, and careful planning. Many renovation projects require contracted work, and the code must be followed to the letter. Careful inspection of the home is important before buying it to renovate. Be sure the house structure is solid, plumbing and electrical systems are sound, and estimated renovation costs are realistic.

Historical preservation involves returning a building to its original condition while maintaining traditional styles, materials, and in some cases, furnishings. Many historic homes are painstakingly restored in every detail with authentic materials, designs, and colors. Preservation through remodeling is sometimes counter to its preservation. Generally, remodeling a residential structure that is undergoing historical preservation only modifies slightly the intended use of the dwelling. Examples are changing room layouts, adding space, or upgrading the plumbing or wiring systems. Adaptive reuse converts old, nonresidential structures into dwelling units.

A good remodeling, renovation, or preservation job must be carefully planned before any work begins. Frequently, help is needed from an interior designer, architect, or contractor. Each has a particular role to play that will help ensure that the project will be a success.

Review Questions

1. For what reasons do families remodel their homes?
2. Why might a family choose remodeling over buying a new house?
3. What factors should be considered when considering whether to remodel?
4. What are the five main types of remodeling?
5. Which type of remodeling is simplest? most complex?
6. For a family of four living in a two-bedroom house with a basement and attic, what type of remodeling should be considered first for creating a new bedroom? Why?
7. What precautions should be taken when tearing down an exterior wall?
8. When looking for a house to renovate and narrowing the choices to two, what are some possible reasons for *not* buying the less-expensive one?
9. How does adaptive reuse differ from remodeling?
10. What are the steps in planning a remodeling, renovation, or preservation project?
11. How can interior designers, architects, and contractors help with a remodeling, renovation, or preservation project?

Suggested Activities

1. Write a short essay discussing the planning involved when remodeling an attic into a studio workplace.
2. List the reasons that people remodel and the factors they should consider before beginning a remodeling project.
3. Compare the five main types of remodeling according to cost, complexity, and time required. Prepare a chart of your analysis.
4. Find a residence in your community that is a candidate for historic presentation. Take a series of photographs of the building. Research the history of the building and the area in which it resides. Determine if restoration, preservation through remodeling, or adaptive reuse is best for this building. Present your analysis to the class.
5. Explain the role of the family, interior designer, architect, and building contractor in a remodeling project.

Internet Resources

California Closets, customized storage solutions
calclosets.com

Hartco Flooring, An Armstrong Company
hartcoflooring.com

KitchenAid, a manufacturer of home appliances
kitchenaid.com

Lennox Industries Inc., a manufacturer of indoor comfort and air-quality products
lennox.com

Met-Tile, a manufacturer of metal roofing
met-tile.com

North American Insulation Manufacturers Association, a resource for rockwool insulation
naima.org

Old House Journal
oldhousejournal.com

Pozzi Wood Windows
pozzi.com

Preservation, the online magazine of the national Trust for Historic Preservation
nationaltrust.org/magazine

Qualified Remodeler Magazine
qrmagazine.com

The Hoover Company, manufacturer of central vacuum systems and vacuum cleaners
hoovercompany.com

The McGraw-Hill Companies, Inc. construction products marketplace
sweets.com

U.S. Department of Housing and Urban Development
hud.gov

Whirlpool Corporation
whirlpool.com

Note: Web addresses may have changed since publication. For some entries, reaching the correct Web site may require keying *www.* into the address.

Part Eight
Presentation Methods

Chapter 27
Presenting Housing Ideas
Chapter 28
Computer Applications

Chapter 27
Presenting Housing Ideas

Objectives

After studying this chapter, you will be able to
- explain how presentation methods can help the design professional communicate ideas.
- list the seven types of drawings used to present design ideas and describe how each is used in clarifying a design.
- identify the materials and methods used to make a rendering.
- determine how presentation boards, models, slides, and PowerPoint® presentations can help a client visualize a finished project.

Key Terms

exterior perspective
vanishing point
interior perspective
presentation floor plans
presentation elevation
presentation plot plan
presentation landscape plan
section drawing
renderings
appliqué
presentation boards

Professionals in design use presentation techniques to communicate their ideas. Presentation methods allow a designer to present ideas to a client in nontechnical language, 27-1. Presentation drawings, boards, models, and other methods may be used with prospective clients and investors, or they may be used for advertising. They are seldom seen by building contractors. Designers must know how to visually present their ideas in order to communicate them to others.

Presentation Drawings

Presentation drawings help give a client a clear picture of how a finished project will appear. Several types can be used to depict a house's exterior, interior, and surroundings. They include: exterior perspectives, interior perspectives, presentation floor plans, presentation elevations, presentation plot and landscape plans, and presentation sections. Each type of drawing features different aspects of a plan or uses a different presentation approach.

Exterior Perspectives

An **exterior perspective** is a pictorial drawing of the outside of a house. It shows how the building

Sater Design Collection, Inc.

27-1 Presentations can be used to communicate with prospective owners, lending agencies, and the media.

will appear in its completed form, 27-2. The drawing shows more than one side of the home for a three-dimensional appearance. Elements further away from the viewer are reduced in size for a realistic representation.

Drawings are given perspective by using **vanishing points**, which are imaginary points used to create the illusion of a perspective. The part of the drawing meant to appear closest to the viewer is drawn in the largest scale, while parts meant to appear farther are drawn gradually smaller. Vanishing points are reached by extending lines from the closest parts of a drawing past the farthest parts, until the lines meet. A drawing may have one, two, or three vanishing points.

Most exterior perspectives have two or three vanishing points. A two-point perspective usually features two sides of a building. One corner appears close while the walls extending from that corner are drawn in perspective to a different vanishing point. By changing the level of the vanishing points in relationship to the building, more or less of the roof can be shown, 27-3. Three-point perspective is sometimes used for very tall buildings. A third vanishing point is placed above the building to give an appearance of height. Three-point perspective is the most difficult type of perspective drawing to master.

Interior Perspectives

An **interior perspective** is a pictorial drawing of a room or other area inside a house. It generally includes the furnishings and decorations planned for the finished room. One-point perspective is used most often for interior drawings. Generally, the pictorial shows three walls, the floor, and the ceiling, 27-4. Interior perspectives can be drawn fairly easily using a grid designed for one-point perspective.

Sater Design Collection, Inc.

27-3 By using vanishing points at a low level compared to the height of the house, the tallness of the structure is emphasized.

Helmuth A. Geiser, Member AIBD

27-2 Using two-point perspective for an exterior gives the drawing a realistic appearance.

Presentation Elevations

A **presentation elevation** shows a view perpendicular to a surface. It may represent any one side of an object, but it shows no depth. Any interior or exterior wall may be shown with this type of drawing. It can be drawn quickly and contains the same basic information shown in a perspective drawing, 27-7.

Kitchens, bathrooms, and walls with built-in cabinets are interior areas frequently shown by using presentation elevations, 27-8. Exterior elevations often include plants and other surrounding features to give the illusion of depth. Scale is usually *¼ in. equals 1 ft.* or larger.

Presentation Plot Plans

A **presentation plot plan** is used to show the relationship between the site and the structure. It may also include important topographical features such as trees, walks, streets, and soil contour. This

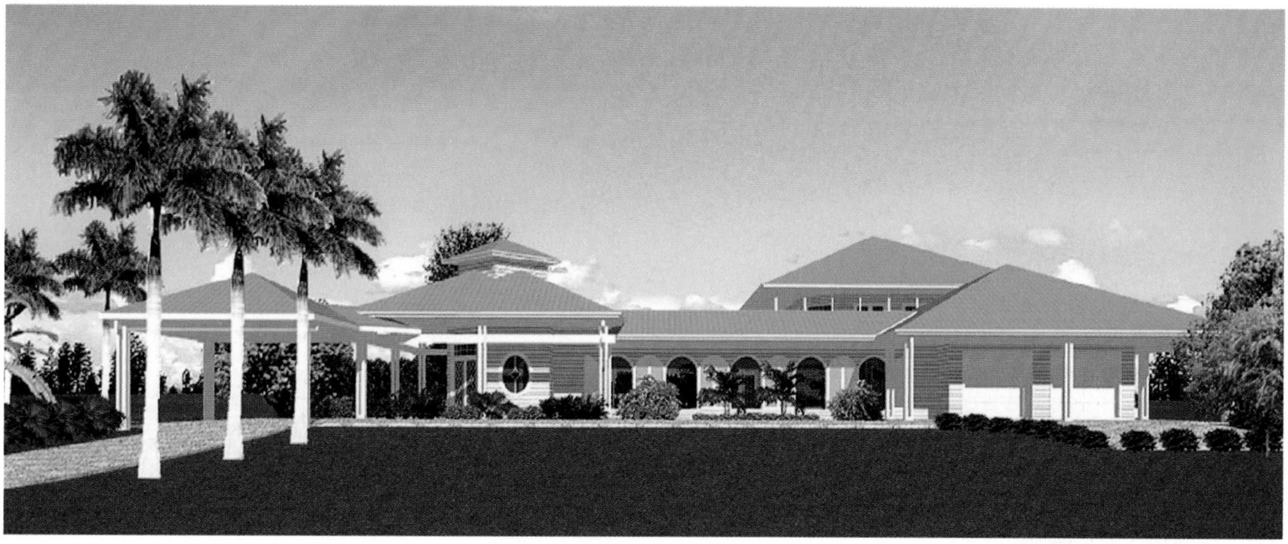

Helmuth A. Geiser, Member AIBD

27-7 The presentation elevation does not use perspective, but it communicates the same basic design elements featured in a perspective.

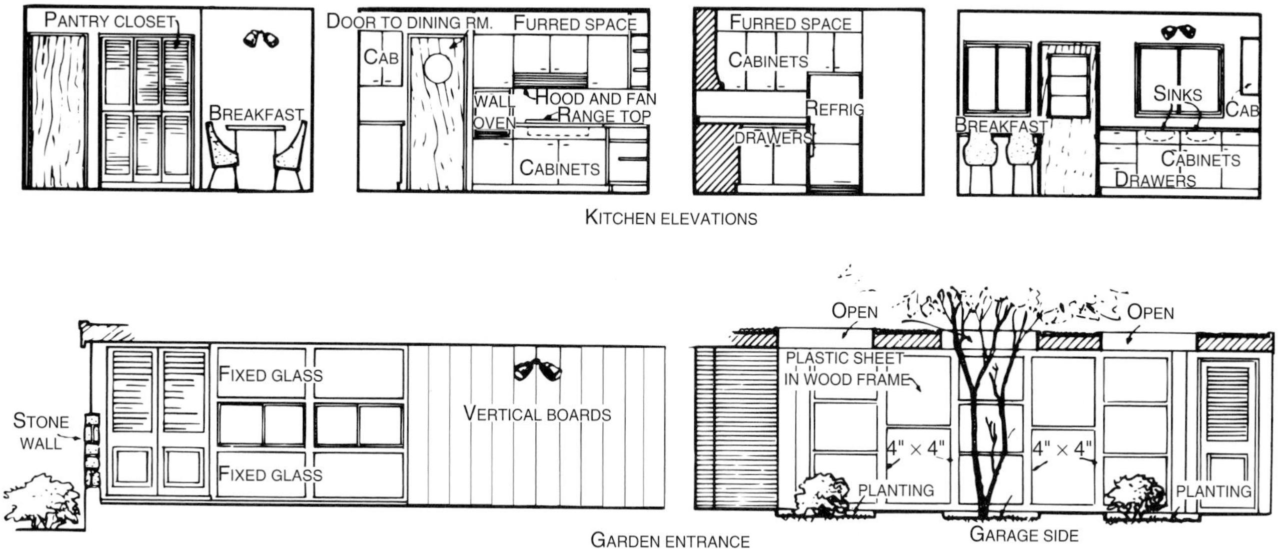

27-8 Interior wall elevations are frequently used to show the arrangements of built-in cabinets and appliances.

drawing shows a top view of the property with all elements in place. Color is often used to distinguish different features, 27-9. Different scales may use 1 in. to represent 10, 20, or 30 ft. or more if the property is very large.

Presentation Landscape Plans

The **presentation landscape plan** shows an entire landscape plan in one presentation. It includes the placement of trees, shrubs, flowers, pools, walks, fences, drives, the house, and any other important features. A north directional symbol is generally included. Plant symbols may be varied to represent different species planned for the landscape. Plant symbols should be in proper scale to the measurements of full-grown plants. See 27-10. Color may be used to define elements and show how space is used. The scale is similar to that used for presentation plot plans.

Presentation Sections

Section drawings can be used to show the interior and exterior of a house. They can also be used to show more than one interior room in one drawing. A **section drawing** shows a cutaway view of a house or series of rooms in a house. Sections can be used to help the client better understand the internal layout of the structure. Often a floor plan is used to show what part of the house is featured in the section drawing. Use of color is common on presentation sections to give the illusion of depth and define features, 27-11.

Rendering

Rendering is the addition of shades, shadows, texture, and color to a line drawing to achieve a realistic appearance. Many materials and techniques are used for rendering, including: pencil, ink, colored pencil, felt-tip marker, watercolor, appliqué, and airbrush. The design professional should have several techniques mastered to offer flexibility in communicating with the client.

Pencil Rendering

Pencil rendering is accomplished by using a soft lead pencil. It is the most popular form of rendering, and beginning students can master the technique with some practice. Renderings can be done quickly and errors can be easily corrected. No special materials or equipment are required. Shading and the appearance of texture can be accomplished with pencil rendering. However, care must be taken to prevent the soft lead from smudging.

Renderings in pencil may range from rough, freehand sketches to precise line drawings executed with drafting instruments, 27-12. The degree of

Midwestern Consulting, Inc.

27-9 A presentation plot plan shows the physical properties of a site and the location of structures on the site.

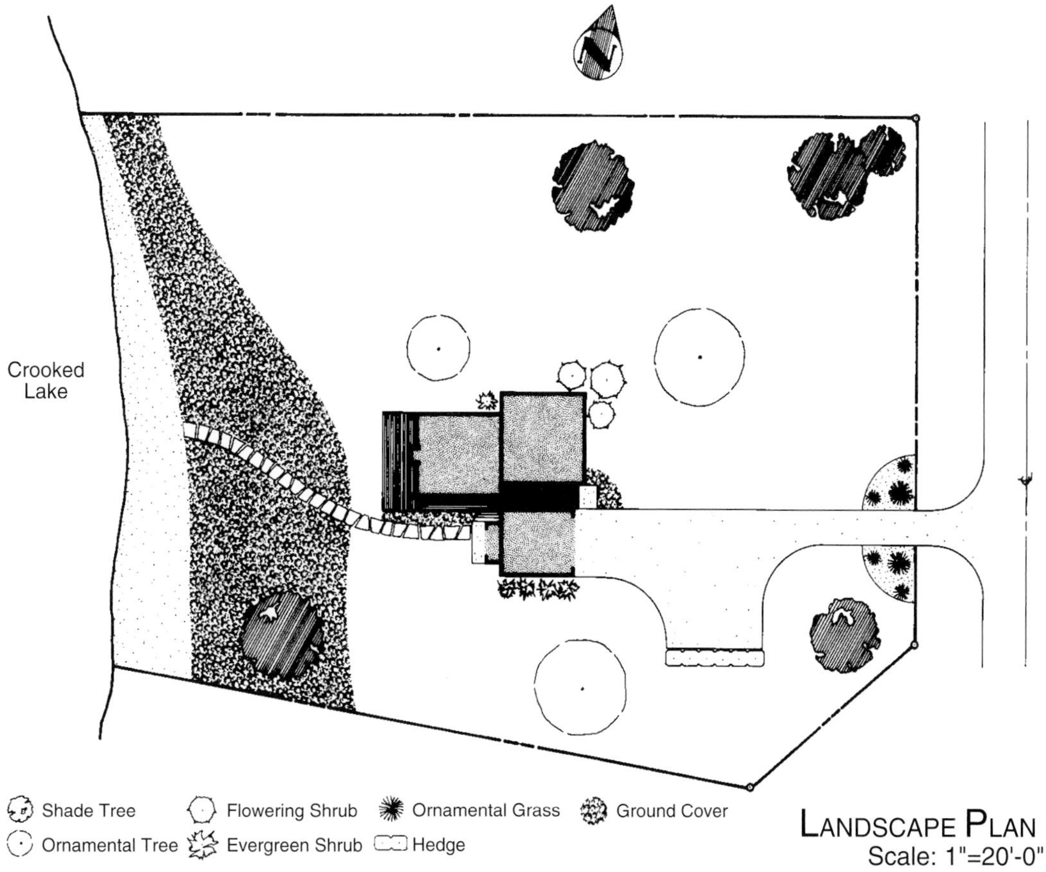

27-10 A presentation landscape plan features plants and other elements that will be included in a landscape.

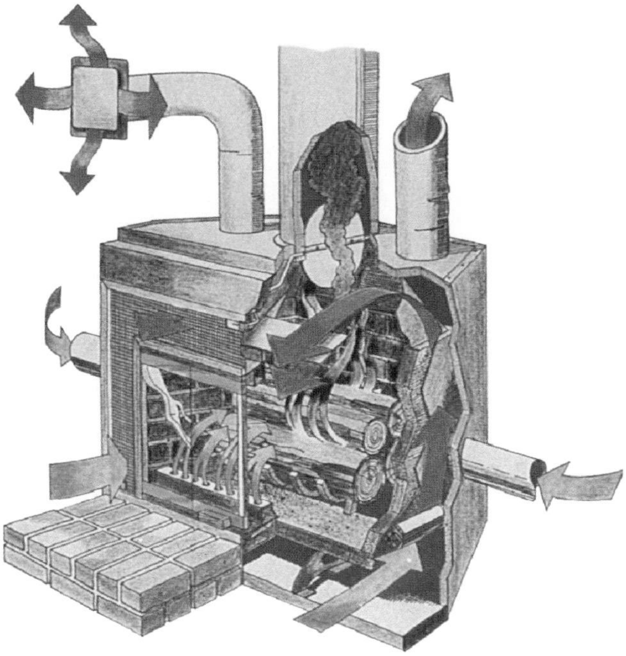

Heatilator, Inc.

27-11 Presentation sections help clients see the relationship between the interior and exterior of an object.

Stuart Resor, Architect

27-12 Pencil renderings are quickly drawn, but they can show precise architectural features.

refinement depends on the purpose of the drawing and the stage of the project. In the early stages of design, rough sketches are usually enough to convey the general concept. More precise renderings are used in presenting final designs and in advertising.

Ink Rendering

Ink renderings are more suitable for reproduction than pencil renderings. Ink produces a sharper line and finer detail than pencil, 27-13. Skill is needed to produce good ink renderings because mistakes are not easily corrected. Shading and texturing is possible with ink by using a series of dots, parallel lines, or other types of markings. Technical fountain pens, lettering pens, poster pens, or brushes may be used to produce ink renderings.

Good ink renderings require paper that takes ink without producing a feathered edge. Recommended materials include mat boards, bristol boards, tracing paper, and overlay paper. Colored mat boards can be used with black or colored ink for special effect. Ink may be used for the object lines in a drawing with some other rendering technique used for shades, shadows, and colors. Waterproof ink is required if felt-tip markers or watercolors are used.

The Garlinghouse Company

27-13 Ink renderings have clear lines that reproduce well.

Watercolor Rendering

Good watercolor rendering gives a realistic appearance to a presentation, 27-14. The technique is difficult and may require some formal art training. Vivid colors or light washes of colors are characteristic of watercolor renderings. Subjects

Sater Design Collection, Inc.

27-14 A watercolor rendering has an appearance similar to that of a photograph.

requiring precise details may be inked and then watercolored. Brushes of various sizes are used. Boards and papers should be compatible for use with watercolors.

Colored Pencil Rendering

Color renderings can also be produced with colored pencils, which are available in a wide range of colors in standard and watercolor forms. Shading techniques are easily accomplished, even by the beginning student, 27-15. Adding water with a brush to a watercolor pencil rendering gives the appearance of a watercolor rendering. Most types of boards and paper can be used for colored pencil renderings.

Felt-Tip Marker Rendering

Felt-tip markers are used to produce colorful, dramatic renderings, 27-16. Such renderings are popular for preliminary drawings and completed project drawings. Errors are very difficult to correct with this technique. A wide range of colors is available and ink may be used for fine detail. Board products and thin tracing paper are recommended for felt-tip marker renderings.

Appliqué Rendering

This type of rendering supplies color, shading, or texture to the image. An **appliqué** is a pressure-sensitive transfer material with a printed pattern or color on one side. Appliqué may be cut to the size

27-15 Colored pencil rendering is easily mastered by the beginning student.

Ken Hawk

27-16 Felt-tip markers can be used in a variety of colors and shades to produce a realistic rendering.

needed and transferred onto a rendering. The use of appliqué assures bold, uniform color and patterns, 27-17. It is popular for use in magazines because it reproduces well. Many common rendering symbols, such as trees, people, furniture, building materials, and doors, are available in appliqué form.

Airbrush Rendering

Professional illustrators generally prefer the airbrush technique to other rendering methods. It produces smooth gradation of tones and a realistic appearance, 27-18. Special equipment and much practice are required to produce good renderings. Colored inks are often used over black ink drawings. The airbrush produces subtle shading by using very small dots of color. Areas that should not be sprayed are covered with rubber cement or other masking.

Other Presentation Methods

Presentation drawings are valuable for communicating the details of a design, but frequently more information is desirable. Such details as fabrics, color schemes, furniture styles, and textures are difficult to represent accurately and completely on

Progress Lighting

27-18 Very realistic pictures can be made by using an airbrush and ink pen.

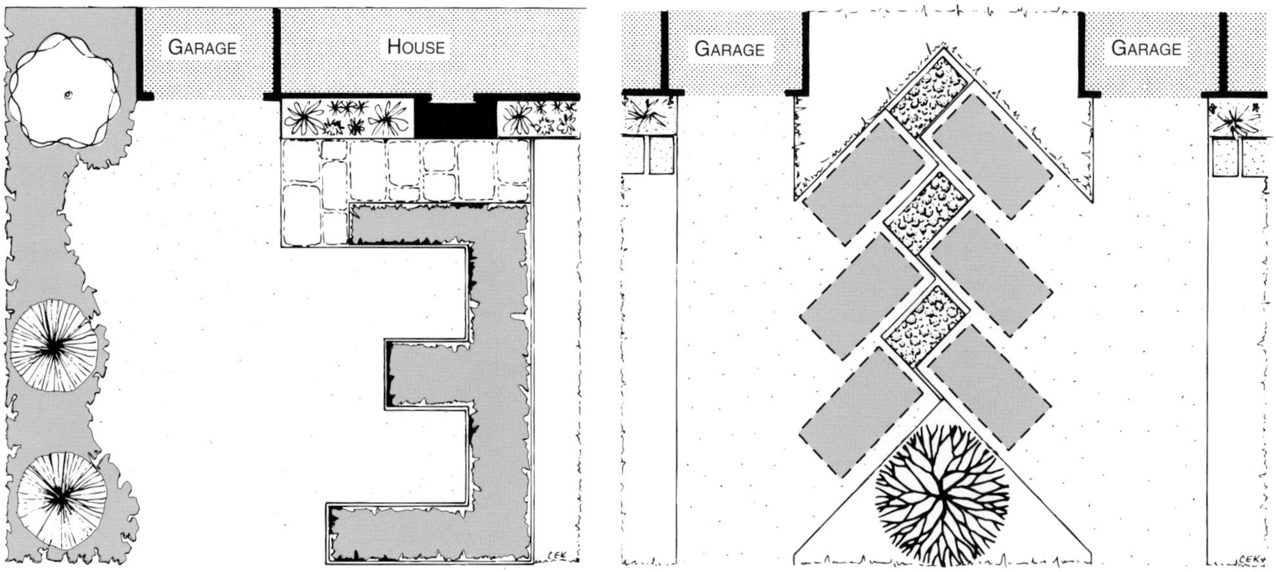

27-17 Colored appliqués can be used over ink renderings to direct attention to specific areas.

rendered drawings. Other presentations may help clients picture a finished product more clearly. These include presentation boards, models, or slides.

Presentation Boards

Presentation boards contain drawings, such as floor plans and elevations, and any other information necessary and samples of materials to help the client visualize a finished product. A large piece of mat board or illustration board is used for mounting samples, drawings, and photos in a logical, attractive format, 27-19. Manufacturers' samples of carpeting, draperies, upholstery, and paint may be included.

Various schedules may also be part of the presentation board. For example, a furniture schedule

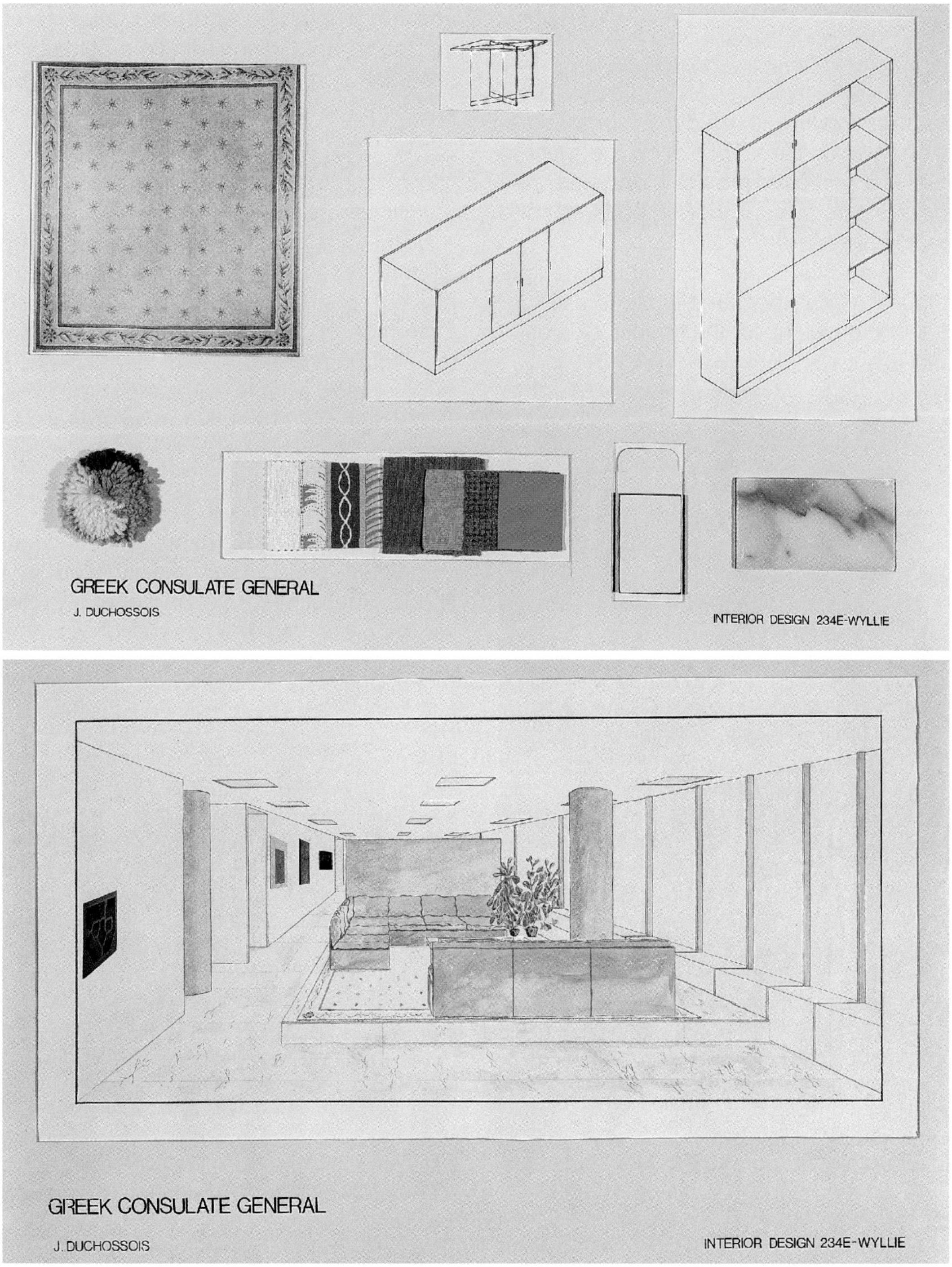

Janet Duchossois, ASID, Flossmoor, Illinois

27-19 Presentation boards should be designed to communicate information in a way that clients will understand.

may identify individual pieces, manufacturer, dimensions, finishes, and any other important information. Specifications for walls, floors, and ceilings may also be placed in a schedule.

The presentation board helps the client form a better picture of the proposed finished product. It should help the client see how the various colors, textures, and designs will coordinate in a room. The board should contain any information necessary to answer questions the client may have about a project.

Models

Models are miniature, three-dimensional representations of a design idea. They allow the client to view all sides of a proposed project. Models are also used by the designer to solve design problems and double-check a plan for flaws, 27-20.

Models can be built to any scale, but less time and effort is involved if the same scale is used for the model as the drawings for the project. Copies of the floor plan can be used as a base for the model. If a model is used simply as a development tool to inspire additional ideas for a design, appearance is not important. This type of model is generally not preserved after a design is completed. Dimensions, however, should be accurately represented, 27-21.

Final models meant for clients to view should be precisely detailed and properly scaled. They can be as elaborate as needed or desired. Final models should not be constructed until a design is accepted and renderings are approved because changes in the model are difficult and time-consuming. Models are most commonly used for very large structures and complex designs that are difficult to visualize.

Slide Presentations

Slides are used to effectively communicate with a client. For example, in the early stages of the design process, slides can be used to show examples of previous work. They can also present examples of designs used in situations similar to the client's. A wide range of ideas can be presented to determine what features the client likes.

Slides are also used to preserve examples of past work accomplished by a design professional. Renderings, models, and presentation boards require storage space and eventually deteriorate over time. Color slides of presentation materials and completed projects are easily filed in very little space. Specific information about a project or slide can be preserved in a companion document.

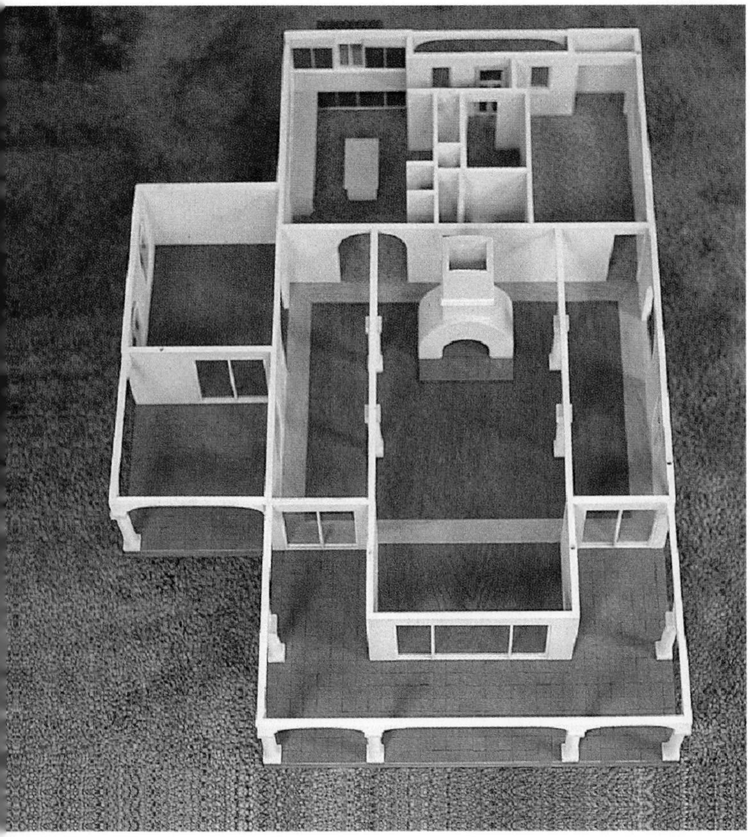

27-20 A presentation model shows how each architectural and design feature will look in the finished project.

27-21 Rough models used by design professionals to develop ideas are not usually seen by the client.

PowerPoint Presentations

PowerPoint® is a software application used to create presentations. A presentation may use different media such as slides, overhead transparencies, or automated shows viewed on a computer or over the Web. A PowerPoint presentation allows mixing text, graphs, charts, clip art, templates, and digital images, 27-22. PowerPoint also provides for the creation of outlines, printed handouts, and speaker notes.

A PowerPoint presentation can be displayed on a computer screen by running a slide show that presents one slide at a time. The slides can be advanced manually or a timed sequence can be used. PowerPoint presentations are frequently used to communicate with a larger group of individuals who have an interest in a given project.

27-22 PowerPoint presentations may include written information as well as digital images.

Chapter Summary

Professionals in design use presentation techniques to communicate their ideas in nontechnical language. An exterior perspective shows a pictorial of the outside of a house when it is completed, usually in two-point perspective. An interior perspective is a drawing of a room or other area inside a dwelling, generally with the furnishings and decoration. A presentation floor plan shows the room arrangement, usually with major furniture pieces. A presentation elevation shows a view perpendicular to one side of the structure. A presentation plot plan shows the relationship between the site's topographical features and the structure. A presentation landscape plan shows the design of the structure's exterior surroundings. A presentation section can show the interior and exterior of a house when a structure has several levels within the dwelling.

Rendering is the addition of shades, shadows, textures, and color to a line drawing to achieve realism. Pencil rendering uses a soft lead pencil and is an easy technique. Ink rendering is more suitable for reproduction. Watercolor rendering gives a very realistic appearance to a presentation. Colored pencil produces an acceptable presentation in color. Felt-tip marker rendering may be used to produce colorful, dramatic renderings. Appliqué rendering supplies color, shading, or texture to an image. Airbrush rendering permits subtle shading.

Presentation boards contain drawings, such as floor plans or elevations, and other information or samples to help a client visualize the design. Models are miniature, three-dimensional representations of a design idea. They allow the client to view all sides of the project. Slide or PowerPoint presentations are frequently used to communicate with a larger group of individuals who have an interest in a given project. Storage of this information should be organized for future reference.

Review Questions

1. What are the seven types of presentation drawings?
2. Which of the presentation drawings are used primarily to show exteriors? to show interiors?
3. What is the difference between a perspective drawing and an elevation?
4. How does a drawing in two-point perspective differ from one with a one-point perspective?
5. What types of drawings use a one-point perspective versus a two-point perspective?
6. What are the seven main materials or techniques used to produce renderings?
7. Which type of technique used to produce renderings is simplest to master? most complex?
8. Why is ink rendering preferred over pencil rendering for reproduction?
9. What type of color rendering is recommend for a beginning design student? Why?
10. What is the preferred method of rendering for professional illustrators?
11. What methods other than drawings can be used to present housing ideas?
12. How are the two basic types of models used to present housing ideas?

Suggested Activities

1. Draw an exterior perspective of your school or home to demonstrate the use of a vanishing point. Display your drawing to the class.
2. Using Figure 27-5 as a guide, create a presentation floor plan by applying interior design ideas to either Figure 3-10 or 3-15 from Chapter 3 of this text.
3. Select a simple detail on a local building, such as a column, window trim, or overhang, and prepare a rendering of it. Use any one of the techniques described in the text. Display it to the class.
4. Using cardboard, illustration board, or balsa wood, build a scale model of a room in your house. Include doors, windows, and furniture.

Internet Resources

American Society of Interior Designers
interiors.org

Architectural Digest Magazine
archdigest.com

ART Inc., publisher of Chief Architect software
chiefarch.com

Better Homes and Gardens Magazine
bhg.com

Design Basics, Inc., a home design service
designbasics.com

Homes of Elegance
homesofelegance.com

SoftPlan Systems, Inc. residential design program
softplan.com

The Sater Design Collection, Inc.
saterdesign.com

Note: Web addresses may have changed since publication. For some entries, reaching the correct Web site may require keying *www.* into the address.

Chapter 28
Computer Applications

Objectives

After studying this chapter, you will be able to
- identify the four basic categories of computer applications in housing.
- list several benefits of computer applications in housing design and analysis.
- determine several applications of the computer in the selection of construction elements and processes.
- describe how the computer is used to serve clients and customers.
- explain how the computer is useful in project management.

Key Terms

computer-assisted drafting and design (CADD)
computer simulation
CD-ROM
interactive
virtual reality models
Project Evaluation and Review Technique (PERT) chart
Gantt chart

Computers and specialized software have had a significant impact on planning, designing, constructing, and furnishing modern housing units. The computer provides the potential for powerful analyses and graphic representations of many aspects of housing, architecture, and construction. Computers are now used for various tasks, such as the following:
- drafting, designing, and rendering plans
- adding color and shading to layouts
- displaying plans in three dimensions
- touring building interiors from a walk-through perspective
- analyzing a housing unit's energy use
- generating all the necessary reports

With the widespread availability of the personal computer, practically any architect, builder, and interior designer can have access to powerful, time-saving tools that make work easier and more efficient, 28-1.

28-1 This computer has all the necessary hardware and software to produce complex figures and reports.

The computer allows the housing professional to "test" designs, retrieve previously designed components, and choose just the right element for a particular application. It also helps the professional locate sources of current and archival information about a project, perform cost estimates, market a product, present design plans to a client, and produce work schedules and financial records.

This chapter provides an introduction to computer applications. With further study, you may become proficient in using and applying the computer and its associated software to plan, design, and present quality solutions to real housing challenges.

The computer is only as useful as the software program and the computer skill of the user. Many commercial computer programs are readily available, but software can also be developed to address specific circumstances. The four basic categories of computer applications in the housing field are: design and analysis, selection of construction elements and processes, service to clients and customers, and project management.

Design and Analysis

Presently, design and analysis functions in all areas of housing account for the greatest use of computer applications. This category includes four primary areas: computer-assisted drafting and design (CADD); plot, site, and landscape planning; kitchen and bath design; and energy analysis. The number and type of software programs for these topics are rapidly increasing and, in many cases, are tailored to address a specific feature, such as fireplace or stair design.

Computer-Assisted Drafting and Design

The largest and most familiar area of computer application in housing is computer-assisted drafting and design. **Computer-assisted drafting and design (CADD)** is a computer program that automatically draws objects to scale or exact measurements. By being able to retrieve standard components or drawings from the computer's memory, the designer is able to save time and improve accuracy. Previously, traditional drawings were done by hand, which is very labor intensive and costly for large-scale projects.

By using the computer to draw plans and insert uniform components, the drafting and design process has harnessed the computer's powerful speed and accuracy. One example of a computer-generated architectural drawing is shown in 28-2. This elevation drawing is an example of a planning document that can be developed quickly by a skilled operator of CADD equipment.

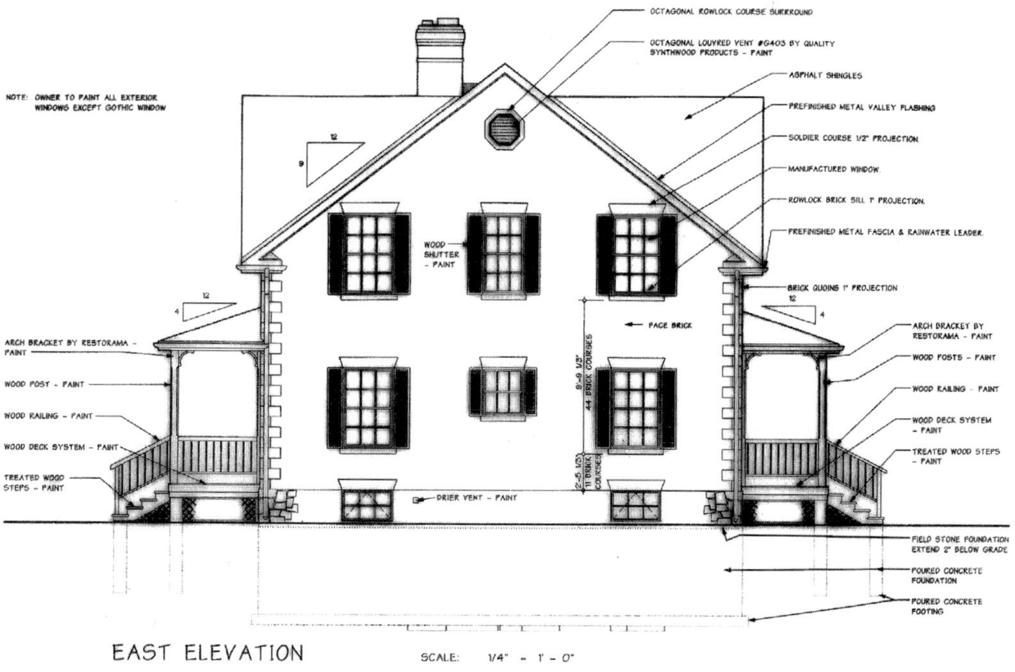

Graphisoft: ArchiCAD Software

28-2 The computer is very useful in creating elevations of buildings. Notice the precise details and realistic representation, a major strength of CADD.

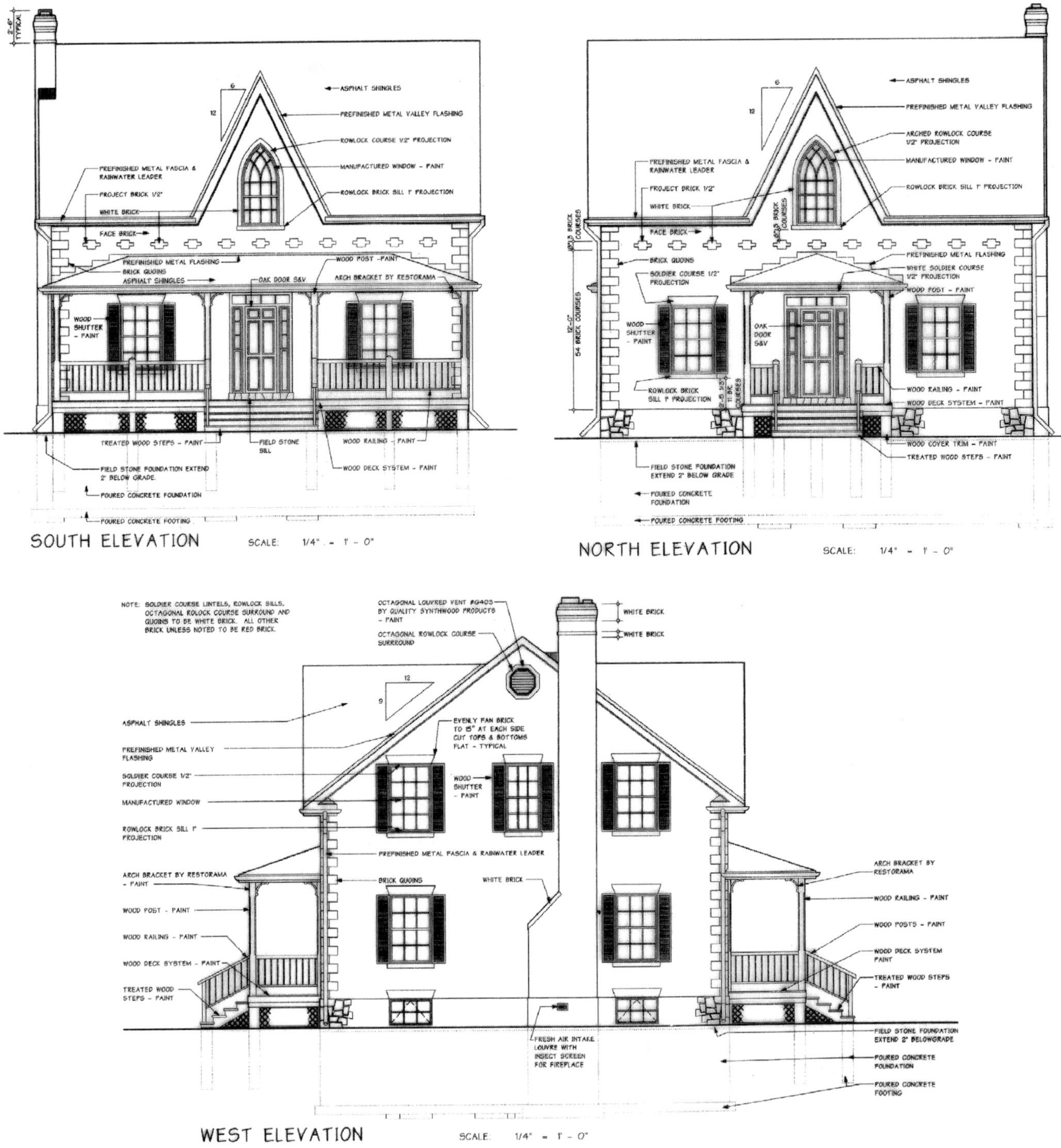

28-2 *Continued*

Figure 28-3 shows a typical menu of standard symbols that a designer can use when creating a drawing. Rapid access to such menu items permits the operator to complete complex drawings quickly. Once a design has been completed and stored in the computer, it can be retrieved whenever needed for copies or revisions. Revising CADD drawings is where true time savings is realized.

Another benefit of CADD is its computerized symbols library. Inserting standard symbols and shapes is quick, easy, and accurate. Once a standard symbol is stored in the library, it can be retrieved and added to as many drawings as needed. For example, symbols for trees, furniture, doors, windows, and common appliances are usually included in an architectural symbols library. When inserting an image in a

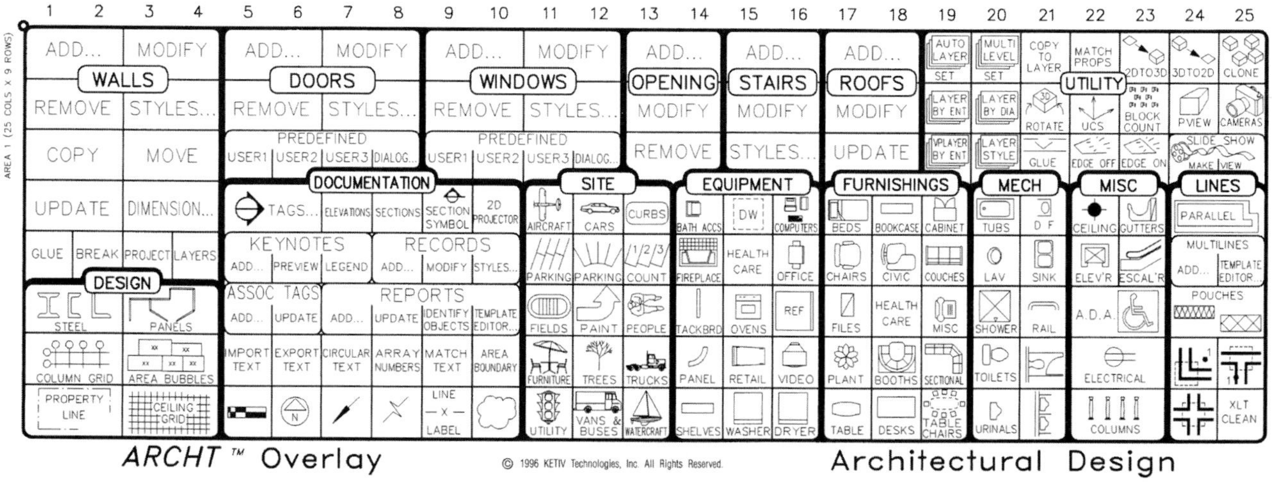

ArchT Architectural Software template courtesy of Ketiv Technologies, www.ketiv.com

28-3 This digitizing template includes a representative selection of symbols included in the symbols library.

document, it can be enlarged, reduced, rotated to a different angle, or flipped to its mirror image to meet a specific need. See 28-4. In addition, specialized symbols may be designed and added to the library for individualized applications.

Some of the many other CADD applications to drawings include the following:

- addition of visual definition to specific lines and shapes
- easy adjustment of dimensions
- application of color and shading treatments
- quick calculation of square footage, materials quantities, and cost estimates

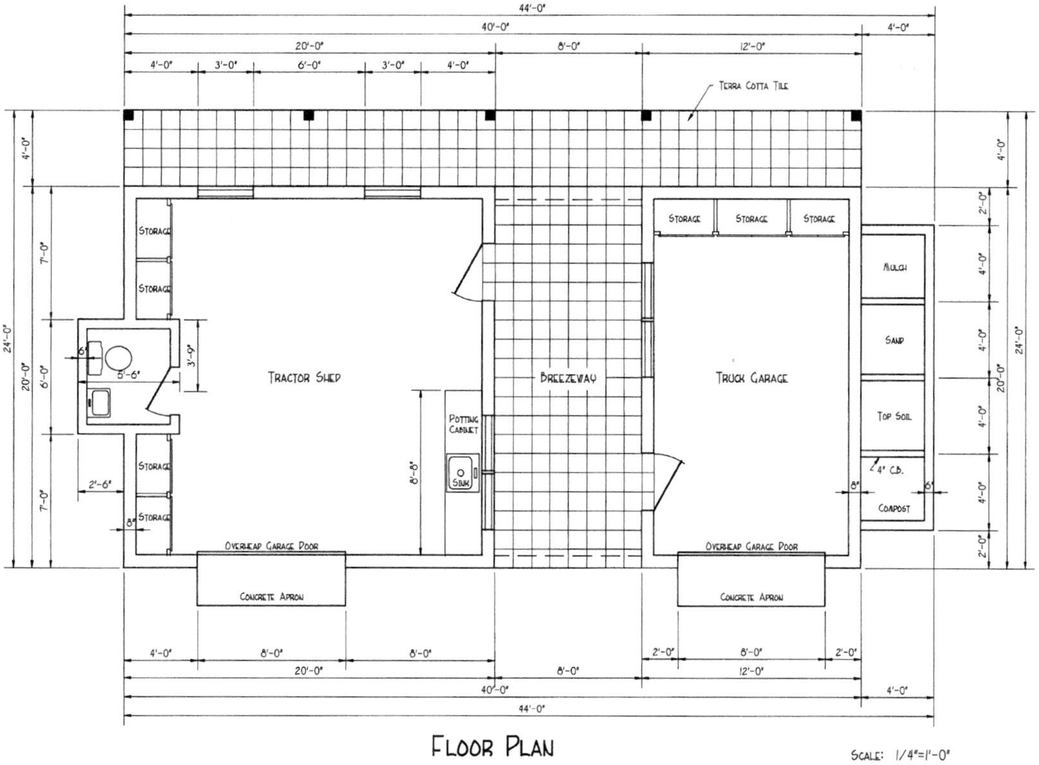

28-4 Symbols from the symbols library have been used to create this CADD-generated floor plan. Note that window, door, and bathroom symbols have been scaled and oriented as needed.

Plot, Site, and Landscape Planning

Plot plans, site plans, and landscape plans are required for most homes, apartment buildings, and subdivisions. The plot plan shows the site and location of the buildings on the property. A site plan includes a complete description of the shape, size, and important features on the site. The landscape plan shows all plants on the site as well as the paved areas, fences, and other landscape elements, 28-5.

The computer is very useful in converting topographical data collected by land surveyors into property boundaries, contour lines, and accurate location of features on the site. Another computer application is the generation of site-grading plans for the contractors of the development, 28-6. Some landscape programs even have an aging feature to show how the landscape will change over time as plants mature.

Site Planning and Mapping
Design and evaluation of water treatment systems
Solutions of complex geometry problems
Earthwork cost optimization
Automated contour mapping
Water-surface profile analysis
Calculation of cut, fill, and mass-haul volume quantities
Generation of earth sections and profiles
Generation of site grading plans
Calculation and plotting of points, bearings, distances, and elevations
Assessment of delays and congestion
Subdivision planning and mapping

Auto-trol Technology Corporation

28-6 The preliminary site layout and generation of a site-grading plan is an interactive process that requires the melding of land form and structure with a CADD system.

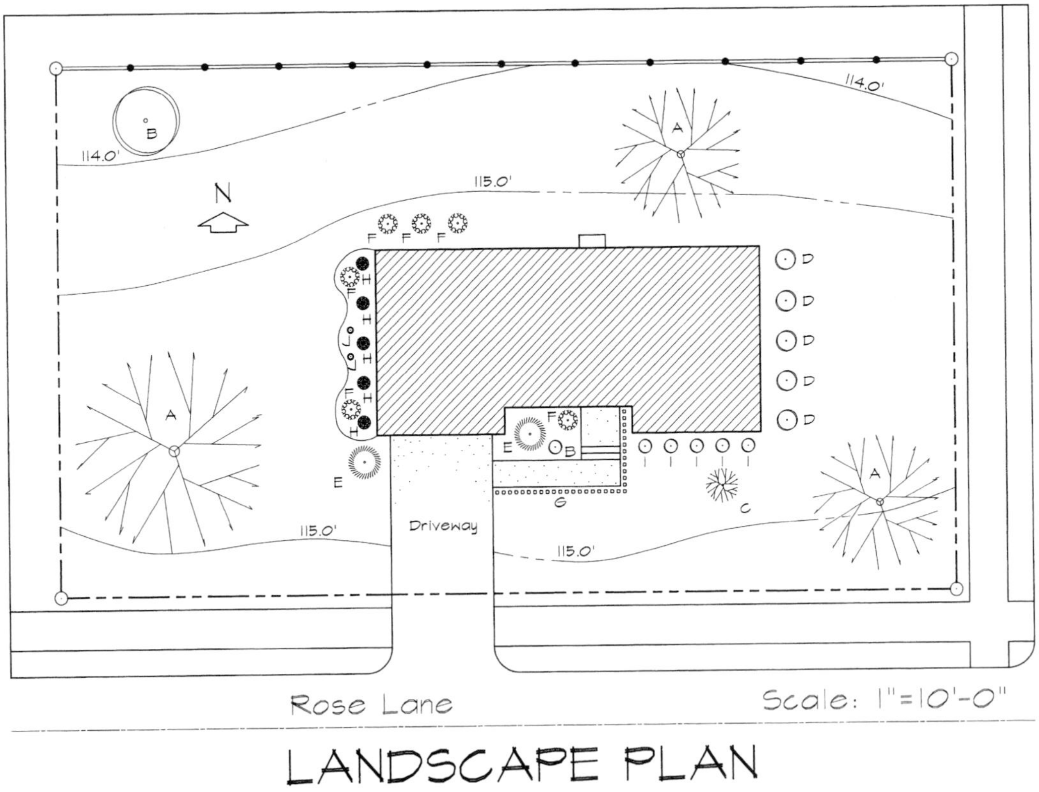

LANDSCAPE SCHEDULE

KEY	QUAN.	PLANT DESCRIPTION
A	3	SHADE TREE
B	2	ORNAMENTAL TREE
C	1	FLOWERING CRAB
D	4	RHODODENDRON
E	2	FLOWERING SHRUB

KEY	QUAN.	PLANT DESCRIPTION
F	6	VIBURNUM
G	33	PRIVET
H	5	UPRIGHT JUNIPER
I	5	FORSYTHIA
J	2	BAXUS

28-5 This is a typical computer-generated landscape plan, created by using AutoCAD software from Auto Desk, Inc.

Other computer applications used in plot, site, and landscape planning include the following:

- design and evaluation of water treatment systems
- water surface profile analysis
- calculation of the volume quantities of earth that must be removed from the site or brought in for fill
- generation of earth sections, profiles, and site-grading plans
- automated contour mapping
- subdivision planning and mapping

Kitchen and Bath Design

Kitchens and bathrooms are usually the two most expensive areas per square foot in the home. Both require careful planning to achieve maximum efficiency. As a result, numerous software programs are available to assist in designing these rooms and selecting standard appliances, cabinets, and fixtures, 28-7.

A

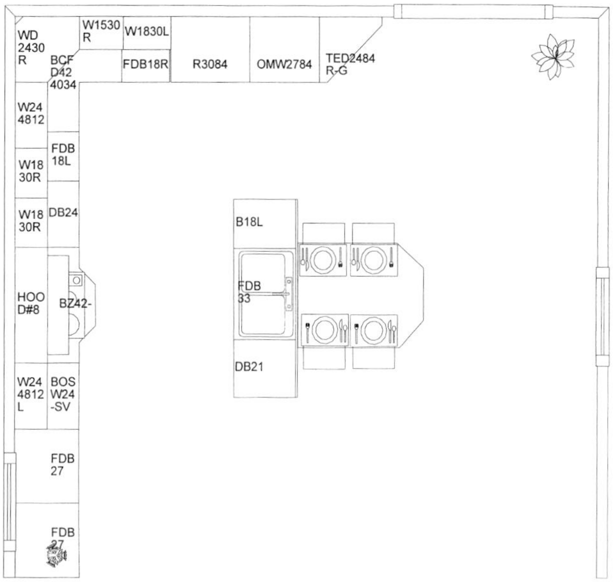

B

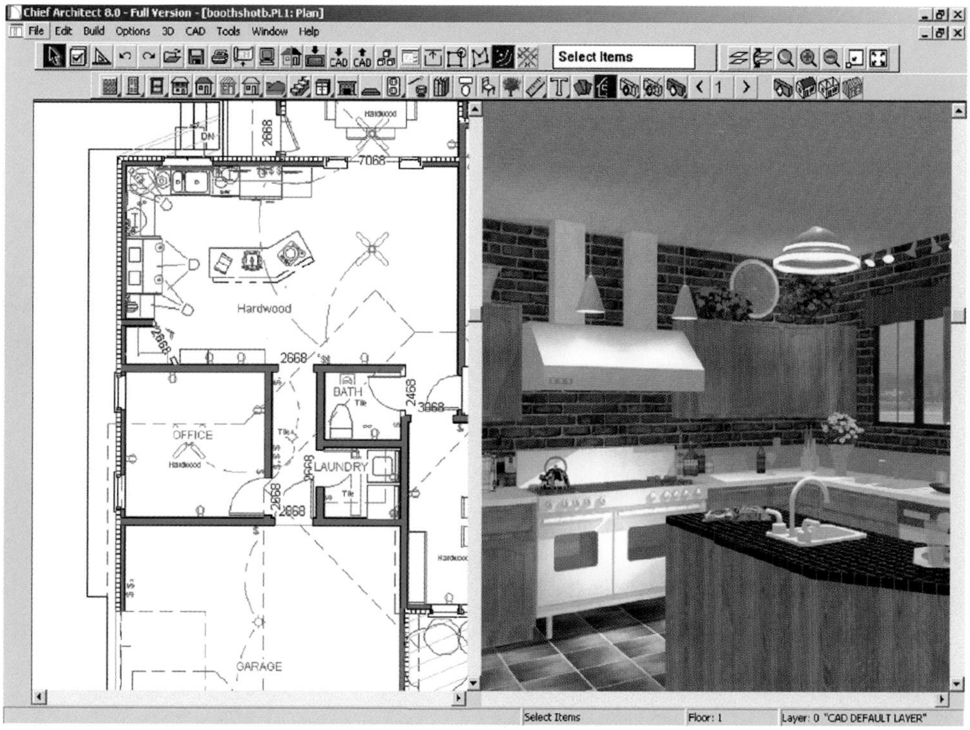

C

©ART, Inc.

28-7 This computer-generated pictorial shows a very realistic representation of the kitchen design components. It communicates the design to the client (A) and confirms the design plan for the designer (B). It compares the floor plan to a pictorial image (C).

Most kitchen cabinet manufacturers have software programs that include all of their standard models. These programs allow users to select specific units, place them on a floor plan, and generate one or more views of the total arrangement, 28-8. The resulting picture is immediate and it permits a quick revision of any disappointing elements in the plan. Once the design is approved, a cabinet specification sheet and an order form can be generated by the software to eliminate costly ordering mistakes.

Many of the larger bathroom-fixture companies also have software programs for their products. Just as with kitchen software, these programs facilitate the rapid and accurate design of baths. Each fixture can be selected and placed in the floor plan in its proper orientation and scale. A bath can be planned in just a few minutes using one of these programs. A list of the fixtures chosen is generated automatically by most of these programs.

Energy Analysis

Since energy costs today are so significant, a complete energy analysis should be performed for most planned structures. An energy analysis is also important for all remodeling construction projects. Using these programs, the designer is able to analyze all aspects of energy use and plan energy-efficient structures. One example of the type of information that can be provided by a computer is the outdoor temperature ranges for a certain geographic location. Using this information, the designer can design a building with the most efficient combinations of insulation and heating/cooling system.

Other computer applications of energy analyses include the following:

- examination of alternative building configurations and materials for increased energy efficiency
- performance analysis of mechanical and lighting systems
- evaluation of thermal and economic aspects of solar energy systems
- evaluation of energy reflection and transmission from various surfaces

Selection of Construction Elements and Processes

The design process frequently involves one or more areas not generally included in typical CADD software that are associated with the drafting and design of plans. These include: structural component analysis and selection, and preferred techniques for construction and/or installation.

SoftPlan Systems Inc.

28-8 The bath design was developed using application-specific software created for this purpose. The result is photo-realistic.

Application-specific software is available to aid the designer in making decisions that will improve the use, function, efficiency, and safety of a design, 28-9. Much of this software is provided by manufacturers or associations whose purpose is to ensure the proper use of materials, products, or construction techniques.

Structural Analysis

Structural analysis is an important aspect of every housing design from single-family residences to commercial complexes. Structural analysis allows the designer to design building components able to withstand the building's own stress and weight plus the impact of outside forces. As an example, structural analysis is used to design the massive concrete shells used in earth-sheltered homes. Most nontraditional building designs require structural analysis to ensure design integrity.

The designer may use structural analysis to assist in designing components by using step-by-step model generation. An architect uses descriptive analysis to calculate stress forces in unique residential structures or structural elements, 28-10. Other common computer applications of structural analysis focus on the following:

- strength and elastic stability of building materials
- heat transfer
- pipe rupture and fluid-flow analysis
- conditions that exert force and stress

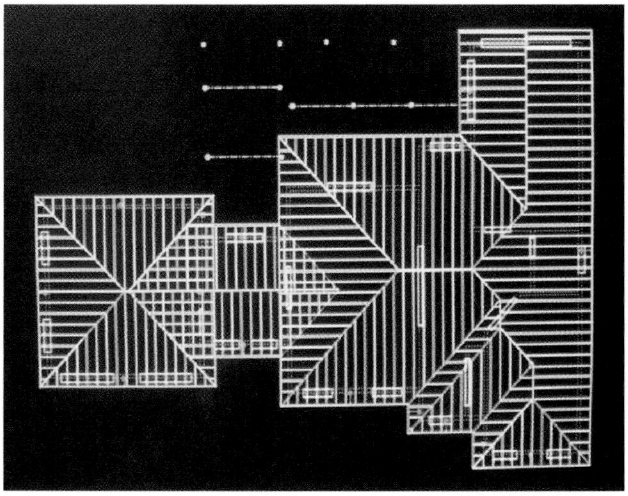

SoftPlan Systems, Inc.

28-9 The computer image clearly describes the structural elements of this residential dwelling. Problems can be identified and solved before construction begins.

Structural Component Selection

As the model building codes become more specific and restrictive, greater assurance is required that the structural components have enough strength to support the intended loads. Many of these structural components are available in new engineered-wood products, 28-11, which are unfamiliar to many designers and builders. As a

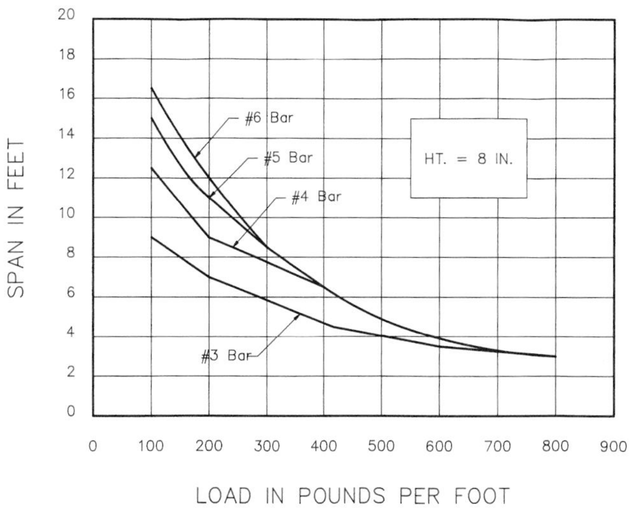

NOTES: Lintels may be 5 or 6 inches nominal width.
Lintels must be grouted solid over entire height.
f'm = 4000 psi, Em = 2,400,000 psi.

28-10 This computer-generated chart will assist the designer in selecting the proper-size reinforcing bars.

The Engineered Wood Association

28-11 New engineered wood products such as these require extensive analysis before users feel confident in choosing them for specific applications.

result, both do-it-yourselfers and professionals are turning to application-specific software programs to accurately select components of the proper size and type for a particular application.

Some common computer programs related to analyzing and selecting structural components focus on the following areas:

- fixed arches and other supports
- steel-structure design
- structural members and frames, including cables, beams, and columns

Computer Simulation

One of the more useful functions of the computer is its ability to simulate, or illustrate, results before the structure or system is built. This is accomplished with **computer simulation**, which means using application-specific software to illustrate how the final result will appear. In this way, the planner or designer can see the outcome of various design options. By altering the impact of one or more options, the operator can view all possible design changes and determine which is best.

One example of simulation is the arrangement of living room components shown in 28-12. By changing the layout and/or mixing furniture of different dimensions, the living/dining area can be tailored to satisfy the client's needs while fitting the designated space. A wide variety of computer simulation applications are available to show the ultimate results of changing various materials, designs, and systems affecting the home's interior and exterior.

Window Selection

All housing structures have windows for the obvious reasons and because building codes require them. As a result of the enormous number of windows used each year, many companies produce them in a wide variety of styles and materials. Therefore, window ordering must be precise to avoid expensive mistakes.

Most window manufacturers have software programs specific to their products. These programs generally allow the designer or prospective homeowners to select the particular windows they like and indicate their intended locations on the floor plan. The program then draws the proper window symbols on the plan and creates an elevation view as well, 28-13. Window details are generally drawn for the builder and a window schedule may also be created as part of the construction drawings.

These software packages help reduce specification errors and improve the overall plan by showing how the completed structure will appear. They also reduce mistakes in ordering by generating a companion order form for each plan.

Helmuth A. Geiser, Member AIBD

28-12 This sophisticated computer simulation represents the capabilities of realistic model generation provided by application-specific software.

Andersen Dealer: ASSOCIATED DOOR & PLYWOOD P O BOX 486 TERRE HAUTE, IN 47808 Salesperson: MIKE PORTER	Today's Date: 08/03 Date Quoted: 08/03	Project: Quote Name: Quote No.: 1363 Report: Design: Right View Window Schedule

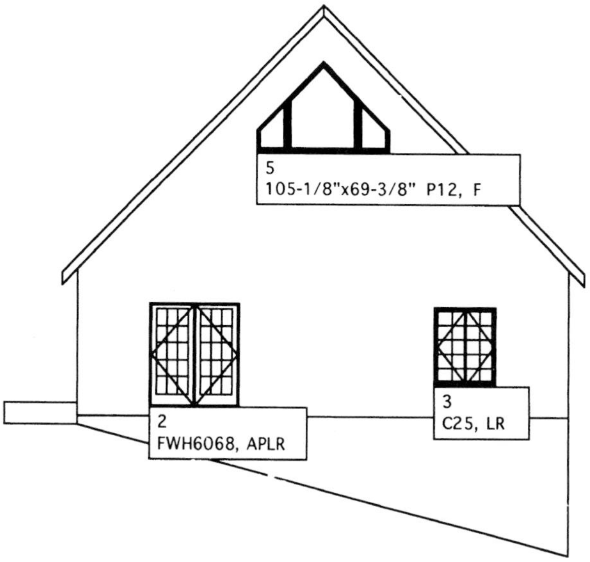

		Unit		Rough Opening	
Code	Andersen Unit Size	Width	Height	Width	Height
1	CTC3/C35	5′ 11 7/8″	8′ 2 1/4″	6′ 3/8″	8′ 2 3/4″
2	FWH6068	5′ 11 1/4″	6′ 7 1/2″	6′	6′ 8″
3	C25	4′	4′ 11 7/8″	4′ 1/2″	5′ 3/8″
4	AFFW608	5′ 11 1/4″	8′ 9 9/16″	5′ 11 3/4″	8′ 10 1/16″
5	105-1/8"x69-3/8"P12	8′ 9 1/8″	5′ 9 3/8″	8′ 9 5/8″	5′ 10″

Andersen Corporation

28-13 This is a typical printout from Andersen's "Window of Knowledge" system.

Preferred Construction and Installation Techniques

In construction, as in many other fields, it is important to disseminate information about preferred practices to the practitioners. Companies and associations have taken the lead in codifying these practices, but the challenge is to deliver the information to everyone who needs it.

Now that the computer is becoming a universal learning tool, using it to teach these techniques and practices will become more common. The most promising teaching tool is the CD-ROM, 28-14. A **CD-ROM** is a compact disc containing data that can be read by a computer. It can contain text, photographs, sound, and video.

Many CDs are **interactive**, too. This is a type of CD-ROM that communicates information specific to the user's response to questions or options. The CD allows users to skip to the sections pertinent to their situations. As the cost of developing a CD-ROM drops, more manufacturers are recognizing the value of this medium and including them with their products.

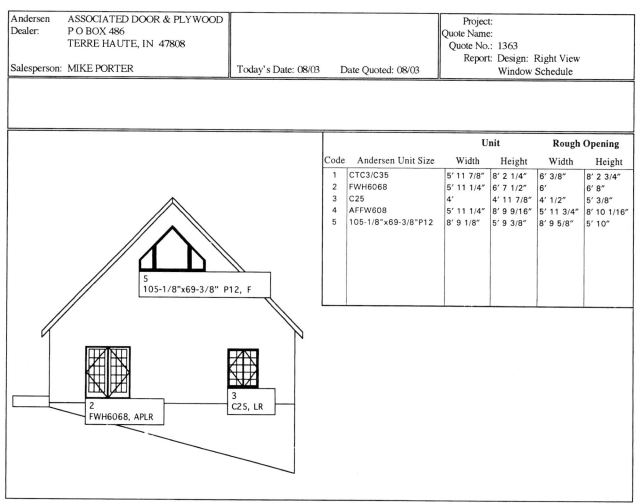

CarCAD Computer Aided Design System by Caradco

28-14 This CD-ROM from a window and door manufacturer allows the user to configure any of its products, design combination units, schedule individual projects, and use a special symbols library.

Service to Clients and Customers

Providing more service to consumers is an important objective for everyone employed in the housing industry. Through a wide variety of software programs, the computer has significantly addressed the challenge of helping consumers better visualize plans for their home. Software programs include subjects, such as home security, home entertainment systems, color coordination, and carpet selection, to name a few.

The basic categories of software programs designed for clients and potential customers include: home planning aids, interior design packages, CD-ROM marketing tools, Internet sources, and virtual reality models.

Home Planning Aids

Many new software programs are available to represent products, designs, and layouts in a more realistic manner, 28-15. Since visualizing the completed structure from a set of construction drawings has always been difficult for most people, hand-drawn pictorials and three-dimensional models were provided. However, these methods frequently failed to give enough detailed information for decision making.

With the computer and application-specific software, that no longer is the case. Now designers can show clients photo-quality representations that display every detail of a building plan. This approach eliminates surprises and results in fewer disgruntled clients. It also helps planners and designers better understand each client's unique wishes and preferences.

Interior Design Programs

To make an apartment, condo, or single-family residence livable, it must have the right colors, furnishings, and accessories to satisfy the family's needs and wishes. Pulling all the elements of the interior together into an attractive, efficient design requires careful thought and planning.

Numerous, easy-to-use software programs help customers select home furnishings, arrange them in a living space, and see the arrangement in a realistic fashion. Other programs are commercially available to help consumers select flattering color schemes for their home and apply the principles of design, 28-16.

SoftPlan Systems Inc.

28-15 This high-quality computer graphics representation of a residential structure was created using SoftPlan software. It provides an image of the house as it will appear upon completion.

Helmuth A. Geiser, Member AIBD

28-16 Solids-modeling software was used to create this image.

CD-ROM Marketing Tools

The CD-ROM has become a useful marketing tool in cases where a large amount of information is needed to make an informed choice or when many choices are available. See 28-17. A typical CD-ROM disc can store all the information contained in an entire encyclopedia. Therefore, a large company can include its entire products catalog, installation details, and servicing procedures on a single disc. For example, a company that produces cedar log homes has recorded its entire line of home packages in the form of a multimedia presentation on CD-ROM. The CD is more effective than videotape because the viewer can determine the viewing sequence and exclude topics of little or no interest.

Rather than publishing thick documents and heavy manuals, this medium is also a logical choice for large compilations of information. Such data collections include model building codes, the National Electrical Code, and research reports from the American Plywood Association and other trade groups.

National Home Builders Association

28-17 This CD-ROM contains more than 12,000 products from 2,500 manufacturers. Included are product catalogs, videos, specifications, product literature, interactive displays, and much more.

Internet Sources

Finding good sources of information is always necessary when planning, designing, constructing, furnishing, or decorating a home. Many types of information are needed about local and coded requirements, new products and services, and technological advances. In the past, sources such as the phone book, manufacturers' catalogs, trade associations, and professionals in the field could be contacted for help. Now, an individual can access countless sources by using a computer linked to the Internet and the World Wide Web, 28-18.

The Internet is composed of millions of computers around the world sharing information. The Web, which is one part of the Internet, is very popular because it can deliver messages with colorful graphics, video, and sound in addition to text. Documents from other Internet sources, on the other hand, only contain single-color text and graphics. With the right hardware, software, and Internet link-up, access to information sources is practically unlimited.

Virtual Reality Models

Virtual reality models, also called virtual models, are usually created from a drawing to show the client how the exterior or interior of a dwelling will appear. The result is a very lifelike representation of the finished structure, 28-19. The amount of detail is dependent on the designer, but may include furniture, carpeting, pictures on the wall, flowers in a vase, and all other objects in the space. Textures, colors, lighting, shades, and shadows may be included as well, 28-20.

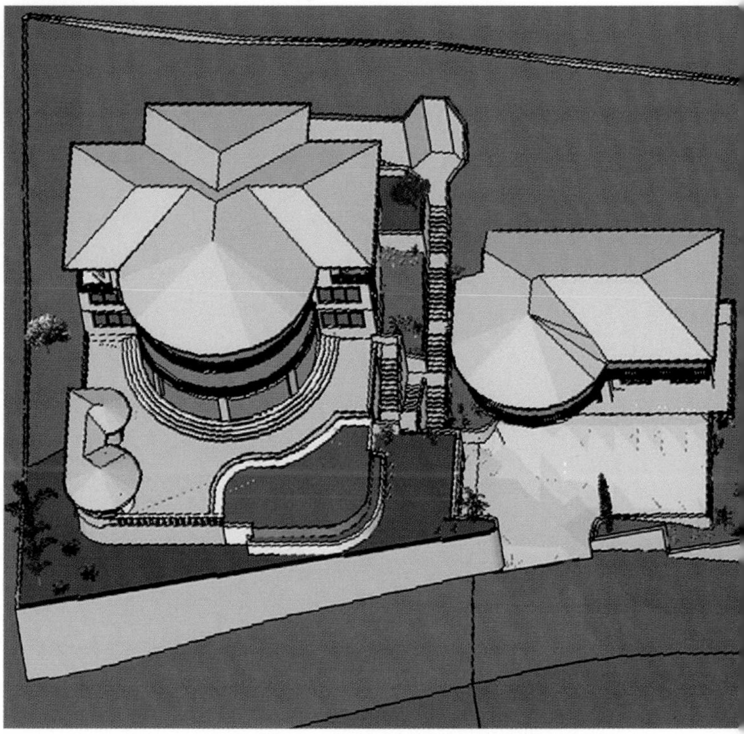

Helmuth A. Geiser, Member AIBD

28-19 This virtual model shows the client how the exterior of a house will look when completed.

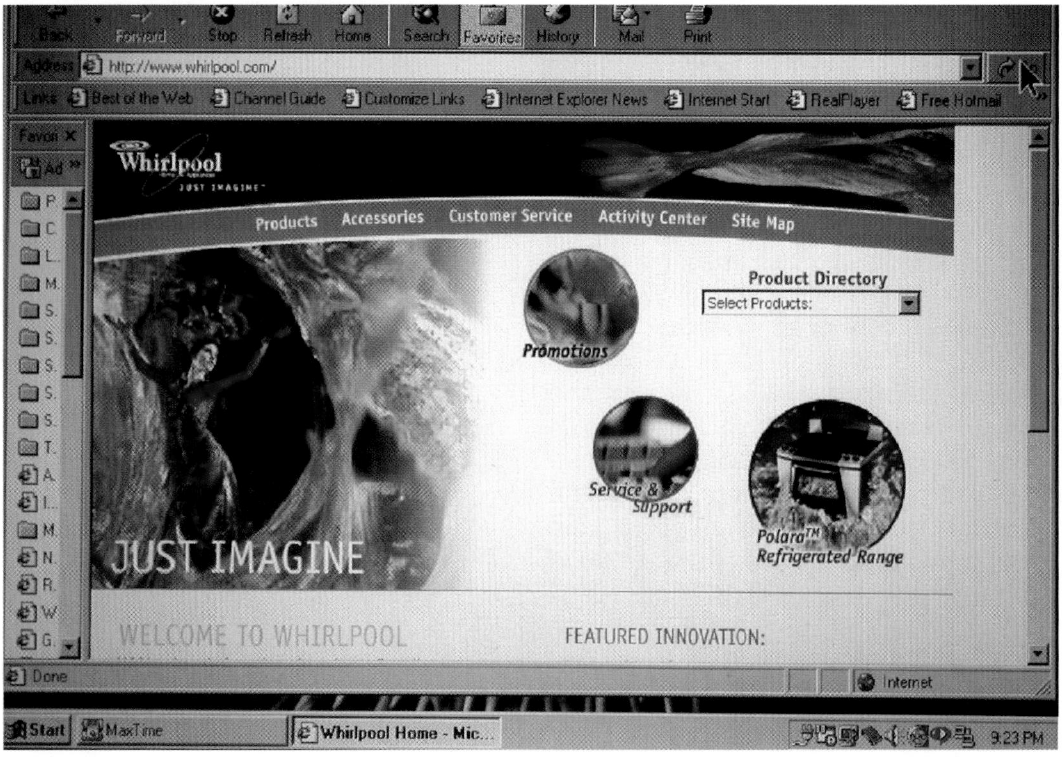

28-18 This is a screen photo of a typical Web site. Most companies are providing similar information to advertise their products on the Internet.

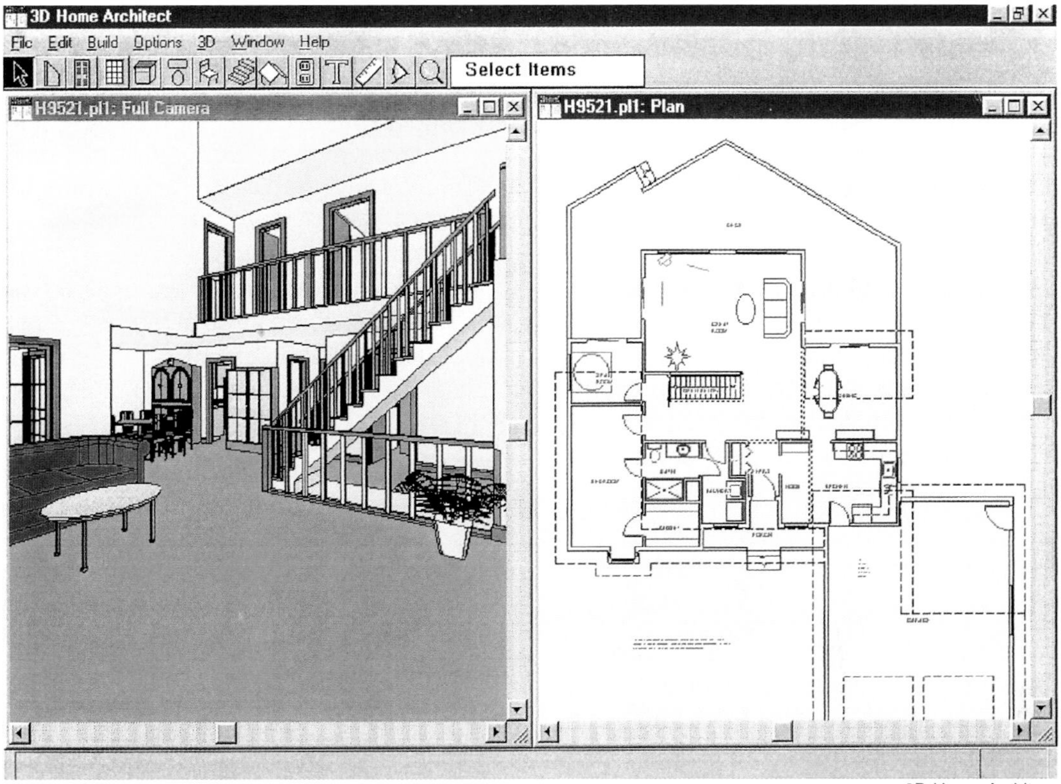

3D Home Architect

28-20 This virtual model allows the designer and client to view the interior space of a home before it is built.

The most impressive part of a virtual reality model is its ability to let a person "walk" through a house and "see" its finished appearance before any construction begins. The client can enter any room, look out a window, or see how a bedroom would look as a den or music room instead.

This tool is especially attractive to builders of expensive houses who, in the past, had to build several full-scale model homes so prospective buyers could decide among the different features. Now, the builder needs only to build one or two models to demonstrate the quality of workmanship and materials used. Then, the computer "shows" clients how the models can be customized to incorporate different features.

Another advantage of the virtual model is the ease of modifying elements in the interior, such as removing a wall or changing carpet colors, with the click of the computer's mouse. Some builders give CD-ROMs containing their virtual models to customers so they can examine them more thoroughly after leaving the office. Companies are also adding their virtual models to the Internet to take advantage of the relocation market.

Project Management

The computer may be used to assist in planning the management, cost estimates, financial models, and scheduling for the construction. Frequently, the difference between profit and loss on a project lies in the area of project management. The three basic types of software programs discussed here are: PERT and Gantt charts for scheduling, cost estimates and financial models, and project data management.

PERT and Gantt Charts for Scheduling

It takes tens of thousands of parts and pieces, brought together over several months, to complete a residential structure. The system is complex, timing is extremely important, and coordination and sequencing is crucial. Most builders agree that "as the building schedule goes, so goes the whole operation." When scheduling is bad, everything else suffers, especially quality, efficiency, employee relations, and customer satisfaction. A poor schedule results from poor planning, poor design, or poor management. The costs to suppliers and subcontractors from poor scheduling are enormous.

The two techniques that are widely used in the field to aid in better scheduling are the PERT and Gantt charts. A **Project Evaluation and Review Technique (PERT) chart** provides step-by-step guidance in the construction of a project. See 28-21. The PERT chart provides both a plan to complete the project and checkpoints to monitor progress. The larger the project, the more valuable is the PERT chart.

The **Gantt chart** is a graphic representation that compares estimated timetables for progress with actual progress performance. See 28-22. It helps contractors keep their projects on schedule.

Cost Estimates and Financial Models

Estimating is one of the most important aspects of a building contractor's business. To be able to accurately and sensibly bid jobs, a contractor must know the limitations of his organization, accurately estimate construction costs, and prepare bid proposals for projects that he or she would like to undertake.

Estimating accurately is founded on a thorough understanding of the construction process, the construction drawings, and specifications, 28-23. An accurate and up-to-date database of unit prices is a must. Most estimators use standard databases that are regularly updated for each section of the country.

Financial models are needed for larger, complex projects involving millions of dollars. Keeping track of financing, cash flow, and payment schedules can directly affect the project schedule as well as profit margin. A financial model provides a road map for the project that ensures a smooth, uninterrupted construction schedule.

Project Data Management

Hundreds of drawings, specifications, contracts, photos, letters of understanding, receipts, and other important documents are accumulated for each project. Often this vital information is piled into a box and not managed at all. Consequently, data stored in this fashion is virtually lost as a database for future projects.

Computer software programs for data management keep information organized and easily retrievable. The programs also provide additional benefits such as the following:

- improved customer service
- increased productivity

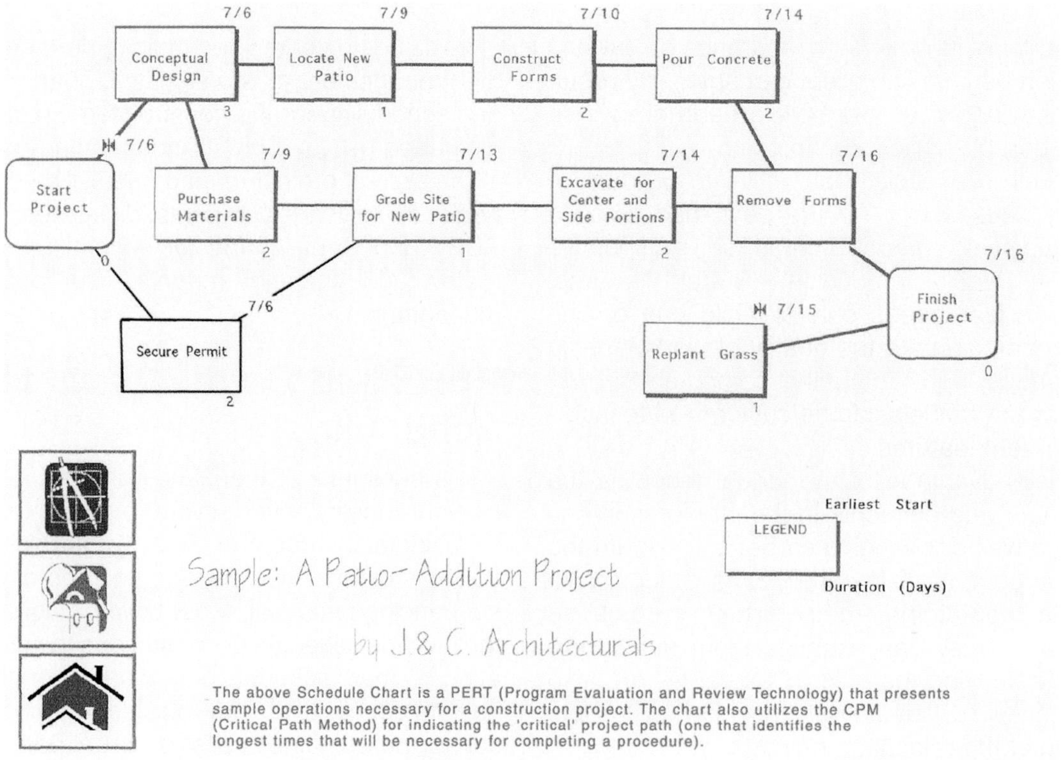

Provided by David P. Beach

28-21 This simple PERT chart shows the important steps in building a patio.

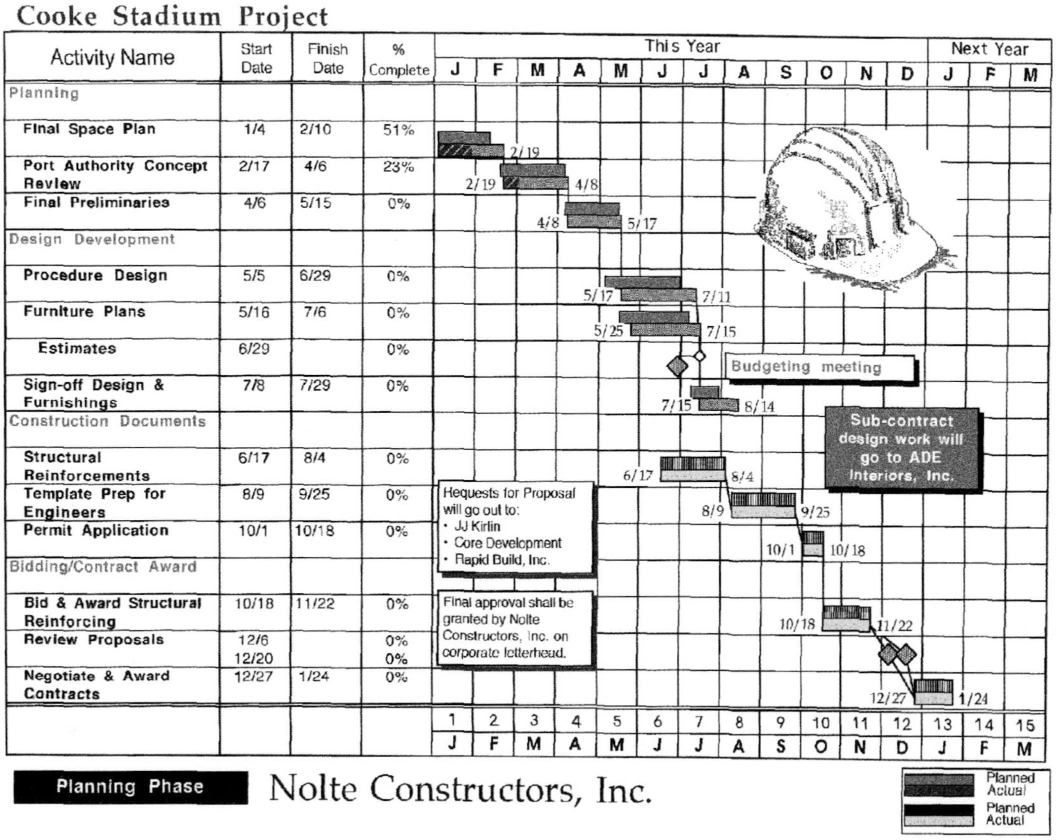

Provided by David P. Beach. Fast Track ScheduleTM Software by AEC Software, Inc.

28-22 A Gantt chart shows the amount of time planned for each phase of a construction project. Both actual time and planned time are shown.

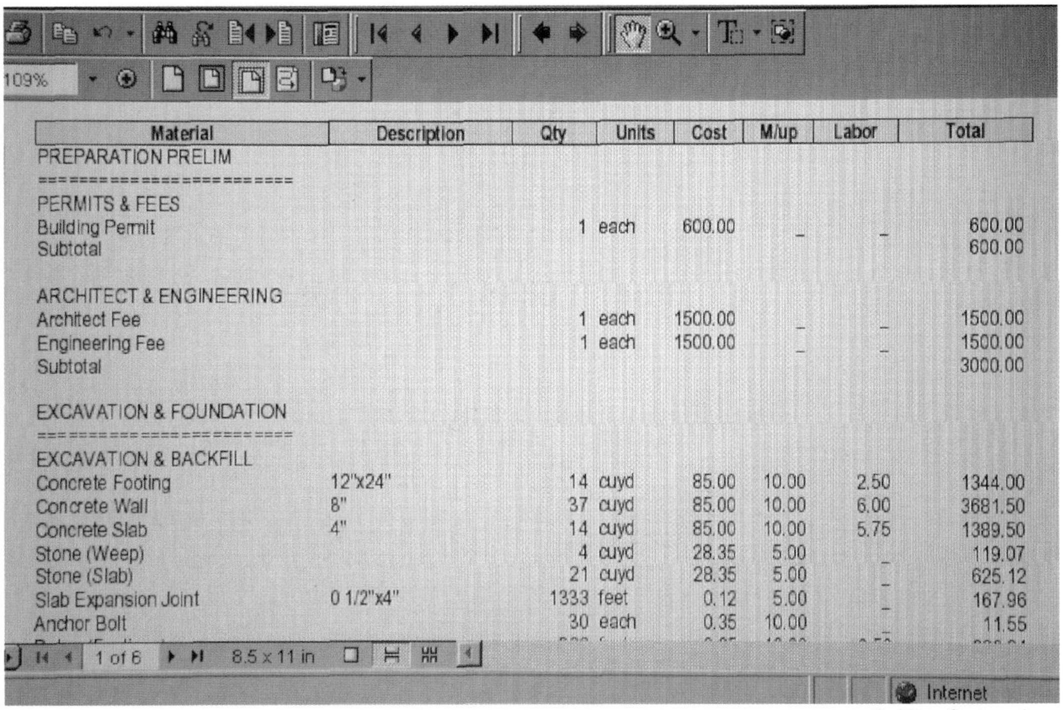

Material	Description	Qty	Units	Cost	M/up	Labor	Total
PREPARATION PRELIM							
=========================							
PERMITS & FEES							
Building Permit		1	each	600.00	_	_	600.00
Subtotal							600.00
ARCHITECT & ENGINEERING							
Architect Fee		1	each	1500.00	_	_	1500.00
Engineering Fee		1	each	1500.00	_	_	1500.00
Subtotal							3000.00
EXCAVATION & FOUNDATION							
=========================							
EXCAVATION & BACKFILL							
Concrete Footing	12"x24"	14	cuyd	85.00	10.00	2.50	1344.00
Concrete Wall	8"	37	cuyd	85.00	10.00	6.00	3681.50
Concrete Slab	4"	14	cuyd	85.00	10.00	5.75	1389.50
Stone (Weep)		4	cuyd	28.35	5.00	_	119.07
Stone (Slab)		21	cuyd	28.35	5.00	_	625.12
Slab Expansion Joint	0 1/2"x4"	1333	feet	0.12	5.00	_	167.96
Anchor Bolt		30	each	0.35	10.00	_	11.55

SoftPlan Systems Inc.

28-23 This is part of an estimate for the construction of a residential structure. The total report is several pages long.

- better cost control
- quicker response time
- timely correction of conditions causing errors
- more accurate pricing
- clear picture of profit/loss situation

Many of these data management programs enable analyses of the final project details for future decisions and convert the drawings and photos to digital data to reduce storage space. It is conceivable, then, to have the records of an entire project stored on a CD.

Computer Usage by Housing Professionals

The computer is now commonplace in the housing field. Designers and drafters use CADD systems to formulate design ideas and make drawings to apply for construction permits, secure funding, gain client approval, and guide the construction process. The hardware and software of CADD systems enable a designer to create designs, drawings, and presentations to meet clients' needs. CADD allows quick adjustments to accommodate the client's wishes, and it presents solutions in forms that the client understands.

Building inspectors use computers to keep track of code compliance as a building is constructed. Builders use computers in all aspects of their business, including scheduling, bidding, management, accounting, and reporting. Interior designers use computers to check the availability of furnishings, record design ideas, and make presentations to clients. Real estate agents use the computer to see listings, compare prices, and communicate sales.

Virtually all parts of the housing and construction industry depend on the computer. Designs are now modified in minutes instead of the hours or days associated with manual drafting. Realistic views of the proposed design can quickly communicate the most complex design details to clients. "Walk-throughs" or "fly-overs" present the inside as well as the outside of a dwelling. Some presentations have a look so realistic as to resemble photographs, 28-24.

Computers are also used to design roof and floor trusses, analyze structural components, and plan the actual construction process. All types of schedules, reports, and documentation are created by computer to keep the building process on schedule and on budget. Landscape designers use computers to generate landscape designs, perform soil studies, and plan landscape lighting. This is just a brief glimpse of the many uses of the computer in the housing and construction industry. One thing is sure—applications will continue to increase as more professionals are trained to use the computer to solve their problems.

Helmuth A. Geiser, Member AIBD

28-24 Almost anyone could mistake this computer-generated image for a photograph of the actual home. Yet, this image was produced before the home was built.

Chapter Summary

Computers and specialized software have greatly impacted planning, design, constructing, and furnishing modern housing units. Computers are now used for: drafting, designing, and rendering plans; adding color and shading to layouts; displaying plans in three dimensions; touring building interiors from a walk-through presentation; analyzing a housing unit's energy use; and generating all the necessary reports.

Design and analysis functions account for the greatest use of computer applications. Through the use of computer-assisted drafting and design, construction drawings have greater accuracy and uniformity. Revision is easier and much quicker. Plot plans, site plans, and landscape plans are easier to produce from topographical and survey data. Also, producing analyses about water-surface profiles, earth sections, and contour mapping is almost automatic with advanced software. Kitchen and bath design speeds the design process and reduces errors, which is particularly helpful in the remodeling sector. Energy analysis is required in many U.S. areas, and application-specific software has greatly impacted the area.

Structural analysis allows the designer to specify building components that will perform as required. Computer simulation allows the designer to "test" various components or designs before the structure is built. The computer is also useful in teaching good construction practices.

The computer has played an important role in improving service to clients and customers through the use of home planning aids, interior design packages, CD-ROM marketing tools, Internet sources, and virtual reality models. As a group, these products are powerful tools for designers to serve their clients better.

The computer and application-specific software has played a very active role in project management. It has provided assistance in planning the management, cost estimates, financial models, and scheduling for construction functions involved in constructing a building. The role of the computer in the design and construction of dwellings will continue to increase as more professionals learn to use these tools.

Computer usage by housing professionals—drafters, designers, builders, architects, and contractors—is so commonplace that virtually every part of the housing and construction industry depends on them.

Review Questions

1. How is a computer symbols library useful?
2. How is computer simulation useful to the designer of a residential structure?
3. How are software programs from window, door, and furniture manufacturers useful to the designer?
4. What two forces are causing design professionals and do-it-yourselfers to depend on application-specific software for the selection of structural components?
5. Why is a CD-ROM a useful medium for information storage?
6. What functions may be performed using modern computer software programs in the area of landscape planning?
7. Why is an interactive CD-ROM an advantage to the user?
8. When making drawings on a CADD system, where is the greatest time savings realized?
9. Why might an energy analysis be performed when designing a new home?
10. What is a virtual reality model?
11. In housing construction, on what is accurate estimating based?
12. Identify several advantages of project data management.

Suggested Activities

1. Identify and describe the four basic categories of computer applications in housing. Prepare a brief oral report.
2. List several benefits of computer applications in housing design and analysis.
3. Write a report about several applications of the computer in the selection of construction elements and processes.
4. Describe in a short essay how the computer is used to serve clients and customers.
5. Identify project-management steps in which the computer is useful.
6. Using a computer, locate at least three Web sites that provide useful information about residential housing. Share them with the class.
7. Using a CADD system, draw a presentation bath or kitchen floor plan that would be appropriate to show a client.

Internet Resources

Autodesk, Inc., publisher of AutoCAD
autodesk.com

Bently Systems Inc., publisher of MicroStation engineering design software
bentley.com/products

Cadalyst Magazine
cadalyst.com

Compaq Computers, a Hewlett-Packard Company
compaq.com

Dell Inc.
dell.com

Hewlett-Packard Development Company, L.P.
hewlettpackard.com

SoftPlan Systems, Inc. residential design program
softplan.com

Note: Web addresses may have changed since publication. For some entries, reaching the correct Web site may require keying *www.* into the address.

Part Nine
Career Opportunities

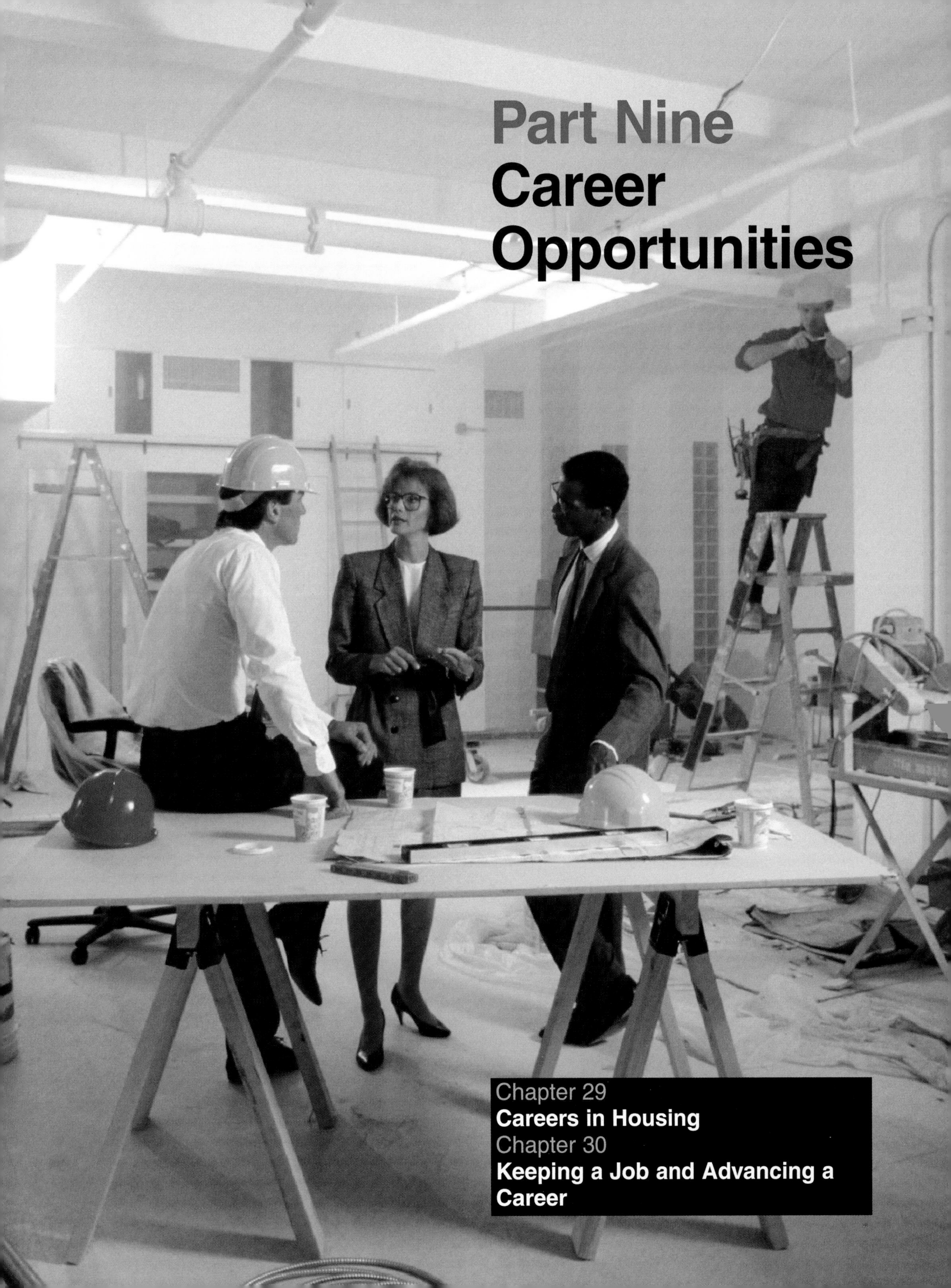

Chapter 29
Careers in Housing
Chapter 30
Keeping a Job and Advancing a Career

Chapter 29
Careers in Housing

Objectives

After studying this chapter, you will be able to

- list various career options within the housing field.
- compare the duties and educational requirements of various occupations related to housing.
- determine typical career paths for entry-level, midlevel, and professional level positions.

Key Terms

architect
bachelor's degree
master's degree
associate degree
architectural drafter
architectural illustrator
interior designer
model maker
landscape designer
trade
building contractor
construction technologist
apprentice
journeyman
land surveyor
career path

Housing is a broad field that includes many occupations. Perhaps the most well-known career associated with housing is carpentry, since carpenters are a familiar sight on most construction jobs. However, there are numerous other skilled professionals involved with housing construction. These professionals generally fall into three career categories: planners and designers, building tradespeople, and allied professionals.

Planners and Designers

Long before a building is built, planners and designers are hard at work developing the plans for it. These occupations usually require creative ability and problem-solving skills as well as knowledge and training in housing design. Planners and designers include: architects, architectural drafters, architectural illustrators, interior designers, model makers, and landscape designers.

Architect

The architect's job requires creativity with forms and materials. An **architect** designs structures by having a thorough understanding of construction technology, building codes, laws pertaining to construction, and the use of modern CADD equipment.

The architect works closely with a client, making preliminary sketches, suggesting materials, and helping choose a satisfactory final design for a structure, 29-1. Working drawings are then prepared. The architect may also help the client with choosing a building contractor and dealing with the contractor during construction. Sometimes an architect checks that construction and materials meet specifications.

To become a registered architect, a person must fulfill the educational training requirements for the state in which he or she will work. In addition, all states require an examination to obtain a license. Most states require at least a bachelor's degree from a college with an accredited architecture program. A **bachelor's degree** is a college or university degree

29-1 An architect often meets with clients at a building site to show them features that will be incorporated into their home.

VICA

29-2 Architectural drafters often add details to working plans that have been drawn by architects.

that generally requires four years of full-time study. Many architects also obtain a **master's degree**, which is an advanced degree involving one to two years of study beyond a bachelor's degree.

In some areas, education and training requirements can be met with completion of a specified number of years of practical experience and an associate degree. An **associate degree** is a college degree that usually requires two years of full-time study. Most areas require that building designs be certified by a registered architect before construction can begin.

Architectural Drafter

An **architectural drafter** draws the details of working drawings and makes tracings from the original drawings prepared by the architect or designer. These professionals often begin as junior drafters, 29-2. As they gain experience, they may move into drafting positions requiring more responsibility.

An architectural drafting position usually requires at least a high school diploma with some courses in architectural drawing and CADD. Further education at a community college, technical school, or university may assure better job placement. Architectural drafters sometimes use this position to gain experience and eventually become registered architects.

Architectural Illustrator

An **architectural illustrator** prepares presentation drawings, sketches, and illustrations for advertising and for client presentations. These professionals usually begin study in architectural drawing or commercial art and then branch into this specialized field, 29-3. Much of their work today is performed on a CADD system. Architectural illustrators need a high degree of artistic skill to be readily employable.

Educational requirements for this type of work are similar to requirements for the architectural drafter. A natural talent for freehand drawing is important because of the artistic ability expected in this position. Large architectural firms generally employ architectural illustrators.

Interior Designer

An **interior designer** plans and supervises the design, decoration, and furnishings of building interiors. Often these interiors are private homes, restaurants, and offices, but interior designers also apply their expertise to retail establishments, hospitals, hotels, and government and other public buildings. They also plan new interiors when existing structures are renovated or expanded.

29-3 Courses in art and drafting are usually needed to become an architectural illustrator.

29-4 Interior designers work closely with clients to learn their needs and desires, then translate that information into a design plan.

Most interior designers specialize. For example, some concentrate in residential design, while others further specialize by focusing on particular rooms, such as kitchens or baths. Creativity and a full knowledge of design principles, materials, furnishings, and accessories are needed for this type of work. An understanding of computers and CADD is a necessity, 29-4.

Interior designers work from prints to prepare presentation plans, presentation boards, and models. They help clients choose furnishings and materials to meet their needs and tastes. Interior designers may select and estimate the costs of furniture, floor and wall coverings, and other needed items. They may also arrange purchases and hire and supervise various workers. Interior designers must design space to conform to federal, state, and local laws including building codes. Designs for public areas must also meet accessibility standards for the disabled and elderly.

A four-year degree in interior design is recommended for professional designers as well as membership in the American Society of Interior Designers (ASID), the organization representing the profession. Formal training, however, can also be obtained through a professional school or community college.

Interior design is the only design field subject to government regulation. According to the American Society for Interior designers, 19 States and the District of Columbia require interior Designers to be licensed or registered. Passing the National Council for Interior Design qualification examination is required for licensure. To take the exam, one must satisfy the following minimum requirements: two years of postsecondary education in design, two years of practical work experience, and additional related education or experience to total six years of combined education and experience in design. Because licensing is not mandatory in all states, membership in ASID is an indication of an interior designer's qualifications and professional standing, which can aid in obtaining clients.

Knowledge of art and design principles plus an awareness of design innovations and technologies is fundamental to the job of the interior designer. Meeting client needs by applying that knowledge to create a pleasing style is the challenge. Besides working as independent design consultants, interior designers are also employed by architectural and design firms, and manufacturers and retail stores specializing in paint, furniture and other decorating materials.

Model Maker

A **model maker** builds scale models of objects, such as planned communities, individual buildings, room layouts, or pieces of furniture. Model makers work from construction drawings or conceptual design renderings. Architects and other types of designers often employ model makers, 29-5.

Model making requires a thorough knowledge of materials and an ability to read drawings. The model maker must also be creative and skilled in operating the machinery used to make models. There are no special educational requirements for this job, but considerable experience and manual dexterity is needed.

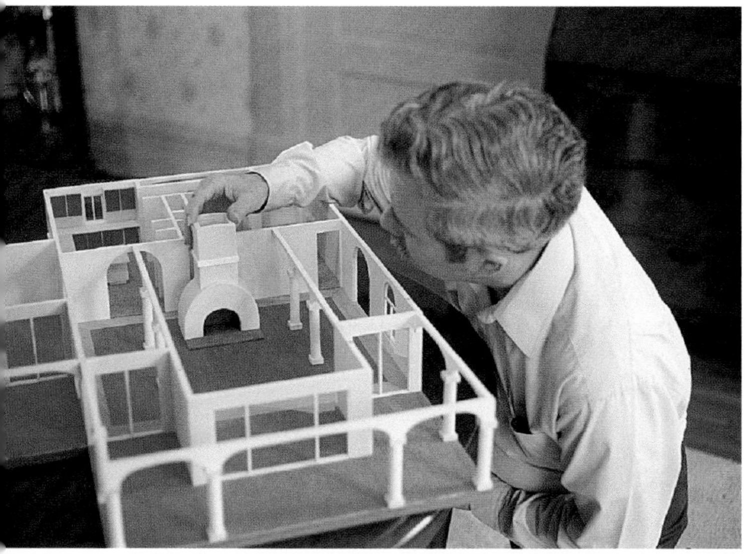

29-5 Architects often employ model makers to make three-dimensional representations of their plans.

Landscape Designer

The **landscape designer** plans the arrangement and composition of landscape elements on a site. This involves working with clients to prepare a design plan, selecting landscape materials, and supervising the installation of elements. See 29-6.

The landscape designer generally has a bachelor's degree or at least some formal training and practical experience in landscaping. Landscape designers need a thorough knowledge of soil science, horticulture, design principles, and construction materials and techniques.

Building Tradespeople

Another large category of jobs related to the housing industry involves people who work in an occupation that requires manual or mechanical skill. This is the definition of a **trade**. Sometimes a tradesperson is called a craftsperson.

Workers of various trades are involved in housing, including building contractors, construction

29-6 Developing a landscape that meets clients' needs and complements the exterior of their home is the landscape designer's goal.

technologists, skilled tradespeople, and construction machinery operators. These positions require concentrated training to develop the needed skills.

Building Contractor

The **building contractor** plans and coordinates the construction of buildings. This involves working with or supervising subcontractors, inspectors, and designers. Contractors are responsible for scheduling work, obtaining materials and equipment, and checking that materials and construction comply with building codes. They also make sure the specifications of the architect and owner are met, 29-7. Computers are used in all phases of the building contractor's work.

A contractor must obtain a license to do contracting work. Generally, years of experience in several areas of construction are needed. Course work in management, accounting, economics, construction law, and labor relations is helpful because most contractors are self-employed.

Construction Technologist

A **construction technologist** is qualified for both technical and supervisory roles in the construction industry. Specialty areas within construction technology include estimating and bidding, quality control, site supervision, specifications writing, expediting, purchasing, and managing construction, 29-8. A construction technologist must be able to utilize the computer in all aspects of the work.

A construction technologist typically has a bachelor's degree in construction technology. A strong science background and knowledge of construction are needed for this major. Experience in construction is helpful, but not necessary.

Skilled Tradesperson

Skilled tradespeople include painters, paperhangers, electricians, plumbers, carpenters, and masons, 29-9. Trades are highly specialized, and seldom does a person work in more than one trade. Classroom education is available through career/technical programs in some high schools and community colleges as well as through programs offered by trade unions. On-the-job training is required for positions in most trades.

Most trades recognize three positions, designated by skill and experience—apprentice, journeyman, and master. Generally, a high school diploma is sufficient to begin as an **apprentice**. This

29-7 The contractor coordinates all the jobs necessary to construct a building.

29-8 A construction technologist is qualified to perform several roles in the management of construction.

Associated General Contractors of America

29-9 Cement finishers are just one of several categories of skilled tradespeople needed to construct a building.

person learns a trade by working under the direction and guidance of a skilled worker. A **journeyman** is an experienced, reliable worker who knows the trade, while a master has demonstrated the highest level of expertise. Tradespeople may work for one contractor, or they may obtain work through their respective trade unions.

Construction Machinery Operator

Many large, expensive machines, such as cranes, bulldozers, backhoes, and forklifts, are used in modern construction. Competent machinery operators are needed to run machines safely and efficiently. See 29-10. Operators must have good eyesight and physical coordination. Jobs require a high school diploma and on-the-job training.

Land Surveyor

A **land surveyor** locates property boundaries, measures distances, establishes contours, and makes maps and reports of the site surveyed. See 29-11.

29-10 Operators of large, complex construction equipment are vital to the construction industry.

29-11 Surveyors measure distances and contours of a construction site.

Computer expertise is expected. The registered surveyor supervises a survey party consisting of one or more survey technicians and helpers.

A land surveyor must be licensed to practice as a registered surveyor. Formal training in surveying is needed, and some states require a bachelor's degree. Land surveying is highly technical work requiring skill in trigonometry and drawing. Registered surveyors receive training in other positions on the surveying team before receiving a license.

Allied Careers

Government and real estate positions are also related to housing. These positions usually require knowledge and skills beyond the housing field as well as a general knowledge of housing fundamentals.

Government Positions

Many positions in local, state, and federal government involve aspects of the housing industry. Building inspectors examine construction in progress to verify that local codes are followed. Health inspectors check soil, water, and sewer components on a lot. Inspectors are employed at all levels of government and may do highly specialized work on complex construction sites. Inspection covers nearly all materials, equipment, and workmanship on a construction site.

Government agencies monitor housing trends, provide loans, underwrite financing for low-cost housing, and sponsor research to improve housing. They employ housing professionals as well as accountants, field representatives, and community planners. Technical expertise is required for these positions.

Real Estate Positions

Several careers are possible in the field of real estate. The real estate agent assists people in appraising, buying, selling, renting, and leasing property, 29-12. Brokers are professionals that must know building codes and laws relating to real estate transactions. They also must be familiar with local communities.

Brokers generally have college degrees, but this is not a requirement. They must, however, pass a test to obtain a brokerage license.

Real estate management is another career in the field of real estate. Large housing units, such as apartments, condominiums, and mobile home courts, often employ property managers. Management duties involve interviewing prospective tenants, maintaining the property, and reporting to the building owner. There are no specific educational requirements for these types of positions. However, a manager must be responsible and able to deal with people.

Preparing for a Career Path in Housing

The previous sections of this chapter acquainted you with well-known jobs in the housing industry, but there are many others. Learning what types of jobs are available in the housing field is the first step to finding suitable work and a rewarding career.

What Is a Career Path?

A **career path** is a series of related work experiences of increasing responsibility and/or expertise. A job, on the other hand, is work a person does to earn money. The purpose of a career path is to advance in a field. A career path includes both paid and unpaid work since projects undertaken as a volunteer can also expand a person's skills and knowledge. Often favorite courses, extracurricular activities, and volunteer work in the community can play a big role in helping students recognize suitable career areas for themselves.

Depending on the specific profession, there is usually more than one way to pursue a career path. For example, a person working in a retail furniture store with an interest in decorating who gains further education could advance to a position as an interior design consultant. A high school student working as a waitress part-time may develop an interest in the restaurant's décor and recommend design ideas. If they increase business, she may be inspired to pursue commercial interior design as a career. Consider the model maker who, after creating numerous room layouts for others, decides to study interior design and use his model-making skill in his own kitchen-design business.

Typically, workers start at entry-level positions. Then, with experience gained on one job and additional education, they are ready to advance to a more challenging job, often with better pay. Senior positions with an employer and self-employment opportunities usually require many years of work to achieve.

29-12 The real estate broker plays a key role in buying, selling, and renting house properties.

Entry-Level Positions

Entry-level positions provide access to the profession. People in these positions follow the directions of supervisors and managers. The tasks they perform are generally more repetitive with less opportunity for independent action, 29-13. Their duties almost never involve supervising or managing anyone else. Some entry-level positions teach workers all they need to know in order to do their jobs. Moving to a better job, however, usually requires more education or training.

Midlevel Positions

Workers who hold midlevel positions are often *support* personnel. They support or assist the professionals in the organization by supervising entry-level workers. For example, a foreman of a

29-13 Members of a landscaping crew provide the manual labor that is needed to execute a landscaping design.

masonry crew is responsible for getting the work done on time and at a prescribed level of quality. He or she might work as a member of the crew, but has supervisory authority over other crewmates. There may be several tiers of midlevel positions in a given field depending on the size and/or complexity of the work to be done, 29-14. Progressing to a higher level almost always requires more education, experience, and ability to handle greater responsibility.

Professional Positions

People who occupy the professional positions have the highest level of education and experience in their chosen field. Some of the professional-level positions in the construction and housing industry are architects, engineers, interior designers, land use planners, and building contractors. These professionals handle countless responsibilities as they make decisions that affect the lives of many people, 29-15. They may work for themselves or as part of a larger enterprise. However, they must be able to coordinate their activities and responsibilities with others in the industry. Without this cooperation, work does not get done.

29-14 Midlevel positions exist among professionals as newer leaders learn from more-experienced leaders.

29-15 This design professional is planning the interior for a new apartment complex.

For What Jobs Are You Suited?

Answering this question requires relatively in-depth knowledge of yourself. If you have experience in summer or part-time jobs or with volunteer projects, you already know some jobs that appeal to you and some that do not.

Asking trusted family members, teachers, and friends can help you know what traits others see in you and what jobs use those traits. Your school or guidance counselor can help you evaluate your personality, natural talents, and abilities. Counselors will also acquaint you with the following valuable U.S. Department of Labor resources:

- *Occupational Outlook Handbook*—describes what workers do on a job, its working conditions, the training and education required, and average earnings. It is available as a publication and accessible online.
- *Guide for Occupational Exploration*—helps people understand what traits are required for certain occupations and how well their abilities and interests match job requirements. It is only available as a publication.

- O*NET, the Occupational Information Network—helps people explore careers, related job skills, and trends, and provides tools for assessing personal abilities and interests. It is only accessible online.

These and other resources can help you judge what type of work is best. Above all, it is important to know that only you will be able to determine the perfect job for you.

How Do You Get the Job You Want?

After identifying the type of work that interests you and getting the required training and education, you will want to find a job. Where will you begin? Figure 29-16 shows sources to explore for information about job openings.

When workers look for employment, one of the primary features to seek in any new position is the opportunity for further advancement or promotion. Eventually your curiosity and evolving interests will lead you into new directions and to the desire for another job. Ideally, opportunities will exist with your current employer.

Choosing your next job should be easier since you will have a clearer idea of what work you enjoy doing. Often workers need to learn new skills and/or increase their education to qualify for a higher position. Usually that position will involve increased responsibility and a corresponding increase in pay.

It is always important to show interest in taking on the new responsibilities associated with your position and demonstrate maturity and trust. This is accomplished by starting work on time, showing enthusiasm toward the job's responsibilities, and accepting new challenges in a positive manner.

Leads to Job Openings

- Personal contacts, such as family members, teachers, neighbors, and friends
- School career planning and placement offices
- Internet networks and resources
- Companies and businesses
- Classified ads in national and local newspapers, professional journals, and trade magazines
- State employment service offices and the federal government's Office of Personnel Management
- Professional and trade associations
- Labor unions
- Nonprofit organizations and agencies
- Private employment agencies and career consultants

29-16 Finding the right job often involves searching many sources.

Chapter Summary

The housing field comprises many occupations in three broad categories: planners and designers, building tradespeople, and allied professionals. Planners and designers are hard at work before a building is constructed. These occupations usually require creative ability, problem-solving skills, and training in housing design. This group includes architects, drafters, illustrators, interior designers, model makers, and landscape designers.

Building tradespeople comprise the second largest category of jobs related to housing construction. Some of the jobs in this category include: contractors, technologists, tradespeople, and machinery operators.

Allied careers related to housing include government and real estate positions. These positions usually require knowledge and skills beyond the housing field as well as a general knowledge of housing fundamentals. Government positions are available in local, state, and federal governments that relate to housing. Some include inspectors, housing research, and community planners.

Employees use career paths to advance in their fields. To advance to new jobs, workers need to improve their present skills, learn new skills, and/or increase their education. There are numerous career paths to follow depending on the profession. Entry-level positions provide access to the profession. Those holding midlevel positions often serve as support personnel. People who occupy the professional positions have the highest level of education and experience in their chosen field.

Review Questions

1. What are the responsibilities of an architect?
2. What background is needed to become a registered architect?
3. Besides a career as an architect, what other career areas are available in architecture?
4. What skills and knowledge should the interior designer possess?
5. What background is needed to become a licensed interior designer?
6. What positions are available in the field of construction?
7. How do positions in construction vary in responsibilities and educational requirements?
8. What government positions are available in the field of housing?
9. What real estate positions are available in the field of housing?
10. What is the purpose of a career path?

Suggested Activities

1. Select a job in the housing field that interests you and research it to learn the following: the job's duties, working conditions, required education and training, average earnings, and employment outlook. Write a summary of your findings.
2. Interview a professional in the housing field to learn about his or her job. Share your findings with the class.
3. Borrow the *Occupational Outlook Handbook* from your school counselor and demonstrate to the class how to use it.
4. Explore your likely career choice on the O*NET. Report to the class what information you find.

Internet Resources

American Institute of Architects
aia.org

American Institute of Building Design
aibd.org

American Institute of Constructors
aicnet.org

American Society of Interior Designers
interiors.org

American Society of Landscape Architects
asla.org

Federal Emergency Management Agency
fema.gov

National Association of Industrial Technology
nait.org

National Institute of Building Sciences
nibs.org

U.S. Department of Labor's Occupational Information Network (O*NET)
onetcenter.org

U.S. Department of Labor's *Occupational Outlook Handbook*
bls.gov/oco/

Note: Web addresses may have changed since publication. For some entries, reaching the correct Web site may require keying *www.* into the address.

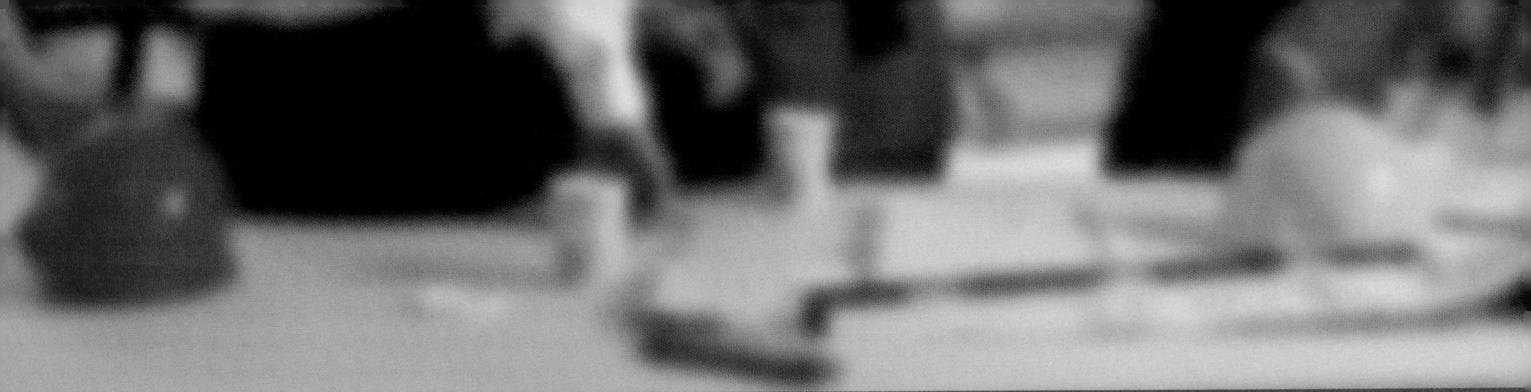

Chapter 30
Keeping a Job and Advancing a Career

Objectives

After studying this chapter, you will be able to

- identify factors that affect job performance.
- list the steps in meeting a client's needs through a functional plan.
- determine why ethics is an important consideration to the workplace.
- list common characteristics of a good leader.
- describe the typical process of conflict resolution.
- explain the concept of entrepreneurship.
- explain the need to manage home and work responsibilities.

Key Terms

Occupational Safety and Health Administration (OSHA)
empathic listening
structural model
prototype
ethics
work ethic
manager
delegate
conflict
mediation
entrepreneur

Whether the job you hold is your dream job or one step to achieving it, you will want to do the very best work possible. This chapter is designed to help employees in the housing field enjoy job and career success, regardless of their specialty area.

First and foremost, success requires an ability to do a job well and conduct yourself appropriately in the workplace. While there are many definitions of career success, the only true success flows from behaving ethically. A successful employee also works well with coworkers, taking charge of situations and resolving conflict as needed. For some, success means working for themselves instead of others. For all, career success can only result when there is harmony between their personal and professional lives.

Job Performance

You will probably start your job with a training or orientation period that explains your job responsibilities and how you are expected to perform them. For a time, you will likely work closely with an experienced coworker until your employer feels confident of your ability to handle the job alone, 30-1.

During this initial period, your performance will be closely watched, but throughout your career, your work will be observed and evaluated. People who work in the trades and perform poorly are not called back for other jobs. People who work in an office setting can expect an annual or semi-annual *performance review,* which consists of a written evaluation of accomplishments that stays on file with the employee's record.

The evaluation is generally based on two areas: competence in work skills and an ability to display the proper personal qualities on the job. These qualities include demonstrating good work habits, safety-mindedness, good communication techniques, an ability to meet client needs, and a desire to keep learning. Career advancement is linked to possessing these important qualities and showing increased competence in your field of expertise.

30-1 This new employee with a design firm will need to demonstrate good design and communication abilities to his supervisor before he gets an assignment that involves working with a client.

Developing Good Work Habits

General work habits play a large part in progressing on the job. You should always strive to improve your performance and the quality of your work. You might begin by asking yourself the following questions about your general work habits:

- *Do you know your employer's policies and observe them?* On the first day of work, many employees receive a copy of the company's employee handbook. Policies are established to inform employees of work rules and standards of behavior that all must follow. Adherence to policies is vital to the smooth operation of the business.
- *Do you always give your best effort to each job?* One way to improve your performance is to practice good work habits. Always try to improve your skills and take pride in your work.
- *Do you plan and execute your work efficiently?* A professional comes to the job ready to work and has the necessary tools and attitude to perform the prescribed tasks. Time is not wasted on daydreaming, chatting, joke telling, and other work interferences. Such distractions steal time from the workday and can actually cause an accident.
- *Do you keep the work area clean and organized?* A cluttered workplace encourages accidents and slows the work.
- *Do you observe safety rules?* Staying safety-minded means safeguarding your personal safety as well as the safety of others. See 30-2. Safety, which is discussed more fully in the next section, is everyone's business.

These are some questions to ask yourself about your general work habits, but you can probably think of others. Paying attention to your work habits could result in greater appreciation of you and your work, increased pay, and possibly a promotion.

Practicing Safety on the Job

Have you ever seen people stand on top of a ladder, struggle to lift heavy boxes, or leave drawers hanging open? All were acting unsafely. Given the right set of circumstances, each could have caused an accident, possibly involving others.

Statistics show that 5 percent of all accidents are caused by unsafe conditions, while the other 95 percent are caused by unsafe actions. Carelessness, laziness, impatience, and outright disobedience are

30-2 Does this scaffolding look sturdy enough to pass an OSHA inspection?

some reasons for unsafe actions. Fatigue and lack of sleep can also cause accidents as well as impaired thinking due to illness, drugs, or alcohol. Erroneously believing that your workplace is perfectly safe, as many office workers do, is another cause of accidents. Here the cause is indifference, or lack of concern.

Construction is a particularly dangerous business. In fact, construction is cited by the **Occupational Safety and Health Administration (OSHA)** as the most dangerous occupation in the country. The OSHA keeps job-injury statistics, provides job safety information, and enforces rules to protect worker safety. When all construction occupations are considered, an injury is recorded every 18 seconds and a death every 47 minutes. Job safety must, by necessity, be a primary concern for every employer, employee, and visitor to a construction site.

People involved in accidents may experience suffering, medical bills, physical disabilities, and even death. For employers, accidents can involve fines, lawsuits, production losses, and the permanent loss of capable employees. Is there any wonder why safety is a top priority in the workplace?

Worker safety requires frequent training sessions so all employees understand how to properly do their jobs and handle related tools, equipment, and materials. See 30-3. Safety training also teaches employees to remain safety-conscious and correct (or report) unsafe conditions. Refresher courses are given to reinforce the training. Methods for preventing the most common accidents involve the following actions:

- properly using machines and tools, such as ladders
- wearing prescribed clothing, such as hard-toed shoes on a construction site
- using protective equipment, such as eye or ear protectors around machinery
- lifting heavy items properly to prevent strains and back injury
- keeping work areas neat to prevent tripping, slipping, or being struck by falling objects
- following fire prevention guidelines

30-3 Is this worker thinking "safety"? He is not wearing safety glasses or gloves while cutting metal fabric.

If an accident should occur, you may need to handle it until help arrives. If the accident is serious and you are alone, call *911* or the local emergency number. Always stay on the line until the emergency provider gets all the needed information, such as the type of accident involved and its location. If possible, have bystanders help with placing the call, assisting the injured, or controlling traffic.

Always follow company policy regarding the steps to take following an accident. One or more people at your workplace should be trained in accident procedures. Rely on him or her, especially when the accident involves loss of blood. After an accident, everyone should participate in a discussion of the details to determine how it happened and what could have prevented it.

Using Good Communication Techniques

Effective communication is crucial on the job and in the business world. Good verbal communication includes techniques such as speaking clearly, maintaining eye contact, and conveying an understandable message. Ambiguous language confuses coworkers, supervisors, and clients, so choose your words carefully. Consciously work to sharpen your communication skills. Listen to what you say and how it sounds to others.

With good communication skills, you can communicate information and ideas that are clear and precise. Meetings, presentations, seminars, videoconferencing—these activities all demand good communication skills, 30-4. Good communication can do the following:

- reduce conflict due to misunderstandings
- save time
- increase customer satisfaction

30-4 Only when good communication is practiced throughout the workplace can projects be accomplished well. Here employees are evaluating plans for advertising a new housing development.

- enhance your professional image and status
- contribute to business success

Most people are trained to read, write, and speak well, but few have learned how to listen. Listening usually occurs at one of four levels—barely listening, pretending to listen, selective listening, and attentive listening. The highest level of listening is often called **empathic listening,** which is listening with the intent to understand. This involves listening attentively from the other person's frame of reference and truly understanding all expressed views.

Most people listen with the intent to reply, not to understand. Empathic listening takes time, but it takes less time than correcting misunderstandings. Good listening skills are vital to good job performance.

Meeting Client Needs

An important job responsibility for professionals employed in the housing field is being able to satisfy client needs. The need may be as simple as repainting the house or as complex as designing a one-of-a-kind dream home. Good communication is essential for understanding what a client needs. Creating a functional plan to address those needs involves the following steps.

Determine Client Needs

The first step in developing a new design or altering an existing one is to determine the needs of the client and the ultimate purpose or goal of the design plan. This is usually accomplished through a series of interviews to develop information for formulating a preliminary design. The following factors will affect the nature of the interviews:

- the client's knowledge and ideas
- size and complexity of the proposed project
- time schedule and cost estimate

With smaller projects or when the client envisions a specific solution, the interview often focuses on the client's ideas. With more complex projects or when the client has few specific ideas, the discussion may cover several possible solutions to judge the client's reaction to various design proposals. In any case, the first step is to gather information from the client about what purpose the design will serve.

Research Potential Design Elements

When creating a design, professionals often begin by researching the desired design characteristics, such as size, shape, weight, color, materials to use, cost, ease of use, fit, and safety. Using the interview information as a starting point, identify the elements that must be considered and develop options and alternatives for each. This reservoir of information can be used to generate possible design solutions. Some of this information may be shared with the client for the purpose of determining which designs to eliminate or possibly include when developing the design plan.

Researching possible design elements expands the range of possibilities, but it also forms the basis for eliminating some design considerations. This step moves the design closer to an acceptable solution.

Formulate a Preliminary Plan

Designers prepare sketches—by hand or with the aid of a computer—to illustrate the design they envision. A preliminary plan may take the form of a presentation drawing, sketch, or model. It is important to present the design ideas in a form that communicates well to the client.

Many designers increasingly are using computer-aided design (CADD) tools to create and better visualize the final design. Computer models allow greater ease and flexibility in exploring various design alternatives, thus reducing design costs and cutting the time it takes to create the preliminary plan. To show the client a range of possibilities, the proposal may actually include several plans that have different costs and time lines. Remember the goal is to move toward a final solution.

Present a Preliminary Plan

When the preliminary plan is ready, you will meet with the client to present your proposal, 30-5. As you present your ideas, be aware of the client's reaction to each aspect. Explain how the plan addresses the design needs, desires, and goals expressed at the start of the project.

Keep in mind that no one will ever agree with all your ideas except you. Expect to make changes to the designs you create for others. Also, recognize this—the person who must live with the final plan is the client. Therefore, do not act defensively, but present your plan as another step in the process toward formulating the final design solution.

Seek Client Input

Probe deeper into the client's reaction to uncover additional feelings, perceptions, and concerns about the preliminary plan. Be sure to associate all alternatives with costs, time, advantages, and disadvantages. Share any concerns you may have with suggested alternatives.

Ultimately, you will know what aspects of the plan the client wants to keep and which should change. Summarize your understandings verbally at the end of the presentation meeting. Later, present to the client a written summary of agreements made during the meeting. Record the strengths and weaknesses as the client sees them. Keep a written record of everything pertinent to the project.

30-5 This rough floor plan is one of several items the designer will use to convey his design proposal to the client

Modify the Plan to Incorporate Client Input

After consulting with the client, designers define and describe the plan by creating detailed designs using drawings, a structural model, computer simulation, or a full-scale prototype. A **structural model** is used to show the construction of a product. A computer simulation uses application-specific software to illustrate how the final result will appear. A **prototype** is a model on which later stages are based or judged. It is suitable for complete evaluation of form, design, and performance.

Because computer-aided design is increasingly common, you should become familiar with using it as a design tool. Interior designers use CADD to create numerous versions of interior space designs since images can be inserted, edited, and replaced easily without added cost. This makes it possible for a client to see and choose among several designs. Remember, the drawings and presentations may be used for other purposes, such as seeking funding, advertising the project, securing permits, or constructing the project.

Present the Final Plan

Once all input has been collected, analyzed, and incorporated into the design plan, it is time to present the final plan to the client. During this presentation, it is important to point out how the suggestions and concerns pertaining to the earlier plan are addressed in the final design solution, 30-6.

The goal of the meeting is to demonstrate how the final plan fully addresses the client's needs and wishes. This will involve a comprehensive presentation of the plan, covering all aspects of the design as well as the costs and timing of execution.

Seek Client Approval

If the designer has listened carefully to the ideas and concerns discussed earlier and modified the plan to include them, client acceptance of the design is likely. On the other hand, if the client does not accept the plan, the modification process must begin again.

The ultimate goal of the professional designer is to please the client with an acceptable design solution. Word-of-mouth from satisfied customers can be a great asset to future business and your career success.

Manufactured Housing Institute

30-6 The designer points out all the important features of a design plan during the presentation to the client.

Continuing Your Education

When a person obtains a diploma or college degree, the educational process should not stop. Professionals and workers who want to advance their career must continually update their knowledge and skills regardless of their position within the organization.

Continually learning new knowledge and acquiring new skills is called *lifelong learning.* The term means your need for learning will never end. Rapid advances in science and technology have created the need for lifelong learning in all professions. Those who enjoy learning are likely to experience more opportunities for job growth, career advancement, and better-paying jobs, 30-7. Those who consider learning a chore will doom themselves to low-paying jobs that require little more than following orders. It is important for managers to keep their workers apprised of new products and systems and the reasons for changing the way work is done.

Organizations at the national, regional, state, and local level provide abundant opportunities for those who wish to continue their education. These opportunities include technical seminars and training sessions, university classes, technical publications, directories, informational CDs, Internet resources, and construction-information telephone lines. Many of these are available from industry associations and manufacturers.

30-7 Taking additional courses will help you advance your career and identify you as a dedicated worker.

Ethics

Ethics can be defined as the rules or standards governing the conduct of the members of a profession. Essentially, ethics is a guiding philosophy that focuses on truth and honesty. Ethical practices are the foundation of a good reputation. Such practices can be expected from businesses and professionals who wish to be successful over the long term.

Many organizations list their goals as a means of stating their intention to do business ethically. For example, refer to the ethical code of the National Association of Home Builders, 30-8.

Work Ethic

The belief or guiding philosophy that motivates a person to do a good job is called a **work ethic**. This is a very important factor in keeping a job or receiving a promotion. A person who has no work ethic tries to avoid doing work and will eventually suffer serious consequences.

Employers are very concerned about the attitudes employees bring to the workplace. A good work ethic is demonstrated by enthusiasm for the

Sample Ethics Code

These are the objectives of the National Association of Home Builders' code of ethics.

1. To conduct business affairs with professionalism and skill.
2. To provide the best housing value possible.
3. To protect the consumer through the use of quality materials and construction practices backed by integrity and service.
4. To provide housing with high standards of safety, sanitation, and livability.
5. To meet all financial obligations in a responsible manner.
6. To comply with the spirit and letter of business contracts, and manage employees, subcontractors, and suppliers with fairness and honor.
7. To keep informed regarding public policies and other essential information which affect your business interests and those of the building industry as a whole.
8. To comply with the rules and regulations prescribed by law and government agencies for the health, safety, and welfare of the community.
9. To keep honesty as our guiding business policy.
10. To provide timely response to items covered under warranty.
11. To seek to resolve controversies through a non-litigation dispute resolution mechanism.
12. To support and abide by the decisions of the association in promoting and enforcing this Code of Ethics.

30-8 What is your reaction to an organization that fosters ethical conduct among its employees?

work and a willingness to work hard for the company's success. A person with a good work ethic also shows self-management skill because he or she has the discipline to do what is needed. Employers need independent thinkers who can recognize what needs to be done and do it, rather than wait for constant reminders.

Teamwork and Leadership

Being able to work as a member of a team is an expectation in today's workplace. Employees with vast technical knowledge and skill are of little value to an employer if they cannot get along with others and work as part of a team, 30-9. Improving a site, planning a structure, building it, and designing its interior demand the cooperation of many people.

30-9 Teamwork is necessary to accomplish this task of placing roofing tiles for installation.

Teamwork accomplishes more work than could be done if individuals acted alone. Usually, a team consists of people of varying skills, ages, and backgrounds, and this wide range of experiences can inspire and motivate the members.

Much wasted time and confusion can result when everybody on the job takes charge. The same is true when no one takes charge. In a smooth-running operation, different people are in charge of different things at different times. Your performance should reflect this recognition. Ideally, members of a work team should know the steps of a project well enough to take a leadership role when circumstances call for it. *Leadership* is the ability to guide and influence others. To gauge your ability in the areas of teamwork and leadership, ask yourself the following questions:

- *Are you a team player?* Team players are valued more in the workplace than solo artists because few jobs exist that only need one person. Teamwork is two or more people working together for a common goal. Presenting yourself as a respectful, trustworthy, likeable person will help you become accepted by your coworkers.
- *How well do you accept instructions from others?* If you cannot accept instructions well from others, the chances are pretty good that your instructions to others will not be accepted very well either.
- *Do you get into personality conflicts with other workers?* Naturally, you cannot completely

ignore your personality traits, but they can be controlled. Avoid viewing every situation as a crisis or a threat. Learn to take matters in stride, and place events in their total context. For example, put yourself in the other person's place, and consider how you would act.

- *Are you a good communicator?* Many conflicts are the result of poor communication. Frequently, people take more offense at *how* something is said than *what* is said. Think about what you wish to communicate and put your thoughts into non-threatening words that are clearly understood. See 30-10.
- *Do you keep your supervisor or employer informed of potential problems?* Alerting leaders to a potential problem will be appreciated and help to establish you as a valued member of the team.
- *Do you have the ability to manage others?* Your coworkers will most likely know the answer to this question even before you do. Seek their advice about improving your leadership skills. Study leadership styles or take a course in developing leadership skills. Learn from others.

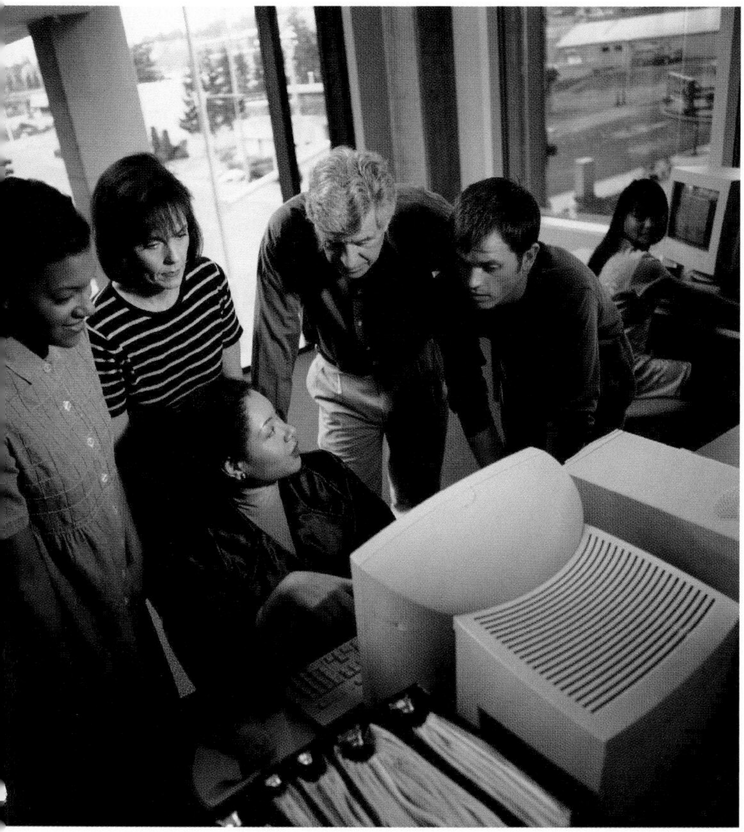

30-10 When giving instructions, present yourself as a helpful coworker who wants all team members to do a good job.

Employers always need people who can lead and manage others. A **manager** is a person who makes and implements decisions and who accomplishes desired results through others. Some people have skill in managing a large number of people, while most are capable of supervising a few. If you wish to have the opportunity to manage, you should observe the traits in others that make them good managers and practice these behaviors.

As you progress to a job or position that involves managing others, you will be expected to show *leadership*, which is the ability to lead and influence others. Contrary to old-fashioned beliefs, a leader is not someone who does all the thinking and barks out orders. Instead, today's leader is someone who directs others to use their full capabilities. The key qualities of a leader are described as follows:

- *Vision.* This is the ability to know what needs to be done now and in the future. Vision also includes the ability to set a schedule to achieve goals.
- *Communication.* A good leader is able to share information clearly and understandably. In addition, a strong leader is able to create an atmosphere of communication in the group so everyone is comfortable enough to speak honestly and directly.
- *Persistence.* This is the ability to stay focused on overall goals and avoid distractions. Persistent leaders meet problems head-on and do whatever is necessary to meet deadlines.
- *Organizational ability.* An important trait for good leadership is organizing and allocating resources, which include workers, materials, time, and money. Organized leaders are capable of making changes based on past mistakes. They are tactful, but can command cooperation of the group when necessary. They stay mindful of all details.
- *Responsibility.* A responsible leader willingly takes the blame, or credit, for his or her actions. In addition, a responsible leader gives credit to those who deserve it.
- *Ability to delegate authority.* **Delegate** means to assign authority or responsibility to another. Good leaders are eager to give capable workers the tasks that will increase their leadership skills.

Leaders value their employees as people as well as members of the team. Most importantly, they lead by example and never expect more from their teammates than from themselves. For a more complete list of qualities that good leaders possess, see 30-11.

Qualities of a Good Leader
Primary Qualities
• Having vision • Communicating well • Staying persistent • Having good organizational ability • Showing responsibility • Delegating authority
Additional Qualities
• Being positive • Being optimistic and enthusiastic • Avoiding sarcasm • Being friendly, not a friend • Controlling emotions • Always being truthful • Treating everyone fairly • Criticizing constructively, not destructively • Always being a role model • Having fun when appropriate

30-11 Which of these qualities of a good leader do you possess?

Conflict Resolution

Conflict is hostility resulting from opposing views. It involves one or more parties wanting to change the present system or relationship because they believe it is not working. In the housing industry, conflict can arise between employees, a manager and employees, or a professional and his or her client.

Some people think immediately of going to court to resolve a conflict, but that should be seen as the last resort. Instead, the parties should try to find their own solution, and if that does not work, they should consider mediation. **Mediation** is negotiation with the impartial assistance of someone who is not affected by the outcome of the dispute. It is a step to take when the parties cannot find a solution by themselves.

People bring different perceptions and beliefs to every situation. The beliefs of one person may not be identical to that of another. It is the mediator's responsibility to create an atmosphere in which all parties can comfortably express themselves. Each person should be able to state thoughts regarding the situation and the preferred outcome. Once all conflicting views are heard, the parties should be receptive to considering new ways of resolving the conflict.

Mediators can start the negotiation, keep it on track, encourage a discussion of solutions, or help parties continue working cooperatively when communication has broken down. Mediators work to increase the trust and understanding between the parties, 30-12.

Communication is the key to managing conflict, solving problems, and producing a desired outcome. Listening is an excellent way to increase communication skills. It is imperative that each party understands what the others are saying. This helps everyone feel they are being heard, and as a result, good rapport starts to develop.

When the conflict is viewed as an opportunity for positive change and growth, a positive outcome is likely. When no resolution can be found, damage to the relationship will likely occur.

Suggestions for Resolving Conflict

To be successful in managing conflict, it is important to state negative feelings honestly, but tactfully, in person or over the phone. E-mails and answering machines are too impersonal, while letters or faxes, unless given great thought, may not fully express what or how you wish to communicate.

When you feel threatened by what someone says, do not be defensive or ignore the message. Listening to others' criticisms will help you become a more open and trusting communicator. Try to restate what is said. This technique will help both parties stay focused in a difficult conversation.

Avoid anger when making requests of others. If an employee is always late to meetings, discuss the problem with the employee. If you say nothing and let your anger build, it will be expressed in some

30-12 A mediator does not bring emotion to the discussion, which helps diffuse tension among conflicting parties.

other way that damages the relationship. Be responsible for your own feelings instead of blaming others. "I feel angry when you are late for a meeting" is better than saying, "You make me angry when you arrive late."

Practice using self-control in negotiations. The more often you are challenged to control your emotions, the easier it becomes to remain calm in high-tension situations. Then, allow a period of time to "cool off." You will become more objective afterward, and the facts will seem clearer.

A mediator is usually able to resolve a conflict more quickly. For example, if responding to an employee's request for an increase in pay, a mediator could respond, "I appreciate that you need the increase, but our company cannot afford it at this time. However, I will see what I can do to improve your compensation package." In conflicts, the mediator looks for a compromise position that considers both parties' limits and needs.

Entrepreneurship

Some day, instead of working for an employer, you may prefer to work for yourself in your own business. An **entrepreneur** is a person who starts, manages, and assumes the risks of a new business. If you think about being your own boss, you are not alone. Many new businesses are started every year, but most fail. The reasons generally cited include inadequate financing, poor management, or lack of knowledge.

There are positive and negative aspects of owning your own business. Some advantages include: being in charge of your work, the chance to make more money, and the satisfaction of building a successful business. Disadvantages include: the enormous responsibility of making correct decisions, long hours, and the risk of failure. If the business has employees, there is the added responsibility of controlling the livelihood of others.

Unfortunately, some business opportunities are not opportunities at all. If it is too good to be true, it probably is. Be sure to ask questions such as those in 30-13.

Every business should have definite, well-defined goals. Goals provide direction and help in making decisions concerning the product or service you offer for sale. The questions in 30-14 can help an aspiring entrepreneur formulate well-defined goals.

Just having a good idea or quality product or service is not enough to have a successful business. It needs solid planning and constant attention to detail. Risk of failure is always present and may be brought about by forces beyond your control. Running a business requires an enormous amount of time and energy and frequently presents a hardship for the family. However, the rewards of running a successful business generally outweigh the liabilities.

Considering Entrepreneurship as a Career
When checking business opportunities, the following questions should be answered:
What business skills and knowledge do you have?
What type of business organization should you choose?
Is the location good?
How much overhead will there be in the business (utilities, taxes, insurance)?
How strong is the competition?
Where will you find good employees?
Can you manage the work force?
Can you get financing?
What government regulations apply to the business?
What are your goals?
How will you advertise your products (or service)?
Where can you get good advice?
What governmental agencies offer help?
Do you have the strength and determination to own and manage a business?
What are the long-term consequences to yourself and your family?
Are you prepared to risk failure?

30-13 Do you think the failure rate for new businesses would be so high if all these questions were honestly answered early in the planning process?

Characteristics of Entrepreneurs

A person should possess certain characteristics before considering becoming a successful entrepreneur. The following list summarizes the major entrepreneurial traits identified by experts:

- *Goal oriented.* An entrepreneur likes to set goals and work hard to achieve them.
- *Good health.* Long hours, stress from deadlines, and dealing with clients place heavy demands on the owner of a business.

Shaping a Business Plan
When developing a business, the following questions should be answered:
What kind of image do you want your company to convey to others?
Will the product (or service) be conventional or unique?
Who will purchase the product (or service)?
How much should you charge?
How will you gain the support and respect of your employees?
How will you reward productive workers?
How will you protect your workers against injury on the job?
What activities will help meet your goals?
How will you organize the business to maintain high efficiency and quality?

30-14 If you considered owning a business, how would you answer these questions?

- *Knowledgeable.* To make a profit, the owner must know all aspects of the business. In addition, the person must understand the industry, its products, and how technological advances will shape them.
- *Good planner.* Running a successful business means that nothing is left to chance. The owner must be able to foresee difficulties as well as plan how to take advantage of opportunities.
- *Willing to take calculated risks.* Once a good business plan is developed, the entrepreneur must have the courage to risk his or her money and future on making the plan work.
- *Innovative.* A business owner must be successful in finding ways to improve and produce better work and thus gain the confidence of customers.
- *Responsible.* Whether good or bad, a business owner must be willing to accept the consequences for decisions made. This includes paying debts, keeping promises, and accepting the responsibility for mistakes of the employees.

As the population ages, it will demand many services. Housing is one of the areas predicted to be in great demand. Thus, a business designed to offer services such as home construction, home rehabilitation, or interior design services would have a good chance of success.

Self-Employment

A self-employed worker without partners and assistants is an entrepreneur on a small scale. According to the *Occupational Outlook Handbook*, self-employment for housing professionals has a brighter outlook than similar work in many other industries. Only a moderate financial investment is needed to run a business from home, but the field is very competitive and the rate of business failure is high.

Self-employment is often a natural extension of accumulated experience and a way to advance in the field, 30-15. Some self-employed housing

30-15 This self-employed professional produces high-quality work so his services are in high demand. Consequently, he can be choosy about which projects to take.

professionals prefer the independence and personal satisfaction of running a business. Many enjoy working unusual hours, working with customers, estimating jobs, and gaining respect as a business owner in the community.

The self-employed individual must be ready to assume the risks that accompany owning a business. These workers are usually self-starters with high confidence levels. If a housing professional decides to run a business independently, he or she must be prepared to provide the service advertised.

A self-employed housing professional must make daily decisions and accept the responsibility for them. Will the business be a one-person operation, or will additional employees need to be hired? If other people will be hired to work in the enterprise, what work assignments must be made, and what supervisory work must be conducted? Will a working space be rented or purchased? Where will the business be located? Will you work out of your home? What equipment will be required? How will advertising be carried out?

A self-employed housing professional must investigate the requirements for a business license in the community where the business will be located and must comply with the laws of that community. Anticipated expenses for startup should be calculated. A business plan is required in preparation for borrowing startup money. Generally, the investment is relatively small since a limited amount of equipment is required to begin operation.

Due to the highly competitive nature of the housing business, a self-employed person needs to actively explore ways of creating and maintaining a customer base. Using personal referrals, networking, affiliating with organizations, and advertising all help promote the development of an active customer base.

A decision must be made if the business will specialize in a narrow aspect of the field or offer broad-based services. While specialization may help you gain recognition over the competition, limiting a business to one service might cause the business to fail if the market changes.

The entrepreneur should match the business to his or her own strengths and personality so the services offered are distinct from others. The needs of the customer and the community should be considered so the services provided can fill local needs. Using available technology allows the self-employed housing professional to stay current. It is also important to price work accurately and deliver quality services. Many challenges face the self-employed, but the rewards can also be great.

Managing Home and Work Responsibilities

Good management of home and work responsibilities enables a career person to work effectively on the job and lead a pleasant home life. A harmonious home life helps the individual handle the challenges at work, and a fruitful career increases that person's satisfaction with life at home. Good management of the many related responsibilities eliminates the stress that can build and helps individuals handle the multiple roles of responsible worker and family member so neither role suffers.

Careers help families financially by increasing the family income, but they take time away from family life. With good management of resources, the many responsibilities involved in maintaining a home and family can be accomplished. These include keeping an organized home, making sure the home is in good repair, taking care of the lawn, and seeing that everyone has nourishing meals. Managing a home also involves providing emotional support to a spouse, the children, and sometimes elderly parents, too. All family members need to work together to provide a pleasant home atmosphere.

Meeting the needs of work and family can be challenging for all families. Sometimes extra challenges are faced by *dual-career families,* since both parents work outside the home, and by single-parent families. Decisions will need to be made regarding how to maintain the home and provide care for the child while parents are at work.

Some businesses provide on-site child care, but this is not a common option. Usually parents must find competent child care within their community. Employers may help parents by allowing them to adjust their work schedules to drop off and pick up children or care for them when ill.

All family members may be expected to help with the care of the home, 30-16. Additional help may come from hiring professionals to maintain the lawn, make house repairs, clean the house, and prepare food. Other families may rely more on using convenience foods or buying ready-to-eat meals on the way home from work.

Families with dual careers need to make an effort to keep the lines of communication open. It is important to schedule quality time together as a family and allow members to take turns deciding how to spend the time. An evening spent at home playing games or listening to music can strengthen family ties while refreshing and energizing workers for a productive workday tomorrow.

At times parents may feel guilt and stress when work responsibilities prevent them from attending a child's function at school. Children may feel resentment as well. When this occurs, parents need to find ways to solve this problem. Friends and extended family members may provide extra support. In addition, parents may look to adjusting work responsibilities in order to spend more family time. Working part-time, working out of the home, or starting a home-based business may be viable options.

30-16 When family members share the task of maintaining the home, the atmosphere is friendlier and no one is overly burdened.

Chapter Summary

Job performance plays a large part in work satisfaction and career advancement. Job performance can be measured by evaluating a person's general work habits, safety record, and ability to communicate well. Good communication reduces conflict, saves time, increases customer satisfaction, and contributes to business success. A key job responsibility for designers is meeting client's needs through a step-by-step process that creates a functional plan. Continuing education helps employees stay abreast of new techniques, equipment, and materials so they can provide greater value to their employer.

Businesses and professionals concerned about long-term success focus on ethics. A positive work attitude is a sign of a good work ethic.

Employee teamwork and leadership may be more important to an employer than basic skills. Most jobs require teamwork, and many offer leadership opportunities.

As people with different backgrounds and beliefs are put together to accomplish tasks that require cooperation and teamwork, conflict may result. Mediation is one method of conflict resolution.

Entrepreneurship provides many opportunities and challenges, but it takes certain personal qualities to achieve success. Self-employment is entrepreneurship on a small scale. It is a natural extension of many positions in the housing industry.

Managing home and work responsibilities require a concerted effort on the part of all family members to achieve a solution. A harmonious home life helps a person handle challenges at work, and a fruitful career increases the person's satisfaction with life at home.

Review Questions

1. Why should a new employee in the workforce be concerned about his or her work habits?
2. According to the Occupational Safety and Health Administration, what is the most dangerous occupation in the country?
3. Name the four levels of listening.
4. What is the first step in developing a new design for a client?
5. Besides their definitions, how do the terms *ethics* and *work ethic* differ?
6. Identify five qualities commonly found in all good leaders.
7. What is the process called when a disinterested individual helps settle a conflict between two parties?
8. What is the greatest risk in owning your own business?
9. Name five characteristics of successful entrepreneurs.
10. Name two actions that might be taken to better manage home and work responsibilities.

Suggested Activities

1. Interview a local business owner who employs at least three or four people. Ask the business owner to describe the most important attributes that he or she desires in an employee. Prepare a report of your findings.
2. Select a job or position in the housing field and research it to determine the types of continuing education opportunities that exist. Describe these opportunities in a report.
3. Prepare a code of ethics for your class and present it to your classmates for discussion. If possible, adopt a code of ethics for your class following input from all class members.
4. Research the topic *Entrepreneurs in America*. Narrow the topic to a subject that interests you and write a report. Summarize the report in a five-minute presentation to the class.

Internet Resources

Institute for Business and Home Safety
ibhs.org

Insurance Information Institute
iii.org

LookSmart Ltd.
findarticles.com

Qualified Remodeler Magazine
qrmagazine.com

U.S. Department of Housing and Urban Development
hud.gov

U.S. Department of Labor's *Occupational Outlook Handbook*
bls.gov/oco/

U.S. Occupational Safety and Health Administration (OSHA)
osha.gov

Note: Web addresses may have changed since publication. For some entries, reaching the correct Web site may require keying *www.* into the address.

Appendix

A-1 Weights and Measures

English	Metric
Length	
12 inches = 1 foot	1 kilometer = 1000 meters
36 inches = 1 yard	1 hectometer = 100 meters
3 feet = 1 yard	1 dekameter = 10 meters
5280 feet = 1 mile	1 meter = 1 meter
16.5 feet = 1 rod	1 decimeter = 0.1 meter
320 rods = 1 mile	1 centimeter = 0.01 meter
6 feet = 1 fathom	1 millimeter = 0.001 meter
Weight	
27.34 grains = 1 dram	1 ton = 1,000,000 grams
438 grains = 1 ounce	1 kilogram = 1000 grams
16 drams = 1 ounce	1 hectogram = 100 grams
16 ounces = 1 pound	1 dekagram = 10 grams
2000 pounds = 1 short ton	1 gram = 1 gram
2240 pounds = 1 long ton	1 decigram = 0.1 gram
	1 centigram = 0.01 gram
	1 milligram = 0.001 gram
Area	
144 sq. inches = 1 sq. foot	100 sq. millimeters = 1 sq. centimeter
9 sq. feet = 1 sq. yard	100 sq. centimeters = 1 sq. decimeter
43,560 sq. ft. = 160 sq. rods	100 sq decimeters = 1 sq. meter
160 sq. rods = 1 acre	10,000 sq. meters = 1 hectare
640 acres = 1 sq. mile	

Temperature

32 degrees Fahrenheit	Water freezes	0 degree Centigrade
68 degrees Fahrenheit	Reasonable room temperature	20 degrees Centigrade
98.6 degrees Fahrenheit	Normal body temperature	37 degrees Centigrade

Angular and Circular Measures

1 minute =	60 seconds
1 degree =	60 minutes
1 right angle =	90 degrees
1 straight angle =	180 degrees
1 circle =	360 degrees

A-2 Topographical Symbols

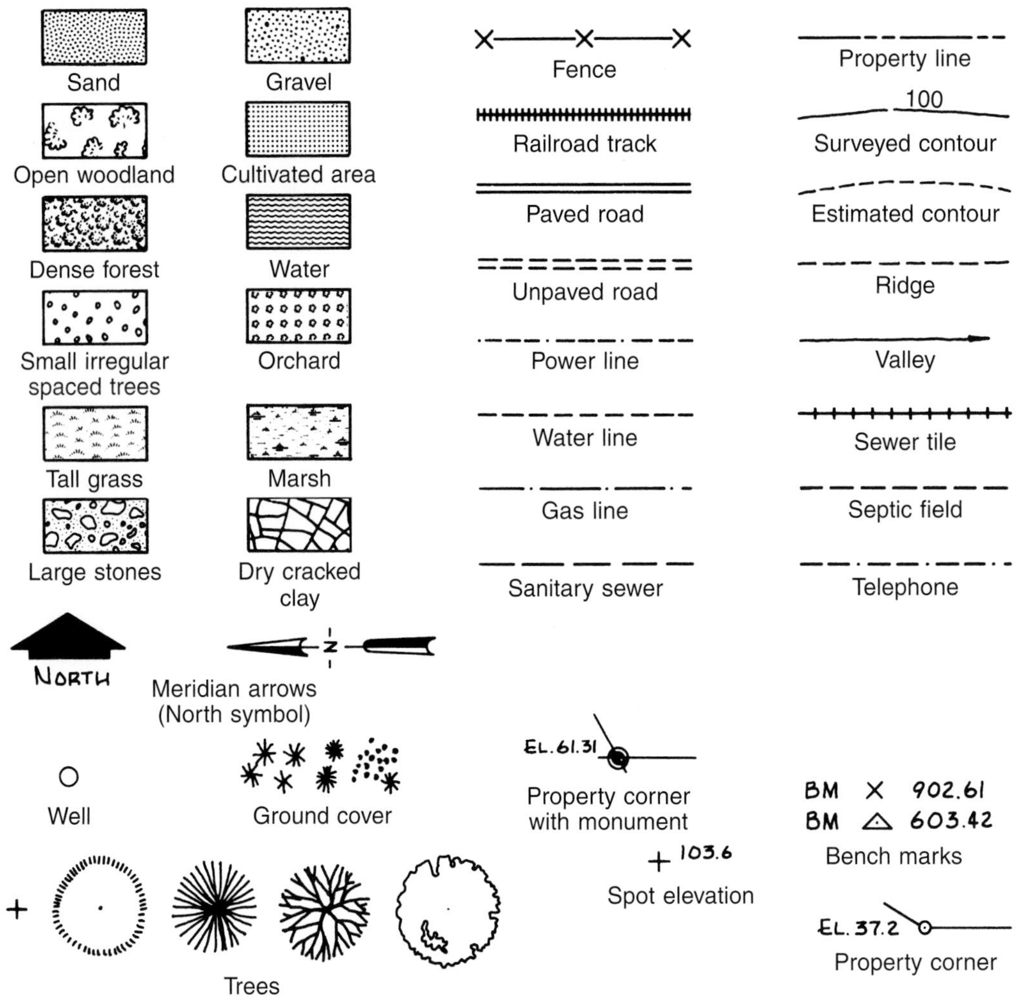

A-3 Plumbing Symbols

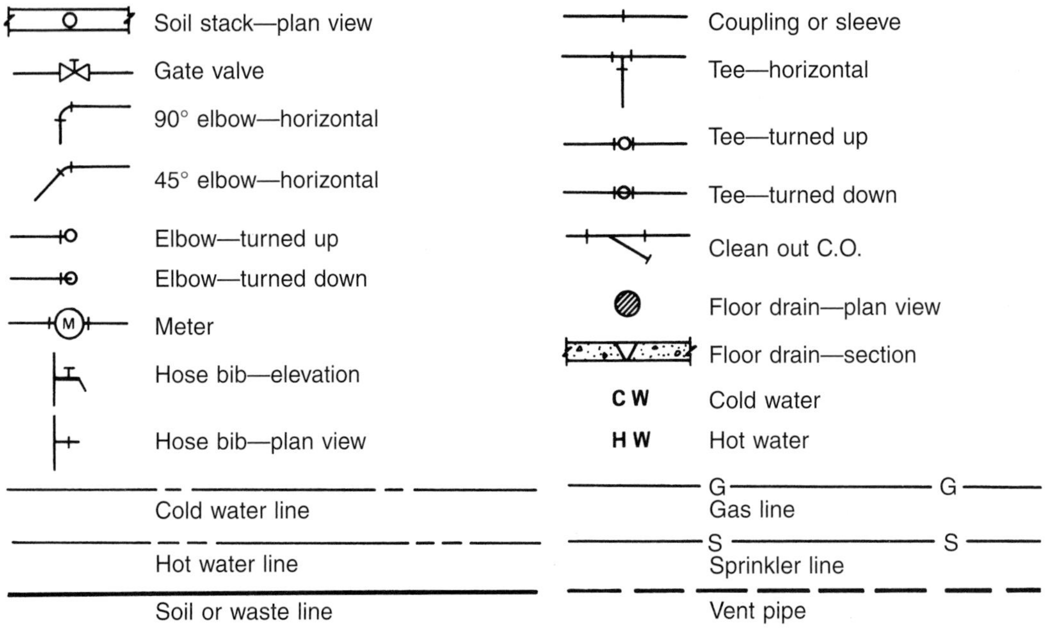

A-4 Electrical Symbols

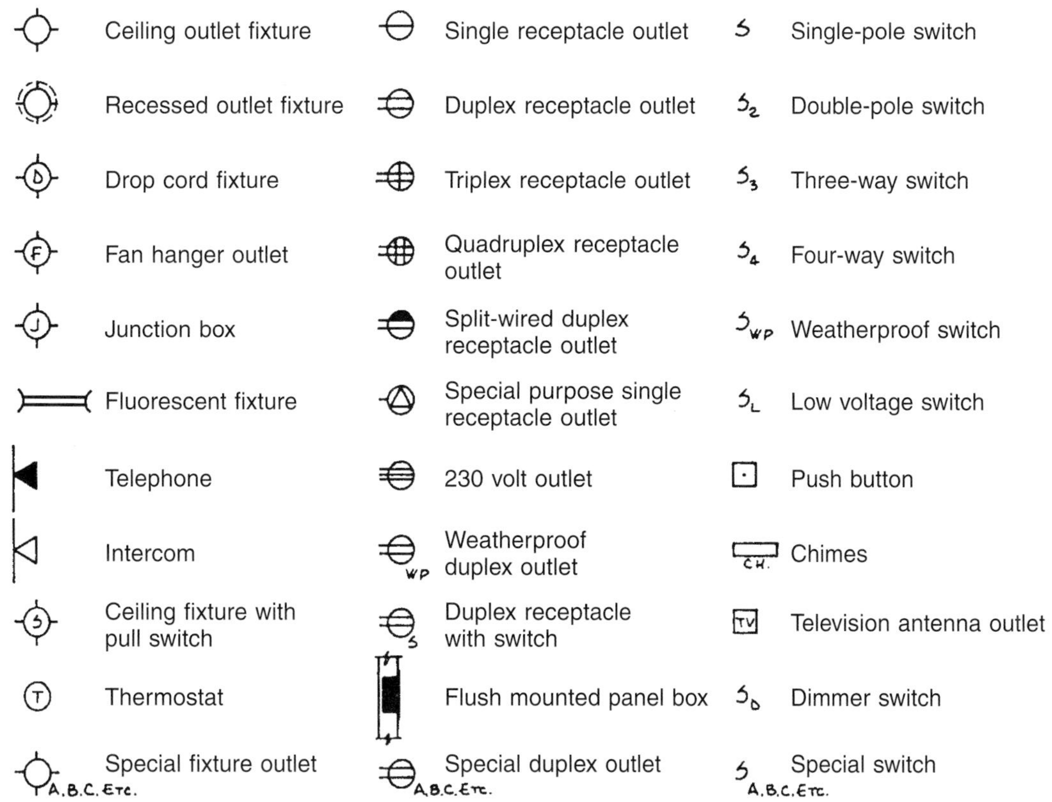
Ceiling outlet fixture
Recessed outlet fixture
Drop cord fixture
Fan hanger outlet
Junction box
Fluorescent fixture
Telephone
Intercom
Ceiling fixture with pull switch
Thermostat
Special fixture outlet
A.B.C. Etc.
Single receptacle outlet
Duplex receptacle outlet
Triplex receptacle outlet
Quadruplex receptacle outlet
Split-wired duplex receptacle outlet
Special purpose single receptacle outlet
230 volt outlet
Weatherproof duplex outlet
WP
Duplex receptacle with switch
Flush mounted panel box
Special duplex outlet
A.B.C. Etc.
Single-pole switch
Double-pole switch
Three-way switch
Four-way switch
Weatherproof switch
Low voltage switch
Push button
Chimes
CH.
Television antenna outlet
TV
Dimmer switch
Special switch
A.B.C. Etc.

A-5 Climate Control Symbols

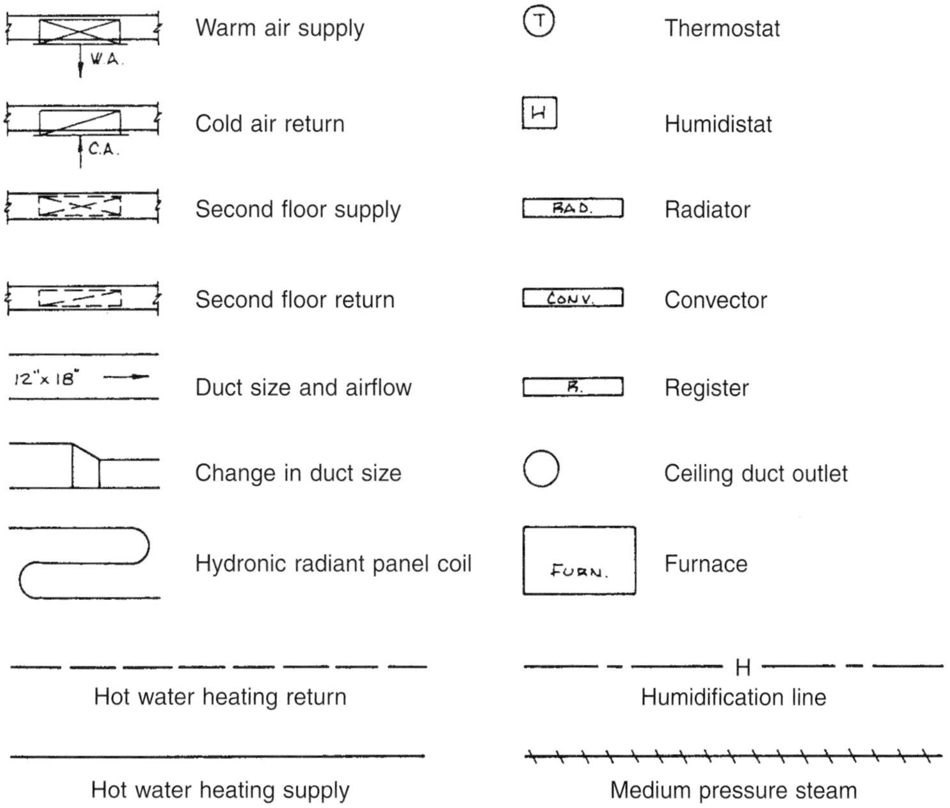
Warm air supply
W.A.
Cold air return
C.A.
Second floor supply
Second floor return
Duct size and airflow
12" x 18"
Change in duct size
Hydronic radiant panel coil
Thermostat
Humidistat
Radiator
RAD.
Convector
CONV.
Register
R.
Ceiling duct outlet
Furnace
FURN.
Hot water heating return
Hot water heating supply
Humidification line
H
Medium pressure steam

A-6 Abbreviations

Acoustic	ACST
Actual	ACT
Addition	ADD
Adhesive	ADH
Aggregate	AGGR
Air conditioning	AIR COND
Alternate	ALT
Aluminum	AL
American Society of Interior Designers	ASID
American Institute of Architects	AIA
American Society for Testing and Materials	ASTM
Amount	AMT
Ampere	AMP
Anchor bolt	AB
Approximate	APPROX
Architectural	ARCH
Area	A
Asbestos	ASB
Asphalt	ASPH
Assembly	ASSY
Automatic	AUTO
Average	AVG
Balcony	BALC
Basement	BSMT
Bathroom	B
Beam	BM or BMS
Bedroom	BR
Bench mark	BM
Between	BET
Blocking	BLKG
Board feet	BD FT
Bottom	BOT
Bracket	BRKT
British thermal unit	BTU
Broom closet	BC
Building	BLDG
Buzzer	BUZ
Cabinet	CAB
Casing	CSG
Cast iron	C I
Caulking	CLKG
Ceiling	CL
Cement	CEM
Center line	CL or ℄
Center to center	C to C
Ceramic	CER
Circuit	CKT
Circuit breaker	CIR BKR
Closet	CLOS or CL
Clothes dryer	CL D
Column	COL
Composition	COMP
Concrete	CONC
Concrete block	CONC B
Construction	CONST
Copper	COP or CU
Counter	CTR
Cross section	X-SECT
Cubic feet	CU FT
Cubic yard	CU YD
Damper	DMPR
Decorative	DEC
Detail	DET
Diagram	DIA
Dimension	DIM
Dining room	DR
Dishwasher	DW
Door	DR
Double hung	DH
Down	DN
Downspout	DS
Drain	D or DR
Drawing	DWG
Elbow	ELL
Electric	ELEC
Elevation	EL or ELEV
Entrance	ENT
Estimate	EST
Excavate	EXC
Exterior	EXT
Family room	FAM R
Finish	FIN
Firebrick	FBRK
Fireproof	FP
Fitting	FTG
Fixture	FIX
Flange	FLG
Flashing	FLSHG
Floor	FL
Floor drain	FD
Flooring	FLG
Footing	FTG
Foundation	FDN
Frame	FR
Full size	FS
Galvanized	GALV
Glass	GL
Grade	GR
Gypsum	GYP
Hall	H
Hardware	HDW
Header	HDR
Heater	HTR
Horizontal	HORIZ
Hose bibb	HB
Inside diameter	ID
Insulation	INS
Interior	INT
Joint	JT
Joist	JST
Kiln dried	KD
Kitchen	K
Kitchen cabinets	KC
Kitchen sink	KS
Laminated	LAM
Landing	LDG
Laundry	LAU
Lavatory	LAV
Leader	LDR
Level	LEV
Light	LT
Linen closet	L CL
Linoleum	LINO
Living room	LR
Lumber	LBR
Maximum	MAX
Medicine cabinet	MC
Metal	MET
Minimum	MIN
Modular	MOD
Molding	MLDG
North	N
Number	NO
Office	OFF
On center	OC
Opening	OPG
Outside diameter	OD
Painted	PTD
Panel	PNL
Parallel	PAR
Partition	PTN
Perpendicular	PERP
Plaster	PLAS
Plate glass	PL GL
Platform	PLATF
Plumbing	PLMB
Plywood	PLY
Polyvinyl chloride	PVC
Prefabricated	PREFAB
Property	PROP
Push button	PB
Radiator	RAD
Range	R
Receptacle	RECP
Recessed	REC
Reference	REF
Refrigerator	REF
Register	REG
Reinforce	REINF
Return	RET
Riser	R
Roof	RF
Roofing	RFG
Rough	RGH
Round	RD
Schedule	SCH
Section	SECT
Self-closing	SC
Service	SERV
Sewer	SEW
Sheet metal	SHT'G
Shelves	S M
Shower	SHVL'S
Siding	SH
Sink	SC
Socket	SOC
Soil pipe	SP
Specification	SPEC
Square	SQ
Stairs	ST
Standpipe	ST P
Steel	STL
Structural	STR
Surface	SUR
Surface four sides	S4S
Surface two sides	S2S
Suspended ceiling	SUSP CLG
Switch	S or SW
Symbol	SYM
Tee	T
Telephone	TEL
Television	TV
Temperature	TEMP
Terra-cotta	TC
Thermostat	THERMO
Thickness	THK
Tongue and groove	T&G
Tread	TR
Unfinished	UNFIN
Vanity	VAN
Ventilation	VENT
Ventilator	V
Vertical	VERT
Wall cabinet	W CAB
Wall vent	WV
Water	W
Water closet	WC
Water heater	WH
Waterproof	WP
Weep hole	WH
Wide flange	WF
Window	WDW
With	W/
Wood	WD
Wrought iron	WI

A-7 Common Sizes of Living Room Furniture

Sofa

Width	Depth	Height
72"	36"	28"
76"	35"	35"
84"	36"	37"
87"	31"	31"
88"	32"	29"
91"	32"	30"

Sofa

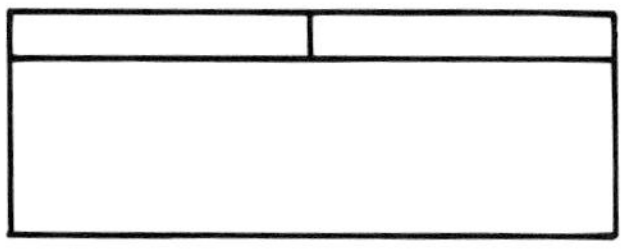

Width	Depth	Height
72"	30"	30"
74"	30"	30"
90"	30"	30"

Lounge Chair

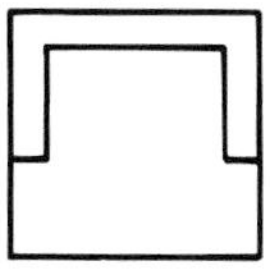

Width	Depth	Height
28"	32"	29"
33"	31"	31"
33"	32"	30"
34"	36"	37"
35"	35"	35"

Recliner Chair

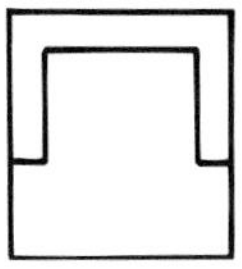

Width	Depth	Height
31"	30"	40"
32"	34"	40"
32"	35"	41"
36"	37"	41"

Recliner Chair

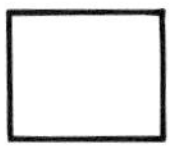

Width	Depth	Height
22"	18"	13"
22"	22"	16"
24"	19"	16"

Love Seat

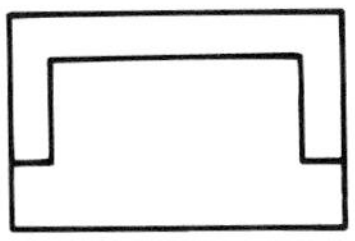

Width	Depth	Height
47"	28"	36"
54"	30"	36"
59"	36"	37"

Small Arm Chair

Width	Depth	Height
18"	18"	29"
21"	22"	32"

Corner Chair

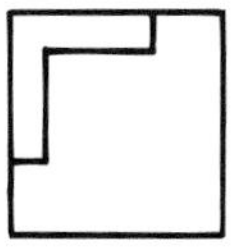

Width	Depth	Height
30"	30"	25"
36"	36"	25"

Sofa Table

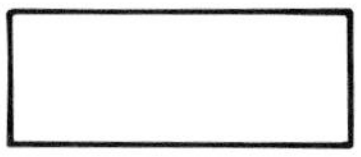

Width	Depth	Height
30"	30"	25"
36"	36"	25"

End Table

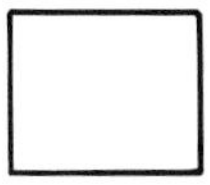

Width	Depth	Height
21"	28"	20"
22"	28"	21"
26"	20"	21"
27"	19"	22"
28"	28"	20"

Round Cocktail Table

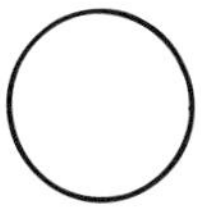

Diameter	Height
18"	20"
24"	20"
26"	20"

Cocktail Table

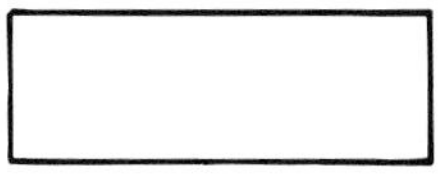

Width	Depth	Height
35"	19"	17"
50"	18"	15"
54"	20"	15"
56"	21"	16"
57"	19"	15"
58"	20"	15"
61"	21"	17"
66"	20"	15"

Bunching Table

Width	Depth	Height
20"	20"	15"
19"	19"	15"
21"	21"	16"

Step Table

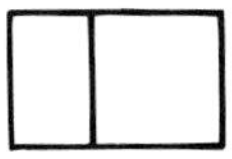

Width	Depth	Height
15"	27"	21"
19"	30"	21"
20"	30"	23"

Corner Table

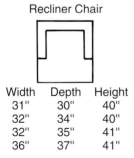

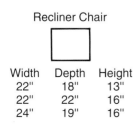

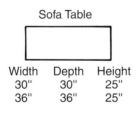

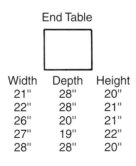

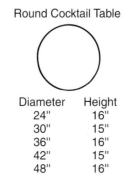

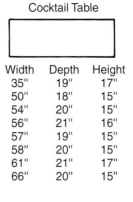

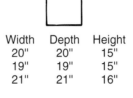

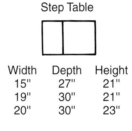

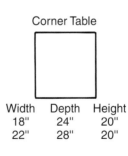

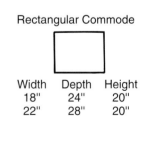

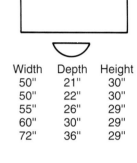

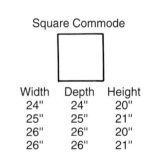

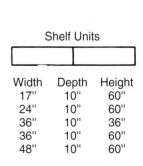

Width	Depth	Height
18"	24"	20"
22"	28"	20"

Round Cocktail Table

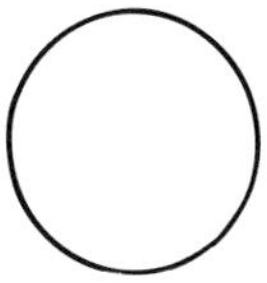

Diameter	Height
24"	16"
30"	15"
36"	16"
42"	15"
48"	16"

Hexagonal Commode

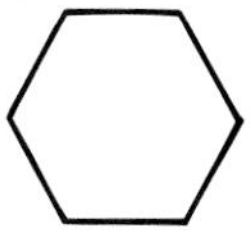

Width	Depth	Height
27"	27"	20"
28"	28"	22"

Desk

Width	Depth	Height
50"	21"	30"
50"	22"	30"
55"	26"	29"
60"	30"	29"
72"	36"	29"

Square Commode

Width	Depth	Height
24"	24"	20"
25"	25"	21"
26"	26"	20"
26"	26"	21"

Rectangular Commode

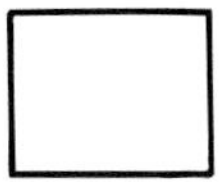

Width	Depth	Height
18"	24"	20"
22"	28"	20"

Shelf Units

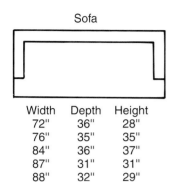

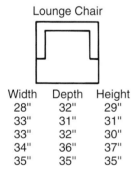

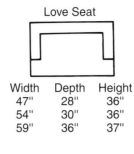

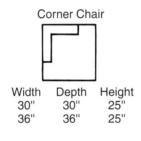

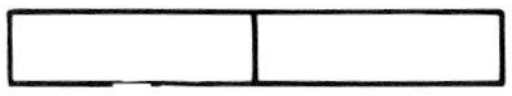

Width	Depth	Height
17"	10"	60"
24"	10"	60"
36"	10"	36"
36"	10"	60"
48"	10"	60"

A-8 Common Sizes of Bedroom Furniture

Telephone Table

Length	Width	Height
12"	12"	26"
12"	14"	25"
17"	23"	22"

Night Stand

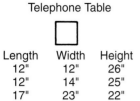

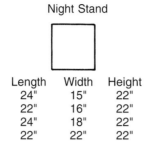

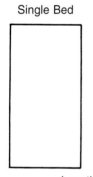

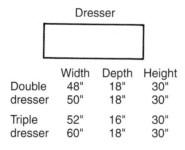

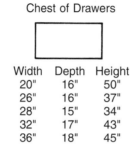

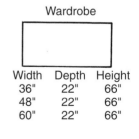

Length	Width	Height
24"	15"	22"
22"	16"	22"
24"	18"	22"
22"	22"	22"

Double Bed

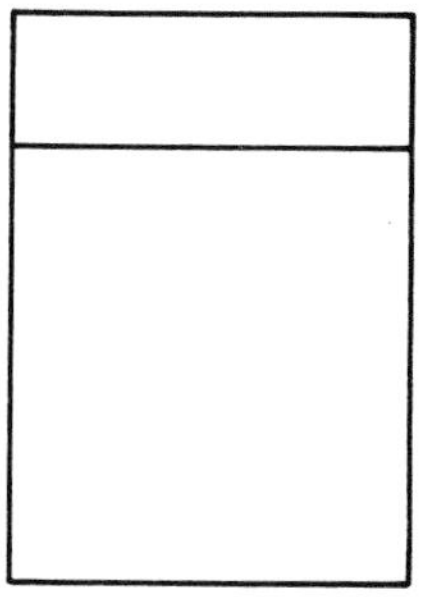

	Length	Width
Double bed	75"	54"
	80"	54"
	84"	54"
Queen-size bed	80"	60"
	84"	60"
King-size bed	80"	72"
	80"	76"
	84"	72"
	84"	76"

Desk

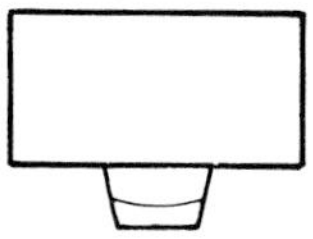

Width	Depth	Height
33"	16"	29"
36"	16"	29"
40"	20"	30"
43"	16"	30"

Chest of Drawers

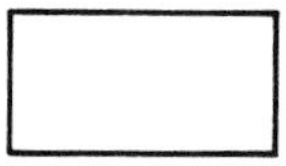

Width	Depth	Height
20"	16"	50"
26"	16"	37"
28"	15"	34"
32"	17"	43"
36"	18"	45"

Single Bed

	Length	Width
Bunk bed	75"	30"
	75"	33"
Dormitory bed	75"	33"
	80"	36"
Twin bed	75"	39"
	80"	39"
	84"	39"
Three-quarter bed	75"	48"
	80"	48"

Dresser

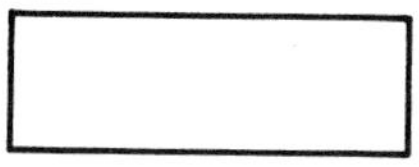

	Width	Depth	Height
Double dresser	48"	18"	30"
	50"	18"	30"
Triple dresser	52"	16"	30"
	60"	18"	30"

Recliner

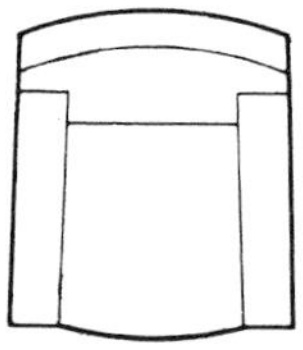

Width	Depth
30"	31"
32"	35"
36"	38"

Sofa Bed

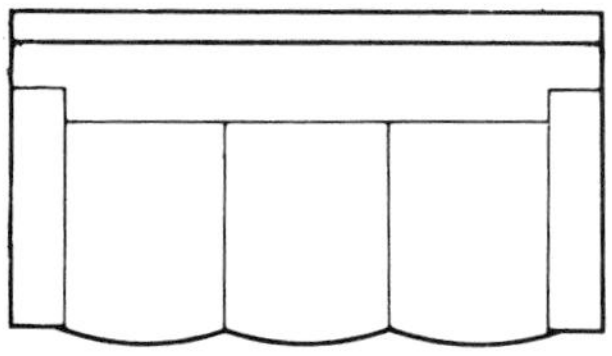

Length	Width
87"	31"
91"	32"
79"	34"

Wardrobe

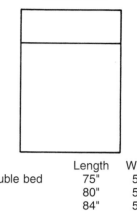

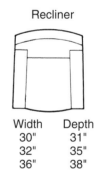

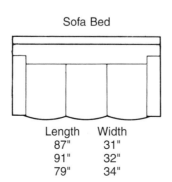

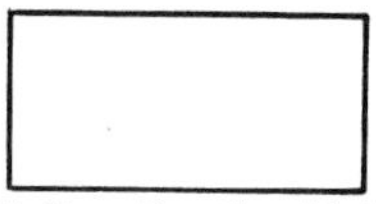

Width	Depth	Height
36"	22"	66"
48"	22"	66"
60"	22"	66"

A-9 Minimum Clearance Requirements

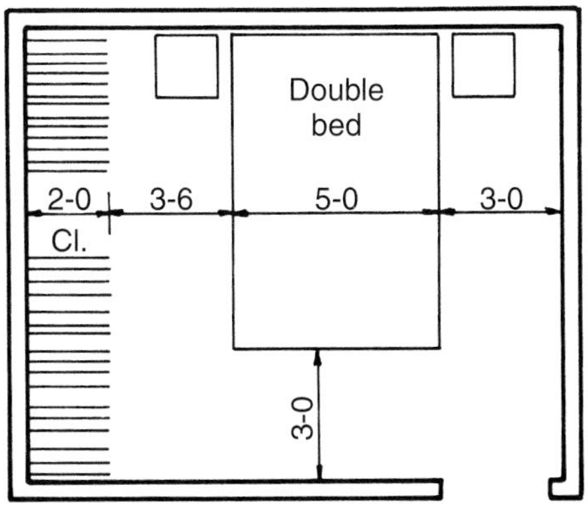

Bedroom

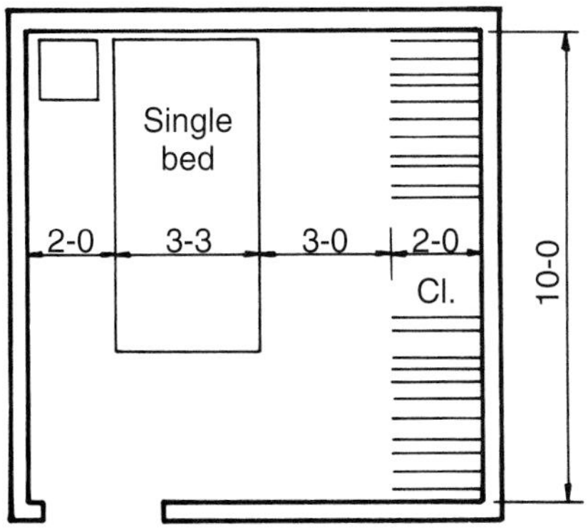

Bedroom

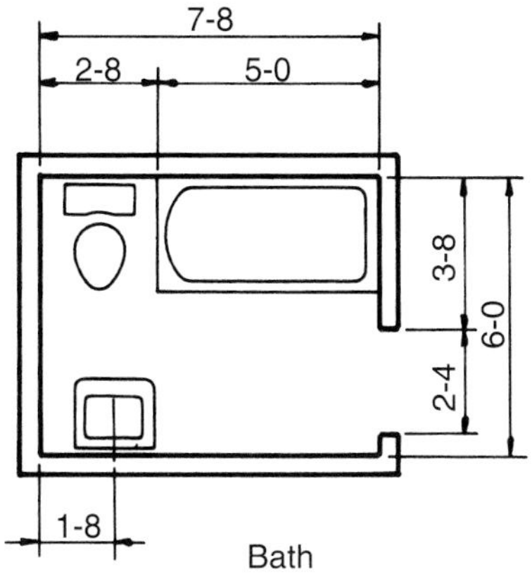

Bath

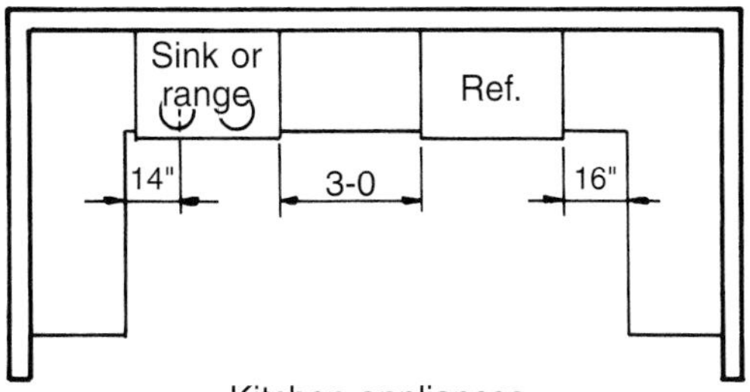

Kitchen appliances

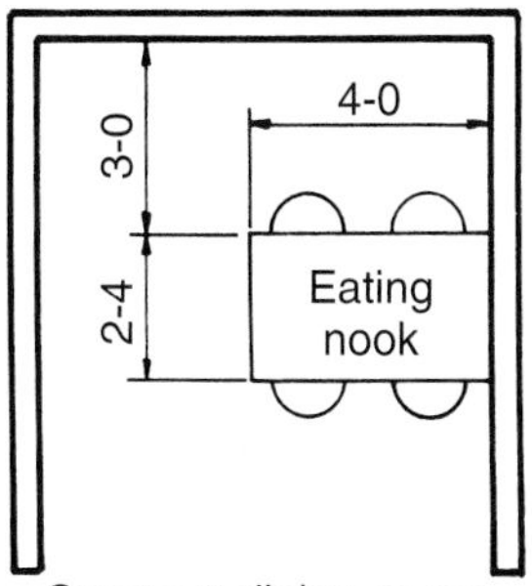

Compact dining space

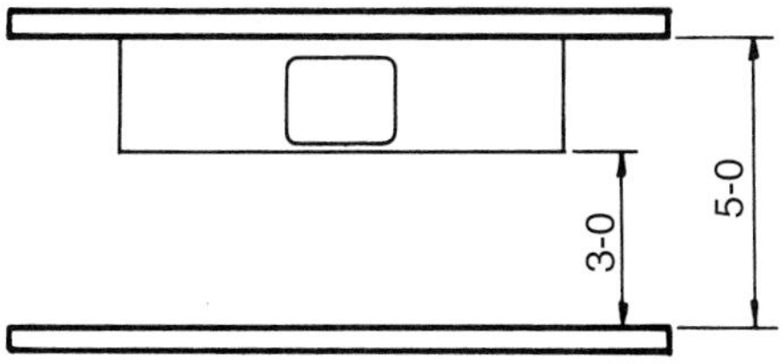

Kitchen walking space

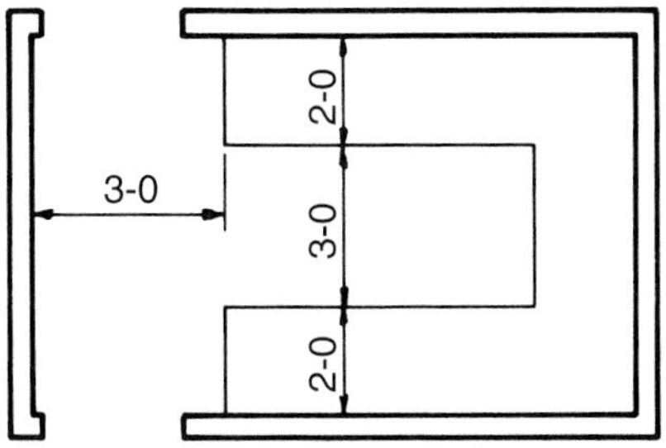

Kitchen walking space

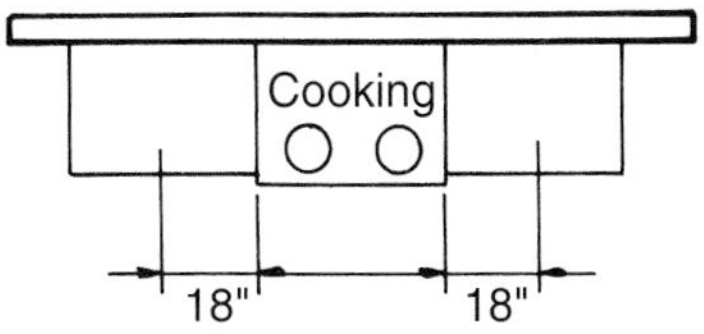

Minimum counter space on either side of a cooking unit

Counter space

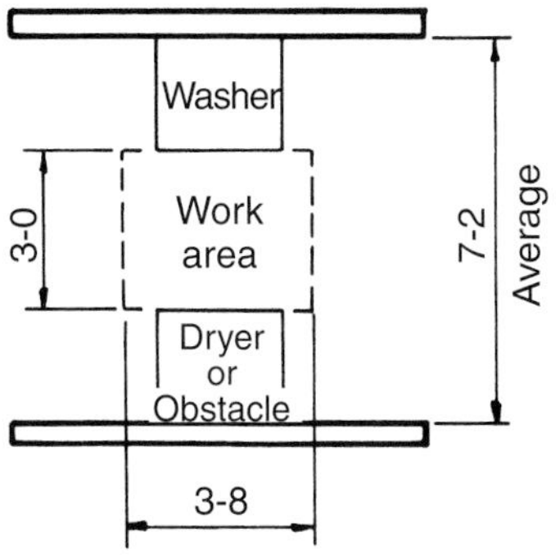

Laundry area

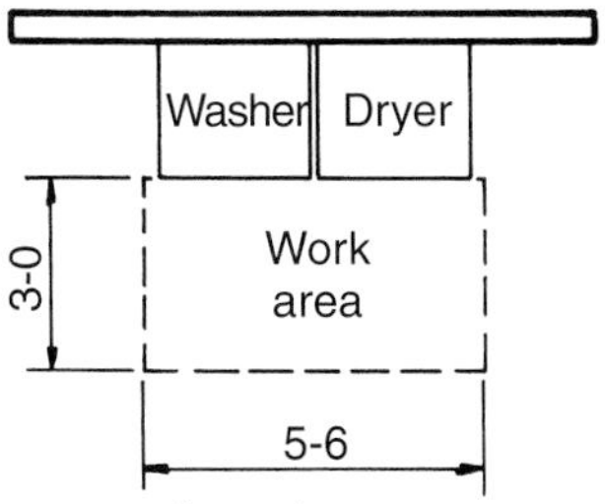

Laundry area

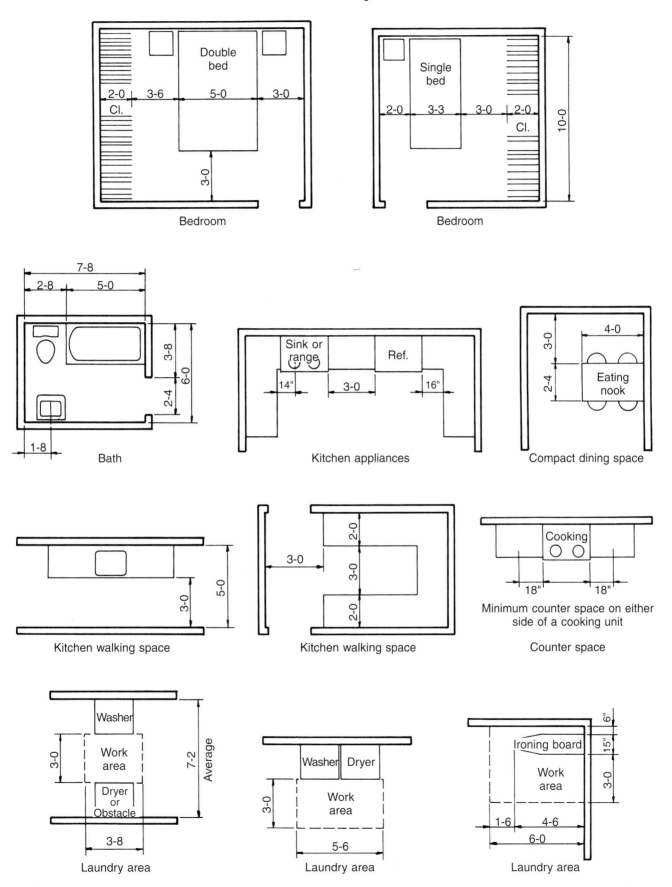

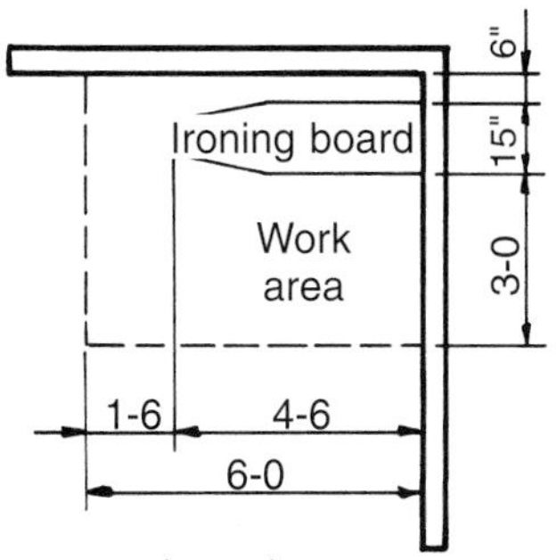

Laundry area

A-10 Common Sizes of Bathroom Fixtures

Standard Tub

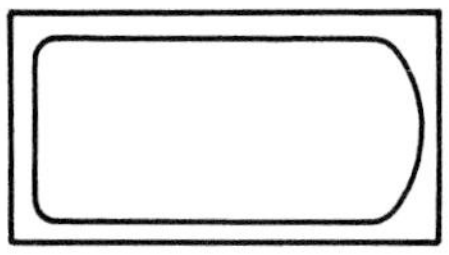

Width	Length	Height
30¾"	54"	16"
30"	60"	14"
30"	60"	16½"
31"	60"	15½"
31½"	60"	16"
31½"	66"	18"
30¾"	72"	16"

Bidet

Width	Depth	Height
15"	22"	15"

Vanity Bases

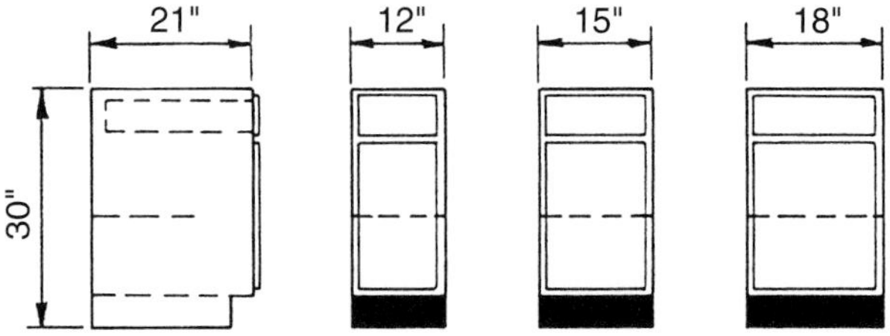

Square Tub

Width	Length	Height
37"	42"	12"
42"	48"	14"

Wall-Hung Sink

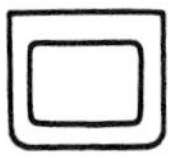

Width	Depth
19"	17"
20"	18"
22"	19"
24"	20"

Drawer Vanity Bases

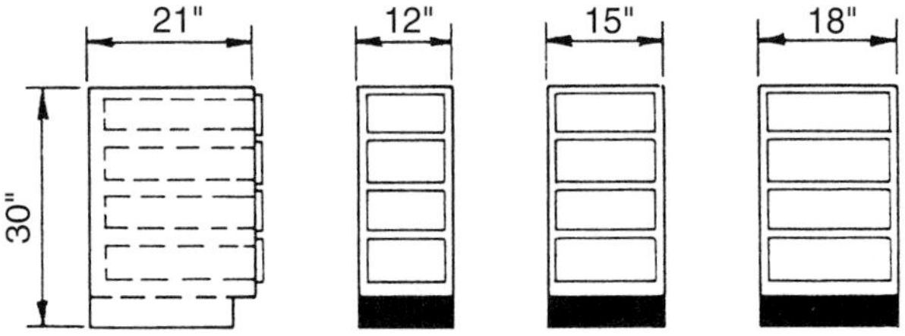

Water Closet

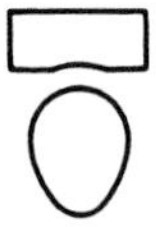

Floor-mounted, two-piece

Width	Depth	Height
17"	25½"	29½"
21"	26¾"	28"
21"	28¾"	28"

Floor-mounted, one-piece

Width	Depth	Height
20⅜"	27¾"	20"
20⅜"	29¾"	20"

Wall-hung, two-piece

Width	Depth	Height
22½"	26"	31"

Wall-hung, one-piece

Width	Depth	Height
14"	24¼"	15"

Circular Lavatory

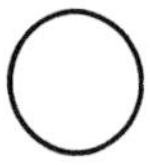

18" Diameter

Vanity Bowl Bases

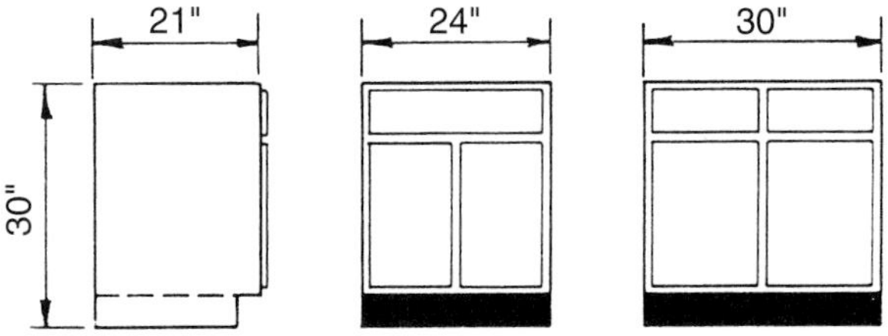

Vanity Hamper Base

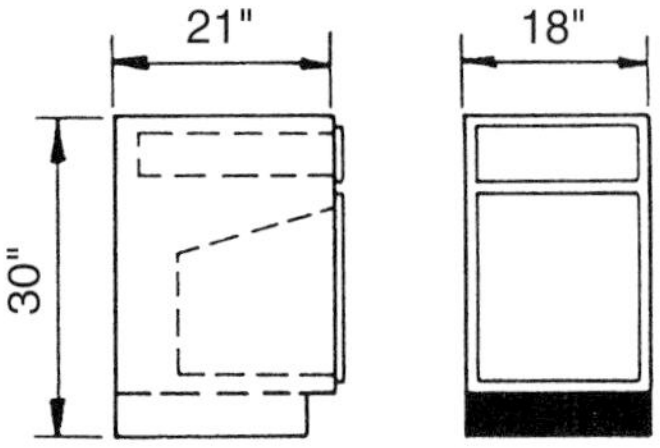

Vanity Wall Cabinet

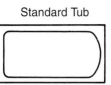

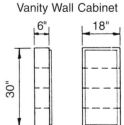

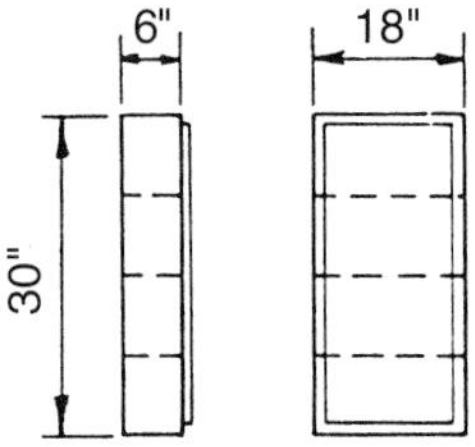

A-11 Common Sizes of Kitchen Base Cabinets

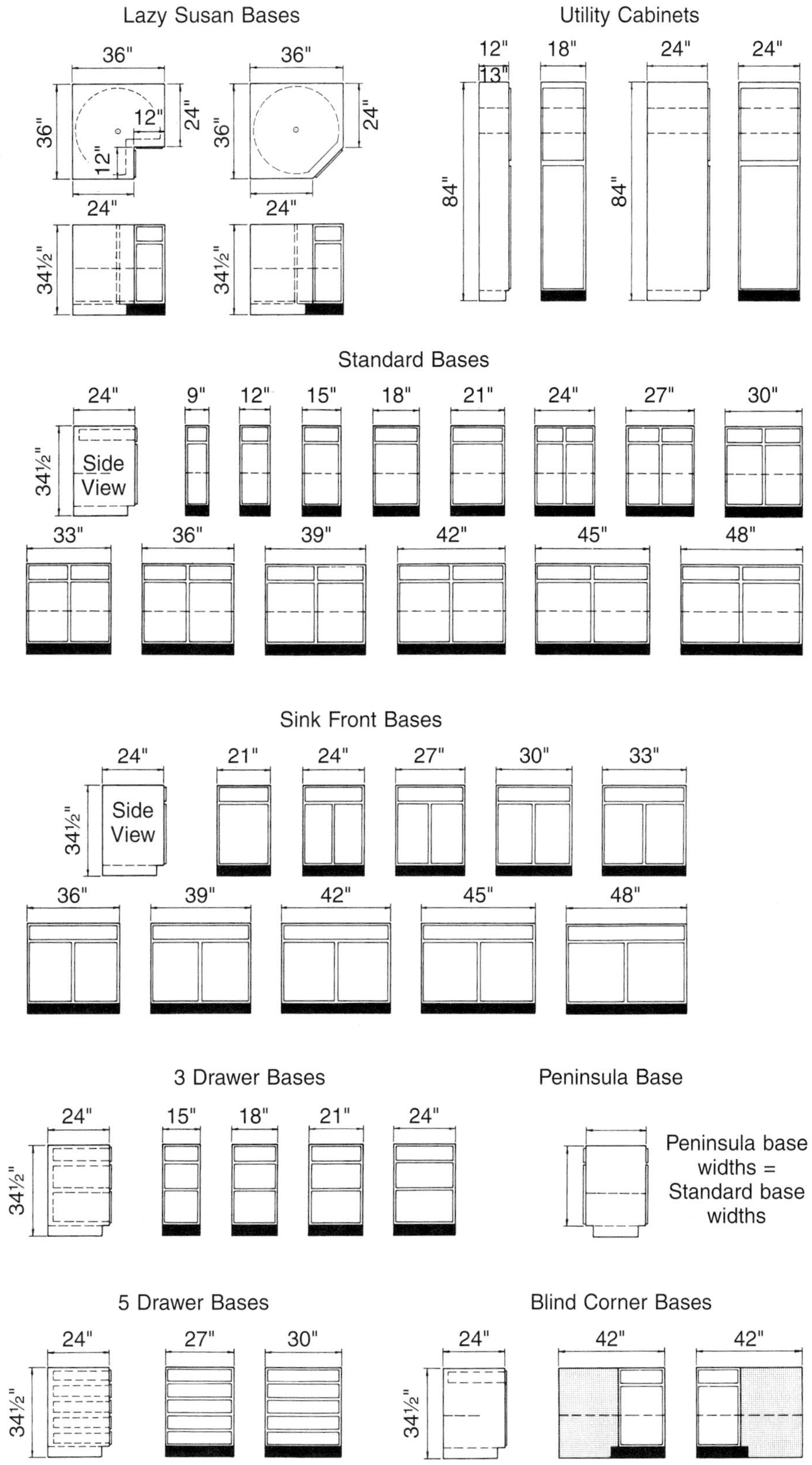

A-12 Common Sizes of Kitchen Wall Cabinets

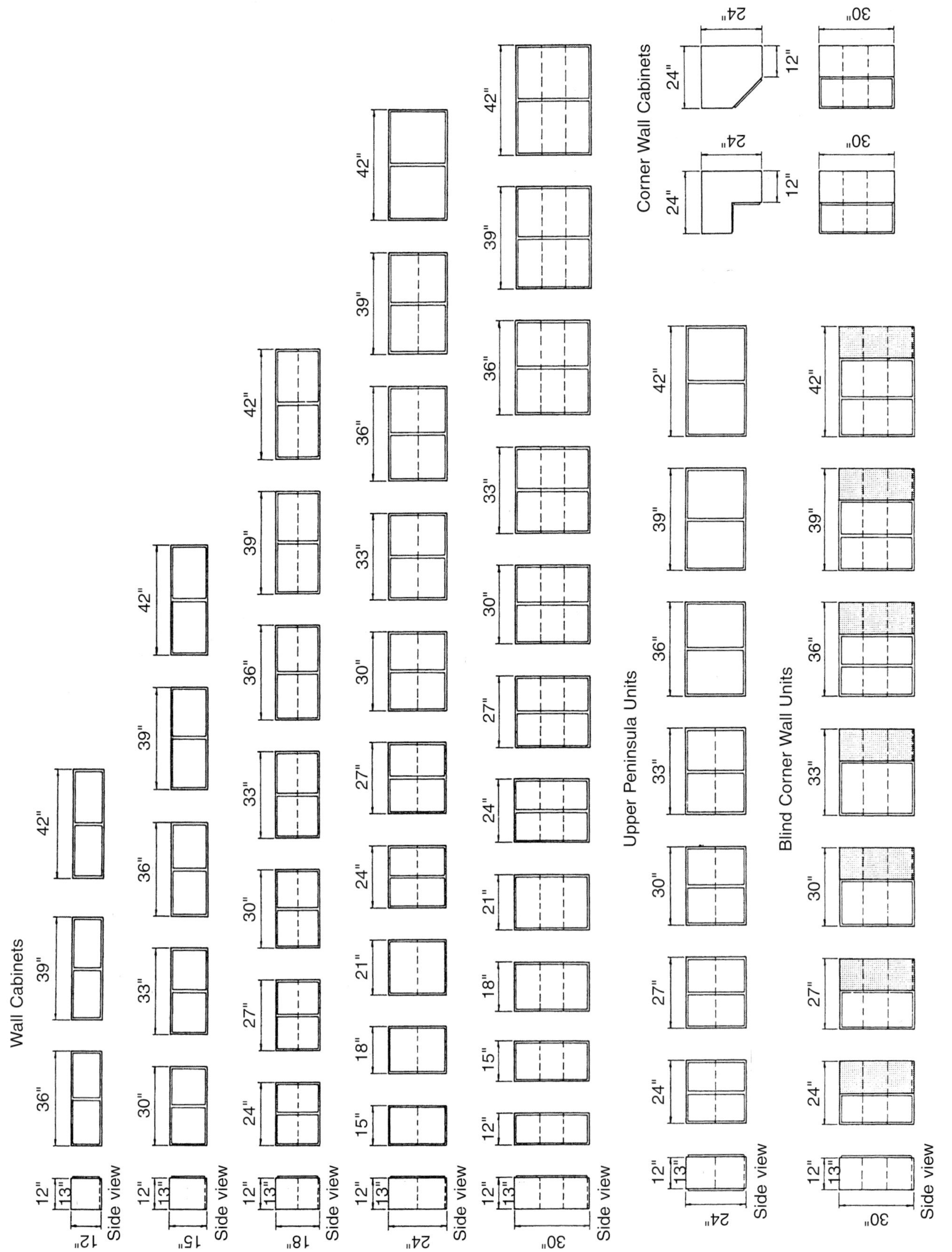

A-13 Common Sizes of Kitchen Appliances

Refrigerator

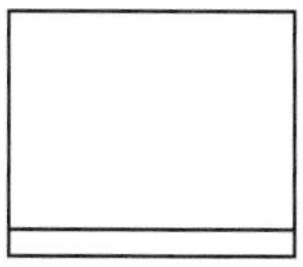

Ft^3	Width	Height	Depth
9	24"	56"	29"
12	30"	68"	30"
14	31"	63"	24"
19	34"	70"	29"
21	36"	66"	29"

Upright Freezer

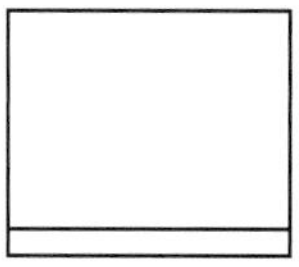

Ft^3	Width	Height	Depth
9	26"	47"	26"
13	28"	58"	28"
15	28"	64"	27"
16	30"	66"	30"
20	33"	66"	28"
31	36"	73"	32"

Free-Standing Range

Width	Height	Depth
20"	30"	24"
21"	36"	25"
30"	36"	26"
40"	36"	27"

Drop-In Range

Width	Height	Depth
23"	23"	22"
24"	23"	22"
30"	24"	25"

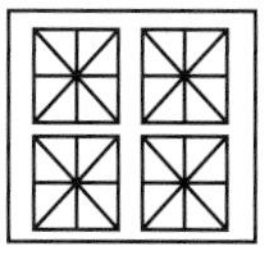

Double-Oven Range

Width	Height	Depth
30"	61"	26"
30"	64"	26"
30"	67"	27"
30"	71"	27"

Built-In Cooktop

Width	Height	Depth
12"	2"	18"
24"	3"	22"
48"	3"	25"

Range Hood

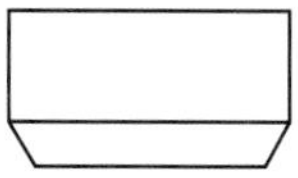

Width	Height	Depth
24"	5"	12"
30"	6"	17"
66"	7"	26"
72"	8"	28"

Double-Compartment Sink

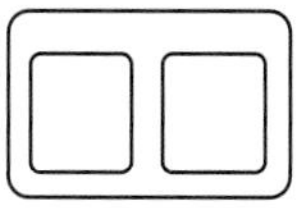

Width	Depth
32"	21"
36"	20"
42"	21"

Dishwasher

Width	Height	Depth
18"	34½"	24"
21"	34½"	24"
24"	34½"	24"

Single-Compartment Sink

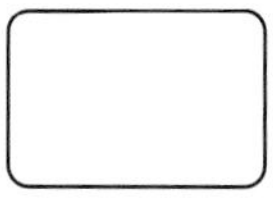

Width	Depth
21"	21"
24"	20"
30"	21"

Trash Compactor

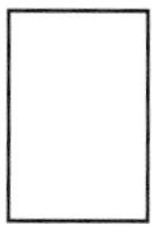

Width	Height	Depth
15"	34½"	24"
18"	34½"	24"

A-14 Common Sizes of Brick

Unit Designation	Nominal Dimensions (inches)			Manufactured Dimensions (using $\frac{3}{8}$ in. mortar joints)		
	t	h	l	t	h	l
Standard Modular	4	$2\frac{2}{3}$	8	$3\frac{5}{8}$	$2\frac{1}{4}$	$7\frac{5}{8}$
Engineer	4	$3\frac{1}{5}$	8	$3\frac{5}{8}$	$2\frac{13}{16}$	$7\frac{5}{8}$
Economy 8 or jumbo closure	4	4	8	$3\frac{5}{8}$	$3\frac{5}{8}$	$7\frac{5}{8}$
Double	4	$5\frac{1}{3}$	8	$3\frac{5}{8}$	$4\frac{15}{16}$	$7\frac{5}{8}$
Roman	4	2	12	$3\frac{5}{8}$	$1\frac{5}{8}$	$11\frac{5}{8}$
Norman	4	$2\frac{2}{3}$	12	$3\frac{5}{8}$	$2\frac{1}{4}$	$11\frac{5}{8}$
Norwegian	4	$3\frac{1}{5}$	12	$3\frac{5}{8}$	$2\frac{13}{16}$	$11\frac{5}{8}$
Economy 12 or jumbo utility	4	4	12	$3\frac{5}{8}$	$3\frac{5}{8}$	$11\frac{5}{8}$
Triple	4	$5\frac{1}{3}$	12	$3\frac{5}{8}$	$4\frac{15}{16}$	$11\frac{5}{8}$
SCR brick	6	$2\frac{2}{3}$	12	$3\frac{5}{8}$	$2\frac{1}{4}$	$11\frac{5}{8}$
6-in. Norwegian	6	$3\frac{1}{5}$	12	$5\frac{5}{8}$	$2\frac{13}{16}$	$11\frac{5}{8}$
6-in. jumbo	6	4	12	$5\frac{5}{8}$	$3\frac{5}{8}$	$11\frac{5}{8}$
8-in. jumbo	8	4	12	$7\frac{5}{8}$	$3\frac{5}{8}$	$11\frac{5}{8}$

A-15 Building Material Symbols

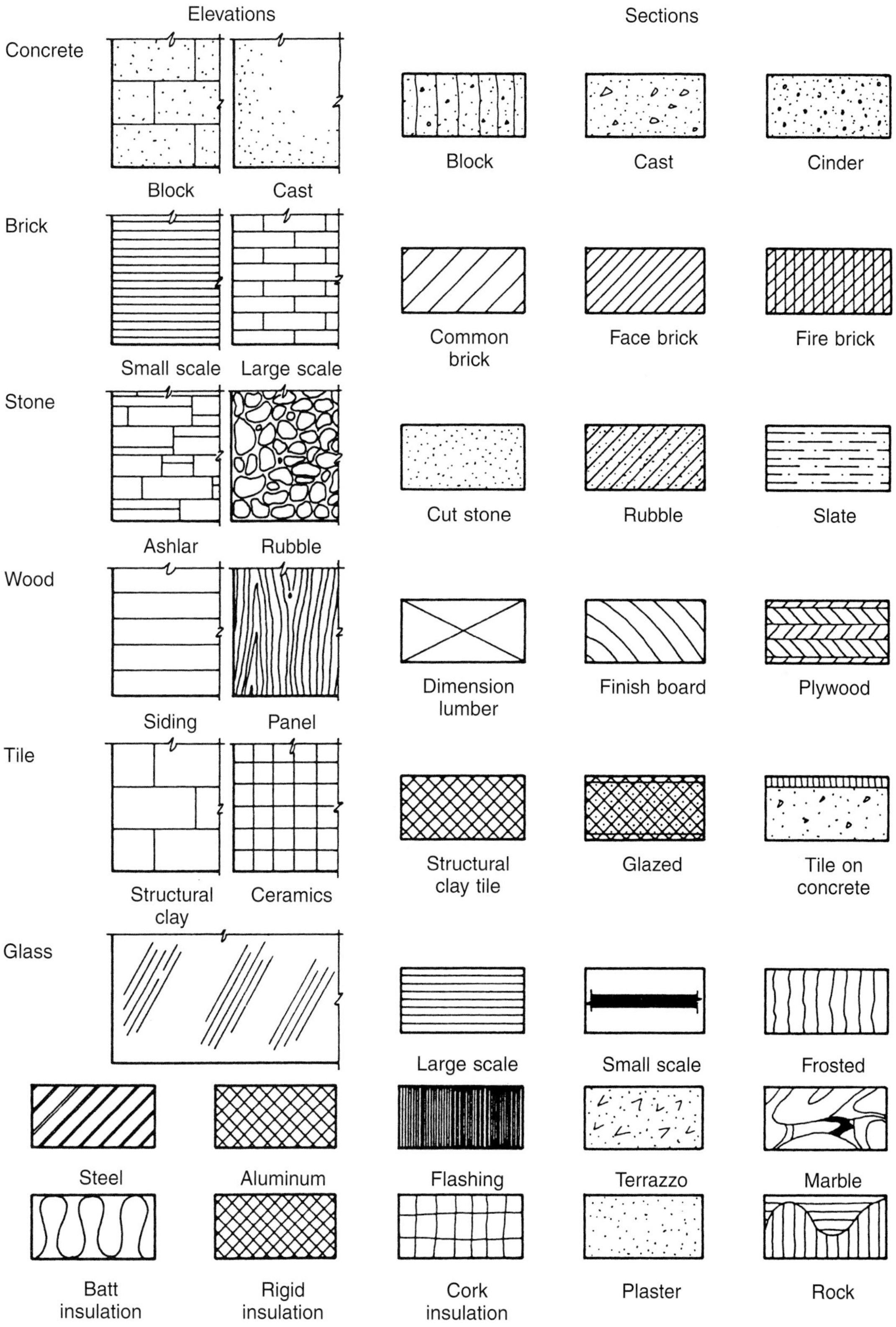

A-16 Thermoplastics

Family	Important Properties	Applications
Acrylics	Weather resistant, colorable, transmits light, cements well, good electrical properties, good surface luster	Skylights, translucent panels, lenses, carpeting, draperies, lighting fixtures, containers
Polystyrene (PS)	Transparent, water resistant, softens at 212 degrees F., brittle, yellows with exposure, tasteless and colorless	Tile, sheets for wall coverings, building insulation, molded furniture parts, appliance housings, packaging containers
Polypropylene (PP)	Off-white in color, lightweight (will float), good flex life, good electrical and chemical resistance, easily colored, scratch resistant	Bottles, fibers for carpeting, housewares, electrical parts, appliance housings, hoses, containers with integral hinges
Vinyls	Good strength and toughness, average chemical resistance, can perform well at low temperatures, begins to soften at 130 degrees F.	Pipe and tubing, simulated leather, gutters, siding, storage tanks, adhesives, upholstery, outdoor furniture
Polyamides (Nylon)	Tough, resists abrasion and chemical attack, not recommended for outdoor exposure, high surface gloss, colorable	Textiles, drawer slides, rollers, hinges
Cellulosics (CA) (CAB)	Very tough, good electrical properties, moderately heat resistant, good surface luster, colorable	Household appliances, tool handles, safety glasses, plumbing fittings
Tetrafluorethylene (TFE)	Highly resistant to chemical attack, wide temperature range, "anti-stick" quality	Lining for pots and pans, electrical insulation, gaskets, tape
Polycarbonates (PC)	Transparent, high impact strength, good heat resistance, weathers well, good chemical resistance	Window glazing, lighting globes, bottles, housings for tools and appliances, covers for electrical panels
Acrylonitrile-Butadiene-Styrene (ABS)	Chemical resistant, rigid, rough, will tolerate high temperatures, medium chemical resistance, tan in color, will burn. Thermoplastics can be softened with heat and hardened with cooling.	Plumbing fittings and pipe, hardware, furniture, appliances
Polyethylene (PE)	Flexible, tough, chemically resistant, feels waxy, fair weatherability, easily colored	Vapor barriers in walls and floors, containers, electrical insulation, housewares, ice trays, bottles

Thermoplastics can be softened with heat and hardened with cooling.

A-17 Thermosetting Plastics

Family	Important Properties	Applications
Alkyds	Opaque, may be colored, good weather resistance, tough, moisture resistant	Paints and enamels, circuit breakers, electrical insulation
Melamines (MF)	Hard, durable, abrasion resistant, chemical resistant, easily colored	Decorative laminates, countertops, switch plates, dinnerware, doorknobs, appliance housings, adhesives for wood
Polyesters	Weather and chemical resistant, stiff and hard, colorable, heat resistant	Textile products, bathtubs and shower stalls, tool handles, appliance housings, prefabricated sections for roof and wall panels
Silicones (SI)	Very stable, excellent corrosion resistance, good insulating properties, will stretch, wide temperature range, odorless, tasteless, nontoxic	Coatings and sealants, fuel lines, gaskets, transformer insulation, masonry waterproofing
Phenolics (PF)	Hard and brittle, low cost, chemically inert, excellent heat and insulating properties	Fabrics, laminating veneers, telephones, tool housings, handles, impregnated wood
Epoxies	Will adhere to most any building material, good chemical and moisture resistance	Protective coatings for walls and floors, adhesive, high strength mortar
Polyurethanes (UP)	Excellent thermal insulating properties, lightweight, resistant to moisture and decay, can be made fire resistant	Sponges, insulation, gaskets, shock impact devices, synthetic leather, furniture cushions
Ureas	Good scratch resistance, low to medium chemical and heat resistance	Molded hardware, electrical fittings, adhesive, insulating foam

A-18 Common Furniture Sizes

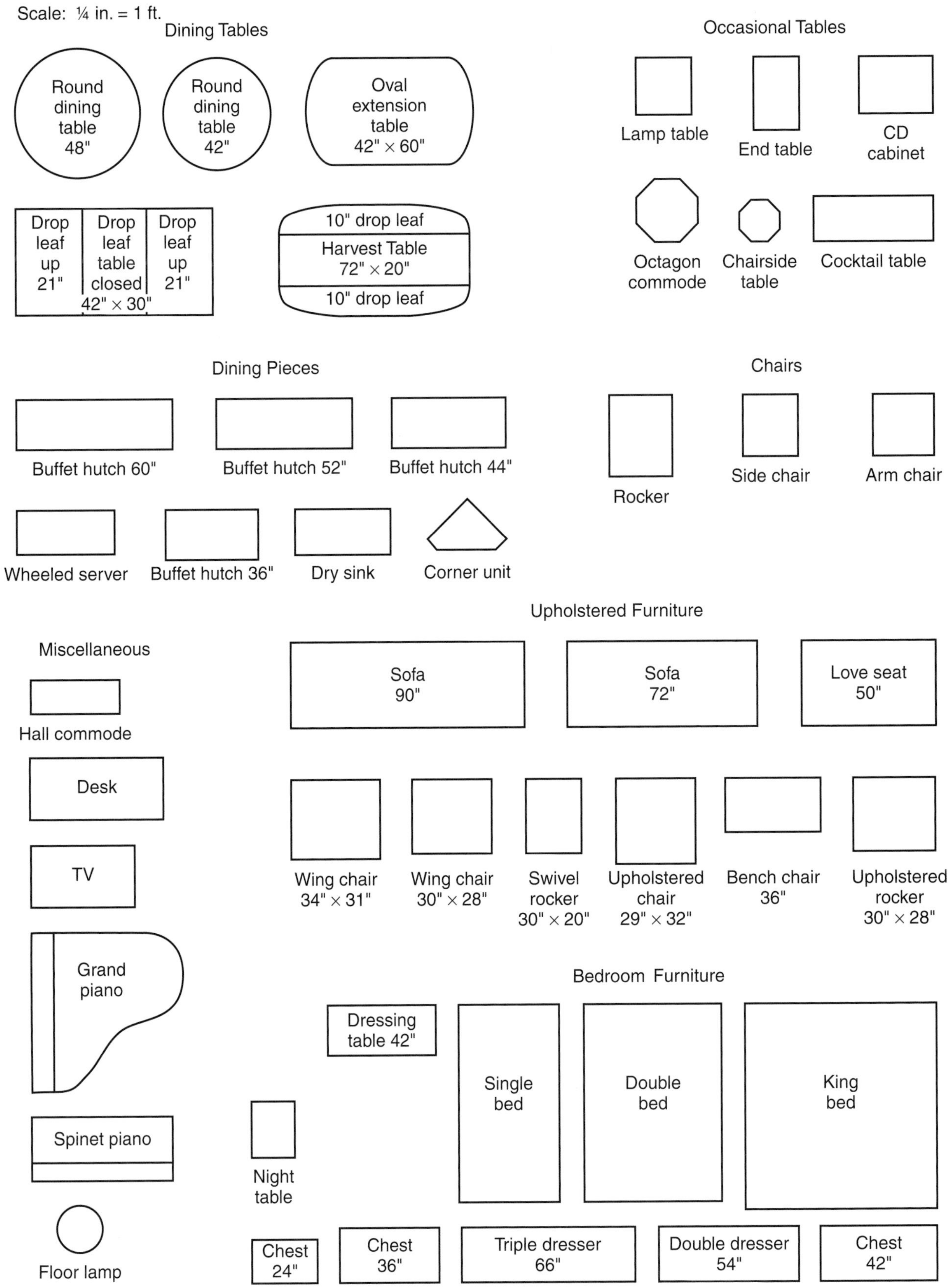
Scale: ¼ in. = 1 ft.
Dining Tables
Round dining table 48"
Round dining table 42"
Oval extension table 42" × 60"
Drop leaf up 21"
Drop leaf table closed 42" × 30"
Drop leaf up 21"
10" drop leaf
Harvest Table 72" × 20"
10" drop leaf
Occasional Tables
Lamp table
End table
CD cabinet
Octagon commode
Chairside table
Cocktail table
Dining Pieces
Buffet hutch 60"
Buffet hutch 52"
Buffet hutch 44"
Wheeled server
Buffet hutch 36"
Dry sink
Corner unit
Chairs
Rocker
Side chair
Arm chair
Upholstered Furniture
Sofa 90"
Sofa 72"
Love seat 50"
Wing chair 34" × 31"
Wing chair 30" × 28"
Swivel rocker 30" × 20"
Upholstered chair 29" × 32"
Bench chair 36"
Upholstered rocker 30" × 28"
Miscellaneous
Hall commode
Desk
TV
Grand piano
Spinet piano
Floor lamp
Bedroom Furniture
Dressing table 42"
Night table
Single bed
Double bed
King bed
Chest 24"
Chest 36"
Triple dresser 66"
Double dresser 54"
Chest 42"

A-19 Common Sizes of Double-Hung Windows

A-20 Common Sizes of Horizontal Sliding Windows

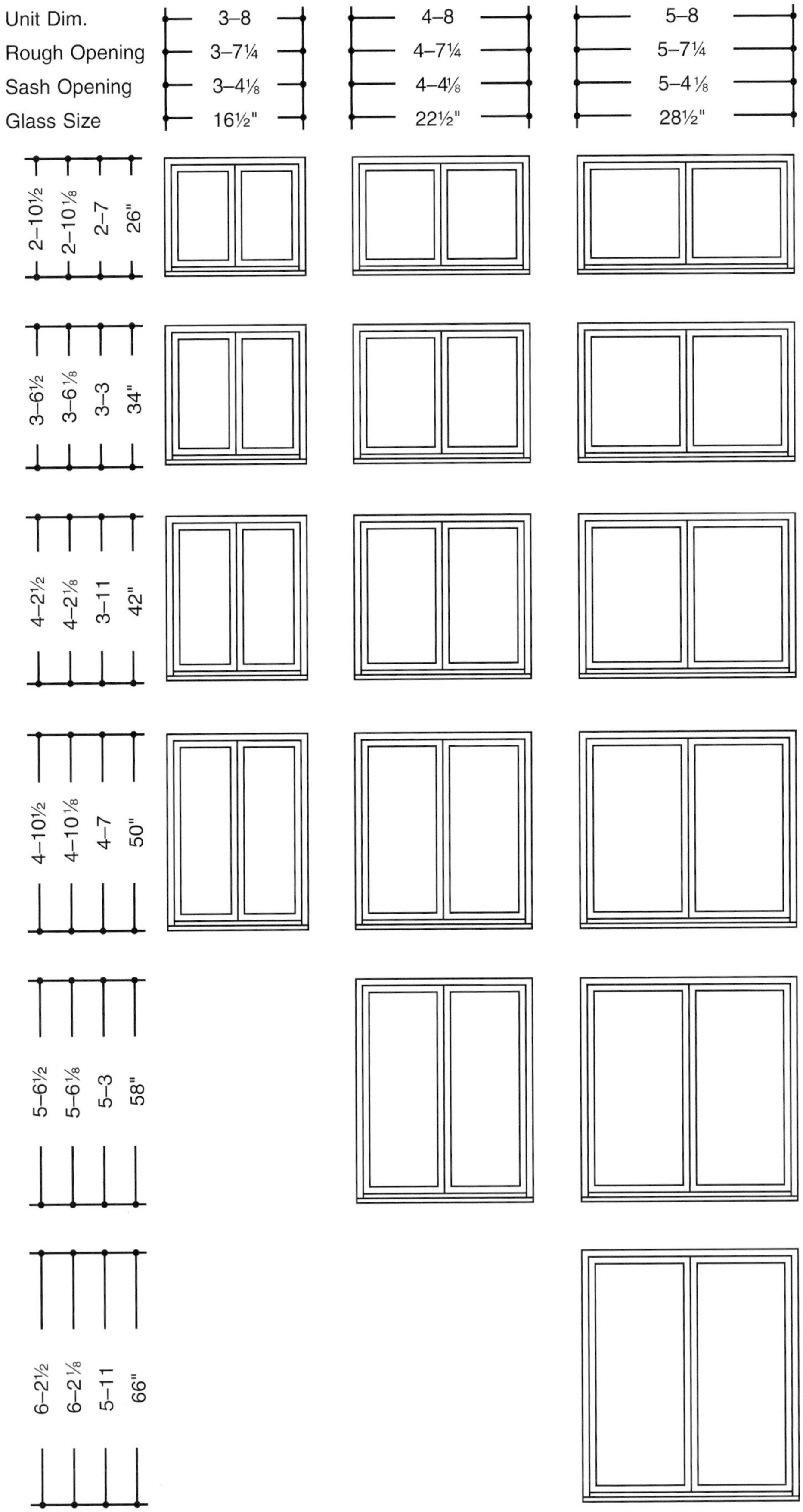

A-21 Common Sizes of Casement Windows

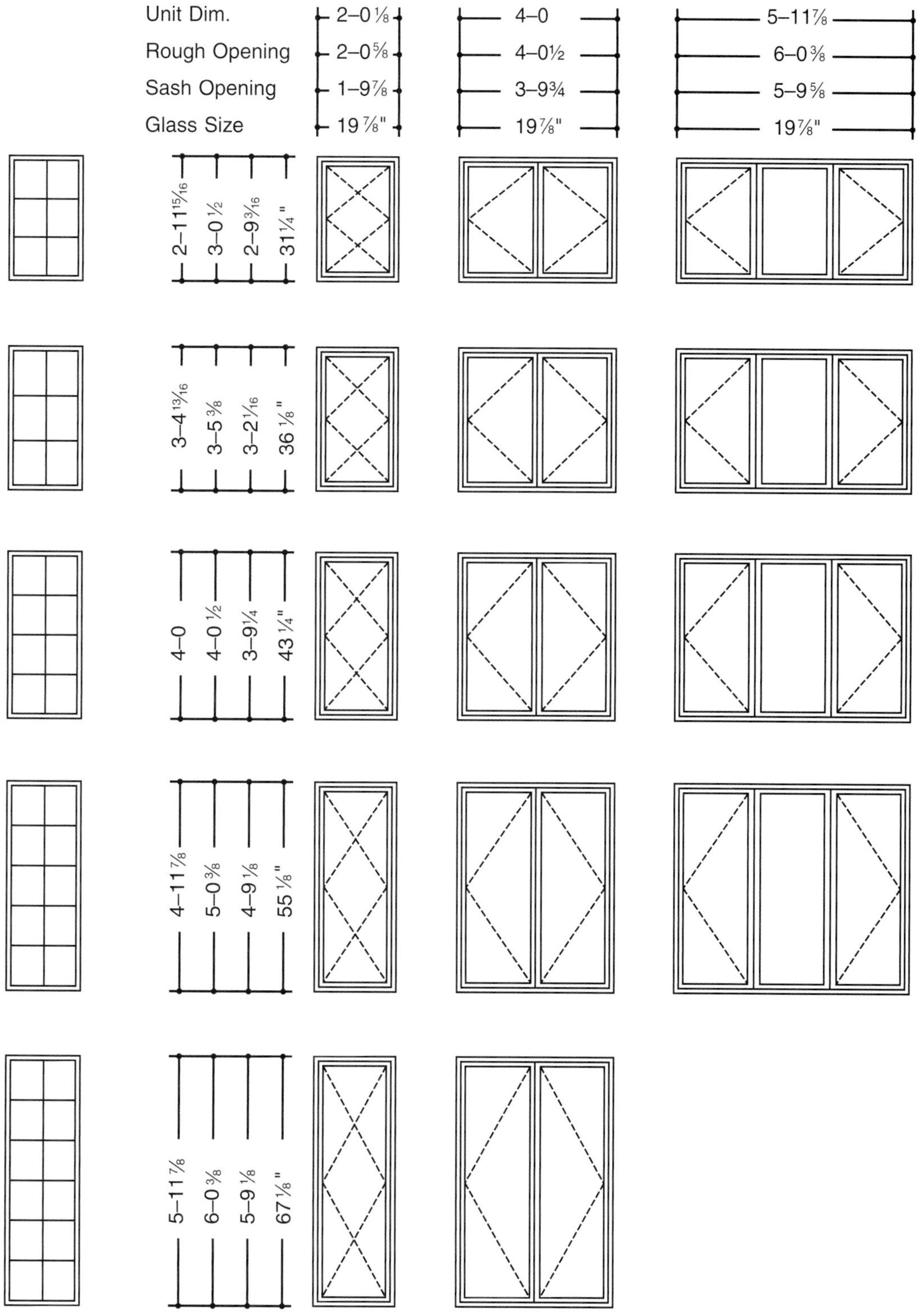

A-22 Common Sizes of Awning and Hopper Windows

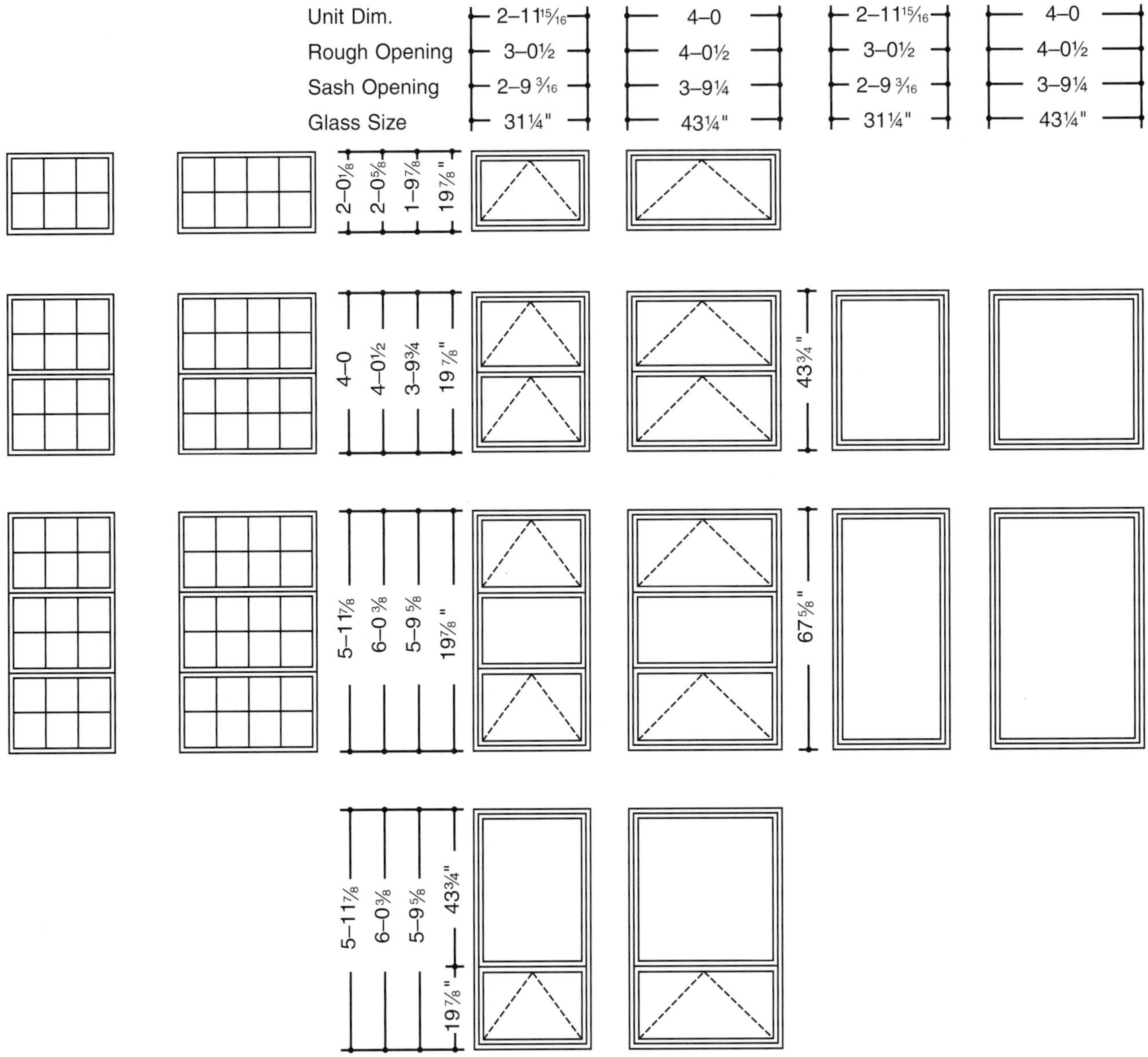

Hopper Windows

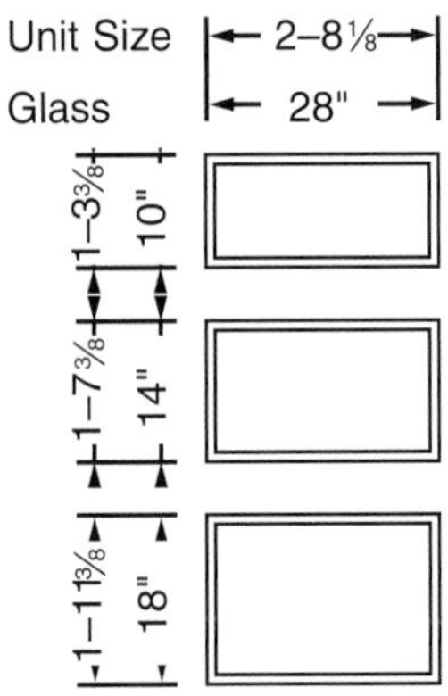

A-23 Common Sizes of Picture Windows

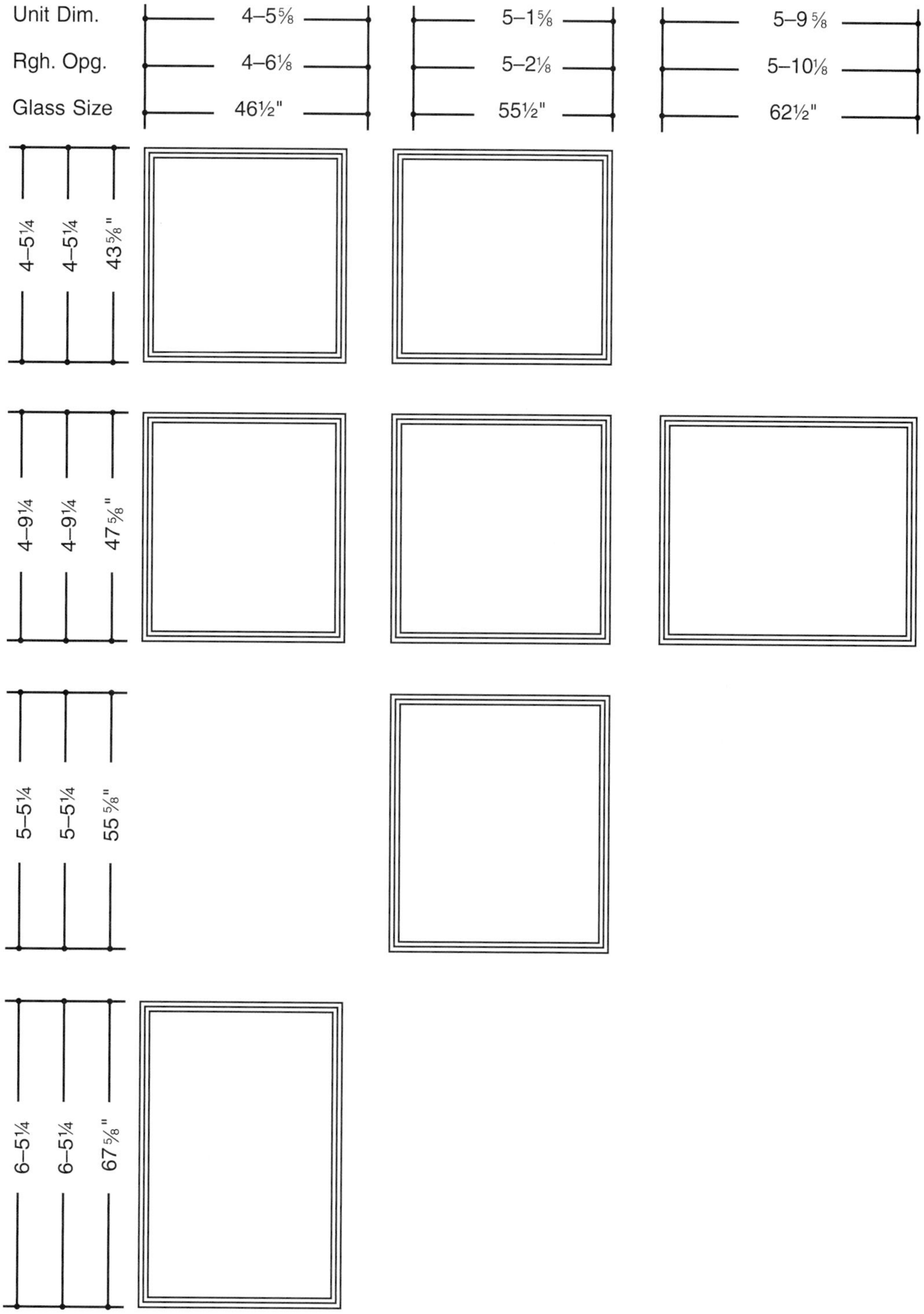

A-24 Common Sizes of Glass Sliding Doors

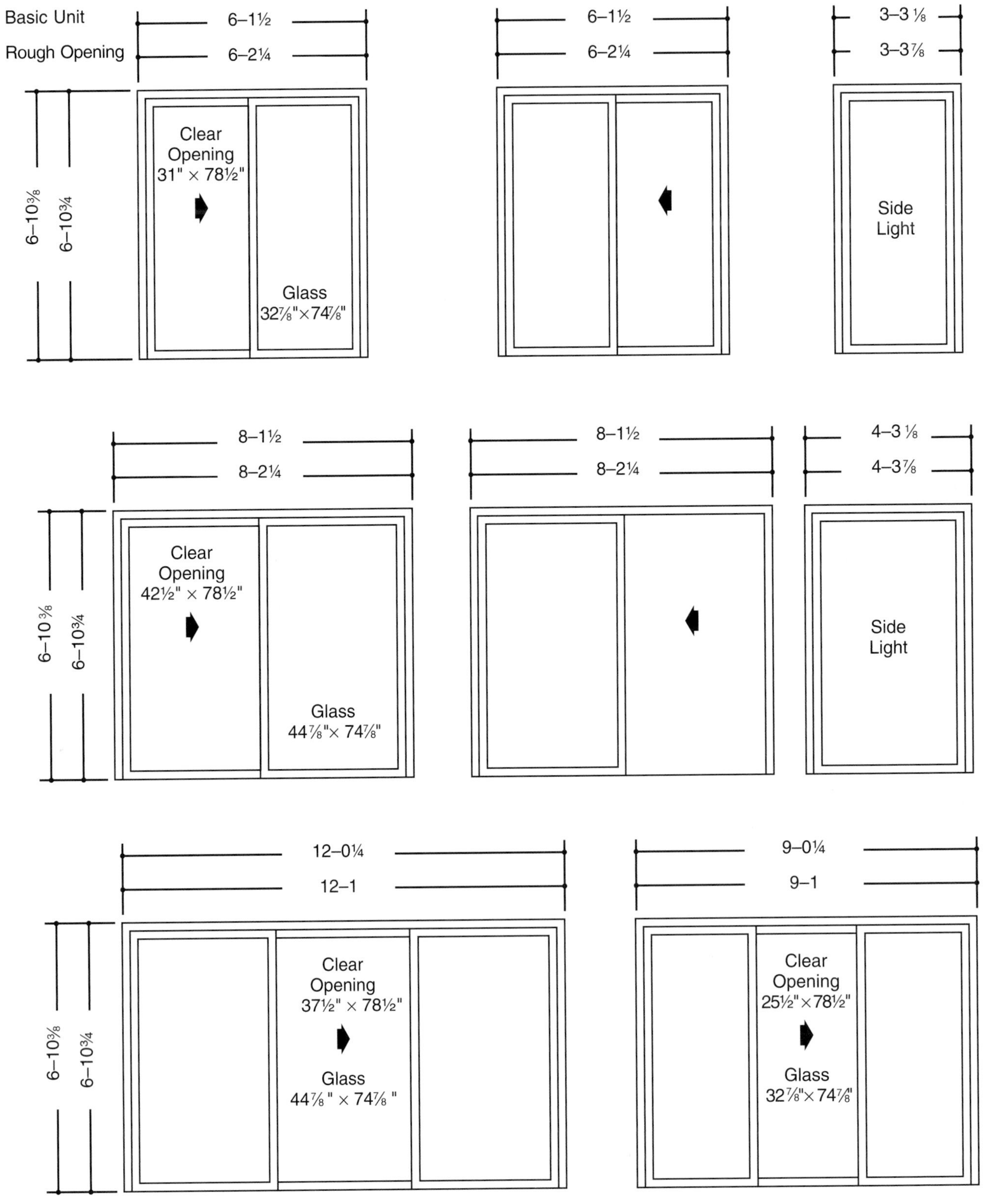

A-25 Percentage of Light Reflected by Color

Color	Percentage of Light Reflected
Natural Wood Tones	
Mahogany & black walnut	5-15
Cherry & dark oak	10-15
Light maple	25-35
Light oak	25-35
Beech & birch	35-50
Dark Colors & Tones	
Forest green	7
Blue green & dark blue	5-10
Olive green	12
Dark gray & dark brown	10-15
Medium gray	20
Medium blue & medium gray	21
Mauve & cocoa brown	24
Medium Colors & Tones	
Rose	29
Old gold	34
Medium light blue	42
Yellow-green	45
Light gray	35-50
Yellow, gold, tan	55
Apricot	56-62
Buff	63
Pink	64
Light Tints	
Light peach & soft pink	69
Cream gray & beige	70
Sky blue, light green & orchid	70-75
Pale yellow & pale pink	75-80
Ivory	75
Eggshell or cream	79
Whites	
Flat or dull white	75-90

Glossary

A

accent lighting. A type of lighting that uses a highly concentrated beam to highlight an area or object. (18)

activating functions. Another term for *switching functions.* (21)

active wall. A wall that suggests movement and attracts attention. (13)

adaptive reuse. The process of changing the function of a building. (26)

addition. New space built onto a home. (26)

adobe. A building that has exterior walls of adobe brick, which is made of soil and straw and baked in the sun. (24)

air chamber mattress. Type of mattress with a series of air chambers made from puncture-resistant flexible rubber. (12)

alarm functions. Performed by devices that alert the homeowner or a home security agency to potential dangers based on a signal from a monitoring device. (21)

alkyd. A category of paints that are oil based. (13)

alloy. Mixture of metals. (9)

analogous color harmony. Color harmony based on combining three to five adjacent hues on the color wheel. (7)

appliqué. A pressure-sensitive transfer material with a printed pattern or color on one side. (27)

apprentice. A person who learns a trade by working under the direction and guidance of a skilled worker. (29)

architect. A person who designs structures by displaying creativity with forms and materials as well as a thorough understanding of construction technology, building codes, laws pertaining to construction, and the use of modern CAD equipment. (29)

architectural drafter. A person who draws the details of working drawings and makes tracings from original drawings that the architect or designer has prepared. (29)

architectural illustrator. A person who prepares pre-sentation drawings, sketches, and illustrations for advertising and client presentations. (29)

artificial light. Light produced by incandescent, halogen, or fluorescent bulbs. (18)

associate degree. A college degree that usually requires two years of full-time study. (29)

attic. The space between the ceiling and roof structure of a building. (26)

B

bachelor's degree. A college or university degree that generally requires four years of full-time study. (29)

balance. In design, a sense of equilibrium. (6)

balance point. The temperature at which the amount of energy required by a heat pump is equal to the amount of energy produced. (22)

balloon framing. A type of floor framing in which the wall is continuous from the sill to the top of the wall and the floor joists are attached to the studs. (14)

bearing wall. A wall that supports some weight from the ceiling or roof of a structure. (13)

blanket insulation. Thick, flexible insulation made from mineral wool. (22)

blend. Yarn formed by spinning at least two different staple fibers into a single yarn. (10)

block printing. Method of hand-printing fabric by stamping a pattern with a dye-covered block. (10)

branch circuits. Individual electrical circuits from the service-entrance panel. (19)

broad conical. An evergreen tree that tapers gradually from a wide base to a single erect stem. (25)

brown coat. The second coat of a three-coat plaster finish. (15)

building brick. A structural clay product used mainly as a structural material where durability and strength are more important than appearance; also called common brick. (8)

building contractor. A person who plans and coordinates the construction of buildings. (29)

bulbous form. A melon-shaped carving used to decorate furniture supports of Elizabethan furniture. (11)

bundled cable. A cable that has several types of conductors inside one PVC jacket. (21)

C

cable pair. The two wires of a telephone line. (21)

cabriole leg. A carved furniture support in the shape of an animal leg. (11)

cafe curtains. Straight curtains hung from rings that slide along a rod. (16)

carbon monoxide (CO). A colorless, odorless, potentially deadly gas that forms when carbon in fuel is not burned completely. (23)

career path. A series of related work experiences of increasing responsibility and/or expertise. (29)

case goods. Pieces of furniture that are made primarily of wood. (12)

cast iron. Iron containing 2 to 3.75 percent carbon that is melted in a blast furnace and cast into different shapes. (9)

cathedral ceiling. A type of ceiling that has exposed beams and a surface covering that is attached to the rafters. (15)

CD-ROM. A compact disc containing data that can be read by a computer. (28)

cellulosic fibers. Fibers derived from plants. (10)

ceramic mosaic tile. Small, decorative tile, usually no larger than 2 sq. in., made of porcelain or natural clay. (9)

check. A small split that runs parallel to the grain of the wood. (12)

chest. Sturdy box with a lid and sometimes a lock that is used for storing and protecting items. (11)

circular stairs. A custom-built, curved stairway made of trapezoid-shaped steps. (17)

circulating stove. A stove that uses airflow and radiant heat to distribute warmth throughout a room. (20)

circulation. Routes that people follow as they move from one place to another in the home. (2)

circulation frequency. Number of times a route within a home is repeated in any given period. (2)

climate control plan. A plan sometimes found in a set of construction drawings that shows the location of the heating, cooling, humidification, and air cleaning equipment in a structure. (2)

closed plan. Design plan in which rooms in the living area are basically cubicles that permit little sharing of activities between them. (3)

coil spring. A spring used in upholstered seat bases that has a three-dimensional spiral shape. (12)

color spectrum. The full range of all existing colors. (7)

columnar. An evergreen tree with nearly vertical branches that tapers only slightly at the top. (25)

combination. Yarn formed by twisting two single yarns of different fibers into a single yarn. (10)

combination system. Home automation system that selects from hard-wired systems, power line technology, and structured wiring systems, providing the opportunity to design a very high-tech, customized system. (21)

combustion. Refers to the process of burning. (23)

communication/recording functions. Performed by devices that record, play back, and/or allow live voice, video, or data communication. (21)

complement. On the color wheel, the color directly opposite another color. (7)

complementary color harmony. A combination of two hues that are directly opposite each other on the color wheel. (7)

composite board. Wood panels that are fabricated from wood particles. (8)

compressor-cycle system. A type of cooling system in which highly compressed refrigerant is used to cool air. (20)

computer-assisted drafting and design (CADD). A computer program that automatically draws objects to scale or exact measurements. (28)

computer simulation. Using application-specific software to illustrate how the final exterior or interior space will appear. (28)

concrete building brick. Concrete brick that is similar in size, function, and appearance to clay brick. (8)

condensation. Water vapor that has returned to a liquid state; generally forms on cool or cold surfaces. (23)

condominium. Dwelling wherein the owner buys an apartment and a share of the common ground. (1)

conflict. Hostility resulting from opposing views. (30)

construction details. Drawings included in a set of construction drawings that provide detailed information to fully describe the construction of special architectural features. (2)

construction technologist. A person who specializes in areas of construction such as managing, purchasing, expediting, specification writing, estimating and bidding, quality control, and site supervision. (29)

cooperative. Dwelling that is managed and run as a corporation. (1)

cornice. The overhanging area of the roof. (15) In draperies, a horizontal decorative treatment across the top of the window generally made of wood that is padded and covered with fabric. (16)

corridor kitchen. A kitchen design consisting of work centers along two walls divided by an aisle 4 to 5 ft. wide. (5)

Cotswold cottage. A compact-size house with very steep gable roof; has casement windows and recessed-arched doorways. (24)

court. Patio-like structure that is partially or completely enclosed by walls. (3)

cove molding. A continuous strip of decorative trim that usually borders a room. (13)

custom house. A house designed and built to meet the needs of a specific household. (1)

D

deciduous. A plant that sheds or loses its foliage at the end of the growing season. (25)

deck. Uncovered porch. (3)

dehumidifying system. Removes moisture vapor from the air to reduce the relative humidity in the space. (26)

delegate. To assign authority or responsibility to another. (30)

direct lighting. Lighting that focuses strong illumination directly on an object. (18)

door jamb. A door frame that fits inside the rough opening of a wall, allowing the door to fit and close securely into the wall. (16)

dormer. A window set in a small projection from a slanted roof. (24)

double-complementary color harmony. A combination of two sets of complementary colors. (7)

double house. A colonial house with two rooms on the main floor and a centrally located fireplace. (24)

double-L stairs. A stairway with two landings along the flight, each with a 90 degree turn. (17)

draft. The upward flow of air that draws sufficient oxygen for a fire to burn well. (20)

drywall. Common name for gypsum wallboard. (13)

ductile. The ability of metal to be drawn into a wire. (9)

Dutch Colonial. A housing style whose most notable feature is the gambrel roof that flares out at the bottom and extends to cover an open porch; usually constructed of fieldstone or brick. (24)

E

earth berm. A ledge or mound of earth that helps to direct prevailing winds up and over a house. (22)

earthquake zone. An area that is prone to earthquakes. (23)

eclectic. A mix of different styles. (11)

electrical plan. A plan found in a set of construction drawings that shows the location and types of electrical equipment to be used in the structure. (2)

Elizabethan. A structure that has both Gothic and Dutch influences; usually a stone, brick, or half-timber construction standing two or three stories high. (24)

empathic listening. Listening with the intent to understand. (30)

emphasis. In design, the center of interest or attention. (6)

EnergyGuide. A yellow label required on certain new major appliances to identify the energy used and how it compares to that used by similar models. (22)

Energy Star label. Indicates a product is at least 10 percent more energy efficient than similar products. (22)

entrepreneur. A person who starts, manages, and assumes the risks of a new business. (30)

ergonomics. The study of humans and their response to various working conditions and environment. (5)

ethics. The rules or standards governing the conduct of the members of a profession. (30)

evergreen. A plant that has foliage that remains green throughout the year. (25)

exterior elevations. Series of drawings found in a set of construction drawings that show the finished appearance and height dimensions of one side of a building. (2)

exterior perspective. Pictorial drawing of the outside of the structure. (27)

F

facing brick. A structural clay product with an attractive appearance for use on exposed surfaces. (8)

felt. A fabric made by applying heat, moisture, agitation, and pressure to wool fibers. (10)

fiber. Basic element of most textiles. (10)

filaments. Fibers that are continuous strands. (10)

films. Fabrics made from synthetic solutions that are formed into thin sheets. (10)

firebrick. A structural clay product designed for use in places that become very hot, such as the inner lining of a fireplace. (8)

flash flood. A high volume of fast-moving water that develops suddenly. (23)

flashing. Sheet metal or a wide strip of other material used in roof and wall construction to shed water away from areas of potential leakage. (15)

float glass. Glass produced by floating molten glass over a bed of molten metal. (9)

floating floor. Flooring that is fastened together using clips that add resiliency, while allowing for the slight expansion that occurs with solid wood flooring. (14)

floating slab. A concrete floor that is separate from the foundation wall. (14)

floodplains. Regions identified by the average number of years between flooding, as in a 100-year or 500-year floodplain. (23)

floor coverings. Floor treatments that are attached to the floor's surface, but are not a structural part of it. (14)

flooring materials. Floor treatments that are structurally part of a floor and serve as its top surface. (14)

floor plan. A section drawing for each floor of a structure taken about 4 ft. above the floor. (2)

fluorescent light. Light produced in a glass tube by releasing electricity through a mercury vapor to make invisible ultraviolet rays. (18)

foams. Fabrics made from a rubber or polyurethane substance into which air is incorporated. (10)

footcandle. The amount of illumination produced by a standard plumber's candle at a distance of one foot. (18)

footing. A wide projection at the base of a foundation wall. (13)

form. The outlined edges of a three-dimensional object. (6)

formal balance. Visual equilibrium achieved through the placement of identical objects on both sides of a central point. (6)

foundation/basement plan. A plan found in a set of construction drawings that shows the location and size of footings, piers, columns, foundation walls, and supporting beams of the structure. (2)

foundation wall. The part of a dwelling that extends from the first floor down to the footing base. (13)

foyer. Entry hall that functions as a place to greet guests and, in colder climates, remove coats and boots. (3)

frame. On upholstered furniture, the wood support beneath the textile covering. (12)

French doors. Doors with large areas of paned glass. (24)

French Normandy. A housing style that is usually one and one-half to two and one-half stories high with brick, stone, or stucco walls and a central turret. (24)

full bath. Bathroom containing a water closet, lavatory, and tub with or without a shower. (4)

function. The intended use or purpose of a structure, room, or object. (6)

furring strip. A strip of wood about the width of a stud used on concrete walls as a base for the attachment of another wall surface such as drywall or paneling. (13)

G

gable end. The horizontal extension of a gable roof beyond the end wall of the house; also called the rake. (15)

Gantt Chart. A graphic representation that compares estimated timetables for progress with actual progress performance. (28)

gauge. Wire thickness. (12)

general lighting. An application of lighting to provide a comfortable, even level of brightness throughout a room. (18)

general-purpose circuit. A branch circuit designed to supply power to permanently installed lighting fixtures and to receptacle outlets for devices that use little wattage in operation. (19)

geodesic dome. An engineered system of triangular frames that create self-reinforcing roof and wall units based on mathematically precise divisions of a sphere. (24)

glazed tile. Ceramic tile with a glossy, stain-resistant finish produced by finishing the tile with one, two, or three coats of glazing. (9)

gradation. In design, creating rhythm by making a gradual change in form or color value. (6)

grade level. The level of the land surrounding the building. (3)

grain. In wood, the pattern of the fibers. (8)

grasses. Plants that typically have narrow leaves, hollow jointed stems, and spikes. (25)

green building. A way for builders to minimize the environmental impact of their construction projects; both a design/building process and the resulting structure. (22)

ground covers. Low, thick foliage used in place of grass. (25)

ground fault circuit interrupter (GFCI). A safety device that continually monitors the amount of electricity flowing in the circuit and opens it if an imbalance occurs. (4)

group plan. Layout plan that clusters bedrooms in one area of the home. (4)

grout. A substance used to fill the joints between tiles. (14)

gunmetal bronze. The strongest bronze possible, containing 90 percent copper and 10 percent tin.

gypsum wallboard. A sheet material used to cover wall studs that is made of a gypsum core covered with heavy paper surfaces; also called drywall. (13)

H

half bath. Bathroom containing a water closet and a lavatory. (4)

half house. A colonial house having one main-floor room with a tiny entrance and a steep stairway leading to an attic. (24)

half-timber. Wall construction with large, rough, wood support beams that are filled with masonry or plaster. (24)

halogen bulbs. Type of lighting with tungsten filaments that produce bright, white light matching the quality of pure daylight. (18)

hardboard. A type of composite board made from refined wood fibers that are pressed together. (8)

hard-wired systems. Home automation systems that are dedicated (stand-alone), self-contained systems, which are part of the infrastructure of the building. (21)

hardwoods. Classification of woods from deciduous (broadleaf) trees. (8)

harmony. In design, an agreement among parts. (6)

header course. A row of bricks or blocks that are placed across two rows to hold them together. (13)

helical. Tiny, coiled spring used to link serpentine springs together. (12)

highboy. A tall chest on long legs with drawers generally divided to resemble a chest-on-chest. (11)

hillside ranch. A ranch-style house built on a hill with part of the basement exposed. (24)

historic preservation. Returning a building to its original condition while maintaining traditional styles, materials, and in some cases, furnishings. (26)

hollow-core flush door. A door made of a framework core covered with a wood, metal, or vinyl veneer. (16)

horizontal axis washer. A washer that reduces water and energy use, opens in front, and agitates the load on its side, lifting and dropping the clothes in water no higher than the door opening. (22)

housing. The structural dwelling, its contents, and its surroundings. (1)

hue. The name of a color; the characteristic that makes each color different. (7)

hurricane. A tropical storm with winds at a sustained speed of 74 miles per hour (64 knots) or more; also called a cyclone or typhoon. (23)

hurricane codes. Building restrictions designed to reduce damage to property during a hurricane. (23)

I

incandescent light. Light produced when electricity is passed through a fine tungsten filament in a vacuum bulb. (18)

independent evaporator unit. A unit consisting of a blower, cooling coils, and filter used with the compressor/condenser unit in a cooling system independent of the furnace. (20)

indigenous. A plant living naturally in a given area. (25)

indirect lighting. Diffused light produced by directing the light toward an intermediate surface that reflects the light into the room. (18)

individual-appliance circuit. A branch circuit designed to serve a permanently installed appliance that uses a large amount of electricity or has an automatic starting motor. (19)

informal balance. Visual equilibrium achieved by placing different, but equivalent, objects on either side of a central point. (6)

inlay. A technique whereby pieces of wood, metal, ivory, or shell of contrasting color or texture are inserted in a background material to provide surface decoration. (11)

innerspring mattress. A type of mattress containing a series of springs covered with padding. (12)

insulation. A material that efficiently resists the flow of heat through it. (20)

insulation boards. Rigid panels of insulation made of foamed plastics. (22)

intensity. Brightness or dullness of a hue. (7)

interactive. A type of CD-ROM that communicates information specific to the user's response to questions or options. (28)

interior designer. A person who plans and supervises the design, decoration, and furnishings of building interiors. (29)

interior perspective. Pictorial drawing of a room or other area inside a house. (27)

intermediate colors. Colors made by mixing a primary color with a secondary color. (7)

island kitchen. A kitchen design with a counter unit that stands alone. (5)

J

japanning. A relatively inexpensive technique of finishing woods with an appearance similar to Oriental lacquer. (11)

joist. A construction board with a cross-section ranging from 2 by 8 in. to 2 by 12 in. (14)

journeyman. An experienced, reliable worker who knows a trade well. (29)

K

kit houses. Factory models of houses available in kits. (1)

L

lacquer. A wood finishing material that forms a tough, glossy finish. (8)

ladder-back chair. Early American chair with a back consisting of two upright posts connected by horizontal slats. (11)

lambrequin. A cornice that extends down the side of windows. (16)

laminated timber. Wood that is constructed by combining layers of wood with grains running in the same direction. (8)

landing. A flat floor area that may be placed at any point along a stairway. (17)

landscape designer. A person who plans the arrangement and composition of landscape elements on a site. (29)

land surveyor. A person who establishes areas and boundaries of real estate property. (29)

latex. A category of paints that are water based. (13)

lath. A base material to which plaster is applied. (15)

lavatory. A sink. (4)

leaded glass. Transparent, colorless glass made by setting small pieces of glass into strips of lead or copper foil. (9)

leather. A material made from the hides of animals for use as fabric. (10)

line. The visual direction of a design. (6)

lintel. A heavy member of a wall frame used over openings in the wall to support the weight above. (13)

live load. Weight of furniture, people, and their household possessions. (14)

living areas. Places in the home for family members to relax, entertain guests, dine, and meet together. (3)

loose-fill insulation. Insulation in the form of small pieces of mineral fiber, cellulose fiber, or expanded materials such as perlite and vermiculite. (22)

Louisiana French. A housing style having a raised brick or stone basement and balconies with lacy ironwork railings that originated in New Orleans. (24)

lowboy. A low chest of drawers on short legs. (11)

L-shaped kitchen. A kitchen design consisting of work centers forming a continuous line along two adjoining walls. (5)

L stairs. A stairway with one landing at some point along the flight of stairs that changes direction at the landing. (17)

lumber. Wood sawed from logs into boards of various sizes. (8)

luminous ceilings. A structural fixture consisting of transparent or translucent ceiling panels lighted from above. (18)

M

main entry. Entry that opens to the living area of the house, usually the foyer. (3)

main stairway. A stairway between the first and second floors of a house. (17)

malleable. The ability of metal to be formed into sheets. (9)

manager. A person who makes and implements decisions and who accomplishes desired results through others. (30)

manufactured houses. Types of houses that are produced in a factory, shipped to the site, and put into place with a crane. (1)

manufactured stone. A veneer made from lightweight concrete to give the appearance of natural stone. (8)

master's degree. An advanced degree involving one to two years of study beyond a bachelor's degree. (29)

mastic. Thick type of adhesive. (14)

mediation. Negotiation with impartial assistance of someone who is not affected by the outcome of the dispute. (30)

microfiber. The name given to ultrafine manufactured fibers. (10)

millwork. Processed lumber such as doors, window frames, shutters, trim, panel work, and molding. (8)

model maker. A person who builds scale models of objects, such as planned communities, individual buildings, room layouts, or pieces of furniture. (29)

moisture barrier. A membrane that retards the flow of moisture vapor and reduces condensation. (26)

molds. Types of fungus that reproduce through the production of spores. (23)

monitoring functions. Performed by devices that examine certain aspects of the house to determine their status. (21)

monochromatic color harmony. Color harmony based on a single hue. (7)

motif. A repeated figure or element in design or architecture. (11)

motion detectors. Detect the movement of an intruder that is inside the home after bypassing the perimeter system. (21)

muntins. Small vertical and horizontal bars that separate the total glass area into smaller units. (16)

N

narrow conical. An evergreen tree that tapers sharply from base to tip. (25)

natural light. Sunlight. (18)

network. Several computers that share information through joined wiring; also, the process of sharing information. (21)

neutral color harmonies. A combination of black, white, and gray; or shades of brown, tan, and beige. (7)

nonbearing wall. A wall that does not support any weight from a structure beyond its own weight. (13)

nonwoven fabrics. Fabrics made by bonding nonwool fibers, yarns, or filaments by mechanical or chemical means. (10)

O

Occupational Safety and Health Administration (OSHA). The government agency that keeps job-injury statistics, provides job safety information, and enforces rules to protect worker safety. (30)

one-wall kitchen. A kitchen design consisting of appliances and cabinets on one wall. (5)

open plan. Design plan in which rooms in the living area use minimal walls to encourage a sharing of activities across the space. (3)

open standard. A system that is free for all interested parties to implement and use. (21)

orientation. The placement or alignment of an object. (22)

ornamental. A plant grown for its beauty. (25)

overcurrent devices. Devices that prevent excessive flow of current in a circuit such as fuses or breakers. (19)

P

panic button. Sets off an audible siren or sends an "alarm" message silently to a monitoring station. (21)

particleboard. A type of composite board made from wood flakes, chips, and shavings that are bonded together with resins or adhesives. (8)

passive wall. A wall used as a background element that does not attract attention. (13)

patina. On wood surfaces, a mellow glow with richness and depth of tone. (12)

patio. Outdoor extension of a home's living area usually built at grade level, but not structurally connected to the house. (3)

pattern bond. The pattern formed by the masonry units and mortar joints on the exposed parts of construction. (8)

paver. Ceramic tile made from natural clay and shale, generally rectangular and designed for heavy-traffic floors. (9)

paving brick. A hard structural clay product hat is highly resistant to abrasion and moisture absorption. (8)

peninsula kitchen. U-shaped kitchen with a counter extending from one end of the U. (5)

Pennsylvania Dutch Colonial. A housing style having thick, fieldstone walls with a pent roof and an unsupported hood over the front entrance. (24)

pent roof. A small roof ledge between the first and second floors of a house. (24)

perimeter system. A home security system in which all doors and windows are wired with magnetic switches inside the frame that activates an alarm when a switch is disturbed by opening a door or window. (21)

pictorial presentation. Realistic rendering, often in color and proper perspective, used to better communicate the finished appearance of a structure. (2)

pilaster. A thickened section built into a foundation wall from the footing to the top of the wall. (13)

pilling. The formation of tiny balls of fiber, called pills, that form on fabrics from abrasion. (10)

pitch. A natural resin common in softwoods that absorbs stains and other finishes differently from the wood fibers. (12)

platform framing. A type of floor framing in which the floor is placed on a sill that is connected to the top of the wall below it. (14)

plating. A thin coating of metal over another material for added protection or attractiveness. (12)

plot plan. A plan found in a set of construction drawings that shows the location of the structure on the site. (2)

plumbing plan. A plan sometimes found in a set of construction drawings that shows the freshwater supply lines, wastewater lines, and plumbing fixtures of the structure. (2)

plywood. A wood panel made from thin sheets of wood that are glued together so the grain of one layer is at a right angle to the grain of the next. (8)

pocketed. Coil springs in a mattress that are covered with individualized padding. (12)

polyurethane. A synthetic, clear wood finish commonly used on floors. (8)

porch. Outdoor extension of a home's living area that is structurally connected to the house, built above grade level, and covered by a roof. (3)

portable fixtures. Light fixtures that are not a part of the home's architectural structure. (18)

power line technology. Sending home-automation signals over existing electrical wiring to control almost any electrical device. (21)

precuts. Packaged materials used to build a house that are already cut to size for a customer's plan. (1)

prefab housing. Housing units delivered as preassembled panels ready for erecting on the site. (1)

presentation boards. Contain drawings such as floor plans and elevations and any other information and samples of materials necessary to help the client visualize a finished product. (27)

presentation elevation. Pictorial drawing showing a view perpendicular to a surface. (27)

presentation floor plans. Drawings that show the basic room layout inside a structure, sometimes including traffic flow analysis or placement of furniture and appliances. (27)

presentation landscape plan. Pictorial drawing showing the entire landscape plan including plants and other elements to be included. (27)

presentation plot plan. Pictorial drawing showing the relationship between the site and the structure. (27)

primary colors. Red, yellow, and blue; colors from which all other colors are made. (7)

programming functions. Performed by devices that can control a sequence of planned events. (21)

Project Evaluation and Review Technique (PERT) chart. A step-by-step plan to complete a construction project with checkpoints to monitor progress. (28)

proportion. The ratio of one part to another part or of one part to the whole. (6)

protein fibers. Fibers derived from animals. (10)

prototype. An original type, form, or instance that serves as a model on which later stages are based or judged. (30)

Q

quarry tile. Large, strong ceramic tile made from natural clay and shale, and designed for heavy-traffic floors. (9)

R

radiant floor. Floor with imbedded heating elements, such as electrical resistance wires or copper tubing. (14)

radiant heat. Heat that passes through the air with no assistance from airflow. (20)

radiation. In design, creating rhythm by making lines flow outward from a central point. (6)

radon. An invisible, odorless, tasteless radioactive gas that comes from the natural decay of uranium found in soil, rock, and water. (23)

raised ranch. A ranch-style house with part of the basement aboveground. (24)

rattan furniture. Furniture made from a vinelike, climbing form of palm. (11)

recessed lights. Structural fixtures that are small, circular lights installed in the ceiling. (18)

relays. Electronically operated switches. (21)

relief. A projecting detail, ornament, or figure. (11)

remodeling. Changing an existing space into a new form. (26)

rendering. The addition of shades, shadow, texture, and color to a line drawing to achieve a realistic appearance. (27)

renovation. Returning an old home to its previous condition, not necessarily its original condition, without changing the space. (26)

repetition. In design, creating rhythm by repeating color, line, form, or texture. (6)

resilient floor covering. Smooth, hard material in sheet or tile form that returns to its original shape. (14)

restoration. Returning a structure to its original condition. (26)

rhythm. A principle of design that leads the eye from one part of a design to another. (6)

ribbon windows. Wide, short windows that are often used on the first floor to provide ventilation and privacy. (4)

ridge. The highest horizontal line at which two sections of roof meet. (15)

rise. The vertical distance of a roof measured from the top of the wall plate to the underside of the rafters. (15)

roller printing. Method of printing fabric in which color is transferred directly to a fabric as it passes between a series of rollers. (10)

romayne work. Caricatures of human heads used for decoration on furniture. (11)

rotary screen printing. Method of printing fabric in which dye is transferred through a cylinder-shaped screen that rolls over the fabric, printing the design. (10)

ruffled curtains. Curtains that are edged with ruffles on the hems and sometimes on the sides. (16)

run. One-half the distance of the clear span of a roof. (15)

R-value. Level of resistance to heat. (20)

S

safe room. A room within the house that is constructed to withstand tornado-force winds. (23)

sash. A main glass area of a window. (16)

scale. The size of an object in relation to a standard or familiar size. (6)

scratch coat. The first coat of a plaster finish applied directly to the lath. (15)

seasoned. Term describing wood after a drying process that removes moisture to help prevent shrinking, warping, splitting, and rotting in finished products. (8)

seat base. The part of an upholstered chair or sofa that serves as the platform for cushioning materials. (12)

secondary colors. Orange, green, and violet; colors made by mixing equal amounts of two primary colors. (7)

secretary. A type of chest with drawers and a hinged writing surface. (11)

section drawing. Shows a cut-away view of a house or series of rooms in a house. (27)

seismic. Refers to earth vibrations. (23)

serpentine spring. A long, flat spring used in upholstered seat bases that repeats the shape of an S. (12)

service area. The parts of the home that sustain all others; includes the kitchen, laundry facilities, basement, garage (or carport), service entries, special-purpose rooms, and storage. (5)

service-entrance panel. The main distribution box that receives the electricity and distributes it to various points in the house through branch circuits. (19)

service entry. House entrance that usually leads to the work area, often the kitchen. (5)

service stairway. A stairway between the first floor and the basement, generally leading to a service area on the first floor. (17)

shade. A darkened value of a hue made by adding black to a hue. (7)

shape. A flat or silhouette image. (6)

shirred curtains. Curtains that are gathered directly on rods, sometimes at both top and bottom. (16)

shrub. A woody plant of relatively low height that has several stems. (25)

signaling circuits. Supply the electrical power to buzzers, doorbells, chimes, signal lights, or warning devices. (21)

single-face fireplace. A fireplace with one opening in the firebox. (20)

slatback chair. Straight, upright Early American chairs with flat or caned seats and backs with vertical posts. (11)

sleepers. Furring strips embedded in a concrete slab floor so a floor treatment can be fastened to it. (14)

sleeping area. The bedrooms, baths, dressing rooms, and nurseries. (4)

slump brick. A type of concrete brick with an irregular face that has the appearance of stone. (8)

small-appliance circuit. A branch circuit designed to power appliances that require a lmoderate amount of current, such as fry pans and blenders. (19)

smoke detector. A small appliance that signals the presence of smoke. (23)

soffit. The underside of the cornice. (15)

softwoods. Classification of woods from coniferous or cone-bearing trees. (8)

soil stack. Tall, vertical drain pipes that collect waste from fixtures on all floors of the house. (19)

solar collector. Part of an active solar heating system designed to absorb heat from the sun. (20)

solid-core flush door. A door made of solid particleboard or tightly fitted blocks of wood covered with veneer. (16)

solution dyeing. Method of dyeing involving adding dye to a solution for making manufactured fibers before extruding it into filaments. (10)

space. The area provided for a particular purpose. (6)

span. The distance from the outside of one exterior wall to the outside of the opposite exterior wall. (15)

special-purpose entry. Entry that provides access to patios, decks, and courts. (3)

special-purpose room. Separate room dedicated to a single purpose; examples include a home office, exercise room, darkroom, library, sewing room, arts and crafts studio, hobby room, workshop, music room, greenhouse, and billiard room. (5)

spiral stairs. A stairway consisting of a set of wedge-shaped steps fastened together to form a cylindrical shape. (17)

split balusters. Short, turned pieces of wood split in half used to decorate furniture; also called split spindles. (11)

split-bedroom plan. Bedroom-layout plan that separates the master bedroom from other bedrooms to provide greater privacy. (4)

split-complementary color harmony. A combination of one hue with the two hues on both sides of its complement. (7)

Stachybotrys atra. A potentially dangerous greenish-black mold that grows on materials with high-cellulose and low-nitrogen content; commonly called black mold. (23)

stained glass. Glass colored by pigments or metal oxides that are fused to the glass. (9)

stainless steel. Steel that contains chromium to make it hard and corrosion resistant over a wide temperature range. (9)

staple fibers. Fibers that are short; a characteristic of all natural fibers except silk. (10)

stock dyeing. Method of dyeing involving adding dye to loose natural fibers. (10)

storm surge. A dome of ocean water fueled by a hurricane that can be 20 ft. at its highest point and up to 100 miles wide. (23)

straight-run stairs. A stairway with no turns or landings between the ends. (17)

strip lighting. A structural fixture consisting of a strip of receptacles to hold a series of incandescent bulbs or fluorescent tubes. (18)

structural fixtures. Light fixtures that are permanently built into the home. (18)

structural model. An architectural model frequently used to show construction features of a residence. (30)

structured wiring. An organized arrangement of high-quality cables and connections that distribute services throughout the home. (21)

structured wiring systems. Provide for complete home security and home automation in one package. (21)

stucco. The final finish coat of the plastering process on an interior or exterior surface. (13)

style. A distinctive manner or type of design. (11)

suspended ceiling. A ceiling system supported by hanging from the overhead structural framing. (15)

switching functions. Performed by devices that initiate an action based on an input; also called activating functions. (21)

T

tactile. The perception of touch. (6)

task lighting. An application of lighting to provide strong light to a small area. (18)

tensile strength. In glass, the amount of force it can withstand before breaking. (9)

terrazzo. A type of floor surface made of marble chips bound together with Portland cement. (14)

texture. A surface's tactile quality. (6)

thermoplastic. Plastic material that can be repeatedly softened with heat and hardened by cooling. (9)

thermosetting plastic. Plastic products that are permanently shaped during the manufacturing process and cannot be softened again by reheating. (9)

thickened-edge slab. A concrete floor with the floor slab and foundation combined into a single unit. (14)

three-face fireplace. A fireplace that is open on three sides. (20)

three-quarters bath. Bathroom containing a water closet, lavatory, and shower. (4)

timber. Lumber at least 5 in. wide and thick. (8)

tint. A lightened value of a hue made by adding white to the hue. (7)

topography. The configuration of the land's surface with all its features, such as trees, streams, rocks, and manufactured structures. (24)

tornado. A swirling column of air extending from a thunderstorm cloud to the ground. (23)

tornado warning. An alert issued when a tornado has been sighted or detected on radar. (23)

tornado watch. A warning issued when conditions are favorable for tornado formation. (23)

track lighting. Structural lighting mounted in a metal strip that allows fixtures to be placed anywhere along the strip. (18)

tract houses. Several houses built from a few basic plans on land that is divided into lots. (1)

trade. An occupation requiring manual or mechanical skill. (29)

transition. In design, creating rhythm by using curved lines to carry the eye over an architectural feature or rounded parts of furniture. (6)

trap. U-curved pipe installed below plumbing fixtures that holds water to prevent sewer gases from backing into the living space. (19)

trees. Tall, woody plants with a single trunk. (25)

triadic color harmony. The combination of any three colors equally distant from each other on the standard color wheel. (7)

truss. An assembly of structural members designed to span longer distances than a common joist. (14)

turned chair. A chair typical of the Elizabethan period with a triangular seat and heavy, thick turnings for the back, arms, and legs. (11)

two-face adjacent fireplace. A fireplace that is open on the front side and on one adjacent side. (20)

two-face opposite fireplace. A fireplace that is open on the front and back sides. (20)

U

unity. In design, the appearance of all parts seeming to belong together. (6)

U-shaped kitchen. A kitchen design consisting of work centers forming a continuous line along three adjoining walls. (5)

U stairs. A stairway consisting of two flights of steps parallel to each other with one landing between them. (17)

V

valance. A horizontal decorative, fabric treatment across the top of draperies to provide a finished appearance and hide hardware and cords. (16)

value. Lightness or darkness of a hue. (7)

vanishing point. Imaginary points used to create the illusion of a perspective; are reached by extending lines from the closest parts of a drawing past the farthest parts until the lines meet. (27)

variety. In design, the use of contrasting features to prevent monotony. (6)

varnish. Clear wood finishes used to emphasize wood grain and deepen tones. (8)

veneer. A thin slice of wood cut from a log. (12)

veneer wall. A frame wall with brick or masonry used as a covering for it. (13)

ventilation. The circulation of fresh air. (23)

vines. Plants having a flexible stem supported by climbing, twining, or creeping along a surface. (25)

virtual reality models. Three-dimensional images created from a drawing to show how the exterior or interior of a dwelling will appear; also called virtual models. (28)

W

wainscot. The lower 3 or 4 ft. of a wall when it is finished differently from the rest of the wall. (13)

wainscot chair. A chair typical of the Elizabethan period with a rectangular, wooden seat, turned or column legs, and a carved or inlaid wooden back. (11)

warp knitting. Type of knitting in which loops are formed vertically by machine, one row at a time. (10)

wastewater-removal system. Carries wastewater from the structure to the sanitary sewer or private septic tank. (19)

water closet. A toilet. (4)

water-supply system. The source and provider of water to residences, such as a city water main or private well. (19)

water vapor. Invisible moisture contained in air. (23)

weathering steel. Steel that produces a protective oxide that resists rust and corrosion. (9)

weft knitting. Type of knitting in which loops are formed by hand or by machine as yarn is added in a crosswise direction. (10)

welting. Cording sewn into the seams of upholstery to add strength. (12)

wicker furniture. Furniture made by weaving various natural or synthetic materials such as willow, reed, rattan, or spirally-twisted paper around a frame. (11)

winder stairs. A stairway with wedge-shaped steps that are substituted for a landing. (17)

window shades. Screens of fabric or other material that filter or block light. (16)

wiring closet. The central hub of a structured wiring installation. (21)

wood foundation. A basement wall made of pressure treated wood. (13)

work center. Area for performing related tasks and storing the necessary tools. (5)

work ethic. The belief or guiding philosophy that motivates a person to do a good job. (30)

work triangle. Route that connects the sink, refrigerator, and range, ideally no longer than 22 ft. (5)

wrought iron. Nearly pure iron that is worked into various shapes. (9)

Y

yarn. Fibers twisted together to form a continuous strand. (10)

Index

D

F

G

H

I

J

K

L

Q

R

S

Y